Philosophy and
Computer Science

EXPLORATIONS
in philosophy

Philosophy and Computer Science

Timothy R. Colburn

James H. Fetzer, Series Editor

M.E. Sharpe
Armonk, New York
London, England

Library of Congress Cataloging-in-Publication Data

Colburn, Timothy R., 1952–
Philosophy and computer science / Timothy R. Colburn.
p. cm. — (Explorations in philosophy)
Includes bibliographical references and index.
ISBN 1-56324-990-1 (hc : alk. paper). — ISBN 1-56324-991-X (pbk. : alk. paper)
1. Computer science—Philosophy. 2. Artificial intelligence.
I. Title. II. Series
QA76.167.C65 1999
004—DC21   99-28936
CIP

Printed in the United States of America

The paper used in this publication meets the minimum requirements of
American National Standard for Information Sciences
Permanence of Paper for Printed Library Materials,
ANSI Z 39.48-1984.

BM (c) 10   9   8   7   6   5   4   3   2   1
BM (p) 10   9   8   7   6   5   4   3   2   1

To Carrie, for leading me back to the academy,
and to Jim, for lighting the way.

Contents

Part III The Philosophy of Computer Science 127

Series Preface

The series, *Explorations in Philosophy*, is intended to provide undergraduates and other readers with quality introductions not only to the principal areas of philosophy, including traditional topics of investigation—epistemology, ethics, and social and political philosophy—but also to contemporary subjects of importance—such as computer science, feminist studies, and the ethics of reproduction. In each case, the editors have chosen authors who could not only explain the central problems encountered within their respective domains but who could also propose promising solutions to those problems, including novel approaches and original analyses.

The present volume, *Philosophy and Computer Science*, provides a lucid and stimulating introduction to some of the most fascinating ideas explored in contemporary philosophy and science, which concern the scope and limits of computers and their powers. The author, Timothy Colburn, who is both a philosopher and a computer scientist, supplies a framework that is historical and analytical, explaining the philosophical origins of many problems that are raised by modern computing machines. Anyone with an interest in artificial intelligence, reasoning by machines, and the theoretical foundations of computer science will find it rewarding.

James H. Fetzer

Acknowledgments

This book would not have been possible without the support and encouragement of my brilliant mentor and friend, Jim Fetzer. He provided me with the seminal ideas that first began to unite my distinct intellectual lives in philosophy and computer science, and he offered me myriad opportunities to express myself. I cannot thank him enough.

I would also like to thank Kluwer Academic Publishers for permission to use parts of my papers appearing in the journal *Minds and Machines*, and for permission to use part of my contribution to the volume *Program Verification: Fundamental Issues in Computer Science* (1993). Thanks are also due the editors of *The Monist: An International Quarterly of General Philosophical Inquiry*, for permission to include part of my contribution to the January, 1999, issue on philosophy of computer science.

Philosophy and
Computer Science

– 1 –
Introduction

"Philosophy and computer science ... isn't that a rather odd combination?" Such is the typical cocktail-party response when learning of my academic training in the discipline Socrates called "the love of wisdom" and my subsequent immersal in the world of bytes, programs, systems analysis, and government contracts. And such might be the reaction to the title of this book. But despite its cloistered reputation and its literary, as opposed to technological, image, the tradition of philosophical investigation, as all of us who have been seduced by it know, has no turf limits. While few but the truly prepared venture into philosophy's hard-core "inner circle" of epistemology, metaphysics, (meta)ethics, and logic, literally anything is fair philosophical game in the outer circle in which most of us exist. And so we have the "philosophy *of*s:" philosophy of science, philosophy of art, of language, education. Some of the philosophy *of*s even have names befitting their integration into vital areas of modern society, for example, medical ethics and environmental ethics, which we can say are shorter names for the philosophies of ethical decisions in medicine and ecology. One of the aims of this book is to make an early contribution to a nascent philosophy *of* computer science.

Which is not to say that there has not been a vast amount of work done which can be described as the cross-disciplinary encounter of philosophy with computer science. Despite the typical cocktail-party reaction to this combination, the solutions to many problems in computer science have benefited from what we might call *applied* philosophy. For example, hardware logic gate design would not be possible without boolean algebra, developed by the nineteenth-century mathematician George Boole, whose work helped lay the foundation for modern logic. Later work in logic, particularly the development of predicate calculus by Gottlob Frege, has been drawn upon extensively by researchers in software engineering who desire a formal language for computer program semantics. Predicate calculus is also the formal model used by many of those who implement automated reasoning systems for mechanical theorem proving. These theorem proving techniques have even formed the basis for a style of general-purpose computer programming called *logic programming.*

Furthermore, the application of philosophical methods to computer science is not limited to those in logic. The study of ethics, for example, has found broad application to computer-related issues of privacy, security, and law. While these issues are not regarded as germane to the science of computing *per se*, they have arisen directly as a result of the drastic changes society has undergone due to the ubiquity and power of computers. In 1990, a major U.S. software vendor attempted to openly market a large mailing list compiled from public sources, but was forced to withdraw it when the public outcry over invasion of privacy became too great. While the scaling back of the U.S. Strategic Defense Initiative in the 1980s could be seen as a response to technical feasibility questions, a major underlying moral concern was whether a nation *ought* to entrust its security, to such a large extent, to machines. And now, with the pervading influence of the World Wide Web, society has been forced to confront issues regarding freedom and decency in the digital world.

Within the field of law, many sticky ethical questions related to computers have arisen: Is unauthorized use of a computer from the privacy of one's own home, without damaging any files or programs (i.e., hacking), the same as breaking and entering? Can authors of programs that are experts in medicine or law be sued for malpractice? Should computer programs be copyrightable, or should they be free, like air? Should programmed trading be allowed on the stock exchange? Answers to the last two questions, and others like it, would have significant effects on the conduct of our economy. None of these questions could have been predicted a mere few decades ago. Today, it would be difficult to find a college curriculum that did not include, in either the computer science or the philosophy department, a course entitled "Computers and Society," "Values and Technology," or the like.

But our inquiry in this book goes beyond the application of philosophical method to specific issues like those just mentioned. Our inquiry attempts to seek a *new* encounter between philosophy and science by examining the ways they can *change one another* in the context of one of science's newest disciplines. This type of inquiry is in addition to the traditional concern of philosophy of science, which, in its analyses of concepts like explanation, theory, and the ontological status of inferred entities, is typically unaffected by the content of *particular* scientific discoveries. This insular nature of philosophical content and method is being challenged by work in the area of computer science known as *artificial intelligence* (AI), particularly in the traditional philosophical areas of logic, philosophy of mind, and epistemology.

Although even the *definition* of the field of AI is fraught with philosophical debate, genuine philosophical questions come to the fore as researchers attempt to model human intelligence in computer programs: What is the structure of human knowledge (so that we may represent it in computer memory)? What is the process of human thought (so that we may model reasoning, learning, and creativity in computer programs)? Interestingly, while AI researchers must ask the same sorts of cognitive questions as philosophers do, they usually agree with the pervasive assumption, stated by Hobbes in the seventeenth century, that "cognition is computation," a point of view certainly not shared by all philosophers. One of the fascinating aspects of AI is its concern for both computer scientists and philosophers. As a subfield of computer science, it is a young discipline, but the questions it raises have been the objects of philosophical investigation for centuries. There is no dearth of writing on this confluence of concerns from seemingly disparate disciplines, but Part I of this book, "Philosophical Foundations of Artificial Intelligence," provides a fresh treatment of their relationship by returning to historical philosophical problems and looking at them in the light of how they would set the stage for an age when people would begin pronouncing certain computer programs "intelligent."

This retro-treatment of historical philosophy is an interesting exercise, because it allows us to imagine an epochal sweep of philosophical musings through the ages, in which concepts of mind and reasoning are first rooted in the formal or the divine, then become powers of humanity's own individuality, and finally are manifest in humanity's own artifacts. However one feels about the inexorability of this sweep, one thing is clear: The construction of models of mind and reasoning have today forced many philosophers out of the cloistered confines of their *a priori* worlds.

One reason for this emergence is consistent with the traditional role of philosophy as a guiding beacon, a giver rather than receiver of wisdom in its encounter with science. AI underwent a resurgence in the 1980s that was primarily the result of its switching focus from systems for doing merely automated reasoning to so-called *knowledge-based* systems. Prior to this the most important theoretical tool for the AI researcher was logic, and it was thought that by automating formal and well understood patterns of inference, one could emulate human intelligent behavior in a computer program. Insofar as logic had been the province of philosophers and mathematicians, it was obvious that previous work by them had a bearing on AI. However, many AI researchers began to believe that the role of reasoning in machine intelligence had been overemphasized at the expense of knowledge. Early AI programs were very good at proving theorems in first-order predicate logic, but such programs proved hugely inefficient when used to implement nontrivial systems for reasoning in specific areas. It became obvious that more effort spent on acquiring and digitally representing knowledge in a specific area, combined with even a minimal reasoning mechanism, would pay off with programs more accurately emulating human expertise in that area, and the first truly successful applications in AI became known as *expert systems*. Such programs were said to be knowledge-based because much of the intense effort in their development centered around the representation and manipulation of specific knowledge, as opposed to the efficient modeling of mechanisms of pure reason.

Thus AI researchers became interested in the concept of knowledge as well as logic, and it seemed reasonable to suppose that they could learn something from philosophers, who have been thinking about knowledge for a long time. The most important area of AI directly related to epistemology became known as *knowledge representation*. But it was clear that, to truly emulate intelligent behavior, not only models of knowledge representation but also models of *coming to know* were necessary. In other words, AI programs had to be able to learn. So there are several important aspects of knowledge with which AI researchers and practitioners must be concerned.

This question of how philosophy can help us do AI is couched in the language of interdisciplinary cooperation, in which one discipline perhaps serendipitously benefits another by offering relevant work already done or an insightful outlook previously unseen. That this relationship is even possible between AI and philosophy is due to the overlap of subject matter: philosophy is concerned with issues of human knowledge and reasoning, and AI is concerned with *modeling* human knowledge and reasoning.

But philosophy, in its general role of critically evaluating beliefs, is more than merely a potential partner with AI. Perhaps the most visible role philosophy has played in this relationship is that of watchdog, in which it delineates the limits, and sometimes even attempts to destroy the foundations, of AI.

These critiques proceed by taking to task the claim that computation is even an appropriate model for human thought or consciousness in the first place. Their primary focus is not logic or knowledge, but of mind. Here the primary question is whether philosophy can tell AI what it can do. Many philosophers believe the answer to this question is yes, but they are largely ignored by AI researchers and practitioners, because the latter's focus is not mind but logic and knowledge. While this ignoring is done at their peril, it is becoming clear that a swing in the opposite direction has occurred, to the point where it is claimed that technological advances, especially those in computer science, can shed light on traditional philosophical problems.

To claim this was unthinkable within many philosophical circles just two decades ago, and there are still those who will steadfastly resist countenancing the possibility. But since certain questions traditionally thought to be philosophical—such as: How do we come to know things? What is the structure of knowledge? What is the nature of the mind?—are now being asked by AI and cognitive science researchers as well, it is inevitable that these researchers will offer answers in the technical terms with which they are familiar. In short, the rapid growth in the speed and complexity of computing machines is tempting people to put forth models of the human mind in terms of computer science. But why are computer science models so tempting? To answer this, it helps to discuss something about the relation between science and philosophy in general.

Science and philosophy are often distinguished by pointing out that science seeks explanation while philosophy seeks justification. To ask what causes the tides is a scientific question, while to ask what would constitute adequate grounds for believing that I see the moon is a philosophical one. "What reason do you have for believing X?" is a typical question asked by philosophers, and the nature of X determines the kind of philosophy undertaken. For example, "What reason do you have for believing that mercy killing is wrong?" is a question for normative ethics, "What reason do you have for believing in the existence of disembodied minds?" is a question for philosophy of mind, and "What reason do you have for believing that this argument is valid?" is a question for philosophical logic. So philosophy has been characterized as the critical evaluation of beliefs through the analysis of concepts in a given area of inquiry.

Of course, science is *also* concerned with critically evaluating beliefs and analyzing concepts. But when one looks at the kinds of things X is in the questions above, one notices that none of them lend themselves to empirical study. One need not witness actual cases of mercy killing to come to a conclusion about whether it ought to be done. By definition, a disembodied mind is one that cannot be substantiated through physical observation. And the validity of an argument form is not determined by looking for instances of the form in the world. So philosophy has also been characterized as a nonempirical, or *a priori*, discipline, in distinct contrast with science.

Computer science, being a science, would seem to be distinguished from philosophy just as any other science. But computer science is unique among the sciences in the types of *models* it creates. In seeking explanations, science often constructs models to test hypotheses for explaining phenomena. For example, it might be hypothesized that the phenomenon of the northern lights is caused by the interaction of solar atoms with the earth's magnetic field. To test this hypothesis, a model of the earth and its magnetic field could be created in a laboratory, complete with appropriate magnets and gaseous elements. Then, if, under the right conditions, luminosity is observed, the hypothesis may be said to be confirmed. This model, in the form of experimental apparatus, is of course a physical object, like many models built and manipulated in any of the natural sciences. The models built and manipulated in computer science, however, are not physical at all.

Computer science is a science concerned with the study of *computational processes*. A computational process is distinguished from, say, a chemical or electrical process, in that it is studied "in ways that ignore its physical nature."[1] For example, the process by which a card player arranges cards in her hand, and the process by which a computer sorts names in a customer list, though they share nothing in common physically, may nevertheless embody the same computational process. They may, for example, both proceed by scanning the items to be arranged one by one, determining the proper place of each scanned item relative to the items already scanned, and inserting it into that place, perhaps necessitating the moving of previously scanned items to make room. This process (known as an *insertion sort* in computer science terms) can be precisely described in a formal language without talking about playing cards or semiconducting elements. When so described, one has a *computational model* of the process in the form of a computer program. This model can be tested, in a way analogous to how a hypothesis is tested in the natural sciences, by executing the program and observing its behavior. It can also be reasoned about abstractly, so that we may answer questions about it, such as, are there other processes which will have the same effect but do it more efficiently? Building computational models and answering these kinds of questions form a large part of what computer scientists do.

The explosive growth in the number of computer applications in the last several decades has shown that the kinds of real world processes amenable to modeling by computer are limitless. Not only have traditional activities, like record keeping, investing, publishing, and banking, been simply converted to control by computational models, but whole new kinds of activity have been created that would not be possible without such models. These are the by-now-familiar "virtual" activities we describe in the language of cyberspace: e-mail, chat rooms, Web surfing, on-line shopping, Internet gaming, and so on. But long before computers came to dominate everyday life, computational models were employed to describe processes of a special sort, which have existed as long as modern *Homo sapiens* has existed. These are the processes associated with human reasoning and knowledge organization, and computational models of them are the concern of AI.

The study of the nature of human reasoning and knowledge, in the form of logic and epistemology, has, of course, been a focus of western philosophy since Plato and Aristotle. However, not until the latter part of the twentieth century and the advent of the digital computer did it become possible to actually *build* models of reasoning that contained alleged representations of human knowledge. Before that time, if you wanted to study human reasoning or the structure of human knowledge, you remained for the most part in the *a priori* world of philosophy, utilizing perhaps a datum or two from psychology. With computers, however, it became possible to *test* one's epistemological theory *if* the theory was realizable in a computer model. It therefore became reasonable to at least ask: Can AI, as an empirical discipline concerned with building and observing models of human cognitive behavior, help us do philosophy?

If we take seriously the characterization of philosophy given above, namely, that it is by definition a nonempirical discipline, then we may regard the asking of this question as a category mistake. Roderick Chisholm is a primary proponent of this view:

> Contemporary interest in the nature of knowledge pertains not only to that branch of philosophy called "theory of knowledge" or "epistemology," but also to the fields of information theory, artificial intelligence, and cognitive science. The latter disciplines are not alternatives to the traditional theory of knowledge because they are branches of empirical science and not of philosophy. For the most part, the facts with which they are concerned are not relevant to the traditional philosophical questions.[2]

However, many contemporary researchers, both philosophers and computer scientists, would take issue with this view, finding it a methodological dogma that may have seemed reasonable in an earlier time when it was not possible to build digital models of human reasoning and knowledge, but which is questionable and naive in the Information Age. This is a genuine dispute, and may extend to what some would regard as the very foundations of philosophy. But it is the case, for better or worse, that computer science is beginning to affect how we do philosophy, and Part II of this book, "The New Encounter of Science and Philosophy," describes this reverse effect in deeper detail, suggesting a continuing new symbiosis in the future.

While it is a new revelation for *some* philosophical thinking to be affected by the running of computer programs, "independent" philosophers are by no means out of business. AI is but a subfield of computer science, and the consideration of mind and reason notwithstanding, computer science is ripe for the good old-fashioned analysis that philosophy provides. Thus, Part III of this book, "The Philosophy of Computer Science," attempts to place computer science within the broad spectrum of inquiry that constitutes science. The concern here is to deal with the inevitable identity crises that crop up in the self-image of any adolescent, which computer science certainly is. We will ask philosophical questions like: What is the relation between mathematics and computer science? Is there a sense in which computer science is experimental science? Is a computer programmer merely a data wizard, or can she also engage in information modeling? What is the nature of abstraction in computer science? What are the ontological implications of computer science concepts?

In short, this book is about the philosophical foundations of artificial intelligence in particular and computer science in general, and it is about the contributions that philosophy and computer science can make to each other. It asks where computer science fits in as a science, how philosophy can guide computer science, and how work in computer science can shape one's philosophy. I do advise the reader that chapters 7 and 8 on models of reasoning and the naturalization of epistemology may impose more demands upon readers than do the other chapters. Still, by the conclusion of this book, I hope that readers will be sufficiently enlightened to begin to answer these questions for themselves.

Part I

Philosophical Foundations of Artificial Intelligence

– 2 –

The Definition and Scope of AI

Since the first two parts of this book use AI as their focus for examining the relation between philosophy and computer science, I will open this part with a description of what AI is, and a short survey of the kinds of things that AI programs do.

The lure and promise of computer science has always been the ability to model digitally the objects and processes which occur in everyday life. Whether it be bank accounts, basketball games, or shopping malls, the digital modeling of any entity is possible due to ever more sophisticated mediums of description available to programmers in the form of programming languages and software development environments. As I will show in chapter 11, programmers' modeling power increases as their ability to represent real-world entities in software is facilitated, and this is accomplished with abstraction tools. The less they need to be concerned with computer-specific details like memory management and machine address manipulation, the more they can concentrate on representing and managing real-world information and objects.

At the dawn of the digital age, a group of visionary thinkers speculated that the real world objects capable of being modeled include the intelligent reasoning processes exhibited by humans. At a small conference at Dartmouth in 1956 these thinkers gathered to discuss the following theme: *Every aspect of learning or any other feature of intelligence can in principle be so precisely described that a machine can be made to simulate it.*[1] John McCarthy, one of the attendees, came up with the term *artificial intelligence* to describe the field committed to this theme, and this label has stuck. One way to "precisely describe" intelligence is by carefully characterizing it as a kind of symbol processing governed by strict rules of symbol manipulation. McCarthy realized that in order to test this *symbol system* hypothesis he needed a programming tool that would allow him to think in terms of symbols and lists of symbols, rather than in terms of bytes, registers, and memory addresses. So he created the list processing language called *Lisp* that continues as the dominant AI research language today.

Marvin Minsky, another of the Dartmouth conference attendees, has defined AI as "the science of making machines do things that would require intelligence if done by men."[2] This definition does not presuppose a theory of human intelligence such as the symbol system hypothesis, but characterizes AI as being concerned only with machine *behavior* insofar as it mimics human intelligent behavior. Thus we can describe two different approaches to AI, one that attempts to make machines *think* like humans, and one that attempts to make machines *act* like humans.[3] The former approach is today placed within the interdisciplinary field of *cognitive science*, in which the objects of study are the cognitive processes of actual humans and animals. To test theories about these processes, it is often expedient to write programs that model human or animal cognitive architecture, and then to observe whether the programs behave (cognitively) in the way that humans and animals do. The latter approach also observes the cognitive behavior of programs, but ignores the issue of whether AI faithfully emulates the actual structure and process of human reasoning, measuring its success solely against the behavior of a computing artifact. This approach has the advantage of avoiding both controversies over how humans think and criticisms that machines will never be able to think like humans.

But there is another dimension along which approaches to AI can be distinguished. Whether it is thought or behavior that is emulated, some approaches to AI do not use *humans* as their models, opting instead for the notion of an ideal *rational agent*. Realizing that human thought and behavior are both mysteriously complex and at times unreliable, these approaches model intelligence on a notion of ideal rationality. The resulting systems are judged to be not humanlike in their behavior, but agentlike, where an agent is nothing more than a system that perceives and acts.[4] One type of agent that has received large amounts of research attention in the 1990s is the *software agent*, or *softbot*. Motivated by the need to filter useful knowledge from enormous amounts of information available by electronic mail and the World Wide Web, software agents have since been applied in many other areas including electronic commerce and spacecraft control.

Whatever their approach, AI practitioners are taking advantage of four decades of research to produce systems within a wide variety of applications. These applications have found their way into all corners of society that are dependent upon technology, including the military, medicine, science, manufacturing, commerce, and finance. The kinds of things that AI systems do mirror the kinds of actions that humans take in their capacity as reasoners and decision makers in specific areas requiring intellection. These areas include planning, scheduling, recognition, classification, diagnosis, prediction, and maintenance. The reasoning emulated by a machine can be either in conjunction with humans, in which the machine acts as an assistant, or alone, in which the machine acts as an autonomous intelligent agent.

The AI areas just mentioned are very broad, and thus techniques devoted to them are applicable to multiple activities. For example, efficient planning and scheduling are vital to the productivity and profitability of large manufacturing companies, so the design, construction, and deployment of computer programs to perform automated job-shop scheduling is a focus of many companies, including automobile manufacturers. But planning and scheduling are also especially important within military environments, in which the ability to generate logistical plans for, say, the rapid mobilization of combat forces at an air base in the face of unpredictable, ambiguous, and rapidly changing environments, is critical to national security. In fact, the Defense Advanced Research Projects Agency (DARPA) works with the U.S. Air Force to fund AI projects in force planning and aircraft deployment, among others.

One of the largest areas of AI research in recognition is natural language processing, of which there are many subareas. Among the early hopes for AI was the ability to perform natural language translation, say from Russian to English. This proved notoriously difficult, and pointed out the need for knowledge of context when dealing with machine representations of natural language. (AI folklore tells the story of an early system that attempted to translate simple sentences from English to Russian and then back to English. When the system was given "The spirit is willing but the flesh is weak," it responded with "The vodka is good but the meat is rotten.") But successes have emerged, to the point now where there are usable front ends to database systems supporting natural language queries. There is also now limited vocabulary commercial dictation software available, in which the spoken word is converted to text.

In the area of diagnosis, perhaps what first comes to mind is medicine. Indeed, some of the most dramatically successful AI programs take as input descriptions of the symptoms and background of an afflicted patient, say one suffering from lymph node problems, and produce as output a correct diagnosis, along with a detailed explanation of the factors used in the program's reasoning.[5] But the methods used to create such a program are equally applicable to other areas in which correct diagnosis is required, both within medicine and in areas not even remotely similar. This is because AI programmers have learned that the best way to design programs is by distinctly separating the program's *knowledge* from its *control*. In the same way that the control mechanism of a compact disk player can accept and read many different disks, a well-designed AI program's control mechanism can accept and process knowledge from many different areas. Thus the lymph node program's control mechanism might be applied to knowledge of, say, cardiological disorders, to produce a new program for diagnosing diseases of the heart. But beyond that, the program's control mechanism might just as well be applied to nonmedical domains, from the troubleshooting of complex machinery to even the *debugging* (uncovering programming mistakes) of computer programs.

Programs that are able to perform diagnoses or otherwise analyze in an area normally regarded as requiring human expertise are examples of *expert systems* mentioned earlier. They first became widespread in the 1980s and now there are thousands in everyday use. To give just a taste of the types of expert system applications being created today, here are some recently reported in an international journal on expert systems:

- Evaluating and monitoring the level of air pollution.

- Aiding probation officers in sentence recommendation.

- Predicting payment performance on consumer loans.

- Auditing tasks in a large public accounting firm.

- Diagnosing equine cough.

- Assisting in accounting education.

- Process selection and costing of the hole-making operation in manufacturing.

The focus in expert systems is on emulating human expertise by representing expert knowledge in a language that both machines and humans can understand. This language is often symbolic logic, but it can also be one of a variety of other well-specified and unambiguous languages for representing the facts and rules that can be elicited from human subjects. Currently, there is even an effort at Stanford University to create a knowledge *interlingua*, or universal language for representing facts and rules.[6] The use of these languages is central to what has come to be regarded as the *classical* approach to AI, in which the symbolic representation of facts and rules, along with their manipulation via logic or logic-like control mechanisms, is paramount.

Nowhere in the classical approach is there any concern with the way in which the brain *physiologically* goes about the process of thinking and reasoning. There was a time, in the infancy of modern AI, when brain neurophysiology was considered as a model of computational thought, but for various reasons it was largely abandoned in favor of the classical approach.[7] In the 1990s, however, a resurgence of the brain model for AI occurred, due largely to the success of *artificial neural networks*, or programs that operate on the principle of parallel distributed processing (PDP). In PDP, computation is accomplished through the work of many small processing elements taking input from and emitting output to one another in much the same way that neurons communicate with one another in a biological brain. Because of the massive connectivity exhibited among neurons in the brain, this approach to AI is sometimes called *connectionism*.

It turns out that artificial neural networks (ANNs) are good at one thing that brains do very well, and that is complex pattern recognition, whether the pattern be an image of a face, typed characters, a voice print, or quantitative properties of chemical compounds. ANNs can be made to recognize these patterns through training techniques that are partially borrowed from what we know about brain physiology. Thus ANNs constitute one facet within a large area of AI concerned with *machine learning*. Although ANNs are not the only model for machine learning, they have proved successful enough at low-level tasks to warrant an explosion of current research. Among the many current applications of this research are:

- Classification of biological particles from electron-microscopy images.

- Classification of seismic events.

- Learning to factor polynomial equations.

- Detecting credit card fraud.

The success of ANNs and other machine learning techniques in the processing and assimilating of large amounts of data in the training process has spurred current interest in an area of AI known as *knowledge discovery in databases* (KDD; also called "data mining"). KDD tries to automate the process of extracting from the large amounts of data, typically produced by scientific and business endeavors, useful knowledge that was previously unknown. Potential applications include analyzing purchases to determine customer profiles, discovering patterns in health care, or even discovering galaxies.

There are many other areas of AI that I have not mentioned here, among them computer vision and robotics, but I hope this section has described the field adequately enough so that we may now return to our focus on the relation of philosophy to computer science. While computer science is a young field even within the modern era, it turns out that through AI philosophy has for thousands of years been pondering questions that many computer scientists are concerned with now. In the next chapter we will look at AI through the ages in the history of philosophy.

– 3 –

AI and the History of Philosophy

Whether AI is concerned with creating computer systems that think and act like humans, or that think and act rationally, it must address the modeling of reasoning in computer programs. The programming part of this endeavor, however, is secondary to the problem of conceptualizing a model of reasoning in the first place. The availability of digital computers in the twentieth century has only allowed the *testing* of human reasoning models; the conceptual *creation* of such models has been the topic of philosophical investigation for centuries, in the form of logic. In a real sense, then, logicians have since antiquity been laying some of the foundations of AI, although without any foreknowledge of electronics they never could have imagined the purposes to which their work would ultimately be put in machines.

The historical foundations of AI lay not only in the work of those interested in formalizing reasoning through logic. Just as important to AI are two underlying philosophical theories concerning the mind and its thought processes, namely, that they are understandable within both a *physical* and a *computational* model. The first theory involves taking a stand on the traditional philosophical problem of the relationship between mind and body. For if, as in the theory of mind/body dualism, the mental events making up conscious thought and reasoning are not necessarily dependent upon certain physical events for both their existence and content, then to pursue the artificial creation of thought and reasoning processes in a physical medium (like a computer) may not be easy to justify. It should be noted, however, that a successful defense of a physicalistic view of the human mind does not necessarily imply that it is possible to artificially produce thought and reasoning processes in a computer. It is possible to be an antidualist regarding the mind/body relationship, yet still deny the possibility of something like thought or consciousness in such *nonbiological* matter as what makes up computers.

The second theory involves a commitment to the manner in which mental events responsible for thought and reasoning take place, whether their medium is physical or not. If these events are not computational in nature, with their processing achieved through rulelike, algorithmic control, then to attempt to realize the nature of human reasoning in a computational environment (like a computer program) may be similarly misguided. A full understanding of the philosophical foundations of AI requires some knowledge of the context provided by both logic and philosophy of mind.

It is interesting that theories on logic and philosophy of mind hospitable to the modern AI project can be seen as flourishing in Greek antiquity, then either relegated to secondary status or reviled through medieval times, and finally restored to respectability in modern times in preparation for the great scientific and technological advancements of the twentieth century.

Ancient Views of the Mind

With respect to the relationship of mind to matter, it is accepted that the first major figure to frame the problem philosophically was Plato (c. 427–347 b.c.). That a person could be regarded simply as a body was repugnant to Platonism, as illustrated in the following dialogue between Socrates and Alcibiades:

> Soc: [T]he user and the thing he uses are different, are they not?
> Alc: How do you mean?
> Soc: For instance, I suppose a shoemaker uses a round tool, and a square one, and others, when he cuts.
> Alc: Yes.
> Soc: And the cutter and user is quite different from what he uses in cutting?
> Alc: Of course.
> Soc: And in the same way what the harper uses in harping will be different from the harper himself?
> Alc: Yes.
> Soc: Well then, that is what I was asking just now–whether the user and what he uses are always, in your opinion, two different things.
> Alc: They are. ...
> Soc: And man uses his whole body too?
> Alc: To be sure.

Soc: And we said that the user and what he uses are different?
Alc: Yes.
Soc: So man is different from his own body?
Alc: It seems so.
Soc: Then whatever is man?
Alc: I cannot say.
Soc: Oh, but you can–that he is the user of the body.
Alc: Yes.
Soc: And the user of it must be the soul?
Alc: It must.
Soc: And ruler?
Alc: Yes.[1]

By the "user and ruler" of the body, we can take Socrates' *soul* to be the reasoning *mind* with which we are concerned. The strict separation of humans' essences from their bodies is consistent with the celebrated Platonic Theory of Forms, which stratifies reality into the mutable objects of ordinary experience and the immutable, timeless, and transcendant realm of the Forms, like *justice, equality,* or *unity,* with which the mind is concerned when it reasons or philosophizes. Certainly, the mind or soul has knowledge of ordinary objects like people, trees, and stones, through the deliverances of sight, hearing, touch, and so on. But neither the mind nor the concepts it reasons about are themselves part of this corporeal world. It would have been impossible for Plato to conceive of an artifically created mind, for anything so fabricated could exist only in the imperfect material world, while reasoning occurs in the realm of the Forms.

That the workings of the mind are not to be couched in physical, corporeal terms is also born out by Plato's view that learning, a primary activity of the mind, is really the recollection of knowledge acquired outside the physical life of human beings and within the realm of the Forms. As Socrates remarks to Meno:

> Thus the soul, since it is immortal and has been born many times, and has seen all things both here and in the other world, has learned everything that is. So we need not be surprised if it can recall the knowledge of virtue or anything else which, as we see, it once possessed. All nature is akin, and the soul has learned everything, so that when a man has recalled a single piece of knowledge—*learned* it, in ordinary language—there is no reason why he should not find out all the rest, if he keeps a stout heart and does not grow weary of the search, for seeking and learning are nothing but recollection.[2]

Intimations of reincarnationism in Platonism notwithstanding, the commonalities between Platonism and later Christian doctrine regarding the relationship of mind and body are clear, in that materialism, or any associated view that allows thought or reasoning to be predicated of material things, is to be rejected.

But while Christian theology would dominate medieval philosophy for centuries, it is important to point out that antiquity had its materialists and skeptics with regard to the mind. Hippocrates (c. 460–357 b.c.) was born before Plato and is best known for the medical oath. He was fascinated by epilepsy, which at the time was given the name "sacred disease." Hippocrates understood that the disease was granted a divine origin due both to its strange manifestations and to general public ignorance concerning its cause, but he also understood the primary role played in the disease by the brain. Most importantly, he extended the brain's role from a mere causer of certain disorders to a central factor in all aspects of mental life:

> Men ought to know that from the brain, and from the brain only,
> arise our pleasures, joys, laughter and jests, as well as our
> sorrows, pains, griefs and tears. Through it, in particular, we
> think, see, hear, and distinguish the ugly from the beautiful, the
> bad from the good, the pleasant from the unpleasant ...[3]

Beyond understanding the central role played by the brain, Hippocrates even ventured physical, causal explanations of madness and intelligence:

> Madness comes from its moistness. When the brain is abnormally
> moist, of necessity it moves, and when it moves neither sight nor
> hearing are still, but we see or hear now one thing and now
> another, and the tongue speaks in accordance with the things
> seen and heard on any occasion. But all the time the brain is still
> a man is intelligent.[4]

Although views of the mind or soul as incorporeal in nature persisted through the classical ages in the Platonist and Stoic schools, there were also well developed systems of materialist philosophy post-Plato, particularly in the Epicurean school. Epicurus (341–270 b.c.), an advocate of atomism, envisioned the soul as being composed of the same atoms that make up air, wind, and heat, as well as a fourth kind of atom made sensually undetectable due to its minute size. One's soul, which is the center of the self, is therefore an empirical object because one's body is. The soul is intertwined with body and cannot exist without it.

Although most of Epicurus' writings have been lost, tenets of the Epicurean school survive in the writings of later devotees and followers.

One of them, born over one hundred and seventy years after Epicurus' death, was the Roman poet Lucretius (c. 99–55 b.c.), whose didactic poem *On the Nature of Things* was a celebration of Epicureanism. It is described as "the fullest surviving exposition of the most coherent and influential system of materialistic philosophy produced in classical antiquity."[5] It is materialist in that it attempts to locate the mind within a physical substratum:

> Now I assert that the mind and the soul are kept together in
> close union and make up a single nature, but that the directing
> principle which we call mind and understanding, is the head so to
> speak and reigns paramount in the whole body. It has a fixed
> seat in the middle region of the breast: here throb fear and
> apprehension, about these spots dwell soothing joys; therefore
> here is the understanding or mind.[6]

While modern materialism would find the mind misplaced in the breast, the message is clear that the faculties of understanding are not to be disembodied, but to find their seat in matter. When confronted with explaining the relationship of the mind and body as they interact to wake a man from sleep, for instance, Lucretius refuses to countenance the possibility of a connection between things corporeal and noncorporeal in nature, choosing instead a materialist stance:

> [T]he nature of the mind and soul is bodily; for when it is seen to
> push the limbs, rouse the body from sleep, and alter the
> countenance and guide and turn about the whole man, and when
> we see that none of these effects can take place without touch nor
> touch without body, must we not admit that the mind and the
> soul are of a bodily nature?[7]

So here is a repudiation of the strict Platonic dualism that would come to dominate both philosophy and theology in the middle ages and later find its fullest metaphysical flowering in Cartesian dualism. It serves to remind us that AI's materialist intuition, far from being a product of the modern analytical approach to philosophy buttressed by neurophysiological science, is found in diverse ages and intellectual environments.

The Age of Modern Philosophy

The foundations of the modern approach to AI were laid by philosophers who were concerned with general characterizations of human understanding. These philosophers regarded as fundamental the question of what is the nature of consciousness, including how humans think and perceive, how ideas and concepts are represented in the mind, and how ideas give rise to others. Of course, understanding these problems is crucial to any attempt to create artificial intelligence, although the western philosophers of the seventeenth and eighteenth centuries who were interested in these matters had no idea that three hundred years later these issues would be central to the debate over whether machines could think.

It is generally agreed among historians of philosophy that the era of modern philosophy began with the seventeenth century. This was a time following several centuries of marked changes in science, art, and literature associated with the Renaissance, and more recent changes in religion associated with the Reformation. It is no surprise that a profound change in the method of doing philosophy also occurred at this time, due to a general parting of the ways of theology and philosophy. While the ancient Greek philosophers succeeded in separating out the philosophical questions with which they were concerned from dogmatic theology, the rise of Christianity in the Middle Ages brought with it a pervading intellectual context in which knowledge with certainty is attributable only to divine revelation. Such knowledge, for example, a simple truth of mathematics, was something that a Middle Ages thinker could not conceive of gaining simply on one's own, purely as a result of rational thought and without the help of God. At the time of St. Augustine (354–430 a.d.), the idea among Christians of a discipline of philosophy as separate from theology was not possible, although throughout the succeeding centuries a separation began to take shape. As the philosophical historian F.C. Copleston describes it:

> In the early Middle Ages the distinction between theology and
> philosophy had not been clearly worked out, partly owing to the
> rudimentary character of philosophical development at the time.
> In the thirteenth century the distinction was clearly recognized;
> but the leading figures in the intellectual world of the period
> were, for the most part, primarily theologians; and they
> constructed great syntheses of theology and philosophy, in which
> the two sciences were harmonized. In the fourteenth century this
> synthesis tended to fall apart.[8]

Some medieval theologians, most notably St. Thomas Aquinas (1224–1274) and William of Ockham (c. 1285–1349), succeeded in separating the concerns and methods of philosophy and theology. The fundamental assumption that distinguishes their systems from modern philosophy, however, was their notion of divine revelation of knowledge, as opposed to the later ideas that the source of all human knowledge is reason and/or experience. The concept of an "artificial" intelligence would have been completely anathema to them, since even humans, much less any kind of fabricated beings, were not responsible for many of the important things they know. The falling apart of the theology/philosophy syntheses mentioned by Copleston proceeded during the European Renaissance of the fifteenth and sixteenth centuries. The thinker who gave the first complete voice to post-Renaissance philosophy was the Frenchman René Descartes.

Cartesian Dualism

The Renaissance was typified by the spread of humanism, a return to the classical values of Greece and Rome, and the beginning of objective scientific inquiry. Like other thinkers of his time, Descartes (1596–1650) was not a theologian using philosophical concepts and methods to advance dogma, but a scientist and mathematician who was also interested in putting human reason to the task of justifying theological beliefs. In a letter to the dean and doctors of the Sacred Faculty of Theology of Paris, Descartes describes his motivation for writing his *Meditations on the First Philosophy*:

> I have always been of opinion that the two questions respecting
> God and the soul were the chief of those that ought to be
> determined by the help of philosophy rather than theology; for
> although to us, the faithful, it be sufficient to hold as matters of
> faith, that the human soul does not perish with the body, and
> that God exists, it yet assuredly seems impossible ever to
> persuade infidels of the reality of any religion, or almost even any
> moral virtue, unless, first of all, those two things be proved to
> them by natural reason.[9]

Thus the general significance of Descartes for modern AI is that he is the first post-medieval philosopher to clearly use the method of *starting with the individual self and its ideas* and going from there to ascertain (or not ascertain, as the case may be) knowledge of external entities such as God and matter. Before Descartes, the method was just the opposite: *start with God and matter as givens*, and work from there to determine truths about the world and mathematics. The new method clearly concedes more power and autonomy to the human mind, opening the way to scrutinizing and understanding how it works, and possibly leading to a time when the mind is well enough understood to be modeled.

But Descartes's significance for AI goes beyond philosophical method and reaches into the very content of his *Meditations*. For along with the existence of God, Descartes wanted to demonstrate another theological claim, namely, the immortality of the soul, using philosophical methods.

He did this by investigating the nature of the mind and coming to the conclusion that it is a substance independent of any physical substance:

> [A]lthough I certainly do possess a body with which I am very closely conjoined; nevertheless, because, on the one hand, I have a clear and distinct idea of myself, in as far as I am only a thinking and unextended thing, and as, on the other hand, I possess a distinct idea of body, in as far as it is only an extended and unthinking thing, it is certain that I (that is, my mind, by which I am what I am) is entirely and truly distinct from my body, and may exist without it.[10]

It was therefore clear to Descartes that a mind is a thing that thinks, and that whatever thinks is not a physical body. And although as a scientist he was well aware of the role the brain plays in feeling pain, causing thirst, and so on, he was adamant that a brain is not a thinking thing. Since he was convinced that physical bodies cannot think, he had a remarkably prescient outlook on the possibility of AI. He not only anticipated what would three hundred years later come to be regarded as a test of intelligence in artificially created beings, but he also claimed that no such artifact could ever pass such a test:

> [I]f there were machines bearing the image of our bodies, and capable of imitating our actions as far as it is morally possible, there would still remain two most certain tests whereby to know that they were not therefore really men. Of these the first is that they could never use words or other signs arranged in such a manner as is competent to us in order to declare our thoughts to others. ... The second test is, that although such machines might execute many things with equal or perhaps greater perfection than any of us, they would, without doubt, fail in certain others from which it could be discovered that they did not act from knowledge, but solely from the disposition of their organs; for while reason is an universal instrument that is alike available on every occasion, these organs, on the contrary, need a particular arrangement for each particular action; whence it must be morally impossible that there should exist in any machine a diversity of organs sufficient to enable it to act in all the occurrences of life, in the way in which our reason enables us to act.[11]

Descartes argues here that the diversity in quality of types of human reasoning is great, in fact too great for such reasoning to be attributable to the physical arrangement of organs in an artificial being. For nowhere near enough such arrangements are possible to match all types of reasoning. Of course, Descartes did not have the benefit of what we know today about the enormous neurological complexity of the brain, and the distinct role the brain plays in thinking. But it is still a matter of debate whether the models of thought put forth in AI research are correct, and Descartes can legitimately be thought of as AI's first critic.

While Descartes's deemphasis of the role of the brain in thought seems misguided today, his work brought the analysis of the human mind to the forefront of philosophical research. As pointed out earlier, this work marked the birth of modern philosophy with its emphasis on the nature of human understanding. Western philosophy in the seventeenth and eighteenth centuries would play out as a point and counterpoint between the two great traditions of Rationalism and Empiricism, and their encounter would produce not only criticisms, but also the very foundations, of modern artificial intelligence.

Hobbes and the Computational Model of Thought

Thomas Hobbes, a British contemporary of Descartes who lived from 1588 until 1679, was less concerned than Descartes with rationally deriving theological truths, and more concerned with politics and ethics (although at the time even these could not be completely divorced from theology). In his *Leviathan*, Hobbes tried to lay the foundation for a "science of natural justice," and part of the foundation was Hobbes's view of man, nature, and art. By *art* Hobbes did not mean fine art or performing art, but what we would today think of as design for fabrication. Hobbes thought of nature as the artwork of God, and since natural life is created by God, why would it not be possible for artificial life to be created by man?

> Nature, the art whereby God has made and governs the world, is by the *art* of man, as in many other things, so in this also imitated—that it can make an artificial animal. For seeing life is but a motion of limbs, the beginning whereof is in some principal part within, why may we not say that all *automata* (engines that move themselves by springs and wheels as does a watch) have an artificial life? For what is the *heart* but a *spring*, and the *nerves* but so many *strings*, and the *joints* but so many *wheels* giving motion to the whole body such as was intended by the artificer?[12]

The point of this comparison between nature and art, for Hobbes, is to point out that the commonwealth or state can be conceived of as an artificial man. However, this anthropocentric metaphor for political organization illustrates, along with Descartes, another profound shift for the source of human understanding from God alone to man himself.

For Hobbes, philosophy is the same thing as *natural reason*, a power born to all humans and in need of development and flowering in the same way in which a seed turns into a plant. What reason is, and what it is not, were central questions for Hobbes as a basis for the larger social and political project in his *Leviathan*. In his *Elements of Philosophy*, he took up these questions, among others. A primary element of natural reason is *ratiocination*:

> Philosophy [or natural reason] is such knowledge of effects or appearances, as we acquire by true ratiocination from the knowledge we have first of their causes or generation: And again, of such causes or generations as may be from knowing first their effects.[13]

Ratiocination is thus the gaining of new knowledge, either of effect on the basis of cause, or of cause on the basis of effect. This rules out certain activities of the mind in which new knowledge is not gained on the basis of established knowledge:

> [W]e must consider, first, that although Sense and Memory of things, which are common to man and all living creatures, be knowledge, yet because they are given us immediately by nature, and not gotten by ratiocination, they are not philosophy.

> Secondly, seeing Experience is nothing but memory; and Prudence, or prospect into the future time, nothing but expectation of such things as we have already had experience of, Prudence also is not to be esteemed philosophy.[14]

So sense, memory, and experience, though they can be sources of knowledge, are not ratiocination or reason because they do not use knowledge of cause and effect to produce new knowledge. What, then, exactly comprises the ability to ratiocinate, or reason from cause to effect or vice versa? Hobbes's answer is at once the most celebrated and the most controversial statement in modern AI, made all the more remarkable by the fact that it is over three hundred and forty years old:

> By ratiocination, I mean *computation*. Now to compute, is either to collect the sum of many things that are added together, or to know what remains when one thing is taken out of another. *Ratiocination*, therefore, is the same with *addition* and *subtraction*.[15]

Hobbes should not be interpreted as holding the simple-minded view that computation involves only numbers. If this were the case, there would be no AI controversy, since ratiocination, or reasoning, clearly does not proceed only through numbers. What makes Hobbes's claim both tenable and debatable is his generalization of the notion of computation so that the concepts of *adding together* or *taking away from* apply in nonnumeric contexts as well:

> We must not therefore think that computation, that is,
> ratiocination, has place only in numbers, as if man were
> distinguished from other living creatures ... by nothing but the
> faculty of numbering; for *magnitude, body, motion, time, degrees*
> *of quality, action, conception, proportion, speech and names* (in
> which all the kinds of philosophy consist) are capable of addition
> and subtraction.[16]

It is this claim, that any kind of reasoning at all can be understood in the computational terms of adding together or taking away, that is the cornerstone of modern AI. While it was not Hobbes' intent to carefully characterize this computational sense of human reasoning, it was indeed his intuition, as it is today for anyone working in AI.

However, a computational model of the mind is not all that is necessary to pave the way for AI attempts. Perhaps not as obvious, but just as important, is a *physical* model. Descartes recognized this in his unwitting role as first AI critic when he argued that because it is a *disembodied* mind that thinks, it will never be possible to build a physical object that does so. Today, most of us regard the mind as inextricably linked to the brain, to the point of arguing in many cases that mental events are to be *identified* with physical processes occurring in the brain. But post-Renaissance European thought, although it found itself free to give the human mind great autonomy in the pursuit of truths about itself and the world, was nevertheless constrained by the dogma of Judeo-Christian theism.

To square their philosophies with religious doctrine, which included the existence of a deity interacting with humans in history and providing them with an afterlife, great thinkers like Descartes and Hobbes couched their arguments within these parameters. For Descartes, this manifested itself in a detailed defense of platonic dualism, the philosophical underpinning of the Judeo-Christian doctrine of immortality of the soul. For Hobbes, it resulted in polemical criticism of scholastic Aristotelianism and its associated abstract essences and substantial forms, which he regarded as antithetical both to the tenets of the Church of England, and to his vision of society in the *Leviathan*. It is easy for a reader today to conclude that most of the early modern philosophers were selling out to the prevailing religious authorities of their times, but we must remember the extent to which these authorities held sway, even over the dawn of modern science, in which Galileo was forced to recant his Copernican views. Despite the fact that Hobbes was a devout man, the *Leviathan* argued for absolute sovereignty without appealing to divine right, and he was suspected of atheism, causing him to fear for his life at an advanced age.

It would take a courageous thinker to break the spell of religious authority and question concepts like disembodied minds, but that is what would be necessary for intellectual history to prepare for a discipline such as AI. The best example of such an early pioneer is the Scottish philosopher David Hume (1711–1776).

In the grand scheme of modern philosophical history, Hume is seen as one of the "big three" of *British Empiricism*, the other two being John Locke and George Berkeley. British Empiricism as a philosophical movement is contrasted with the *Continental Rationalism* of the same time, which was also represented by three influential philosophers, namely Descartes, Gottfried Leibniz, and Benedict Spinoza. The empiricist and rationalist movements differed radically in their methodologies, which naturally brought about highly contrasting philosophical results. But both were responses to the post-Renaissance liberation from the medieval thought models that limited the source of all knowledge primarily to divine revelation.

The rationalist response was to give the mind free reign over its imaginative impulses, and to see what it can come up with, *by pure reasoning alone*, in regard to knowledge about God, mind, substance, space, time, and so on. Descartes's *Meditations* are a paradigm of this method, starting as they do in a philosophical environment of total doubt and methodically reconstructing, in a completely *a priori* manner, knowledge of God and disembodied minds.

The empiricist response was also to recognize the powers of the mind, but to limit what it can know to the *deliverances of experience only*. Taking their cue from the successes of the great scientists of their time, like Francis Bacon, Galileo, and Isaac Newton, the empiricists also attempted to methodically reconstruct the world and humanity's place in it, but they did so in a completely *a posteriori* manner through analysis of their experience as presented by sense perception and memory. By contrast, the model of discovery employed by the rationalists was not science but pure mathematics, in particular, axiomatic geometry. Indeed, Spinoza's great work, *Ethics*, has the organization of an immense geometrical proof, and a similar character infuses much of the work of Descartes and Leibniz. So while the source of all knowledge for the empiricists was experience, for rationalists reason itself could produce knowledge, and not just in science but in metaphysics as well. As Bacon described the difference, "Empiricists are like ants, they collect and put to use; but rationalists, like spiders, spin threads out of themselves."[17]

Berkelian Idealism

It is interesting that the experience constraint resulted in quite different philosophical systems even within the British empiricist camp, and it is a testament to the extent to which personal inclinations regarding religion can influence the outcome of philosophical investigation. For Berkeley (1685–1753), an Anglican bishop, experience gives knowledge only of our sensations, perceptions, ideas, and so on, all of which exist only in the mind. Conspicuously missing from this list of knowable things is anything which presumably exists outside the mind, like the *matter* of which physical objects are composed. In fact, for Berkeley, the empiricist program forces him to conclude that the concept of matter is incoherent:

> By *matter* ... we are to understand an inert, senseless substance, in which extension, figure, and motion do actually subsist. But it is evident from what we have already shown, that extension, figure, and motion are only ideas existing in the mind, and that an idea can be like nothing but another idea, and that consequently neither they nor their archetypes can exist in an unperceiving substance. Hence, it is plain that the very notion of what is called *matter*, or *corporeal substance*, involves a contradiction in it.[18]

Since for Berkeley the concept of matter existing outside the mind is incoherent, he must somehow explain the nature of what we take to be physical objects, including our own bodies. His answer was a version of *idealism*, or the view that matter, like all ideas, cannot exist except by being perceived. The argument runs as follows. What we perceive with the senses can be nothing but our own ideas or sensations of shape, color, sound, and so on. Since houses, mountains, rivers, and so on are things we perceive with our senses, they are nothing but our own ideas or sensations. Now, since ideas or sensations cannot exist unperceived (they go away when we are not employing our sense modalities), then houses, mountains, rivers, and so on cannot exist unperceived either. Thus for everything that there is, including physical objects, *Esse est percipi*, or, "To be is to be perceived."

While Berkeley was regarded as something of an eccentric, even he recognized the disastrous consequences his doctrine would have for science, which relies on physical objects existing in a stable manner regardless of whether they are actually being perceived by anyone at any given time. It must be the case that the objects of science exist independently of the minds of the scientists who study them, and so Berkeley turns to religion to ensure this:

> To me it is evident ... that sensible things cannot exist otherwise than in a mind or spirit. Whence I conclude, not that they have no real existence, but that seeing they depend not on my thought, and have an existence distinct from being perceived by me, *there must be some other mind wherein they exist.* As sure therefore as the sensible world really exists, so sure is there an infinite, omnipresent Spirit who contains and supports it.[19]

The Skepticism of Hume

We see then that both rationalists and empiricists could be heavily influenced by matters of religion in their philosophy. David Hume's philosophy was a reaction against both the rampant idealism of Berkeley and the speculative metaphysics of the rationalists. His was one of the first important accounts in the modern era which neither sought to justify religious claims through philosophical analysis, as Descartes did, nor to appeal to religious concepts to solve philosophical problems, as we saw in Berkeley.

Hume was an empiricist who divided what humans can know into two types of propositions. The first, what he called *matters of fact*, are typically those with which the natural sciences are concerned and which are supported by experience (including memory) and observation. He called the second type *relations of ideas*, which can be known simply by consideration of the concepts involved. This category includes the statements of mathematics and logic, for example, "Triangles have three sides" and "Either p is the case or it is not." It was primarily by his analysis of how we come to know matters of fact that Hume came to embrace a thoroughgoing skepticism, or doubt, about the existence of any unexperienced objects including God and disembodied minds. Interestingly, Descartes's agenda was just the opposite: to begin with doubt about everything he knows other than that he thinks, and to spin from this a complex metaphysical web involving God and disembodied minds.

Hume acknowledged that reason combined with the imagination could produce vast and coherent systems of metaphysical philosophy, but he doubted that such systems had any correspondence with reality. When he tried to use experience and observation to reveal the peculiar and intimate relationship between the mind (or alternatively, the *will* or the *soul*) and the body, he came up completely empty:

> The motion of our body follows upon the command of our will. Of this we are every moment conscious. But the means by which this is effected, the energy by which the will performs so extraordinary an operation—of this we are so far from being immediately conscious that it must forever escape our most diligent inquiry. ... [I]s there any principle in all nature more mysterious than the union of soul with body, by which a supposed spiritual substance acquires such an influence over a material one that the most refined thought is able to actuate the grossest matter?[20]

Hume's skepticism concerning the existence of the mind apart from the material body was part of a more overreaching condemnation of all inquiry that was not supported by either logic, mathematics, or experience. He was insistent on these empiricist constraints and came down hard on anything outside their purview with a passion:

> When we run over libraries, persuaded of these principles, what havoc must we make? If we take in our hand any volume—of divinity or school metaphysics, for instance—let us ask, *Does it contain any abstract reasoning concerning quantity or number?* No. *Does it contain any experimental reasoning concerning matter of fact and existence?* No. Commit it then to the flames, for it can contain nothing but sophistry and illusion.[21]

If Berkeley was an empiricist to a fault, producing as he did a most counterintuitive idealism, Hume also was an empiricist to a fault, being committed to a skepticism that was debilitating in its scope. The same unbending commitment to the deliverances of experience required by his condemnation of rampant metaphysics would also reduce concepts central to science to ones with unsatisfyingly weak meanings. Physical objects become bundles of perceptions, for example. Just as troubling is what becomes of our knowledge of the relationship between *causes* and their *effects*:

> I shall venture to affirm, as a general proposition which admits of no exception, that the knowledge of this relation [cause and effect] is not, in any instance, attained by reasonings a priori, but arises entirely from experience, when we find that any particular objects are constantly conjoined with each other.[22]

Thus, the causal relation expressed by "the sun causes the stone to become warm" is not knowable through any connection *between* the events of the sun shining on the stone and the stone becoming warm, but through the mere constant conjunction of events of these types. So causality becomes reduced in meaning to the constant conjunction of events. But how could the mere constant conjunction of events justify the sweeping causal laws of science, whereby precise predictions of not yet observed events are routinely and accurately made? In our simple example, Hume would claim that our knowing that in the past the event of the sun shining on the stone is constantly conjoined with the stone growing warm justifies our belief that the sun shining on the stone tomorrow will be accompanied by the stone becoming warm. But why do we make this prediction of the future if all that causality involves is a constant conjunction of events which we have experienced in the past? Is there not more to causal laws than what we can glean from experience? For Hume, ever the empiricist, the answer is of course no, and moreover he has an explanation for why we make judgments about the unobserved on the basis of the observed: the principle of *custom* or *habit*.

Of course, the basing of the vast causal structure of science on a tenuous psychological mechanism was and is more than most philosophers could tolerate, and for them Hume's analyses, as brilliant as they were, amounted to a telling example of the excesses of thoroughgoing empiricism. But though his view shakes out as one of studied skepticism, his method would lay the groundwork for materialist accounts of the relationship between mind and body. While it is the nature of skepticism to *doubt*, it is likewise incumbent on skepticism to *not rule out*, and though Hume's empiricist strictures can seem scientifically suffocating, they also allowed him to imagine scenarios unheard of for his day. In an essay on the immortality of the soul published posthumously, Hume would muse about mind/body materialism:

> Matter, therefore, and spirit, are at bottom equally unknown,
> and we cannot determine what qualities inhere in the one or in
> the other. They likewise teach us that nothing can be decided *a
> priori* concerning any cause or effect, and that experience being
> the only source of our judgements of this nature, we cannot know
> from any other principle, whether matter, by its structure or
> arrangement, may not be the cause of thought.[23]

Musings of this sort would open the way for computational and physicalistic models of the mind required by AI. But the seedbeds of modern AI are not to be found *exclusively* in empiricist soil.

Unfortunately for Hume, his radically empiricist views would not be taken seriously until more than one hundred years following his death. The rationalism inspired originally by Descartes would find adherents in various forms during the centuries leading to 1900. But fresh ideas relevant to modern AI would be found in the rationalist systems of Hume's contemporaries, and with the benefit of hindsight we see now that both movements, empiricism and rationalism, contributed to fertilizing the fields for AI. As we have seen, the rationalists were willing to give the mind more powers in arriving at *a priori* knowledge of reality. This would give philosophers valuable hypotheses about the mind's own structure and operation, which could not help but be useful in artificially modeling it. As Santillana remarked: "The true scientist has an empiricist conscience and a rationalist imagination."[24] This is certainly true about many of today's computer scientists who are involved in AI.

In his unwitting role as AI critic, Descartes had observed that since the mind, a thing that thinks, is wholly independent of the body, then it would not be possible to create a reasoning, thinking being only out of extended matter. It is possible to debate this claim on two grounds. First, one could deny that the dualism asserted in the premiss actually implies the conclusion. So, a counterargument would go, just because human thought does not depend on matter, this does not mean that some other kind of thought, perhaps something akin to human thought but not the same as it, could not be created exclusively in matter. While it would be possible to argue this way, a perhaps easier approach is to answer Descartes in the second way, which is to deny the premiss asserting dualism.

Descartes's brand of dualism has been called *dualistic interactionism* because, although the mind and body are separate kinds of entities, nevertheless they affect one another in a manner tantamount to causal interaction. So, for example, the bodily event of burned flesh causes the mental event of pain, which in turn causes removal of the hand from the fire, again a bodily event. Now natural science regards a causal chain of events as occurring within a physical realm only, but here we have a chain of events made up of a mental event sandwiched between two physical events. Since dualism holds that mental events are independent of physical events, how then can mental events cause physical events and vice versa? For many philosophers today, this is a major problem with dualistic interactionism, regardless of whether they think that dualism is a problem for AI, and it is cause for dualism's rejection.

But many great post-Renaissance philosophers took alternative approaches as well. We have already seen how Hume's extreme empiricism compelled him to adopt a consistent epistemological skepticism regarding the self, matter, God, afterlife—anything that is not immediately perceived. While radical, and a definite attack against dualism, skepticism as a philosophical attitude amounts to general agnosticism, and does not offer a positive system on which to base an account of either the mind or the world.

Leibniz and Preestablished Harmony

Some early modern philosophers wanted to maintain dualism, but not the interactionist variety advocated by Descartes. The greatest example of such a thinker was Gottfried Leibniz (1646–1716), the German philosopher, scientist, mathematician, and historian. Like many thinkers of his time, Leibniz was committed to a mind/body distinction, but he did not think that mental and physical events could have causal effects on one another. In his *Discourse on Metaphysics*, he purports to give

> the explanation of that great mystery "the union of the soul and
> the body," that is to say how it comes about that the passions
> and actions of the one are accompanied by the actions and
> passions or else the appropriate phenomena of the other. For it is
> not possible to conceive how one can have an influence upon the
> other.[25]

Leibniz's "explanation" involves a conception of mental and physical events as realms which *appear* to us to causally influence one another, but which in actuality are independent realms whose actions are contrived to behave in a manner apparently exhibiting mutual influence by a force external to the persons whose lives involve the mental and physical events. As Leibniz describes it,

> I believe that those who are careful thinkers will decide favorably
> for our principles because of this single reason, viz., that they are
> able to see in what consists the relation between the soul and the
> body, a parallelism which appears inexplicable in any other way.[26]

Thus *parallelism* has come to be known as a version of dualism which denies that the mind can influence the body or vice versa. It then becomes incumbent upon the parallelist to explain the apparent influence between the mental and physical realms.

The only explanation, if there is no causal link between apparently intimately related events like the burning of flesh and the feeling of pain, is divine. In the version of parallelism known as *occasionalism*,[27] there is continuous divine intervention in the mental life of people, such that, for example, on the occasion of the flesh being burned, God causes a feeling of pain in the subject. Leibniz, like many philosophers today, found this view just as counterintuitive as interactionist dualism, remarking,

> [I]t is unreasonable to have recourse at once to the extraordinary
> intervention of the universal cause [God] in an ordinary and
> particular case.[28]

Thus, while God may participate as an originating cause of all things, he
cannot be thought of as everywhere causing all the routine and mundane
mental events of all persons' lives.

Still, Leibniz adhered to parallelistic dualism, only he attributed the
apparent close connection between the parallel lives of the mind (or soul,
as he termed it) and body to a *preestablished harmony* between them. In
The Monadology, Leibniz considers the decomposition of all substance,
both physical and mental, into its simple, indivisible, parts, and calls
these simple substances *monads*. Though simple, monads nonetheless
reflect multiplicity by the relations they bear to all other monads:

> Now this interconnection, relationship, or this adaptation of all
> things to each particular one, and of each one to all the rest,
> brings it about that every simple substance has relations which
> express all the others and that it is consequently a perpetual
> living mirror of the universe.[29]

Now this is a difficult step for many to fathom—that all monads, including
those that are minds and those that make up bodies, contain within them
representations of all there is. But it is enough for Leibniz to formulate
his version of parallelism:

> The soul follows its own laws, and the body likewise follows its
> own laws. They are fitted to each other in virtue of the
> preestablished harmony between all substances, since they are all
> representations of one and the same universe. Souls act in
> accordance with the laws of final causes through their desires,
> ends and means. Bodies act in accordance with the laws of
> efficient causes or of motion. The two realms, that of efficient
> causes and that of final causes, are in harmony, each with the
> other.[30]

This harmony, of course, is not accidental and must be brought about by
God:

> In the case of simple substances, the influence which one monad
> has upon another is only ideal. It can have its effect only through
> the mediation of God. ... For since one created monad cannot
> have a physical influence upon the inner being of another, it is
> only through the primal regulation that one can have dependence
> upon another.

To the modern mind, dualistic parallelism seems even more indefensible than dualistic interactionism. But we have seen that important philosophers even from antiquity adopted a stance against both. This stance, which we now call *monism*, asserts that persons are made up of a singular kind of stuff, thereby immediately sidestepping both the problem of the causal interaction of mental and bodily events, and the divine intervention required by parallelism. For, according to monism, our linguistic categorization of events into "the mental" and "the physical" does not reflect distinct ontological categories; our use of these terms simply facilitates practical discourse about persons. Monistic theories differ in the nature of the substance of which persons are actually composed. *Materialistic* monism holds that this substance is matter, the same kind of thing studied by natural scientists. We saw how Epicurus and Lucretius of antiquity were proponents of materialism. On this view, material things can think, since persons, who think, are material things.

While few of the empiricist or rationalist philosophers of the seventeenth and eighteenth centuries can be classified as materialists, there are other kinds of monism besides materialism. We have seen that Berkeley, who held that the only things that exist are ideas, was an advocate of *idealism*, which denies the existence of matter. While the strict removal of the mind as a thinking thing from the realm of extended bodies represented for Descartes an obvious reason for thinking material things could not think, there is no corresponding conclusion to draw from idealism. In fact, since according to Berkelian idealism all sensible things, including both persons and computer programs, "cannot exist otherwise than in a mind or spirit," then presumably computer programs, which exist and thus are part of a mind, could participate in what a mind does, which is think. A justification for AI would come pretty easy if it were based on Berkelian idealism, but the price for holding such a nonscientific view today would be high.

Spinoza and Monism

Another monistic view was advocated by the Dutchman Benedict Spinoza (1632–1677). Spinoza's monism is sometimes called *double-aspect theory*, because it characterizes mind and matter as two aspects of a substance which is in essence neither mental nor material. This substance, whose essence is existence, is called God. Since this substance is all that there is, God is all that there is, and everything that we think or perceive is an attribute of God. In his great work, *The Ethics*, Spinoza says:

> [T]he human mind is part of the infinite intellect of God; thus
> when we say, that the human mind perceives this or that, we
> make the assertion, that God has this or that idea.[31]

But for Spinoza God is also the totality of all matter, including our bodies.
So while the human mind in a sense thinks with God, it is also intimately
connected to the activities of the body:

> [O]ur mind can only be said to endure, and its existence can only
> be defined by a fixed time, in so far as it involves the actual
> existence of the body.[32]

And also:

> The mind is, only while the body endures.[33]

Double-aspect theory is discredited today because of problems with describing the "third," but primary, kind of stuff of which the mental and
the physical of ordinary discourse are aspects. If the substance of all that
there is is neither mental nor physical, then what is it?

But regardless of the metaphysical underpinnings of what there is for
Spinoza, he is important to modern AI for a reason which is subtle yet
evident throughout the entire work of *The Ethics*. The organization of
this work is modeled on a vast system of geometry complete with definitions, axioms, postulates, proofs, and lemmas. More than simply reflecting a methodological or didactic preference, this choice of presentation, as
much as the content of Spinoza's work, exposes his fundamental intuitions
about human thought. In the introduction to part III, "On the Origin
and Nature of the Emotions," he justifies his presentation "to those, who
would rather abuse or deride human emotions than understand them":

> Such persons will, doubtless think it strange that I should
> attempt to treat of human vice and folly geometrically, and
> should wish to set forth with rigid reasoning those matters which
> they cry out against as repugnant to reason, frivolous, absurd,
> and dreadful. However, such is my plan. ... [N]ature's laws and
> ordinances, whereby all things come to pass and change from one
> form to another, are everywhere and always the same; so that
> there should be one and the same method of understanding the
> nature of all things whatsoever, namely, through nature's
> universal laws and rules. ... I shall, therefore, treat of the nature
> and strength of the emotions according to the same method, as I
> employed heretofore in my investigations concerning God and the
> mind. I shall consider human actions and desires in exactly the
> same manner, as though I were concerned with lines, planes, and
> solids.[34]

Spinoza's commitment to understanding the universal order, therefore, necessarily extends to human thought, and the model he chooses to describe it, geometry, is decidedly *computational*. So while his version of monism may be difficult to justify, his model of the mind in geometric and computational terms is a crucial early indication of the attitude that would one day compel people to claim intelligence for certain computer programs.

AI and the Rise of Contemporary Science and Philosophy

Historical Interest in Robots and Automata

The contributions of philosophy to what would become modern AI accelerated in the mid to late 1800s with the beginnings of the development of logic as we know it today. As we shall see in chapter 5, there was ancient interest in symbolic representations of reasoning, but the disciplined study of the forms of reasoning then languished for centuries. Still, humankind's fascination with artificial emulations of other aspects of life often revealed itself in both deceptively real artifacts and mythical fabricated beings. This anticipated today's science of *robotics*, a branch of artificial intelligence concerned with emulating physical action rather than conscious thought.[1] The *Iliad* mythologizes artificial creatures like gangly walking tripods forged by the divine blacksmith Hephaestus, and the patrolling copper giant Talos molded by Daedalus. Egyptian mythology mentions the god Amon being embodied in a moving and speaking statue, who would decide among eligible heirs of a departed pharoah as they were marched before it. Of course, a concealed priest controlling levers was responsible for the movement and speech, but there would come attempts at creating truly autonomous artificial beings based on mechanisms. In the Greek city of Alexandria, for example, we are told of mechanical moving and singing ravens powered by the force of water.

Public appetite for automata surged in the late Middle Ages and the Renaissance:

> Roger Bacon reportedly spent seven years constructing talking
> figures. To honor Louis XII, Leonardo da Vinci built an
> automaton in the shape of a lion. During the sixteenth and
> seventeenth centuries, Italian and French designers, such as Gio
> Battista Aleotti and Salomon de Caus, elaborated on designs of

the Alexandrian school: gardens and grottoes resonated with the songs of artificial birds and mechanical flutists, while fully animated nymphs, dragons, and satyrs pepped up aristocratic receptions. René Descartes built in 1649 an automaton that he called "my daughter Francine." But on one of Descartes' trips, a superstitious ship captain happened to open the case containing Francine and, frightened by her lifelike movements, threw case and contents overboard.

By the eighteenth century, the French artisan Jacques de Vaucanson could assemble his celebrated duck, which provided an almost complete imitation of its model. One prospectus described it as an "artificial duck of golden Copper that Drinks, Eats, Croaks, Splashes in water and Digests as a live duck." Life-sized, the animal rested on a waist-high case containing a drum engraved with cogs and grooves. Control rods passing through the duck's legs caused it to move in a manner programmed in the cogs: today we would call the drum a Read Only Memory (ROM) device.[2]

Of course, the automating of lifelike action is but a feat of engineering, however impressive, and has nothing to do with automating or modeling reasoning or any other cognitive activity. But success with cogs, gears, and cams would soon encourage attempts in the nineteenth century to automate a most definitely cognitive activity, namely computation. Certainly, devices for alleviating the mental burden of counting and adding, like the abacus, had been around for centuries. And later aids like navigation tables would assist even more complex calculations. Even general-purpose calculating machines were conceived and built by Leibniz and Pascal. But all these devices suffered from the drawback of being able to specify and perform only one calculation at a time.

Charles Babbage (1792–1871) is credited, one hundred years before the first electronic digital computer, with conceiving what we today call the *stored program computer*. He had the idea that the mechanical workings of a device can be both conceptually and physically separated from its control by strictly distinguishing the device's *store* from its *mill*.[3] Babbage had a design for such a device, called the *analytical engine*, which would perform complex arithmetic calculations using its mill by following instructions encoded in its store. These instructions, which would be transmitted to the store through the use of punched cards, amounted to a *program* for the mill. Since different programs could be devised for different calculations without changing anything about the device's mill, the analytical engine could be regarded as a flexible and general purpose calculating machine. The person responsible for creating the punched cards for the analytical engine was Ada, countess of Lovelace and daughter of the poet Lord Byron. Babbage and Ada were therefore the world's first computer programmers. Unfortunately, the design of the analytical engine was beyond the capability of anyone to build, and it remained just that, a design. Today, of course, Babbage's notions of *store* and *mill* find embodiment in millions of computers as *memory* and *processor*.

While Babbage was just about one hundred years ahead of his time as far as the actual creation of programmable calculating machines, in his time there could be heard the rumblings of what would become explosive growth in the development of symbolic logic. From his time on up to the first digital electronic computer, mathematicians and logicians would begin formalizing impressive systems of logic which would provide the bases for the first artificial intelligence programs. But at the same time thinking about the mind began to take on a contemporary look.

Challenges to Dualism

Scientific advances in the nineteenth century in biology, medicine, and physiology began to change the outlook and vocabulary begun by Descartes in framing the metaphysical problem of the relation between mind and body. Such advances changed the terms of discussion from the more general "mind/body" problem to the more specific "consciousness/brain" problem, namely, what role does the brain play in conscious thought? And conversely, what effect can states of consciousness have on brain activity? Of the first question, that there was a strict dependence of mental action on neural change was becoming obvious. The effects on consciousness of blows to the head, epileptic seizures, alcohol and coffee consumption, and so on had always been known, but new discoveries involving the effects of damaged or diseased brains on memory and motor control, as well as detailed studies of the nervous systems of nonhuman animals, were beginning to make the relationship between certain brain states and states of consciousness determinate and predictable. The American philosopher and psychologist William James (1842–1910) put it clearly in 1892:

> *The immediate condition of a state of consciousness is an activity of some sort in the cerebral hemispheres.* This proposition is supported by so many pathological facts, and laid by physiologists at the base of so many of their reasonings, that to the medically educated mind it seems almost axiomatic. ... [T]he simple and radical conception dawns upon the mind that mental action may be uniformly and absolutely a function of brain-action, varying as the latter varies, and being to the brain-action as effect to cause.[4]

James used the term *medical materialism* to refer to the view that, in principle, any mental state of consciousness, from a feeling of pain to a spiritual revelation, can be explained in terms of an underlying state of the brain's neural system. It is not, however, true mind/body materialism, because it does not commit anyone who holds it to metaphysical monism. In fact, holding this view amounts to dualistic interactionism if one also believes that states of consciousness can exert causal influences on brain processes. Thus, one would still be a Cartesian dualist if one agreed with James's quote above, and also with the view that states of consciousness in the form of acts of volition, for example, one's intending to move one's arm, can cause the appropriate brain processes that ultimately result, via a chain of neurophysiological events, in the motion of one's arm.

However, the success of science in identifying sufficient causal conditions for bodily processes and events simply in terms of *other* bodily processes and events, led some to deny that states of consciousness, though they exist and are caused by brain events, have any causal efficacy themselves at all. This view has come to be known as *epiphenomenalism*, since according to it all mental events are mere *epi*phenomena, in the sense that they depend for their existence on brain events, like shadows depend for their existence on the objects casting them, but they are enjoined from having any physical effects themselves, just as shadows are. So when my hand is burned by fire, there is pain and I remove my hand from the fire, but the removal need not be causally explained by the feeling of pain. Rather, a complete causal chain of neurophysiological events, starting with the burning of nerve endings and the transmission of an electrochemical message to the brain, and ending with a similar transmission from the brain to the muscles of my arm, is all that is necessary to explain the removal of my arm. My feeling of pain is only incidental, an ontological parasite which comes into being then passes away with no effect. It has as much ontological significance, the philosopher C.J. Ducasse put it, as a halo on a saint.

Huxley and Epiphenomenalism

Epiphenomenalism was the view of nineteenth century biologist Thomas Huxley (1825–1895), who was convinced of it by experiments on animals and experience with neurophysiological injuries in people. By studying the results of elaborate spinal cord severings and brain separations in frogs, Huxley came to believe that Descartes was correct in describing animals as marvelously complex and efficient machines, that is, as automata, but incorrect in thinking that animals are not conscious. He was thus compelled to conclude that nonhuman animals are conscious automata. To square the notion of an organism's being a machine with its also being conscious, Huxley regarded conscious states as epiphenomena:

> It may be assumed, then, that molecular changes in the brain are the causes of all the states of consciousness of brutes. Is there any evidence that these states of consciousness may, conversely, cause those molecular changes which give rise to muscular motion? I see no such evidence. The frog walks, hops, swims, and goes through his gymnastic performances quite as well without consciousness, and consequently without volition, as with it. ... The consciousness of brutes would appear to be related to the mechanism of their body simply as a collateral product of its working, and to be as completely without any power of modifying that working as the steam-whistle which accompanies the work of a locomotive engine is without influence upon its machinery.[5]

That the notion of a conscious automaton even made sense would have been good news for anyone trying to create artificial intelligence in the nineteenth century, for this seems to allow that it is at least in principle possible to build a machine that thinks. But genuine AI is the attempt to artificially create behavior that we would regard as requiring intelligence if observed in *humans*. For Huxley, who agreed with Darwin's theory of evolution, it was no great leap to argue by analogy from nonhuman to human animals:

> It is quite true that, to the best of my judgement, the argumentation which applies to brutes holds equally good of men; and therefore, that all states of consciousness in us, as in them, are immediately caused by molecular changes of the brain-substance. It seems to me that in men, as in brutes, there is no proof that any state of consciousness is the cause of change in the motion of the matter of the organism. ... [T]he feeling we call volition is not the cause of a voluntary act, but the symbol of that state of the brain which is the immediate cause of that act. We are conscious automata.[6]

Although epiphenomenalism is consistent with the idea of a conscious automaton, which itself is consistent with the idea of AI, epiphenomenalism is open to two basic philosophical objections. The first is that it *arbitrarily* singles out one of the two "causation directions" between mental and physical events as being untenable. After all, if it is perfectly legitimate to admit of a causal relationship, across categories, between a brain event (the cause) and a feeling of pain (the effect), why should it not be legitimate to go in the other direction, across the same categories, and admit of a relationship between a feeling of pain (the cause) and the first brain event (the effect) triggering the sequence of events resulting in moving the hand?

The second objection to epiphenomenalism is that, even if singling out one of the causation directions is not arbitrary, it is nevertheless indefensible, for there remains a causal relationship across categories, one of which is not physical. There is nothing in our physiological description of the brain that affirms a causal connection between objective patterns of neural activity and the subjective content of inner experience. The only things that patterns of neural activity can be said to cause are *other* patterns of neural activity. Indeed, so this objection goes, the subjective content of inner experience, in terms of pains, ideas, and perceptions, is not even part of the *language* describing the patterns of neurophysiological cause and effect in brains, and it would be a logical mistake to include such terms in this language.

While this objection has force, it is undeniable that there is a correlation, if not an outright causal connection, between states of the brain and the subjective states of consciousness. As twentieth-century science continued to discover more about the organization and function of the brain, the nagging question of how the mind and body are related continued to vex scientists. As the scientist Lord Adrian put it:

> The part of our picture of the brain which may always be missing is, of course, the part which deals with the mind, the part which ought to explain how a particular pattern of nerve impulses can produce an idea; or the other way round, how a thought can decide which nerve cells are to come into action. ... My own feeling is that before the trouble comes to a head it will have been solved by some enlargement of the boundaries of natural science.[7]

In a continuing optimism begun through the enlightening effects of the birth of modern science three hundred years before at the time of Descartes, this was typical of a new attitude which held that simply by delving deeper into brain research, we would sooner or later uncover the mysterious connection between brain states and the subjective states of consciousness, like finding treasure in the back of a deep cave. Indeed, Descartes even speculated that the seat of human consciousness would turn out to be in the location of the pineal gland.

But while Descartes will always be regarded as pivotal in intellectual history's move from medieval to modern thought in science and philosophy, his framing of the mind/body problem in terms of material versus immaterial "substance" would cause some twentieth-century philosophers to regard the problem as intractable. So at the same time that science was making headway in understanding the brain, some philosophers began to seriously doubt that the so-called problem of mind and body was even being correctly posed.

Ayer, Logical Positivism, and the Identity Theory

In the 1920s, a movement that would become known as *logical positivism* began in Europe. Seeking the same sort of progress in philosophy that was being witnessed in science, particularly physics, logical positivism wanted to succeed where Immanuel Kant (1724–1804) had failed "to set philosophy upon the sure path of a science." The positivists saw Hume's admonition to "commit to the flames" any work which does not reason either abstractly about quantity or experimentally about matters of fact, as their founding principle in bringing this about. Its modern positivist form ran like this: For any proposition to have any meaning, either it must be a tautology of mathematics or logic, or its truth must be empirically verifiable; a proposition which fails either of these criteria is literally meaningless or nonsensical. One of the most eloquent spokespersons for this point of view was A.J. Ayer (1910–1989), who described the positivist approach as follows:

> A great deal of philosophical talk was held to fall into this
> category [the nonsensical]: talk about the absolute, or
> transcendent entities, or substance, or the destiny of man. Such
> utterances were said to be metaphysical; and the conclusion
> drawn was that if philosophy was to constitute a genuine branch
> of knowledge it must emancipate itself from metaphysics.[8]

Included in the category of nonsensical talk was anything having to do with the mind characterized as immaterial substance being affected by material events. Positivism was thus a direct attack on Cartesian dualism as well as its one-way derivative constituting epiphenomenalism. The positivists believed that interactionist dualism in any form could be discounted simply by analyzing the meaning of the terms involved:

> [S]ince the mind has no position in space—it is by definition not
> the sort of thing that can have a position in space—it does not
> literally make sense to talk of physical signals reaching it.[9]

While it may be true that it makes no sense to speak of a causal connection between the material and the immaterial, it is still the case that our language permits us to *correlate* events described physically and events described mentally. Hume's admonition that correlation of events does not justify the ascription of causal power of one toward the other, even if it was difficult to accept within the pure physical realm, was very persuasive when the causation was held to cross the boundary between the physical and mental. Still, the evident correlation of events described physically and events described mentally needed to be explained. Any twentieth-century philosopher of mind who accepted the positivist critique of interactionist dualism seemed forced either to revert to the excesses of parallelist dualism or to accept a monist account. Parallelism was regarded as a step backward that virtually no analytic philosopher would take. Thus many philosophers who could not countenance the cross-category causation from brain state to conscious state chose to eliminate the categorical distinction entirely and *identify* the brain state with the conscious state. This is the essence of modern materialism, also called the *identity theory.* If this theory is correct, the argument for AI becomes easier to make, since the arena of thought and consciousness is entirely physical.

Ryle and the Ghost in the Machine

However, the relegation of all metaphysical talk, in particular talk about immaterial minds, to meaninglessness as intoned by the positivists, was regarded by many twentieth-century philosophers as an overreaction to the perplexities presented by the mind/body problem. There are at least two ways to react against the Cartesian hypothesis of the existence of an immaterial mode of being in which the properties of mind, including thought, consciousness, and reasoning, are supposed to inhere. The positivist way, we have seen, is to write off all talk of the immaterial mind causally affecting material objects as simply linguistically incoherent, or meaningless. Another way is to regard such talk not as meaningless, but as a victim of the fallacy of committing a *category mistake.* This was the view proposed by Gilbert Ryle (1900–1976) in the middle of the century. A category mistake is committed when an entity of one sort, or category, is incorrectly included in another category, resulting in an improper predication of properties for that entity. A classic example is that of a child, taken for the first time to view a parade, who witnesses a procession of marching bands, floats, and clowns. When it is over the child asks, "Where is the parade?" The child incorrectly includes the concept of a parade within the category of objects that make up a parade.

Ryle believed that Descartes committed a category mistake by regarding humans both as machines, as described by causal mechanical laws, and as minds, as described by equally causal but paramechanical laws in an immaterial realm. Ryle derisively called the Cartesian view "the dogma of the ghost in the machine" and attributed to it the origins of the modern mind/body problem. For it views the mind and body as polar opposites of the same sort, rather than as objects in totally different categories. To even ask how the mind can cause bodily events is to commit the same sort of mistake as the child asking where the parade is, because the language we use to describe the behavior of bodily events is no more appropriately applied to the realm of the mental than the term "parade" is appropriately applied to the individual objects which in their totality make up a parade.

While it is an abuse of language to commit a category mistake, for Ryle this does not necessarily have ontological significance. There *are* things like parades and marching bands and floats, but it is a mistake to include them in the same category. Similarly, there *are* instances of correct linguistic usage of physical and mental terms, but it is a mistake to use them as though they referred to objects in one category of thing. Consider: "She came home in a flood of tears" and "She came home in a sedan chair." Each sentence makes sense when considered singly; but "She came home in a flood of tears and a sedan chair" is an abuse of language because it does not distinguish two separate uses of the preposition "in," one of which describes an emotional state, while the other indicates physical containment. Similarly, according to Ryle our reaction to the mistake of positing a "ghost in the machine" should not be to radically change our ontology:

> [T]he hallowed contrast between Mind and Matter will be dissipated, but dissipated not by either of the equally hallowed absorptions of Mind by Matter or of Matter by Mind. ... [B]oth Idealism and Materialism are answers to an improper question. The "reduction" of the material world to mental states and processes, as well as the "reduction" of mental states and processes to physical states and processes, presuppose the legitimacy of the disjunction "Either there exist minds or there exist bodies (but not both)." ... It is perfectly proper to say, in one logical tone of voice, that there exist minds and to say, in another logical tone of voice, that there exist bodies. But these expressions do not indicate two different species of existence.[10]

We see in Ryle, then, a modern incarnation of the double-aspect theory, a monistic theory that is neither idealist nor materialist concerning minds. If pressed for what exactly a man is, Ryle is careful not to betray any metaphysical prejudice:

> Man need not be degraded to a machine by being denied to be a
> ghost in a machine. He might, after all, be a sort of animal,
> namely, a higher mammal. There has yet to be ventured the
> hazardous leap to the hypothesis that perhaps he is a man.[11]

For many, any double-aspect theory begs the question of what a person is. If not mind and not matter, then what? Materialism at least offers an answer, and with the advent of digital electronic computers it also offered a test bed through AI. But it is important to realize that while a materialist theory of the mind might make arguing for AI easier, it is by no means sufficient for AI to succeed. The AI enthusiast must also defend a model of reasoning that is *computational* in nature, and on top of that must defend the particular *cognitive architecture* within that model. In the middle of the twentieth century, at the dawn of modern AI, computers were judged to be the ideal means for implementing such a cognitive model based on mathematical logic. Before that time, however, it would be necessary for philosophers and mathematicians to lay more foundational groundwork in the development of logic. The better understood logic became, the more tempting it proved to be as the language of artificial intelligence.

Part II

The New Encounter of Science and Philosophy

– 5 –
AI and Logic

Logic is sometimes characterized normatively as the study of *correct* as opposed to *fallacious* reasoning, that is, as the study of how one *ought* to think in argumentation. For example, I.M. Copi starts his book on logic with "Logic is the study of the methods and principles used to distinguish good (correct) from bad (incorrect) reasoning."[1] However, in order to know what good reasoning even is, we must first investigate the means by which we draw conclusions based on the things we already know. Therefore, logic is often alternatively characterized as the study of the *consequence relation*, which is the relation that holds between the things we know as antecedents in a case of reasoning, and anything we can know on the basis of these antecendents, that is, the conclusion. On this view, logic is like a science in that it studies things that occur in nature, namely instances of actual reasoning, and explicates the underlying relation of logical consequence.[2]

Note that this distinction between logic as the study of the consequence relation and logic as a normative activity is somewhat analogous to the distinction between AI as the pursuit of emulating *human* thought and AI as the pursuit of emulating *rational* thought. In the former cases the focus is on studying and describing a natural process, while in the latter cases the focus is on creating a normative standard. From the point of view of AI, the descriptive approach to logic as a study of the consequence relation is most valuable, because it provides something concrete, namely the natural phenomenon of human reasoning, on which to base a model. The normative approach, rather than simply studying how it is that humans in fact draw conclusions, must *compare* human reasoning against an idealized model of correct reasoning. The construction of such an idealized standard is difficult and also unnecessary if one's goal is the construction of models of how humans actually reason, regardless of whether they do it as an idealized agent would. This counterpoint, and sometimes tension, between the normative and the descriptive arises in other aspects of the relation between philosophy and AI, as we shall see.

Most modeling activities include two primary objectives: (1) the creation of the model and (2) the testing of the model. For example, the ocean-going vessel designer first creates a replica and then places it in a tank where its reaction to waves and how it drafts can be observed. Or, the demographer first creates a formula for specifying a mathematical series intended to mirror population growth, and then applies it to actual past generations to determine whether it correctly predicts successive population numbers. As a final example, the large-scale integrated circuit designer first builds a model of, say, a next generation microprocessor, using a formal hardware description language. Then, she observes the input/output behavior of this "virtual" microprocessor by simulating its running on a number of hypothetical electrical inputs.

The modeling of human reasoning through logic is no different. It's just that work on the first objective, the creation of the model, began over two millenia ago, while realizing the second objective, the testing of the model, was not possible until the advent of digital electronic computers. Until the time of electronic computers, we can reasonably characterize attempts at building models of human reasoning through logic as *historic* AI. Since computers, we can characterize the attempts to test such models as *modern* AI. Perhaps the at once greatest discovery and greatest disappointment of early modern AI was how inadequate certain logics were as models of actual human reasoning. So we shall see that today, work in AI is often characterized by the creation of new reasoning models through extending old logics or creating new ones. Thus, every time philosophers or logicians throughout history attempted to describe the consequence relation with a symbolic language, they unknowingly contributed to the foundations of modern AI.

Ancient Views of Logic

Nearly all philosophers would agree that the first known attempt to study and formally analyze patterns of human reasoning is due to Aristotle (384–322 b.c.), who defined a *syllogism* as "a piece of discourse in which, certain things being posited, something else follows from their being so."[3] As such, a syllogism seems like any valid argument, but in fact the kind of discourse to which it applies is restricted to very specifically defined types of sentences that predicate something P of a subject S. Such sentences can be either affirmative or negative, and either universal or particular. They must assume one of the following forms:

(A) Every S is P.
(E) No S is P.
(I) Some S is P.
(O) Not every S is P.

(The A, E, I, and O designations were given to these forms after Aristotle's time.) Aristotle realized that some sentences were consequences of others. For example, if no S is P, then no P is S (E is a consequence of E). For another, if every S is P, then some S is P (I is a consequence of A). Furthermore, Aristotle categorized all the ways in which sentences of these forms can be placed in groups of three such that one of the sentences is a consequence of the other two taken together, as in,

(E) No S is P. (E.g., No penguin is a flyer.)
(A) Every Q is S. (Every antarctic bird is a penguin.)
(E) Therefore, no Q is P. (No antarctic bird is a flyer.)

Aristotle determined all such valid forms (the syllogisms) and, moreover, showed some to be reducible to others, which therefore could assume the status of axioms. "Thus, not only did Aristotle introduce variables and use them to formulate, for the first time, a number of formally valid laws of logic, but by means of the first axiom system in history he managed to demonstrate some of the interrelationships among those laws."[4]

As impressive as Aristotle's feat was, it did not account for all types of sentences used to express thoughts. It did not, for example, admit of singular sentences like "Fred is a penguin," which is not strictly of any of the forms A, E, I, or O. More importantly, it was not amenable to forms of reasoning in which the basic linguistic entities are sentences themselves, rather than simple general terms like "penguin" and "flyer." Thus the theory of the syllogism could not countenance arguments like:

Fred is not both a penguin and a flyer.
Fred is a penguin.
Therefore, Fred is not a flyer.

Which is of the form:

Not both the first and the second.
The first.
Therefore, not the second.

The ancient philosophical school of Stoicism, led by Chrysippus, identified and studied reasoning patterns like this, in which expressions such as "the first" and "the second" can be understood to be variables ranging over sentences. Together with another philosophical school known as the Megarians, the Stoics were concerned with understanding the sense of the sentential connectives "if ... then ____ ," "and," and "or." They can be thought of as inventing, in the third and fourth centuries b.c., the sentential calculus that is part of what we regard as symbolic logic, and therefore part of the reasoning systems of many of today's artificial intelligence programs.

However, it would be more than two millenia before anyone would pick up where Aristotle and the Megarians and Stoics left off and even attempt a full-blown development of symbolic logic. For more than a thousand years after Chrysippus, authors concerned themselves primarily with preserving the ancient doctrine. In medieval times, particularly from the twelfth to the fourteenth centuries, there occurred a resurgence in what we would call "philosophy of logic," in which emphasis is placed on the relationship between language and universals, on the nature of identity and existence, etc. Following this, the long dry spell for logic proper continued, and no real contributions to the study of reasoning were made until the nineteenth century.

However, it is interesting to note a seventeenth-century vision of Leibniz as it relates to the modern goals of logic and AI. Although most modern logicians characterize logic as the study of the consequence relation, a requisite activity of this study is the formalization of the patterns of human discourse in symbolic models. This is done to eliminate the ambiguity and vagueness that attends natural language, so that the notions of consequence and proof can be studied in their formal purity. Thus a modern side effect of the study of the consequence relation is a procedure for the translation of statements made in natural language into equivalent statements in a formal language. Now the language of modern AI is the language of digital computers, which, like the language of logic, is artificial and formal. The reason that modern AI is interested in logic is that logic offers a ready-made language into which the natural language of discourse and reasoning can be translated for representation in machines.

The Influence of Leibniz

Although the most significant developments in logical formalism would not occur until two centuries after his time, Leibniz as a young man conceived of a grand attempt to construct a *"lingua philosophica* or *characteristica universalis*, an artificial language that in its structure would mirror the structure of thought."[5] Of course, Leibniz's motivation for such a language did not have anything to do with its application to modern digital computers, but it *did* have to do with a desire to mechanize through artificial language the processes of logical discovery in thought. This desire is shared by modern AI researchers, and it displays the bias, first stated by Hobbes, toward the computational view of the mind. But it goes beyond Hobbes in that it proposes a project of actually mapping natural concepts and forms of reasoning to an artificial language. In his *De arte combinatoria*, Leibniz foresaw the goals of modern logicians and philosophers to reduce complex terms of discourse to totalities of simple ones:

> Analysis is as follows: Let any given term be resolved into its
> formal parts, that is, let it be defined. Then let these parts be
> resolved into their own parts, or let definitions be given of the
> terms of the (first) definition, until (one reaches) simple parts or
> indefinable terms.[6]

The decomposition of propositions into their primitive or basic constituents is an underlying theme of modern logical analysis, but just as important is the attachment of mathematical symbols to these constituents for representation in a calculus. Leibniz also anticipated such formalism, as noted by Copleston:

> These simple or indefinable terms would form an alphabet of
> human thoughts. For, as all words and phrases are combinations
> of the letters of the alphabet, so can propositions be seen to
> result from combinations of simple or indefinable terms. The
> second step in Leibniz's plan consists in representing these
> indefinable terms by mathematical symbols. If, then, one can find
> the right way of "combining" these symbols, one will have formed
> a deductive logic of discovery, which would serve not only for
> demonstrating truths aready known but also for discovering new
> truths.[7]

Leibniz would be frustrated in his attempt to complete such a project, but as we shall see, he anticipated later, more successful, attempts.

Leibniz's desire for an artificial and universal language to assist in knowledge discovery was closely related to another of his philosophical visions which interestingly presaged one of the primary goals of AI today. It involves the notion of human knowledge as a *commodity*, and the extraction and storage of expertise as a *product*, the use of which could make life better. In the words of Leibniz historian L.J. Russell:

> Leibniz held that there already exist vast stores of experience
> held by groups of skilled workers, or by individuals, that are not

fully utilized. These must be collected and systematically
arranged, if their full fruits are to be obtained for understanding
and practical application.[8]

In the parlance of modern AI, Leibniz proposed an encyclopedic *knowledge base* of known facts, and rules by which new facts could be inferred
from them. Leibniz's idea of storing the valuable expertise of individuals would reach its zenith in the 1980s with the concept of an *expert
system*, which, as we saw in chapter 1, is a computer program encoding the experience and skill of a human expert in some well-defined area
of knowledge, for use as a consultant or aid by others. The AI mantra
of the 1980s, "Knowledge is power," testifies to how the *engineering* of
knowledge by AI is seen to benefit humankind. Leibniz, however, would
not have described the value of the knowledge endeavor in this way. For
he saw full knowledge of the world as the best way to put *divine* power
on display, and thus to increase the level of piety and devotion to God.
Still, there are remarkable parallels between Leibniz's and modern AI's
visions concerning the value of storing and extracting human knowledge
by means of formal representation and manipulation.

Modern Logic

Boole and De Morgan

The age of modern logic began with an examination of the foundations of
mathematics. This inquiry, initiated primarily by the British mathematicians and logicians George Boole (1815–1864) and Augustus De Morgan
(1806–1871), would have as an ultimate effect the positioning of logic as
the basis for mathematics. Since mathematics can be regarded as knowledge in its most abstract and nonempirical form, many philosophers and
scientists would adopt its language in their attempts to analyze and for-
malize knowledge in empirical domains. Boole and De Morgan began
an extended tradition of promoting logic as the language of talk about
reasoning and knowledge, and so it would inevitably become, for many,
the language of AI as well.

Up until the time of Boole and De Morgan, the language of algebra was
taken to be about specific objects in traditionally mathematical domains,
like positive numbers. Thus an expression like $a(x + y) = ax + ay$ was
taken to involve the numerical relations of multiplication and addition.
De Morgan was among the first to consider expressions like this without
regard for any particular interpretation. Boole noticed that many numerical algebraic expressions, such as the law of distribution in this case,
had very similar counterparts in the logic of *classes*. Thus, if pq is taken

to denote the intersection of the classes p and q, and $p + q$ is taken to denote their union, then the expression $a(x + y) = ax + ay$ is also true as a law about classes. This led Boole to consider the notion of a purely *symbolic* algebra, using the generic notion of a class for its interpretation. His investigations would embolden him to surmise that he had discovered principles for the characterization of all reasoning, and his publication of *An Investigation of the Laws of Thought* would place him as an early founder of modern logic.

The eventual repercussions for AI of Boole's work would be dramatic in two ways. First, in attempting to determine the laws common to both numerical and class algebra, Boole discovered that, considering only the numerical values 0 and 1, all the operations of his algebra of classes were also valid operations in the algebra of numbers. This means that the binary number system conforms to the same laws as the symbolic algebra of classes. Thus, to the extent that the algebra of classes could be understood, the algebra of binary numbers could also be understood. This relationship would be exploited enormously in the twentieth century when the logic of switching circuits, modeled by the binary number system, would be investigated in the design of digital computers. In fact, the laws governing the behavior of such circuits would come to be known as *boolean logic*, now required material for all students of machine organization and computer engineering.

The second effect of Boole's work would be in the area of AI software, which would owe much to the logic of *sentences*. Boole was the first to notice the relationship between the algebra of classes and a sentential calculus. By letting 1 and 0 stand for truth and falsity, x and y for sentences, and xy for the logical conjunction of x and y, an expression like $x(1 - y) = 0$ could be taken to mean "the conjunction of x and the negation of y is false," or in other words, "not both x and the negation of y." Such expressions would come to be known as *truth functions*, and would later form the basis of a full logic, or calculus, of sentences. This basis would prove fundamental in the semantics of programming languages, which would require the ability to specify logical conditions for the execution of machine operations. In fact, these conditions would come to be known as *boolean expressions*, the linguistic apparatus for which are included in all important programming languages today.

Logic's early modern era would also witness the analysis of conditional sentences of the form "if x then y" truth-functionally as "not both x and the negation of y" or "either the negation of x or y." Conditional sentences would prove fundamental in early attempts at automated reasoning in AI, and they would become primary constituents of the knowledge bases processed by inference mechanisms in expert systems. But sentences of the form "if x then y" are truly useful as representations of human knowledge only if their constituent sentences x and y can be broken down into simple predicates and relations signifying corresponding concepts about the world. That is, a complete decomposition of the mechanics of thought of the sort envisaged by Leibniz would be necessary. By the end of the nineteenth century, such machinery would be forthcoming in the brilliant work of Gottlob Frege.

Frege

Historians of logic are in virtually unanimous agreement that Frege (1848–1925), a German mathematician and philosopher, single-handedly founded modern mathematical logic. To understand the significance of his contributions, it helps to look at examples of how simple patterns of reasoning lend themselves to symbolic formalization under logical systems before and after Frege. We have already noted that the ancient Megarians and Stoics investigated patterns of reasoning in which the basic element is the sentence. Boole and De Morgan continued this tradition, with Boole in particular discovering the relationship between sentential logic and the logic of classes. The understanding gained by the analysis of sentences and their connectives "and," "or," "if ... then ___ ," and "not" works perfectly well for symbolizing some patterns of reasoning. For example, consider the argument:

If the Knicks lose today, then their season is over. The Knicks lose today. Therefore, the Knicks' season is over.

This sort of argument is well handled by considering the sentence as basic. We can symbolize the sentence "The Knicks lose today" as p and "The Knicks' season is over" as q, and render the argument in sentential logic as:

$$p \to q$$
$$\underline{p}$$
$$q$$

Here, the "$\to$" symbol is used to symbolize an "if ... then ___ " (conditional) sentence, and the horizontal line separates the argument's premisses from its conclusion. The argument thus symbolized is valid because it has the long-recognized form called *modus ponens*, in which a conditional and its antecedent are affirmed and the consequent of the conditional is inferred.

But the machinery of sentential logic is inadequate for faithfully symbolizing many types of reasoning patterns. Consider the following argument, together with sentential letters for its components:

> Mary is the mother of Bill (p). Bill is the father of Sue (q).
> Therefore, Mary is the grandmother of Sue (r).

In sentential logic, this argument has the form:

$$\frac{\begin{array}{c} p \\ q \end{array}}{r}$$

which is not valid; there is no logical connection between the premisses and the conclusion. Of course, one could trivially *make* there be a connection by including an explicit conditional relating the premisses and the conclusion:

$$\frac{\begin{array}{c} p \\ q \\ p \wedge q \to r \end{array}}{r}$$

Here the "$\wedge$" symbol is used to indicate logical conjunction. Thus the added premiss states, "If Mary is the mother of Bill and Bill is the father of Sue, then Mary is the grandmother of Sue." While the new argument is valid in sentential logic, it is unsatisfying as a symbolization of the original reasoning pattern, for when we conclude that Mary is Sue's grandmother, we do so by appealing to a general rule that *anyone* who is the mother of the father of another person is that person's grandmother, and not just Mary. The generality of such a rule can be captured with *variables*, as in "If x is the mother of y and y is the father of z, then x is the grandmother of z." But the constraints of sentential logic do not allow us to take advantage of such a rule. Since none of the components of this rule, call it s, are the same as p, q, or r, the argument would have to be symbolized in sentential logic as

$$\frac{\begin{array}{c} p \\ q \\ s \end{array}}{r}$$

which is invalid. What is needed is the ability to further break up sentences into their component parts, and to match up those parts with variables. This essentially is what Frege accomplished. His book *Begriffsschrift* was the first fully formalized axiomatic development of the sentential calculus, consistent and complete. ... Even more important is Frege's introduction of quantifiers into his formal system; by including additional axioms and rules, he expands it to a complete system of first order predicate calculus.[9]

Predicate calculus, the heart of all systems of mathematical logic today, would be the closest thing to Leibniz's ideal of a universal symbolic language for deductive reasoning. It recognizes that sentences *predicate* properties of individuals, represented either as logical constants or variables. It provides mechanisms by which variables can be made to *quantify* over all or some of the individuals in the domain of discourse, and by which variables are *instantiated* in the drawing of conclusions. Through its provisions, our argument which resists adequate symbolization in sentential logic is easily represented as the following valid argument in predicate calculus:

$$\text{Mother-of(Mary,Bill)}$$
$$\text{Father-of(Bill,Sue)}$$
$$(\forall x)(\forall y)(\forall z) \, (\text{Mother-of}(x,y) \, \wedge \, \text{Father-of}(y,z) \rightarrow$$
$$\text{Grandmother-of}(x,z)$$

$$\overline{\text{Grandmother-of(Mary,Sue)}}$$

The third premiss is interpreted as "For all x, y, and z, if x is the mother of y and y is the father of z, then x is the grandmother of z."

Because it was designed as a model of human reasoning and thought, predicate calculus would turn out to be one of the preferred languages of AI. Both its representational and its deductive powers would prove irresistible to AI's early pioneers. Indeed, the following description of Frege's system by Mates could easily describe many of the AI systems of today:

> The entire presentation is in accord with his [Frege's] own rigorous conception of a satisfactorily formulated theory: it should be framed in an artificial, formalized language, for which the concept of (well-formed) formula is explained by reference solely to the shapes of the expressions involved; the primitive symbols must be explicitly listed, and all others defined in terms of them; all formulas to be asserted without proof are to be listed as axioms; other asserted formulas are to be derived from these by the application of formal inference rules, all of which are to be stated in advance.[10]

The formal rigor of Frege's predicate calculus is of the same sort as required by the language of computers, which is concerned only with formal symbols and their manipulation, and because predicate calculus explicitly and unambiguously states the manner in which new formulas can be inferred from others, it lends itself perfectly to the "input and output" model of digital machines. The correspondence would appear so perfect to some that the "physical symbol system hypothesis" mentioned in chapter 2 would begin to take shape and ignite a fierce debate about the relationship between minds and machines.

Machines for Doing Logic

The calculating devices of the first third of the twentieth century were all *analog* devices whose principal media of operation were cogged wheels, shafts, and gears.[11] The accuracy of such calculators was dependent on the precision with which their parts were manufactured, and their speed was limited due to the motion of mechanical parts. In 1938, a Massachusetts Institute of Technology (MIT) research assistant named Claude Shannon had the inspired idea to exploit Boolean algebra and replace the cogs and gears of calculators with electromechanical relays, or switches which could be either on or off (1 or 0). While calculators made of electromechanical relays were shown to be many times faster than human beings, they still relied on and were therefore limited by the mechanical motion of the relays. The first truly *electronic* calculators replaced electromechanical relays with vacuum tubes, and therefore they had no moving parts. They were developed independently during World War II by Germany, the United States, and Great Britain, for very specific purposes related to these countries' war efforts, such as airplane design, ballistics calculations, and code breaking. The American machine, called ENIAC (for Electronic Numerical Integrator And Calculator), contained thousands of tubes, weighed many tons, and consumed enormous amounts of power, but it was a thousand times faster than any calculator based on electromechanical relays.

In peacetime it became clear that machines like ENIAC were difficult to apply to purposes for which they were not constructed, because this required a massive, laborious, and error-prone rewiring of the machine's connections. Although the wartime electronic calculators were single purpose, they were useful because, like mechanical calculators, they could apply their functions to arbitrary sets of data. This data could be encoded in the machine's storage elements, in binary form, without having to physically wire any of the machine's components. All that was necessary was to turn on (or off) the relevant storage elements by supplying power to them (or not). In 1945, the Hungarian-born mathematician

John von Neumann made the pivotal observation that, not only an electronic calculator's data, *but also its programmed instructions*, could be stored, in what von Neumann now called the machine's *memory*. This seemingly simple idea would prove revolutionary, because it replaced the notion of a *special-purpose calculator* with that of a *general-purpose computer*. Now, the function of a computing device could be altered in radical ways without touching a single wire; just devise a new program for it and "load" it into the device's memory. This approach brought with it the clear separation within a computer's architecture between its memory and its *central processing unit*, a distinction still fundamental to every computer produced for mass consumption today.

The new *von Neumann architecture*, as this stored-program computer was called, combined with the replacement of vacuum tubes by transistors, led to the availability in the 1950s of general-purpose electronic computers to researchers at certain elite academic and government institutions. Some were eager to test theories of human problem solving, and the first AI programs were written. One of these attempted to mimic how humans prove theorems of mathematical logic.

Besides his invention of first-order predicate calculus, Frege had also discovered that arithmetic and other large parts of mathematics can be reduced to logic. The complete success of this project was thwarted by the discovery by Bertrand Russell of a paradox involving classes, but in 1910, Russell and fellow British philosopher Alfred North Whitehead took up where Frege left off and published *Principia Mathematica*, which largely succeeded in deriving mathematics from logic. The project involved proving a number of theorems of mathematical logic, so in 1955 a team of researchers composed of Allen Newell, J.C. Shaw, and Herbert Simon devised a computer program to determine whether a machine could prove any of the theorems from *Principia*. The program, called Logic Theorist,[12] was able to prove thirty-eight of the first fifty-two theorems from chapter 2. (Simon and Newell were attendees at the Dartmouth AI conference in 1956.)

Other successes, including a program to prove theorems in additive arithmetic in 1954 (unpublished) and the Geometry Theorem-Proving Machine,[13] produced a general feeling of AI euphoria at the time. In 1958, Simon and Newell predicted that within ten years digital computers would become the world chess champion, would discover and prove an important new theorem, and would write music with aesthetic value. Simon and Newell were willing to extrapolate from the success of the Logic Theorist that computers would rival humans in every area of intellectual endeavor. As Simon wrote:

It is not my aim to surprise or shock you—if indeed that were possible in an age of nuclear fission and prospective interplanetary travel. But the simplest way I can summarize is to say that there are now in the world machines that think, that learn and that create. Moreover, their ability to do these things is going to increase rapidly until—in a visible future—the range of problems they can handle will be coextensive with the range to which the human mind has been applied.[14]

With forty years of hindsight since Simon and Newell made these predictions, it is clear that the predictions were overstated and made hastily. But just because their timeline was too optimistic does not mean that the predictions will never come to pass. After all, the current world chess champion has already been beaten by an IBM computer and admits that before long it will consistently beat him. But the philosophically interesting aspect of all this is not whether and how long it will take for predictions like this to come true, but rather the underlying conception of the human mind which causes extremely bright people like Simon and Newell to make them.

Physical Symbol Systems

The development of mathematical logic in the nineteenth and twentieth centuries by philosophers and mathematicians can be regarded as the creation of a formal model of certain aspects of human thought. Since the model is fundamentally composed of symbols and rules for their manipulation, the availability of modern digital computers, which are at bottom symbol processing machines, paved the way for the testing of a hypothesis concerning the nature of human thought, namely, that it too is essentially described as symbol processing according to definable rules. It created an opportunity to truly flesh out Hobbes' intuition, skeletally stated as it was, that ratiocination, or intelligent thought, is computation. Here now was a way to explicitly describe the nature of cognitive intelligence in the computational terms of actual, physical symbol processing machines, and to test Hobbes' intuition with computer programs.

Computers thus became the experimental test bed for the hypothesis that human intelligence itself can be accounted for by the action of a physical symbol system. For, so the reasoning goes, if intelligent behavior can be observed in symbol processing computing machines, then physical symbol processing is sufficient to explain intelligent behavior in humans as well. This hypothesis, called the physical symbol system hypothesis by Simon and Newell, is subject to confirmation or falsification through experience in the world, just as were, for example, the atomic theory of the elements, the germ theory of disease, and later the theory of plate techtonics in geology:

> This is an empirical hypothesis. We have defined a class of
> [physical symbol] systems; we wish to ask whether that class
> accounts for a set of phenomena we find in the real world.
> Intelligent action is everywhere around us in the biological world,
> mostly in human behavior. It is a form of behavior we can
> recognize by its effects whether it is performed by humans or not.
> The hypothesis could indeed be false. Intelligent behavior is not
> so easy to produce that any system will exhibit it willy-nilly.
> Indeed, there are people whose analyses lead them to conclude
> either on philosophical or on scientific grounds that the
> hypothesis *is* false. Scientifically, one can attack or defend it only
> by bringing forth empirical evidence about the natural world.[15]

Early AI researchers believed that the way to defend the physical symbol system hypothesis was to consistently create physical symbol systems that exhibit behavior that we would say requires intelligence if shown in humans. Thus, Newell and Simon's Logic Theorist was the first in a line of programs using logic or other symbolic systems as their model of intelligent behavior. Newell and Simon themselves followed up Logic Theorist with a grand project called the General Problem Solver (GPS)[16] which claimed to mimic thought by representing problems to be solved in terms of goal states and current states, and undertaking strategies to eliminate the differences between them through the invoking of subgoals. Less general approaches were taken by programs like Symbolic Automatic Integration (SAINT),[17] that symbolically represented calculus integration problems and implemented symbol manipulation rules to transform integrals into evaluable forms. The success of the symbol system approach reached one of its most notorious levels with ELIZA,[18] a program that duped many observers into thinking its output was that of a real psychotherapist.

One of the ways that early AI researchers discovered they could show impressive results was by limiting the complexity of actions and objects that their systems could reason about. Writing programs that could play games like checkers[19] thus became popular, because their reasoning environments could be strictly and unambiguously defined, unlike the environments in which we find ourselves in everyday life. For nongame applications, it became customary to define simple and precisely described worlds for the program to represent and reason about, worlds inhabited by geometrical shapes, tables and blocks, or robots operating in nearly empty rooms. Such worlds came to be known as *microworlds*, and they were the scenes of several early and successful AI programming endeavors involving planning and natural language understanding.

As AI researchers began trying to bring their techniques into the real world of common sense, however, they began to discover that mere logic and/or other symbolic methods of representation were inadequate. The most famous manifestation came to be known as the *frame problem*, which revealed itself when AI was applied to instances requiring reasoning over time. The problem was finding a way to program a commonsense principle that all humans have, namely, that when a change to our world occurs over a given time interval, although that change causes us to alter *some* of our beliefs, typically almost all our beliefs *remain unchanged* during that interval. So, it takes no great intellectual power for me to know that, despite my picking up my coffee cup and putting it down in a different place, nevertheless all the other dozens of objects in my office have not moved.

While this seems even laughably trivial, it is difficult to represent using only logic in an AI program. This is because it is necessary to reason about the results of performing actions at particular times, and thus times must somehow be attached to the facts represented. So if I represent to an AI reasoning system that all the objects in my office are in particular places at time t, then after picking up and moving my coffee cup, the system must reestablish that these objects are in the same places at time $t + 1$. While this can be accomplished through the use of *frame axioms*,[20] it results in clumsy and cluttered representations that are not faithful to how humans actually think. Of course, if, as an AI researcher, you are concerned only with machine behavior, and not with how the machine gets its reasoning done, then the clumsiness and clutter of frame axioms is not an issue for you.

Some AI researchers began in the 1960s to look to philosophical approaches to analyzing the problems resulting from representing knowledge and reasoning patterns in symbol systems. McCarthy and Hayes described the *epistemological adequacy* of AI representation schemes. If any scheme cannot express beliefs that one actually has about the world, it is not epistemologically adequate. Also, if the language of the representation scheme does not match the efficiency of actual reasoners in the world, then the representation fails to be *heuristically adequate*. In the 1970s it came to be acknowledged that the language of deductive logic was both epistemologically and heuristically inadequate for representing much of the knowledge and reasoning of everyday life. It also became evident to some that the physical symbol system hypothesis was philosophically impoverished as a theory of the human mind.

– 6 –
Models of the Mind

Underlying all our treatments so far has been the assumption that it even makes sense to describe mental processes in computational terms. As I pointed out in chapter 3, more than three hundred years ago the interpretation of cognition as computation was given clear expression by Hobbes. Modern AI not only provides the *experimental apparatus* to test Hobbes's hypothesis through suitably constructed computer programs, but is also seen by many as an *elaboration* of the hypothesis by making explicit the nature of the computation involved in cognition. One explicit elaboration we already mentioned in chapter 5 is the physical symbol system hypothesis, which claims that cognitive processing, whether human or not, is characterized by the representation and manipulation of symbols, governed by rules, in a physical system. Such a hypothesis has deep implications for the traditional *philosophy of mind*, because it makes assumptions that have been and are contentiously arguable by philosophers. In this chapter we will take a closer look at these assumptions from a philosophical point of view, and we will close with an alternative mind model which challenges the physical symbol system hypothesis.

Metaphysical Misgivings

One of the assumptions of the physical symbol system hypothesis is that thinking things are physical things. While Descartes initiated the tradition of strictly separating physical from mental processes by characterizing them as arising within distinct physical and mental *substances*, most philosophers and scientists today regard this ontological dualism as a mistake. The principle reasons for this are two. The first reason is a logical one. Granting for the sake of argument that physical and mental events are ontologically distinct, there nevertheless are cases where they causally interact, as when burning one's hand causes pain. But mental events are, by the definition of dualism, not to be located in space or time at all, so the sense in which the mental event of pain is caused by a physical event is incoherent. Thus ontologically separating out a mental category from the physical is incorrect. The second reason dualism is largely rejected is scientific. Throughout the last century overwhelming evidence has accumulated that correlates various aspects of "mental" life with processes in the brain. In the face of this, it is much more parsimonious to retain the language of physical description when describing the events of conscious life, and to call on the language of mental entities only for the sake of convenience.

But then what *are* we to make of what we have till now called mental events? It is still necessary to account for the *relation* between brain events and events like being in pain, no matter how well correlated they are. Two responses to this need are either to deny that mental events exist (*eliminative materialism*) or to reduce them to some other type of thing (*identity theory*). The former is difficult to comprehend for anyone who has had as much as a toothache. The latter does not deny that mental events exist, but *identifies* them with brain processes.[1] While the identity theory makes the relationship between mental events and brain processes explicit, doubts are immediately raised by this identification. Many mental states are characterized as having phenomenal qualities that cannot be attributed to processes of neurons firing away in grey matter. For example, I may have a vivid dream of a gold mountain, but there is nothing gold or mountainish about the specific location in my brain that is to be identified with this image. Identity theory has been described by H. Putnam as "another instance of the phenomenon of 'recoil' in philosophy, this time from Cartesian dualism all the way to 'the absence of phenomenology.' "[2]

The birth and development of the digital computer has given rise to an alternative to eliminative materialism and mind/brain identity theory in the general recoil against dualism, and it constitutes the foundation of AI. This is *functionalism*, or the view, put succinctly by R. Burton, that

> mental states and processes are the embodiments of abstract
> functional states and processes that mediate between
> environmental inputs and behavioral outputs. Thus the mind is a
> computational system, and psychological explanation consists of
> developing a functional analysis of mental processes on the model
> of a computer program that would enable a suitably designed
> computer to process the environmental inputs to achieve the
> behavioral outputs in question.[3]

Functionalism is still a type of identity theory, but rather than identifying mental processes with certain kinds of brain processes, it identifies them with computational properties described abstractly through functions on inputs yielding outputs. What then is the role of the brain? It carries out the computations specified abstractly through functions, in a way which at present we do not understand. Mental states and processes therefore exist, but the best we can do to characterize them are as *abstractions* of computational properties of the brain. While it may still seem difficult to fathom the characterization of, say, a toothache, or an image of a gold mountain, as simply a computational property rendered abstractly, functionalism has many adherents in AI, philosophy, and cognitive psychology, because of the success of computationally modeling nonphenomenal activities like reasoning and learning.

What are the computational properties of the brain which functionalism makes abstract? In a way, every theory of functionalism is a hypothetical answer to this question. For it is a fact that we do not know, except at a very low level, how the brain computes, so by proposing an abstract functional model of, say, reasoning or problem solving, one thereby has a hypothesis that can be tested in a computer program. If the program behaves in the way in which a human would, that is, arrives at the same conclusion in reasoning or at the same answer in problem solving, then we have some evidence for thinking the brain computes in a similar way. But would one also thereby have evidence for thinking that human mental states are merely "the embodiments of abstract functional states and processes that mediate between environmental inputs and behavioral outputs"? Some philosophers who look closely at this issue say no.

Putnam, who was once a functionalist, changed his view when he concluded that identity theory, whether based on neurophysiology or on computational functionalism, was simply "Cartesianism *cum* materialism." Although materialism of any sort disavows entities like disembodied minds and sense-data (*qualia*) that have perceptible qualities but do not exist in space, the materialism of philosophy and cognitive psychology retains other assumptions that are not dualistic but are nevertheless associated with dualism. "These include the assumption that there is a self-standing realm of experiences or mental phenomena; that these experiences take place in the mind/brain; that the locus of this drama is the human head; and, finally, that perception involves a special cognitive relation to certain of these 'inner' experiences, as well as the existence of 'causal chains of the appropriate type' connecting them to 'external' objects."[4] While the last clause of this quote speaks specifically to the philosophy of human perception, it is equally applicable to a more general philosophy of human thought. For just as this account of perception is committed to the existence of an "inner" experience that amounts to a mysterious interface between the outer world and ourselves, so too is a functionalist account of the mind committed to an "inner" process of computation of which we are largely unaware but which amounts to an interface between the environment from which we take our input and our brains, and to which we have intimate access when we are reasoning and solving problems.

The "inner" process of computation posited by functionalist accounts of the mind are well described in the semantics of computer programs that are put forth as able to reason or solve problems. Each such program is an instantiation of the physical symbol system hypothesis, and it is based on logic, rules, or some other symbolic model of cognitive computation. Because the syntactical rules of such a system regulate the ways in which symbolic representations beget others while reasoning, some have proposed that the inner process of computation is governed by a *language of thought*.[5] It is as though there are two distinct realms in which languages are supposed to work. One is the normal, everyday realm in which natural language is employed to facilitate communication through speech and written text. The other is the purely abstract realm in which symbolic models of computational brain events grind away in response to outer stimuli.

One might hold that what the identity theory in any form gains for us by displacing dualism, it gives up by violating parsimony in another way. A functionalist theory of the mind which presupposes an inner language of thought in addition to the ordinary language of human communication, might be thought of as multiplying entities despite its antidualist stance. A parallel complaint can be lodged against a materialistic theory of perception. In such a theory my experience of a red statue, say, is identified with an appropriate brain event that has as its initial cause light reflecting from the statue. But the causal chain which starts with the reflection of light from the statue and ends with the appropriate brain event commits the theory to some kind of "inner" experience of that brain event which is *other* than my experience of the statue. This is because the statue is not in my brain; but in my brain, presumably, is where the causal chain ends and my experience begins. For many this inner experience is as puzzling as dualism and is reason for rejecting identity theory in any form. Putnam puts it this way:

> Much of the appeal of the "identity theory" has always had its
> source in the fear of being driven to the supposed opposite horn

of a specious dilemma—the dilemma that either we must opt for
some form of identity theory (or perhaps eliminative
materialism), or else be forced to the dark old days of dualism.
But does abandoning "identity theory" commit us to a dualism?
Not at all. ... Mind talk is not talk about an immaterial part of
us, but rather is a way of describing the exercise of certain
abilities we possess, abilities which supervene upon the activities
of our brains and upon all our various transactions with the
environment, but which do not have to be reductively explained
using the vocabulary of physics and biology, or even the
vocabulary of computer science.[6]

While modern science would regard a return to dualism as a return to
"the dark old days," some philosophers claim that despite calling the relation between mental processes and computationally characterized functional processes one of "identity," AI enthusiasts are really closet dualists.
John Searle, for example, believes that, like it or not, dualism is at the
heart of the attempt to construct intelligent machines:

If mental operations consist of computational operations on
formal symbols, it follows that they have no interesting
connection with the brain. ... This form of dualism is not the
traditional Cartesian variety that claims there are two sorts of
substances, but it is Cartesian in the sense that it insists that
what is specifically mental about the mind has no intrinsic
connection with the actual properties of the brain.[7]

The kind of dualism that Searle seems to be alluding to here is the dualism between the abstract and the concrete,[8] where the concrete is the
physiological activity of the brain, while the abstract is the characterization of mental events through functionalism. Now to call someone a
dualist in this sense is not pejorative. After all, logic and mathematics as well as computer science are based on abstractions. What Searle
claims is that to try to conceive of the mental in terms of the abstract
is doomed to fail, because of the *causal* properties the brain enjoys in its
role in mental life. For Searle the *formal* properties that we may be able
to ascribe to the brain via analyses of the way humans reason, learn, and
solve problems are not useful in trying to create intelligence:

What matters about brain operation is not the formal shadow
cast by the sequence of synapses but rather the actual properties
of the sequences. All the arguments for the strong version of
artificial intelligence that I have seen insist on drawing an outline
around the shadows cast by cognition and then claiming that the
shadows are the real thing.[9]

Thus for Searle causal powers of the sort possessed by brains are essential for intelligence. But what are these causal powers? Certainly, computers have causal powers. They have the ability to move enormous numbers of electrons around at very high speeds, to turn driveway lights on and off as well as to shut down entire power grids, to land airplanes and control planetary rovers, and so on. What sort of causal power does the brain have that a computer does not? Perhaps Searle means the power to produce other brain events. But brain events can be produced by external means through electrical or chemical stimulation, and one can certainly imagine computers having this power. Perhaps Searle means the power to produce mental events. But if these mental events are not themselves brain events then we are back to dualism. It does not seem that an appeal to the brain's causal power is enough to deny functionalism as a theory of the mind.

But even if it were, computer scientists are not likely to be swayed by the metaphysical musings of philosophers brought on by dualism and various forms of identity theory. After all, philosophers themselves differ widely in their ontological commitments to the kinds of things they take to be. While some prefer, in W.V.O. Quine's terms, the entanglement of "Plato's beard," others long for "desert landscapes" in their ontologies. Whether "mind talk" can be successfully reduced to the vocabulary of any discipline is of secondary interest to AI researchers who are trying to produce artificial but rational behavior. What will make them straighten up and listen, however, are claims that the ultimate assumptions about the mind on which functionalism is based are fundamentally misconceived. No one has presented the issues involved here, while arguing for functionalism, better than the British mathematician Alan Turing.

The Legacy of Turing

In 1936, before the first digital electronic computer, Turing set out to characterize the general notion of computability. He was motivated to do so because of Kurt Gödel's famous *incompleteness theorem*, which showed, in the case of mathematics, that there are some functions on the integers that cannot be computed; that is, they cannot be implemented by an effective procedure or algorithm. Turing wanted to define the set of functions on integers that *are* computable, and so for the purposes of theoretical consideration he devised an abstract computing machine that is now called a Turing machine.[10] It is visualized as an indefinitely long tape divided linearly into cells, into which a moving read/write head can write a 1, a 0, or a blank (writing a blank amounts to erasing). At any time, the machine is in one of a finite number of states, each of which has a unique name. The action of the read/write head is specified by a control function which takes as input the state the machine is in and the symbol under the read/write head. The output of the function is an action to take (for example, move the head right, or write a "1") and a new state for the machine to go into.

Turing produced simple examples of his machines that could, for example, add any two integers represented on the tape as strings of "1"s. If, say, a string of three "1"s and a string of two "1"s are written on the tape and presented to the adding Turing machine, the machine will employ its control function to move its read/write head and write symbols in such a way that when it halts only a string of five "1"s will be on the tape. Similar machines could perform the other operations of subtraction, multiplication, and division. More complex machines could be constructed to compute arbitrarily complex functions on the integers.

Turing discovered that his machines, through a painstaking encoding scheme, could themselves be represented as patterns of "1"s, "0"s, and blanks. This meant that an encoding of the Turing machine described above for adding two arbitrary integers could be written on a tape and itself presented as input to another Turing machine. This other Turing machine's control function could then be devised to read the encoded machine presented to it *as a program*, and simulate completely the encoded machine's action, writing its simulated output onto the real tape. Not only could this machine be defined to "execute" the addition machine; it could be defined to take *any* specific machine as input and execute it. This special machine, called the *universal* Turing machine, is an abstract model of today's general-purpose stored-program computer.

The success of the Turing machine as a model of computation, and the inability of any competing model to be shown to compute a function that a Turing machine could not compute, contributed to Turing's speculation, now called the "Church-Turing thesis," that a Turing machine can be constructed for any integer function which is computable. The reason this can only be speculated, and not conclusively proved, is that our notion of "computable" is only an intuitive one. But as mathematicians and philosophers began to accept the Church-Turing thesis, the power of the Turing machine model seduced some into applying it in areas seemingly far removed from the world of number theoretic functions for which it was originally created. In particular, if you believed that the brain is a computing device, and you were convinced that there is no model of computing that is better than a Turing machine,then you might conclude that the best chance for emulating the computational powers of the brain is through devices based on Turing machines.

Turing himself reasoned in this way. In 1950 he published a paper[11] in which he considered the question "Can machines think?" Believing this question too vague, he couched the problem instead in terms of "What would a computer program have to do in order to convince us it was intelligent?" He gave an answer which is still debated half a century later. It was based on an activity called the "imitation game," in which a man A and a woman B are physically separated from a third player C who has no indication of A's or B's gender other than through their written responses to C's questions. C knows that one of the two is a woman, and it is A's objective to convince C that he is the woman. B (the woman) has the same objective. If after detailed questioning A succeeds then he wins the imitation game.

Turing modified this game by replacing A with a computer, so that C knows that one of A and B is a computer and the other is a human, and making the computer's objective to convince C that it is the human. Turing contended that, if, after serious and well thought out questioning of both the computer and the human, the computer succeeded in convincing C that it was the human, then one would have to admit that the computer was intelligent. The key to Turing's conception here is that literally anything can be asked of the computer in an attempt to get it to reveal an "Achilles heel." He envisaged the following kind of exchange[12]:

> Q: Please write me a sonnet on the subject of the Forth Bridge.
> A: Count me out on this one. I never could write poetry.
> Q: Add 34957 to 70764.
> A: (Pause about 30 seconds and then give as answer) 105621.
> Q: Do you play chess?
> A: Yes.
> Q: I have K at my K1, and no other pieces. You have only K at K6 and R at R1. It is your move. What do you play?
> A: (After a pause of 15 seconds) R-R8 mate.

The question and answer format of this game offered, for Turing, the ideal environment to test intelligence, because it excluded abilities that are not germane to thought. "We do not wish to penalize the machine for its inability to shine in beauty competitions, nor to penalize a man for losing in a race against an airplane. The conditions of our game make these disabilities irrelevant. The 'witnesses' can brag, if they consider it advisable, as much as they please about their charms, strength or heroism, but the interrogator cannot demand practical demonstrations."[13]

Turing's criterion of intelligence based on the imitation game, which is also called the *Turing Test*, reveals a bias toward functionalism as a theory of mental events. For just as functionalism essentially ignores the qualitative character of mental events in favor of regarding them as "black boxes" abstractly characterized through functions, so too does the Turing Test ignore the manner in which a computer's answers are arrived at in favor of regarding intelligence as a "black box" whose measure is the practical effect of an artifact's behavior. Still, the appeal of the Turing Test is that, were a machine to be able to consistently win the modified imitation game, it is difficult to come up with any theory other than machine intelligence to explain it. Because there currently are no computers that come close to satisfying the Turing Test, its status is similar to an Einsteinian thought experiment, which due to technological limitations cannot actually be carried out, but which can be reasoned about *a priori*. Turing masterfully reasoned *a priori* about the notion of computability, and he truly believed that intelligence could be reduced to this notion. It was just a matter of time and availability of memory:

> I believe that in about fifty years' time it will be possible to program computers, with a storage capacity of about 10^9, to make them play the imitation game so well that an average interrogator will not have more than 70 per cent chance of making the right identification after five minutes of questioning. The original question, "Can machines think?", I believe to be too meaningless to deserve discussion. Nevertheless I believe that at the end of the century the use of words and general educated opinion will have altered so much that one will be able to speak of machines thinking without expecting to be contradicted.[14]

Turing was correct about the notion of "machines thinking" creeping into our popular language. Whether or not any of today's programs can be said to be intelligent, we loosely but routinely describe many of them as "thinking" while we wait for them to crunch away at this or that task. We use epistemic terms as well, for example, when we say that a program or system "knows about" uppercase and lowercase when prompting for input. Software and hardware marketers know that describing machines as thinking is good public relations, as witnessed by the names of actual companies like Thinking Systems Software and Thinking Machines Corporation.

Fifty years have passed and a typical desktop computer has on the order of a gigabyte (more than 10^9 bytes) of storage. But so far machines have been able to pass only very limited versions of the Turing Test, in which the realm of discourse is vastly restricted compared to the unfettered questioning envisioned by Turing. In 1990, Hugh Loebner, a university director of computing, offered a prize of $100,000 for the first computer to pass the unrestricted Turing Test. Although no program has yet claimed the prize, each year one program wins $2,000 for coming the closest.[15]

Fundamental Attacks

Some regard functionalism, and its particular embodiment in the physical symbol system hypothesis, as too ruthless of an abstraction away from what is essential about mental phenomena. Specifically, critics contend, it ignores the element of *intentionality*, or the bringing of one's focus of attention onto an object of thought. It ignores, for example, the peculiarly intimate relation between me and an unrealized state of affairs when I hope that it won't rain tomorrow. It also ignores the relation that holds between me and a nonphysical concept when I am thinking about Pegasus. For those who think that these relations, called *intentional attitudes*, cannot be captured by a mere symbol manipulation system, a machine's passing of the Turing Test will not be evidence of intelligence, no matter how impressive its performance.

In chapter 5 we mentioned ELIZA,[16] a program written over thirty years ago which mimicked the interaction with a psychotherapist. Following is an excerpt from a script of a dialogue with ELIZA. The responses in capital letters are made by the program.

```
Men are all alike.
IN WHAT WAY
They're always bugging us about something or other.
CAN YOU THINK OF A SPECIFIC EXAMPLE
Well, my boyfriend made me come here.
YOUR BOYFRIEND MADE YOU COME HERE
He says I'm depressed most of the time.
I AM SORRY TO HEAR YOU ARE DEPRESSED
It's true. I am unhappy.
DO YOU THINK COMING HERE WILL HELP YOU NOT TO BE UNHAPPY
I need some help, that much seems certain.
WHAT WOULD IT MEAN TO YOU IF YOU GOT SOME HELP
```

```
Perhaps I could learn to get along with my mother.
TELL ME MORE ABOUT YOUR FAMILY
```

Viewed in isolation, this exchange seems to reveal impressive powers of insight into interpersonal relations. It seems to be able to make reasonable associations among the patient's various concerns, and it makes no obvious gaffes that reveal it is a program. But after the publicity gathered by ELIZA, Joseph Weizenbaum, the program's principle developer, was quick to reveal that the program was able to appear to understand and converse in natural language only through a very rudimentary knowledge of grammar and no knowledge at all of meaning. He felt obliged to take the air out of AI's sails:

> It is said that to explain is to explain away. This maxim is nowhere so well fulfilled as in the area of computer programming, especially in what is called heuristic programming and artificial intelligence. For in those realms machines are made to behave in wondrous ways, often sufficient to dazzle even the most experienced observer. But once a particular program is unmasked, once its inner workings are explained in language sufficiently plain to induce understanding, its magic crumbles away.[17]

Weizenbaum was critical of what he felt were exaggerated claims for AI in the early decades, and he later described his misgivings in detail.[18]

The programming sleight of hand in ELIZA involved appealing to symbolically rendered rules of response that depended only on some simple pattern matching techniques. For example, the first two machine responses in the script above are general "canned" responses, chosen from a pool of available responses to use when the input matches nothing in the program's rule base, that is, the input was not understood in any sense. The third response is simply an echo of the input, also indicating no understanding. The fourth response keys on the input "I'm depressed," changes it to second person—"YOU ARE DEPRESSED"—and dresses it up in a response about being sorry. Nearly all responses are either canned, or modified reformulations of the input. Some responses key off of simple terms ("my mother") to elicit a specialized canned response.

It is part of the folk history of AI that one time a version of ELIZA was left running on an office worker's desk. Another worker, not knowing that the ELIZA program was running, assumed instead that the terminal was running a communication program that allowed him to converse via the keyboard with a colleague. He sat down at the terminal and had the following interaction:

```
Do you think that I can use the computer this morning?
WHY DO YOU ASK?
I might be able to make some additional telecomp sales.
WHY AREN'T YOU SURE?
My prospective customers have never seen a demonstration
of this system.
DOES THAT MEAN VERY MUCH TO YOU?
Of course it does.
YOU SEEM VERY POSITIVE ABOUT THAT.
This is ridiculous.
WHAT DO YOU MEAN THIS IS RIDICULOUS?
Is there any reason I can't use the computer now?
TELL ME MORE ABOUT YOUR PROSPECTIVE CUSTOMERS.
```

This exchange shows how much ELIZA depends upon its interlocutor being someone who expects to be talking with a psychotherapist, for that is one of the few contexts in which it can appear to be holding a conversation.

ELIZA may be thought of as performing well in a severely restricted Turing Test, where the context is psychotherapy or something like it. But a thoroughgoing opposition to the physical symbol system hypothesis would hold that, despite a system's performance, if its operational paradigm were merely symbol manipulation then it would not be exhibiting intelligence or understanding. This is the view of Searle, who shook up the AI world in the early 1980s with his famous "Chinese room argument." [19]

The Chinese room argument is Searle's proposed counterexample to the claim that mere formal symbol manipulation in a program can result in understanding. The argument was in response to a program by Roger Schank[20] which was able to represent general knowledge about typical scenarios, for example walking into a restaurant and ordering lunch. The program could then be given as input a specific restaurant story, like: "A man went into a restaurant and ordered a hamburger. When the hamburger arrived, it was burned to a crisp, and the man stormed out of the restaurant angrily without paying for the hamburger or leaving a tip." When then asked a question like "Did the man eat the hamburger?" the program would give the correct answer, "No, he did not."

Searle claims that in no sense does the program understand the story or the question, despite its unfailing ability to answer correctly. His argument is based on an analogy and goes like this. Suppose I am locked in a room with many pieces of paper filled with Chinese writing, and I understand nothing of Chinese. I can recognize the symbols on the paper only by their shapes. Then, in English, which I understand, I am given explicit rules stating what I should do when given additional pieces of paper with unintelligible Chinese on them. These rules tell me things such as: given input symbols of such-and-such a form, go to the pile of papers and find the same symbols, correlate them with certain other symbols, make copies of certain pages, make so-and-so changes to the symbol shapes on them, and so on. I am then given a paper with a bunch of Chinese symbols on them and after processing the symbols on this paper by following all the rules, I write the resulting string of symbols on a piece of paper and shove it out the door. Now, unknown to me, some of the papers in the room contain Chinese descriptions of general restaurant knowledge, and some contain a Chinese description of a particular story, like the one above about the man who stormed out of the restaurant. The input papers I am given contain questions in Chinese about the story, and, because I faithfully follow all the rules of symbol manipulation, the output symbols I create constitute correct answers in Chinese to the input questions. Now Searle claims that Schank's question-answering program does not understand English stories and questions any more than I understand Chinese in this example. In fact, Searle claims that the Turing Test is invalid as a criterion for intelligence, because the example is one in which the test is satisfied but there is no intelligence.

A standard reply to Searle from the AI community, called the *systems reply*, is that, while it is true that in the Chinese room example I do not have an understanding of Chinese, the *totality* of me, the representation in Chinese of restaurant knowledge, and the rules for how to respond to input, together constitute a *system* that understands. Searle thinks that this reply involves an abuse of the meaning of "understands," saying, "It is not easy for me to imagine how someone who was not in the grip of an ideology would find the idea [the systems reply] at all plausible."[21]

If the idea that mental processing can be explained by computational models of symbol manipulation is an AI ideology, there seems to be a countervailing ideology, embodied by Searle and many others,[22] that no matter what the behavior of a purely symbol manipulating system, it can *never* be said to understand, to have intentionality. Still, Searle admits that if the system is *not* a formal symbol system but merely mimics the brain and its causal powers, and the result is system behavior that cannot be distinguished from human, then the only explanation for the behavior is that it *is* intentional. This seems to say that the Turing Test is acceptable as a criterion for intelligence or understanding in an artificially created system as long as it is not a *formal* symbol system. For

Searle, it appears that the Turing Test is only selectively applicable to systems deemed to be sufficiently like brains.

To AI workers this selective applicability of the Turing Test smacks of biological anthropocentrism and dogmatism. But to philosophers like Searle, the claim that the Chinese room system understands Chinese is to beg the question of what understanding is. The debate has the markings of one in which the two sides completely talk past one another. Many people in AI choose to avoid this standoff by conceiving of their work as creating rational behavior in agents, and not as replicating human thought in machines. Others have coined the term *android epistemology*[23] to make it clear that human thought systems are not all that AI and computational cognitive psychology are concerned with. Still others, however, continue to stand their ground against philosophical attacks. The American Association for Artificial Intelligence, for example, presents a yearly award for "the silliest published argument attacking AI."[24] The award is named after Simon Newcomb, an astronomer who claimed to prove that heavier-than-air flight is impossible.

Opposition from Within

The physical symbol system hypothesis, as a hypothesis about the mind, has been opposed not only by philosophical watchdogs who object on theoretical grounds, but also by some AI researchers themselves. Their opposition is not against the general functionalist view that the mind can be modeled on the abstract notion of computational processes described by input/output behavior—in fact they accept this general characterization of the mind. What they object to is (1) the insistence that the computational processes must involve formal symbols in a language of thought paralleling actual human language, and (2) the wedding of traditional AI's computational models to the structure of general purpose computing machines. We will return to the nature of these objections in more detail, but first I will briefly consider the conditions that motivated them.

The success of the first digital computers in the middle of the century was impressive at the time, and resulted in computers being popularly called "electronic brains." But this appelation was due more to the wonder computers engendered in performing high-speed arithmetic than to any similarity they had to actual brains. Some of the terminology, for example, "memory" to refer to data storage, supported the computer/brain comparison, but other than that little about how computers were organized was brainlike. The most fundamental difference was in how a computer executed a program. As you may recall, John von Neumann had revolutionized computer design by conceiving of the *stored-program* machine, in which programs were represented in memory just as data was. This allowed computers to run arbitrary programs without rewiring, and led to the first truly general-purpose machines. But with this advantage came a commitment to a model of processing which was truly nonbrainlike. This model, called the *fetch-execute cycle* model, picks one instruction at a time from memory (called a *fetch*), places it in a special part of the processor called the *instruction register*, decodes the ones and zeros that constitute what the instruction means (like add the contents of two locations, or move a value to memory, etc.), *executes* the instruction, and then starts the cycle anew by fetching another instruction from memory. Half a century later, this is still the processing model used in virtually every computer in general use.

The fetch-execute cycle is exceedingly complex, requiring millions of interacting and synchronized circuits working together. The downsizing of microprocessors to small chips using very large scale integrated (VLSI) circuitry and the continual increases in speed and performance of new generations of microprocessors (in hardware generations measured in months) tend to obscure the basic fact that programs are executed sequentially one instruction at a time. This is a fundamentally limiting factor in computer organization and has come to be known as the *von Neumann bottleneck*. The bottleneck metaphor arises from the fact that in many computational situations, there is no inherent reason why a number of program instructions cannot be executed in parallel. For example, a process for multiplying two matrices can be written in a sequential way, computing dot products cell by cell, but it could just as well be specified as a number of parallel processes working independently on different parts of the matrices at the same time.

While designing and building computers that are composed of large numbers of processors that can be programmed to act in parallel has long been an area of computer science research, the computational model employed by each of the processors is, but for their ability to share data with each other, largely the same as that employed by a classically designed single-processor computer. Some researchers in AI, cognitive science, and philosophy believe that this classical computer architecture prejudiced the manner in which functionalism has been conceived in the physical symbol system hypothesis, for it has forced the computational model of cognition to assume the form of a sequential, linear, formal language processing paradigm. To be sure, this paradigm has provided the basis for some AI successes, including theorem proving, expert systems, data mining, and now software agents. But at the same time, AI approaches based on the physical symbol system hypothesis have been beset by well-known problems. One is the frame problem (chapter 5), brought on when trying to reason about change over time. Another is brittleness, or the tendency of systems, particularly expert systems, to perform inadequately or "break" when given intuitively reasonable input for which they were not specifically designed. The symbol processing paradigm is also particularly poor at sensory-level pattern recognition and learning problems that humans solve with ease, such as learning to recognize a face and interpreting handwriting.

While solutions to these kinds of problems have proven notoriously difficult to model symbolically, these problems are of a kind that the human brain handles readily. This has motivated some researchers to look for functional models of cognition at a *sub*symbolic level, and to exploit what is known about parallelism in a biological brain. But this sort of parallelism eschews the notion of a stored-program computer entirely in favor of emulating the way neurons in the brain are connected.

This approach to modeling cognition is called *connectionism*, and today it is regarded by many as offering a major alternative to symbol systems as a theory of the mind.[25] It is not a new idea, having been proposed in earlier forms,[26] but it was not until the early golden years of classical symbolic AI had run their course and its challenges clearly expressed that the connectionism bandwagon of the 1990s took hold. Briefly, the basic tenets of connectionism are the following. The mind is to be modeled computationally, but the computational paradigm is not the stored-program computer, nor even many stored-program computers working in parallel. Instead, the processing elements are simplified models of actual neurons, connected to one another by communication channels modeled on the way in which axons and dendrites pass chemical messages across synapses. Although each element is thought of as an input/output device, it produces output not through the execution of a stored program but by combining the inputs from each of its connected neighbors and determining whether the combined input reaches a certain threshold. If the threshold is reached, the processing element emits a certain output, otherwise it does not. Its input/output behavior is thus mathematically modeled on the way in which actual neurons in the brain "fire," or electrochemically transmit messages to their adjacent neighbors.

In practice, this *parallel distributed processing* (PDP) paradigm is usually not, at the present time, implemented in actual physical machines whose architecture resembles that of human brains. Instead, the connectionist architecture is simulated on traditional machines through software that implements *artificial neural networks* (ANNs). Programming an ANN bears little resemblance to programming a traditional machine. In fact, "programming" may not even be an appropriate description of the task, which is to define the geometry of how the artificial neurons are connected to each other, and to describe the nature of these connections through the use of numerical weights. There is no describing what the computer is supposed to do through statements in a formal programming language, nor is there any encoding of knowledge or inference patterns in a representation language using logic or rules. Thus there is no inner symbolic language of thought involved in this computational model of cognition.

How does an ANN exhibit behavior that can be called intelligent if it is not modeled on the manipulation of formal symbols? Through its ability to *learn*, or redefine the numeric weights of its connections to change the way in which its neurons emit output in response to input. This feature, called *back-propagation*, has been used to immense advantage in the automatic training of ANNs to recognize patterns, learn input/output relationships, classify features, and predict properties. Some of the many applications that have benefited from the ability to train by backpropagation are "character recognition, speech recognition, sonar detection, mapping from spelling to sound, motor control, analysis of molecular structure, diagnosis of eye diseases, prediction of chaotic functions, playing backgammon, [and] the parsing of simple sentences."[27] While some of the results have been impressive, there remain significant drawbacks to ANN technology using backpropagation, including sometimes excessive time required to train a network, and the propensity of some networks to *overlearn*, or memorize specific patterns at the expense of being able to generalize to unseen patterns.

These drawbacks, as well as the fact that ANNs have only been successfully applied to low-level cognitive tasks and not yet to those we would regard as high-level abstract reasoning, have not prevented some theorists from putting forth connectionism as a thorough-going theory of mental activity. For them, it is irresistible to claim that the symbols and rules of classical AI are abstract and unnecessary fictions that were created to perhaps *describe* certain types of reasoning but that do not *prescribe* mental behavior in any sense that implies they are actually used by our cognitive equipment. According to the alternative gospel, knowledge is not represented in any form that can be described as a symbolic language of thought; instead, "all the knowledge is *in the connections*,"[28] and the connections are completely described by the topology of the network and its associated weights. Rumelhart goes on to put the matter very clearly:

> [A]lmost all knowledge is *implicit* in the structure of the device that carries out the task, rather than *explicit* in the states of units themselves. Knowledge is not directly accessible to interpretation by some separate processor, but it is built into the processor itself and directly determines the course of processing.[29]

Just as hindsight has tempered the early claims and predictions of AI success made by those such as Simon and Turing, many writers have taken the excited pronouncements of connectionism with a grain of salt. J.F. Rosenberg, for example, felt compelled "to preach a modest sermon against the medieval sin of *Enthusiasm*."[30] While praising the "brilliance of the connectionist achievement"[31] in modeling the discriminatory powers of the organic brain, Rosenberg insists, I think rightly, that the *connectedness of neurons* in the connectionist paradigm cannot account for the essential *connectedness of concepts* that is at the bottom of the human ability to make inferences within what Wilfrid Sellars[32] has called "the logical space of reasons." As Rosenberg describes it,

> What differentiates the exercise of a mere discriminative capacity, a systematic propensity to respond differentially to systematically different stimuli, from a conceptual representing properly so called, is that the latter has a place and a role in a system of *inferential* transformations, a web of consequences and contrarieties in terms of which the representational state admits of being (more or less determinately) located in a "logical space" with respect to *other* representations.[33]

Rosenberg's appeal to Sellars here is entirely appropriate, and it is interesting to note that over forty years ago Sellars unknowingly anticipated the polarity within AI between the connectionist and classical views of the mind. For he distinguished between a piece of knowledge's *description* and its *justification*:

> The essential point is that in characterizing an episode or a state as that of *knowing*, we are not giving an empirical description of that episode or state; we are placing it in the logical space of reasons, of justifying and being able to justify what one says.[34]

Now, knowing and reasoning are not being modeled at all if the model of the mind is simply a slavish imitation of the structure of the brain, for the geometric space of neurons is categorically different from the logical space of reasons. But we cannot do without this logical space, because only within it can we ask the Socratic questions "What can we know?", "How can I be sure that my beliefs are justified?", and "How can I improve my present stock of beliefs?"[35] It is the nature of being human, and a distinguishing feature of scientific thought, to assess one's beliefs and to take steps to add to or change them. If we cannot ask the Socratic questions, then we cannot do either science or epistemology.

So we seem to be standing at a crossroads. Functionalism, as expressed by classical AI, suffers at once from the ontological poverty of not accounting for intentionality and the ontological excess of relying on a language of thought. Connectionism embraces only the functionalism of neurons and avoids this ontological excess but does so at the expense of an epistemological poverty of not explicitly representing the inferential transformations inherent in all reasoning.

Should one reject functionalism as a paradigm of the mind at all? Perhaps, but if so, one should not regard this as a repudiation of AI. To the extent that a cognitive theory of the human mind is based on functionalism, the rejection of functionalism is a repudiation of that theory. But recall that AI need not be concerned with making machines think like humans. Instead, the goal may simply be to make machines act rationally, and the paradigm used can be either classical AI or connectionism. While the standard for such action may be human rational action, this does not commit one in any way to a theory of human thought, no matter how badly philosophers or psychologists may desire such a theory.

The similarities and differences between human thought and computational procedures has been suppressed in much of the work in this area in the past. Much work has presupposed—actually taken for granted—that thought processes *are* computational procedures. But there is substantial opposition to this idea. For example, in addition to Searle's earlier work, J. Fetzer has identified what he refers to as "static" and "dynamic" differences between thinking and computing, which he views as completely undermining computational conceptions of the mind.[36] But philosophy can still learn from AI, even if AI is only concerned with rational action. For example, experiments in the machine modeling of reasoning and problem solving behavior may be relevant to epistemology, as we see in the next two chapters.

– 7 –

Models of Reasoning

One of the goals of computer science is the formalization of methods by which both simple and complex tasks can be automated by machine. Understanding a task well enough to automate it invariably requires that a *model* of a phenomenon be constructed, and in this regard computer science is as much an engineering discipline as a pure scientific one. But computer science differs from traditional engineering disciplines (and agrees with mathematics) in that the models it deals with are abstract. If I want to write a program that plays a game of chance, then I might simulate the tossing of a die by writing a procedure to return a random number. To fully understand how this procedure should behave, I need a model in mind of the natural phenomenon of dice tossing. Such a model is available, for example, as an abstract uniform probability density function.

If we regard the tasks computer science seeks to automate as involving "natural" phenomena, like tossing a die, as opposed to the digital phenomena which take place in the machine solutions to them, we can see the progression of steps in computer problem solving as suggested in Figure 1. As another example, if we want to automate the task of sorting

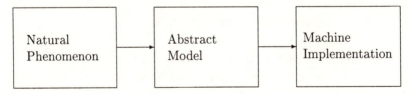

Figure 1. General Steps in Computer Problem Solving

a list of names alphabetically, we can regard physically sorting a list as a natural phenomenon, and model it abstractly through an *algorithm*, or effective sequence of steps, which we can convince ourselves works for any list. We then convert the algorithm into a program in a computer language and, with the help of system tools, produce binary code, which is the ultimate machine implementation.

Of course, algorithms are not the only abstract models with which computer scientists are concerned, and the modeling of physical events is not what they are always concerned with. Of particular interest to researchers in artificial intelligence today is the creation of artificial rational agents for drawing conclusions and making decisions. The natural example on which to base an artificial rational agent is the human reasoner, but the full range of quality of human reasoning involving even simple common sense has proven enormously difficult to model. Thus early successes were achieved in restricted and well-defined domains of mathematical theorem proving.[1] In terms of the dimensions of the problem solving process given in Figure 1, it is easy to explain the early success of theorem proving programs. It was not difficult for researchers to come up with an abstract model of the reasoning process they wished to automate, as they had been using the model themselves for years, namely predicate calculus. Insofar as human deductive reasoning is concerned with proving mathematical theorems, machine implementations are relatively straightforward (if not terribly efficient), since the required abstract model is both readily available and *formal*. Figure 2 shows these high-level relationships in an instantiation of Figure 1.

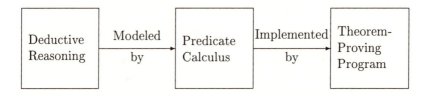

Figure 2. Modeling Deductive Reasoning

An unexpected offshoot of automated theorem-proving research was the discovery that predicate calculus could be used not only as a model of mathematical theorem proving, but also as the semantical basis for a programming language.[2] By imposing restrictions on the form of the axioms and the method of inference to shrink the search space, a procedural interpretation of the axioms can be given which allows them to be collectively viewed as a *logic program*. These restrictions amount to using a subset of predicate logic called Horn clause logic, with the resulting theorem-proving program amounting to a logic programming system.

Figure 3 depicts this instantiation of the general idea of mechanical theorem proving.

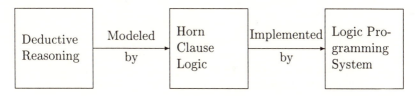

Figure 3. A Restricted Model of Deductive Reasoning

The restriction to a *specific kind* of inference on a *specific kind* of logical clause had the somewhat serendipitous effect of producing a *general-purpose* AI programming paradigm. Since its inception in the early 1970s, logic programming has been used to considerable advantage well outside the narrow bounds of mathematical theorem proving, in natural language processing, intelligent database systems, and knowledge-based expert systems.

Despite logic programming's early successes, predicate calculus still proved inflexible for modeling the many everyday inferences which are justified but *non*deductive, including *defeasible* inferences. The classic example of a defeasible inference is concluding that Fred is a flyer on the basis of Fred's being a bird, taking into account that additional information about Fred—for example, his being a penguin—would defeat this conclusion. Philosophers were the first to study and understand defeasible reasoning, but this work went unnoticed by most AI researchers.

The Truth-Based Approach to Defeasible Entailment

In the early 1980s the computer science community saw a flurry of activity in research on what was called *default* or *non-monotonic* reasoning. Artificial intelligence researchers hurried to investigate the structure of this reasoning in hopes of uncovering an underlying logic.[3] Judging by the interest generated, an observer might well conclude that this was the first time this kind of reasoning had been seriously investigated. In fact, however, epistemologists had already recognized this type of reasoning, called it defeasible, and begun to study its structure at least as early as the early 1970s. Some philosophers even regard defeasible reasoning as a species of *inductive* reasoning,[4] the study of which, of course, has been ardently pursued in the philosophy of science for decades. But John Pollock, a philosopher, in providing a taxonomy of the types of reasons involved in epistemic justification, first described the kind of reasoning with which AI researchers had become concerned. This is the kind of reasoning that we would call rational but not conclusive:

> Logical reasons that are not conclusive are particularly interesting because they have been largely overlooked by philosophers bent upon finding reductive analyses. ... Let us call such reasons *logically good reasons*. Whereas conclusive reasons guarantee truth, logically good reasons only guarantee justification. ... Many logically good reasons have a certain kind of structure which makes it reasonable to call them *prima facie reasons*. A prima facie reason is a logical reason that is *defeasible*. In other words, a prima facie reason is a reason that by itself would be a good reason for believing something, and would ensure justification, but may cease to be a good reason when taken together with some additional beliefs.[5]

While it may seem obvious that any characterization of defeasible reasoning must be based on the notion of a justification-preserving, and not truth-preserving, relationship, much of the more visible research of the 1980s attempted to characterize it model-theoretically using familiar tools of predicate calculus semantics. An illuminating attempt to unify these approaches to defeasible reasoning, including various versions of circumscription,[6] default logic,[7] and autoepistemic logic,[8] was given by Shoham. He argued that the basic idea behind each of these is a changing of "the rules of the game" of first-order predicate calculus, not by introducing the idea of justification, but by doggedly clinging to the notions of truth and satisfiability:

> In classical logic $A \models C$ if C is true in all models of A. Since all models of $A \wedge B$ are also models of A, it follows that $A \wedge B \models C$, and hence that the logic is monotonic. In the new scheme [defeasible logic] we have that $A \models C$ if C is true in all *preferred* models of A, but $A \wedge B$ may have preferred models that are not preferred models of A.[9]

Thus defeasible entailment is to be understood through a new logic, but the semantical basis for what such an entailment means remains rooted in the idea of truth in a model. A closer look at the idea of a preferred model reveals an epistemological poverty of this approach.

Shoham uses the symbol $\models_C$ for defeasible (or what he calls "preferential") entailment. Consider then $Bird(Fred) \models_C Flyer(Fred)$. According to Shoham, this entailment means that *Flyer(Fred)* is true in all preferred models of *Bird(Fred)*. Now a preferred model of *Bird(Fred)* is a model M for which there is no interpretation M' such that M' is preferred over M

and *Bird(Fred)* is true in M' (p. 231). An interpretation M_2 is preferred over another M_1 if $M_1 \sqsubset M_2$ in a strict partial order $\sqsubset$ on interpretations for the language. While Shoham does not specify this strict partial order, the idea is that it arranges interpretations such that preferred ones are "more specific" in their predicate assignments.

Now consider an interpretation X in which *Bird* means "bird that is not a penguin." Since X is more specific than an interpretation Y in which *Bird* means simply "bird," X is therefore preferred over Y. Also, *Bird(Fred)* is true in X. Thus by the definition of a preferred model, in the preferred model of *Bird(Fred)*, *Bird* means *at least* "bird that is not a penguin." By parity of reasoning, the preferred model of *Bird(Fred)* is one in which *Bird* means *at least* "bird that is not a penguin and not an ostrich and not dead and not ... ." For all practical purposes, the preferred model of *Bird(Fred)* is one in which *Bird* means "bird that is a flyer." So we have $Bird(Fred) \models_{\sqsubset} Flyer(Fred)$ means that *Flyer(Fred)* is true in all preferred models of *Bird(Fred)*, that is, models in which *Bird* means, for all practical purposes, "bird that is a flyer."

Such a semantics of defeasible entailment suffers from an epistemological poverty of the model-theoretic language it employs. When we reason about an arbitrary bird, we may conclude that it flies, but we do not alter our concept of birdness to include flight in order to make that conclusion, as the above account implies. Instead, we are willing to make a slight epistemic "leap of faith" from the concept of birdness to the concept of flight. The reason there is faith involved is that there is only justification, and not truth, to countenance the leap. This should be at the heart of a semantics of defeasible entailment.

The philosopher J. Hawthorne, for example, presented a theory which recognized the inadequacy of truth as a basis for defeasible entailment:

> Truth-value semantics is inadequate as a basis for non-monotonic
> [i.e., defeasible] entailments because the concept of truth it
> explicates is monotonic to the core. ... Non-monotonic logic
> presumes that there is more to the meaning of a sentence than the
> determination of truth-values at possible worlds. The meaning of
> a sentence (and, perhaps, the state-of-the-world) imbues a
> sentence with an inferential connection to other sentences.[10]

Here Hawthorne characterizes defeasible entailment ultimately in terms of the meaning, not the truth, of the sentences involved. In his theory he proposes a set of plausible semantic rules which define a class of general entailment relations. These relations are autonomous with respect to classical logical entailment in that monotonicity and transitivity do not in general hold. In fact, Hawthorne shows how each relation can be thought of as a way of *extending* the classical logical entailment relation to permit additional defeasible entailments.[11]

Thus, philosophers taught AI how it ought to approach modeling defeasible reasoning—not by forcing it into a deductive paradigm ruled by logical entailment, but by describing a wholly different type of entailment based on the meaning of constituent statements. For example, knowing the meaning of *Bird(Fred)* imbues it with a justificatory connection to *Flyer(Fred)*.

Of course, quarrels with semantic foundations of a theory, as I have been expressing here with regard to truth-based approaches to defeasible entailment, can pale in significance if computational models based on the theory turn out to adequately model the human reasoning we wish to simulate. For if we wish to create a rational agent, then semantics fades as a concern if the agent's cognitive behavior is indeed rational. In this case, however, the computational model required to implement the theory faces difficult challenges. Consider the approach to modeling defeasible reasoning offered by McCarthy's circumscription. Recognizing that the first-order axiom $\forall x(Bird(x) \rightarrow Flyer(x))$ is false, this approach amends it to say that all birds that are *not abnormal* are flyers: $\forall x(Bird(x) \land \neg Ab(x) \rightarrow Flyer(x))$. So, if *Bird(Fred)* is true, how can it be inferred that *Flyer(Fred)* is true without also proving that Fred is not abnormal, a sort of fact which, if explicitly included as an axiom would hopelessly clutter any reasonable size database? The answer according to circumscription is to introduce another axiom, called a circumscription formula, which when added to the database says that the *only* objects which are abnormal are those which can be proved to be so; any others are not abnormal. Such a database is said to be a circumscription of the predicate Ab. Defeasible entailment from *Bird(Fred)* to *Flyer(Fred)* can then be handled with entirely deductive machinery.

Unfortunately, this deductive machinery is unwieldy to implement. For one thing, the circumscription formula is second order, quantifying over the predicate Ab, making it very difficult to automate the deriving of logical consequences from the augmented database.[12] For another, typical applications will want to countenance many instances of defeasible entailment, requiring the circumscription of a separate abnormality predicate for each. This requires the invocation of the circumscription process, across the entire database, each time a new rule representing defeasible entailment is added.

Another problem with this proliferation of abnormality predicates is that they may conflict during the process of deduction. For example, birds which are not abnormal ($Ab1$) fly. But antarctic birds which are not abnormal (*Ab2*) do not fly. Showing that Fred, an antarctic bird, is neither *Ab1* nor *Ab2* then results in the inference that Fred is both a flyer and not a flyer. This can be avoided in circumscription only by prioritizing the predicates *Ab1* and *Ab2* and advising the deduction apparatus to prefer one of the inferences based on this prioritization. A more intuitive solution to this general problem, however, is recognizing the natural relation between the corresponding predicates for which the abnormality predicates are given, namely *Bird* and *Antarctic-bird*. The conflict is eliminated by noticing that *Antarctic-bird(Fred)* logically implies *Bird(Fred)* but not *vice versa*.

Rather than trying to prove abnormality under a complicated ordering of abnormality predicates, a system would be better off looking for defeaters inferrable from common axioms such as $\forall x(Antarctic\text{-}bird(x) \rightarrow Bird(x))$.

A Justification-Based Approach to Defeasible Entailment

Suppose $p =$ "Fred is a bird and all birds are vertebrates" and $q =$ "Fred is a vertebrate." By appropriately translating p and q into a predicate calculus representation, we have that p logically entails q, or $p \models q$, the meaning of which is adequately captured model-theoretically as in the quote from Shoham earlier. Now suppose $p =$ "Fred is a bird and most birds are flyers," and $q =$ "Fred is a flyer." Although $p \not\models q$, it is possible for someone S (a rational agent) to be justified in believing q on the basis of p. It is also possible for S *not* to be justified in believing q on the basis of p, particularly if S believes something which when added to p does not constitute a good reason for believing q, like "Fred is a penguin and no penguins are flyers." There is, however, a measure of support which p provides for q *not considering any other information that might be available*, and this is what we should mean by defeasible entailment. We will use the notation $p \overset{S}{\rightarrow} q$ to stand for p *defeasibly entails* q, or alternatively, *p supports q*.

Using the concept of justification, the definition of defeasible entailment (or support) is fairly straightforward:

Definition 1 $p \overset{S}{\rightarrow} q$ *if, and only if, for any subject S, if S were to only believe p, then S would be justified in believing q.*

Now the question becomes, what does it mean to be justified in believing something? Fortunately, there is a long epistemological tradition in the analysis of justification from which to borrow. Here I will cite Chisholm's description of the terms of epistemic appraisal.[13] In this description, the notions of belief and reasonableness are used to build a hierarchy of epistemic states in which a subject S may be with respect to a proposition. These states range from a proposition having *some presumption in its favor* for S, to being *certain* for S. Each is defined in terms of belief (or, derivatively, disbelief or withholding) and the notion of epistemic preferability, or the idea of one proposition being "more reasonable than" another proposition for S. We are interested in that epistemic state S is in when believing a proposition q is more reasonable for S than withholding belief about it. (In this case Chisholm calls q *beyond reasonable doubt* for S.) We may regard this description as adequate for characterizing justification:

Definition 2 *S is justified in believing q if, and only if, believing q is more reasonable for S than withholding belief about q.*

In a model of defeasible reasoning, an account of defeasible *nonentailment* is just as important as an account of defeasible entailment, for it is the former which signals the presence of defeat. Whatever support p might provide for q through defeasible entailment is canceled if there is an r such that $p \wedge r \stackrel{S}{\not\to} q$. More precisely:

Definition 3 *r defeats p as support for q if, and only if, $p \stackrel{S}{\to} q$ and $p \wedge r \stackrel{S}{\not\to} q$.*

A defeasible reasoning system, though entitled to use defeasible entailments to draw conclusions, must also check for the presence of defeaters. To do this requires an understanding of the nature of defeat.

The Nature of Defeat

This understanding is due to Pollock, who first pointed out that there are two general ways in which r can defeat p's support for q.[14] First, r may be a good reason for *dis*believing q, that is, for believing the negation of q. In this case r provides contradicting evidence against q. Second, r may somehow render p irrelevant as support for q. In the first case, r is a reason for believing $\neg q$; in the second, r is a reason for doubting the connection between p and q. Pollock initially called these Type 1 and Type 2 defeaters, respectively, and later changed these designations to *rebutting defeaters* and *undercutting defeaters*, respectively.

We are concerned with characterizing the general conditions of rebutting and undercutting defeat in such a way that they can be recognized in a defeasible reasoning system. We shall find that the conditions of defeat involve the notion of true logical implication. When necessary we will employ the notation $A \vdash q$ to mean "q is deductively provable from axiom set A." In the case where I want to emphasize q's being deductively provable from a specific sentence p, or $\{p\} \vdash q$, we will invoke the deduction theorem, drop the $\vdash$, and simply write $p \to q$.

Note that $p \overset{S}{\to} q$, being an expression of defeasible entailment, is not intended to be a formula in an extended first-order language. Similarly, x in $F(x) \overset{S}{\to} G(x)$ is not intended to act as a free variable. Rather, $F(x) \overset{S}{\to} G(x)$ is intended to be a schema, using a variable-like placeholder, just as certain deductive inference rules are. Thus it can be regarded as the set of all defeasible entailments $F(i) \overset{S}{\to} G(i)$, where i is an individual name in the language. We call an expression like $F(x) \overset{S}{\to} G(x)$ a *support rule*.

What then are the conditions of defeat? Consider rebutting defeat first. Suppose $p \overset{S}{\to} q$. A sentence r defeats p in the rebutting sense if r is a reason for believing $\neg q$. But there are two ways in which r could be a reason for believing $\neg q$. First, r might be a deductive reason for believing $\neg q$, that is, both $A \vdash r$ and $A \vdash r \to \neg q$, giving $A \vdash \neg q$. I will call this *strong* rebutting defeat:

Defeat Principle 1 (Strong Rebutting Defeat) *For any p and q, if $A \vdash \neg q$ then $p \wedge \neg q \overset{S}{\not\to} q$.*

In other words, if $\neg q$ can be shown with certainty, it defeats anything as a reason for believing q.

But $\neg q$ might not be known with certainty, yet still be involved in rebutting defeat. Specifically, the reason for believing $\neg q$ might be r where $r \overset{S}{\to} \neg q$. I call any defeat that may arise here *weak* rebutting defeat since the reason for believing $\neg q$ is defeasible. This is characterized by the situation where the following are all true:

$$p \overset{S}{\to} q$$
$$r \overset{S}{\to} \neg q$$
$$p$$
$$r$$

What to conclude in this case depends upon whether there is auxiliary knowledge about the relationship between p and r. For example, suppose that most of the people in a room are programmers but most of the people near the room's window are not. Suppose also that Alonzo is in the room and near the window. Then we have the following support rules and axioms:

$In\text{-}room(x) \overset{S}{\to} Programmer(x)$

$Near\text{-}window(x) \overset{S}{\to} \neg Programmer(x)$

$In\text{-}room(Alonzo)$

$Near\text{-}window(Alonzo)$

Intuitively, Alonzo's being near the window, since it is more specific than his merely being in the room, should defeat his being in the room as a reason for thinking he is a programmer, allowing the justified inference that he is not a programmer. This is explained by the fact that his presence in the room is *implied* by his presence near the window (but not *vice versa*), and ought to be represented as a further axiom:

$(\forall x)(Near\text{-}window(x) \to In\text{-}room(x))$

Thus weak rebutting defeat occurs when competing reasons are related by implication:

Defeat Principle 2 (Weak Rebutting Defeat) *For any p, q and r, if $p \overset{S}{\to} q$ and $r \overset{S}{\to} \neg q$ and $r \to p$ then $p \wedge r \overset{S}{\not\to} q$.*

An implication of this principle is that if p and r happen to be equivalent, that is, $(p \to r) \wedge (r \to p)$, then the situation degrades to mutual defeat. This is what one would expect; if there are equivalent sentences, one of which supports q and the other $\neg q$, then the reasonable response is to believe nothing on the basis of them.

There may, however, be no relationship at all between p and r. Let us alter the above example to read that most engineers are programmers while most of the people in a certain room are not programmers. Suppose also that Alonzo is an engineer in the room, but there is no general relation between being an engineer and being in the room:

$Engineer(x) \overset{S}{\to} Programmer(x)$

$In\text{-}room(x) \overset{S}{\to} \neg Programmer(x)$

$In\text{-}room(Alonzo)$

$Engineer(Alonzo)$

Clearly, in this case the evidence for Alonzo being a programmer is *counterbalanced* by the evidence for his not being a programmer. While no defeaters are inferrable by principle 2, no conclusions are justified either. In general we might say that when p and r are independent, that is, $p \not\to r$ and $r \not\to p$, the situation is one of *ambiguous defeasible inference*, with the reasonable response being to withhold belief about q—to believe neither it nor its negation. We can summarize weak rebutting defeat in Figure 4.

Relationship of p, r	Defeaters	Justified Conclusion
$(p \rightarrow r) \wedge (r \nrightarrow p)$	$r \wedge p \overset{S}{\nrightarrow} \neg q$	q
$(r \rightarrow p) \wedge (p \nrightarrow r)$	$p \wedge r \overset{S}{\nrightarrow} q$	$\neg q$
$(p \rightarrow r) \wedge (r \rightarrow p)$ (p, r equivalent)	$p \wedge r \overset{S}{\nrightarrow} q$ $r \wedge p \overset{S}{\nrightarrow} \neg q$	None (mutual defeat)
$(p \nrightarrow r) \wedge (r \nrightarrow p)$ (p, r independent)	None	None (ambiguous defeasible inference)

Figure 4. Weak Rebutting Defeat, Where $p \overset{S}{\rightarrow} q$ and $r \overset{S}{\rightarrow} \neg q$

We now ask whether we can similarly characterize undercutting (originally Type 2) defeat in a property about support. Let us look at two examples of undercutting defeat. In each case, $p \overset{S}{\rightarrow} q$ and $p \wedge r \overset{S}{\nrightarrow} q$ yet r is neither a strong nor weak rebutting defeater.

> p = Fred is a bird.
> q = Fred is a flyer.
> r = Fred is an antarctic bird (either a penguin or a tern).

> p = Most U.S. citizens in a random survey favor nuclear power.
> q = Most U.S. citizens favor nuclear power.
> r = Coincidentally, most U.S. citizens in the survey are Republicans and all Republicans favor nuclear power.

In these cases, if r is true it does not constitute a reason for disbelieving q. Rather, r in a sense adds to p, making the information more specific, in such a way that r makes p irrelevant to q. In each case r clearly does *not* support q, but r *implies* p. This suggests the principle:

Defeat Principle 3 (Undercutting Defeat) *For any p, q and r, if* $p \overset{S}{\rightarrow} q$ *and* $r \overset{S}{\nrightarrow} q$ *and* $r \rightarrow p$ *then* $p \wedge r \overset{S}{\nrightarrow} q$.

This is very similar to principle 2. If all else is equal, nonsupport $(r \overset{S}{\nrightarrow} q)$ has just as much power to defeat $p \overset{S}{\rightarrow} q$ as support of negation $(r \overset{S}{\rightarrow} \neg q)$.

Note that $r \overset{S}{\nrightarrow} q$ is implied by $r \overset{S}{\rightarrow} \neg q$, but not conversely. The distinction is important, as it permits the characterization of undercutting defeat, a type of defeat which poses a problem for circumscription. Consider how circumscription would model the defeasible entailment in Fred's case where the only "abnormal" birds we know about are penguins:

$$\forall x(Bird(x) \land \neg Ab(x) \rightarrow Flyer(x))$$
$$\forall x(Penguin(x) \rightarrow \neg Flyer(x))$$
$$Bird(Fred)$$

When an appropriate circumscription axiom is added to this database, the effect is that *failing* to prove *Ab(Fred)* is equivalent to proving ¬*Ab(Fred)*, allowing the conclusion *Flyer(Fred)* to be drawn. Now if *Penguin(Fred)* is added to the database we have a case of rebutting defeat, which is detected by the fact that *Ab(Fred)* is provable. But if instead *Antarctic-Bird(Fred)* is added, the resulting undercutting defeat is not detected, since *Ab(Fred)* is not provable. Still something must be added to block the conclusion *Flyer(Fred)*. The only way for circumscription to work would be to add:

$$\forall x(Antarctic\text{-}Bird(x) \rightarrow \neg Flyer(x))$$

which is false since some antarctic birds are terns. As indicated in principle 3, what accounts for the defeat is a natural and true statement of nonsupport:

$$Antarctic\text{-}bird(x) \overset{S}{\nrightarrow} Flyer(x)$$

By incorporating the $\overset{S}{\rightarrow}$ operator into a system based on these three defeat principles, defeasible reasoning can be adequately modeled.

One of the ways that both philosophers and computer scientists have gone about building systems that incorporate defeasible reasoning is by syntactically and semantically extending the Horn clause logic of logic programming systems to accommodate the main varieties of defeasible inference. The extension amounts to relaxing the entailment relation to allow justification-preserving as well as truth-preserving inferences. Corresponding extensions to the declarative semantics of Horn clauses and the procedural semantics of logic programming systems offer a method of implementing defeasible reasoning on a machine. Figure 5 shows the extensions in all three dimensions of Figure 3. To see how this is possible we must understand the value of logic programming for AI.

Logic Programming

As mentioned, logic programming owes its power in part to the ability to give a *procedural interpretation* to a set of Horn clauses. This is in addition to their standard *declarative interpretation*, which lies in the ability, inherited from predicate calculus in general, to precisely represent sentences in natural language. Any well-formed formula in predicate calculus

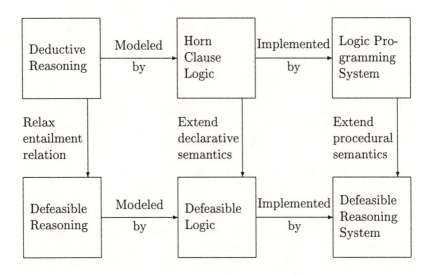

Figure 5. Extending Logic Programming for Defeasible Reasoning

can be converted, through various syntactic transformations, to an equivalent conjunction of disjunctions of literals, or conjunctive normal form. For example, $\forall x(Bird(x) \rightarrow Vertebrate(x))$ can be rendered in conjunctive normal form as the single disjunction $\neg Bird(x) \vee Vertebrate(x)$, where each side of this disjunction is a literal. It must be assumed here that the variable x is universally quantified. When a disjunction of literals, called a *clause*, has exactly one positive literal it is called a *Horn clause*. (Clauses with no positive literals are also regarded by logicians as Horn clauses, but for the purposes of describing logic programs I shall restrict my attention to Horn clauses having exactly one positive literal.) It can be shown that Horn clauses with at least one negative literal are equivalent to implications involving a single positive literal as the consequent and a conjunction of positive literals as the antecedent. For example, the Horn clause

$$\neg Rectangle(x) \vee \neg Equilateral(x) \vee Square(x)$$

can, by the application of various logical identities, be made equivalent to

$$Rectangle(x) \wedge Equilateral(x) \rightarrow Square(x)$$

(where $\wedge$ has higher precedence than $\rightarrow$). The key insight for logic programming, made by Kowalski[15] and others, is that "implications" like this latter formula can be seen as embodying a proof *procedure*. In this case the procedure is: to show that something is a square, it is sufficient to first show that it is a rectangle and equilateral. It is this sort of procedural interpretation which Horn clauses embody, and which logic programming exploits.

For the purposes of logic programming, Horn clauses are written with the consequent first and any antecedents following a "reversed implication" arrow. Consider the following set of Horn clauses:

$$Animal(x) \leftarrow Vertebrate(x) \quad \text{(A1)}$$
$$Vertebrate(x) \leftarrow Bird(x) \quad \text{(A2)}$$
$$Bird(Fred) \quad \text{(A3)}$$

A Horn clause's procedural interpretation lies in considering it a *procedure* with its set of antecedents the *body*, and each individual antecedent a procedure *call*. Thus A1 is the procedure *Animal* whose body includes a call to the procedure *Vertebrate* (A2). A procedure's body is executed whenever its *head*, that is, the consequent, is matched by a *query*. A query is a literal usually containing one or more variables. The desired output of a logic program is a set of query variable substitutions which make the resulting grounded literal (i.e., the query with values substituted for variables) deducible from the Horn clauses. The process of logic program execution is a series of matching steps to produce these substitutions. If such substitutions can be found, the query is considered to succeed; if not, to fail.

Consider the query $Animal(y)$. Declaratively, it can be regarded as a request for all substitutions for y which make $Animal(y)$ deducible from A1–A3. Procedurally, it can be regarded as a call to the *Animal* procedure. The call proceeds by matching the pattern $Animal(y)$ with the head of A1. The match succeeds under the substitution of x for y. (The process of matching a formula under a variable substitution is called "unification.") Remembering this substitution, the procedure *Vertebrate* is called, with $Vertebrate(x)$ becoming the new query. This query unifies with the head of A2, but to avoid variable name clashes the occurrences of x in this clause must be consistently renamed for uniqueness. Thus the call $Vertebrate(x)$ unifies with the head of A2 under the substitution of, say, x_2 for x. Now the call becomes $Bird(x_2)$, which unifies with the head of A3 under the substitution of *Fred* for x_2. Since A3 has no body, the computation is complete. By a chain of substitutions—*Fred* for x_2, x_2 for x, and x for y—we have a substitution of *Fred* for y in the original query, and the query succeeds with this substitution as the output of the logic program. This ability to answer questions posed as queries containing variables have made logic programming systems one kind of basis for *intelligent databases.*

Limitations of Logic Programming for Defeasible Reasoning

As a model of deductive reasoning, logic programming works very well. For defeasible reasoning, however, Horn clause representation is inadequate. Consider the following Horn clause representation involving Fred the penguin:

$$Flyer(x) \leftarrow Bird(x) \qquad \text{(B1)}$$
$$Nonflyer(x) \leftarrow Penguin(x) \qquad \text{(B2)}$$
$$Bird(x) \leftarrow Penguin(x) \qquad \text{(B3)}$$
$$Penguin(Fred) \qquad \text{(B4)}$$

Given the query $Flyer(y)$, executing B1–B4 as a logic program would result in a substitution of *Fred* for y. Clearly, this is not an adequate model of the reasoning involved, since Fred's being a penguin *defeats* his being a bird as a reason for thinking Fred is a flyer. Indeed, logic programming apparatus is oblivious to any epistemic defeat at work here, and can make no distinction between the strengths of evidence for competing conclusions. In fact, given the query $Nonflyer(y)$, executing B1–B4 also results in the substitution of *Fred* for y.

The shortcomings of Horn clauses to represent defeasible reasoning are apparent from both a declarative and a procedural point of view. Declaratively, B1 represents the sentence "All birds are flyers," but of course this is not what we mean when we assert that birds are flyers. Instead, we mean to express the defeasible entailment $Bird(x) \overset{S}{\rightarrow} Flyer(x)$. This suggests extending the declarative semantics of logic programming to allow such entailments using a $\overset{S}{\leftarrow}$ operator. In addition, a nonsupport operator $\overset{S}{\nleftarrow}$ can provide representational power for undercutting defeat.

Another problem for Horn clauses is the handling of negated consequents. B1 and B2 are competitors only if B2 is fully translated as $\neg Flyer(x) \leftarrow Penguin(x)$. The problem with a clause like this for logic programming is that it is not a Horn clause with exactly one positive literal, for its conjunctive normal form is $\neg Flyer(x) \vee \neg Penguin(x)$. Without a positive literal, the clause cannot be naturally interpreted as a procedure to prove anything, so it can serve no role in a logic programming system. But clauses with negated consequents are essential for the representation and detection of rebutting defeat. Negated consequents can be handled in a way similar to how negated antecedents are handled in standard logic programming systems. In such systems, for example, Prolog, negated calls like *not(f(X))* in a procedure *body* are interpreted not as involving full-blown negation as in theorem-proving systems, but as calls to a special built-in procedure called *not*. Similarly, in a defeasible reasoning system based on Horn clauselike representation, we can indicate negation in a consequent as in $Neg(Flyer(x)) \leftarrow Penguin(x)$.

The procedural shortcoming of logic programming from the point of view of defeasible reasoning is that the execution of a procedure does not include the notion of a defeat check. Suppose we implement the language changes to allow a set of clauses which looks like:

$$Flyer(x) \overset{S}{\leftarrow} Bird(x) \qquad (C1)$$
$$Neg(Flyer(x)) \leftarrow Penguin(x) \qquad (C2)$$
$$Bird(x) \leftarrow Penguin(x) \qquad (C3)$$
$$Penguin(Fred) \qquad (C4)$$

Given the query *Flyer(y)*, a logic programming system extended for defeasible reasoning must not only unify with the consequent of C1 and call the *Bird* procedure successfully; it must also determine whether the application of C1 is defeated. The concept of a defeat check on a procedure can be integrated into logic programming. In straight logic programming a procedure succeeds if its head successfully unifies and its body succeeds; in the expanded defeasible reasoning system a procedure succeeds if its head unifies and its body succeeds *and* survives a defeat check. The defeat check is itself just a series of unification attempts on literals, controlled by a process embodying the defeat principles we have identified.

The relationship between logic programming and defeasible reasoning has been explored by both philosophers and computer scientists.[16] Nute's contribution is particularly interesting because the created system is described by Nute both as a computer program *and* as a philosophical analysis. It is an example of some philosophers' tendency to move away from the traditional view of philosophy as a totally nonempirical endeavor, and toward the view that philosophical analysis can benefit from the construction and study of reasoning artifacts. But to couch defeasible reasoning in the framework of logic programming necessarily limits artificial defeasible reasoning agents to the paradigm of Horn clause logic. The philosopher who has done the most toward creating a complete theory of rationality based on defeasible reasoning, without any programming language restrictions, is John Pollock.

Pollock's Quest to Build a Person

Pollock is a philosopher and cognitive scientist whose objective is "the construction of a general theory of rationality, and its implementation on a computer."[17] He has an ongoing project called OSCAR to do just that. OSCAR is a computer program that puts into practice Pollock's work as an epistemologist in the 1970s, but more importantly, the more Pollock works on OSCAR, the more OSCAR informs and changes his views on just what constitutes rationality. Pollock is passionate about the value for philosophy of building reasoning models:

> Philosophers may wonder whether there is any philosophical point to actually carrying out ... computer modeling. To them, it may seem that all that is important is the *possibility* of building an automated reasoner that models the theory of reasoning. Their view would be that actually building the system is the business of AI, not philosophy. However, the refining and the modeling of theories of reasoning go hand in hand in a way that philosophers have generally overlooked. I recommend this as *the* proper way to pursue philosophical investigations of reasoning. It is probably the only way to get theories of reasoning wholly right. One does not have to spend long constructing computer models of theories of reasoning to discover that they almost never do precisely what we expect them to do, and sorting out why leads to the discovery of subtle errors in the theories. ... I cannot emphasize too strongly how important this is. Computer modeling has led me to make profound changes in my own theories. Philosophers may not fully appreciate what a powerful technique this is until they try it, but once they try it they will never be content to do without it. I predict that this will become an indispensable tool for philosophy over the next twenty years.[18]

Pollock comes from an epistemological tradition of *foundationalism*, which holds that the justificatory structure of empirical knowledge is hierarchical, with higher-level beliefs supported by justification chains of other beliefs, with these chains ultimately ending in a foundational level. For example, beliefs about physical objects are ultimately supported by deliverances of sense and memory, which are not supported by anything other than themselves. The foundationalist view of the structure of knowledge invites a corresponding view about how knowledge is acquired through reasoning, for the justificatory relationship by which beliefs stand to each other can be held up against the inferential relationship by which premisses and conclusions stand to each other in proofs. And, as we have seen in this chapter, the model of reasoning offered by symbolic logic is conveniently suited for implementation on computers.

But Pollock's OSCAR is unique in AI because it is not wedded to deductive logic or programming paradigms based on it, like logic programming. The cognitive architecture of OSCAR[19] is designed to reflect

Pollock's theory of rationality, which is heavily dependent upon his analysis of defeasible reasoning. By contrast, a defeasible logic implemented as an extension of logic programming might compromise the cognitive architecture of the theory by being shoehorned into a particular logical paradigm. By formalizing a language of thought based on an epistemological theory of rationality, OSCAR is not influenced by any preconceived languages of logic.

It will be interesting to observe the outcome of Pollock's prediction that computer models will become indispensable tools for philosophers, at least those who are interested in reasoning. Doubtless, some will resist. R.M. Chisholm, for example, who agreed with Pollock on the important fundamental aspects of epistemology, would not agree that writing computer programs and observing their behavior can be related to philosophizing. In the next chapter, we will examine this possibility more closely in the context of heuristics and justification.

The Naturalization of Epistemology

A guiding principle of epistemology, and indeed of common sense, is that in order for a true belief to count as knowledge, it must be justified in an appropriate way. Chief among the objectives of classical contemporary epistemology has been to identify the criteria for such justification. Since terms like "justified," "warranted," and "reasonable" are clearly normative terms, until the last two decades epistemology was regarded as an exclusively normative enterprise. Concomitant with the rise of artificial intelligence and cognitive science, however, there has been a movement among some philosophers to change the role of epistemology from a normative to a descriptive one. In this new guise, epistemology would retreat from its *a priori* role of pure argument analysis and take on an empirical character, studying instead the actual cognitive and physiological processes involved in an agent's coming to know things. Since these are natural processes to be known *a posteriori*, this transition has come to be called the "naturalization" of epistemology.

Extremely influential philosophers have varied widely in response to this movement. W.V.O. Quine, one of its earliest and most radical proponents, saw the old epistemology as mired in the Carnapian "rational reconstruction" of physical statements in terms of statements of sense experience, logic, and set theory:

> But why all this creative reconstruction, all this make-believe?
> The stimulation of his sensory receptors is all the evidence
> anybody has had to go on, ultimately, in arriving at his picture of
> the world. Why not see how this construction really proceeds?
> Why not settle for psychology?[1]

Hence,

> Epistemology, or something like it, simply falls into place as a
> chapter of psychology and hence of natural science. It studies a

> natural phenomenon, viz., a physical human subject. This human
> subject is accorded a certain experimentally controlled input –
> certain patterns of irradiation in assorted frequencies, for instance
> – and in the fullness of time the subject delivers as output a
> description of the three dimensional world and its history.[2]

Other philosophers of the old school, like R. Chisholm, regard this
movement as a profound mistake. While it is true that the nature of
knowledge is now of interest to fields outside of philosophy, Chisholm
admits, that does not thereby make those fields contributors to the *theory*
of knowledge (or "epistemology") proper:

> The latter disciplines [i.e., information theory, artificial
> intelligence, cognitive science, psychology, etc.] are not
> alternatives to the traditional theory of knowledge because they
> are branches of empirical science and not of philosophy. For the
> most part, the facts with which they are concerned are not
> relevant to the traditional philosophical questions. Unfortunately,
> however, this relevance has been exaggerated by many writers
> who do not seem to have grasped the traditional problems.[3]

It is clear that Quine and Chisholm have fundamentally different views
about the methods and goals of epistemology, which put them in a position of talking past each other on this issue and many others. Others,
however, like A. Goldman, find a rich and exploitable middle ground in
which the study of cognitive processes may offer insights to traditional
questions of normative epistemology:

> Why is epistemology interested in these processes? One reason is
> its interest in epistemic justification. The notion of justification is
> directed, principally, at beliefs. But evaluations of beliefs, I
> contend, derive from evaluations of belief-forming processes.
> Which processes are suitable cannot be certified by logic alone.
> Ultimately, justificational status depends (at least in part) on
> properties of our basic cognitive equipment. Hence, epistemology
> needs to examine this equipment, to see whether it satisfies
> standards of justifiedness.[4]

Since Goldman believes that epistemology needs help from the cognitive sciences in determining standards of justifiedness, he disagrees with
Chisholm and agrees with Quine. But also, to the extent he believes
in standards of justifiedness at all, epistemology for him still has a normative component. With Goldman, I believe that the proper extent of
the naturalization of epistemology lies somewhere between the somewhat
radical extremes of Chisholm and Quine.

Epistemology, as the theory of knowledge, is not, on the face of it, limited in the types of knowledge that are open to study. In practice, however, epistemologists tend to focus their scrutiny on so-called knowledge of the external world. Such knowledge can be direct, through perception, or indirect, through the application of principles of scientific reasoning. But there is more to knowledge than perceptual and scientific knowledge. In particular, there is the knowledge humans need to acquire through the conscious or unconscious reasoning processes they employ just to solve problems in everyday life. While the formalization of reasoning has been well studied through logic, many AI researchers have discovered that the Carnapian rut here is the overemphasis on logic as a modeling tool for reasoning. The patterns of continual discovery that need to be made just to plan a trip to the store or open a window are not nearly as well known as the principles of logic. Perhaps this is because these activities at first blush seem too trivial to study. But if research in artificial intelligence has shown anything, it is that the simplest of human problems are notoriously difficult to model computationally, despite a heavy reliance on logic as a representational tool. This seems to be a clear signal that the empirical study of problem-solving agents can tell us something which logic cannot about the structure and representation of human knowledge.

But I do not believe it is possible to fully follow Quine's suggestion to merely study the input/output behavior of human beings as they solve problems and to thereby learn what constitutes, say, empirical justification. Such a study would be vain because even if one fully understood the firings of neurons and the brain state transitions involved in complex problem solving, one would not thereby understand the cognitive architecture of the mind, or the patterns of reasoning that are required. Simply understanding behavior cannot reveal the patterns of reasoning that motivates behavior. However, hypothesizing patterns of reasoning and implementing them on a machine might produce the behavior we are trying to understand. Thus I will agree with Quine that we should observe input/output behavior, but I suggest that the empirical domain of inquiry should be machine problem solving, not that of humans. We can already recognize rational behavior in humans when we see it, even if we do not have a complete theory of what human rationality is. But if we can recognize rational behavior in a computer model, then we will have truly learned something about what rationality is, because we had to articulate the patterns of reasoning in order to build the model.

When I say that the study of machine *behavior* can give us better insight into rationality than the study of human *behavior*, I do not mean to belittle the role that human *introspection* has in traditional epistemology's understanding of epistemic terms. The *internalist* versus *externalist* debate in epistemology argues over the value of "armchair philosophizing" in attempting to grasp these terms. As Chisholm, an internalist, puts it, "The internalist assumes that, merely by reflecting upon his own conscious state, he can formulate a set of epistemic priciples that will enable him to find out, with respect to any possible belief he has, whether he is *justified* in having that belief."[5] On the other hand, an externalist with regard to justification holds that for one to understand what justifies a belief depends on relations that are external to one's own conscious state. While there are several different accounts of what these relations are, they share a standard form, which in the words of R. Fumerton, "will typically be a complex nomological property, such as the property of being caused by a process which satisfies a certain description."[6] Goldman, therefore, is an externalist.

Any admonition to consider the mechanism and behavior of artificial reasoners in inquiring about epistemic matters would seem to side with the externalist, but there is still a place for introspecting into one's internal state. We can regard the introspective epistemologist as being in the same relationship to the cognitive scientist as the theoretical physicist is to the experimental physicist. Just as the theoretical physicist can in isolation produce theories for the experimental physicist to test in a laboratory, the introspective epistemologist can in isolation adduce principles of justification for the cognitive scientist to test in a machine. An excellent example of this is Pollock's characterization, through introspection, of defeasible reasoning, and his subsequent testing and refinement of this account through the OSCAR system.

Thus, epistemology can still be normative, because the patterns of reasoning we build into models are motivated by how we think a rational agent *ought* to reason; but done this way, epistemology is also descriptive, because in an iterative process of refinement our proposed patterns of reasoning are informed by the behavior we observe in our artificially constructed agents. One way of elucidating this further is by studying the role of *heuristic search* in AI.

AI and Search

Problem solving is modeled on machines as patterns of search. This is an entirely plausible model, since human problem solving is often characterized by weighing possible next moves against each other, by trial and error, and by backtracking. But to model problem solving as *unconstrained* search is impossible even for modest problems. Consider a robot R which must plan a sequence of moves from its current location to a goal location G in a world represented by the grid in Figure 6. If P

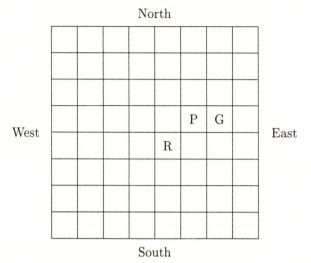

Figure 6. *Grid Representation of Robot Planning Problem*

represents a pillar to be avoided, and the available moves are to move one cell in any of the directions *north, south, east,* or *west,* it is clear that the optimal sequence of moves is *east-east-north.* But at any point during the construction of such a sequence, the robot is faced with a number of alternative possible actions. If the search is unconstrained, the problem is that every action must be considered when deciding on a move. That is, for every possible state of affairs (or simply "state") the robot finds itself in, there are four possible next moves and thus four possible next states to decide among when making a plan. Figure 7 depicts the combinatorial explosion of states necessary to search for even this simple three-step solution in terms of a graphical tree structure called a *state space.*

Each node in this structure represents a state like that depicted in Figure 6. The node labeled "Root" would actually be the state in Figure 6, and each of its direct descendants would be the state resulting from the move specified on the corresponding connecting arc. If the robot just blindly searches through this structure, then depending upon the order in which it considers moves, it would have to search through a maximum of $4^3 = 64$ different sequences. A simple change in the starting configuration of this problem (Figure 8) increases the number of sequences to be searched to $4^4 = 256$.

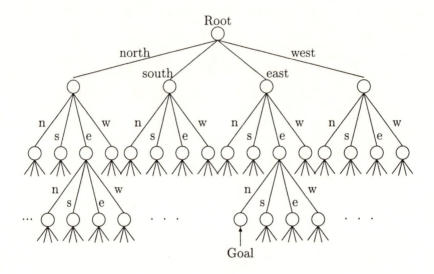

Figure 7. *State Space*

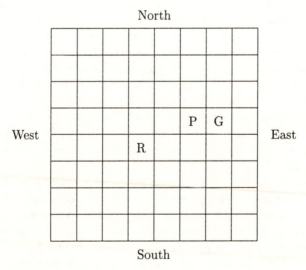

Figure 8. *Another Robot Planning Problem*

For realistic problems of moderate size, solvable by humans with no great effort, the number of states necessary to search becomes too large even for the most powerful computer to handle in a reasonable amount of time. When faced with a decision at the outset to go *north, south, east,* or *west,* the robot should not just arbitrarily try one direction in hopes of fortuitously choosing the correct one. The choice must be guided by a *heuristic,* or rule for choosing actions. A heuristic effectively rank-orders the possible actions, which pays off if the higher-ranked action indeed does eventually lead to a good solution. This is due to the fact, as put by R. Korf, that "a small amount of knowledge often buys a large improvement in solution quality and/or computation time."[7] The problem is to embody this knowledge in a heuristic rule.

An obvious rule for choosing actions in our robot problem is to pick a direction that decreases the distance, measured rectilinearly (called the "Manhattan" distance), between the current robot location and the goal. So the heuristic might be stated:

(**H1**)   Choose a move that decreases the Manhattan distance between R and G.

Given the state depicted in Figure 8, **H1** would eliminate the consideration of going *south* or *west.* In then choosing between going *north* and *east,* another heuristic should be invoked, one which recognizes that going *north* introduces the pillar into the path while going *east* does not. One way of making a rule of this is:

(**H2**)   Choose a move that places R on the same horizontal row or vertical column as G, unless there is a P in that row or column.

Thus, all consequences of initially going *north, south,* or *west* are ranked lower and the search is constrained from the start.

From an epistemological point of view, a heuristic amounts to a *justification* for acting in a certain way, and so it is normative. It is normative not in the sense that a moral imperative justifies the action, but in the sense that a pragmatic imperative requires a minimal use of system resources. To describe the situation doxastically, a heuristic provides justification for the *belief* that one next move in a problem-solving scenario results in a more efficient plan of action than all its competitors. The performance of machine models of problem solving can be measured by their use of system resources. One that minimizes such use is better at justifying its intermediate beliefs about courses of action. So a study of the use of heuristics in machine models of problem solving may help us to understand just what it is that justifies beliefs in certain empirical arenas.

Heuristics in State Space Pruning

A *quantitative* heuristic is a criterion that simplifies a state space search via a function by which competing next states can be compared and judged according to a numerical cost determination. **H1** is clearly such a heuristic, ranking going *north* or *east* better than going *south* or *west* in Figure 6 or 8 on the basis of Manhattan distances. **H2** can also be regarded as a quantitative heuristic, although devising a numerical function to compute it would not be as straightforward as a Manhattan distance.

The justification provided by heuristics in problem solving can perhaps be made clearer through another example. Artificial intelligence researchers often test theories by modeling problems in a "blocks world," where state representation is simplified and possible actions are well defined. Consider a world in which there are two blocks, A and B, and three places, p, q, and r, where blocks may be placed. A block can be moved (by an idealized robot arm, say) and placed on another place or block provided the other block is not on top of it. Suppose the problem is to change the initial state to the goal state as depicted in Figure 9. It is immediately obvious that the minimal solution to this problem is a

Initial   Goal

Figure 9. *Initial and Goal States in Blocks World*

three-step solution that moves A from atop B to r, moves B from p to q, and then moves A from r to atop B. Each of these moves reflects a belief that it will move the problem solver closer to a solution. With Goldman, we may then ask, How do we come to believe this? By studying the behavior of computer programs that solve this problem, we may be able to understand how these moves are both formulated and justified during the formation of the overall plan.

Programs simulating planning must navigate through the possible states that can be reached via the legally defined moves or actions. In the blocks world problem the possible states are as shown in Figure 10. In the diagram, the initial state is labeled S1 and the goal state S12.

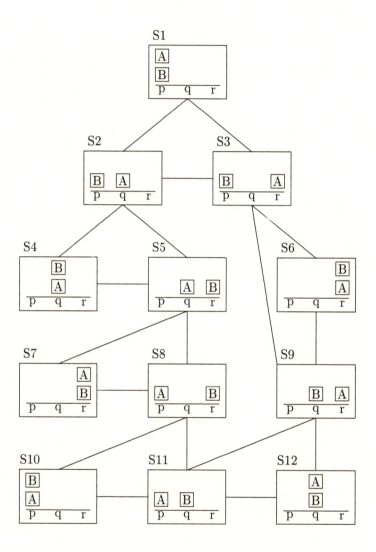

Figure 10. *Possible States in Blocks World Problem*

Legal transitions from one state to another and vice versa are indicated by a connecting arc between them. There are forty nonrepetitive ways to get from S1 to S12. (A nonrepetitive solution is one in which no state repeats itself.) The minimal solution is represented by the path through the structure beginning at S1, moving through S3 and S9 and ending at S12. It is relatively easy to write a computer program that exhaustively generates all solutions, but there is no guarantee that the minimal solution would be found first. In this simple problem, generating all forty solutions using a backtracking algorithm would require a hundred and thirteen state visitations. During this algorithm many silly solutions would be generated which a human would not even entertain, for example, the ten-move solution S1, S3, S2, S4, S5, S7, S8, S10, S11, S9, S12. For a program to model human problem solving in this case, heuristics must be employed.

To attempt to come up with a heuristic in a problem-solving domain is to attempt to codify knowledge of that domain. A simple but naive bit of knowledge in our blocks world is that a state Si is "closer" to the goal state than another state Sj if more of the places p, q, and r in Si have the correct block on them than in Sj. Thus, the heuristic might be stated as:

(H3)   Choose the state that has the fewest number of places with incorrect blocks on them.

For example, S9 is to be chosen ahead of, say, S6, since in S9 only place r has an incorrect block, while in S6 both q and r are incorrect. We say that S9 has a heuristic value of one while S6 has a heuristic value of two.

Computer scientists have developed a "best-first" algorithm[8] whereby a state graph like that in Figure 10 is searched using a method that considers both the heuristic value of a state and its depth in the state space. The algorithm uses the sum of these values to prioritize the consideration of states during search. It accomplishes this through a list of states organized as a *priority queue*, which is a data structure used by programmers to rank-order pending actions. The algorithm processes the priority queue by picking the best-ranked state from it and determining which states it can legally "get to" from it. It then creates representations of these possible next states and places them in the priority queue on the basis of their heuristic values. The algorithm then picks the new best-ranked state and repeats the process until the goal state is found. If we apply this best-first algorithm using heuristic **H3** to our blocks world problem, the number of states created by the program before finding the minimal solution is cut substantially. Figure 11 shows the states created with the heuristic value given on the top right of each state.

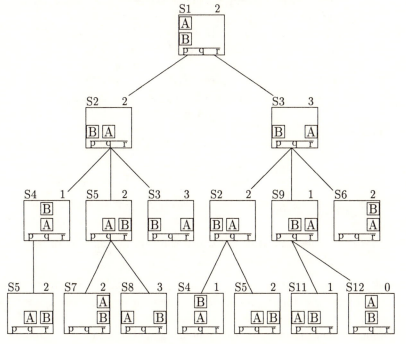

Figure 11. *States Created Using Heuristic* **H3**

The number of states explored is sixteen compared with the maximum number of a hundred and thirteen that a nonheuristic approach might require. Still, the heuristic is naive in that in evaluating the descendants of S1 it assigns a lower cost to S2 than to S3, leading the algorithm to momentarily consider the left subtree in a fruitless search for the minimal length solution. The problem with **H3** is that it only considers the status of the places p, q, and r, without also considering the status of the blocks on top of them. We might try to remedy this by taking into account the number of blocks that would have to be moved onto or off of a place in order to get it into its goal state. So with an eye toward coming up with a reasonably general heuristic which can work in situations with more than just two blocks, we can recursively define the *cost* of a place or block X in state S using the algorithm given in Figure 12. Now we can use the following more sophisticated heuristic:

> **IF** X has no blocks on it in the goal state **THEN**
> > **IF** X has no blocks on it in S **THEN** the cost of X in S is zero
> > **ELSE** the cost of X is the number of blocks on it in S
> **ELSE** (X does have at least one block on it in the goal state)
> > **IF** X has the correct block on it in S **THEN**
> > > the cost of X in S is the cost of the block on X
> > **ELSE IF** X has an incorrect block on it in S **THEN**
> > > the cost of X in S is the number of blocks on it in S +
> > > > > the number of blocks on it in the goal state
> > **ELSE** (X has no blocks on it in S)
> > > the cost of X in S is the number of blocks on it in the goal state

Figure 12. *Algorithm for Computing Blocks World Costs*

(**H4**)   Choose the state for which the sum of the costs of its places is least.

When the best-first algorithm is run using this heuristic the number of states created is reduced from sixteen to the eleven shown in Figure 13 along with their computed heuristic values.

Another measure of comparative heuristic performance is the number of times that the best-first search algorithm needs to retrieve states from the priority queue. With **H3** the number of such retrievals is six and with **H4** the number of retrievals is four. But while **H4** is preferable to **H3** on these counts, **H4** still indicates no clear preference when evaluating the descendants of S1; both S2 and S3 receive heuristic values of four. Thus there is no way of keeping the program from considering the left subtree (although it is a smaller subtree than before) before finding the minimal length solution on the right, and it would probably be inaccurate to claim that **H4** adequately models human problem solving in this case.

It is tempting to try to repair **H4** so that S3 will have a lower estimated cost than S2. We might recognize, for example, that by finding the *sum* of the costs of the places in S3, **H4** overestimates the number of moves to get to the goal since the two moves required to clear places p and r are the same two moves required to get place q in the correct state. Rather than adding the costs of the three places, we can consider taking the *maximum* of the costs of them:

(**H5**)   Choose the state for which the maximum of the costs of its places is least.

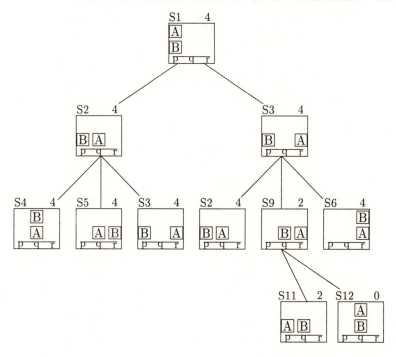

Figure 13. *States Created Using Heuristic* **H4**

Under **H5**, S3 is given a heuristic value of 2 and S2 is given a value of 3, forcing the program to not consider the left subtree and instead zero in directly on the solution on the right. Figure 14 shows that only eight states need to be created for this problem using **H5**. Moreover, only three priority queue retrievals are required, the minimum necessary to find the solution.

However, lest we be seduced into thinking that we have discovered a model of human blocks world problem solving in quantitative terms of a priority queue, our cost function and the concept of a maximum, let us consider how this model performs for more complicated problems. Figure 15 shows the performance of the best-first search algorithm using the three heuristics on five blocks world problems of increasing complexity. Despite the promise shown by **H5** for the simplest problem, it performs the best on only three of the five problems, and on the most difficult problem its performance is dismal. Clearly, a heuristic's performance cannot be extrapolated from simple problems, despite the not insignificant ef-

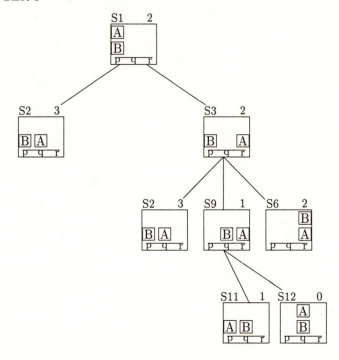

Figure 14. *States Created Using Heuristic* **H5**

fort that can go into analyzing them for clues to human problem solving ability.

Problem Decomposition and Simplified Models

Depending on the level of problem solving we wish to model, the performance of these heuristics may or may not live up to human abilities. What they have in common is a simple ability to compare a current state and a goal state and to estimate the "distance" the current state is from the goal state through a comparative measure. This may very well model the approach some humans take in solving problems such as these. Others, however, might take more sophisticated approaches involving the identification of *subgoals* in an effort to simplify the search.[9] None of the heuristics **H3**, **H4**, or **H5** can be said to do this, though they might still be involved in the overall effort at a lower level.

When solving problem 5 in Figure 15, for example, a thoughtful human is likely to recognize that the problem can be broken down into

Problem		Solution length	Number of Priority Queue Retrievals		
Initial state	Goal state		H3	H4	H5
1 — A / B / p q r	A / B / p q r	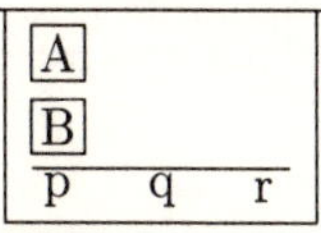 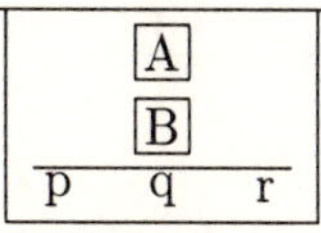 3	6	4	3
2 — A / B / C / p q r	A / B / C / p q r	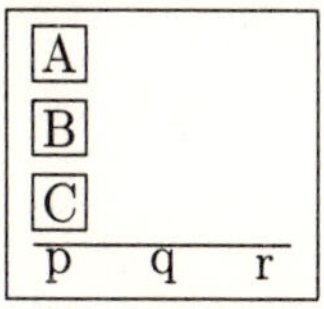 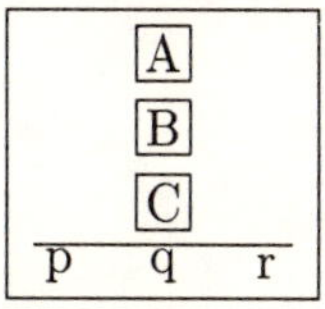 5	8	8	5
3 — A C / B D / p q r	A C / B D / p q r	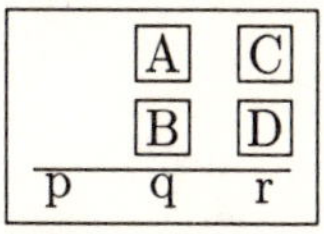 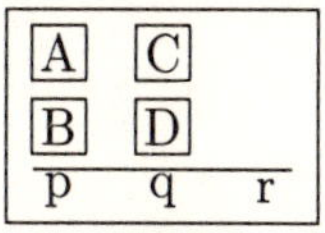 6	46	7	14
4 — A / B / C / D / p q r	B / C / A / D / p q r	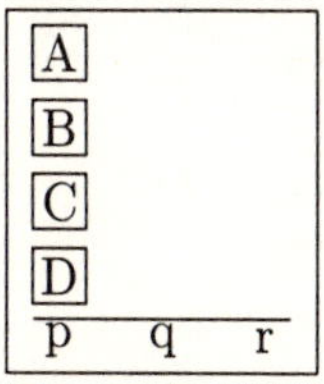 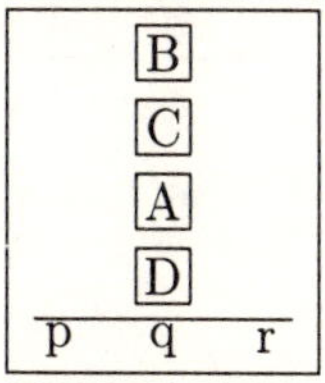 8	125	30	25
5 — A B C / D E F / p q r	D E F / A B C / p q r	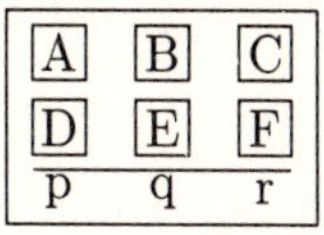 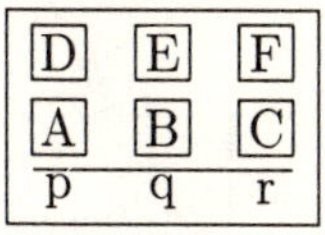 12	7615	25	1321

Figure 15. *Other Blocks World Problems*

three subproblems: first interchange blocks A and D, then interchange blocks B and E, and finally interchange blocks C and F. Each of these subproblems can still be guided by a heuristic. The total number of priority queue retrievals required for solving these three subproblems (15) using **H4** is less than the number required for the overall problem (25), as Figure 16 shows.

One might take the idea of problem decomposition further by considering that even the subproblems can be decomposed into simpler problems, and so on until the problem is solved. For example, subproblem 5a of problem 5 from Figure 16 can be subdivided into the simpler problems 5a-1 and 5a-2 in Figure 17. The total number of priority queue retrievals required to solve problem 5a when broken down like this (four) is less

| Subproblem | | Solution length | Number of Priority Queue Retrievals |
Initial state	Goal state		
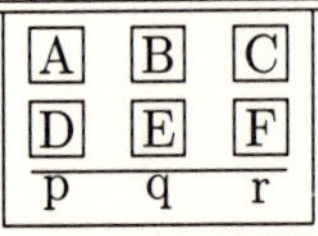 5a A B C / D E F / p q r	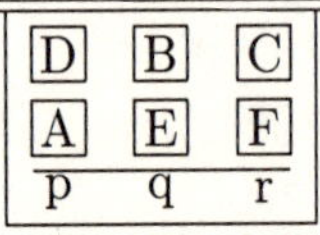 D B C / A E F / p q r	4	5
5b D B C / A E F / p q r	D E C / A B F / p q r	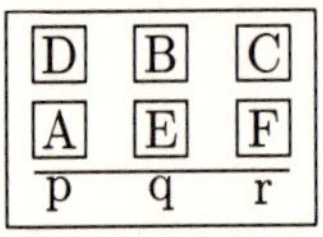 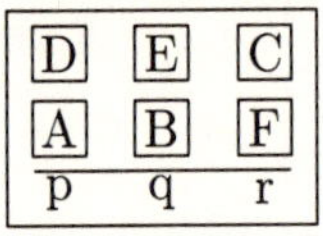 4	5
5c D E C / A B F / p q r	D E F / A B C / p q r	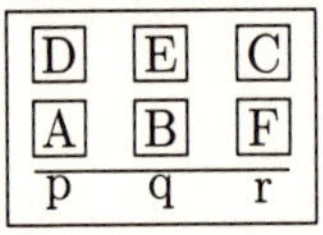 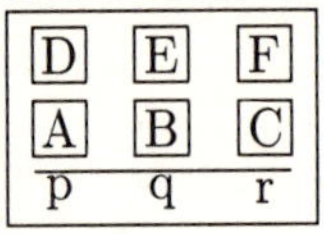 4	5
		12 total	15 total

Figure 16. *Subproblems of Problem 5 Using* **H4**

| Subproblem | | Solution length | Number of Priority Queue Retrievals |
Initial state	Goal state		
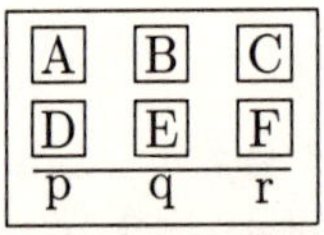 5a-1 A B C / D E F / p q r	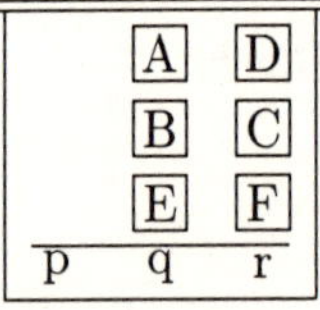 A D / B C / E F / p q r	2	2
5a-2 A D / B C / E F / p q r	D B C / A E F / p q r	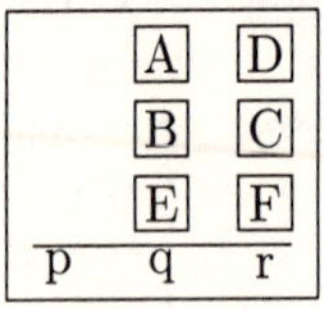 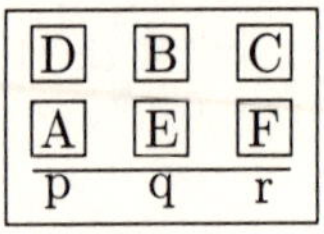 2	2
		4 total	4 total

Figure 17. *Subproblems of Problem 5a Using* **H4**

than the number required without decomposition (5) and equal to the minimum necessary to find the solution.

It is a natural final step to observe that problem 5a-1 (and also 5a-2) can also be broken down into two subproblems, each of which can be solved with one move. One might argue from this that problem decomposition into subproblems is the major factor in human problem solving, with heuristic comparison of next states retreating into a minor role. We must ask, however, what justifies the decomposition of a problem into subproblems in the first place. For this is itself a search process, requiring decisions as to how to abstract a sequence of moves at the lowest level of detail into subproblems. We can understand the process better through the notion of simplified models.[10] A simplified model of a problem is one in which one or more constraints on legal moves is removed, with the result that the newly modeled problem is easier to solve. Simplified models of problems are used by computer scientists to generate heuristics that are guaranteed to find minimal length solutions. But simplified models can also be used to decompose a problem into subproblems.

For example, in the blocks world model we might relax the constraint that only one block can be moved at a time by allowing two blocks to exchange positions simultaneously in one move. This makes for an easier problem. For example, under this constraint problem 5 in Figure 15 can be solved in three moves rather than 12. See Figure 18.

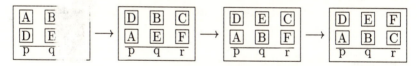

Figure 18. *Problem 5 with Relaxed Constraint*

Note that these moves correspond to the subproblems 5a, 5b, and 5c in Figure 16. Thus, moves in a solution for a simplified model of the problem are equivalent to the specification of subproblems in the nonsimplified model of the problem.

Similarly, problem 5a, which requires four moves under the unrelaxed block rules, is simplified when the constraints are changed to allow the simultaneous moving of two blocks *excluding* exchanging them. Note that this constraint is a relaxation of the original problem's rules, but more stringent than allowing block exchanges. Figure 19 shows a two-move solution of problem 5a using this constraint. These two moves are equivalent to the subproblems 5a-1 and 5a-2 in Figure 17. Note that a decomposition of 5a-1 into two moves involves tightening the two-block

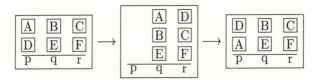

Figure 19. *Problem 5a with Relaxed Constraint*

movement constraint so that only one block can be moved, which is the rule for the fully constrained problem. So the more relaxed the problem constraint (or the more simplified the model), the higher the level of problem decomposition that results.

Thus the determination of subproblems can be thought of as a search through a space whose problem constraints have been relaxed. However, this search must itself be guided, or much processing could be wasted on considering subproblems which have no promise in solving the overall problem. For example, the first move in the solution of Figure 18 is just one of fifteen possible block exchanges that can be performed on the initial state. Thus the solution shown is one of $15^3 = 3375$ possible three-move paths from the initial state. Clearly, a heuristic such as **H4** must still be involved in the problem decomposition process. It seems a reasonable conjecture that while humans may use problem decomposition extensively, heuristic estimates of "distance" from the goal are used in any case.

Heuristics in Defeasible Reasoning

We would be straying from our purpose of studying human justificatory principles if we only considered quantitative heuristics in our models of problem solving. While quantitative comparisons are clearly involved in much of the decision making in state space search, we just as clearly depend upon qualitative considerations. One way of characterizing a *qualitative* heuristic is not as a function, but as an assumption that simplifies a reasoning process by limiting the number of premises required to be established in an argument. Let us alter our original robot example as in Figure 20 so that P does not represent a nonmoving obstacle like a pillar, but a roving obstacle like a penguin. Recall heuristic **H2**:

> **(H2)**   Choose a move that places R on the same horizontal row or vertical column as G, unless there is a P in that row or column.

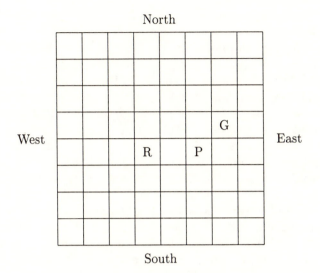

Figure 20. *Another Robot Planning Problem*

In the situation depicted in Figure 20, the decision to go north would be prescribed by **H2** only given an added assumption that the penguin P is not also at some time going to move north into the row occupied by R and G. If the action of the penguin cannot be predicted, then some such assumption as this must be made in order to plan the moves. This assumption would take the form of another heuristic:

> (**H6**)   If P is not an obstacle to G at time t, then assume P will not be an obstacle to G at time $t + 1$.

H6 differs fundamentally from **H2** in that it provides a pervading basis for the application of **H2**. **H6** allows **H2** to be applied by not requiring that the future position of P be ascertained. Given that the future position of P may not even be ascertain*able*, this is a greatly simplifying assumption. But the simplification gained by its use is not through pruning a state space *while* it is being searched, as is the case with quantitative heuristics, but by simplifying the problem's representation scheme. Without it, it would be necessary to explicitly represent sets of facts like "P is not in row i and column j at time t," "P is not in row i and column j at time $t + 1$," "P is not in row i and column j at time $t + 2$," and so on. With it, a problem solver can ignore the future position of P and get on with the problem of planning a solution.

What is the epistemological status of a heuristic like **H6**? While it has the form of a conditional: "If A, then assume B," it is certainly not expressing a truth-preserving connection between A and B. Rather, if spelled out, it expresses a justification-preserving connection between beliefs about the location of penguins: "If P is not an obstacle to G at time t, and there is no independent reason to suppose that P will be an obstacle to G at time $t+1$, then it is justified to believe that P will not be an obstacle to G at time $t+1$." This is an example of a *defeasible rule* of the type described in chapter 7. It allows the tentative introduction of its consequent until new information is learned which defeats its application. Thus defeasible rules provide justification for qualitative heuristics.

The formalization and mechanization of reasoning using defeasible rules, an area of research in artificial intelligence, is an example of the bilateral contributions that can be made by epistemology and AI to each other. Much of the early work in AI can be regarded as testing the hypothesis that human knowledge can be adequately modeled by deductive logic, and the experiments failed in a quagmire of representational problems. This motivated attempts by computer scientists to begin developing more expressive logics around 1980.[11] While these attempts were for the most part a step in the right direction, we have seen that work in knowledge representation in the last decade has benefited from the insights of epistemologists like Pollock who had already studied defeasible reasoning. By studying the nature of the justification relation rather than forcing defeasibility to be explained by extending the truth conditions of standard logic, they were able to produce systems which more accurately model the mechanisms of defeat.

The study of heuristics is an example of a confluence of artificial intelligence and epistemology, since heuristics can be regarded as justifying the actions and beliefs of problem-solving agents. One type of heuristic attempts to quantify the justifiedness of actions and beliefs. The study of justified belief in problem solving benefits from computer models employing quantitative heuristics, for these models can be evaluated for their performance against human problem solving. Qualitative heuristics embody the justifying ability of defeasible rules. Since the modeling of defeasibility is critical for the creation of intelligent programs, artificial intelligence researchers attempting to do knowledge representation must do some epistemology in order to understand what they are modeling.

I have tried to show that a benign naturalization of epistemology can be accomplished in a way that combines its traditional philosophical nature peaceably with the empirical and experimental methods of artificial intelligence. Researchers in artificial intelligence must ask themselves, when modeling human problem solving processes, how inferences in such processes are justified and what form the justification takes. On the other hand, epistemological theories, because their subject matter is human knowledge, are subject to the testing and falsifying that attends the study of any natural artifact, since human knowledge can be modeled in computer programs. The "naturalization" of epistemology, therefore, should go hand in hand with the "philosophization" of artificial intelligence.

Part III

The Philosophy of
Computer Science

– 9 –
Computer Science and Mathematics

The first two parts of this book have explored the interplay of philosophy and computer science through the field of artificial intelligence. I hope it is clear that this interplay is marked by give-and-take, at least as far as the suitability of various models of mind, reasoning, and justification are concerned. But of course, there is much more to philosophize about in computer science than these specific sorts of models. There is also the entire foundation of the discipline to worry about, as evidenced by a number of debates that have arisen in the absence of an agreed-upon framework for such a foundation.

But there has been little sustained work in the investigation of the philosophical foundations of computer science *qua* science. As we come upon a new millenium, fully half a century after the birth of computer science, it is time to address theoretical questions about the nature of the discipline. Although theoretical, our inquiry here is not to be confused with theoretical computer science, in which, for example, models of computation are reasoned about in an effort to analyze and increase the efficiency of computational processes. Rather, our investigation will have the typical *meta*-flavor characterizing the philosophy *of*s, and we will inquire into areas such as whether computer science can be reduced to mathematics, the proper role of formal models, and the nature of abstraction in computer science. My hope is that this discussion will kindle an ongoing tradition of a philosophy *of* computer science.

Toward a Philosophy of Computer Science

Are there philosophical foundations of computer science? Before contemplating this, we should ask what makes any philosophy a philosophy *of* something else. Here is one point of view. Epistemology, metaphysics, and (meta)ethics constitute core philosophical areas in that they take for their subject matter the most "generic" of concepts, stripped of flavor and color: knowledge (in general, not necessarily knowledge *of* anything in particular), existence (of *kinds* of entities, not anything in particular), and values (the meaning and possibility of value-laden or moral terms, not the morality of acts per sé). We might even call these areas the foundations of philosophy. See the bottom level in the taxonomy presented in Figure 21, which is by no means intended to be exhaustive, only illustrative.

When philosophical investigation is concerned with any of these concepts laced with a particular slant, it is a philosophy *of*. A philosophy *of* can involve questions and problems in one or several of the foundational areas of philosophy. So, philosophy of mind is concerned with the existence and knowledge of *particular* kinds of entities, namely mental objects and mental events. Philosophy of art analyzes the existence and value of *aesthetic* objects. Normative ethics (philosophy of moral decisions) is concerned with the morality of *particular* acts. Finally, more relevant to our current problem, philosophy of science is concerned with the logic of *scientific* concept formation in the analysis of *scientific* knowledge—how we come by it and what it means. (See the second tier of Figure 21.)

We can describe a third tier of philosophical investigation, essentially a level of specialization in relation to the second tier. This is a level in which questions of knowledge, existence, and value are posed within a quite specific context, demanding expertise at least in the language of a specific field of inquiry. Thus, medical ethics is a specialization of normative ethics concerned with the morality of medical acts, like abortion or euthanasia. Philosophies of, say, cinema and dance are specializations of philosophy of art. Philosophy of psychology poses questions for both philosophy of science and philosophy of mind, while philosophies of other social or natural sciences are restricted studies in the philosophy of science. Such specializations are depicted in the third tier of Figure 21, which illustrates philosophy's appeal for both pure generalists and focused specialists, as well as many falling in between.

Clearly, the philosophy of computer science should take a place alongside other specific philosophies of science in the third tier. Work in this tier is typically characterized by one or more Central Questions. A Central Question in the philosophy of biology, for example, is whether the science of the organic can be reduced to the science of the inorganic (the reduction of biological to physical laws). A Central Question in the philosophy of the social sciences is whether the social sciences can or should be value-free. A Central Question in philosophy of physics concerns the function and ontological status of inferred entities like quarks and strings.

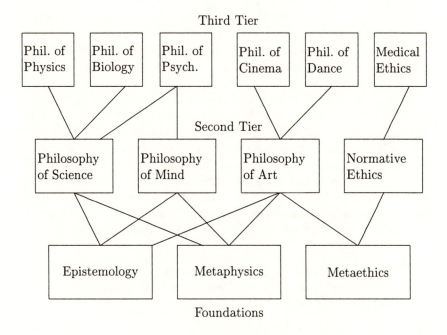

Figure 21. A Taxonomy of Philosophy

What are the Central Questions in the philosophy of computer science? As in all philosophy, the philosophy of science is sustained by controversy. Following World War II, much of the discussion regarding theory building centered on the role of observation. The view, commonplace at the time, of theory building as the mere generalization of observation came under attack by scientists and philosophers alike who objected to the empiricists' reductive analysis. More specific philosophies *of* are also often born of controversy over reductionism. In biology, it was vitalism, or belief in a unique "vital force" in organic life, versus mechanism, or the belief that all talk about such a force can be reduced to talk about inorganic processes. In psychology, it was behaviorism, or the belief that talk about consciousness can be reduced to talk about stimuli, percepts, and responses, versus the view that entities such as the self are unique, irreducible, and impossible to study without processes such as introspection.

So it seems that there may be a pattern in the birth and sustenance of philosophy *of*s involving reductionist attempts. The philosophy of computer science may be no exception, for if the history of philosophy ever looks back and identifies an early Central Question in the philosophy of computer science, it may be this: Can computer science be reduced to a branch of mathematics? This is one of the broad questions around which the last part of this book is arranged. The range of perspectives from which this question can be addressed is as wide as the difference between the following view, expressed by C.A.R. Hoare:

> Computer programs are mathematical expressions. They
> describe, with unprecedented precision and in the most minute
> detail, the behavior, intended or unintended, of the computer on
> which they are executed.[1]

and this alternative, offered by C. Floyd:

> Programs are tools or working environments for people. [They]
> are designed in processes of learning and communication so as to
> fit human needs.[2]

While these quotes express views on the function and status of computer programs, the differences of opinion extend to the broader notion of computing as a science, in which the task of actually creating a program is but one aspect. Of related concern, for example, are the activities of program *specification* and *verification*. A program specification is a detailed description of a program's input and output, ignoring the details of how the program actually accomplishes its task. Program verification is the process of determining whether a program actually conforms to its specification. These activities are just as germane to the software process as writing the program itself, and there is no agreement on whether or not program specifications should be mathematical entitities and whether or not program verification can be a purely mathematical activity.

As it turns out, it is the latter question concerning verification which has generated the most debate, contested by computer scientists since the appearance of a paper by R. DeMillo, R. Lipton, and A. Perlis in 1979.[3] But I think that a starting point for best understanding the issues involved is at the level of computer programs themselves and what they mean. The view expressed by Hoare, above, is unequivocal: Computer programs *are* mathematical expressions. The quote by Floyd is less precise, but it expresses a view on the *function* of programs for humans in decidedly nonmathematical terms. While these views do not necessarily contradict one another, they can most definitely signal contrasting values as to how computer programs *ought* to be designed, built, and used.

Not until 1988 did these questions draw the attention of a "pure" philosopher. J. Fetzer resurrected the program verification/social process debate of a decade earlier and subjected it to genuine philosophical analysis.[4] Before this time, however, debate on the issues was evidenced mainly by differences in visionary accounts, given not by philosophers but by computer science practitioners and teachers, of how the young discipline of computer science ought to proceed.

As a practicing computer scientist trained in philosophy, I find myself compelled to frame some of these issues in historical philosophical perspective. Many philosophers have long held there to be a clear distinction between formal science (mathematics and logic) and factual science (any empirical discipline, including physics, biology, sciology, etc.), offering criteria for the distinction between the two as well as an account of their interplay. Quite possibly we can use this distinction to throw some light on the question of whether computer science can be reduced to a branch of mathematics.

According to one widespread philosophical opinion, the difference between formal and factual sciences is based upon the distinction between *analytic* and *synthetic* statements. For R. Carnap, for example, an analytic statement is one that is valid according to the syntactic rules of a pertinent language "independently of the truth or falsity of other statements."[5] The idea is that the truth of an analytic statement can be determined by virtue simply of a language's formation and transformation rules, so that "it is a consequence of the null class of statements." Thus, statements of mathematics ("5 is a prime number") and logic ("It is either the case that x is F or it is not") are analytic; they are derivable entirely within the rules of their respective languages. A synthetic statement, on the other hand, is one which is not analytic (and also not contradictory). A synthetic statement therefore is one whose truth or falsity does not follow from the syntactic transformation rules of a pertinent language but depends upon extra-linguistic states of affairs. "Chicago is on Lake Michigan" is synthetic because it is a consequence of geographical statements such as, "At such-and-such a place there is a conjunction of such-and-such a city and such-and-such a lake."

Now, according to Carnap, "The distinction between the formal and the factual sciences consists then in this: the first contains only analytic, while the second also contains synthetic statements."[6] We might try to put this criterion to the test in the case of computer science. We have the claim, championed by Hoare, that "computer programs are mathematical expressions." Presumably, this would be accompanied by the claim that computer programming is a formal (mathematical) science. Are the statements of a computer program all analytic, or are some synthetic? Take a typical statement in a programming language, like

   (S)   A := 13*74.

The problem with analyzing **S** is that it can have either an imperative sense, as in

   (I)   Compute the value 13 times 74 and place it in
         memory location A,

or a declarative sense, as in

   (D)   Memory location A receives the value of computing
         13 times 74.

Imperative statements, as such, are neither true nor false and thus cannot be classified as analytic or synthetic. Let us focus, then, on the declarative sense.

Statement **D** hides an ambiguity concerning the ontological status of the entity described by "memory location A." This ambiguity, as Fetzer observed, arises because A can be either a *physical* memory location or an *abstract* one. If A is a physical memory location in an executing computer, then **D** should read

   (DP)   Physical memory location A receives the value
          of physically computing 13 times 74.

DP is actually a *prediction* of what will occur when statement **S** is ultimately executed. In reality, **S**, as marks on a piece of paper, or character codes in a computer memory, is not executed *per se*. Instead, it is translated into or interpreted as a set of more primitive operations to be executed when the program is run. But whatever the level of a computer operation, its representation in a statement like **S** is at best a static prediction of its later dynamic execution. As such, it cannot be analytic, since the validity of no nontrivial prediction can be ascertained via syntactic transformation rules alone.

So let us turn to an interpretation of **D** with memory location A in its abstract sense. But what *is* an abstract memory location? In computer science there is the notion of an *abstract* machine, that is, a complete description of the operations of a machine which, were it built to certain specifications and run in certain conditions, would exhibit certain ideal behavior in terms of its state changes and output when given certain input. An abstract machine can be thought of as a specification, realizable either in hardware, through circuit fabrication, or in software, through simulation, of a physically executing machine. As Fetzer points out, physical machines are subject to the problems of reliability and performance that attend any causal systems. Abstract machines, however, do not fail; they are ideal and thus simply *supposed* not to fail. In discourse about programs and their behavior, we tend to unknowingly flip back and forth between reference to abstract and physical machines. When talking about a program and its *intended* behavior, as when predicting that it will run correctly, we assume that the machine on which it runs does not fail its specifications, and thus we are talking about an abstract machine. When talking about a program and its *actual* behavior, say after it is run in analyzing its efficiency, we are talking about a physical machine.

Mathematics, of course, abounds with abstract entities like geometric forms, numbers, structures, and operations, and if Carnap is right mathematics consists of analytic statements. Does an interpretation of computer programs as running on abstract machines result in their statements being analytic? Consider the statement

> **(DA)** Abstract memory location A receives the value
> of abstractly computing 13 times 74.

How does one analyze the validity of such a statement as **DA**? Specifying what an abstract memory location shall receive after abstractly performing a computation is rather like a mathematician *stipulating* the contents of a variable, for example "let $a = 962$." But such a statement is not true analytically; it is true merely by virtue of its being made, like an Austinian performative utterance. Thus **DA** is very much like a mathematical statement, but not in any interesting way—no more interesting than a mathematician incanting "let ..." without a "therefore ... ." Any statement in any programming language can be construed in an abstract sense as in **DA**. Thus any program can be regarded as a series of stipulations in an abstract world. As such, a program, like a series of mathematicians' "let"s, is not a mathematical expression in any interesting sense.

What is mathematical, however, is *reasoning* about programs in their abstract sense. For example, given a program P consisting of the statements $S_1, \ldots, S_n$, and interpreting each S_i as an abstract machine statement s_i, it is possible to construct statements like

(**T**)   Let s_1, s_2, ..., and s_n be an abstract representation of program P. Then P has property R,

where R describes some aspect of the execution of P in the abstract sense. For example, R might describe limits on the time it would take P to run, or the amount of memory P would require to execute. By giving precise interpretations to the s_i in a pertinent language and appropriately choosing R, it may be possible that **T** is a theorem in the language and thus analytic. This is in fact the approach taken by modern researchers in computer science who are concerned with reasoning about algorithms and data structures.

While I have just given a justification of how reasoning *about* programs can be regarded as mathematical, it is yet a much broader claim to say that computer science is, or ought to aspire to be, a branch of mathematics. For there are still the issues of whether the specification, generation, or maintenance of programs (apart from reasoning about completed ones) is or ought to be like a mathematical activity. The issue which motivates and underlies much of the tension in philosophical discussion of computer science is formal verification, or mathematically reasoning about a program's outcome.

The Mathematical Paradigm

Several early thinkers on these issues laid the foundations of what we shall call the mathematical paradigm for computer science. While these authors no doubt would have conceded Fetzer's later point about the causal properties of physical systems versus the mathematical properties of abstract systems, they probably would not have had a problem with relegating their arguments to programs running on abstract machines. Instead, they found their greatest challenge in somehow establishing an exploitable mathematical link between the *static* properties of programs and the *dynamic* properties of running it (albeit in an abstract sense).

One of the earliest contributions in this area was written by J. McCarthy in 1962,[7] who is also given credit for coining the term "artificial intelligence" in the 1950s. While much of McCarthy's work has been driven by a philosophical opinion concerning the relation of human thought and computation, this paper is as much concerned with establishing a basis for a theory of computation which is free of any dependence on a particular computational domain, for example, integers or character strings. Thus, while his contribution here was not directly concerned with reasoning about programs, it *was* overtly concerned with establishing a language for talk about the abstract activity of computation itself. Because, it might be argued, the most general talk about any computation is always in terms of its bare *function*, the best mathematical framework for discussing computation is that of recursive function theory. Such a framework, however, by itself lacks the essential power of programming languages, namely the ability to conditionally execute a statement based on the outcome of some test. McCarthy, therefore, added *conditional expressions* to the standard mathematical lexicon and showed how typical programming features can be described in terms of recursive functions. Since recursive functions can be reasoned about, for example, to show that two sets of functions are equivalent, corresponding programs can also be reasoned about. Thus the static-to-dynamic bridging problem is crossed, for McCarthy, through the intermediary of recursive functions. Not coincidentally, McCarthy is also the designer of a programming language, called Lisp, whose chief programming element is the function and whose effective use relies heavily on recursion.

Still, McCarthy's motive was not just the promotion of a programming language. The question of which programming language to use is moot, so long as the language's syntax and semantics are well specified, since the theory of computation he envisioned would allow, among other advantages, the automatic translation from one linguistic paradigm to another. We can, in fact, look back now after nearly thirty years and confirm that automatic program translation, with the help of precise language specification, has been accomplished in the case of language *compilers*. These are programming tools which translate programs written in familiar human languages like Basic, C++, and Java, into the machine language of computers, which is composed only of zeroes and ones. However, that a compiler, however automatically, in all cases *correctly* translates programs into an assembly or machine language, is something that no compiler builder ever guarantees, as every language reference manual's warranty disclaimer demonstrates. Thus, there is the distinction between (1) using mathematical methods during language translation to produce highly reliable machine language code, and (2) using mathematical methods to prove that a machine language program behaves on its abstract machine exactly as a source language program behaves on its abstract machine.

This distinction between the use of mathematics as an engineering tool versus the use of mathematics to conclusively prove statements in formal systems fairly accurately characterizes the polarity underlying the contrasting quotes from Floyd and Hoare cited above. It also provides the undercurrent for the program verification debate, in which is contrasted the distinction between (1) using mathematical methods during program development and testing to produce highly reliable code and (2) using mathematical methods to prove that a program's execution on its abstract machine is correct. McCarthy, seeing no obstacle to (2), wrote:

> It should be possible almost to eliminate debugging. Debugging is the testing of a program on cases one hopes are typical, until it seems to work. This hope is frequently vain. Instead of debugging a program, one should prove that it meets its specifications, and this proof should be checked by a computer program.[8]

While McCarthy was one of the first to express this opinion, it was shared by others in the 1960s who strove to describe what such a proof would be like. P. Naur, in an effort to cross the static-to-dynamic bridge in reasoning about programs,[9] recognized that one way to talk about a program both as a static, textual entity and as a dynamic, executing entity, was to conceive of the program as executing, but from time to time to conceptually "halt" it and make statements about the state of its abstract machine at the time of halting. By making a number of these "snapshots" of a conceptually executing program, and providing justifications for each on the basis of the previous one, a proof about the state of the abstract machine upon termination could be constructed.

Naur envisioned the use of mathematical thinking not only to prove the correctness of programs, but also to aid in the actual construction of program elements, particularly loops. He prescribed a disciplined approach to loop construction that involves the use of snapshots and painstaking attention to the limits and parameters of the loop–all of which are activities actually preparatory to writing the loop, which, it is hoped, simply "falls out" as a result of the conceptual work involved in the mathematical description of snapshots. That Naur believes the mathematical component of programming to be essential is evident when he writes:

> It is a deplorable consequence of the lack of influence of
> mathematical thinking on the way in which computer
> programming is currently being pursued, that the regular use of
> systematic proof procedures, or even the realization that such
> proof procedures exist, is unknown to the large majority of
> programmers.[10]

Naur's work and that of R. Floyd formed the basis of much of the contemporary work on proving properties of programs through program semantics. Independently of Naur but at about the same time, Floyd investigated the idea of assigning meanings to programs in terms of *interpretations* placed on their flowcharts.[11] Like Naur's snapshots, Floyd's interpretations are propositions labeling various points in the control flow of a program (called *tags*) which, if proved, may constitute a proof of correctness:

> It is, therefore, possible to extend a partially specified
> interpretation to a complete interpretation, without loss of
> verifiability, provided that initially there is no closed loop in the
> flowchart all of whose edges are not tagged and that there is no
> entrance which is not tagged. This fact offers the possibility of
> automatic verification of programs, the programmer merely
> tagging entrances and one edge in each innermost loop; the
> verifying program would extend the interpretation and verify it,
> if possible, by mechanical theorem-proving techniques.[12]

Though this idea held much promise for believers in the mathematical paradigm, it came under attack in the above-mentioned essay by DeMillo, Lipton, and Perlis. They argued passionately that mechanically produced program verifications, which are long chains of dense logical formulas, are *not* what constitute mathematical proofs. In coming to be accepted, a mathematical proof undergoes social processes in its communication and peer scrutiny, processes that cannot be applied to unfathomable pages of logic. While DeMillo, Lipton, and Perlis did not subscribe to the mathematical paradigm (i.e., that computer science is a branch of formal mathematics), they also did not deny that programming is *like* mathematics. An analogy can be drawn between mathematics and programming, but "the same social processes that work in mathematical proofs doom verifications."[13] Social processes, they argued, are critical:

> No matter how high the payoff, no one will ever be able to force
> himself to read the incredibly long, tedious verifications of
> real-life systems, and unless they can be read, understood, and
> refined, the verifications are worthless.[14]

The main focus of DeMillo, Lipton, and Perlis's attack laid in the practicality and social acceptance of the method of formal verification. They hinted, however, at another, nonsocial, reason for deemphasizing verifiability in software design, having to do with conceptual confusion over the ultimate significance of mathematical models:

> For the practice of programming, ... verifiability must not be allowed to overshadow reliability. Scientists should not confuse mathematical models with reality—and verification is nothing but a model of believability.[15]

Fetzer's paper, mentioned above, once more brought the debate over formal verification to the forefront, but by elaborating this conceptual confusion in great detail. Fetzer argued, in fact, that the presence or absence of social processes is germane to neither the truth of theorems nor program verifications:

> Indeed, while social processes are crucial in determining what theorems the mathematical community takes to be true and what proofs it takes to be valid, they do not thereby make them true or valid. The absence of similar social processes in determining which programs are correct, accordingly, does not affect which programs are correct.[16]

DeMillo, Lipton, and Perlis hit upon, for example, the boredom, tedium, and lack of glamor involved in reviewing proofs produced by mechanical verifiers. But for Fetzer, if this is all there is to their criticism of formal verification, it is not substantial. As Fetzer pointed out, social processes are characterized by transitory patterns of human behavior which, one could imagine, in different circumstances would reserve for program verification the same sort of excitement and collegial collaboration which marks the best mathematical research. Thus DeMillo, Lipton, and Perlis have identified a difference "in practice" between mathematical research and formal program verification, but not "in principle":

> What this means is that to the extent to which their position depends upon this difference, it represents no more than a contingent, *de facto* state-of-affairs that might be a mere transient stage in the development of program verification within the computer science community.[17]

Like DeMillo, Lipton, and Perlis, Fetzer believes that formal program verification cannot fulfill the role that some of its advocates would assign to it within software engineering. But he attacks it from a nonsocial, more strictly philosophical perspective, hinted at but not elaborated by

DeMillo, Lipton, and Perlis above. This has to do with the relationship between mathematical models and the causal systems they are intended to describe. Close scrutiny of this relationship reveals, for Fetzer, the relative, rather than absolute, nature of the program correctness guarantee that formal verification can provide, leaving the indispensability of empirical methods (i.e., program testing) in the software development process intact.

Despite the criticisms brought by DeMillo, Lipton, and Perlis, elaboration of the mathematical paradigm continued throughout the 1980s. An example of a grand but incompletely specified vision of mathematically basing the process of programming was provided by W. Scherlis and D. Scott in 1983. They not only responded to the objections of DeMillo, Lipton, and Perlis with respect to formal verification, but they gave a proposal for an overall approach to programming as concerned primarily with a process rather than a product:

> The initial goal of research must be to discern the basic structural elements of the process of programming and to cast them into a precise framework for expressing them and reasoning about them. This understanding must be embodied in a *logic of programming*—a mathematical system that allows us not only to reason about individual programs, but also to carry out *operations* (or transformations) on programs and, most importantly, to reason about the operations.[18]

The objects of reasoning, in this vision, are not programs themselves, but program *derivations*. Scherlis and Scott are therefore guided by the following analogy[19]:

Mathematics		*Programming*
problem	...	specification
theorem	...	program
proof	...	program derivation

where a process of program derivation produces a program precisely as a proof mathematically supports a theorem. A program derivation is thus somewhat akin to a formal derivation in logic and can be reasoned about mechanistically. Note however that there is a basic disanalogy in Scherlis and Scott's comparison of mathematics and programming. While in mathematics a theorem is stated and then a proof discovered to support it, in Scherlis and Scott's view of programming the program would not be stated and then supported by a derivation; rather, the program is a by-product of the derivation process. This process, though supported by mathematical tools, is nevertheless a scientific one.

Since the derivation is guided by the program specification, it should be possible at all times during the derivation to reason about the process and demonstrate that the development history so far has conformed with the specification. Scherlis and Scott envisioned this process as a formal one aided by a mechanical theorem prover, and thus they described the desired process of program development as "inferential" programming. While they granted that formal verification is not feasible *after* programs have been produced, they claimed that this is not a problem under a paradigm of inferential progamming, since verification would be built into the very process of programming.

One of the most consistent champions of the mathematical paradigm since the 1960s has been Hoare. In 1969, he presented the beginnings of a system of axioms and rules that can be used in proofs of program properties.[20] Essentially, these axioms and rules described principles of general program behavior. By substituting statements about specific programs into the axiom schemata and applying the rules to obtain new statements, proofs of terminating conditions of the program could be obtained, allegedly ensuring correctness of the program. Hoare realized, however, that the correctness of a running program depends on more than verification of the program itself and involved a system of supporting software and hardware:

> When the correctness of a program, its compiler, and the
> hardware of the computer have all been established with
> mathematical certainty, it will be possible to place great reliance
> on the results of the program, and predict their properties with a
> confidence limited only by the reliability of the electronics.[21]

Hoare's admission understates the vastness of the software and hardware systems supporting programs, however, and in the thirty years since his pronouncement, no program nearly as large as any production compiler has been mathematically verified. Some progress has been made in the mathematical proving of hardware circuit designs, but even practitioners in this field are aware of the limits of proving hardware.[22]

But Hoare has persistently believed in "the principle that the whole of nature is governed by mathematical laws of great simplicity and elegance,"[23] and the governance of software engineering practices is no exception. He developed an analogy between operations on natural numbers and the "sequential composition" of commands that make up final programs. Through this analogy, he provided strict mathematical foundations for familiar software engineering practices, for example, procedural abstraction (the practice of separating a program into independent procedures) and stepwise refinement (iteratively adding functionality of a program until it is complete). However, his aim was not merely to theoretically base these practices on mathematics, but to inject mathematics *into* the practices: "I would suggest that the skills of our best programmers will be even more productive and effective when exercised within the framework of understanding and applying the relevant mathematics."[24] Though he gave detailed attention to the arithmetic analogy and the mathematical reasons for good software engineering practice, he was less specific about what the relevant mathematics is and how it should be used in the process of creating programs.

The mathematical paradigm has its adherents in other aspects of programming besides development and verification. In particular, the *specification* of programs is seen by many as an area in which natural language's vagueness and ambiguity have contributed to problems in program development, and thus that a formal approach is preferable. An early example of an actual formally stated program specification was proposed by B. Meyer.[25] As evidence of the need for formalism, Meyer described the deficiencies of a fairly meticulously stated specification, in natural language, of a program implementing a very simple text formatter. In a careful analysis, Meyer uncovered numerous instances of the "seven sins of the specifier," as he called them, including noise, overspecification, contradiction, and ambiguity. Meyer's recommendation:

> In our opinion, the situation can be significantly improved by a reasoned use of more formal specifications. ... In fact, we'll show how a detour through formal specification may eventually lead to a better English description. This and other benefits of formal approaches more than compensate for the effort needed to write and understand mathematical notations.[26]

This effort can be considerable. In order to comprehend Meyer's proposed formal specification for the text formating program, a thorough understanding of functions, relations, sets, sequences, and predicate calculus is required, all in order to make precise the intuitively clear idea of "filling" text into paragraphs with a given width specification. Meyer made a point of saying, however, that he was not proposing to replace natural language as a specification vehicle. He showed, for example, how one might go about producing a precisely stated natural language specification from the formal one. Whether the translation process is effective and the resulting product worth the formal effort, however, is open to question.

It is clear then that the elaboration of the mathematical paradigm for computer science has gone far beyond the vision embodied by our schema **T**, in which mathematical reasoning is employed to reason merely about the properties of programs running on abstract machines. In addition, we have the mathematical modeling of computation through recursive functions (McCarthy), deductive reasoning about program derivations with the help of mechanical theorem provers (Scherlis and Scott), mathematical justification of software engineering practices (Hoare), and a strict formal mode for program specification writing (Meyer).

Challenges and Limits

Just as clearly, however, a movement away from the mathematical paradigm could be discerned. Naur, despite his role as an early supporter of using mathematical proof procedures in the programming process, later warned of problems in swinging radically to the formal side: "[T]he emphasis on formalization in program development may in fact have harmful effects on the results of the activity."[27] For Naur the formal/informal antinomy is not germane to the program development problem:

> Instead of regarding the formal mode of expression as an
> alternative to the informal mode we must view it as a freely
> introduced part of the basic informal mode, having sometimes
> great advantages, mostly for the expression of highly specialized
> assertions, but having also great disadvantages, first and foremost
> in being limited to stating facts while being inapplicable to the
> many other shades of expression that can be reached in the
> informal mode.[28]

In a counterpoint predating Meyer, Naur denied the claim that a formal mode of expression in specification writing necessarily removes errors and inconsistencies. As evidence, he took a very small part of a formal specification for an early programming language and uncovered several problems which the formal mode cannot thereby preclude. But most of all, Naur supported the unique intrinsic value of the informal, intuitive mode: "In fact, an important part of any scientific activity is to express, discuss, criticize, and refine, intuitive notions. In this activity formalization may be very helpful, but it is, at best, just an aid to intuition, not a replacement of it."[29]

With this paper by Naur, we see a backing away from the treatment of mathematics as a *paradigm* for computer science, and toward its use as a *tool* for those who specify, code, and verify programs. As B. Blum wrote:

> It should be clear that success in computer science rests on
> formal methods. Instruction sequences in a computer can only be
> understood in terms of formal abstractions. Programming

languages and their compilers are consistent and reliable to the extent we have good formal models for them. The issue is not one of having formalisms. It is one of identifying when and how they contribute to the software process and of understanding their limitations.[30]

This view strikes a conciliatory tone for any perceived formal/informal polarization in computer science. Blum argues for the acceptance of *prototyping* within an overall fairly rigorous software process. Software prototyping is the building of a software product that may be far from the final product. One prototypes typically as a learning process, with the product itself being secondary. According to Blum, prototyping is necessary when one understands that the software creation process consists of two very general and fundamentally different subprocesses. *Abstraction* is the process of producing a precise specification S of a problem statement from a real world application domain, and *reification* is the process of transforming S into a software product P. The pivotal object in the overall process is therefore the specification S. For Blum, it isn't S being a possibly *formal* object that is objectionable; rather, what can cause problems is that at the start of the reification process, S is normally *incomplete*. For one thing, project sponsors themselves "seldom know enough about the application to define it fully at the start,"[31] but more importantly, S *should not* be complete or the problem will be overspecified. Overspecification results in S being *isomorphic* to P, in which case S includes details of behavior which are irrelevant to the sponsor, and thus not incumbent upon him/her to provide. "Therefore, during reification it may be necessary to augment S as the problem becomes better understood. ... [T]he software process is not simply one of the logical derivation of a product from a fixed specification."[32]

For Blum, the initial incompleteness of S results from the transition from a *conceptual* mode of thinking about the problem to a *formal* mode during the abstraction subprocess. By definition, during an abstraction detail is lost, and it needs to be added to the formal expression of S in a typically iterative process. According to Blum, *rapid prototyping* can facilitate this process, "as a technique to define (or refine) the initial specification."[33] Prototyping as a method of software development has often been distinguished from the linear phase method, in which software is conceived as a product arising from a progression of well-defined phases, from requirements analysis to maintenance. Indeed, prototyping is also often presented as incompatible with the linear phase method, since prototyping is not literally one of the phases. Correspondingly, prototyping has been viewed as an alternative paradigm to the mathematical one being studied here. It is Blum's contention, however, that when viewed as part of the specification phase, rapid prototyping is compatible with the linear phase conception and even necessary for determining the problem specification, which is independent of whether formal methods are used to produce a program from the specification. He provides examples to support his resulting view that "prototyping and formal methods can fruitfully coexist in the same paradigm."[34]

C. Floyd also pleas for coexistence, but of two paradigms, one of which she thinks should assume a new prominence in computer science. In doing so, she does not challenge the mathematical/formal paradigm as we have described it here *per se*, but rather a general paradigm for software engineering in which the mathematical model plays the dominating role. This general paradigm comes from what Floyd calls a *product-oriented perspective* which has dominated the discipline of software engineering since its inception: "The product-oriented perspective regards software as a product standing on its own, consisting of a set of programs and related defining texts."[35] According to this perspective, it is assumed that the problem for which a computerized solution is proposed is so well understood as to allow its software requirements to be infallibly determined before software production, allowing the formal approaches to specification and verification to be applied with deductive precision so that software is simply churned out or "engineered" like complicated electronic hardware components. While a noble goal, it is unrealistic, declares Floyd: "[T]he product-oriented approach ... does not permit us to treat systematically questions pertaining to the relationship between software and the living human world, which are of paramount importance for the adequacy of software to fulfill human needs."[36]

As an alternative paradigm, Floyd sees the need for a *process-oriented perspective* which "views software in connection with human learning, work, and communication, taking place in an evolving world with changing needs."[37] From this perspective, software requirements are never static entities; they change both as the user's needs change and as the software is being developed, through evaluation and feedback from different groups of people. Since a software specification cannot be separated from the people for whom the software is produced, and since communication about the specification is necessary, the essential part of the specification should be written in natural language. Thus Floyd views social processes as crucial in the entire software development process. In this regard she goes beyond DeMillo, Lipton, and Perlis, for whom the existence of social processes was necessary only for arguing against formal verification.

Naur's later thinking in this area was not nearly so conciliatory an attempt to analyze the relationship between formal and informal methods of software development. Instead, it is an indictment of what he considers to be an overemphasis on "minor" issues, as he calls them, in the area of constructed models. One such issue is "the construction of a model M_b, from building elements E_b, when model M_a, built from elements E_a, is given. This is often encountered in a form where E_a is a so-called specification language, M_a is a specification, and E_b is a programming language."[38] Thus he relegates to minor status the actual building of programs from specifications, and with it the verification, formal or otherwise, of a program in relation to its specification.

Major issues, according to Naur, with regard to the modeling of anything, including the modeling of real-world problems in terms of specifications or programs, involve the modelee, or thing being modeled, and thus are not primarily concerned with questions of formalism, or the use of strictly defined notation according to abstract rules. These issues are (1) the *modeling insight*, or "grasping a relation between aspects of the world that have no inherent strictly defined properties and the strictly defined items of the model," and (2) the *model building insight*, or finding a way of "combining the available model building elements so as to arrive at a model having appropriate properties."[39] With regard to software, the major issues are therefore the designing and the building of programs, and the fundamental problems here are not solved by adherence to a formalism. The relationship of a perhaps formally stated design *specification* and a program, while having a role, is a minor one, and does not justify the ignoring of *in*formal concerns which pervades contemporary work in programming logic, including formal verification. Naur gives many examples of research in which informal concerns about formal matters are expressed in passing but given scant attention to make way for formal results and techniques. For Naur, this results in a "deplorable" situation and elicits a scathing assessment of the state of programming logic research:

> It is curious to observe how the authors in this field, who in the formal aspects of their work require painstaking demonstration and proof, in the informal aspects are satisfied with subjective claims that have not the slightest support, neither in argument nor in verifiable evidence. Surely common sense will indicate that such a manner is scientifically unacceptable.[40]

Philosophical foundations of what it means to be a model are also central to an analysis by B.C. Smith.[41] While not arguing *against* formal verification *per se*, he points out that what it really accomplishes is the establishment of the relative consistency between a computer program and an abstract specification of the problem it is supposed to solve. This relation leaves utterly unaddressed the question of whether the program solves the problem in the real world, that is, the question of whether the program (or its specification) is an *accurate* model of some aspect of the real world. Thus his primary observation is very similar to Naur's, but he uses it as a launching point for an analysis of program correctness. The question of program correctness, Smith argues, should not be confused with the question of consistency with its specifications. In fact, "correct" can mean many other things: "Is a program correct when it does what we have instructed it to do? or what we wanted it to do? or what history would dispassionately say it should have done?"[42]

Because "correct" can mean so many things, Smith suggests that "reliable" is the adjective we should attach as our desideratum for programs. Reliability is a concept which we know how to apply to humans, and we should, claims Smith, apply no stricter reliability criteria to computer programs, for they cannot be expected to do better. If anything, a program is destined to perform worse, since the realm it is dealing with is not the real world, but a model of it. Since this model can never be complete, it makes no sense to ask that a program be "correct" as its behavior relates to the real world:

> Plans to build automated systems capable of making a "decision", in a matter of seconds, to annihilate Europe, say, should make you uneasy; requiring a person to make the same decision in a matter of the same few seconds should make you uneasy too, and for very similar reasons. The problem is that there is simply no way that reasoning of any sort can do justice to the inevitable complexity of the situation, because of what reasoning is. Reasoning is based on partial models. Which means it cannot be guaranteed to be correct.[43]

While correctness, in a narrow technical sense, can be seen to be a relation between a program and a model of a problem in terms of abstract specifications, reliability must be a relation between the program and its actual functioning in the real world.

The Formal Verification Debate

Verificationists are concerned with reasoning, in Naur's terms, about a program model M_b, such that it can be shown to be consistent with a specification model M_a. As we have seen, the debate over program verification began with DeMillo, Lipton, and Perlis' insistence on the role of social processes in mathematical proofs and became inflamed with Fetzer's charge that the very notion of program verification trades on ambiguity. There is usually no question that M_a, a program specification, is taken to be a formal model. But it is not clear whether M_b, a program, is also a formal model, so Fetzer's ambiguity comes into play. The lure of formal methods with respect to verification extends beyond the realm of programs and into hardware and system areas. We can assess the appropriateness of formal methods in these areas by learning from the program verification case.

During the 1980s, the National Security Agency funded research in the design of "provably secure" computers, meaning computers that are mathematically guaranteed not to compromise a given multi-level security policy.[44] The goal here was not to prove the consistency of a software specification and program, as in program verification, but to prove the consistency of a security model M_a and a computer system design M_b, thus showing that there are no security leaks inherent in the design. Thus the goal is *design* verification *vis-à-vis* a security model. Since both M_a and M_b are formal models with no causal efficacy, Fetzer's ambiguity charge does not pose a problem here unless one makes the misguided claim that by proving the system design M_b to be secure, any computer built to that design is also secure.

But Fetzer's ambiguity does come into play in another area of verification, namely, hardware verification. One of the most successful application areas for automated theorem-proving techniques has been that of "proving" computer hardware circuits. The formal model M_a is taken to be a hardware circuit specification. From a logic description M_b of a hardware circuit, M_a and M_b are shown to be consistent, verifying the circuit with respect to its specification. But the notion of a hardware circuit, like that of a program, is ambiguous. Is the conclusion, that the circuit is verified, referring to the circuit as a causal or a formal model? If the latter, then the conclusion may be an analytic statement and indeed follow with the logical certainty reserved for conclusions in mathematics. But if the former, then the conclusion is a synthetic statement and follows only in conjunction with accompanying descriptions of further facts concerning the circuit's fabrication and physical environment when it is used.

While distinguishing between entities as causal and formal models may seem to be belaboring the obvious, confusing them can lead to disturbing results. For A. Cohn, a researcher in hardware verification, these manifested themselves in oversold claims made in promotional material concerning a military microprocessor named Viper. According to one

such claim, Viper was called "the first commercially available microprocessor with ... a formal specification and a proof that the chip conforms
to it."[45] Cohn, a member of the Viper project team, carefully showed,
however, that "Neither an intended behavior nor a physical chip is an
object to which the word 'proof' meaningfully applies."[46]While she did
not explicitly refer to the formal model/causal model ambiguity, it un-
derlaid her caution with respect to the meaning of 'verified': "Since any
model is an abstraction of a material device, it is *never* correct to call a
system 'verified' without reference to the level of the models used."[47] The
relative, rather than absolute, nature of hardware verification claims is
as clear for Cohn as the relative, rather than absolute, nature of program
verification claims is for Fetzer:

> A proof that one specification implements another—despite being
> completely rigorous, expressed in an explicit and well-understood
> logic, and even checked by another system—should still be
> viewed in context of the many other extra-logical factors that
> affect the correct functioning of hardware systems. In addition to
> the abstract design, everything from the system operators to the
> mechanical parts must function correctly—and correctly
> together—to avoid catastrophe.[48]

There seems, in the end, to be no way to verify either a program's
or a hardware device's reliability other than by testing it empirically and
observing its behavior. In chapter 10, I try to make this explicit through
a delineation of five different ways programs can be run as tests. Only one
of these, namely, testing a program to determine whether its (abstract)
behavior conforms to its specifications, can conceivably be replaced by
purely deductive, mathematical reasoning. The other ways (for example, testing a program to determine whether its specification actually
solves the given problem) cannot be so replaced because the activities
involved cannot be reduced to proofs of consistency between syntactic
or formal objects; they are fundamentally different from that, employing
the element of empirical discovery common to natural science, and not
to mathematics.

And so we come to a view of computer programming as part of an
overall process of computer science that is analogous to natural or, even
more broadly, experimental science. In this view, objects such as algorithms or program specifications are like hypotheses which can only be
tested by writing and running programs. Such tests provide insight into
the adequacy of the model/real-world relationship that we exploit in the
program. As such, the program is only a tool in an overall process of inquiry, as experiment apparatus and setup is in hypothesis confirmation or

rejection. This is not to say that the programming/mathematics analogy that has dogged the discussion up till now is invalid, but that it should be seen as subordinate to the overall computer science/experimental science analogy which is the primary one. The problem of producing a program with certain specifications must still be solved, and a formal approach may be appropriate, but ordinarily this is a subproblem in an overall problem of, variously, testing an algorithm, or testing the specifications themselves, or explaining a phenomenon through simulation.

Before closing this chapter I would like to return to Fetzer, who aroused such passion in the computer science community in 1988. For the two years following, he became enmeshed in a debate of monumental proportions carried out in multiple venues, including the editorial pages of the *Communications of the ACM* (the flagship periodical of the Association of Computing Machinery), publicly staged counterpoints, and electronic mail discussion groups. Only the most carefully reasoned philosophical position could hold up to this kind of scrutiny (not to mention hysterical diatribes), and in a later work Fetzer recounts the position. His basic charge is the same: "[I]t should be apparent that the very idea of the mathematical paradigm for computer science trades on ambiguity."[49] Strong claims of formal verificationists are victim to this ambiguity through the ignoring of several distinctions: between programs running on abstract machines with *no* physical counterpart and programs running on abstract machines *with* a physical counterpart; between "programs-as-texts" and "programs-as-causes"; and between pure and applied mathematics. Recognizing these distinctions, for Fetzer, reveals that the claim that it is possible to reason in a purely *a priori* manner about the behavior of a program is true if the behavior is merely abstract, false, and dangerously misleading otherwise. Fetzer appeared, then, to emerge from the fracas none the worse:

> [I]t should ... be obvious that the conception of computer science as a branch of pure mathematics cannot be sustained. The proper conception is that of computer science as a branch of applied mathematics, where even that position may not go far enough in acknowledging the limitations imposed by physical devices.[50]

For myself, I see a possible replacement of the mathematical paradigm by an experimental science paradigm for computer science, and I see it in a way that should reconcile heretofore conflicting views. But whether the paradigm be experimental science, or applied mathematics, or engineering, it is interesting to note, and a tribute to the value of philosophizing in any age, that after studying the important contributions of various writers I come finally to an observation by Carnap about the role of mathematics in science:

> All of logic including mathematics, considered from the point of view of the total language, is thus no more than an auxiliary calculus for dealing with synthetic statements. *Formal science* has no independent significance, but is an auxiliary component introduced for technical reasons in order to facilitate linguistic transformations in the *factual sciences.* The great importance of the formal sciences, that is, of logic and mathematics, within the total system of science is thereby not in the least denied but instead, through a characterization of this special function, emphasized.[51]

Although Carnap made this observation well before the Age of Computers, had he lived to take part in the program verification debate, he might have couched his observation thus:

> All of logic including formal verification, considered from the point of view of the total language of computer science, is no more than an auxiliary calculus for dealing with broader issues of computer problem-solving as an experimental discipline. *Formal verification* has no independent significance, but is an auxiliary component introduced for technical reasons in order to facilitate linguistic transformations from formal program-specification models to formal program-execution models. The importance of formal verification within the total system of computer science is thereby not in the least denied but instead, through a characterization of this special function, emphasized.

I couldn't have put it better myself.

– 10 –
Two Views of Computer Science

In this chapter I will cast the program verification debate described in chapter 9[1] within a more general perspective on the methodologies and goals of computer science. This will lead, I hope, to a reconciliation of two views of computer science which on the surface appear to be inconsistent.

I begin by opposing the "mathematical paradigm" for computer science with a view of computer science as a *nonformal* endeavor. This is the view that computer science is, as its name implies, a science, but more importantly, an *empirical* science in the sense which deemphasizes pure mathematics or logic. This sense is meant to cover all and only those experimental disciplines included in the "natural" and "social" sciences. This view is expounded implicitly and explicitly in many standard computer science texts, as in the following:

> Perhaps nothing is as intrinsic to the scientific method as the formulation and testing of hypotheses to explain phenomena. This same process plays an integral role in the way computer scientists work.[2]

This view is also exemplified by the curricula and attitudes of many current academic computer science departments, in which computer science is put forth as the science of problem solving using computers, and not as "mere computer programming."

On the other hand, there is the view that computer science is, again as its name implies, a science, but an *exact* science in the sense which emphasizes the primacy of mathematics or logic. In this sense, there is no role for the testing of hypotheses to explain phenomena, since formal disciplines like mathematics or logic are not concerned with explanation of observable phenomena; they are *a priori*, or prior to experience, rather than seeking to explain experience. This view has as one of its most outspoken proponents C.A.R. Hoare:

Computer programming is an exact science in that all of the properties of a program and all of the consequences of executing it in any given environment can, in principle, be found out from the text of the program itself by means of purely deductive reasoning.[3]

As Fetzer has shown, citing other examples of writers comparing programming to formal mathematics or holding programming up to standards of perfection, this view is not a straw man and actually represents "several decades of commitment to formal methods by influential computer scientists."[4]

These two views would indeed seem to be antithetical if they were both purporting to describe the same thing. However, a closer look at the second view at least as exemplified above by Hoare shows that he is referring to computer *programming* as an exact science, presumably leaving it open whether computer programming is to be identified with computer *science*. I believe these two views can be reconciled through a casting of computer programming within a rather broader context of computer science. This provides an interpretation under which in some circumstances computer science is best viewed as the *engineering*, possibly using mathematical methods, of problem solutions on a computer, while in other circumstances it is best viewed as concerned with the experimental *testing of hypotheses* and the subsequent recording of observations in the real world. As I shall argue, computer science "in the large" can be viewed as an experimental discipline that holds plenty of room for mathematical methods, including formal program verification, within theoretical limits of the sort emphasized by Fetzer and touched on briefly in chapter 9.

Recall that program verification is the attempt to show that a program's behavior corresponds to its specifications, which are explicit statements of what the program should emit as output given certain input. To put the issue of whether computer science is an exact or empirical science in practical perspective, place yourself in the following (admittedly simplified) scenario:

You are responsible for purchasing software for a large institution which has a need to automate a critical task. You specify, in a fairly rigorous way, the requirements that a program must meet, in terms of the kind of input it will accept, the kind of output it will produce, how long it will take for the program to run, and so on, in solving your problem. You find that two software companies have anticipated your need and claim to have programs that meet your requirements, so you invite their sales representatives to your office.

Salesman A: We are offering, for a limited time only, a program that meets your requirements. We know that it meets your requirements because we have painstakingly tested it over many months and on many machines. Although it is not possible to test every combination of inputs, we have failed to uncover any errors. To the extent possible through testing, this is a verified product.

Salesman B: We also are offering a program that meets your requirements. But we know that the program is correct because we have formally *proved* it correct with the most sophisticated mathematical and logical techniques available. We are so sure of its correctness that we did not even need to test it on any specific machine. This is a completely verified product.

Assuming that the programs are comparable in price, which do you buy?

This scenario, besides being simplified, is also hypothetical since there are no large, critical programs that claim to have been formally proved correct. Still, it is a caricature of a scenario the possibility of which some researchers in software reliability are working to bring about. It tends to suggest that formal program-proving methods always provide an alternative to program testing, as though the goals of these two activities were always the same. By taking a closer look at what it means for a program to be run as a test, I shall argue that this is not a realistic portrayal. But before turning to this, we must better understand the limits of both program testing and formal program verification.

The Defeasible Nature of Program Testing

In practice, nontrivial programs are verified by running them and observing their behavior with varying sets of representative input. It has long been recognized that for most nontrivial programs, it is either impossible or impractical to test every possible input configuration. R. Gumb, for example, writes: "testing a program does not always establish its correctness; crucial test cases may be overlooked or there may be too many cases to test."[5] This inherent incompleteness of program testing has led to two different responses. One is to admit that program testing is incomplete but to deny that it must necessarily be *ad hoc*, and to develop rigorous testing methodology which maximizes test case coverage through both static and dynamic program analysis.[6] The other response is to consider the incompleteness of program testing as grounds for eschewing it in favor of another approach to program verification, namely, the mathematical approach. In the same passage, for example, Gumb writes: "Program correctness must be understood in the context of a mathematical theory." Since there are alternative approaches to the problem of the incompleteness of testing, the "must" in this quote cannot be taken to be a logical "must" but rather is a way of advocating the primacy of mathematical methods in both the construction and the verification of programs.

For an advocate of the experimental science approach to computer science, the incompleteness of testing is not grounds for eschewing it, but simply being more careful about it. E. Dijkstra once made a famous remark to the effect that testing can show only the presence, not the absence, of program errors. But this is damning to the whole platform of program testing only if understood in the context of mathematical-style proof. In this context, it is of course true that the fact that *some* specific inputs to a program issue correct output in no way proves the claim that *every* input would issue correct output. But just as observing only black crows serves to *confirm*, but not prove, that all crows are black, observing only correct output during program testing confirms, but does not prove, that the program is correct. In the context of experimental science, the fact that program testing cannot *prove* the absence of errors does not damn the whole effort, any more than the fact that observing black crows cannot prove that all crows are black damns the effort of confirming this fact.

The reasoning involved in program testing is a species of inductive reasoning, since it argues from the observed (the input sets that are actually tested) to the unobserved (those that are not). For example, consider the algorithm in Figure 22 expressed in pseudo-code. It attempts to compute the factorial of a positive integer supplied in the input variable N, returning the result in the output variable M. In testing such a procedure, one typically supplies a value in N, runs the procedure, and checks to see whether the value in M is correct. After repeating this process for various input values, say, integers 0 through 5, and being satisfied of the correctness of the output, one infers that the unchecked input values *would* also issue correct output *were* they tested. As such, this reasoning is no more "incorrect" than that involved in any experimental endeavor attempting to confirm a generalization from observed instances. It does, however, depend in some sense on an assumption of the *typicality* of the unobserved instances in relation to the observed. That is, if an unobserved instance has a property distinguishing it significantly from the

```
factorial (N)
begin
    M ← N
    while N > 1 do
        begin
            N ← N - 1
            M ← M * N
        end
    return M
end
```

Figure 22. *Procedure to Compute Factorial*

observed instances, it may *defeat* the claim that all inputs issue correct output.

The fact that reasoning can involve possibly false assumptions does not thereby make it faulty or incorrect. It does, however, change the nature of the warrant that such reasoning provides. To describe that warrant, we must look again at the distinction between *defeasible* and *indefeasible* reasoning, a distinction first studied by philosophers like Pollock and also by researchers in artificial intelligence and cognitive science.[7] This distinction, as we described in chapter 7, is based upon the concept of a *defeater*, or piece of evidence which can make an ordinarily justified inference no longer justified. The possibility of defeaters pervades empirical reasoning. For example, I may infer that a statue is red on the basis that it looks red to me, but if I later discover that there are red lights shining on it I am no longer entitled to this inference, since the normal connection between the color a statue *looks* and the color it *is* is defeated by this new knowledge. Besides examples of perception, the possibility of defeaters also accounts for the nonabsolute (or "fallible") nature of reasoning in other areas of empirical inquiry, including reasoning on the basis of memory, testimony, and inductive evidence.

The difference between defeasible and indefeasible reasoning is often not immediately obvious from the way in which arguments employing them are stated. Consider, for example, the syntactically similar arguments

(**A**)   1. Birds are vertebrates.

2. Fred is a bird.

3. Therefore, Fred is a vertebrate.

and

(**B**)   1. Birds are flyers.

2. Fred is a bird.

3. Therefore, Fred is a flyer.

Despite the syntactic similarities, arguments **A** and **B** employ different consequence relations and thus provide different warrants for their conclusions. In argument **A**, the formal model of predicate calculus is entirely adequate in characterizing the reasoning as indefeasible:

(**C**)   1. $(\forall x)(Bird(x) \rightarrow Vertebrate(x))$

2. *Bird(Fred)*

3. $\vdash$ *Vertebrate(Fred)*

In argument **B**, however, predicate calculus is not adequate for modeling the argument because (2) quantifiers are not adequate for representing the implicit proposition that only *typical* birds fly, and (2) the warrant given by the argument is not truth preserving, as provided by $\vdash$, but only justification preserving. Any model of the reasoning involved in **B** must provide representation for at least the following premisses in the expanded argument:

1. Typically, birds are flyers.

2. Fred is a bird.

3. There is no reason to suppose that Fred is not typical, that is, that Fred cannot fly.

But even if these premisses are all true—in particular, even if I have no reason to think that Fred is a nonflying bird (I have it on good evidence that Fred is a falcon)—they cannot guarantee that Fred can fly (Fred might, unbeknownst to me, have clipped wings). Thus there is no deductive warrant for the conclusion

4. Therefore, Fred is a flyer.

since the premisses can be true while the conclusion is false. The fact that I am reasoning about a property which not all birds have assures that my reasoning is defeasible. I can at best conclude the *justifiedness* of the intended result:

4′. Therefore, "Fred is a flyer" is justified.

One might wonder, from a purely logical point of view, what warrants even this inference. In this argument and in the argument schemata which follow, we shall assume an implicit conditional premiss simply relating the explicit premisses to the conclusion. In this case the implicit premiss is,

3′. If birds are typically flyers and Fred is a bird and there is no reason to suppose that Fred is not typical, then "Fred is a flyer" is justified.

These implicit premisses can be regarded as instances of general epistemic principles without which we would have no hope of acquiring empirical knowledge.[8] Thus, a full rendering of the reasoning involved in argument **B** is captured in:

(**D**)   1. Typically, birds are flyers.

2. Fred is a bird.

3. There is no reason to suppose that Fred is not typical, that is, that Fred cannot fly.

4. If birds are typically flyers and Fred is a bird and there is no reason to suppose that Fred is not typical, then "Fred is a flyer" is justified.

5. Therefore, "Fred is a flyer" is justified.

Note that the inclusion of premiss 4 does give argument **D** a deductive form: the conclusion is a modal statement in a meta-language about another statement's justifiedness in the object-language.

The reasoning underlying program testing is also defeasible, due, one might say, to the assumption of *typicality* of the unobserved test inputs. For example, after testing my `factorial` procedure with the integers 0 through 5 and being satisfied with the output, I assume that unobserved test inputs also work correctly because the test cases using integers 0 through 5 are typical of the (unrealized) test cases using 6 on up. This is not to say that the *integers* 0 through 5 are typical of the *integers* 6 on up, but that the test cases using them in procedure `factorial` are. That is, the integers 0 through 5 *exercise* the procedure in the same way that larger integers would. Although the simple factorial example does not display much complexity in its flow of control, in more complex programs the set of possible inputs divides naturally into subsets that characterize the different paths of control flow through the program. Rigorous testing attempts to choose test inputs from each of the subsets, reducing the danger of leaving untested any cases that are not typical of those tried, that is, that exercise different parts of the program. Still, for large programs there often is no guarantee that every path of control flow has been anticipated. Reasoning about their untested cases, like reasoning about Fred and flying, carries only a guarantee of justification, not truth:

(E)   1. Program **P** is correct for the test cases observed.

2. There is no reason to suppose that the unobserved cases are not typical (that is, that they exercise **P** differently from the observed cases).

3. Therefore, "Program **P** is correct for the unobserved cases" is justified.

The defeasible nature of this pattern of reasoning in program testing, viewed as a method whereby generalizations are made in empirical science, should not be a problem. But if the goal of program verification is to reason about a program in such a way that arguments about unrealized behavior are truth-preserving (that is, absolute guarantees of program correctness), then testing is not adequate. One approach with this goal in mind is *formal* program verification, but as we shall see, although its methods are entirely different, the reasoning behind it is also defeasible by nature.

The Defeasible Nature of Formal Program Verification

As a representative example of techniques in research on formal program verification, consider the method of *inductive assertions*. Briefly, this method attempts to prove *output assertions* about the program on the basis of *input assertions* as well as assertions concerning the relationships that constantly obtain among variables while the program runs. Most often the program executes a loop, so these latter assertions are sometimes called *loop invariants*. The method of proof is called "inductive" because mathematical induction, a special kind of deductive reasoning, is used on the number of iterations in the loop to prove that some loop invariant holds throughout the loop, establishing the output assertions.

For example, consider again the procedure in Figure 22. By restricting N to positive integers we have the input assertion:

$$N \in \text{positive integers}$$

The output assertion we wish to prove is:

$$M = N!$$

To prove this, we must prove something about the loop, a loop invariant, from which it follows that $M = N!$. Loop invariants typically state a general relationship among variables after an arbitrary number of iterations through the loop. We can let N_i and M_i refer to the contents of N and M, respectively, after i iterations through the loop. The invariant we would like to prove, for all i, is:

(a) $M_i \times (N_i - 1)! = N!$

To see this, suppose the loop requires k iterations. Then when the loop is complete $N_k = 1$ so $(N_k - 1)! = 0! = 1$ and therefore the invariant reduces to

$$M_k = N!$$

This asserts that at the end of the loop M contains $N!$, our original output assertion. To prove the invariant **a**, we use induction on i.

(**F**)   1. (*Base step:*) When $i = 0$, $M_i = N$ and $N_i = N$. Thus $M_i \times (N_i - 1)! = N \times (N - 1)! = N!$

      2. (*Inductive step:*) From $M_i \times (N_i - 1)! = N!$ show that $M_{i+1} \times (N_{i+1} - 1)! = N!$. By observing the program, we see that after any iteration of the loop, M contains what it had before the iteration multiplied by the contents of N after the iteration. Thus $M_{i+1} = M_i \times N_{i+1}$. We can also see that $N_{i+1} = N_i - 1$. Making use of these equalities and the inductive assumption, we can prove the inductive conclusion:

$$
\begin{aligned}
M_{i+1} \times (N_{i+1} - 1)! &= \\
M_i \times (N_i - 1) \times (N_i - 2)! &= \\
M_i \times (N_i - 1)! &= N!
\end{aligned}
$$

F appears to be an ironclad proof of the loop invariant **a**. However, **F** is unusual for mathematical proofs in that what we mean by M and N makes a difference in the type of reasoning **F** involves. That is, as stated, **F** harbors an ambiguity of the type that Fetzer has pointed out.[9] To see this, consider the crucial premise in the inductive step that

(b) ... after any iteration of the loop, M contains what it had
     before the iteration multiplied by the contents of N after the
     iteration.

The ambiguity is over the ontological status of M and N. If M and N
are assumed to be abstract memory locations in an *abstract* machine, the
proof is indeed ironclad since abstract machines are *ideal* in the sense
that their operation is simply assumed never to fail. Recall the difference
between abstract and physical machines described in chapter 9. Abstract
machines are represented and conceived of purely functionally, and not in
terms of physical control units, registers, adders, and memory elements.
Thus if M and N are abstract memory locations, **b** can be conclusively
established simply by observing the program and understanding the language.

However, if M and N are assumed to be physical memory locations
in a given *physical* machine, then **b** can be established only by making
a host of assumptions, including the proper functioning of the hardware
units mentioned above, as well as all the supporting software which results in a program executing in physical memory. So insofar as proof **F**
refers to physical memory locations, these assumptions render the verification provided, in Fetzer's words, as "relative" rather than "absolute."[10]
That is, the significance of proof **F** for the physical behavior of procedure `factorial` on an actual machine is entirely dependent upon the
proper functioning of the underlying software and hardware supporting
the program which manipulates M and N.

Thus, reasoning about physical machine behavior on the basis of **F**
is defeasible. Just as, in the program testing case, I must make the
possibly false assumption that the unobserved cases are in some sense
typical in order to infer that they would result in the correct output, in
formal program verification I must also make possibly false assumptions
about the typicality (proper functioning) of the underlying software and
hardware. Thus, the truth of **a** cannot be inferred by **F**, though its
justifiedness can. So the overall method of reasoning by formal program
verification, as applied to predicted behavior on a physical machine **M**,
also conforms to a general schema of defeasible reasoning:

(**G**)   1. Program **P** has been formally verified.

        2. There is no reason to suppose that the underlying hard-
           ware and software for machine **M** are not typical, *i.e.*,
           that they are not functioning correctly.

        3. Therefore, "Program **P** works correctly on machine **M**"
           is justified.

It is, of course, an epistemic obligation to justify as far as is practical the beliefs in one's underlying assumptions. For me to commit to the belief that Fred can fly, the amount of effort I put into ruling out any abnormalities concerning Fred's flying abilities is proportional to the amount of importance I attach to not being wrong. The amount of importance attached to the correctness of computer programs, of course, can reach enormous levels, in matters of medicine, financial transactions, and national security, so that the obligation to minimize assumptions becomes not merely an epistemic but an ethical one. In the case of formal program verification, the desire to minimize assumptions has led to the movement toward *system* verification, in which the goal is to apply formal methods not only to individual application programs, but also to the system software (operating systems, compilers, assemblers, loaders, etc.) and hardware designs of the components on which they will run.

The Defeasible Nature of Formal Hardware Verification

As programs manipulating abstract memory locations, we might allow that the programs composing system software can theoretically be proved correct, ignoring the practical limitations on proving programs of this size and complexity. But as programs manipulating physical memory locations on a given machine, arguments about them are subject to the same assumptions concerning the "typicality" (correctness and proper functioning) of the integrated circuitry in memory and processor as application programs. Thus significant efforts in "hardware verification" are under way. Here the object of scrutiny in the proving process is not a program but a formal specification of some device. Typically, the proof proceeds by levels, each level being concerned with a more specific description of the device than that provided in the level before it. At each level relevant assertions about the specification are proved, possibly using mechanical tools (theorem-proving programs), the goal being to show that the behavior of the device modeled at some level is the same as that modeled at the next higher level of abstraction. The ultimate objective is to continue this process down to a formal proof of the gate-level circuit design.

It is important to note that in this process of hardware verification we are still talking about the behavior of *abstract* memory locations and processing elements, and not actual devices *per se*. Just as it is a mistake to claim that program proof **F** conclusively establishes the correctness of a program executing on some physical machine, it is a mistake to claim that hardware proofs conclusively establish the correctness of behavior of physical devices. This latter point is even made by the hardware verification practitioner A. Cohn:

> [A] material device can only be observed and measured; it cannot be verified. ... [A] device can be described in a formal way, and the description verified; but ... there is no way to assure accuracy of the description. Indeed, any description is bound to be inaccurate in *some* respects, since it cannot be hoped to mirror an entire physical situation even at an instant, much less as it evolves through time; a model of a device is necessarily an abstraction (a simplification). In short, verification involves a pair of *models* that bear an uncheckable and possibly imperfect relation to the intended design and to the actual device.[11]

Cohn is conceding, in the hardware verification realm, the same point introduced by Fetzer in the program verification realm, namely, that there is a fundamental difference between the nature of the abstract and the nature of the physical, preventing conclusions about the physical from having the same warrant as those in the abstract. Thus even if we were to grant the possibility of proving complicated system software, equally complicated theorem-proving software, and the gate-level circuit designs of the devices that make programs run, we still do not have a mathematical proof of any physical behavior of a given application program.

One might argue that this is quibbling, and that the difference between gate designs and gates themselves is so trifling that the program is as good as formally verified. But to conclude from the formal proof of an abstract hardware specification that the corresponding physical device, say, a chip, will work correctly involves the making of a host of assumptions concerning the conformance of the chip to the specification, including assumptions about the fabrication of the chip, the properties of its materials, the environment in which it runs, and so on. Thus, no matter how rigorous its proofs about formal, abstract designs, for a hardware verification argument to be saying anything about an actual physical device, it must be regarded as defeasible and not conclusive in the sense reserved for arguments in mathematics or logic. As a general schema:

(**H**)   1. The hardware design **D** of physical device **P** has been formally verified.

2. There is no reason to suppose that the fabrication of **P** from **D** is not typical (that is, that **P** does not conform to **D**).

3. Therefore, "The hardware of **P** works correctly" is justified.

So even if a program and its supporting system software "superstructure" can be formally proved correct, the defeasibility of reasoning about the program's physical behavior is ensured by the defeasibility of reasoning about the behavior of the chip on which it runs.

Since reasoning by program testing, formal program verification, and formal hardware verification are all defeasible, it would seem that a combination of them in an overall attempt at verifying program correctness would be desirable. The defeasible assumptions required by the testing point of view might be mitigated by the formalist's methods, while those required by the formalist might be mitigated by testing. On one hand, if you start with the testing point of view, you cannot have the right to be sure about untested cases until you have reasoned correctly and *a priori* about them. On the other hand, if you start with the formalist point of view, you cannot have the right to be sure about the physical behavior of a program until you have tested it. But in what sense of testing: merely to check the underlying functioning of hardware, or to verify the program itself, or for some other purpose? To answer this requires a closer examination of why programs are tested.

The Role of Program Testing in Computer Science

With respect to a simple program like `factorial`, it seems that we might be prepared to admit that, on the basis of proof **F**, one can be justified in assuming that the program is correct, in the sense that it will result in correct physical memory contents given certain inputs, *without actually running it*, provided that (1) we are satisfied that the supporting software has—mathematically or not—been "proved" correct, and (2) the physical chip on which it and the supporting software runs has been extensively tested—whether or not its gate-level design was mathematically proved— to the point where we are satisfied that it carries out instructions without error. Still, owing to the fact that the chip could fail for a number of physical reasons, our justification is not conclusive, so we are in a position of being *defeasibly justified* in predicting what the behavior of the program would be were it run on this chip.

Although we have a (somewhat idealized) situation in which program testing can be foregone in favor of a formal proof, we have seen that, although the proof is mathematical, its warrant is defeasible. The focus has now shifted from the correctness of procedure `factorial` to the operability of the chip on which it runs. The running of the procedure would not be a test of its correctness at all, but of whether the chip was working. So we can distinguish at least two ways in which a program can be run as a test:

Testing Sense 1: We might run a program to determine whether its behavior conforms to its specifications.

Testing Sense 2: We might run a program to determine whether the hardware/software superstructure supporting it is functioning properly.

In the first case the program tests itself, while in the second case it tests its supporting superstucture. These are not independent notions, however, for two reasons. First, one cannot run a program as a test in sense 2 unless one has already determined how the program is supposed to behave. Thus, unless the program's intended behavior has been completely understood and formally verified, it must be tested in sense 1 in advance. Second, the failure of a program test in sense 1, without independent confirmation of the operability of the superstructure, is equally explained by program incorrectness *or* superstructure failure; the same superstructure malfunctioning that can undermine a formal proof of program correctness may also undermine the running of a program to test itself. Thus, testing a program in sense 1 presupposes the proper functioning of the superstructure, which involves testing in sense 2 (though not, of course, via the same program).

Normally, a typical application program is run primarily as a test in sense 1, while only very specialized programs are run to test the superstructure: programs like self-diagnosing routines for memory boards that execute when the machine is booted, or program test suites used in compiler validation. Still, we regard the *positive* outcome of a test in sense 1 as also a positive outcome of a test in sense 2. (This must allow, however, for the highly unlikely possibility that the program as written is *in*correct, but a subtle defect in the superstructure causes their interaction to produce correct behavior—a false positive result!)

It is tempting to conclude that any problems involved in the interdependence of testing in senses 1 and 2 above could be avoided by replacing testing in sense 1 with formal program verification and leaving testing in sense 2 to hardware technicians and hardware testing equipment. But even if we perfected mathematical program-proving techniques, developed more sophisticated mechanical theorem provers, and wrote all our application software in a way amenable to analysis and formal proof, program testing would still be indispensable, not as a method of demonstrating programs' correctness, but in the broader, general role that testing plays in any empirical science. The example we have considered here— the computing of the factorial of a number, not considered in the context of some greater problem—is a mathematical activity whose modeling on a computer is very straightforward and whose verification can easily give way to the same mathematical approach. But in many cases the role of testing cannot be so easily supplanted.

Suppose I am a geneticist trying to understand a process that I suspect involves combinatorial analysis, so I devise a number of methods of modeling it, one of which involves the computing of factorial. I may be able to convince myself of the correctness of my factorial procedure, if not through a proof like **F** then through some mental walk-through, without testing, but that is not what is being tested anyway; I have coded a particular genetic model and *that model* is what I endeavor to test when I run a program, not the factorial procedure, or even the totality of the procedures I have written to implement the model.

Note that this example casts the role of computers in the solving of a problem in a very different light from that exemplified in the opening scenario above. In that scenario, as the data processing manager, I have a problem that I suspect can be solved with a computer program and I provide a complete specification of the program requirements for competing software producers. Once I choose a producer and satisfy myself that its program satisfies my requirements, the primary purpose in running it is to implement a solution to my original problem.

In the genetics example, I also must produce requirements for a program, but rather than implement an already understood solution to a problem, the program will implement a genetic model. Once I am satisfied that the program meets my input/output and performance requirements, the primary purpose in running it is not to implement a problem solution, but to *test* whether the model accurately depicts a genetic process. These examples correspond to two different but *complementary* conceptions of computer science.

Computer Science as Solution Engineering

In the original scenario, a well-designed solution to a problem in terms of rigorous requirements is outlined, and an implementation of the solution is engineered via a computer program. The principal objective is to meet the requirements in a program solution, so the method can be characterized as *solution engineering* with computers. It is tempting to associate this paradigm with the mathematical view of computer programming as an exact science, with formal program verification playing the role (in theory if not in current practice) of defeasibly warranting a program's correct behavior, testing being necessary only to confirm the proper functioning of underlying software and hardware. But even within the restricted paradigm of computer science as solution engineering, with formal program verification playing its role of verifying that a program meets its requirements, there still is a role for program testing.

Our treatment of computer science methodology has so far glossed over the use of algorithms in problem solving, but in practice they play an important role in the process of designing programs. Ordinarily conceived, an algorithm is not a program but an abstraction of a problem solution in the form of a terminating sequence of steps, which when implemented in a programming language issues a list of computer instructions which carry out the solution steps. The role of an algorithm in computer problem solving can be elucidated through an analogy with natural science.

Natural science seeks explanations of observable phenomena through hypothesis construction and subsequent hypothesis testing via experiments. For example, the hypothesis that *aurora borealis* is caused by interaction of the earth's ionosphere with solar atoms can be tested by creating laboratory conditions that imitate this interaction and observing for the *aurora* effect. Thus, the method of natural science can be described as follows:

(I)   1. Formulate a HYPOTHESIS for explaining a phenomenon.

2. TEST the hypothesis by conducting an EXPERIMENT.

3. CONFIRM or DISCONFIRM the hypothesis by evaluating the results of the experiment.

Similarly, we might understand the role of an algorithm in the method of computer science via an analogy between explaining phenomena in natural science and problem solving in computer science. We might say that in computer science we:

(J)   1. Formulate an ALGORITHM for solving a problem.

2. TEST the algorithm by writing and running a PROGRAM.

3. ACCEPT or REJECT the algorithm by evaluating the results of running the program.

So we can add the following to the ways in which a program can be run as a test:

Testing Sense 3: We might run a program to determine whether an algorithm solves a problem.

If this analogy holds up, then just as what is on trial in scientific reasoning is not an experiment but a hypothesis giving rise to an experiment, what is on trial in computer science is not a program but a problem-solving method or algorithm for which a program is produced. To continue the analogy, writing a program is to computer science what experiment construction is to natural science. Just as test implications need to be produced from a scientific hypothesis, one needs to produce a program from an algorithm. Program verification, as an endeavor to make sure that input/output specifications required by an algorithm are enforced by the program, can be viewed as the process of making sure that the program actually does implement the algorithm being tested. This would be analogous to that part of the scientific method which is the process of making sure that the experiment actually does set up the conditions required for a correct testing of the hypothesis. Under this conception, then, program testing is indispensable since an algorithm, and not a program, is on trial.

All analogies inevitably break down, however, and an advocate of the primacy of formal methods in computer science will emphasize a *dis*analogy between the hypothesis/experiment relationship in natural science and the algorithm/program relationship in computer science. The short history of the field has seen programming languages get more and more high level and algorithm description languages more and more formal, so that the distinction between an algorithm and a program gets smaller. This has led to the effort to bring about the *automatic* generation of programs from formal specification languages. Since a program specification tells *what* a program is supposed to do and not *how* it will do it, the possibility of success in this area threatens to obliterate not only the distinction between algorithms and programs, but also the need for human programmers to program in a traditional sense at all.[12] The vision is one of program specification writers replacing programmers, with programs produced mechanically by other programs.

Models of the software development process have changed over the years, from the earliest linear phase models, to the waterfall model, to the rapid prototyping model. But whatever the current model, the trends and research areas just mentioned, including program verification, endeavor either to automate the process of going from program specification to actual program or to make this transition totally straightforward through formal methods. For when a process can be modeled formally, it is more likely able to be achieved mechanically. The desideratum, then, is for the software development process to become a "black box," with program specifications as input and totally correct program as output, with as little need for human involvement as possible. See Figure 23. The under-

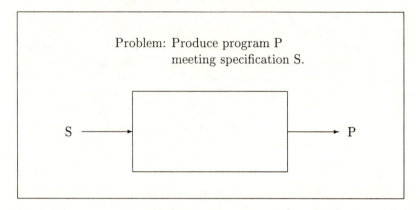

Figure 23. *Software Development as a Black Box*

lying paradigm of computer science as *solution engineering* is upheld in this vision, since the objective is to achieve a computer implementation of a problem whose solution is so well designed and conceived as to admit of formal treatment. But a case can still be made for the necessity of testing, despite the mechanical fabrication of programs from specifications. For *unless there is some sort of independent guarantee that the program specifications, no matter how formally rendered, actually specify a program which solves the problem,* one must run the program to determine whether the solution design embodied by the specification is correct. So there is another sense in which a program can be run as a test:

Testing Sense 4: We might run a program to determine whether a program specification solves a problem.

In this sense the method of computer science can be captured as follows:

(**K**)   1. Formulate a SOLUTION DESIGN, in terms of a program specification, for solving a problem.

2. TEST the solution design by generating and running a PROGRAM.

3. ACCEPT or REJECT the solution design by evaluating the results of running the program.

When a problem application domain is mathematical, as in computing the factorial of an integer, it may be easy to see that a program specification is correct for a problem and obviously solves it. Limiting problem solving to mathematical areas will reinforce the conception of computer science as an exact science. But in other problem areas, for example, involving trial and error or search, it is not at all obvious that a particular program specification results in a program that solves a problem, even if the program is mechanically generated. This point is emphasized even more if the problem includes constraints on the amount of resources the program is allowed to use to solve the problem. To perform computer problem solving in these areas requires a conception of computer science in which its method is held not merely to be *analogous* to that of experimental science but a *species* of it.

Computer Science as Experimental Science

In the genetic modeling example above, the point of writing the program can also be described, albeit innocuously, as implementing a solution to a problem, but it is more appropriately characterized as testing a model of a phenomenon. Here, the method of writing and running the program is best conceived not as implementing a problem solution, but as a bona fide case of hypothesis testing. The only difference between this method and that of experimental science is that experimentation is carried out via a *computer model* of reality in a program. Testing the program in this sense is not at all to make sure it or an algorithm works. So we have yet another way in which a program can be run as a test:

Testing Sense 5: We might run a program to test a hypothesis in a computer model of reality.

In this sense program testing *cannot* be supplanted by formal program verification since it is essential to the whole method of experimental science. See Figure 24.

This is not to say that formal program verification cannot play any role in programming as hypothesis testing. On the contrary, any or all of the methods of computer science as solution engineering come into play within the broader context of computer science as experimental science. The problem of producing a program with certain specifications must still be solved, but it can be seen as a subproblem of the overall problem of explaining a phenomenon. Figure 25 shows the relationship of computer science as experimental science and computer science as solution engineering.

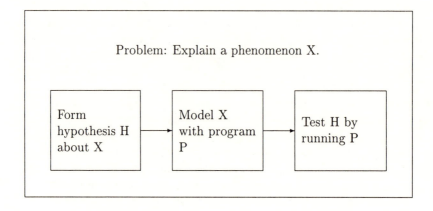

Figure 24. *Hypothesis Testing Using a Program*

The method of "doing" computer science as experimental science is exemplified in many applications involving modeling and simulation. But perhaps the field in which the experimental approach is most pervasive is AI, in which human problem-solving capabilities are not just aided by programs but emulated by them. As we saw in chapter 8, the attempt to emulate problem-solving capability in a program can reveal a dearth of understanding as to the nature of that problem-solving capability, as the program's behavior displays inadequacies in comparison with human problem solving. There is no way, obviously, to tell from an AI program whether its modeling of problem solving is "correct" without running it. This is because the main point of running it is to test a hypothesis about human problem solving, not to check whether it meets its specifications. Thus research in AI is often characterized as the study of human intelligence through attempts to model it in a program.

The question then might be raised, is the AI researcher really doing computer science or something else, say, cognitive science? Similarly, is the genetic model programmer really doing computer science or genetics? These questions, being matters of how to label fields of inquiry, should not be troubling, arising from the unique multidisciplinary nature of computer science. No matter what we choose to call these marriages involving computer methods, they are united in their reliance upon the testing of programs to test hypotheses and sharply distinguished from the "solution engineering" view of computer science, which sees programs as solutions to well specified problems.

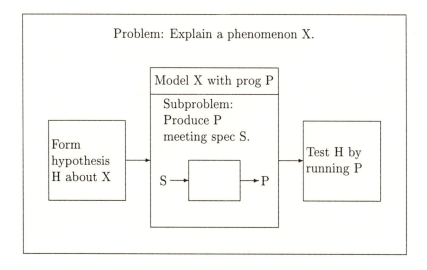

Figure 25. *Computer Science as Experimental Science*

To sum up this chapter, the two views of computer science described here should not be perceived as contraries, since the view of computer science as the engineering of program solutions can be seen as being properly contained in the view of computer science as experimental science (or computer science "in the large"). Formal program verification, as a method of computer science as solution engineering, might, at least in theory if not in current practice, replace program testing as a method of guaranteeing that abstract devices such as memory locations change state correctly in the running of a program. But even combined with formal hardware verification, formal program verification can only defeasibly guarantee the correctness of state changes in physical devices.

Formal program verification may be able to show (defeasibly) that a program meets its specifications, but as such formal program verification only (theoretically) replaces *one* of the ways in which programs are run as tests. Programs are also run as tests of whether a program specification solves a problem, and, in many nonmathematical problem areas, this sort of testing will continue to be indispensable. In particular, when computer programs are used for the modeling and explaining of phenomena, it is only through testing that the correctness of a program can be ascertained, for in these cases the testing of the program also doubles as the testing of a hypothesis.

Abstraction in Computer Science

One of the reasons for the typical incredulous cocktail-party response to any mention of philosophy and computer science in the same breath is that computer scientists are often thought to labor exclusively in a world of bits and bytes, or logic circuits and microprocessors, while philosophers are concerned with knowledge and reality in a world inhabited by people, tables, and other observable objects, as well as loftier objects of inquiry like minds, reason, truth, and beauty. Indeed, the foundational concepts of computer science are described in the language of binary arithmetic and logic gates, but it is a fascinating aspect of the discipline that the *levels of abstraction* that one can lay upon this foundational layer are limitless, and provide the ability to model familiar objects and processes of every day life entirely within a digital world. When digital models are sufficiently faithful to the real thing, we call the environments which they inhabit *virtual worlds*. So today, of course, we have virtual libraries (made possible by the Internet), virtual shopping malls (made possible by the World Wide Web), virtual communities (made possible by e-mail and chat rooms), and even virtual persons, like the digital version of actor Alan Alda created in an episode of PBS's *Scientific American Frontiers*.[1]

Complex virtual worlds such as these are made possible by computer scientists' ability to distance themselves from the mundane and tedious level of bits and processors through tools of abstraction. To abstract is to describe something at a more general level than the level of detail associated with that kind of thing from another point of view. For example, an architect may describe a house by specifying the height of the basement foundation, the location of load-bearing walls and partitions, the R-factor of the insulation, the size of the window and door rough openings, and so on. A realtor, however, may describe the same house as having a certain number of square feet, a certain number of bedrooms, whether the bathrooms are full or half, and so on. The realtor's description leaves out architectural detail but describes the same entity at a more general level, and so it is an abstraction of the architect's description. But abstraction is relative. For example, the architect's description is itself an abstraction when compared to a metallurgist's description of the nails, screws, and other fasteners making up the house, and the botanist's description of the various cellular properties of the wood it contains.

The computer scientist's world is a world of nothing but abstractions. It would not be possible to create the complex virtual worlds described above if the only things computer scientists could talk about were bits, bytes, and microcircuits. In this chapter I will give an idea of what computer scientists do by describing the abstraction tools they use. Now to characterize computer science as involved with abstractions seems to claim for it a place alongside mathematics as a purely formal endeavor. But I will show that the types of abstraction involved in computer science are intended to allow mere *data* to give way to *information* in the programming process. Thus the types of abstraction used in computer science and mathematics are quite dissimilar, and this reinforces the claim that computer science is not merely a branch of pure mathematics. In chapter 12 I close with a discussion of some ontological issues that arise in a consideration of abstraction in computer science.

Data and Information

The distinction between the modeling of information and the modeling of data in the creation of automated systems has historically been important because early development tools available to programmers were wedded to *machine-oriented* data types and processes. That is, they were required to speak in or very close to the language of machines (bits, bytes, numbers, and characters—the language of data) and not in the language of people (customers, accounts receivable, chat rooms, and so on—the language of information). This state of affairs brought about a great emphasis on the *datalogical/infological* distinction,[2] a distinction which is valid in concept, but which has come to also dictate, for some writers, the proper role of software designers.

R. Ashenhurst, for example, describes information modeling as

> the formulation of a model in support of information systems
> development, one in which information aspects of objective and
> subjective reality ("the application") are represented,
> independently of the datasets and processes by which they may
> be realized ("the system").[3]

This is well and good, but Ashenhurst also believes that software designers are concerned *only* with "the system's" data and machine processes, that is, they are engaged only in data modeling, and thus cannot be said to be involved in information modeling in any way. He offers several examples from the literature which indicate that this distinction is appreciated and understood, but he contends that in the end most attempts to model information aspects of objective and subjective reality (that is, attempts to do information modeling) slide surreptitiously into the language and methods of data modeling, with too much emphasis on the "datasets and processes by which they may be realized."

It is clear that Ashenhurst regards the infological/datalogical distinction as sacrosanct, and part of an order of natural kinds in computer science. He says,

> In considering data vs. information/knowledge, the confusion is
> between symbolic artifacts and their interpretation as meaningful
> representations of, or statements about, the real world,[4]

as though it is acceptable for data objects to be *interpreted* as, but forever not acceptable for them to *be themselves*, meaningful representations of the world. In fact, he adopts as a criterion of any appropriate description of information modeling the lack of any reference to "data" or "data structures."[5]

However, I contend that advances in the use of abstraction in software engineering allow activities reasonably described as information modeling to be performed in the software creation process. An examination of the evolution of programming languages and the development of general programming paradigms suggests that while data modeling will necessarily continue to be a programmer's concern, more and more of the programming process itself is coming to be characterized by information modeling activities.

As a software developer and computer science teacher as well as a philosopher, I believe that the infological/datalogical distinction in automated system design is in fact dissolving, due to methods involving *data abstraction* and *procedural abstraction* in the software creation process. These kinds of abstraction, an appreciation for which is now instilled in freshman programmers in every reasonable computer science curriculum, result precisely in the creation of *software* designs, not just *logical system* designs, which are "independent... of datasets and processes by which they may be realized."

In the world of actual software creation, it is not necessary to adamantly continue to drive a wedge between the infological and the datalogical points of view. The software tools and methods of today are allowing programmers to both think and program in infological terms. It is no longer as though the software designer is an unfathomable data wizard to whom are passed the specifications of the information modeler for implementation. The abstraction tools of current and developing programming languages allow the software specialist to design in the language of Ashenhurst's "objective and subjective reality." I believe that the trend, in fact, is to make the term "software specialist" a misnomer, since the successful software developer will need to be a generalist, conversant in the terms of any reality capable of being modeled by a machine. This is not a futuristic prediction, but a natural outcome of the inexorable movement toward *machine independence* in both the design of programming languages and the practice of software construction.

In the rest of this chapter, I show that information modeling is a proper domain for software designers. I support this through a combination of appeals to historical, current, and future software development contexts, maintaining throughout that the trend is toward an infological approach to software design. I start by describing the evolution of software engineering as a discipline whose effect has been to successively free, though not entirely remove, the programmer from machine process and data details. I then place this movement in the modern context of procedural and data abstraction, and I claim that the practice of abstraction, a primary software development tool, is a kind of information modeling. Finally, I describe how the various attempts at abstraction in programs have resulted in the major programming paradigms of today, and how they share the effect of making information modelers out of programmers.

The Evolution of Software Engineering

High-Level Languages

While the history of programming languages may be familiar to some, it is worth briefly describing here. The earliest computers in the 1940s and the early 1950s were programmed directly in the language of the machine's processor, namely, the binary language of zeros and ones, or bits. All data, all machine locations, and all instructions were represented by bits, grouped into eight-bit chunks (or bytes), and loaded into memory (by persons who, justifiably, might be called *wizards*). Every machine manufacturer developed its own binary encoding of data and instructions, so the details of the programming process differed widely from manufacturer to manufacturer. This process, tedious and error-prone at best when performed by humans, became automated in the 1950s by special system programs called *assemblers*, which allowed programmers to write in an *assembly language*, which had at least some of the trappings of English, as in the assembly language instruction "`addb r7,sum`" ("add the byte integer in register 7 to the integer in location `sum` and store the result in location `sum`"), as opposed to the equivalent machine language hexadecimal (base 16) instruction "40571052," or worse, the equivalent binary instruction "01000000010101110001000001010010." While it was an improvement over machine language, assembly language was still tightly related to specific machine architectures. Furthermore, it was still tedious to code even algebraically straightforward quantities like $\sqrt{b^2 - 4ac}$, which could easily require a dozen lines of hard-to-decipher assembly language code.

A breakthrough occurred with the development in the late 1950s and the early 1960s of more special system programs that allowed programmers to write in higher-level languages yet, by automatically translating from these languages to machine or assembly language for a given processor. One of the earliest such languages was called *Fortran* (for *For*mula *trans*lator), and the system program that did the translating from the Fortran language to machine or assembly language was called a Fortran *compiler*. Henceforth, instead of thinking about a square root problem awkwardly in an unnatural machine or assembly language, programmers could work with expressions more familiar to them. For example, the quantity $\sqrt{b^2 - 4ac}$ could be computed in a Fortran program using the expression "`SQRT(B^2 - 4*A*C)`." Also, since the elements of the higher-level programming language are machine independent (devoid of references to registers and memory locations, for example), then a program written in, say, Fortran, will work on any machine that has a Fortran compiler written for it. Programmers are freed from needing to know the architectural details of the machines they are programming (just as realtors are freed from knowing the architectural details of the houses they list). The move from machine language to assembly language and from assembly language to Fortran were the earliest examples of *language abstraction* in computer science. The success of Fortran spawned advances in compiler technology leading to the creation of numerous languages, like Algol, Cobol, APL, Pascal, Modula-2, C, and Ada, many of which are heavily used today.

While the use of these high-level languages frees the programmer from needing to know about specific machine architectures, it does not, obviously, free the programmer from having to think datalogically; after all, these languages are intended to facilitate the manipulation of data through programmer-specified computational processes. In fact, an earmark of all these languages is their widening of the class of strictly defined *data types*—integers, real numbers, characters, strings of characters, arrays of data, records of data, and so on—beyond that offered in the terminology of assembly language. But the movement toward machine independence in programming was followed by another movement in software design which promised to free the programmer in a different way from the strict data types of the computational (modeling) world, toward the natural types of the real (modeled) world.

The "Software Crisis"

The movement began in the late 1960s with the birth of *software engineering* as a discipline in computer science[6] and continued through the 1970s as practitioners and researchers in software creation pronounced their field "in crisis."[7] Despite the liberating effects of compilers for high-level programming languages, software developers found their large projects becoming mired in vastly overrun budgets, poor-quality software products, and maddeningly difficult software maintenance. The situation was all the more frustrating when compared with their hardware counterparts, for whom the advances in semiconductor technology and large-scale integration of circuits were beginning the process, continuing even to this day, of producing ever smaller, faster, and cheaper components. The software industry found itself not able to keep up with the pace set by the hardware industry in introducing new-generation processors and cheaper memory in time periods measured by months and years instead of decades.

The problem was in software complexity, which itself was driven by the rapid growth of both application and computer system complexity. With each introduction of faster processors and more dense memory it became easier to write larger programs. For example, the change from 16-bit to 32-bit processors was accompanied by a change of maximum address space from 64 kilobytes (65,536 bytes) to 4 gigabytes (4,294,967,296 bytes). While programs for 16-bit processors greater than 64K in size could be written, this required the painstaking use of overlays while programming. When the address space increased to 4 gigabytes, and with the introduction of virtual memory techniques, the programmer was freed from the tyranny of overlays and larger programs were the result. Larger programs became notoriously difficult to fix, when the inevitable error was discovered after deployment, and to maintain, when the inevitable change in the end application required modification. It was found that, although typical programming projects budgeted 10-15 percent of their effort and cost for maintenance, the amount actually expended on maintenance in the end was 55-70 percent![8]

Not only program size, but also programming style, contributed to the software maintenance problem. When programs were still relatively small, programmers could be seduced into thinking that to be an expert programmer meant to be able to rely on their wits, their (often bitter) experience with other programs, and "Band-Aid fixes" (or program "hacks") when fixing or maintaining programs. And when creating new programs, the freedom offered by the compiled high-level languages often tempted the programmer to forgo the laborious work of careful design for the more flashy route of quick-and-dirty creation on the fly, as if daring and even welcoming a future nettlesome problem to test his or her mettle as a programmer and a problem solver. This was the culture of the hacker (not in the sense of a security hacker), and it was considered a badge of honor to be clever enough to overcome a program's poor initial design.

Structured Programming

The culture of hacking combined with poor program design resulted in unrestricted locality of reference (that is, inappropriate use of program jumps creating "spaghetti code"), inconsistent use of program constants, inattention to the boundary conditions in loops, and very little attempt to verify the correctness of program code before running it. With larger programs, these problems came to overwhelm programmers, who found that fixing one problem caused another problem someplace else, and so large software projects came to be characterized by crisis management.

The software community recognized the crisis and took steps to deal with it by developing new languages and enforcing certain rules of programming style. The discipline of "structured" programming[9] narrowed a program's locality of reference by replacing loops loosely constructed out of program jumps with *while* and *repeat* statements. The use of structured programming took programmers further from the language of machines, in the sense that transfer of program control was not expressed by jumps and labels, but by ordinary English constructs. By the end of the 1970s the so-called procedural languages became prominent, and programmers were admonished to design and create their programs out of small, relatively autonomous "chunks" of code called procedures, which are programs in their own right, and can be combined and arranged into complex programs by way of strictly defined standard control transfer protocols. The result was software constructed out of modules, much as electronic equipment such as televisions and stereos were being assembled, to the envy of software engineers, as programmers sometimes now referred to themselves. The standard control transfer protocols among procedures enabled their use in more than one program, and the concept of software procedure libraries was more prominent than before, encouraging the practice of software reuse.[10] This idea would have been foreign to many of the early hackers who routinely threw away code when it was no longer useful, and started completely from scratch when they embarked on a new project.

Programmers as Information Modelers

Just as the movement to higher-level languages freed programmers from having to think strictly in terms of machine-oriented computational processes, the accompanying trend toward software creation as an engineering discipline freed programmers from having to think strictly in terms of *data* representation, allowing them to concentrate also on the modeling of *information* for eventual realization in a machine program.

Programmer-Defined Data Types

As a simple and early illustration, the programming language Pascal, besides encouraging structured and procedural programming, allowed programmers to define their own data types, in addition to using the data types, such as integer, real, and array, that were built into the language. When limited to built-in types, programs often had to use awkward codes for real-world concepts, if those concepts were not readily representable through built-in machine types. For example, to check whether a day of the week was a company payday, a program might contain the statement,

```
if Today = 5 then ComputePay;
```

To understand what this statement means, it would be necessary to know which day of the week the integer 5 stood for, as in the mapping of the list of integers 0, 1, ... , 6, to the list of days Sunday, Monday, ... , Saturday. But with programmer-defined types it was possible to augment when necessary the set of types accepted by the language. In this example, it is straightforward in Pascal to declare a type called day, say, where variables of type day can have symbolic values in the range Sunday, Monday, ... , Saturday. Now the program can contain statements that are faithful models of company information, as in,

```
if Today = Friday then ComputePay;
```

This is possible because the Pascal compiler hides the representation of Friday from the programmer. The programmer never has to know, nor should she ever *want* to know, this representation. She is freed from datalogical concerns, at least as regards days of the week, and may program more nearly in the language of real-world information.

The programmer-defined typing mechanism in Pascal, though innovative for languages of its kind, was relatively primitive, and other languages have evolved entirely new programming paradigms. These paradigms all have in common the freeing of programmers from the tyranny of machine-oriented data and processes, allowing them to think in terms of information-oriented abstractions.

Symbol Processing Languages and Artificial Intelligence

Even back in the early 1960s, researchers were designing languages based on computational models not at all related to physical machine architecture. By 1965, the language Lisp had become established as a model of the lambda calculus and recursion. One of the primary data types supported by Lisp was the abstract notion of a *list*, the implementation of which in terms of pointers and pairs was completely hidden from programmers who, without understanding anything about the machines they were using, could easily create a list object through statements like,

```
(setq things-to-get '(milk cheese apples carrots))
```

This example also points out another Lisp data type, namely, the *symbol*, like `things-to-get` or `apples`, which distinguishes Lisp as one of a class of languages called *symbol processing* languages, as opposed to *numeric processing* languages such as Fortran or Pascal. Lisp proved so adept at manipulating lists of both symbols and other lists that many researchers in AI soon adopted it as their vehicle for testing various methods of knowledge representation and automated reasoning. They found that lists of symbols were suitable for representing formulas in predicate logic. For example, the formula

$$\forall x (Human(x) \rightarrow Mortal(x)),$$

representing the fact that all humans are mortal, could be represented by the list

```
(forall ?x (human ?x) -> (Mortal ?x))
```

Such a representation, combined with suitable algorithms implementing the inference rules of logic, allowed researchers to build programs capable of inferring new facts from and answering questions of *knowledge bases*.

By elevating the symbol and the list to the status of full-fledged data type heretofore allowed only objects like integers, reals, and arrays, Lisp allowed programmers to think and write more in terms of the reality that was being modeled in their programs, like milk, apples, and predicate logic formulas. This closeness is why AI researchers are able to engage in the practices of *exploratory programming* and *rapid prototyping*, in which program specifications are not entirely understood at the outset of a software project, and so an implementation is undertaken as part of the design process.[11] In using Lisp, the programmer is not encumbered by decisions about how to implement the necessary underlying data structures or how to manage memory; the built-in lists and symbols along with the Lisp run-time system are sufficient for modeling the information with which the programmer is most concerned.

The capabilities of Lisp did not come without a price. In its early days Lisp was maligned for being slow, and its memory requirements were beyond what many programmers could afford. But this was not surprising given the amount of work Lisp had to do to provide the programming freedom that so distancing the programmer from the machine provided. Programmers could sacrifice that freedom for speed if they wanted, but then they found themselves back at the level of bits and subroutines. Today, compiler technology and cheap memory have combined to make powerful versions of Lisp (in the dialect known as Common Lisp) available on desktop PCs, and price and performance are no longer an issue.

AI may be the best example of an area in which programmers are directly involved in information modeling, by virtue of the fact that they must do *knowledge representation*. Contrary to the picture of a programmer as merely a squeezer of bits and optimizer of loops, the AI programmer must understand an area of human endeavor, symbolically represent knowledge in that area, and transfer it to a machine in this symbolic form. Classical AI software architecture requires that the knowledge remain in this symbolic form, in near-English representation, so that knowledge bases can be easily augmented and modified, and so that familiar logical inference mechanisms can be brought to bear on them.

The symbolic processing language Prolog, the AI language of choice in Europe and Japan, takes the programmer closest to the real world and farthest from the machine yet. In Prolog, a sophisticated symbolic pattern matcher (called *unification*) and a powerful inference mechanism (called *resolution*) are embedded in every machine cycle, and the programmer codes directly in the language of predicate logic. For example, the following definition of *grandparent*:

X is a grandparent of Y if there is a Z such that X is a parent of Z and Z is a parent of Y,

is directly representable by the following Prolog logic procedure:

```
grandparent(X,Y) :- parent(X,Z), parent(Z,Y).
```

When combined with the following facts:

```
parent(pat, priscilla).
parent(priscilla, cecilia).
```

these expressions constitute a logic program which, when invoked by a query asking who is the grandparent of Cecilia:

```
?  grandparent(Who, cecilia).
```

will cause the output:

```
Who = pat
```

This behavior is possible because predicate logic clauses can be regarded as having both declarative and procedural semantics. In effect, a Prolog programmer takes real-world knowledge and translates it into predicate logic clauses that are directly executable on a Prolog machine. He deals almost exclusively with information, and not with the structures and processes required to manipulate it.

Varieties of Abstraction

Of course, not all programmers are AI programmers, and not all languages are AI languages (far from it). But the general trends in all programming are toward higher-quality software by abstracting away from the lower-level concepts in computer science and toward the objects and information that make up the real world. This is a kind of abstraction that is fundamentally different from that which takes place in mathematics. Understanding the difference is crucial in avoiding the persistent misconception by some that computer science is just a branch of pure mathematics.

Abstraction in Mathematics

Both mathematics and computer science are marked by the introduction of abstract objects into the realm of discourse, but they differ fundamentally in the nature of these objects. I will suggest that the difference has to do with the abstraction of *form* versus the abstraction of *content*.

Traditionally, mathematics, as a formal science, has been contrasted with the factual sciences such as physics or biology. As natural sciences, the latter are not concerned with abstraction beyond that offered by mathematics as an analytical tool. The literature is full of strict bifurcations between the nature of formal and factual science in terms of the meanings of the statements involved in them. Recall that Carnap, for example, employs the analytic/synthetic distinction in claiming that the formal sciences contain only analytic statements. Since analytic statements are true only by virtue of the transformation rules of the language in which they are made, Carnap is led to the view that

> *[t]he formal sciences do not have any objects at all*; they are systems of auxiliary statements without objects and without content.[12]

Thus according to Carnap the abstraction involved in mathematics is one totally away from content and toward the pure form of linguistic transformations.

Not all philosophers of mathematics agree with Carnap that mathematics has only linguistic utility for scientists, but there is agreement on the nature of mathematical abstraction being to remove the meanings of specific terms. Cohen and Nagel, for example, present a set of axioms for plane geometry; remove all references to points, lines, and planes; and replace them with symbols used merely as variables. They then proceed to demonstrate a number of theorems as consequences of these new axioms, showing that pure deduction in mathematics proceeds with terms that have no observational or sensory meaning. An axiom system may just *happen* to describe physical reality, but that is for experimentation in science to decide. Thus, again, a mathematical or deductive system is abstract by virtue of a complete stepping away from the content of scientific terms:

> Every [deductive] system is of necessity *abstract*: it is the structure of certain *selected* relations, and must consequently omit the structure of other relations. Thus the systems studied in physics do not include the systems explored in biology. Furthermore, as we have seen, a system is deductive not in virtue of the special meanings of its terms, but in virtue of the universal relations between them. The specific quality of the things which the terms denote do not, as such, play any part in the system. Thus the theory of heat takes no account of the unique sensory qualities which heat phenomena display. A deductive system is therefore doubly abstract: it abstracts from the specific qualities

of a subject matter, and it selects some relations and neglects others.[13]

As a final example, consider Hempel's assessment of the nature of mathematics while arguing for the thesis of *logicism*, or the view that mathematics is a branch of logic:

> The propositions of mathematics have, therefore, the same unquestionable certainty which is typical of such propositions as "All bachelors are unmarried," but they also share the complete lack of empirical content which is associated with that certainty: The propositions of mathematics are devoid of all factual content; they convey no information whatever on any empirical subject matter.[14]

In each of these accounts of mathematics, all concern for the content or subject matter of specific terms is abandoned in favor of the *form* of the deductive system. So the abstraction involved results in essentially the *elimination* of content. In computer science we will see that content is not totally abstracted away in this sense. Rather, abstraction in computer science consists in the *enlargement* of content. For computer scientists, this allows programs and machines to be reasoned about, analyzed, and ultimately efficiently implemented in physical systems. For computer users, this allows useful objects, such as documents, shopping malls, and chat rooms, to exist virtually in a purely electronic space.

Abstraction in Computer Science

Understanding abstraction in computer science requires understanding some of the history of software engineering and hardware development, for it tells a story of an increasing distance between programmers and the machine-oriented entities which provide the foundation of their work. This increasing distance corresponds to a concomitant increase in the reliance on abstract views of the entities with which the discipline is fundamentally concerned. These entities include machine instructions, machine-oriented processes, and machine-oriented data types. I will now try to explain the role of abstraction with regard to these kinds of entities.

Language Abstraction

At the grossest physical level, a computer process is a series of changes in the state of a machine, where each state is described by the presence or absence of electrical charges in memory and processor elements. But as we have seen, programmers need not be directly concerned with

machine states so described, because they can make use of software development tools which allow them to think in other terms. For example,
with the move from assembly to high-level language, computer scientists
can abandon talk about particular machine-oriented entities like instructions, registers and word integers in favor of more abstract statements
and variables. High-level language programs allow machine processes to
be described without reference to any particular machine. Thus, specific
language content has not been eliminated, as in mathematical or deductive systems, but replaced by abstract descriptions with more expressive
power.

Procedural Abstraction

Abstraction of language is but one example of what can be considered the
attempt to enlarge the content of what is programmed about. Consider
also the practice of *procedural abstraction* that arose with the introduction
of high-level languages. Along with the ability to speak about abstract
entities like statements and variables, high-level languages introduced
the idea of *modularity*, according to which arbitrary blocks of statements
gathered into *procedures* could assume the status of statements themselves. For example, consider the high-level language statements given in
Figure 26. It would take a studied eye to recognize that these statements

```
for i ← 1 to n do
    for j ← 1 to m do
        read(A[i,j])
for j ← 1 to m do
    for k ← 1 to p do
        read(B[j,k])
for i ← 1 to n do
    for k ← 1 to p do begin
        C[i,k] ← 0
        for j ← 1 to m do
            C[i,k] ← C[i,k] + A[i,j] * B[j,k]
    end
```

Figure 26. *Multiplying Matrices*

describe a process of filling an $n \times m$ matrix A and an $m \times p$ matrix
B with numbers and multiplying them, putting the result in an $n \times p$

matrix C such that $C_{i,k} = \sum_{j=1}^{m} A_{i,j} B_{j,k}$. But by abstracting out the three major operations in this process and giving them procedure names, the program can be written at a higher, and more readable, level as in Figure 27. These three statements convey the same information about

---

ReadMatrix(A,n,m)
ReadMatrix(B,m,p)
MultiplyMatrices(A,B,C,n,m,p)

Figure 27. *Multiplying Matrices with Procedural Abstraction*

the overall process, but with less detail. No mention is made, say, of the order in which matrix elements are filled, or indeed of matrix subscripts at all. From the point of view of the higher-level process, these details are irrelevant; all that is really necessary to invoke the process is the names of the input and output matrices and their dimensions, given as parameters to the lower-level procedures. Of course, the details of how the lower-level procedures perform their actions must be given in their definitions, but the point is that these definitions can be strictly separated from the processes that call upon them. What we have, then, is the total abstraction of a procedure's use from its definition. Whereas in the language example we had the abstraction of the content of computer instructions, here we have the abstraction of the content of whole computational procedures. And again, the abstraction step does not eliminate content in favor of form as in mathematics; it renders the content more expressive.

Data Abstraction

As a last example, consider the programmer's practice of *data abstraction*. Machine-oriented data types, such as integers, arrays, floating point numbers, and characters, are, of course, themselves abstractions placed on the physical states of memory elements interpreted as binary numbers. They are, however, intimately tied to particular machine architectures in that there are machine instructions specifically designed to operate on them. They are also built into the terminology of all useful high-level languages. But this terminology turns out to be extremely impoverished if the kinds of things in the world being programmed about include, as most current software applications do, objects like customers, recipes, flight plans, or chat rooms.

The practice of data abstraction is the specification of objects such as these and all operations that can be performed on them, without reference to the details of their implementation in terms of other data types. Such objects, called *abstract data types* (ADTs), once they become implemented, assume their place among integers, arrays, and so on as legitimate objects in the computational world, with their representation details, which are necessarily more machine oriented, being invisible to their users. The result is that programs that are about customers, recipes, flight plans, and so on are written in terms that are natural to these contexts, and not in the inflexible terms of the underlying machine. The programs are therefore easier to write, read, and modify. The specification and construction of abstract data types are primary topics in undergraduate computer science curricula, as evidenced by the many textbooks devoted to these topics.[15] But this again is a type of abstraction that does not eliminate empirical content, as in mathematics, but rather enlarges the content of terms by bringing them to bear directly on things in a nonmachine-oriented world.

The keys to the nature of ADTs are their encapsuling together of object with operation and the disregarding of machine details in their specification. To be sure, these details must be dealt with *some* time by a programmer, but they will often be satisfied by low-level code already written to perform routine operations like input and output. More important, the programmer will first be thinking about objects in the real world, how to abstractly specify the legal operations on them given the information about them she knows, and last how to translate these operations into computational procedures. She lives comfortably in the infological world, passing into the datalogical world only when necessary.

There is, of course, an element of wishful thinking in this scenario, as any programmer laboring in a pit of antique code (and there is still *lots* of it) will attest. Nevertheless, it is one desideratum of software engineering to allow both infological and datalogical thinking in the programming process, and training in both is a primary objective in computer science education.

Programming Paradigms

The drive toward procedural and data abstraction in software design has resulted in the delineation of various programming paradigms, each with its own story about how it enhances the software development process. These are called "paradigms" because they constitute general models of computer problem solving which any one of a number of particular programming languages may attempt to instantiate. An understanding of the fundamental nature of these paradigms, and how they have evolved, can help to illuminate today's role of the software developer as information modeler. To describe these paradigms, we must start with a working definition of what a programming language actually is. We use one taken from a standard programming languages text:

> A programming language is a language that is intended to be used by a person to express a process by which a computer can solve a problem.[16]

Any process, whether purely physical, computational, or otherwise, is a sequence of actions among objects. A computational process occurring on a computer is a curious entity because it is at once concrete and abstract. It is concrete because it can be described as the passing of electrons in circuits measured in microns, effecting changes in the state of semiconducting memory elements. On the other hand, the description of these state changes is a program that, as an expression in a formal language, is an abstraction of a process the programmer hopes is a correct model of the solution of a problem in the real world. What distinguishes the major programming paradigms is the kinds of object and action that the abstract process involves.

The Imperative Programming Paradigm

The *imperative* programming paradigm is so called because programs written in this paradigm "command" the computer to perform actions on objects, telling it how to behave. Assembly languages are imperative languages in which programs specify processes that involve objects like memory locations and registers, and actions like loading from and storing to memory, adding the contents of registers, shifting bits in registers, etc. Higher-order languages like C, Pascal, and Ada are imperative languages in which programs specify objects like procedures and matrices, and actions like calling a procedure or multiplying two matrices. The objects and actions in these languages are machine-independent, in that they do not directly specify things like memory addresses and register comparisons. But the objects and actions that are provided are only slightly removed from the machine level, and are fairly easily translated to machine level by the language's compilers. If programmers want to specify objects and actions like movies and game strategies, they must create abstract data types for them. With some possible concessions to Ada, higher-order imperative languages are impoverished in their ability to support ADTs, and it is not difficult to see why. Programmers find themselves trying to shoehorn their thinking about a complex real-world object into the language of a paradigm which is only allowed to give step-by-step commands that can be directly translated into machine instructions. It was frustration with the inappropriateness of imperative languages to support abstraction that gave way to alternative paradigms. These paradigms are not restricted to models of computer processor behavior; they are intended to model how we think in realms other than machine-oriented processes.

The Functional Programming Paradigm

Some people, including those who are mathematically inclined, tend to think about the world in functional abstractions. That is, they see objects in the world as subject to actions that can be modeled by the application of functions to arguments resulting in values. The *functional* programming paradigm is so called because programs written in this paradigm are composed entirely of function calls. Many imperative languages allow the definition and calling of functions also, but only as an enhancement to their language of algebraic expressions; their primary objects and actions still are those of the imperative paradigm. But true functional languages, like Lisp, Scheme, and ML, are utterly *unconcerned* about the machine representation of the objects and actions with which they *are* concerned. For functional language programmers, the concepts of function, argument, and value (often couched in the language of the lambda calculus) together constitutute not only the fundamental nature of computation, but of real-world modeling as well. Insofar as mathematics is an appropriate information modeling language for real-world problems, functional programming languages are also appropriate.

The Logic-Oriented Programming Paradigm

For those who would argue that mathematical modeling and information modeling are fundamentally different, the (pure) functional programming paradigm would not suffice as an information modeling tool. It can be argued that this deficiency at least partly explains the development of the *logic-oriented* programming paradigm as a tool for AI programming. In this paradigm, the prime example of which is Prolog, a computational process is expressed entirely in a language whose objects include facts, logic variables, rules, and goals, and whose actions involve goal matching, rule firing, and backtracking in an abstract deduction search space. The logic-oriented programming paradigm is also called a *declarative* programming paradigm, because the programming activity is marked by indicating *what* is the case in a computational world, rather than *how* to accomplish something.

The Object-Oriented Programming Paradigm

While the logic-oriented or declarative programmer is far removed from machine details and can be regarded as programming in an infological domain, the logic-oriented paradigm is not mainstream in the programming world. However, the same desire for extreme machine independence and primacy of real-world concepts in the programming endeavor has given rise to the *object-oriented* paradigm exemplified by current widespread interest in C++ and Java. In this paradigm, computational processes are expressed as actions among objects described as classes and instances of classes. An important aspect of this paradigm is the arrangement of classes of objects in a hierarchy, allowing for the inheritance of both features and operations by one class from another. This feature of inheritance allows for the definition of *generic* operations, having utterly nothing to do with the machine representation of their targeted objects.

As an example, consider the representation of bank accounts.[17] It is natural to consider bank accounts as arranged in a hierarchy, with the most general type of account at the top. General accounts would be defined with familiar features like name, balance, and interest rate, as well as account operations like withdrawing and depositing. More specific types of accounts, like password protected accounts (for use with automated teller machines) and limited withdrawal accounts (for protection against overdrafts) would be defined to inherit all the features and operations (also called "methods") of general accounts, as well as take on their own defining features and methods. Thus the bank account class hierarchy could be visualized as in Figure 28.

Object-oriented software methods allow the creation of data objects to mirror this hierarchy. For example, suppose that the following information describes the general notion of a bank account:

1. The attributes of an account are: name of the account holder, account balance (which defaults to zero if not initially provided), and interest rate (initially 6 percent).

2. To withdraw a given amount from an account, there must be an adequate balance, in which case the amount is deducted from the balance, otherwise an "insufficient funds" error occurs.

3. To deposit a given amount into an account, simply add it to the balance.

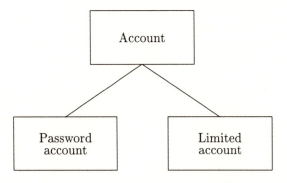

Figure 28. *Bank Account Hierarchy*

4. To accrue interest to an account, multiply the interest rate by the
balance and add the result to the balance.

An object-oriented extension to Common Lisp allows this information
about general bank accounts to be captured by the following class definition:

```
(define-class account (name &optional (balance 0.00))
               ((interest-rate .06))
  (withdraw (amt) (if (<= amt balance)
                      (decf balance amt)
                      'insufficient-funds))
  (deposit  (amt) (incf balance amt))
  (interest ()    (incf balance (* interest-rate balance)))
  (balance  ()    balance)
  (name     ()    name))
```

This defines a class of account objects with instance variables **name** and
balance (which may be omitted at account creation time resulting in a
default opening balance of zero), class variable **interest-rate** with a
default value of 6 percent (called a "class" variable because all accounts
will share it), and methods for withdrawing, depositing, and accruing
interest. (The last two lines specify methods for accessing the balance
and name.) Nowhere in this definition is betrayed any hint of the data
structures and machine processes required to represent these accounts
and carry out their operations. The definition looks very much like an
information model, yet it results in completely executable code. For
example, the form

```
(setf acct1 (account "A. User" 2000.00))
```

will create an account for A. User with an initial balance of $2,000.00. The operation

```
(deposit acct1 42.00)
```

will increase A. User's balance to $2,042.00, and the operation

```
(interest acct1)
```

will cause the balance to increase by 6 percent to $2,164.52.

My choice of Common Lisp as the programming language used in this example is only incidental to the point being made, which is that thinking in terms of real-world objects is possible in object-oriented programming and design. The example does not depend, for example, on one of Lisp's most salient features which sets it apart, namely, dynamic run-time type checking. The same piece of code could be rendered in alternative object-oriented programming languages such as C++, Java, Smalltalk, or Eiffel.

Beyond the obvious advantages of programmers being able to think in terms of real-world objects like bank accounts, object-oriented programming offers the distinct practical advantage of being able to reuse program code. This advantage is a direct result of the hierarchical organization of classes enforced by object-oriented programming and design. For example, a natural way of describing a password account is by specifying how it adds to the notion of a general account:

1. The attributes of a password account are the same as those of a general account, with the addition of a password.

2. For an account user to change her password, she must provide both the current account password and a new password. If the current account password is correct, her account receives the new password, otherwise a "wrong password" error occurs.

3. For any other operation on a password account (that is, a withdrawal, deposit, etc.), the provided password is checked. If it is correct, the operation is performed as with a general account, otherwise a "wrong password" error occurs.

Thus, in our example, a password account can be defined in a straightforward way as a subclass of general account through the following:

```
(define-class password-account (password acct) ()
  (change-password (pass new-pass)
                   (if (equal pass password)
                       (setf password new-pass)
                       'wrong-password))
  (otherwise (pass &rest args)
             (if (equal pass password)
                 (do-operation acct args)
                 'wrong-password)))
```

The distinguishing feature of a password account is the password, indicated here as an instance variable. The inheriting of general account features by password accounts is accomplished by making a general account itself an instance variable (acct) of the password account. Thus, if an operation to change the password is requested, it is carried out directly, but for any other operation (indicated by the otherwise clause), the work is delegated to the general account class (provided the correct password is given). So, in order to make A. User's account password protected, we simply create a new account "wrapped around" the old account, without changing anything done before:

```
(setf acct2 (password-account "secret" acct1))
```

The new account inherits all the features of the old account, but all operations require a password. For example,

```
(balance acct2 "secret")
```

still accesses the correct balance ($2,164.52) of A. User, while

```
(withdraw acct2 "guess" 2000.00)
```

will deny the operation with the response WRONG-PASSWORD.

Similar careful abstraction of features and operations make for the easy definition and creation of limited withdrawal accounts as a subclass of general accounts, as in the following class definition:

```
(define-class limited-account (limit acct) ()
  (withdraw  (amt)
             (if (> amt limit)
                 'over-limit
                 (withdraw acct amt)))
  (otherwise (&rest args)
             (do-operation acct args)))
```

Now we can easily create and use accounts with overdraft protection, but because of the class hierarchy and inheritance features, we get the ability to create a password-protected limited account without having to define any other classes:

```
(setf acct3 (password-account "pass"
            (limited-account 100.00
              (account "A. Thrifty Spender" 500.00))))
```

Now A. Thrifty Spender is subject to all the limits and protections imposed for her:

```
(withdraw acct3 "pass" 200.00) -> OVER-LIMIT
(withdraw acct3 "pass" 20.00) -> 480.0
(withdraw acct3 "guess" 20.00) -> WRONG-PASSWORD
```

The Future

While I believe the example of the previous section clearly illustrates the potential for information modeling in the programming enterprise, it is not intended to support a prediction that the object-oriented programming bandwagon will attract all information modelers of the future. The object-oriented programming paradigm may not turn out to be the software engineering savior that many of its proponents proclaim.

As one reader of this chapter has commented, "Let a thousand paradigms bloom!" I agree and have simply tried to show that the evolution of programming languages is tied to ever-increasing abstraction tools and methods, the current embodiment of which only happens to be object-oriented programming.

Programming paradigms will no doubt continue to come and go, as languages are constantly being modified or completely redesigned to get around their limitations. It is not the paradigm that is important, but the style and discipline of designing and coding in the abstract.

Still, amid the uncertainty about the dominance of future programming languages, one thing seems clear. Whatever programming paradigm a programmer chooses, the trend is toward narrowing the gap between the infological and the datalogical. Moreover, this trend is not a regrettable outcome of sloppy policy, as Ashenhurst would have it, but a welcome benefit of advances in software engineering and programming language design.

It is an endlessly fascinating feature of computer science that the more complex the technology, the more removed from technology's complexity its users become. For users who today are application programmers, this removal will lessen the tyranny of machine data types and processes, and make them information modelers of the future.

Software, Abstraction, and Ontology

Traditional philosophical problems in ontology, that is, problems concerning what kinds of things there are, and how to classify certain individual things, rarely hold more than academic interest. The outcomes of debates over the ontological status of bare particulars, for example, will not make headline news or affect the lives of nonphilosophers very much. Of course, a decision to make an ontological commitment often *does* affect how we do science, as when the conjecture that more than 90 percent of the universe is composed of unobserved "dark" matter prompts lengthy and risky experiments to capture a fleeting glimpse of a neutrino. Still, although the outcomes of these experiments hold enormous implications for cosmology, they will not affect the day-to-day lives of ordinary people whose work involves business, finance, trade, or technology.

However, the ontological status of computer software has emerged as an issue that may hold interest both for academic philosophers and for those involved in the formation of public policy for the international marketplace. As reported in a recent issue of *Scientific American*,[1] the apparent dual nature of software has sparked a debate involving free speech and the applicability of the International Traffic in Arms Regulations. A related controversy concerning policy governing intellectual property rights also appears to have its roots in a perceived dual nature of software.

The aim of this chapter is not to propose solutions to these debates, but to bring to light and analyze the philosophical assumptions underlying them. I will describe the *prima facie* reasons for upholding software's duality, along with the ontological implications. Along the way, I will expose a misconception, namely, that software is a machine made out of text. I will also show how this view is related to the view, already considered in chapter 9, that computer science is merely a branch of pure mathematics. By describing the actual practice and infrastructure surrounding software creation today, I will support a view of software as a *concrete abstraction*, and try to explain what this could mean from an ontological point of view.

The Dual Nature of Software

At the center of one of the debates are cryptography programs. Although the philosophical questions raised by them are also raised by any computer program, they have emerged as a focus because of their value to a wide cross-section of society. Computer cryptography involves both the encryption and the decryption of data that are passed along nonsecure electronic communication lines, so that an eavesdropper on such a line would find only unintelligible data. Encryption and decryption software is essential to ensure the privacy of data such as credit card numbers used in Internet commerce, electronic funds transfers, and personal email messages. The encryption and decryption of data as performed by, say, a *public-key cryptosystem*,[2] proceed through the manipulation of large numbers that function as "keys" for "locking" and "unlocking" the content of the data. As with all software, the computational process that performs this is described by an *algorithm*, or a finite, effective sequence of steps. In this case the steps involve operations like raising large numbers to integer powers and performing modular arithmetic. The medium of an algorithm's description might be a natural language like English, if it is being described informally, or it might be an artificial language like C++ or Java. In the latter case, the algorithm is encoded in the text of a computer programming language.

The controversy reported in *Scientific American* concerns an author of a book on applied cryptography who was prohibited by the State Department from exporting the book because it included as an appendix a floppy disk containing program text expressing algorithms for encryption software. The software was deemed a national security risk, since encryption software that is strong enough could allow unfriendly governments or international terrorists to send one another encrypted messages without the eavesdropping U.S. government being able to decrypt them. On this view, a piece of strong encryption software is a dangerous machine, similar to a cluster bomb or a laser-guided missile. However, were the floppy disk *not* included with the book, the book *would* have been freely exportable even though the program text on the floppy disk was also printed in the book. As text on the printed page, the software was simply a product of every American's right to free speech. But as magnetic representations of the same software on a different medium, it qualified as part of a potentially dangerous mechanism and a threat to national security.

To a technologically informed observer, this double standard for threat assessment of software seems naive, especially since automated optical character readers can eliminate the tedium of typing into a floppy disk the text of a program appearing on a printed page. But there is a philosophically interesting aspect of this controversy, in that the two sides naturally appeal to ontological characterizations of software that appear to be inconsistent: the libertarian side wants to see software as text and therefore freely distributable, while the regulatory side wants to see software as mechanism and therefore subject to export restrictions.

The text/mechanism dichotomy is also at the root of controversies over software copyrighting. At issue is the fairness of the practice of certain software companies quickly "cloning" the look and feel of other companies' successful products, then drastically underselling them to gain quick market share, at the expense of the original companies' large investment in research and development. In "A New View of Intellectual Property and Software," the authors point out that laws implementing copyright and patent policy were written at a time when copyright was considered to apply only to literary work, while patents were considered to apply only to the artifacts of technology, and these were mutually exclusive domains. Software, the authors argue, possesses a unique nature that engenders controversies when placed in this strict categorical scheme, so they propose to relax the constraint that the categories of text and mechanism are mutually exclusive:

> We have attempted to capture some of this conceptual confusion with a pseudo-paradox, pointing out that software is a machine whose medium of construction happens to be text. This captures the inseparably dual nature of software: it is inherently both functional and literary, both utilitarian and creative. This seems a paradox only in the context of a conceptual framework (U.S. law) that cannot conceive of such objects.[3]

The important assertion here is that "software is a machine whose medium of construction happens to be text." As computer scientists, the authors are not concerned with the philosophical implications of this assertion, but rather with urging a new approach to protecting market share for software innovators against underselling by second-comers' software clones. From a philosophical point of view the assertion raises two obvious questions: (1) How can a machine be contructed out of text? (2) How can software, which is constructed using statements written in a formal programming language, be considered a machine?

The first question appears puzzling because ordinarily we associate machines with hardware, not text. But as we saw first in chapter 9, computer scientists often leap back and forth between talking about machines as piles of silicon and wires, and machines as abstractions. Abstract machines are sometimes called *virtual* machines because they have a virtual, rather than a physical, existence. Virtual machines are descriptions of machines that *could* be built in hardware, or emulated in software. They are painstaking descriptions of operations and data structures which may or may not be realized in a particular physical system. The Java Virtual Machine, intended to be a cross-platform description of a language processor for the programming language Java, is a current example. The relationship between a virtual machine and its realizations in hardware or software is similar to the relationship between a blueprint for a house and all the various ways it can be built. Nonvirtual machines are not contructed out of text, but out of central processors, memory elements, input/output devices, and so on. Thus when we distinguish between physical and virtual machines, we see that the first question is not puzzling.

The second question, however, gets to the heart of the purported duality of software and cannot be explained by appeal to the physical/virtual distinction. Software seems to be at once both textual and machinelike. After all, when you look at a printout of a program, you see a lot of statements written in a formal language. But when you hold the same program on a floppy disk in your hand, you feel the weight of a piece of a machine. The nature of software's duality can be illuminated by understanding the distinction between software's *medium of description* and its *medium of execution*.

Strictly speaking, when you look at printed program text, what you see is not the software itself, but the encoding of an algorithm, or formal description of a computational process. As such, what you "see" is an abstraction. The software itself, which causes the machine to execute the computational process, is constructed not out of text, but out of electron charges, magnetic fields, pulses of light, and so on, which are not abstractions, but to which we give an interpretation as binary numbers. The idea that software is a machine built from text gives rise to the notion that software is some kind of mysterious entity which is abstract and which possesses causal power. Fetzer, however, in analyzing the practice of formal program verification, has clearly pointed out the philosophical problems with confusing abstract and causal systems.[4] If we are puzzled by the difference between software's *medium of description*, which is formal language, and its *medium of execution*, which is circuits and semiconducting elements, the response should not be to conflate the categories of text and mechanism into a yet more puzzling category that admits of both. It is not necessary to introduce into our ontology entities such as (nonvirtual) machines constructed out of text if we carefully distinguish between software's medium of description and its medium of execution.

Software's medium of description is, of course, text, constructed out of many possible levels of formal language. As we saw in chapter 11, certain indispensable tools of the software developer are *language translators*, in the form of compilers and assemblers. Thus a simple statement written in C++ such as:

$$c = a + b$$

which instructs the computer to add the values of two variables and assign a third variable the sum, can be translated by a compiler into an assembly language representation such as:

```
copy    a, reg1
add     b, reg1
copy    reg1, c
```

Loosely, these three statements, or, more accurately, *instructions*, describe the process of moving the contents of memory location a into central processor register number 1, adding the contents of memory location b to the value in register 1, and copying the contents of register 1 to memory location c. Prior to the widespread availability of compilers, most programmers had to write in languages like this. Now, hardly any programmer does, because the creation of this type of program is automated. But while this description involves concrete objects like registers and memory locations, it still has no relation to the medium of execution, which is circuits etched in silicon. Also, it is not written in the language of a central processor, which is the binary language of ones and zeros. Assemblers transform assembly language representations of programs into machine language representations, whose elements are ones and zeros. One type of assembler would translate the above assembly language intructions into the following machine language instructions:

```
00010001000100010000011110111000
10000001000100010000011110111010
00010001001100010000011110111100
```

This is the only type of program representation that a central processor "understands." It obliquely refers to operations, registers, and memory locations through a complicated encoding method called a *machine code format*. Prior to compilers and assemblers, programmers were required to write all programs like this. Despite the enormously abstruse expression of such formats, machine language programs are still static, linguistic entities with seemingly no relationship to the dynamic circuitry required to execute them. If you were a programmer in the dark days before language translators, you endured painstaking hours creating a program like this on a piece of paper, and then you had your time with the machine. If the machine did not have a teletype console, you laboriously "loaded" the program into memory by flipping switches on the front panel of the machine, up or down depending on whether you were loading a zero or a one. The physical effect of this was to place bistable memory elements, be they vacuum tubes, magnetic core drum elements, or transistors, into one of two states which, through an act of stipulative definition, could be regarded as a one or a zero. A "category shift" in the programming process between text and mechanism occurred therefore with this at once physical and intentional act of placing some material into one of two states and giving the state an interpretation as a binary digit, or *bit*.

The situation is in principle no different today. Instead of flipping switches or otherwise loading a machine language program full of bits by hand, a program called a *link-loader* does it for you. Each of these bits, representing high or low voltage, is used as the value of an input line, among many, into complex circuits designed to perform binary arithmetic and logic operations. The behavior of enormously complicated larger circuits built out of nothing but combinations of these fundamental ones accounts for all operations called for in any program's text. The incalculable power and utility of tools like compilers, assemblers, and link-loaders masks the fundamental fact that to program a machine is to put its memory into a state which when presented as input to circuits will produce more state of a desired kind. The various levels of formal language that we use today to describe these states are abstract tools for achieving this. The remarkable thing about software is not that it is a machine whose medium of construction is text, but that a textual description of a piece of software is involved in its own creation as states of memory elements. The development over time of tools many programmers take for granted is the reason we can do this relatively easily. Formal languages are indispensable abstractions for thinking about software, but there is no reason to think that software is a machine made of text.

Software as a Concrete Abstraction

The role of formal language in the creation of software does introduce a question of the relationship between the abstract and the nonabstract in computer science. Some accounts are unabashed that an ontological duality is at the heart of the discipline. For example, an undergraduate textbook, *Concrete Abstractions: An Introduction to Computer Science,*[5] freely switches between the poles of this duality right from the start of its preface:

> At first glance, the title of this book is an oxymoron. After all, the term *abstraction* refers to an idea or general description, divorced from actual, physical objects. On the other hand, something is concrete when it is a particular object, perhaps something that you can manipulate with your hands and look at with your eyes. Yet you often deal with concrete abstractions. Consider, for example, a word processor. When you use a word processor, you probably think that you have really entered a document into the computer and that the computer is a machine which physically manipulates the words in the document. But in actuality, when you "enter" the document, there is nothing new inside the computer—there are just different patterns of activity of electrical charges bouncing back and forth between capacitors. ... Even the program that you call a "word processor" is an abstraction—it's the way we humans choose to talk about what is, in reality, yet more electrical charges. Yet at the same time as these abstractions such as "word processors" and "documents" are mere convenient ways of describing patterns of electrical activity, they are also *things* that we can buy, sell, copy, and use.

The juxtaposition of seemingly incompatible ontological categories in a "concrete abstraction" may strike philosophers as puzzling. After all, the similarly curious duality in the nature of microphenomena asserted by the Copenhagen interpretation of quantum mechanics caused philosophical tremors for physicists and philosophers of science alike. In that case the competing characterizations, namely the particle and wave theories of light, ultimately accounted for uncertainty relations in various aspects of microphenomena, for example, the fact that it is impossible to observe simultaneously both the position and the energy of an individual electron. Philosophers immediately asked whether these properties were merely not simultaneously *knowable*, or actually not simultaneously *possessed*, by the electron, since, if the latter, causality as an *a priori* principle would be challenged.[6]

The particle and wave characterizations of light were both *physical* characterizations (albeit ones which nineteenth-century classical mechanics had come to place "in logical opposition to each other.")[7] By contrast, the duality inherent in a "concrete abstraction" crosses *meta*physical categories, and deserves at least as serious philosophical scrutiny as the Copenhagen interpretation. While computer scientists often enthusiastically embrace this duality, a metaphysician will view it as a puzzle to be explained. How can something, namely a computer program, be at once concrete and abstract?

The Ontological Status of Concrete Abstractions

This question brings to mind one of similar form which is also motivated by *prima facie* conflicting kinds of entities. This is the question concerning the mind/body problem: How can something, namely a person, exhibit at once physical and mental properties? I introduce this question into the current discussion not because of a supposed analogy between programs and persons, but because of the methodological framework employed by philosophers to approach the mind/body problem. I believe that the taxonomy of solutions in terms of monism and dualism provides a useful metaphor, if not an entirely appropriate language, for describing programs as concrete abstractions.

Monism

Monism holds that the metaphysical duality apparent in talk about persons in terms of the mental and the physical is an illusion, and that a person is but one kind of entity. Similarly, the computer scientist's contention that a program is both abstract and concrete might be interpreted as a monistic ontology; it is not that there are two different sorts of thing involved in a program whose relationship is mysterious and unfathomable. Rather, a program is one kind of entity only. That it can be described in contrary terms involving abstraction and concreteness recalls a variety of monism in metaphysics called the *double-aspect theory*. This theory asserts with respect to persons that there is but one kind of entity, and it is neither mental nor physical. The mental and the physical are *aspects* of this kind of entity, where the difference in aspects is accounted for by, variously, viewpoints, languages of description, or conceptual schemes. This theory is largely discredited because of problems with describing both this other kind of entity and what exactly an *aspect* is.[8] A double-aspect theory for computer programs would suffer structurally from the same kinds of objections. In fact, the incorrect view expressed above on page 200 is a kind of double-aspect theory of computer programs.

In the other kinds of metaphysical monism, materialism and idealism, one of the two apparent kinds of entity involved in the duality of persons is embraced as "real" while the other is not. Or, talk about one of the two kinds of entity can be eliminated, theoretically if not as a practical matter, in favor of talk about the other. In the case of talking about a computer program as a concrete abstraction, this would involve either eliminating talk about programs as abstract entities in favor of talk about, say, the rearrangement of electrons in a processor, or vice versa. But either of these options would be far more difficult than other reductivist agendas that have proved nettlesome.

Such attempts at reduction, for example, the identity theory in philosophy of mind, or phenomenalism in epistemology, encounter difficulty in trying to characterize the meaning of talk about one kind of entity (for example, physical objects) in terms of a wholly different kind of entity (for example, sense reports). In the case of characterizing the meaning of statements in a formal programming language, even the machine language of zeros and ones, in terms of the physical states of memory elements, the difficulty is even worse. The problem is precisely because the characterization of physical state in machine language as zeros and ones is *itself* an abstraction; the kinds of physical state that this language "abstracts" are limitless. They may be the electronic states of semiconductors, or the states of polarization of optical media, or the states of punched paper tape, or the position of gears in Babbage's eighteenth-century analytical engine, or . . . .

It is worth pointing out, however, that on the abstract side of the abstract/concrete dichotomy lies perhaps the most successful reductivist project ever conceived. As I have tried to describe, the whole history of computer science has seen the careful construction of layer upon layer of distancing abstractions upon the basic foundation of zeros and ones. Each time a programmer writes and executes a high-level program, these layers are stripped away one by one in elaborate translations from talk of, say, chat rooms, to talk of windows, to talk of matrices, to talk of variables, registers, and memory addresses to, finally, zeros and ones. As an abstraction, this translation is complete and flawless. The concrete embodiment of the zeros and ones in physical state, however, is not an abstract process.

Dualism

Since double-aspect or reductivist attempts to characterize the abstract/ concrete dichotomy for computer programs seem destined to fail, we turn to dualism. Within the mind/body problem methodology, dualism asserts that persons are composed of both mental and physical substances, or described by both mental and physical events, accounting for their having both mental and physical properties. The dualistic analog for the computer science problem is that programs are both abstract and concrete. This, of course, sheds no light on *how* a program can be both abstract and concrete; more specifically, it does not say what the *relation* is between the abstract and the concrete. For the mind/body problem, elaborations of dualism emerge in the form of dualistic interactionism, epiphenomenalism, and parallelism.

Dualistic interactionism posits a causal relation between the physical and the mental in both directions. Burned flesh causes a feeling of pain, and a feeling of pain causes removal of the hand from the fire. Epiphenomenalism allows causation in one direction only: Burned flesh causes a feeling of pain, but the removal of the hand from the fire is caused by certain neurophysiological events. The feeling of pain has no causal efficacy, but it exists as an "ontological parasite" on the burned flesh. It should be clear, however, that neither of these accounts is possible with respect to the abstract and the concrete in computer programs. As Fetzer has pointed out, there can be no causal power exerted in either direction between an abstract, formal system and a physical system.

Still, it is tempting to hold that a program expressed in abstract text *does* cause its ultimate execution through physical states of a processor, by considering the complicated sequence of causal events instigated by the text's translation into lower-level language by a compiler. However, it is not *text* that the compiler works on, but just the physical state of a piece of electronic storage media. Program text is simply a way of thinking about that physical state. It can have no causal effect on it. For the mind/body problem, specifying the causal relation between the two sides is merely problematic; for an explanation of concrete abstractions it is in principle impossible.

Preestablished Harmony

That leaves a dualistic account of the concrete and the abstract characterizations of programs without any causal interaction between them. For the mind/body problem, this would be called a parallelistic account, and it would be mentioned only as a historical curiosity. The reason it is not entertained much today is that, without the benefit of a causal relation between mental and physical events, either

1. the observed correlation constantly being affirmed by science between the mental and physical is just a random coincidence, or

2. this correlation is deliberately brought about through a "preestablished harmony," presumably by God.

Both of these alternatives are difficult to justify.

But the preestablished harmony thesis is well suited for explaining the high correlation between computational processes described abstractly in formal language and machine processes bouncing electrons around in a semiconducting medium; for, of course, it is not necessary to appeal to God in accounting for this correlation. It has been deliberately brought about through years of cooperative design of both hardware processors and language translators.

An analogy used to describe parallelism in the mind/body problem imagines two clocks set and wound by God to tick in perfect synchrony forever. For the abstract/concrete problem we can replace God by the programmer who, on the one hand, by his casting of an algorithm in program text, describes a world of multiplying matrices, or resizing windows, or even processor registers; but who, on the other hand, by the act of typing, compiling, assembling, and link-loading, causes a sequence of physical state changes that structurally matches his abstract world. The abstract world of the computer programmer can be thought of as ticking along in preestablished synchrony with the microscopic physical events within the machine.

The "parallel" nature of the abstract and the concrete is a defining characteristic of the digital age. From the notion of cyberspace, to on-line shopping malls, to virtual communities, worlds exist with no impact outside their boundaries. The same is true of the world of the programmer. Programmers today can live almost exclusively in the abstract realm of their software descriptions, but since their creations have parallel lives as bouncing electrons, theirs is a world of concrete abstractions.

A Final Word

It is fitting that we come to the end of this work embracing a theory, preestablished harmony, whose only other claim to fame is as a metaphysical curiosity from the 1700s. I would say that it is a tribute to philosophy that a theory ridiculed this century as an example of untenable mind/body dualism could resurface as a contemporary explanation of a concrete abstraction. While thinkers come and go, philosophy itself endures, even as the objects of its inquiry change from the forms of Plato, to the human understanding, to layers of abstractions in virtual worlds. Despite the inroads that empirical results in artificial intelligence may make onto philosophical turf, the universal value and appeal of philosophizing remain. I hope that the reader carries this appreciation away from these pages, along with the notion that interesting philosophy can be part of what computer science is all about.

Notes

Chapter 1

1. Hailperin, Kaiser, and Knight, *Concrete Abstractions: An Introduction to Computer Science*, 3.
2. Chisholm, *Theory of Knowledge*, 3d ed., vii.

Chapter 2

1. Crevier, *AI: The Tumultuous History of the Search for Artificial Intelligence*, 26.
2. Boden, *Artificial Intelligence and Natural Man*, 4.
3. Russell and Norvig, *Artificial Intelligence: A Modern Approach*, chap. 1.
4. Ibid., 7.
5. Ibid., 26.
6. Genesereth and Fikes, *Knowledge Interchange Format, Version 3.0 Reference Manual*.
7. For a history of the development of AI, see Crevier, *AI: The Tumultuous History of the Search for Artificial Intelligence*.

Chapter 3

1. Plato, *Alcibiades I*, 35–36.
2. Plato, *Meno*, 364.
3. Hippocrates, *On the Sacred Disease*, 32.
4. Ibid., 33.
5. Latham, "Lucretius."
6. Lucretius, *On the Nature of Things*, 86.
7. Ibid., 86–87.
8. Copleston, *Medieval Philosophy*, 15.
9. Descartes, *Meditations on the First Philosophy*, 99.
10. Ibid., 165.

11. Descartes, *Discourse on the Method of Rightly Conducting the Reason and Seeking Truth in the Sciences*, 80–81.

12. Hobbes, *Leviathan*, 23.

13. Hobbes, *Elements of Philosophy*, 2–3.

14. Ibid., 3.

15. Ibid., 4.

16. Ibid., 5–6.

17. Bacon, *Cogitata et Visa*.

18. Berkeley, *A Treatise Concerning the Principles of Human Knowledge*, 154.

19. Berkeley, *Three Dialogues Between Hylas and Philonous, In Opposition to Sceptics and Atheists*, 256.

20. Hume, *An Inquiry Concerning Human Understanding*, 76–77.

21. Ibid., 173.

22. Ibid., 42.

23. Hume, *On the Immortality of the Soul*.

24. de Santillana, "The Development of Rationalism and Empiricism."

25. Leibniz, *Discourse on Metaphysics*, 448.

26. Ibid., 448.

27. See for example Malebranche, *De la Recherche de la vérité*.

28. Leibniz, *Discourse on Metaphysics*, 448.

29. Leibniz, *The Monadology*, 464.

30. Ibid., 468.

31. Spinoza, *The Ethics*, 225.

32. Ibid., 395.

33. Ibid., 399.

34. Ibid., 263.

Chapter 4

1. The following examples are due to Crevier, *AI: The Tumultuous History of the Search for Artificial Intelligence*.

2. Ibid., 2–3.

3. Luger and Stubblefield, *Artificial Intelligence: Structures and Strategies for Complex Problem Solving*, 7.

4. James, *A Textbook of Psychology*, 206–207.

5. Huxley, "Animal Automatism," 203–204.

6. Ibid., 204–205.

7. Adrian, "The Physical Basis of Mind," 232.

8. Ayer, *Logical Positivism*, 10.

9. Ayer, "The Physical Basis of Mind," 244.

10. Ryle, *The Concept of Mind*, as partially reprinted in Morick, ed., *Introduction to the Philosophy of Mind: Readings from Descartes to Strawson*, 37–38.

11. Ryle, *The Concept of Mind*, as partially reprinted in Flew, ed., *Body, Mind, and Death*, 264.

Chapter 5

1. Copi, *Introduction to Logic*, 3.

2. See for example Mates, *Elementary Logic*, among many other treatments.

3. Mates, *Elementary Logic*, 207.

4. Ibid., 210.

5. Ibid., 225.

6. Leibniz, *De arte combinatoria*.

7. Copleston, *A History of Philosophy: Descartes to Leibniz*, 273.

8. Russell, "Gottfried Wilhelm Leibniz," 423.

9. Mates, *Elementary Logic*, 227–228.

10. Ibid., 228.

11. The historical account following is taken from Crevier, *AI: The Tumultuous History of the Search for Artificial Intelligence*.

12. Newell, Shaw, and Simon, "Empirical Explorations with the Logic Theory Machine."

13. Gelernter, "Realization of a Geometry Theorem-Proving Machine."

14. Simon and Newell, "Heuristic Problem Solving: The Next Advance in Operations Research."

15. Newell and Simon, "Computer Science as Empirical Inquiry: Symbols and Search," 42.

16. Newell and Simon, "GPS, A Program that Simulates Human Thought."

17. Slagle, "A Heuristic Program that Solves Symbolic Integration Problems in Freshman Calculus: Symbolic Automatic Integration (SAINT)."

18. Weizenbaum, "ELIZA—A Computer Program for the Study of Natural Language Communication Between Men and Machines."

19. Samuel, "Some Studies in Machine Learning Using the Game of Checkers II—Recent Progress."

20. McCarthy and Hayes, "Some Philosophical Problems from the Standpoint of Artificial Intelligence."

Chapter 6

1. See, for example, Place, "Is Consciousness a Brain Process?"; and Smart, "Sensations and Brain Processes."

2. Putnam, "Sense, Nonsense, and the Senses: An Inquiry into the Powers of the Human Mind," 477.

3. Burton, "Approaches to Mind," 7.

4. Putnam, "Sense, Nonsense, and the Senses," 475.

5. Fodor, *The Language of Thought.*

6. Putnam, "Sense, Nonsense, and the Senses," 483.

7. Searle, "Minds, Brains, and Programs" 304–305.

8. See chapter 12 of this book.

9. Searle, "Minds, Brains, and Programs" 299–300.

10. Turing, "On Computable Numbers, with an Application to the Entscheidungsproblem."

11. Turing, "Computing Machinery and Intelligence."

12. Ibid., 6.

13. Ibid.

14. Ibid., 13–14.

15. Loebner, "The Loebner Prize."

16. Weizenbaum, "ELIZA—A Computer Program for the Study of Natural Language Communication Between Men and Machines."

17. Ibid., 152.

18. See Weizenbaum, *Computer Power and Human Reason.*

19. Searle, "Minds, Brains, and Programs."

20. Schank and Ableson, *Scripts, Plans, Goals and Understanding.*

21. Searle, "Minds, Brains, and Programs," 289.

22. Born, ed., *Artificial Intelligence: The Case Against.*

23. Ford, Glymour, and Hayes, eds., *Android Epistemology.*

24. Ford and Hayes, "The 1996 Simon Newcomb Award," 13.

25. See, for example, Rumelhart, "The Architecture of Mind: A Connectionist Approach"; Smolensky, "Connectionist Modeling: Neural Computation/Mental Connections"; and Churchland, "On the Nature of Theories: A Neurocomputational Perspective."

26. See, for example, McCulloch and Pitts, "A Logical Calculus of the Ideas Immanent in Nervous Activity"; Hebb, *The Organization of Behavior*; and Rosenblatt, *Principles of Neurodynamics.*

27. Rumelhart, "The Architecture of Mind: A Connectionist Approach," 228.

28. Ibid., 208.

29. Ibid., 208.

30. Rosenberg, "Connectionism and Cognition," 293.

31. Ibid., 308.

32. Sellars, "Empiricism and the Philosophy of Mind."

33. Rosenberg, "Connectionism and Cognition," 299.

34. Sellars, "Empiricism and the Philosophy of Mind," 513.

35. Chisholm, *Theory of Knowledge*, 3d ed., 75–76.

36. See, for example, Fetzer, "Mental Algorithms," "Thinking and Computing," and "People Are Not Computers."

Chapter 7

1. See the survey by Loveland, "Automated Theorem Proving: A Quarter Century Review."

2. Kowalski, "Predicate Logic as a Programming Language."

3. See in particular Reiter, "A Logic for Default Reasoning"; McCarthy, "Circumscription—A Form of Nonmonotonic Reasoning"; and McDermott and Doyle, "Nonmonotonic Logic I."

4. Rankin, "When is Reasoning Nonmonotonic?"

5. Pollock, *Knowledge and Justification*, 39–40.

6. See both McCarthy, "Circumscription—A Form of Nonmonotonic Reasoning"; and Lifschitz, "Computing Circumscription."

7. Reiter, "A Logic for Default Reasoning."

8. Moore, "Semantical Considerations on Nonmonotonic Logic."

9. Shoham, "A Semantical Approach to Nonmonotonic Logics," 229.

10. Hawthorne, "A Semantic Approach to Non-Monotonic Entailments," 254.

11. Ibid., 257.

12. Lifschitz ("Computing Circumscription") has presented theorems that, in some cases, allow the replacing of the circumscription formula with an equivalent first-order formula.

13. Chisholm, *Theory of Knowledge*, chap. 1.

14. Pollock, *Knowledge and Justification*.

15. Kowalski, "Predicate Logic as a Programming Language."

16. See, for example, Nute, "Defeasible Reasoning: A Philosophical Analysis in Prolog"; Causey, "The Epistemic Basis of Defeasible Reasoning"; and Marek, ed., *Proceedings of the Workshop on Logic Programming and Non-Monotonic Logic*.

17. Pollock, "OSCAR: A General Theory of Rationality," 189.

18. Ibid., 189–190.

19. For a full account, see Pollock, *Cognitive Carpentry*.

Chapter 8

1. Quine, "Epistemology Naturalized," 68.
2. Ibid.
3. Chisholm, *Theory of Knowledge*, 3d ed., vii.
4. Goldman, *Epistemology and Cognition*, 4.
5. Chisholm, *Theory of Knowledge*, 3d ed.
6. Fumerton, "The Internalism/Externalism Controversy," 444.
7. Korf, "Heuristics," 611.
8. Pearl, *Heuristics*, 48.
9. See, for example, Fikes and Nilsson, "STRIPS: A New Approach to the Application of Theorem Proving to Problem Solving"; Sacerdoti, "Planning in a Hierarchy of Abstraction Spaces"; and Minton, Bresina, and Drummond, "Commitment Strategies in Planning: A Comparative Analysis."
10. See Pearl, *Heuristics* and Korf, "Heuristics."
11. See in particular Reiter, "A Logic for Default Reasoning"; McCarthy, "Circumscription—A Form of Nonmonotonic Reasoning"; and McDermott and Doyle, "Nonmonotonic Logic I."

Chapter 9

1. Hoare, "Mathematics of Programming," 115.
2. C. Floyd, "Outline of a Paradigm Change in Software Engineering," 196.
3. DeMillo, Lipton, and Perlis, "Social Processes and Proofs of Theorems and Programs."
4. Fetzer, "Program Verification: The Very Idea."
5. Carnap, "Formal and Factual Science," 124.
6. Ibid.
7. McCarthy, "Towards a Mathematical Science of Computation."
8. Ibid., 22.
9. Naur, "Proof of Algorithms by General Snapshots."
10. Ibid., 310.
11. R. Floyd, "Assigning Meanings to Programs."
12. Ibid., 25.
13. DeMillo, Lipton, and Perlis, "Social Processes and Proofs of Theorems and Programs, 275."
14. Ibid., 276.
15. Ibid., 279.
16. Fetzer, "Program Verification: The Very Idea," 1049.
17. Ibid., 1053.

18. Scherlis and Scott, "First Steps Towards Inferential Programming," 199.

19. Ibid., 207.

20. Hoare, "An Axiomatic Basis for Computer Programming."

21. Ibid., 579.

22. See Cohn, "The Notion of Proof in Hardware Verification."

23. Hoare, "Mathematics of Programming," 122.

24. Ibid.

25. Meyer, "On Formalism in Specifications."

26. Ibid., 15.

27. Naur, "Formalization in Program Development," 437.

28. Ibid., 440.

29. Ibid., 448.

30. Blum, "Formalism and Prototyping in the Software Process," 225.

31. Ibid., 6.

32. Ibid.

33. Ibid., 13

34. Ibid.

35. C. Floyd, "Outline of a Paradigm Change in Software Engineering," 194.

36. Ibid., 195.

37. Ibid., 194.

38. Naur, "The Place of Strictly Defined Notation in Human Insight," 8.

39. Ibid., 7.

40. Ibid., 14.

41. Smith, "Limits of Correctness in Computers."

42. Ibid., 12.

43. Ibid., 18-19.

44. See Department of Defense document CSC-STD-001-83.

45. Cohn, "The Notion of Proof in Hardware Verification," 135.

46. Ibid.

47. Ibid., 136.

48. Ibid.

49. Fetzer, "Philosophical Aspects of Program Verification," 209.

50. Ibid., 212.

51. Carnap, "Formal and Factual Science," 127.

Chapter 10

1. In addition to the primary reference (Fetzer, "Program Verification: The Very Idea"), see Letters to the Editor, "ACM Forum;" Technical Correspondence, *Communications of the ACM*; and Fetzer and Martin, "'The Very Idea', Indeed! An Intellectual Brawl in Three Rounds (For Adults Only)."

2. Naps, Nance, and Singh, *Introduction to Computer Science: Programming, Problem Solving, and Data Structures*, 5.

3. Hoare, "An Axiomatic Basis for Computer Programming," 576.

4. Fetzer, "Philosophical Aspects of Program Verification."

5. Gumb, *Programming Logics: An Introduction to Verification and Semantics*, 2.

6. See Meyer, "On Formalism in Specifications."

7. See, for example, Nute, "Defeasible Reasoning: A Philosophical Analysis in Prolog"; Kyburg, Loui, and Carlson, eds., *Knowledge Representation and Defeasible Reasoning*; Ginsberg, ed., *Readings in Nonmonotonic Reasoning*; and Reinfrank, ed., *Proceedings of the 2nd International Workshop on Non-Monotonic Reasoning*.

8. Chisholm describes the nature of some of these principles in *Theory of Knowledge*, chap. 4.

9. Fetzer, "Program Verification: The Very Idea."

10. Ibid., 1050–1051.

11. Cohn, "The Notion of Proof in Hardware Verification," 131–132.

12. See Balzer, "A 15 Year Perspective on Automatic Programming," for an example of work in automatic programming.

Chapter 11

1. Hayashi, "Alan Alda Meets Alan Alda 2.0."

2. Sundgren, *Theory of Databases.*

3. Ashenhurst, "Ontological Aspects of Information Modeling," 287.

4. Ibid., 299.

5. Ibid., 300.

6. Naur and Randell, "Software Engineering."

7. See, for example, Brooks, *The Mythical Man-Month*, and Pressman, *Software Engineering: A Practitioner's Approach.*

8. Lientz and Swanson, *Software Maintenance Management.*

9. Dijkstra, "Notes on Structured Programming."

10. Horowitz and Munson, "An Expansive View of Reusable Software."

11. Sheil, "Programming The Uncertain With Exploratory Systems."

12. Carnap, "Formal and Factual Science," 128.

13. Cohen and Nagel, "The Nature of a Logical or Mathematical System," 138–139.

14. Hempel, "On the Nature of Mathematical Truth," 159.

15. For examples of just some of these, see Dale and Walker, *Abstract Data Types: Specifications, Implementations, and Applications*; Carrano, *Data Abstraction and Problem Solving with C++: Walls and Mirrors*; Bergin, *Data Abstraction: The Object-Oriented Approach Using C++*; and Hailperin, Kaiser, and Knight, *Concrete Abstractions: An Introduction to Computer Science*.

16. Dershem and Jipping, *Programming Languages: Structures and Models*, 1.

17. This example is due to Norvig, *Paradigms of Artificial Intelligence Programming: Case Studies in Common Lisp*, 440–442.

Chapter 12

1. Wallich, "Cracking the U.S. Code."

2. Cormen, Leiserson, and Rivest, *Introduction to Algorithms*, 831–836.

3. Davis, Samuelson, Kapor, and Reichman, "A New View of Intellectual Property and Software," 23.

4. Fetzer, "Program Verification: The Very Idea."

5. Hailperin, Kaiser, and Knight, *Concrete Abstractions: An Introduction to Computer Science*.

6. Reichenbach, "The Principle of Anomaly in Quantum Mechanics."

7. Hanson, "Philosophical Implications of Quantum Mechanics," 42.

8. Shaffer, "Mind–Body Problem."

Bibliography

Adrian, E.D. "The Physical Basis of Mind," a talk given on the Third Programme of the British Broadcasting Corporation, as reprinted in A. Flew, ed., *Body, Mind, and Death*, 1974, 231–236.

Anderson, A.R., ed. *Minds and Machines*. Englewood Cliffs, NJ: Prentice Hall, 1964.

Ashenhurst, R.L. "Ontological Aspects of Information Modeling." *Minds and Machines: Journal for Artificial Intelligence, Philosophy, and Cognitive Science* 6, no. 3(1996): 287–394.

Ayer, A.J. "The Physical Basis of Mind," a talk given on the Third Programme of the British Broadcasting Corporation, as reprinted in A. Flew, ed., *Body, Mind, and Death*, 1974, 241–244.

———. *Logical Positivism*, New York: Free Press (Macmillan), 1959.

Bacon, F. *Cogitata et Visa*. 1607.

Balzer, R. "A 15 Year Perspective on Automatic Programming." *IEEE Transactions on Software Engineering* SE-11, no. 11(1985): 1257–1267.

Bergin, J. *Data Abstraction: The Object-Oriented Approach Using C++*. New York: McGraw Hill, 1994.

Berkeley, G. *A Treatise Concerning the Principles of Human Knowledge*, as reprinted in R. Taylor, ed., *The Empiricists*, 1974, 135–216.

———. *Three Dialogues Between Hylas and Philonous, In Opposition to Sceptics and Atheists*, as reprinted in R. Taylor, ed., *The Empiricists*, 1974, 217–305.

Bledsoe, W.W., and Loveland, D.W., eds. *Automated Theorem Proving: After 25 Years*. Providence, RI: American Mathematical Society, 1984.

Blum, B. "Formalism and Prototyping in the Software Process." *Information and Decision Technologies* 15, no. 4(1991): 327–341, as reprinted in T. Colburn *et al.*, eds., *Program Verification: Fundamental Issues in Computer Science*. Dordrecht, Netherlands: Kluwer Academic Publishers, 1993, 213–238.

Boden, M.A. *Artificial Intelligence and Natural Man.* New York: Basic Books, 1972.

Boole, G. *An Investigation of the Laws of Thought.* London: Walton and Maberley, 1854.

Born, R., ed. *Artificial Intelligence: The Case Against.* London: Croom Helm, 1987.

Brooks, F. *The Mythical Man-Month.* Reading, MA: Addison-Wesley, 1975.

Burton, R.G. "Approaches to Mind," in R.G. Burton, ed., *Natural and Artificial Minds,* 1993, 1–20.

Burton, R.G., ed. *Natural and Artificial Minds.* Albany, NY: State University of New York Press, 1993.

Carnap, R. "Formal and Factual Science, " in *Readings in the Philosophy of Science,* edited by H. Feigl and M. Brodbeck, 123–128. New York: Appleton-Century-Crofts, 1953.

Carrano, F.M. *Data Abstraction and Problem Solving with C++: Walls and Mirrors.* Redwood City, CA: Benjamin Cummings, 1995.

Causey, R.L. "The Epistemic Basis of Defeasible Reasoning." *Minds and Machines* 1(1991): 437–458.

Chisholm, R.M. *Theory of Knowledge.* Englewood Cliffs, NJ: Prentice Hall, 1977.

———. *Theory of Knowledge,* 3d ed., Englewood Cliffs, NJ: Prentice Hall, 1989.

Chisholm, R.M., and Swartz, R.J., eds. *Empirical Knowledge: Readings from Contemporary Sources.* Englewood Cliffs, NJ: Prentice Hall, 1973.

Churchland, P.M. "On the Nature of Theories: A Neurocomputational Perspective," in C.W. Savage, ed., *Scientific Theories: Minnesota Studies in the Philosophy of Science,* vol. 14, as reprinted in J. Haugeland, ed., *Mind Design II,* 1997, 251–292.

Codd, E.F. *The Relational Model for Database Management: Version 2.* Reading, MA: Addison-Wesley, 1990.

Cohen, M., and Nagel, E. "The Nature of a Logical or Mathematical System," in H. Feigl and M. Brodbeck, eds., *Readings in the Philosophy of Science.* New York: Appleton-Century-Crofts, 1953, 129–147.

Cohn, A. "The Notion of Proof in Hardware Verification." *Journal of Automated Reasoning* 5, no. 2(1989): 127–139.

Copi, I.M. *Introduction to Logic,* 5th ed. New York: Macmillan, 1978.

Copleston, F.C. *Medieval Philosophy.* New York: Harper, 1961.

———. *A History of Philosophy: Descartes to Leibniz,* vol. IV. New York: Doubleday, 1963.

Cormen, T.H., Leiserson, C.E., and Rivest, R.L. *Introduction to Algorithms.* Cambridge, MA: Massachusetts Institute of Technology Press, 1990.

Crevier, D. *AI: The Tumultuous History of the Search for Artificial Intelligence.* New York: Basic Books (HarperCollins), 1993.

Cummins, R. and Pollock, J., eds. *Philosophy and AI: Essays at the Interface.* Cambridge, MA: Bradford/Massachusetts Institute of Technology Press, 1991.

Dale, N., and Walker, H.M. *Abstract Data Types: Specifications, Implementations, and Applications.* Lexington, MA: Heath, 1996.

Davis, R., Samuelson, P., Kapor, M., and Reichman, J. "A New View of Intellectual Property and Software." *Communications of the ACM* 39, no. 3(1996): 21–30.

DeMillo, R., Lipton, R., and Perlis, A. "Social Processes and Proofs of Theorems and Programs." *Communications of the ACM* 22 (May 1979): 271–280.

Department of Defense. "Trusted Computer Systems Evaluation Criteria." CSC-STD-001-83, August 15, 1983.

Dershem, H.L., and Jipping, M.J. *Programming Languages: Structures and Models.* Pacific Grove, CA: PWS, 1995.

Descartes, R. *Meditations on the First Philosophy,* as reprinted in J. Veitch *et al.,* translators, *The Rationalists,* 1974, 99–175.

———. *Discourse on the Method of Rightly Conducting the Reason and Seeking Truth in the Sciences,* as reprinted in J. Veitch *et al.,* translators, *The Rationalists,* 1974, 39–96.

Dijkstra, E.W. "Notes on Structured Programming," in O.J. Dahl *et al., Structured Programming.* New York: Academic Press, 1971.

Feigenbaum, E.A., and Feldman, J. *Computers and Thought.* New York: McGraw-Hill, 1963.

Fetzer, J. "Program Verification: The Very Idea." *Communications of the ACM* 31, no. 9(1988): 1048–1063, as reprinted in T. Colburn *et al.,* eds., *Program Verification: Fundamental Issues in Computer Science.* Dordrecht, Netherlands: Kluwer Academic Publishers, 1993, 321–358.

———. "Philosophical Aspects of Program Verification." *Minds and Machines* 1, no. 2(1991): 197–216, as reprinted in T. Colburn *et al.,* eds., *Program Verification: Fundamental Issues in Computer Science.* Dordrecht, Netherlands: Kluwer Academic Publishers, 1993, 403–428.

———. "Mental Algorithms: Are Minds Computational Systems?" *Pragmatics and Cognition* 2, (1994): 1–29.

———. "Thinking and Computing: Computers as Special Kinds of Signs." *Minds and Machines* 7, (1997): 345–364.

———. "People Are Not Computers: (Most) Thought Processes Are Not Computational Procedures." *Journal of Experimental and Theoretical Artificial Intelligence*, no. 10(1998): 371–391.

Fetzer, J., ed. *Aspects of Artificial Intelligence*. Dordrecht, Netherlands: Kluwer Academic Publishers, 1988.

Fetzer, J.H., and Martin, C.R. " 'The Very Idea', Indeed! An Intellectual Brawl in Three Rounds (for Adults Only)." National Biomedical Simulation Resource Technical Report No. 1990-2, 1990.

Fikes, R.E., and Nilsson, N.J. "STRIPS: A New Approach to the Application of Theorem Proving to Problem Solving." *Artificial Intelligence* 2(1971): 189–208.

Flew, A. ed. *Body, Mind, and Death*. New York: Macmillan, 1974.

Floyd, C. "Outline of a Paradigm Change in Software Engineering," in *Computers and Democracy: A Scandinavian Challenge*, Hants, England: Gower Publishing Company, 1987, 191–210.

Floyd, R. "Assigning Meanings to Programs." *Proceedings of Symposia in Applied Mathematics* 19(1967): 19–32.

Fodor, J. *The Language of Thought*. New York: Crowell, 1975.

Ford, K., Glymour, C. and Hayes, P., eds. *Android Epistemology*. Cambridge, MA: Massachusetts Institute of Technology Press, 1995.

Ford, K. and Hayes, P. "The 1996 Simon Newcomb Award." *AI Magazine* 17, no. 3(1996): 13–14.

Frege, G. *Begriffsschrift, eine der arithmetischen nachgebildete Formelsprache des reinen Denkens*. Halle, 1879.

Fumerton, R. "The Internalism/Externalism Controversy," in *Philosophical Perspectives, 2: Epistemology*, edited by J.E. Tomberlin, 443–459, 1988.

Gelernter, H. "Realization of a Geometry Theorem-Proving Machine." *Proceedings of the International Conference on Information Processing*, Paris: UNESCO House, 1959, 273–282.

Genesereth, M.R., and Fikes, R.E. *Knowledge Interchange Format, Version 3.0 Reference Manual*. http://logic.stanford.edu/kif/Hypertext/kif-manual.html, 1998.

Gerhardt, C.I. *Die philosophischen Schriften von G.W. Leibniz*, 1875–1890.

Ginsberg, M.L., ed. *Readings in Nonmonotonic Reasoning*. Los Altos, CA: Morgan Kaufmann, 1987.

Goldman, A.I. *Epistemology and Cognition*. Cambridge, MA: Harvard University Press, 1986.

Gumb, R.D. *Programming Logics: An Introduction to Verification and Semantics.* New York: John Wiley and Sons, 1989.

Hailperin, M., Kaiser, B., and Knight, K. *Concrete Abstractions: An Introduction to Computer Science.* Pacific Grove, CA: PWS Publishing, 1999.

Hamilton, E., and Cairns, H., eds. *Plato: Collected Dialogues.* Princeton, NJ: Princeton University Press, 1971.

Hanson, N.R. "Philosophical Implications of Quantum Mechanics," in *The Encyclopedia of Philosophy,* vol. 7, edited by P. Edwards, 41–48. New York: MacMillan, 1967.

Haugeland, J., ed. *Mind Design.* Cambridge, MA: Massachusetts Institute of Technology Press, 1981.

———. *Mind Design II.* Cambridge, MA: Bradford/Massachusetts Institute of Technology Press, 1997.

Hawthorne, J. "A Semantic Approach to Non-Monotonic Entailments," in *Uncertainty in Artificial Intelligence,* vol. 2, edited by J.F. Lemmer and L.N. Kanal, 251–262.

Hayashi, A. "Alan Alda Meets Alan Alda 2.0." *Scientific American* (March 1998). Available at http://www.sciam.com.

Hebb, D.O. *The Organization of Behavior.* New York: John Wiley, 1949.

Hempel, C. "On the Nature of Mathematical Truth," in *Readings in the Philosophy of Science,* edited by H. Feigl and M. Brodbeck, 148–162. New York: Appleton-Century-Crofts, 1953.

Hendel, C.W., ed. *Hume: An Inquiry Concerning Human Understanding,* New York: Bobbs-Merrill, 1955.

Hippocrates. *On the Sacred Disease,* as partially reprinted in A. Flew, ed., *Body, Mind, and Death,* New York: Macmillan, 1974, 31–33.

Hoare, C.A.R. "An Axiomatic Basis for Computer Programming." *Communications of the ACM* 12(1969): 576–583.

———. "Mathematics of Programming." *BYTE* (August 1986): 115–149.

Hobbes, T. *Leviathan,* as reprinted in H.W. Schneider, ed., *Hobbes' Leviathan, Parts I and II,* New York: Bobbs-Merrill, 1958.

———. *Elements of Philosophy,* as reprinted in F.J.E. Woodbridge, ed., *The Philosophy of Hobbes,* 1903.

Horowitz, E., and Munson, J.B. "An Expansive View of Reusable Software." *IEEE Transactions on Software Engineering* SE-10, no. 5(1984): 477–494.

Hume D. *An Inquiry Concerning Human Understanding,* 1750, republished as C.W. Hendel, ed., *Hume: An Inquiry Concerning Human Understanding,* New York: Bobbs-Merrill, 1955.

――――. *On the Immortality of the Soul*, 1783, as reprinted at http://www.utm.edu/research/hume/hume.html.

Huxley, T.H. "Animal Automatism," *Collected Essays*, as partially reprinted in A. Flew, ed., *Body, Mind, and Death*, 1974, 196–205.

James, W. *A Textbook of Psychology*, as partially reprinted in A. Flew, ed., *Body, Mind, and Death*, 1974, 206–211.

Korf, R.E. "Heuristics." *Encyclopedia of Artificial Intelligence*, 2d ed., New York: John Wiley and Sons, 1992, 611–615.

Kowalski, R.A. "Predicate Logic as a Programming Language," in *Proceedings of the IFIP-74 Congress*, New York: North Holland, 1974, 569–574.

――――. Logic for Problem Solving. New York: North Holland, 1979.

Kyburg, H.E., Jr., Loui, R.P., and Carlson, G.N., eds. *Knowledge Representation and Defeasible Reasoning*. Dordrecht, Netherlands: Kluwer Academic Publishers, 1990.

Latham, R. "Lucretius." *The Encyclopedia of Philosophy*, vol. 5, New York: Macmillan, 1967, 99–101.

Leibniz, G. *De arte combinatoria*, as reprinted in C.I. Gerhardt, *Die philosophischen Schriften von G.W. Leibniz*.

――――. *Discourse on Metaphysics*, as reprinted in J. Veitch *et al.*, translators, *The Rationalists*, 1974.

――――. *The Monadology*, as reprinted in J. Veitch *et al.*, translators, *The Rationalists*, 1974.

Lemmer, J.F., and Kanal, L.N., eds. *Uncertainty in Artificial Intelligence*, vol. 2, New York: North Holland, 1988.

Letters to the Editor. "ACM Forum," *Communications of the ACM* 32, 3(1989): 287–290.

Lientz, B., and Swanson, E. *Software Maintenance Management*, Reading, MA: Addison-Wesley, 1980.

Lifschitz, V. "Computing Circumscription," in *Readings in Nonmonotonic Reasoning*, edited by M.L. Ginsberg, 167–173, 1987.

Loebner, H. "The Loebner Prize," http://pascal.acm.org/~loebner/loebner-prize.htmlx, 1998.

Loveland, D.W. "Automated Theorem Proving: A Quarter Century Review," in *Automated Theorem Proving: After 25 Years*, edited by W.W. Bledsoe and D.W. Loveland, 1–45.

Lucretius. *On the Nature of Things*, as partially reprinted in A. Flew, ed., *Body, Mind, and Death*, 1974, 83–90.

Luger, G.F., and Stubblefield, W.A. *Artificial Intelligence: Structures and Strategies for Complex Problem Solving*, 2d ed., Redwood City, CA: Benjamin/Cummings, 1993.

Malebranche, N. *De la Recherche de la vérité* (Search after Truth), reprinted in A. Robinet, *Oeuvres Complétes de Malebranche*, 1958.

Marek, A., ed. *Proceedings of the Workshop on Logic Programming and Non-Monotonic Logic*. Cambridge, MA: MIT Press, 1991.

Mates, B. *Elementary Logic*, 2d ed. New York: Oxford University Press, 1972.

McCarthy, J. "Towards a Mathematical Science of Computation." *Proceedings of the IFIP Congress* 62(1962): 21–28.

————. "Circumscription—A Form of Nonmonotonic Reasoning." *Artificial Intelligence* 13(1980): 27–35.

McCarthy, J., and Hayes, P.J. "Some Philosophical Problems from the Standpoint of Artificial Intelligence," in *Readings in Nonmonotonic Reasoning*, edited by M.L. Ginsberg, 26–45, 1987.

McCulloch, W.S., and Pitts, W.H. "A Logical Calculus of the Ideas Immanent in Nervous Activity." *Bulletin of Mathematical Biophysics* 5(1943): 115–133.

McDermott, D., and Doyle, J. "Nonmonotonic Logic I." *Artificial Intelligence* 13(1980): 41-72.

Meltzer, B., and Michie, D., eds. *Machine Intelligence 4*. Edinburgh, Scotland: Edinburgh University Press, 1969.

Meyer, B. "On Formalism in Specifications." *IEEE Software* (January 1985): 6–26.

Minton, S., Bresina, J., and Drummond, M. "Commitment Strategies in Planning: A Comparative Analysis," in *Proceedings of the Ninth National Conference on Artificial Intelligence*. Menlo Park: AAAI Press, 1991.

Moore, R.C. "Semantical Considerations on Nonmonotonic Logic." *Artificial Intelligence* 25(1985): 75–94.

Morick, H., ed. *Introduction to the Philosophy of Mind: Readings from Descartes to Strawson*. Glenview, IL: Scott-Foresman, 1970.

Myers, G.J. *The Art of Software Testing*. New York: John Wiley and Sons, 1979.

Naps, T.L., Nance, D.W., and Singh, B. *Introduction to Computer Science: Programming, Problem Solving, and Data Structures*, alternate ed. St. Paul, MN: West Publishing, 1989.

Naur, P. "Proof of Algorithms by General Snapshots." *BIT* 6(1966): 310–316.

————. "Formalization in Program Development" *BIT* 22(1982): 437–453.

———. "The Place of Strictly Defined Notation in Human Insight," unpublished paper from Workshop on Programming Logic, Bastad, Sweden, 1989.

Naur, P., and Randell, B. "Software Engineering." *Report on a Conference Sponsored by the NATO Science Committee*, October 7–11, 1969. Brussels: NATO.

Newell, A., Shaw, J.C., and Simon, H.A. "Empirical Explorations with the Logic Theory Machine." *Proceedings of the Western Joint Computer Conference* 15(1957): 218–239.

Newell, A., and Simon, H.A. "GPS, a Program that Simulates Human Thought," in *Computers and Thought*, by E.A. Feigenbaum and J. Feldman, 279–293, 1963.

———. "Computer Science as Empirical Inquiry: Symbols and Search," in *Mind Design*, edited by J. Haugeland, 35–66, 1981.

Norvig, P. *Paradigms of Artificial Intelligence Programming: Case Studies in Common Lisp*. San Mateo, CA: Morgan Kaufman, 1992.

Nute, D. "Defeasible Reasoning: A Philosophical Analysis in Prolog," in *Aspects of Artificial Intelligence*, edited by J. Fetzer, 251–288, 1988.

Pearl, J. *Heuristics*. Reading, MA: Addison-Wesley, 1984.

Place, U.T. "Is Consciousness a Brain Process?" *British Journal of Psychology* 47(1956): 44–50.

Plato. *Alcibiades I*, as partially reprinted in A. Flew, ed., *Body, Mind, and Death*, 1974, 34–71.

———. *Meno*, as reprinted in E. Hamilton and H. Cairns, eds., *Plato: Collected Dialogues*, 1971.

Pollock, J.L. *Knowledge and Justification*. Princeton, NJ: Princeton University Press, 1974.

———. "Defeasible Reasoning." *Cognitive Science* 11(1987): 481–518.

———. "OSCAR: A General Theory of Rationality," in *Philosophy and AI: Essays at the Interface*, edited by R. Cummins and J. Pollock, 189–213, 1991.

———. *Cognitive Carpentry*, Bradford/Massachusetts Institute of Technology Press, 1995.

Pressman, R.S. *Software Engineering: A Practitioner's Approach*. New York: McGraw-Hill, 1982.

Putnam, H. "Sense, Nonsense, and the Senses: An Inquiry into the Powers of the Human Mind." *Journal of Philosophy* XCI, 9(1994): 445–517.

Quine, W.V.O. "Epistemology Naturalized," in *Empirical Knowledge: Readings from Contemporary Sources*, edited by R.M. Chisholm and R.J. Swartz, 59–74, 1973.

Rankin, T. "When Is Reasoning Nonmonotonic?" in *Aspects of Artificial Intelligence*, edited by J. Fetzer, 289–308, 1988.

Reichenbach, H. "The Principle of Anomaly in Quantum Mechanics," in *Readings in the Philosophy of Science*, edited by H. Feigl and M. Brodbeck, 509–520. New York: Appleton-Century-Crofts, 1953.

Reinfrank, M., ed. *Proceedings of the 2nd International Workshop on Non-monotonic Reasoning*. New York: Springer-Verlag, 1989.

Reiter, R. "A Logic for Default Reasoning." *Artificial Intelligence* 13 (1980): 81–132.

Robinet, A. *Oeuvres Complétes de Malebranche*. Paris, 1958.

Rosenberg, J.F. "Connectionism and Cognition." *Acta Analytica*, 6 (1990): 33–46, as reprinted in J. Haugeland, *Mind Design II*, 1997, 293–308.

Rosenblatt, F. *Principles of Neurodynamics*. Washington: Spartan Books, 1962.

Roth, M.D., and Galis, L., eds. *Knowing: Essays in the Analysis of Knowledge*. New York: Random House, 1970.

Rumelhart, D.E. "The Architecture of Mind: A Connectionist Approach," in *Foundations of Cognitive Science*, edited by M.I. Posner, as reprinted in J. Haugeland, *Mind Design II*, 1997, 205–232.

Russell, L.J. "Gottfried Wilhelm Leibniz." *The Encyclopedia of Philosophy*, vol. 4. New York: Macmillan, 1967, 422–434.

Russell, S., and Norvig, P. *Artificial Intelligence: A Modern Approach*. Englewood Cliffs, NJ: Prentice Hall, 1995.

Ryle, G. *The Concept of Mind*. London: Hutchinson Publishing Group, 1949. As partially reprinted in H. Morick, ed., *Introduction to the Philosophy of Mind: Readings from Descartes to Strawson*, 1970, 27–39; and A. Flew, ed., *Body, Mind, and Death*, 1974, 245–264.

Sacerdoti, E.D. "Planning in a Hierarchy of Abstraction Spaces." *Artificial Intelligence* 5(1974): 115–135.

Samuel, A.L. "Some Studies in Machine Learning Using the Game of Checkers II—Recent Progress." *IBM Journal of Research and Development* 11, no. 6(1967): 601–617.

de Santillana, G. "The Development of Rationalism and Empiricism." *International Encyclopedia of Unified Science*, vol. II. Chicago, 1941.

Schank, R.C., and Ableson, R.P. *Scripts, Plans, Goals and Understanding*. Hillsdale, NJ: Laurence Erlbaum Associates, 1977.

Scherlis, W.L., and Scott, D.S. "First Steps Towards Inferential Programming." *Information Processing* 83(1983): 199–212.

Schneider, H.W., ed. *Hobbes' Leviathan, Parts I and II*, New York: Bobbs-Merrill, 1958.

Schrag, R. "Defeasible Reasoning System User's Guide," Technical Report No. CS-R87-001. Minneapolis, MN: Honeywell Systems and Research Center, 1987.

Searle, J.R. "Minds, Brains, and Programs." *The Behavioral and Brain Sciences*, 3: 417–424, as reprinted in J. Haugeland, *Mind Design*, 1981, 282–306.

Sellars, W. "Empiricism and the Philosophy of Mind,", in *Minnesota Studies in the Philosophy of Science*, vol. I, edited by H. Feigl and M. Scriven, Minneapolis, MN: University of Minnesota Press, 1956, as reprinted in R.M. Chisholm and R.J. Swartz, eds., *Empirical Knowledge: Readings from Contemporary Sources*, 1973, 471–541.

Shaffer, J. "Mind-Body Problem." *The Encyclopedia of Philosophy*, vol. 5. New York: Macmillan, 1967, 336–346.

Sheil, B. "Programming The Uncertain With Exploratory Systems." *Computer Design* (March 1985).

Shoham, Y. "A Semantical Approach to Nonmonotonic Logics," in *Readings in Nonmonotonic Reasoning*, edited by M.L. Ginsberg, 227–250, 1987.

Simon, H.A., and Newell, A. "Heuristic Problem Solving: The Next Advance in Operations Research." *Operations Research* 6(1958): 1–10.

Slagle, J.R. "A Heuristic Program that Solves Symbolic Integration Problems in Freshman Calculus: Symbolic Automatic Integration (SAINT)," in *Computers and Thought*, edited by E.A. Feigenbaum and J. Feldman, 191–205, 1963.

Smart, J.J.C. "Sensations and Brain Processes." *Philosophical Review* 68(1959): 141–156.

Smith, B.C. "Limits of Correctness in Computers," Report No. CSLI-85-36. Center for the Study of Language and Information, October 1985.

Smolensky, P. "Connectionist Modeling: Neural Computation/Mental Connections," in *Neural Connections, Mental Computation*, edited by L. Nadel, L.A. Cooper, P. Culicover, and R.M. Harnish. Cambridge, MA: Bradford/Massachusetts Institute of Technology Press, as reprinted in J. Haugeland, ed., *Mind Design II*, 1997, 233–250.

Spinoza, B. *The Ethics*, as reprinted in J. Veitch *et al.*, translators, *The Rationalists*, 1974, 179–408.

Sundgren, B. *Theory of Databases*. New York: Petrocelli/Charter, 1975.

Taylor, R., ed. *The Empiricists*. Garden City, NY: Anchor Books, 1974.

Technical Correspondence. *Communications of the ACM* 32, no. 3(1989): 287–290.

Tomberlin, J.E. *Philosophical Perspectives, vol. 2: Epistemology.* Atascadero, CA: Ridgeview Publishing, 1988.

Turing, A.M. "On Computable Numbers, with an Application to the Entscheidungsproblem." *Proceedings of the London Mathematical Society, 2d Series,* 42(1936): 230-265. Correction published in 43(1937): 544–546.

———. "Computing Machinery and Intelligence." *Mind,* LIX(1950): 236, as reprinted in A.R. Anderson, ed., *Minds and Machines,* 1964, 4–30.

Veitch, J., Elwes, R., and Montgomery, G., translators. *The Rationalists.* Garden City, NY: Anchor Books, 1974.

Wallich, P. "Cracking the U.S. Code." *Scientific American* (April 1997): 42.

Weizenbaum, J. "ELIZA—A Computer Program for the Study of Natural Language Communication Between Men and Machines." *Communications of the ACM* 9(1966): 36–45. Quotes taken from P. Norvig, *Paradigms of Artificial Intelligence Programming: Case Studies in Common Lisp,* 1992, 152–153.

———. *Computer Power and Human Reason.* San Francisco: Freeman, 1976.

Whitehead, A.N., and Russell, B. *Principia Mathematica.* Cambridge: Cambridge University Press, 1910.

Woodbridge, F.J.E., ed. *The Philosophy of Hobbes.* Minneapolis: H.W. Wilson, 1903.

Index

About the Author

Timothy R. Colburn received his Ph.D. in philosophy from Brown University in 1979, and his M.S. in computer science from Michigan State University in 1981. He has worked as a philosophy professor, a computer programmer, and a research scientist in artificial intelligence. He is currently an associate professor of computer science at the University of Minnesota-Duluth. He can be reached via e-mail at tcolburn@d.umn.edu.

972.91064 Cuban
Cuban Missile Crisis

Cuban Missile Crisis

Cuban Missile Crisis

The Essential Reference Guide

Priscilla Roberts, Editor

ABC-CLIO

Santa Barbara, California • Denver, Colorado • Oxford, England

Copyright 2012 by ABC-CLIO, LLC

Library of Congress Cataloging-in-Publication Data

Roberts, Priscilla Mary.
  Cuban Missile Crisis : the essential reference guide / Priscilla Roberts.
    p. cm.
  Includes bibliographical references and index.
  ISBN 978-1-61069-065-2 (hardcopy : acid-free paper) —
ISBN 978-1-61069-066-9 (ebook) 1. Cuban Missile Crisis, 1962. 2. Cuban
Missile Crisis, 1962—Sources. 3. Cuban Missile Crisis, 1962—Chronology.
I. Title.
  E841.R55   2012
  972.9106'4—dc23   2011051907

ISBN: 978-1-61069-065-2
EISBN: 978-1-61069-066-9

16 15 14 13 12   1 2 3 4 5

This book is also available on the World Wide Web as an eBook.
Visit www.abc-clio.com for details.

ABC-CLIO, LLC
130 Cremona Drive, P.O. Box 1911
Santa Barbara, California 93116-1911

This book is printed on acid-free paper ∞

Manufactured in the United States of America

Remembering Des Robinson
(1937–2012)
Spectacular Athlete
Inspiring Teacher
Most Splendid of Friends

Contents

List of Entries

Introduction:
The Cuban Missile Crisis

Priscilla Roberts

Causes

The October 1962 Cuban Missile Crisis was the closest the two Cold War superpowers, the United States and the Soviet Union, ever came to full-scale nuclear war. It represented the convergence of several trends in U.S. foreign policy: the long-time assumption of a hegemonic role in the Western Hemisphere (first enunciated in the Monroe Doctrine); the Cold War policy of containing global communism enshrined in the 1947 Truman Doctrine declaration; post–World War II U.S.-Soviet competition for the loyalties of the developing world; and the nuclear rivalry between the United States and the Soviet Union.

From the early 19th century, successive U.S. governments held it almost axiomatic that their country should rightfully be predominant over the rest of the Western Hemisphere. The Monroe Doctrine was an 1823 declaration that no other power should acquire any further colonies in the Americas nor seek to regain colonies that had become independent. In 1904 President Theodore Roosevelt took this still further, announcing, in what he termed the Roosevelt Corollary to the Monroe Doctrine, that the United States had the right to intervene to restore order in any Latin American nation that failed to conduct its affairs to U.S. satisfaction. U.S. officials treated Latin America as a de facto sphere of influence. Six years earlier, Roosevelt had been among the strongest advocates of war against Spain to end continuing unrest and rebellion in Cuba, then a Spanish colony. In 1898 the United States finally declared war on Spain, winning a quick victory over the European power. At the end of the year, Spain ceded Cuba, together with the Philippines, Guam, and Puerto Rico, to the United States.

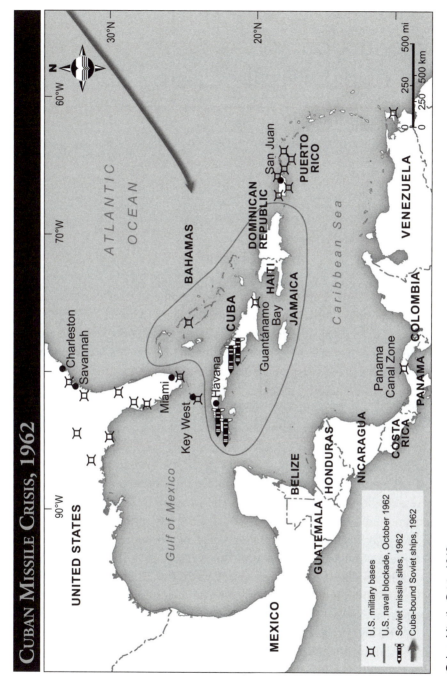

Cuban Missile Crisis, 1962

After four years of U.S. occupation, in 1902 Cuba received independence, with some qualifications. The U.S. Navy obtained a permanent lease on a base at Guantánamo Bay in Cuba. Cuba was also forced to accept the Platt Amendment, whereby the United States retained the right to intervene in Cuba's economic, military, and political affairs should the U.S. government disapprove of Cuban conduct of these. American troops returned again in 1906 for three years, and once more in 1912 to suppress domestic unrest. In 1933 the new government of Ramón Grau, brought to power by a military coup, nullified the Platt Amendment, whereupon U.S. president Franklin D. Roosevelt denied diplomatic recognition to Cuba for a year. Gen. Fulgencio Batista, the military strongman who dominated the new regime and served as president from 1940 to 1944 and again from 1952 to 1958, quickly became a reliable U.S. client, aligning himself with U.S. policies in both World War II and the Cold War. Throughout, Cuba remained heavily commercially and financially dependent on the United States, and American-owned firms dominated the Cuban economy.

From the late 1940s onward, U.S. foreign policy was dominated by the global competition between the United States, the standard-bearer of liberal, democratic, and capitalist values, and the Soviet Union, the world's foremost communist power. In 1947 the Truman Doctrine made containment, the effort to prevent any additional nations becoming communist, the guiding principle of U.S. foreign policy. By the 1950s, the Soviet Union and the United States each possessed horrifically destructive thermonuclear weapons, which meant that unless they exercised great caution conflicts between them had the potential to spiral into devastating war. Rather than confronting each other directly, Soviet and U.S. leaders sought to win the loyalties of developing countries in what was termed the Third World, supporting political groups they considered broadly sympathetic to their own ideological viewpoint. Across Asia, Latin America, and the Middle East, in such countries as Guatemala, Iran, and Vietnam, successive U.S. administrations opposed and tried to overthrow leftist governments while supporting political regimes, however authoritarian, that professed themselves reliably anticommunist.

In 1958 an indigenous revolutionary movement led by Fidel Castro seized power from Batista. Although Castro initially declared that he was not a communist, from spring 1959 he covertly sought Soviet aid and military protection. American economic pressure and boycotts quickly impelled him to move openly into the Soviet camp. In response, the U.S. Central Intelligence Agency (CIA) planned to assist Cuban exiles to attack the island and overthrow Castro. Initiated under President Dwight D.

Eisenhower and inherited by his successor, John F. Kennedy, the April 1961 Bay of Pigs invasion attempt proved a humiliating fiasco for the United States. Kennedy and Secretary of Defense Robert S. McNamara continued to develop plans for invasion, and their CIA and military advisers also devised various ingenious, if often implausible, schemes to overthrow or assassinate Castro, who not unnaturally sought further Soviet aid.

In mid-1961, as the concurrent Berlin Crisis intensified and culminated in the building of the Berlin Wall, military hard-liners in the Kremlin, frustrated for several years, succeeded in implementing a 34-percent increase in spending on conventional forces. Both the Bay of Pigs and Kennedy's bellicose inauguration rhetoric that his country would "pay any price, bear any burden, meet any hardship, support any friend, oppose any foe, in order to assure the survival and the success of liberty," may have energized them. Despite claims of a missile gap between the Soviet Union and the United States, in practice the strategic missile imbalance greatly advantaged the United States, which had at least eight times as many nuclear warheads as its rival. Even U.S. leaders were unaware of just how lopsidedly the nuclear situation favored them, believing the ratio to be only about three to one.

The 1961–1962 U.S. deployment of 15 intermediate-range Jupiter missiles in Turkey, directly threatening Soviet territory, further angered Soviet premier Nikita Khrushchev, making him eager to redress the balance. It seems that Khrushchev also hoped to pressure the United States into making concessions on Berlin. Additionally, installing missiles on Cuba rebutted charges from the People's Republic of China, increasingly the Soviet Union's ideological rival within the communist world, that the Soviets were only paper tigers, unwilling to take concrete action to advance the cause of international revolution. Khrushchev, moreover, apparently felt a romantic sense of solidarity with the new Cuban state, whose emergence reassured him and other old communists that their movement still possessed international vitality.

Early in 1962, Khrushchev offered Soviet nuclear-capable missiles, controlled by Soviet technicians and troops, to Castro, who accepted and oversaw their secret installation. Khrushchev apparently believed that these would deter U.S. plans to invade Cuba. Rather optimistically, he calculated that once the missiles were in place Kennedy and his advisers would find the prospect of nuclear war over them so horrifying that, despite their chagrin, they would accept their presence in Cuba. The Bay of Pigs fiasco, followed by Khrushchev's June 1961 summit meeting with Kennedy at Vienna, apparently convinced the Soviet leader that Kennedy

was weak and could easily be intimidated. So confident was Khrushchev that when Kennedy administration officials warned from July to September 1962 that the United States would respond strongly should the Soviets deploy nuclear or other offensive weaponry in Cuba, he implicitly denied any intention of doing so. Admittedly, by this time the missiles had already been secretly dispatched and their installation was at least a partial fait accompli. At this stage of his career, moreover, Khrushchev's behavior tended to be somewhat erratic. In any case, he miscalculated. Instead of treating the Cuban missiles as deterrent weapons, the Kennedy administration regarded them as evidence of Soviet aggressiveness and refused to tolerate their presence.

Course

On October 16, 1962, Kennedy was provided with photographic evidence, obtained by U-2 reconnaissance planes, that Soviet officials had installed intermediate-range nuclear-capable weapons in Cuba. In response, the president summoned a secret Executive Committee (ExComm) of 18 top advisers, among them Joint Chiefs of Staff chairman Maxwell D. Taylor, CIA Director John McCone, Secretary of State Dean Rusk, Secretary of Defense Robert S. McNamara, national security adviser McGeorge Bundy, Vice President Lyndon B. Johnson, Treasury Secretary C. Douglas Dillon, and the president's brother and closest adviser, Attorney General Robert F. Kennedy, to decide on a course of action. President Kennedy also included senior members of the broader foreign policy establishment, including former secretary of defense Robert A. Lovett and former secretary of state Dean Acheson. Other top officials, such as Adlai Stevenson, U.S. ambassador to the United Nations, and John J. McCloy, Kennedy's disarmament adviser, occasionally joined its deliberations. Technically a committee of the National Security Council, for 13 days ExComm debated how best to respond to Khrushchev's secretive tactic.

Whatever the logical justification for Khrushchev's behavior, politically it would have been almost impossible for any U.S. president to accept the situation. Hard-line Republicans in Congress, such as Senator Barry Goldwater, a potential presidential candidate, were eager to attack Kennedy should he show himself weak on Soviet or communist expansion, especially so close to U.S. shores. The U.S. military calculated that the missiles would increase Soviet nuclear striking force against the continental United States by 50 percent. (In reality the missiles would have

doubled or even tripled Soviet striking capabilities, reducing the existing U.S. numerical advantage to a ratio of merely two or three to one.) Kennedy, however, considered the missiles less a genuine military threat than a test of his credibility and leadership. Taylor, speaking for the U.S. military, initially favored launching air strikes to destroy the missile installations—a scenario that would almost certainly have killed substantial numbers of Soviet troops, was unlikely to eliminate all the missiles, and might well have provoked nuclear war. An invasion of Cuba by U.S. ground forces might also provoke a full-scale war. Discussions continued for several days. Eventually, on October 22, Kennedy publicly announced the presence of the missiles in Cuba, demanded that the Soviet Union remove them, and proclaimed the imposition of a naval blockade around the island, a measure intended to prevent the delivery of any further Soviet weaponry or military personnel to Cuba.

Several tense days ensued, during which (on October 27) Soviet antiaircraft batteries on Cuba shot down—without specific authorization from Kremlin leaders, whom this episode greatly alarmed—a U.S. U-2 reconnaissance plane. Seeking to avoid further escalation, Kennedy rejected Taylor's advice to retaliate militarily and he deliberately refrained from action. After some hesitation, Khrushchev decided not to challenge the naval quarantine and acquiesced in the removal of the missiles. Simultaneously, his ambassador in Washington, Anatoly Dobrynin, secretly obtained an unpublicized pledge from Robert Kennedy that his brother would shortly remove Jupiter missiles in Turkey and Italy. Provided that the Soviet missiles departed and were not replaced, the United States also promised not to mount another invasion of Cuba.

Recently released tapes of conversations among President Kennedy and his advisers reveal that to avoid nuclear war, he was prepared to make even greater concessions to the Soviets, including taking the issue to the United Nations and openly trading Turkish missiles for those in Cuba. In so doing, he parted company with some of his more hard-line advisers. Showing considerable statesmanship, Kennedy deliberately refrained from emphasizing Khrushchev's humiliation, although other administration officials were privately less diplomatic and celebrated their victory to the press.

Newly opened Soviet documentary evidence has demonstrated that the Cuban situation was even more menacing than most involved then realized. Forty-two thousand well-equipped Soviet soldiers were already on the island, far more than the 10,000 troops that U.S. officials had estimated. Moreover, although Kennedy's advisers believed that some of the missiles

might already be armed, they failed to realize that no less than 158 short- and intermediate-range warheads on the island, whose use Castro urged should the United States invade, were already operational and that 42 of these could have reached U.S. territory. The bellicose Castro also hoped to shoot down additional U-2 planes and provoke a major confrontation. The potential for a trigger-happy military officer to spark a full-scale nuclear conflagration almost certainly existed, retrospectively chilling evidence of the dangers inherent in these weapons.

Consequences

The Cuban Missile Crisis had a sobering impact on its protagonists. On Kennedy it had a certain salutary maturing effect, making the once-brash young president a strong advocate of disarmament in the final months before his untimely death in November 1963. His stance induced the Soviet leadership to agree to establish a hotline between Moscow and Washington to facilitate communications and ease tensions during international crises. The two powers also finally reached agreement in 1963 on the Partial Test Ban Treaty (PTBT), which halted nuclear testing in the atmosphere, under water, and in space. From then onward both superpowers exercised great caution in dealing with each other, and subsequently they never again came so close to nuclear war.

Soviet officials felt that they had come dangerously near to losing control of the actual employment of nuclear-capable weapons in Cuba, either to their own military commanders on the ground or even potentially to Castro's forces. Humiliation at U.S. hands was among the factors that propelled Soviet leaders into an expensive major nuclear buildup to achieve parity with the United States, which they reached in 1970. The historian John Lewis Gaddis has even argued that one result of the Cuban Missile Crisis was that the possession of massively destructive nuclear weapons enabled the Soviet Union to command international respect as a superpower for many years longer than it might have otherwise, given the country's increasingly lackluster economic performance.

Khrushchev's fall from power in 1964 was at least partly due to the missile crisis. Politburo colleagues criticized him for recklessness in originally installing the missiles and weakness in subsequently yielding to U.S. pressure. Kennedy's Cuban policies may also have indirectly caused his own assassination. The man arrested for Kennedy's murder, Lee Harvey Oswald, was an unpredictable leftist who had spent some time in the Soviet

Union, sympathized strongly with Castro's Cuba, and opposed Kennedy's efforts to overthrow Castro. Others have suggested that Cuban exiles who resented Kennedy's failure to do more to assist them may have been involved in his death.

The Cuban Missile Crisis tested and perhaps weakened the Western alliance. Western European political leaders, including British prime minister Harold Macmillan, Federal Republic of Germany (FRG) (West German) chancellor Konrad Adenauer, and most notably French president Charles de Gaulle, felt some discomfort that although Kennedy dispatched former secretary of state Dean Acheson to brief them on the crisis, they had not been consulted on decisions of great importance to the survival of their own countries, which were likely to be prime targets for Soviet nuclear missiles in any major war. The Kennedy administration was equally high-handed in ignoring the North Atlantic Council when deciding to remove Jupiter missiles from Italy and Turkey, even though these weapons were supposedly under NATO control. Such behavior on the part of the U.S. government probably confirmed de Gaulle in his decision to take a highly independent foreign policy line in subsequent years.

Although the U.S.-Soviet settlement effectively ensured his regime's survival, Castro, meanwhile, felt deeply humiliated and resentful that the superpowers had settled matters between themselves without consulting him. Before Khrushchev's fall from power, though, the two men were reconciled, and Cuban-Soviet relations remained close until the end of the Cold War. To the chagrin of successive U.S. presidents, most of whom would have welcomed his overthrow, the durable Castro remained in power into the 21st century, eventually becoming the doyen among world political leaders before finally retiring in 2008.

For decades after the Cuban Missile Crisis, new evidence on almost every aspect of these events continued to surface. Robert Kennedy's memoir *Thirteen Days,* posthumously released in 1969, a year after his assassination in June 1968, for the first time confirmed rumors of a U.S.-Soviet understanding on the removal of missiles from Turkey. Aging Kennedy administration officials gradually released new information, greatly qualifying the initial depiction of the crisis as published early on in works by such Kennedy associates as Arthur M. Schlesinger, Jr., and Theodore Sorensen. The release of secret tapes of the deliberations of ExComm, made without the knowledge of any participants except the two Kennedy brothers, demonstrated that to avoid nuclear war President Kennedy was willing to be far more conciliatory than earlier accounts had suggested and also highlighted inaccuracies in the recollections of other participants.

Equally fruitfully, the ending of the Cold War and the consequent relaxation of tensions with the communist world opened the floodgates of recollections from the other side. From the late 1980s onward, several international conferences bringing together Cuban, American, and Soviet participants in the crisis took place in the United States and Cuba. Attendees let slip much new information, including details of just how many Soviet troops and nuclear-capable missiles were already installed on Cuba in October 1962 and accounts of at least one dramatic confrontation between U.S. warships and a nuclear-armed Soviet submarine. Additional documentary evidence released from both Soviet and U.S. archives continued to fill in missing information on aspects of the Soviet-U.S.-Cuban imbroglio, giving historians a far fuller, accurate, and more nuanced understanding of Soviet dealings with Cuba and of the actions of Khrushchev and other Soviet officials before and during the crisis. More is also becoming available from the archives of Western European allies of the United States, illuminating once-obscure episodes and correcting earlier assertions and assumptions on these nations' contributions to the crisis. Undoubtedly, some areas still remain and perhaps always will be murky. Fifty years after the Cuban Missile Crisis, however, our understanding of this terrifying and spectacular international confrontation demonstrates that in hindsight it was even more complex and possessed wider ramifications than appreciated at the time.

A

Acheson, Dean Gooderham (1893–1971)

U.S. secretary of state (1949–1953) and chief architect of U.S. foreign policy in the Cold War's formative years. Born on April 11, 1893, in Middletown, Connecticut, to British parents, Dean Acheson attended the prestigious Groton School, Yale University, and Harvard Law School. In 1921 Acheson joined a Washington, D.C., law firm. He entered public life in 1933 when President Franklin D. Roosevelt named him undersecretary of the treasury. Acheson resigned soon thereafter, however, over a disagreement concerning gold and currency policies. In 1940 he authored a key legal opinion that led to the Lend-Lease program. He became assistant secretary of state in 1941 and then undersecretary of state in 1945. In 1949 President Harry S. Truman appointed him secretary of state, a position he held until 1953.

The possessor of a brilliant legal mind, a regal bearing, and a biting wit, Acheson initially favored a policy of postwar cooperation with the Soviet Union, but he quickly reversed his view and, along with Russian specialist George F. Kennan, became one of the chief proponents of the Cold War containment policy. Unlike Kennan, who believed that the contest with the Soviet Union was primarily political in nature, Acheson stressed the military dimension. Sobered by the failure of democratic nations to halt the Axis powers in the 1930s, Acheson advocated a policy of developing military strength before negotiating with the Soviet Union. Acheson also played a critical role in implementing major Cold War initiatives in Europe, including the Truman Doctrine program of assistance to Greece and Turkey, the Marshall Plan (a program of economic aid to Western Europe), and the North Atlantic Treaty Organization (NATO) security pact.

Acheson retired from public life in 1953 but soon became the main Democratic critic of President Dwight D. Eisenhower's foreign policy. When the Eisenhower administration committed itself to a policy of massive retaliation that emphasized nuclear responses over conventional responses to crises, the former secretary of state reacted with utter disbelief to what he termed "defense on the cheap."

In the 1960s, Acheson returned to public life as the head of NATO task forces, special envoy, diplomatic troubleshooter, and foreign policy adviser for presidents John F. Kennedy and Lyndon B. Johnson. Told by Kennedy in early 1961 of the projected Bay of Pigs invasion of Cuba, an alarmed Acheson hoped, he later recalled, that the president was not "serious" and warned him that "1,500 Cubans weren't as good as 25,000 Cubans." His advice tended to the hawkish. In the 1961 Berlin Crisis, he counseled Kennedy to take a firm stand, and he privately believed that Kennedy should have dismantled the Berlin Wall.

During the Cuban Missile Crisis, Acheson's advice was equally forceful. Included in ExComm's discussions, he invariably advocated air strikes against the missile installations, brushing aside the fears of Attorney General Robert F. Kennedy, the president's brother, that bombing them without warning would constitute another Pearl Harbor. On October 21 President Kennedy dispatched Acheson to Europe to brief President Charles de Gaulle of France, Chancellor Konrad Adenauer of West Germany (FRG), and the North Atlantic Council on the situation. Returning after the implementation of the U.S. naval blockade of Cuba, when the ultimate outcome still hung in the balance, Acheson again advocated air strikes against the missiles. When the confrontation was resolved, Acheson privately felt that President Kennedy had been "out of his depth," disorganized, and insufficiently forceful in handling the crisis and termed his success "homage to plain dumb luck," criticisms he made public in 1969, when Robert F. Kennedy's own account was published. Acheson died of a heart attack on October 12, 1971, in Sandy Spring, Maryland.

Caryn E. Neumann

See also: Bay of Pigs Invasion; Berlin Crises; Containment, Doctrine and Course of; Kennedy, Robert Francis; U.S. Allies

References

Beisner, Robert L. *Dean Acheson: A Life in the Cold War.* New York: Oxford University Press, 2006.

Brinkley, Douglas. *Dean Acheson: The Cold War Years, 1953–71.* New Haven, CT: Yale University Press, 1992.

Chace, James. *Acheson: The Secretary of State Who Created the American World.* New York: Simon and Schuster, 1998.

Isaacson, Walter, and Evan Thomas. *The Wise Men: Six Friends and the World They Made.* New York: Simon and Schuster, 1986.

McMahon, Robert J. *Dean Acheson and the Creation of an American World Order.* Washington, DC: Potomac Books, 2009.

Alekseev (Shitov), Aleksandr Ivanovich (1913–2001)

Soviet diplomat and KGB intelligence officer, Soviet ambassador to Cuba, June 12, 1962–January 15, 1968. Alekseev was born Aleksandr Shitov on January 8, 1913, in Russia's western Komstromskoi Oblast. After studying French and Spanish at Moscow State University, he joined the Soviet intelligence service, the KGB, in 1941. Later that year, as German forces pushed into Soviet territory, the Moscow-based Shitov took the cover name Alekseev, planning to remain in Moscow as an espionage operative should German forces capture the city. From 1941 to 1943 he worked in the Soviet mission in Tehran, Iran; from 1944 to 1951 in French North Africa and in the Soviet embassy in Paris, returning to Moscow in 1951 to work for the Soviet Information Bureau. From 1954 Alekseev was based in Buenos Aires, where, supposedly working as a correspondent for TASS, the Soviet news agency, he was actually recruiting for the KGB. Recalled to Moscow in 1958, he worked on Latin American propaganda activities in the Commission of Cultural Affairs of the Central Committee of the Soviet Communist Party.

On January 10, 1959, the Soviet Union recognized the new radical government of Cuba established under Prime Minister Fidel Castro nine days earlier. Alekseev requested assignment to Havana to establish contact with the new Cuban leaders. The first Russian granted a visa to Cuba, Alekseev arrived on October 1, 1959. Working with covert members of the Cuban Communist Party within the Cuban government, notably Castro's brother Raúl and the Argentinian revolutionary Ernesto "Che" Guevara, Alekseev sought to steer the new regime in a pro-Soviet direction. As Castro initiated radical land reform and nationalized U.S. property in Cuba during 1959 and 1960, Cuban relations with the United States deteriorated. On September 2, 1960, Fidel Castro made a major public proclamation of

radical principles, the Declaration of Havana. The following month, the United States imposed a complete economic embargo. In early January 1961, the United States broke all diplomatic relations with Cuba.

These circumstances facilitated Alekseev's efforts to broker a rapprochement between Cuban leaders and the Soviet Union. At his urging, in February 1960 Anastas Mikoyan, a top Soviet Presidium member, visited Cuba and concluded a Soviet-Cuban trade agreement, whereby the Soviet Union purchased Cuban sugar in exchange for oil and other goods. In May the two countries agreed to resume diplomatic relations. The Soviet embassy in Havana reopened its doors on July 8, 1960, and the following month Ambassador Sergei Mikhailovich Kudryatsev took up his post, with Alekseev as cultural attaché. Kudryatsev never developed good relations with the Cuban revolutionaries. In September 1960 Castro told the ambassador that Alekseev should handle all meetings with top Cuban leaders.

Fearing that the United States was planning military intervention, Castro also turned to Alekseev in a quest for Soviet arms, to supplement existing Cuban purchases from Czechoslovakia and several Western European countries. In July 1960, Soviet premier Nikita Khrushchev publicly stated that if necessary his country would intervene with nuclear weapons to protect Cuba. The Soviet Union gave Cuba increasing quantities of weapons, announcing a major military aid program, including tanks, rifles, and artillery, during Raúl Castro's July 1960 visit to Moscow. Soon afterward, as rumors of a forthcoming U.S. invasion attempt on Cuba circulated internationally, a total of 41 military aircraft (MiG-19 and MiG-15 fighter jets and reconnaissance planes) were promised to Cuba, together with enhanced quantities of other weapons. The Soviet Union also began training 17 Cuban intelligence operatives for espionage against the United States and the Cuban émigré community. After the U.S.-backed April 1961 Bay of Pigs invasion attempt on Cuba, Fidel Castro moved even closer to the Soviet Union in his search for protection, requesting additional KGB operatives and assistance in training Cuban intelligence agents, a request Alekseev supported. On April 16, 1961, Castro announced that he himself was a communist, and on December 1, 1961, he confirmed his adherence to Marxism-Leninism.

Alekseev had little if any input into the Soviet decision to base nuclear-capable missiles in Cuba. In early May 1962, Khrushchev and the KGB summoned him to Moscow and informed him that he was to be appointed ambassador to the island, to supervise the deployment of substantial Soviet forces equipped with conventional weapons. Later in May, Khrushchev enhanced this plan by including substantial numbers of short-, medium-, and

intermediate-range nuclear-capable missiles and warheads, together with a nuclear-armed submarine squadron. Alekseev unavailingly suggested that Castro would refuse the offer of such armaments, reminding Khrushchev that the Cuban leader sought to expel the Americans from their Cuban base of Guantánamo Bay by demanding the removal of all foreign outposts in Latin America.

As the Cuban Missile Crisis escalated, especially after President John F. Kennedy's October 22 public statement, Alekseev served as Castro's principal Russian confidant, warning Khrushchev early on October 27 that Castro believed U.S. intervention to be inevitable and translating a cable from the Cuban leader to Khrushchev that apparently urged a nuclear first strike against the United States. The same day the Kremlin, in turn, sought to use Alekseev's privileged access to Castro to persuade Cuba's prime minister to endorse publicly Khrushchev's proposal that the United States trade Turkish for Cuban missile bases and assure the United Nations that all work on Soviet missile installations in Cuba had ceased. On October 28, Alekseev was instructed to deliver a letter from Khrushchev to Castro, explaining the Soviet position, but Castro refused to meet him. In the following days Alekseev, a textbook example of an ambassador who had gone native, largely embraced Castro's defiant attitude toward both superpowers, questioning the good faith of Washington's pledge not to invade Cuba and warning his Kremlin superiors not to pressure or irritate the volatile Cuban leader.

Hardly surprisingly, Alekseev survived the October 1962 debacle. His cordial relationship with Cuban officials, Castro included, made him too valuable to sacrifice to political expediency. In spring 1963, Alekseev successfully encouraged Castro to visit the Soviet Union and repair his relations with Khrushchev and others. Weathering Khrushchev's fall 1964 ouster by Leonid Brezhnev, Alekseev remained ambassador to Cuba until January 1968. He subsequently served as an adviser to the leftist President Salvador Allende of Chile, who died following a military coup in 1973. Alekseev retired in 1980 and then became an official adviser to the Soviet embassy in Cuba. In 1992 he attended a major conference in Havana marking the 40th anniversary of the missile crisis, where 30 prominent Cuban, Soviet, and U.S. official participants in the crisis pooled their recollections. Alekseev died in 1998.

Priscilla Roberts

See also: ANADYR, Operation; Castro, Fidel; Castro, Raúl; Guantánamo Bay Naval Base; Guevara de la Serna, Ernesto "Che"; Khrushchev, Nikita Sergeyevich; Mikoyan, Anastas Ivanovich

References

Andrew, Christopher, and Vasili Mitrokhin. *The World Was Going Our Way: The KGB and the Battle for the Third World.* New York: Basic Books, 2005.

Dobbs, Michael. *One Minute to Midnight: Kennedy, Khrushchev, and Castro on the Brink of Nuclear War.* New York: Knopf, 2008.

Fursenko, Aleksandr, and Timothy Naftali. *One Hell of a Gamble: Khrushchev, Castro, and Kennedy, 1958–1964.* New York: Norton, 1997.

Polmar, Norman, and John D. Gresham. *DEFCON-2: Standing on the Brink of Nuclear War during the Cuban Missile Crisis.* New York: John Wiley, 2006.

Alliance for Progress

A financial aid program devised by the United States in March 1961 to promote social reform in Latin America. The program's architects hoped to curb violence and prevent communist-inspired revolutions in the region. When dealing with Latin America after World War II, the United States generally emphasized security imperatives at the expense of social and economic concerns. Rejecting the region's pleas for a Latin American plan similar to the 1947 Marshall Plan that revived the Western European economies, the United States had endorsed private investment and free trade as the keys to Latin America's socioeconomic development. While this approach meshed well with President Dwight Eisenhower's efforts to eschew direct aid, it often conflicted with the prevailing economic climate in Latin America.

Two events in the late 1950s demonstrated the risks in this course. First, in May 1958 Vice President Richard M. Nixon's goodwill tour of South America provoked hostile demonstrations and major rioting in the cities of Caracas in Venezuela and Lima in Peru. Second, Fidel Castro seized control of Cuba's government in January 1959, and by 1960 he was becoming increasingly anti-American and pro-Soviet.

In the late 1950s, therefore, the Eisenhower administration began to direct more attention to Latin America's economic and social problems. Latin Americans had long sought U.S. support for a regional development bank. In August 1958 the United States dropped its long-standing opposition to the bank and in October 1960 supported the establishment of the Inter-American Development Bank. This shift in U.S. policy continued at Bogotá, Colombia, in September 1960 at a special meeting called by the Council of the Organization of American States (OAS) to study new

measures for Pan-American economic cooperation. In signing the Act of Bogotá, the Eisenhower administration laid the groundwork for the Alliance for Progress by pledging $500 million for economic development and social reform in Latin America. In return the Latin American nations agreed to implement sound economic policies and to eliminate obstacles to social and economic progress.

During the U.S. presidential elections of 1960, Democratic nominee John F. Kennedy criticized the Eisenhower administration and Republican candidate Richard M. Nixon for "losing" Cuba and failing to align U.S. policy with Latin Americans' rising aspirations. Kennedy called for an "alliance for progress" between the United States and Latin America in his inaugural address.

In March 1961 the Kennedy administration formally committed itself to an Alliance for Progress with Latin America, a long-term program of U.S. aid linked to social and structural reforms, economic development, and democratization. That program took official form at the inter-American meeting at Punta del Este, Uruguay, in August 1961. The conference proclaimed a lengthy list of objectives for the program, including democratization, acceleration of social and economic development, promotion of education, fair wages and working conditions, health programs, tax reforms, agrarian reform, fiscal stability, and the stimulation of private enterprise. To achieve its goals, the program would need $100 billion during its first decade, $20 billion of which would come from external sources, with the United States pledging to provide a major part of that funding. The remaining $80 billion was expected to come from Latin American sources, both public and private. When launching this program, which was designed to provide peaceful, democratic alternatives to violent social revolution and a "second Cuba" in the hemisphere, the U.S. preoccupation with containing the communist threat was greatly in evidence.

The objectives of the Alliance for Progress soon collided with the harsh realities of international economics and growing domestic pressures in both Latin America and the United States. The program implicitly assumed that most Latin American elites would support reforms to avoid violent revolution. Many of the elites, however, were reluctant to implement major reform, realizing that such changes might strip them of power. With Latin America already experiencing high levels of political instability, U.S. officials hesitated to apply too much pressure for reform, fearing that this would only enhance regional political uncertainty. Should the program promote growth but not structural reforms, traditional elites would naturally reap most of the rewards of increased growth. Much Alliance

for Progress aid went to pay off earlier loans rather than promoting social modernization and economic development. Rapid population growth in Latin America also undermined potential advances in social and economic reform.

Domestic U.S. politics also hindered the success of the Alliance for Progress program. Kennedy's assassination in 1963 removed the leader most closely connected to the program's fate. Projected funding for the program was based on capital needs for a decade, but the annual U.S. congressional appropriations process prevented presidents from guaranteeing long-term aid levels.

In the United States, from the mid-1960s onward a series of problems undercut the Alliance for Progress. Kennedy's successor, Lyndon B. Johnson, was primarily interested in domestic issues, while in foreign policy he became increasingly preoccupied with the deteriorating situation in Vietnam. The ability of the program to uplift Latin America was oversold from its inception. These exaggerated hopes for the program made later disillusionment with it all the easier. Latin American governments were often unwilling or unable to implement the program's structural reforms. The U.S. Congress cut funding for the program, which quickly lost its reform content and evolved into a conventional aid program. Although there was no officially declared ending of the Alliance for Progress, like many other programs of its time, it became subsumed by political pressures and broader Cold War imperatives and thus never fulfilled its original goals.

Don M. Coerver

See also: Eisenhower, Dwight David; Johnson, Lyndon Baines; Kennedy, John Fitzgerald; Mann, Thomas C.; Organization of American States

References

Kaufman, Burton I. *Trade and Aid: Eisenhower's Foreign Economic Policy, 1953–1961.* Baltimore, MD: Johns Hopkins University Press, 1982.

Levinson, Jerome, and Juan de Onis. *The Alliance That Lost Its Way: A Critical Report on the Alliance for Progress.* Chicago: Quadrangle Books, 1970.

Rabe, Stephen G. *The Most Dangerous Area in the World: John F. Kennedy Confronts Communist Revolution in Latin America.* Chapel Hill: University of North Carolina Press, 1999.

Taffet, Jeffrey F. *Foreign Aid as Foreign Policy: The Alliance for Progress in Latin America.* New York: Routledge, 2007.

ANADYR, Operation (1962)

Soviet initiative to base a large military and naval force, equipped with a wide range of conventional and nuclear-capable weapons, on Cuba. In late May 1962, Soviet premier Nikita Khrushchev decided that the best way of preventing the United States from overthrowing Prime Minister Fidel Castro's communist regime on Cuba was to station a large force of troops, with substantial numbers of nuclear-capable arms as well as conventional weapons, on the island. This would have the additional advantage of reducing the massive nuclear imbalance in strategic weapons the United States enjoyed over the Soviet Union. Khrushchev hoped, moreover, that an enhanced sense of nuclear vulnerability might make the United States more accommodating toward Soviet efforts to expel the Western powers from West Berlin. In mid-May, Castro also expressed concerns about Cuba's security from U.S. attack, indicating that he feared that the substantial conventional military assistance the Soviet Union had already offered him earlier that month was inadequate to meet the threat from the United States.

The U.S. destroyer *Barry* pulls alongside the Russian freighter *Anosov* in the Atlantic Ocean, November 10, 1962, to inspect cargo as a U.S. patrol plane flies overhead. The Soviet ship presumably carries a cargo of missiles being withdrawn from Cuba. The interception took place about 780 miles northeast of Puerto Rico. (AP/Wide World Photos)

In late May 1962, Khrushchev prevailed upon other Soviet Presidium members to endorse placing regiments equipped with nuclear-capable missiles on Cuba, even though some, especially Anastas Mikoyan—a senior Presidium member with close ties to Cuba—and Foreign Minister Andrei Gromyko, initially expressed misgivings. To inform Castro of this offer, Khrushchev dispatched a delegation to Cuba, one that included Aleksandr Alekseev, Sharaf R. Rashidov, an agricultural specialist and Presidium candidate member, and Marshal Sergei Biryuzov, head of Soviet Strategic Forces. Castro agreed to accept the proffered military units and equipment, all of which were to be moved to Cuba and installed under conditions of strict secrecy, while Rashidov and Biryuzov erroneously reported that Cuba's tropical forests provided ample cover to conceal the missile installations from U.S. U-2 surveillance overflights during their construction. In July 1962 Raúl Castro arrived in Moscow to negotiate a draft treaty between Cuba and the Soviet Union defining the terms on which Soviet troops would be based on the island. After lengthy negotiations and numerous modifications in Havana, in August 1962 Cuba's Interior Minister Ernesto "Che" Guevara came to Moscow and finalized the Treaty on National Cooperation for the Defense of the National Territory of Cuba in the Event of Aggression, an agreement that he and Soviet Defense Minister Rodion Malinovsky secretly initialed late that month. Fidel Castro wished to announce the treaty openly immediately, in which case he would have traveled to Moscow himself to sign it in August, but he deferred to Khrushchev's wishes. Khrushchev planned to visit Cuba in November 1962, after the politically sensitive U.S. midterm congressional elections, by which time he expected all the missiles to be installed and operational, and then publicly announce both the defense treaty and the presence of Soviet nuclear-capable weapons on Cuba.

By June 1962 the Soviet General Staff, following Malinovsky's instructions, had drawn up plans to send nearly 51,000 military personnel to Cuba. The group would include five nuclear missile regiments, three equipped with a total of 36 R-12 (SS-4) medium-range ballistic missiles (MRBMs) with a range of 1,100–1,400 miles, based at 24 launch sites, and two with 24 R-14 (SS-5) intermediate-range ballistic missiles (IRBMs) with a range up to 2,800 miles, based at 16 launch sites. The group would also comprise four motorized regiments of 2,500 troops each, two tank battalions with the latest T-55 tanks, one wing of MiG-21 fighter jets, 42 Il-28 light bombers, two cruise missile regiments with a total of 80 short-range FKR tactical nuclear warheads with a range around 100 miles, antiaircraft batteries, and 12 surface-to-air missile (SA-2) units with a total of 144

launchers. In addition, Soviet forces would have a substantial naval contingent of 2 cruisers; 4 destroyers, of which 2 would have missile launchers; 12 "Komar" ships with 2 conventional R-15 missiles apiece; and 11 submarines, 7 carrying nuclear-capable missiles. The presence of MRBMs and IRBMs in Cuba would double the number of Soviet warheads capable of reaching the continental United States.

Between June and October 1962, Soviet troops and equipment were shipped in great secrecy to Cuba, where, under the command of Army Gen. Issa Alexandrovich Pliyev, construction of the missile installations and other facilities began. Through Georgi Bolshakov, a Soviet military intelligence operative in Washington with close ties to Attorney General Robert Kennedy, the U.S. president's brother, Khrushchev requested that as a goodwill gesture U.S. aircraft should relax their surveillance and harassment of Soviet shipping, a move he hoped would minimize and deflect U.S. scrutiny. Despite Soviet claims that these forces were specialized agricultural and technical advisers, the massive buildup gave rise to intelligence reports from Cuba that attracted considerable press and political attention in the United States. On September 4, 1962, President John F. Kennedy warned publicly that the United States would not tolerate the presence of Soviet nuclear-capable weapons in Cuba. The Kremlin responded by seeking to accelerate the pace of construction. Khrushchev also added six Il-28s modified to carry atomic bombs, and three detachments of Luna short-range missiles, with a total of 12 two-kiloton warheads, to the forces destined for Cuba, but he canceled the naval squadron, apart from four Foxtrot submarines, each carrying 22 torpedoes. Soviet officials decided that one torpedo on each of these submarines should be nuclear-armed.

By late September, 114 of a projected 149 Soviet shipments had been dispatched to Cuba, 94 of which had already reached their destination. All loading was expected to be completed by October 20, and the final cargo would arrive by November 5. By the end of September all 36 R-12 missiles had arrived in Cuba. On October 4 the Soviet freighter *Indigirka* delivered 45 R-12 one-megaton nuclear warheads, 12 tactical warheads for the Luna weapons, six 12-kiloton bombs for the Il-28s, and thirty-six 12-kiloton warheads for the FKR cruise missiles. On October 22, when President Kennedy publicly announced that the United States would not tolerate the presence of Soviet nuclear-capable weaponry in Cuba, the R-12 MRBM sites had been completed, but those for R-14 IRBMs were still under construction. The Luna weapons and cruise missiles were already in Cuba. After Kennedy's speech, construction of missile sites continued at full

speed, as did uncrating and assembly of Il-28s. One Soviet ship, the *Alex-androvsk,* carrying 24 nuclear warheads for R-14 IRBMs and 44 warheads for FKR land-based cruise missiles, reached Cuba on October 23, hours before the United States imposed a naval quarantine or blockade, though four other Soviet vessels carrying F-14 missiles turned back. By that time, around 41,900 Soviet military personnel were present on the island.

On October 16, Kennedy and most of his senior advisers learned of the presence of medium-range nuclear-capable missile installations on Cuba, and over the following two days U.S. reconnaissance planes also identified intermediate-range missile sites. U.S. officials initially assumed that the warheads had not yet reached the island, and throughout the crisis they remained unaware that short-range tactical nuclear-capable weapons and nuclear-armed Il-28s were deployed on Cuba. In addition, U.S. leaders estimated the number of Soviet troops on Cuba to be only around 10,000. While Khrushchev and Malinovsky in Moscow sought to maintain operational control over all the missiles, especially the R-12s and R-14s, which could be used to attack targets in the continental United States, until October 22 it seems that Pliyev had at least verbal authorization to use the tactical nuclear-capable weapons in combat situations without necessarily consulting Kremlin officials. Whether distant Soviet leaders in Moscow could have reined in military officers in Cuba from using these weapons under battlefield conditions when facing U.S. air strikes or invasion was never tested.

Khrushchev ultimately yielded to Kennedy's demands that the nuclear-capable missiles be withdrawn from Cuba, in exchange for an open promise that the United States would not invade the island and a private agreement that NATO missiles in Turkey would also be removed within six months. Despite efforts by Castro and Malinovsky to retain the cruise missiles and Il-28s, in November and December 1962 all the missiles were dismantled and returned to the Soviet Union. By February 1963 only around 18,000 Soviet troops, armed with conventional weapons, remained on Cuba. Khrushchev indicated to Kennedy administration officials that eventually he hoped to withdraw all Soviet military personnel, but Kennedy's assassination in November 1963 and Khrushchev's fall from power the following year aborted such plans. A substantial Soviet military contingent remained in Cuba until the late 1980s, when the reformist Soviet general secretary Mikhail Gorbachev drastically reduced his country's overseas commitments.

Priscilla Roberts

See also: Alekseev (Shitov), Aleksandr Ivanovich; Bolshakov, Georgi Nikitovich; Castro, Fidel; Castro, Raúl; Gribkov, Anatoli Ivanovich; Kennedy, Robert Francis; Khrushchev, Nikita Sergeyevich; Malinovsky,

Rodion Yakovlevich; Mikoyan, Anastas Ivanovich; Military Balance; Nuclear Arms Race; Pliyev, Issa Alexandrovich

References

Dobbs, Michael. *One Minute to Midnight: Kennedy, Khrushchev, and Castro on the Brink of Nuclear War.* New York: Knopf, 2008.

Fursenko, Aleksandr, and Timothy Naftali. *One Hell of a Gamble: Khrushchev, Castro, and Kennedy, 1958–1964.* New York: Norton, 1997.

Gribkov, Anatoli I., and William Y. Smith. *Operation ANADYR: U.S. and Soviet Generals Recount the Cuban Missile Crisis.* Edited by Alfred Friendly, Jr. Chicago, Berlin, Tokyo, and Moscow: edition q, 1994.

Polmar, Norman, and John D. Gresham. *DEFCON-2: Standing on the Brink of Nuclear War during the Cuban Missile Crisis.* New York: John Wiley, 2006.

Arkhipov, Vasili Alexandrovich (1926–1999)

Soviet naval officer. Vasili Arkhipov was born into a peasant family in the town of Staraya Kupavna, near Moscow, on January 30, 1926. Educated at the Pacific Higher Naval School, in August 1945 he served against Japan in a minesweeper. After graduating from the Caspian Higher Naval School in 1947, Arkhipov saw submarine service in the Soviet Black Sea, Northern, and Baltic fleets. In July 1961, as deputy commander of the Hotel-class submarine K-19, Arkhipov helped prevent a mutiny when there was a major problem with the submarine's nuclear reactor.

During the Cuban Missile Crisis, Arkhipov was second in command on B-59, one of four Foxtrot-class attack submarines ordered to Cuba from Murmansk on October 1, 1962. Each submarine had had its designation number scraped off its conning tower, to hamper identification, and each carried 22 torpedoes, one of which was nuclear-armed. On October 24, as the United States imposed a naval blockade (or quarantine, as it was called) around Cuba, U.S. officials informed their Soviet counterparts of their intention to drop practice depth charges to force submarines to surface. The Kremlin, however, failed to transmit this information to its submarine commanders.

On October 27, a group of 11 U.S. destroyers and the aircraft carrier USS *Randolph* enforcing the blockade located, harried, and trapped B-59 in the West Atlantic near the quarantine line, dropping practice depth charges to persuade the vessel, whose batteries were running low, to surface and identify itself. The submarine's captain, Valentin Grigorievitch Savitsky,

concluding that war had already begun, wished to fire the nuclear torpedo against the attackers, but procedure required that the second in command (Arkhipov) and the political officer (Ivan Semonovich Maslennikov) agree to the action. In heated arguments Arkhipov refused to endorse the launch and eventually persuaded his comrades to surface the submarine and request further orders from Moscow. The U.S. naval vessels surrounding the submarine (the *Beale, Cony, Lowry,* and *Murray*) had been unaware it was carrying any nuclear-capable weapons. To indicate that their intentions were not hostile, the U.S. vessels had a jazz band playing on the deck of one ship when the Soviet submarine surfaced. The Americans suspected that B-59 was suffering some mechanical problems, but Savitsky declined their offer of assistance. B-59 eventually turned around, heading east, accompanied by U.S. naval vessels until it submerged late on October 29. The other three Foxtrot submarines received orders to also abort their voyages to the island.

The full implications of this episode were not generally known until a conference held in Havana in October 2002 to mark the 40th anniversary of the Cuban Missile Crisis. Its organizer, Professor Thomas Blanton of the Washington-based National Security Archive, stated, "a guy called Vasili Arkhipov saved the world."

Arkhipov remained in the Soviet Navy, rising to command first submarines and then submarine squadrons. Promoted in 1975 to rear admiral, when he became head of the Kirov Naval Academy, he rose to vice admiral in 1981, retiring in the mid-1980s. He died in Zheleznodorozhny, near Moscow, in 1999.

Priscilla Roberts

See also: ANADYR, Operation; Nuclear Arms Race

References

Burr, William, and Thomas S. Blanton, eds. *The Submarines of October: U.S. and Soviet Naval Encounters during the Cuban Missile Crisis.* National Security Archive Electronic Briefing Book No. 75. http://www.gwu.edu/~nsarchiv/NSAEBB/NSAEBB75/

Dobbs, Michael. *One Minute to Midnight: Kennedy, Khrushchev, and Castro on the Brink of Nuclear War.* New York: Knopf, 2008.

Huchthausen, Peter. *October Fury.* New York: John Wiley, 2002.

Mozgovoi, Aleksandr. *Kubinskaya Samba Kvarteta Fokstrotov* [Cuban Samba of the Foxtrot Quartet]. Moscow: Military Parade Publishing House, 2002.

Polmar, Norman, and John D. Gresham. *DEFCON-2: Standing on the Brink of Nuclear War during the Cuban Missile Crisis.* New York: John Wiley, 2006.

B

Ball, George Wildman (1909–1994)

International lawyer, undersecretary of state, 1961–1966. George Ball was born on December 21, 1909, in Des Moines, Iowa. He obtained bachelor's and law degrees from Northwestern University and, after a spell as a lawyer in the general counsel's office of the U.S. Treasury Department, practiced law in Chicago until the early 1940s as a lawyer in the general counsel's office of the U.S. Treasury Department. During World War II he took government positions with the Lend-Lease Administration and the Foreign Economic Administration. After the war Ball moved to Washington, where he helped found the international law firm of Cleary, Gottlieb, Steen, and Cox.

In the run-up to the 1960 presidential election, Ball prepared foreign policy position papers for the Democratic candidate, Sen. John F. Kennedy. Once elected, Kennedy made Ball undersecretary of state for economic affairs; in November 1961 Ball rose to undersecretary of state, second only to Secretary Dean Rusk within the State Department. Until November 1961, Ball's responsibilities were primarily economic. Excluded from top-level meetings on political and military strategy, Ball was not involved in planning the unsuccessful April 1961 Bay of Pigs invasion and had no foreknowledge of it. With hindsight, he hoped he would have opposed this enterprise but confessed himself uncertain whether he would have been sufficiently confident to do so.

During the Cuban Missile Crisis, Kennedy included Ball in the Executive Committee (ExComm) of senior officials who met regularly to discuss the U.S. response. Ball forcefully advised the imposition of a naval blockade or quarantine around Cuba, which he believed would give Soviet leaders time to reflect and back down, and he opposed the more drastic option

of launching surprise air strikes against Cuba. He also strongly opposed any unannounced air strike against missile installations, arguing that this would jeopardize the United States' moral standing and alienate its allies. After the crisis, Ball wrote a legal justification for the Kennedy administration's position and made arrangements to inform U.S. allies of this.

Ball remained undersecretary until September 1966. Throughout his tenure, he argued forcefully but unavailingly against the steady expansion of U.S. commitments in Vietnam, first under Kennedy and then under President Lyndon B. Johnson. Weary of publicly defending policies he deplored, eventually he resigned and became a senior partner in Lehman Brothers, the New York investment bank, where he remained—with one three-month spell in 1968 as U.S. ambassador to the United Nations—until retiring in 1982. Ball continued to speak and write extensively on international issues. He died of abdominal cancer on May 26, 1994, in New York City.

Priscilla Roberts

See also: Bay of Pigs Invasion; Kennedy, John Fitzgerald; Rusk, Dean David; U.S. Allies

References

Ball, George W. *The Past Has Another Pattern: Memoirs.* New York: Norton, 1982.

Bill, James A. *George Ball: Behind the Scenes in U.S. Foreign Policy.* New Haven, CT: Yale University Press, 1997.

DiLeo, David L. *George Ball, Vietnam, and the Rethinking of Containment.* Chapel Hill: University of North Carolina Press, 1991.

Batista y Zaldívar, Fulgencio (1901–1973)

Authoritarian Cuban president (1940–1944, 1952–1958). Born in Banes, Cuba, on January 16, 1901, Fulgencio Batista joined the army in 1921, eventually becoming a military stenographer. He first emerged on the national scene during the 1933 revolution that deposed the dictator Gerardo Machado.

During the short-lived Ramón Grau San Martín government (September 1933–January 1934), Batista was the military strongman behind the scenes and was ultimately responsible for the government's collapse.

Batista was the true power figure behind successive puppet governments during 1934–1940. In 1940 he was elected president. His four-year term was noted for its progressive social reforms, links with the Communist Party, and support for the Allied side in World War II. Batista provided the United States with access to naval and air bases and sold it nearly all Cuba's sugar production.

Batista was succeeded by another democratically elected leader, Ramón Grau San Martín, the man he had helped overthrow in January 1934. The increasing corruption of the Grau government and its successor facilitated Batista's return to power in March 1952, when he and elements of the army seized power. The new regime suspended the constitution and declared its loyalty to the United States. Batista now largely repudiated his earlier reformism and consolidated his predecessors' anticommunist measures. In the mid-1950s, with support from the U.S. Federal Bureau of Investigation, Batista established a repressive anticommunist political police force.

Rapid successes by anti-Batista movements, especially among middle-class students and including Fidel Castro's July 26 Movement, brought Batista's fall in late 1958. On January 1, 1959, he fled Cuba for the Dominican Republic as Castro's forces closed in on Havana. Batista died on August 6, 1973, in Estoril, Portugal.

Barry Carr

See also: Castro, Fidel; Eisenhower, Dwight David

References

Argote-Freyre, Frank. *Fulgencio Batista: From Revolutionary to Strongman.* New Brunswick, NJ: Rutgers University Press, 2006.

Gellman, Irving. *Roosevelt and Batista: Good Neighbor Diplomacy in Cuba, 1933–1945.* Albuquerque: University of New Mexico Press, 1973.

Morley, Morris. *Imperial State and Revolution: The United States and Cuba, 1952–1986.* Cambridge: Cambridge University Press, 1987.

Bay of Pigs Invasion (April 15–19, 1961)

Abortive U.S.-backed invasion of Cuba whose failure contributed to the subsequent Cuban Missile Crisis.

On January 1, 1959, an indigenous revolutionary movement led by Fidel Castro seized power from Fulgencio Batista, dictator of Cuba since 1933 and a U.S. client. Although Castro initially declared that he was not a communist, from spring 1959 he covertly sought Soviet aid and military protection. U.S. economic pressure and boycotts quickly impelled him to move openly into the Soviet camp. In response, in March 1960 President Dwight D. Eisenhower authorized the Central Intelligence Agency (CIA) to devise a scheme to train Cuban exiles based in Guatemala to invade the island and overthrow Castro. Eisenhower had no schedule for such an invasion, but he did want a plan to be in place and ready to execute at his decision. In early January 1961, shortly before leaving office, Eisenhower took the measure of ending U.S. recognition of Castro's government.

Eisenhower's successor, John F. Kennedy, inherited this projected invasion operation. Perhaps fearing to appear soft on communism, despite lukewarm assessments from the Joint Chiefs of Staff (JCS) of the risk of failure and over Secretary of State Dean Rusk's misgivings, in March 1961 the newly elected president approved its implementation, with two important modifications. First, notwithstanding evidence that U.S. involvement in the training of Cuban exiles had become widely known throughout Latin America, seeking to maintain the deniability of any U.S. contribution to the operation, Kennedy insisted that no American troops or pilots participate. Second, in order to facilitate an unobtrusive clandestine night-time landing, the invasion site was moved a hundred miles west, from Trinidad, on Cuba's southern coast—which offered an escape route into the nearby Escambray Mountains, where the fighters could live as guerrillas if the operation failed—to the more vulnerable Bay of Pigs (Bahia de Cochinos), south of the city of Matanzas. These changes, unfortunately, jeopardized the invasion's chances of success. Although Kennedy wished the invasion force to recruit only liberal Cubans, their outlook anti-Castro but non-Batista, in practice it included many somewhat reactionary Batista supporters.

Initial air strikes against Cuba's air force bases launched on April 15, 1961, by exile Cuban pilots flying surplus U.S. B-26 bombers inflicted damage but failed to destroy the entire Cuban air force. Alarmed by news reports exposing the deceptive U.S. cover story that, as U.S. ambassador Adlai Stevenson publicly stated in the United Nations, defectors from Castro's military had flown these missions, Kennedy refused to authorize a scheduled second air strike, which had been expected to eliminate the remaining Cuban airplanes.

On April 17, 1961, 1,400 Cuban exiles, known as Brigade 2506, commenced their invasion. Some parachuted in; others used amphibious craft.

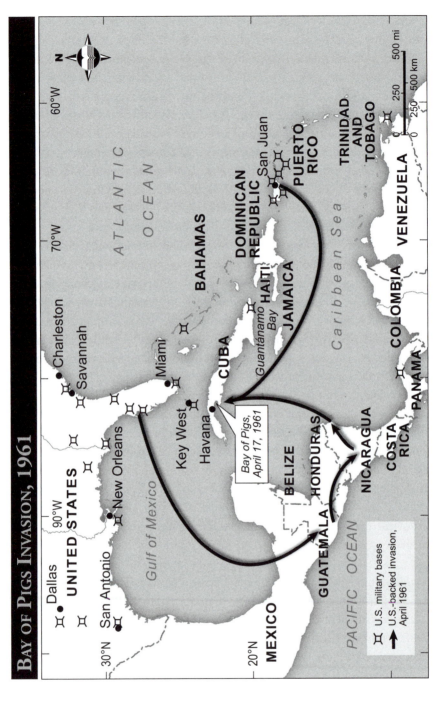

Bay of Pigs Invasion, 1961

Air attacks by Castro's forces slowed the process, destroying one transport carrying vital supplies, and ultimately led the invasion flotilla to put out to sea, while Cuban T-33 fighter jets proved unexpectedly successful in downing the exiles' B-26s. Castro's swift incarceration of one to two hundred thousand potential domestic opponents effectively precluded any internal uprising to support the invasion. Meanwhile, Cuban ground forces, tanks, and artillery wreaked havoc on the invaders. A few escaped by small boat to U.S. naval vessels nearby, but 114 were killed and 1,113 captured. Cuban losses were far greater: approximately 1,650 dead and two thousand wounded. With Kennedy administration backing, 18 months later private sources in the United States provided Cuba with $53 million of food and medicine in exchange for the imprisoned fighters.

The Bay of Pigs represented a humiliating international failure for the United States, vindicating those critics who considered that nation an overbearing, imperialist state that backed unpopular right-wing forces around the globe. Publicly, Kennedy took full responsibility for the operation; privately, he deeply resented what he perceived as CIA mismanagement, and the following year he replaced both Allen W. Dulles, the CIA's near-legendary director, and Richard Bissell, the head of its Clandestine Service. From then onward the CIA placed greater emphasis on intelligence collection as opposed to flamboyant but risky covert operations. Kennedy's reckless authorization and half-hearted implementation of this operation may have helped convince Soviet premier Nikita Khrushchev that he was a lightweight without the resolve to confront the Soviet Union. Undoubtedly, the botched invasion and fear of another subsequent attempt were major reasons impelling Khrushchev to offer and Castro and other leaders in Havana to accept the deployment in Cuba of those Soviet missiles whose presence provoked the Cuban Missile Crisis.

Priscilla Roberts

See also: Batista y Zaldívar, Fulgencio; Bissell, Richard Mervin, Jr.; Castro, Fidel; Central Intelligence Agency; Dulles, Allen Welsh; Eisenhower, Dwight David; Joint Chiefs of Staff; Kennedy, John Fitzgerald; Kennedy, Robert Francis; Khrushchev, Nikita Sergeyevich; Rusk, Dean David; Stevenson, Adlai Ewing II; United Nations

References

Bissell, Richard M., Jr.; with Jonathan E. Lewis and Francis Pudlo. *Reflections of a Cold Warrior: From Yalta to the Bay of Pigs.* New Haven, CT: Yale University Press, 1996.

Blight, James, and Peter Kornbluh, eds. *Politics of Illusion: The Bay of Pigs Invasion Reexamined.* Boulder, CO: Lynne Rienner, 1998.

Higgins, Trumbull. *The Perfect Failure: Kennedy, Eisenhower, and the CIA at the Bay of Pigs.* New York: Norton, 1987.

Jones, Howard. *The Bay of Pigs.* New York: Oxford University Press, 2008.

Kornbluh, Peter, ed. *Bay of Pigs Declassified: The Secret CIA Report on the Invasion of Cuba.* New York: New Press, 1998.

Paterson, Thomas G. *Contesting Castro: The United States and the Triumph of the Cuban Revolution.* New York: Oxford University Press, 1994.

Rabe, Stephen G. *The Most Dangerous Area in the World: John F. Kennedy Confronts Communist Revolution in Latin America.* Chapel Hill: University of North Carolina Press, 1999.

Rasenberger, Jim. *The Brilliant Disaster: JFK, Castro, and America's Doomed Invasion of the Bay of Pigs.* New York: Scribner, 2011.

Welch, Richard E., Jr. *Response to Revolution: The United States and the Cuban Revolution, 1959–1961.* Chapel Hill: University of North Carolina Press, 1985.

Berlin Crises (1958–1961)

Continual disagreement over the control of Berlin between the Soviet bloc and the Western Allies began in earnest in the late 1940s, culminating in the Berlin Blockade (1948–1949). Then, following a period of relative—if tense—calm, renewed Cold War tensions transformed the city into one of the world's potential flash points during 1958–1961.

With Soviet prestige dramatically boosted by the launch of *Sputnik 1* in 1957, Soviet premier Nikita Khrushchev decided to revive the issue of Berlin. On November 10, 1958, he sought to end the joint-occupation agreement in the city by demanding that Great Britain, France, and the United States withdraw their 10,000 troops from West Berlin. He also declared that the Soviet Union would unilaterally transfer its occupation authority in Berlin to the German Democratic Republic (GDR) (East Germany) if a peace treaty were not signed with both East and the Federal Republic of Germany (FRG) (West Germany) within six months. West Berlin would then become a free city. Khrushchev couched his demands by portraying West Berlin's proposed free-city status as a concession because it lay in East German territory and therefore properly belonged to the GDR. None of the Western powers, however, formally recognized East Germany, viewing it as a mere subsidiary of the Soviet Union.

President Dwight D. Eisenhower flatly rejected Khrushchev's demands, although other Western leaders initially tried to make some concessions by proposing an interim Berlin agreement that placed a limit on Western forces and curtailed some propagandistic West Berlin activities, such as radio broadcasts targeting East German audiences. These Allied proposals would have given the Soviets and East Germans some degree of power in West Berlin, a measure that many West Berliners considered a highly dangerous step toward neutralization and, ultimately, abandonment. In December 1958, the Allies issued a North Atlantic Treaty Organization (NATO) declaration rejecting Soviet demands and insisting that no state had the right to withdraw unilaterally from an international agreement.

Khrushchev gradually retreated from his hard-line stance on Berlin. U.S. overflights of the Soviet Union by U-2 reconnaissance planes indicated that the West had an accurate count of the comparatively small number of Soviet nuclear missiles, and the Soviet leader obviously feared starting a war that he could not win. The Soviets now envisioned a gradual crowding out of the Western powers without bloodshed. Meanwhile, East Germany's economic situation continued to deteriorate, with vast numbers of refugees continuing to flee to the West.

In 1961, the newly elected U.S. president, John F. Kennedy, abandoned the demand for German unification that had been U.S. policy since the 1940s, after his foreign policy team concluded that this position was not only impractical but might actually provoke a U.S.-Soviet war. Kennedy and his advisers decided that only three interests were worth risking nuclear war: the continued Allied presence in West Berlin, Allied access to West Berlin by land and by air, and the continued autonomous freedom of West Berlin. Realizing that a rather inconsequential event and a sequence of mutually threatening and unnecessary mobilizations had led to World War I in 1914, Kennedy worried constantly that a relatively minor incident in Germany could escalate into World War III.

Meanwhile, GDR leader Walter Ulbricht decided to close the East Berlin borders in an attempt to exercise control over all traffic to and from Berlin, including Allied military as well as German civilian travelers. On August 13, 1961, East German authorities began construction of the Berlin Wall, essentially sealing off East Berlin from West Berlin and permanently bisecting the city. Ulbricht sought to control both what went into East Berlin and what came out, including thousands of East Germans who sought refuge in West Berlin. The Soviets and the East Germans had wagered that the West would not react to the wall's construction. Kennedy, in accordance with his policy, offered little resistance. In a symbolic incident on

October 22, 1961, the Chief of the U.S. Mission in Berlin asserted the right of U.S. officials to travel freely between West and East Berlin and return, a stance backed up by U.S. tanks.

Throughout the Cuban Missile Crisis, U.S. leaders suspected that West Berlin was the real Soviet target and feared that, should they launch military action against Cuba, the Soviet Union would respond by forcibly seizing West Berlin. Research in Soviet archives has not substantiated these apprehensions. Khrushchev and other Soviet officials apparently had no wish to expand the confrontation by taking such action. On a broader level, the two crises were, it seems, closely connected. When deciding to offer to install missiles in Cuba, Khrushchev apparently hoped that, once these were in place, the Americans would be intimidated into abandoning West Berlin.

Caryn E. Neumann

See also: Eisenhower, Dwight David; Kennedy, John Fitzgerald; Khrushchev, Nikita Sergeyevich; Military Balance; U-2 Overflights; U.S. Allies; Warsaw Pact

References

Ausland, John C. *Kennedy, Khrushchev, and the Berlin-Cuba Crises, 1961–1964.* Oslo, Norway: Aschehoug Publishing House, 1996.

Flemming, Thomas. *Berlin in the Cold War: The Battle for the Divided City.* New York: Berlinica Publishing, 2010.

Harrison, Hope M. *Driving the Soviets up the Wall: Soviet-East German Relations, 1953–1961.* Princeton, NJ: Princeton University Press, 2003.

Kempe, Frederick. *Berlin 1961: Kennedy, Khrushchev, and the Most Dangerous Place on Earth.* New York: G. P. Putnam's Sons, 2011.

Murphy, David E., Sergei A. Kondrashev, and George Bailey. *Battleground Berlin: CIA vs. KGB in the Cold War.* New Haven, CT: Yale University Press, 1997.

Smyser, W. R. *From Yalta to Berlin: The Cold War Struggle over Germany.* New York: St. Martin's Press, 1999.

Taylor, Frederick. *The Berlin Wall: A World Divided.* New York: Harper, 2007.

Bissell, Richard Mervin, Jr. (1909–1994)

Head of the Central Intelligence Agency's (CIA) Directorate of Plans from 1958 to 1962. Born on September 18, 1909, in Hartford, Connecticut,

Richard Mervin Bissell, Jr. graduated from Yale University in 1932 with a BA in history, then studied at the London School of Economics before obtaining a doctorate of economics from Yale in 1939. During World War II, Bissell served in the Office of Strategic Services (OSS), beginning his career in intelligence. After working in the Department of War Mobilization and Reconversion and the Economic Cooperation Administration, in 1954 Bissell joined the CIA, becoming head of the Directorate of Plans (or covert operations) in 1958.

The operations of the Directorate of Plans were soon dubbed "Black Operations" for their clandestine mandate to eradicate world leaders unfriendly to the United States. Bissell and his deputy, Richard Helms, engineered the ouster of Guatemala's Jacobo Arbenz in 1954 and later became nearly obsessed with overthrowing Cuban leader Fidel Castro after his 1959 revolution. During Bissell's CIA tenure, he was also instrumental in developing the U-2 reconnaissance plane and the Corona spy satellite. It was, however, the unsuccessful 1961 Bay of Pigs invasion that won Bissell greatest notoriety.

In March 1960 CIA director Allen W. Dulles was tasked with devising a strategy to remove Castro from power, a mission he turned over to Bissell and Helms, who devised and organized a plan for a paramilitary invasion of Cuba involving nearly 400 CIA officers as well as some 1,400 Cuban exiles, who were to carry out the attack itself. The invasion force, trained and armed by the CIA, landed at Cuba's Bay of Pigs on April 17, 1961. Castro's forces quickly routed them, blowing the cover on the operation and greatly embarrassing the Kennedy administration. As the invasion attempt faced disaster at Cuban hands, Bissell begged Kennedy to allow intervention by U.S. airplanes and naval forces, but Kennedy refused. The Bay of Pigs fiasco effectively ended Bissell's CIA career, as he was forced to leave the agency in February 1962. He subsequently worked for a think tank and then held positions in a number of private corporations. Bissell died in Farmington, Connecticut, on February 7, 1994.

Valerie Adams

See also: Bay of Pigs Invasion; Castro, Fidel; Central Intelligence Agency; Containment, Doctrine and Course of; Dulles, Allen Welsh; Eisenhower, Dwight David; Kennedy, John Fitzgerald; U-2 Overflights

References

Bissell, Richard M., Jr. *Reflections of a Cold Warrior: From Yalta to the Bay of Pigs.* New Haven, CT: Yale University Press, 1996.

Thomas, Evan. *The Very Best Men: Four Who Dared: The Early Years of the CIA.* New York: Simon and Schuster, 1995.

Bohlen, Charles Eustis (1904–1974)

U.S. diplomat. Born in Clayton, New York, on August 30, 1904, Charles "Chip" Bohlen was educated at St. Paul's School in Concord, New Hampshire, and at Harvard University. He joined the U.S. Foreign Service in 1929, becoming one of the small initial group of U.S. diplomats trained as Soviet specialists. When the United States resumed diplomatic relations with the Soviet Union in 1933, Bohlen became one of three Russian-language officers in the U.S. embassy in Moscow.

In 1942 Bohlen became assistant chief of the Russian Section of the State Department's Division of European Affairs and in 1944 was promoted to chief. He attended the Moscow Conference of Foreign Ministers in 1943 and the Tehran and Yalta summits of the Allied leaders in 1944 and 1945. Although later criticized by Sen. Joseph McCarthy of Wisconsin for acquiescing in the decisions at Yalta, Bohlen in fact had reservations as to the wisdom of U.S. policies. Deeply suspicious of Soviet actions and intentions, he advocated firm diplomatic pressure in an effort to win Soviet concessions on Eastern Europe. Appointed political adviser to the secretary of state in 1946 and State Department counselor in 1947, Bohlen helped develop Cold War containment policy.

Bohlen spent 1953 to 1957 as U.S. ambassador to the Soviet Union, and two further years as ambassador to the Philippines. In 1959 he became special assistant to Secretary of State Christian A. Herter. Preparing for the June 1960 U.S.-Soviet Paris summit, Bohlen advised President Dwight D. Eisenhower to remain resolute over West Berlin, then under considerable Soviet pressure. Bohlen accompanied Eisenhower to this meeting, which was cut short by the U-2 Affair.

In their first 18 months in office, President John F. Kennedy and Secretary of State Dean Rusk relied heavily on Bohlen's expertise. In his administration's first weeks, Kennedy consulted Bohlen on plans inherited from the Eisenhower administration to mount an invasion of Cuba and overthrow the anti-American and pro-communist government of Fidel Castro, the leader of the recent revolution. To his subsequent regret, Bohlen did not inform Kennedy and other officials of his private reservations over this venture, misgivings that derived in part from his belief that revolutionary fervor in Cuba was still strong and the Cuban people were

therefore unlikely to support the invasion. Instead, in response to specific queries Bohlen merely stated that, given the island's strategic insignificance to the Soviet Union, the Soviet Union was unlikely to intervene militarily, though it might provide Castro with arms and supplies and would undoubtedly exploit any invasion for propaganda purposes. His failure to oppose the invasion plan forthrightly, perhaps because he believed its momentum was now unstoppable, revealed the occasional limitations of Bohlen's belief that professional diplomats should function primarily as technical experts rather than policymakers.

In October 1962, when Soviet nuclear-capable missiles were discovered in Cuba, Kennedy consulted Bohlen, who counseled a mixture of firmness and restraint, suggesting that Kennedy first correspond sternly but privately with Soviet premier Nikita Khrushchev—advice the president ignored—and then declare a naval blockade of the island, the course ultimately chosen. Bohlen urged that an ultimatum demanding the removal of the missiles should precede any air strike, and he warned Kennedy in writing that an air strike "will inevitably lead to war." Bohlen was scheduled to leave for France, where Kennedy had appointed him ambassador, so attended only the first two days of meetings of the Executive Committee (ExComm) of senior advisers who handled the crisis, for fear that postponing his departure would alert the Soviets to the missiles' discovery.

Bohlen retired in 1969, warning President Richard M. Nixon not to try using China against the Soviet Union. Bohlen was publicly skeptical of both the emerging U.S. policy of détente and West German chancellor Willy Brandt's Ostpolitik opening to East Germany. He died of cancer in Washington, D.C., on January 1, 1974.

Priscilla Roberts

See also: Bay of Pigs Invasion; Castro, Fidel; Containment, Doctrine and Course of; Eisenhower, Dwight David; Kennedy, John Fitzgerald; Khrushchev, Nikita Sergeyevich; Rusk, Dean David; U-2 Overflights; U.S. Allies

References

Bohlen, Charles E. *Witness to History, 1929–69.* New York: Norton, 1973.

Isaacson, Walter, and Evan Thomas. *The Wise Men: Six Friends and the World They Made.* New York: Simon and Schuster, 1986. Mayers, David. *The Ambassadors and America's Soviet Policy.* New York: Oxford University Press, 1995.

Ruddy, T. Michael. *The Cautious Diplomat: Charles E. Bohlen and the Soviet Union, 1929–1969.* Kent, OH: Kent State University Press, 1986.

Bolshakov, Georgi Nikitovich (1922–1989)

Soviet military intelligence operative. From 1941 to 1943 Georgi Bolshakov, who was born in 1922, served in the Red Army as a Finnish-language interpreter and then a division-level intelligence officer on the northwest front. In 1943 he joined the GRU, the army intelligence service, spending three years at the General Staff High Intelligence School and four in the Soviet Army's Military-Diplomatic Academy. Graduating in 1950 with impressive English-language skills, in 1951 he went to Washington, D.C., on his first foreign assignment, remaining there for four years, ostensibly as a correspondent for the Soviet news agency, TASS. From 1955 to 1957 Bolshakov worked in Moscow as an officer for special missions on the staff of Marshal Georgi Zhukov, the Soviet defense minister, briefing him on intelligence information. Zhukov's dismissal temporarily derailed Bolshakov's career. Bolshakov's personal friendship with Aleksei Adzhubei, son-in-law of Soviet premier Nikita Khrushchev, rescued him from obscurity, and in fall 1959 he returned to Washington, supposedly a cultural attaché at the Soviet embassy. Outgoing and gregarious, unlike many of his colleagues Bolshakov socialized easily with Americans and had numerous personal contacts among the political, diplomatic, and media elite.

Through an intermediary in the press, in late April 1961 U.S. Attorney General Robert F. Kennedy, the brother of President John F. Kennedy, contacted Bolshakov. On more than 40 occasions over the next 15 months, Bolshakov served as a back-channel conduit for private messages between Khrushchev and the Kennedy administration, on the June 1961 Vienna summit meeting, the Berlin situation, and the terms of a possible nuclear test ban treaty. Seeking to conceal the dispatch of Soviet troops and weaponry to Cuba, in July 1962 the Soviet government used Bolshakov to transmit a request to the Kennedy administration to decrease its surveillance of Soviet shipping. When the Americans complied, in August Khrushchev sent thanks through Bolshakov and suggested their two countries should accelerate their efforts for a nuclear test ban treaty. As U.S. apprehensions over Soviet arms shipments to Cuba intensified throughout September and into October, on the Kremlin's instructions Bolshakov met Robert Kennedy on October 5, to assure him that the weapons the Soviet Union had dispatched were "only … of a defensive character" and could not threaten the United States, a message he repeated to leading American journalists.

Despite Robert Kennedy's anger over this disinformation, on October 23, at the height of the crisis, he apparently contacted Bolshakov

through emissaries to sound out Soviet officials on the possibility of removing NATO Jupiter nuclear missiles in Turkey and Italy, in exchange for the Soviet nuclear-capable weapons on Cuba, and to encourage the Soviets to halt further arms shipments to Cuba immediately. On November 9, when dismantling of nuclear-capable missiles was already in progress but the continued presence of Il-28 light bombers had become a sticking point, Robert Kennedy met Bolshakov in person, to request that the bombers leave Cuba in the near future, a message Kennedy repeated with harsh emphasis on November 18 when he encountered Bolshakov at a performance by the visiting Bolshoi ballet. Three days later Bolshakov delivered a message from Khrushchev that Soviet officials would remove the Il-28s.

After the Cuban Missile Crisis, the Kennedys blew Bolshakov's cover, allowing journalists friendly to them, in articles on the episode that they authorized, to reveal his role as a liaison with Khrushchev and a conduit for Soviet disinformation in October 1962. Khrushchev complained to U.S. officials that these leaks compromised his use of such channels. In December 1962, hostile embassy officials engineered Bolshakov's recall to Moscow. Relegated to a bureaucratic limbo of routine office chores, Bolshakov sought consolation in alcohol and the company of women. In a rather bizarre footnote to their relationship, after his brother's assassination Robert Kennedy sent a close family associate, William Walton, to meet with Bolshakov in Moscow. Walton told Bolshakov that the president's death was due to a right-wing plot by Americans who sought to undermine his policies of U.S.-Soviet détente and that Lyndon B. Johnson, the new president, lacked his predecessor's commitment to improving relations between their two countries, information that undercut Johnson's own efforts to reassure Soviet leaders that he would continue Kennedy's approach to international affairs. The convivial Bolshakov survived until 1989, but his career never regained its former momentum.

Priscilla Roberts

See also: ANADYR, Operation; Berlin Crises; Johnson, Lyndon Baines; Jupiter Missiles (Turkey and Italy); Kennedy, John Fitzgerald; Kennedy, Robert Francis; Khrushchev, Nikita Sergeyevich; Partial Test Ban Treaty; Vienna Conference

References

Fursenko, Aleksandr, and Timothy Naftali. *One Hell of a Gamble: Khrushchev, Castro, and Kennedy, 1958–1964.* New York: Norton, 1997.

Polmar, Norman, and John D. Gresham. *DEFCON-2: Standing on the Brink of Nuclear War during the Cuban Missile Crisis.* New York: John Wiley, 2006.

Bundy, McGeorge (1919–1996)

U.S. special assistant for national security affairs, 1961–1966. Born on March 30, 1919, in Boston, McGeorge Bundy came from a prominent Boston family with a strong tradition of public service. He excelled academically at Groton School, Connecticut, and Yale University. From 1941 to 1945 he served in the army. After helping former secretary of state and secretary of war Henry L. Stimson write his memoirs, *On Active Service in Peace and War* (1948), laying out that influential statesman's worldview for future generations, in 1950 Bundy began teaching government and international affairs at Harvard University, where in 1953 he became dean of Arts and Sciences.

In 1961 President John F. Kennedy, whom Bundy had advised during his presidential campaign, appointed him special assistant for national security affairs, a position in which he greatly overshadowed Secretary of State Dean Rusk. Bundy shared with Kennedy a strong faith in the centrality of U.S. power and the need to employ it. Bundy was known for intellectual brilliance, energy, swift assimilation of information, and wit, though critics subsequently suggested that as dean and public official these superficial qualities masked an absence of deeper reflection or any firm moral compass, and tendencies to accept prevailing conventional Cold War wisdom and accord overly high priority to pragmatic considerations of political expediency. Bundy thought it his function to be a competent manager, rather than an innovative formulator of policy; to ensure that the president was briefed on both sides of issues, he sometimes played devil's advocate. As Kennedy's gatekeeper on foreign affairs, Bundy controlled the access of both information and individuals to the president, prepared agendas for National Security Council meetings, and selected personnel for task forces Kennedy established to handle specific foreign policy problems.

A few weeks after taking power, Bundy voted for the disastrous April 1961 Bay of Pigs invasion attempt against Cuba, which brought international humiliation on the United States. Bundy proffered his resignation to Kennedy, which the president refused, and conducted postmortems on the abortive operation. During the Cuban Missile Crisis, when the U.S. government discovered Soviet nuclear-capable missiles in Cuba and

demanded their withdrawal, it was Bundy who informed Kennedy that U.S. overflights had detected the presence of these weapons. Surprisingly indecisive, in Executive Committee (ExComm) meetings of Kennedy's top advisers, Bundy initially supported air strikes to destroy the missiles, subsequently endorsed the naval quarantine option Kennedy eventually selected, yet then switched once more to air strikes. When Soviet premier Nikita Khrushchev sent two somewhat contradictory responses to Kennedy's ultimatum on Cuba on October 26 and 27, it was Bundy who suggested replying only to the first, less confrontational message. Reflecting later on this crisis, in his book *Danger and Survival* (1988), Bundy suggested that Kennedy employed "a certain excess of rhetoric," when Americans would have found more moderate language less alarming.

By far the most controversial aspect of Bundy's government service was his responsibility for the escalation of U.S. involvement in Vietnam. Despite some personal misgivings, Bundy acquiesced in the expansion of U.S. commitments to South Vietnam under both Kennedy and his successor, Lyndon B. Johnson. In 1966 Bundy left Johnson's administration to head the Ford Foundation, which he did until 1979. The issue of his responsibility for U.S. intervention in Vietnam perennially dogged Bundy, effectively destroying his chances of becoming secretary of state or president of a major university. Following the gentleman's code in which he was reared, Bundy refused either to defend his record or to criticize Johnson administration policies publicly, and for the rest of his life he rarely even discussed them. By late 1967 Bundy supported gradual troop withdrawals from Vietnam. After the massive early 1968 Tet offensive, Bundy and most of the other "Wise Men" the administration consulted told a shocked Johnson that victory was unattainable and recommended that the United States open peace negotiations with North Vietnam. For 10 years from 1979 Bundy taught at New York University, writing on nuclear policy and in 1982, together with George F. Kennan, Robert S. McNamara, and Gerard Smith, calling for no U.S. first use of nuclear weapons. On September 10, 1996, he died suddenly of heart failure in Boston.

Priscilla Roberts

See also: Bay of Pigs Invasion; Containment, Doctrine and Course of; Johnson, Lyndon Baines; Kennedy, John Fitzgerald; Khrushchev, Nikita Sergeyevich; McNamara, Robert Strange; Military Balance; Nuclear Arms Race; Rusk, Dean David; U-2 Overflights

References

Bird, Kai. *The Color of Truth: McGeorge Bundy and William Bundy, Brothers in Arms; A Biography.* New York: Simon and Schuster, 1998.

Bundy, McGeorge. *Danger and Survival: Choices about the Bomb in the First Fifty Years.* New York: Random House, 1988.

Goldstein, Gordon M. *Lessons in Disaster: McGeorge Bundy and the Path to War in Vietnam.* New York: Times Books, 2008.

Halberstam, David. *The Best and the Brightest.* New York: Random House, 1973.

Kabaservice, Geoffrey. *The Guardians: Kingman Brewster, His Circle, and the Rise of the Liberal Establishment.* New York: Henry Holt, 2004.

Nuenlist, Christian. *Kennedys rechte hand: McGeorge Bundys rolle als national sicherheitsberater, 1961–63* [Kennedy's Right Hand: McGeorge Bundy's Role as National Security Adviser, 1961–63]. Zurich: Center for Security Studies, 1999.

Preston, Andrew. *The War Council: McGeorge Bundy, the NSC, and Vietnam.* Cambridge, MA: Harvard University Press, 2006.

C

Castro, Fidel (1926–)

Cuban communist revolutionary guerrilla fighter and leader of Cuba, January 1959–July 2006. Fidel Alejandro Castro Ruz was born on August 13, 1926, in the municipality of Mayarí (Oriente Province). His father was a wealthy sugarcane planter of Spanish origin. Castro studied at the University of Havana. Here his political formation began in the action-oriented and often violent student politics of the period. As part of a movement by those disaffected with government corruption, he joined the new Ortodoxo (Orthodox) Party led by Eduardo Chibás and in 1947 participated in actions to overthrow Dominican Republic dictator Rafael Trujillo. In 1948 Castro attended a student congress in Bogotá, Colombia, where major disturbances erupted after the assassination of the popular radical politician Jorge Gaitán. In 1950 he earned his law degree.

After Gen. Fulgencio Batista's 1952 Cuban military coup, Castro and his Orthodox Party allies initiated a campaign of resistance against the newly installed dictatorship. On July 26, 1953, the youthful rebels attacked the Moncada military barracks in Santiago de Cuba, the country's second-largest city. The assault failed, and Castro was ultimately imprisoned on the island of Pines. His defense speech at his trial, titled "History Will Absolve Me," was a powerful denunciation of social and economic injustice that would subsequently become a rallying cry in his struggle against the Batista regime.

In 1955 Castro, released from prison as part of a general amnesty, took refuge in Mexico. There he and his comrades, who would eventually establish the July 26 Movement, connected with Argentinian physician and revolutionary Ernesto "Che" Guevara. In December 1956

Cuban president Fidel Castro, the epitome of a romantic revolutionary leader, eloquently criticizes the Eisenhower administration's economic policies toward Cuba during a televised address on July 19, 1960. His fear of the United States led Castro to turn to the Soviet Union for assistance. (AP/Wide World Photos)

Castro, Guevara, and their followers sailed from Mexico on board the yacht *Granma* and landed in southeastern Cuba, beginning a two-year military and political campaign to overthrow the U.S.-supported Batista regime. In the last days of 1958 Batista fled the island, and Castro entered Havana in triumph in January 1959.

From then onward, Castro steadily increased his influence. In February 1959 he made himself prime minister. In April 1959, Castro visited the United States, where his radical views and uncompromising behavior alarmed prominent U.S. officials, including Vice President Richard Nixon. Increasingly, Castro based his regime on anti-Americanism. During 1959–1962 he moved Cuba radically to the Left. His agrarian reforms and their consequences—confrontation with the United States over American investments in Cuba and U.S. support for counterrevolutionary movements culminating in the 1961 Bay of Pigs invasion—caused a break in diplomatic relations with the United States. In December 1961 Castro declared that he was a Marxist-Leninist. He strengthened Cuba's economic, political, and military ties with the Soviet Union steadily throughout the 1960s.

In summer 1962, Castro accepted a Soviet offer to install assorted short-, intermediate-, and medium-range nuclear-capable missiles in Cuba, as a deterrent against future U.S. invasions. In October 1962 U.S. overflights revealed the presence of missile installations to U.S. President John F. Kennedy, who publicly demanded that the Soviet Union withdraw these missiles. Castro urged Soviet leader Nikita Khrushchev to refuse these demands and if necessary to defend Cuba by initiating a nuclear first strike on the United States, counsel Khrushchev rejected. Indeed Castro was

excluded from negotiations over the missiles, and the fact that he learned of the eventual settlement through the media deeply humiliated him, provoking Cuban anger over the perceived Soviet betrayal of Cuban interests.

As talks among Soviet, U.S., and UN representatives on the details of removing the missiles and other military hardware proceeded in November 1962, Castro turned recalcitrant. He issued his own proposals for a settlement, including the return to Cuba of the U.S. military base at Guantánamo Bay and the cessation of all U.S. sanctions against Cuba. He refused to allow on-site inspections of missile bases in Cuba, unsuccessfully attempted to retain tactical nuclear-capable missiles and several squadrons of Soviet Il-28 light bombers, and threatened to shoot down U.S. aircraft conducting reconnaissance overflights to ensure that the missiles had indeed departed. Seeking to mollify Castro, in April and May 1963 Khrushchev hosted him on a month-long visit during which he toured the Soviet Union, met top military and political leaders, and received substantial quantities of armaments, including tanks and antiaircraft equipment. Castro also persuaded Khrushchev to station a brigade of Soviet troops indefinitely on the island, forces that Khrushchev had originally hoped to remove.

The aftermath of the missile crisis initiated a complex period in Cuban-Soviet relations characterized by Castro's suspicion of the Soviet Union's motives tempered by a growing reliance on Soviet economic assistance. While Cuba became a member of Comecon and received important Soviet military aid in the 1960s, Castro's foreign policy, especially in Latin America, embraced the strategy of armed revolution conducted by guerrilla movements in Guatemala, Venezuela, Peru, and Bolivia. This challenged Soviet support for policies of peaceful coexistence with the West.

As the 1960s ended, the failure of the first wave of Castro-inspired guerrilla wars and the collapse of his ambitious plans to industrialize Cuba and produce a record 10 million–ton sugar crop in 1970 led to an accommodation with Soviet economic and strategic goals in the 1970s. Steady economic growth and institutionalization weakened Cuba's commitment to continental and even worldwide revolution. However, adjustment to Soviet economic orthodoxy did not completely erode Castro's commitment to socialist liberation movements.

As he had with Guevara's 1967–1968 revolutionary expedition in Bolivia, Castro assisted revolutionary movements and left-wing governments in the 1980s in Grenada, El Salvador, and Nicaragua. He began sending Cuban military forces to Angola in November 1975, which helped turn the tide there against South Africa's attempt to defeat the left-wing Movimento Popular da Libertação de Angola (MPLA) (Popular Movement for the

Liberation of Angola) in Angola. Some see the Cuban victory in the 1988 Battle of Cuito Carnavale as the beginning of the end of the apartheid regime.

The renewed Cold War of the 1980s ended with the defeat of the Cuban-supported Sandinista government in Nicaragua and a negotiated settlement ending the civil war in El Salvador, which pitted Cuban-supported Farabundo Martí National Liberation Front (FLMN) forces against a series of U.S.-backed governments. The collapse of communism in Eastern Europe and the dissolution of the Soviet Union itself in 1991 were serious setbacks for Castro both economically, with a sharp falloff in foreign aid, and diplomatically. In the 1990s Castro announced the launching of "The Special Period in Times of Peace," inaugurating a shift away from Soviet-style economic institutions toward limited tolerance of private economic enterprises. It also embraced tourism and encouraged investments from Europe, Asia, Canada, and Latin America.

The end of the Cold War did not, as most observers anticipated, precipitate the demise of Castro's regime. Notwithstanding his adoption of many Soviet models, the indigenous, nationalist roots of Cuba's noncapitalist path since 1959 continued to confound predictions. Suffering from health problems, on July 31, 2006, Castro transferred his responsibilities as president of Cuba, commander-in-chief, and Communist Party secretary to his younger brother Raúl on an acting basis. On Castro's initiative, in February 2008 Raúl formally succeeded to these positions in his own right. Although in his 80s, Fidel continued to write for the press and deliver occasional public speeches.

Priscilla Roberts

See also: Alekseev (Shitov), Aleksandr Ivanovich; ANADYR, Operation; Batista y Zaldívar, Fulgencio; Bay of Pigs Invasion; Castro, Raúl; Central Intelligence Agency; China, People's Republic of; Containment, Doctrine and Course of; Eisenhower, Dwight David; Guevara de la Serna, Ernesto "Che"; Kennedy, John Fitzgerald; Kennedy, Robert Francis; Khrushchev, Nikita Sergeyevich; Nuclear Arms Race; U-2 Overflights; United Nations

References

Balfour, Sebastian. *Castro.* 3rd ed. Harlow, England: Longmans, 2009.

Castro, Fidel, and Ignacio Ramonet. *My Life: A Spoken Autobiography.* Translated by Andrew Hurley. New York: Scribner, 2007.

Pérez, Louis A. *Cuba: Between Reform and Revolution.* 4th ed. New York: Oxford University Press, 2011.

Paterson, Thomas G. *Contesting Castro: The United States and the Triumph of the Cuban Revolution.* New York: Oxford University Press, 1994.

Szulc, Tad. *Fidel: A Critical Portrait.* New York: William Morrow, 1986.

Welch, Richard E., Jr. *Response to Revolution: The United States and the Cuban Revolution, 1959–1961.* Chapel Hill: University of North Carolina Press, 1985.

Castro, Raúl (1931–)

Gen. Raúl Castro, the younger brother of revolutionary and longtime Cuban leader Fidel Castro, became Cuba's second president and commander in chief in 2008. A longtime fixture in the government, he was the chosen successor to his elder brother, whose trusted confidant he had been since boyhood.

Raúl Castro Ruz was born on June 3, 1931, near the city of Biran in Oriente Province, the fifth of seven children of a Spanish immigrant father and a Cuban Creole mother. After attending Jesuit schools, he entered the University of Havana, where he became a passionate socialist, even traveling to Europe to attend communist youth rallies. After returning to Cuba, he joined his brother Fidel in an unsuccessful 1953 attempt to overthrow the government of Fulgencio Batista. For his efforts, Castro was sentenced to 15 years in prison. He received amnesty, was released from jail in 1954, and fled with Fidel to Mexico to organize a second coup against the Cuban government.

The Castro brothers, joined by other revolutionaries, trained in Mexico for 18 months and in November 1956 launched another attack, which was foiled by government soldiers. Thirty of the 82 rebels who had sailed in from Mexico escaped into the mountains of the Sierra Maestra. Assisted by Oriente peasants, Fidel and Raúl organized a new army, which succeeded in ousting Batista on January 1, 1959. When Fidel was sworn in as Cuba's prime minister on February 16, 1959, Raúl replaced him as commander of the armed forces. In October that year, his position became a cabinet-level ministership. His place in the government was secure from then onward, and he remained minister for the armed forces until 2008.

With fellow revolutionary Ernesto "Che" Guevara, like him already a committed communist, Raúl Castro was among the more radical members of the Cuban revolutionary government, which by 1961 was clearly orienting itself to the Soviet Union and adopting communist policies. The two men developed close ties with Aleksandr Alekseev, a KGB (Soviet espionage) agent who established himself in Cuba in October 1959 and became Soviet ambassador to Cuba in May 1962. In July 1960 Raúl Castro visited Moscow, meeting Soviet premier Nikita Khrushchev and other

top leaders, and signing a joint communiqué whereby the Soviet Union affirmed its opposition to "an armed United States intervention against the Cuban republic." He also obtained promises of Soviet weaponry for Cuba. Raúl Castro was outspoken against the United States, which further disrupted Cuban-U.S. relations. His tirades grew in intensity after the April 1961 Bay of Pigs invasion attempt and the U.S. imposition of an even tighter economic embargo. As 1961 ended, he helped Fidel establish the single-party system of Marxist-Leninist ideology and what would eventually become the Cuban Communist Party.

Raúl Castro was elated when Soviet officials offered in June 1962 to base nuclear-capable missiles in Cuba. On a July 1962 visit to Moscow, he helped negotiate the draft Cuban-Soviet defense treaty detailing the terms governing the operations of the new Soviet forces in Cuba. Although he would have preferred an immediate public announcement of their deployment, as opposed to their surreptitious installation, the arrival of the missiles in September 1962 gave Raúl and other Cuban leaders a new sense of invulnerability to U.S. attack. In the aftermath of the crisis, he tried to repair Cuban-Soviet relations and defuse his brother Fidel's bitter resentment over Soviet concessions to the United States and the withdrawal of the missiles. In subsequent years, Raúl Castro often assumed the duties of foreign minister, traveling to the Soviet Union for meetings and to Africa to offer military support to emerging communist nations.

A government reorganization in 1972 made Castro—who served concurrently as minister for the armed forces from 1959 to 2008—first vice-premier; in 1976, he was appointed first vice president of both the Council of State and the Council of Ministers. He also served as deputy general secretary of the Communist Party. At the October 1997 party congress, Fidel made it clear that Raúl would succeed him as party leader. The first step toward this succession was taken in July 2006, when Raúl assumed de facto control of the presidency, the party, and the military as Fidel underwent surgery. As Fidel recovered over the next two years, Raúl quietly held power in Cuba, largely avoiding the limelight as Fidel's health remained a major story internationally and domestically. On February 18, 2008, Fidel publicly declared that, given his poor physical condition, he would resign the presidency. Six days later, the National Assembly of People's Power elected Raúl president by a unanimous show of hands, making him the second president of Cuba since the Cuban Revolution.

Raúl was regarded as more practical than Fidel on economic issues: in 1993 he helped push for economic reforms after the collapse of the Soviet Union. He was not, however, considered Fidel's equal in terms of charisma

or diplomacy, which might handicap his effectiveness in a country where a cult of personality had been fostered since 1959.

Priscilla Roberts

See also: Alekseev (Shitov), Aleksandr Ivanovich; ANADYR, Operation; Bay of Pigs Invasion; Castro, Fidel; Guevara de la Serna, Ernesto "Che"; Khrushchev, Nikita Sergeyevich

References

Font, Mauricio A., with Scott Larson, eds. *Cuba: In Transition? Pathways to Renewal, Long-Term Development and Global Reintegration.* New York: The Bildner Center for Western Hemisphere Studies, City University of New York, 2006.

Fursenko, Aleksandr, and Timothy Naftali. *One Hell of a Gamble: Khrushchev, Castro, and Kennedy, 1958–1964.* New York: Norton, 1997.

Pérez, Louis A. *Cuba: Between Reform and Revolution.* 4th ed. New York: Oxford University Press, 2011.

Pérez-Stable, Marifeli. *The Cuban Revolution: Origins, Course, and Legacy.* New York: Oxford University Press, 1993.

Rosendahl, Mona. *Inside the Revolution: Everyday Life in Socialist Cuba.* Ithaca, NY: Cornell University Press, 1997.

Wright, Thomas C. *Latin America in the Era of the Cuban Revolution.* Rev. ed. Westport, CT: Praeger, 2001.

Central Intelligence Agency (CIA)

Principal intelligence and counterintelligence agency of the U.S. government, formally created in 1947. The Central Intelligence Agency's roots were in a World War II espionage organization, the Office of Strategic Services (OSS). The OSS was disbanded in October 1945, but the developing Cold War soon persuaded the administration of President Harry S. Truman that the United States' greatly expanded postwar international role demanded a much enhanced coordinated intelligence establishment as part of the growing defense bureaucracy.

A January 1946 presidential executive order created a Central Intelligence Group and National Intelligence Authority, whose personnel attempted to centralize postwar intelligence activities. These were disbanded when in 1947 Congress passed the National Security Act, which formally established the National Security Council (NSC) and, under it, the Central Intelligence Agency. According to this act, the CIA's mandate included

Aerial view of the San Cristobal medium range ballistic missile launch site number two, Cuba, November 1, 1962. In the immediate aftermath of the crisis, American overflights continued to monitor the presence on Cuba of Soviet missiles and their eventual removal. (U.S. Air Force)

advising the NSC on intelligence activities and making recommendations as to their coordination; the correlation, evaluation, and dissemination of intelligence; and the performance of such intelligence functions and other activities as the NSC might assign to it.

As the Cold War intensified, from December 1947 through 1948 the NSC promptly ordered an immediate and drastic expansion of the CIA's covert operations, and in September 1948 it established the agency's Office of Policy Coordination, to handle such activities with overall guidance from the State and Defense departments. The Central Intelligence Agency Act of 1949 exempted CIA activities from most accounting and procedural limitations on federal expenditures, enabling it to keep its budget secret.

The CIA's failure in June 1950 to predict North Korea's invasion of South Korea led its second director, Gen. Walter Bedell Smith, appointed the following October, to strengthen intelligence collection and analysis within the agency. He established the Office of National Estimates to provide coordinated intelligence analysis; the Office of Research and Reports

to predict economic changes within the Soviet bloc; and the Directorate for Intelligence to furnish finished intelligence.

Allen Welsh Dulles, Smith's successor as director from 1953 to 1961 and the brother of Dwight D. Eisenhower's Secretary of State John Foster Dulles, was a lawyer and flamboyant former OSS operative who presided over what was perhaps the CIA's heyday. Apart from gathering and analyzing intelligence, the CIA launched a wide variety of sometimes spectacular clandestine operations, including the organization of successful pro-American coups in Iran and Costa Rica in 1953 and Guatemala in 1954 and less effective covert activities in Indonesia, Tibet, and Cuba. These culminated in the disastrous U.S.-backed Bay of Pigs invasion of Cuba in April 1961—a humiliating failure marked by inadequate planning and resources and wishful thinking, which brought about the resignation of Dulles and his deputy, Richard Bissell.

The CIA's new director, John A. McCone, put more emphasis on intelligence-gathering and analysis, though the agency still undertook a wide range of covert activities. Prominent among these was Operation MONGOOSE, a range of secret operations—some so far-fetched as to be comically fantastic—intended to destabilize and discredit Fidel Castro's government in Cuba and assassinate Castro himself. In summer 1962 a CIA group concluded that these ventures were unlikely to succeed, but sabotage and paramilitary operations continued, as the CIA infiltrated various anti-Castro guerrilla groups into Cuba.

During the Cuban Missile Crisis, U.S. intelligence was generally far more accurate than it had been during the Bay of Pigs invasion. Alerted by reports of growing deliveries of Soviet weaponry to Cuba, from August 1962 McCone suspected these might include nuclear armaments, and he pressed the White House to authorize surveillance overflights. On October 14 a high-flying U-2 reconnaissance plane produced photographic evidence of potential nuclear-capable missile sites on Cuba.

McCone was a frequent presence at the subsequent Executive Committee (ExComm) meetings of top U.S. officials convened to handle the situation. His preferred option was a full-scale U.S. invasion of Cuba, preceded by air strikes on the missile installations. Other CIA officials who attended in order to give briefings included Arthur C. Lundahl, head of the National Photographic Interpretation Center, who notified his superiors of the probable existence of missile sites on October 15. Ray Cline, CIA deputy director of intelligence, a strong advocate of a hard line against Cuba, also briefed ExComm members. As the crisis continued, the CIA flew additional U-2 missions over Cuba, which returned with evidence

suggesting the presence of substantially more installations than those first detected. The only fatality of the Cuban Missile Crisis occurred on October 27, when Soviet surface-to-air missile batteries shot down the U-2 piloted by Maj. Rudolf Anderson.

Throughout the crisis, CIA officials continued to receive information from sources within Cuba. Unknown to ExComm members and without their authorization, during the crisis the CIA also sent several anti-Castro teams into Cuba, one of which was captured by Cuban forces on October 25. On November 8, with the process of dismantling the missile bases well under way, a CIA sabotage unit attacked and destroyed a Cuban industrial plant, adding a further level of tension to the last days of the crisis. Perhaps alarmed that the program was out of control and jeopardizing any potential rapprochement with Cuba, in spring 1963 the federal government closed down many training camps for Cuban exiles in the United States. Sabotage and assassination plots against Castro continued until April 1964, when the Johnson administration called a halt to them.

Throughout the 1960s the CIA mounted extensive covert operations in Southeast Asia in support of U.S. intervention in Vietnam. Growing opposition to the Vietnam War brought new congressional and public demands for CIA accountability. During the 1970s and 1980s books scathingly critical of CIA activities regularly appeared. In 1974 CIA director William E. Colby responded by providing Congress with a detailed list of all illegal domestic and overseas CIA covert operations. For decades, however, additional evidence and revelations of CIA involvement in a wide range of illicit or clandestine activities within and beyond the United States, of which Cuba-related operations were representative but by no means unique, continued to surface.

Priscilla Roberts

See also: Bay of Pigs Invasion; Bissell, Richard Mervin, Jr.; Castro, Fidel; Containment, Doctrine and Course of; Dulles, Allen Welsh; Dulles, John Foster; Eisenhower, Dwight David; Kennedy, John Fitzgerald; Kennedy, Robert Francis; Lansdale, Edward Geary; McCone, John Alex; MONGOOSE, Operation; U-2 Overflights

References

Brugioni, Dino. *Eyeball to Eyeball: The Inside Story of the Cuban Missile Crisis.* Edited by Robert F. McCort. New York: Random House, 1991.

Cline, Ray S. *Secrets, Spies and Scholars: Blueprint of the Essential CIA.* Washington, DC: Acropolis Books, 1976.

Dobbs, Michael. *One Minute to Midnight: Kennedy, Khrushchev, and Castro on the Brink of Nuclear War.* New York: Knopf, 2008.

Higgins, Trumbull. *The Perfect Failure: Kennedy, Eisenhower, and the CIA at the Bay of Pigs.* New York: Norton, 1987.

Jeffreys-Jones, Rhodri. *The CIA and American Democracy.* 2nd ed. New Haven, CT: Yale University Press, 1998.

Kornbluh, Peter, ed. *Bay of Pigs Declassified: The Secret CIA Report on the Invasion of Cuba.* New York: New Press, 1998.

McAuliffe, Mary S., ed. *CIA Documents on the Cuban Missile Crisis, 1962.* Washington, DC: Central Intelligence Agency, 1992.

Prados, John. *Presidents' Secret Wars: CIA and Pentagon Covert Operations from World War II through the Persian Gulf.* Rev. ed. Chicago: Ivan R. Dee, 1996.

Ranelagh, John. *The Agency: The Rise and Decline of the CIA.* London: Weidenfeld & Nicolson, 1986.

Weiner, Tim. *Legacy of Ashes: The History of the CIA.* New York: Doubleday, 2006.

China, People's Republic of (PRC)

The People's Republic of China was founded in 1949 when communists won control of the Chinese mainland in a civil war, restricting the former government to the island of Taiwan (Republic of China, or ROC). By 1959, when Fidel Castro established a leftist government in Cuba, Chinese Communist Party Chairman Mao Zedong was at odds with the Soviet Union. Disdaining Soviet premier Nikita Khrushchev's policies of peaceful coexistence with the West, Mao argued that armed struggle was the necessary precondition for the spread of communism. Mao advanced his own radical brand of communism as a rival to Soviet ideological theories. Mao's readiness to risk nuclear war with the United States by threatening Taiwan, a U.S. ally and client, also alarmed Khrushchev. In the late 1950s the Soviet Union ceased assisting China's nuclear program, and in 1960 Khrushchev recalled almost all Soviet technical advisers and experts from China. Both China and the Soviet Union publicly denounced each other's positions at a 1960 Romanian Communist Party Conference, and vitriolic mutual criticism continued throughout the 1960s.

The Sino-Soviet split intensified Khrushchev's eagerness to demonstrate his revolutionary bona fides by supporting Cuba. He also sought to keep Cuba in the Soviet rather than the Chinese camp, a concern Castro exploited to extract additional Soviet aid. From September 1960 onward, when

Cuba withdrew diplomatic recognition from Taiwan and opened diplomatic relations with the People's Republic, the first Latin American nation to do so, China sent substantial quantities of military technology to Cuba. In fall 1961, Castro asked the Soviet Union for much larger arms shipments than previously, especially of antiaircraft missiles. When Khrushchev proved slow to respond, Castro purged his government of several pro-Moscow communists and opened talks with China on possible economic assistance. He also began setting up partisan guerrilla groups to spread revolution throughout Latin America. When Soviet KGB officers cautiously declined to establish a training camp for this purpose in Cuba, Castro's representatives made unfavorable comparisons between Soviet and Chinese approaches to popular insurgencies. Khrushchev's desire to emphasize that he could champion international revolution more effectively than Mao was one factor impelling him to offer nuclear-capable missiles to Cuba in May 1962.

During the Cuban Missile Crisis, China enthusiastically supported the Soviets, publishing laudatory editorials in the state-controlled press, and Khrushchev responded by backing China in the concurrent Sino-Indian War. The U.S. military included the Chinese embassy in Havana, which had already featured as a possible target for clandestine U.S.-backed sabotage operations, among potential air strike objectives. The rapprochement was short-lived. Chinese leaders responded with disappointment to the peaceful resolution of the crisis. On October 29, 1962, the Chinese apparently sent a note to the Cubans "implying that the U.S.S.R. was an untrustworthy ally," one that had since 1959 refused to provide China with information on the production of nuclear arms. The Chinese privately urged Castro to withstand Soviet pressure for a swift settlement. At a World Peace Council meeting in Stockholm, Chinese delegates characterized the Soviet decision as "cowardly." Khrushchev, meanwhile, complained that the only Chinese assistance during the confrontation had been an offer by Chinese embassy staff in Cuba to donate blood to Cuba's hospitals.

As U.S.-Soviet negotiations on the details of removing missiles from Cuba proceeded, China vigorously supported demands by Castro for a complete U.S. withdrawal from Cuba, including the Guantánamo Bay military base, and the cessation of all U.S. measures against Cuba, including economic sanctions. Publicly, Chinese officials condemned the Soviet decision to withdraw the missiles as a Soviet Munich, criticizing Khrushchev's action in installing them as "adventurist" and their removal as "appeasement." In Beijing, Mao refused to meet the Soviet ambassador. With Cuban revolutionaries deeply divided and some siding openly with China, Castro proclaimed that Cuba would remain "neutral" toward the Sino-Soviet conflict.

In late 1962 and 1963 the war of words escalated. Khrushchev attacked the Chinese for tolerating the existence of colonial enclaves on their own territory, in Macau and Hong Kong. The Chinese responded by claiming that over 1 million square miles of Chinese territory in Siberia ceded to Russia in the 1860s likewise constituted a colonial enclave, implying they might no longer accept its loss. When Soviet officials embarked on "ideological consultations" with Chinese officials in July 1963 to repair the breach, the Chinese delegation, led by Deng Xiaoping, responded with further invective, again charging Khrushchev with rashness in deploying the missiles and "capitulationism" in ultimately withdrawing them. Chinese polemics also targeted the nuclear test ban treaty Khrushchev and U.S. president John F. Kennedy negotiated at that time, which the Chinese interpreted as directed at their own nuclear program. Kennedy and his advisers believed that the added strains the missile crisis and the treaty placed on Sino-Soviet relations did much to make the split permanent.

Priscilla Roberts

See also: Castro, Fidel; Guantánamo Bay Naval Base; Khrushchev, Nikita Sergeyevich; Partial Test Ban Treaty

References

Freedman, Lawrence. *Kennedy's Wars: Berlin, Cuba, Laos, and Vietnam.* New York: Oxford University Press, 2000.

Fursenko, Aleksandr, and Timothy Naftali. *Khrushchev's Cold War: The Inside Story of an American Adversary.* New York: Norton, 2006.

Fursenko, Aleksandr, and Timothy Naftali. *One Hell of a Gamble: Khrushchev, Castro, and Kennedy, 1958–1964.* New York: Norton, 1997.

Lüthi, Lorenz M. *The Sino-Soviet Split: Cold War in the Communist World.* Princeton, NJ: Princeton University Press, 2008.

Radchenko, Sergey. *Two Suns in the Heavens: The Sino-Soviet Struggle for Supremacy, 1962–1967.* Washington, DC, and Stanford, CA: Wilson Center Press and Stanford University Press, 2009.

Containment, Doctrine and Course of

Fundamental controlling U.S. Cold War strategy, designed to prevent further expansion of Soviet power.

As relations between the United States and the Soviet Union deteriorated in the months after World War II ended, in February 1946 the administration of President Harry S. Truman requested George F. Kennan, counselor in the U.S. embassy in Moscow and a Soviet expert, to explain the rationale behind Soviet policies. In perhaps the seminal document of the Cold War, Kennan replied with the 8,000-word "Long Telegram." He stated that, since Soviet antagonism toward the West arose from the need of Russian rulers to justify their oppressive domestic rule as essential to combat hostility from foreign powers, Western states could do little to alter Soviet policies. Instead, they must adopt policies of "long-term, patient but firm and vigilant containment," firmly resisting attempts to expand Soviet influence while awaiting internal changes to the nature of Soviet government. Kennan's telegram, circulated throughout the higher echelons of the U.S. government, and his subsequent article "The Sources of Soviet Conduct," published in the influential quarterly *Foreign Affairs,* quickly became definitive documents of U.S. Cold War strategy. From then until the early 1990s the word "containment" described the underlying U.S. policy toward the Soviet Union.

Kennan, who returned to Washington to head the newly created Policy Planning Staff, charged with the long-range planning of U.S. foreign policy, soon deprecated the increasingly military emphasis of containment, subsequently claiming he had envisaged that the United States would rely primarily upon peaceful economic and cultural counterpressure to check Soviet expansion. In a March 1947 address (the "Truman Doctrine" speech), President Harry S. Truman publicly pledged to assist any country where democracy was threatened either externally or internally by communism, simultaneously extending substantial economic and military aid to both Greece and Turkey, and some months later announcing the massive Marshall Plan or European Recovery Program to assist with Europe's economic rebuilding.

By 1950 prominent civilian and military officials sought to expand U.S. defense budgets substantially, considering this essential to enable the country to meet increasing international obligations, including membership in the 1949 North Atlantic Treaty Organization (NATO) West European security pact, it had assumed, and to counter the recent Soviet acquisition of atomic weapons and the establishment of a communist state in mainland China. Various State and Defense Department representatives, led by Paul H. Nitze, Kennan's successor on the Policy Planning Staff, argued that, should war break out, the United States lacked the military resources even to fulfill its existing commitments. Implicitly, they endorsed the 1947 Truman Doctrine. The planning paper NSC-68, which

they drafted and delivered to Truman in April 1950, demanded massive enhancements in U.S. conventional and nuclear military capabilities, including substantially enhanced U.S. troop contributions to NATO forces in Europe, stating, "Without superior aggregate military strength, in being and readily mobilizable, a policy of 'containment' … is no more than a policy of bluff." NSC-68 envisaged increasing the existing $13.5 billion U.S. defense budget to anywhere between $18 and $50 billion, recommendations the economy-conscious Truman initially rejected.

The outbreak of the Korean War in June 1950 proved crucial to both the implementation of NSC-68 and the effective globalization of the Cold War, broadening its initial primarily European focus. U.S. defense spending soared in Europe as well as Asia, reaching $48 billion in fiscal 1951 and $61 billion the following year, and after the armistice it still remained far higher than previously. In June 1950 the United States had 1,460,000 military personnel, of whom 280,000 were stationed abroad; four years later the totals were 3,555,000 and 963,000 respectively. The Mutual Security Program, instituted in 1951, furnished military assistance to a wide array of U.S. clients and allies. By the late 1950s the United States had established numerous additional security pacts, including the Rio Pact covering Latin America, the Central Treaty Organization (CENTO) in the Middle East, the Southeast Asian Treaty Organization, the ANZUS defense pact with Australia and New Zealand, and bilateral treaties with South Korea, Japan, and the Republic of China on Taiwan. Covert operations by the Central Intelligence Agency often ensured that any new overseas government unsympathetic to the United States proved short-lived, as in Iran, Guatemala, and later Chile.

Despite rhetorical pronouncements in the 1950s by the administration of President Dwight D. Eisenhower that the United States would "roll back" communism in Eastern Europe and elsewhere, in practice, after Communist Chinese intervention balked U.S. efforts to "liberate" North Korea in autumn 1950, U.S. strategy sought primarily to prevent further communist gains, particularly in countries undergoing decolonization, that were often perceived as subjects for U.S.-Soviet competition. In the late 1950s and early 1960s this outlook led successive U.S. presidents to increase incrementally aid to the southern portion of Vietnam, where communist takeover by the north threatened the existing regime. After 1975 the effective U.S. defeat in this costly conflict, the greatest military humiliation in U.S. history, led the United States to avoid further large-scale interventions, relying instead upon surrogates, such as anti-Soviet guerrilla forces in Afghanistan during the 1980s. Exploiting the Sino-Soviet split,

from the early 1970s onward U.S. leaders differentiated between Chinese and Russian communism, using each socialist big power's distrust of the other to win concessions for the United States.

U.S. military strategy in the 1950s relied heavily on nuclear weapons—because they could inflict far greater casualties at much less cost than conventional forces—a policy termed the "New Look," whose potential to risk nuclear war over relatively minor issues aroused heavy criticism. In the 1960s U.S. strategic thinking emphasized flexible response, enhancing both conventional and counterinsurgency capabilities. The expansion of the United States' international commitments did not preclude efforts from the mid-1950s onward to reach an understanding with the Soviet Union that would prevent an accidental war and place ceilings on ever more expensive and destructive nuclear weapons. These attempts, culminating in the Strategic Arms Limitation Treaties of 1972 and 1979, demonstrated the fundamentally cautious nature of U.S. military strategy.

Alarmed by what he perceived as increasingly assertive Soviet foreign policies of the 1970s, during the 1980s President Ronald Reagan initially increased U.S. defense budgets dramatically, adopted a firmly anti-Soviet posture, and announced the development of a new antimissile shield that would render the United States invulnerable to Soviet attack. By the late 1980s, growing economic weakness led to the collapse of both the Soviet Union and the Soviet empire, which many Americans interpreted as validating the premises of the containment strategy adopted over 40 years earlier. As the 21st century began, no other strategic paradigm had yet attained similar intellectual dominance in the conceptualization of U.S. post–Cold War policy.

Priscilla Roberts

See also: Acheson, Dean Gooderham; Central Intelligence Agency; Dulles, John Foster; Eisenhower, Dwight David; Johnson, Lyndon Baines; Kennedy, John Fitzgerald; Military Balance; Nitze, Paul Henry; Nuclear Arms Race

References

Friedberg, Aaron L. *In the Shadow of the Garrison State: America's Anti-Statism and Its Cold War Grand Strategy.* Princeton, NJ: Princeton University Press, 2000.

Friedman, Norman. *The Fifty-Year War: Conflict and Strategy in the Cold War.* Annapolis, MD: Naval Institute Press, 2000.

Gaddis, John Lewis. *Strategies of Containment: A Critical Appraisal of Postwar American National Security Policy.* Oxford: Oxford University Press, 1982.

Hogan, Michael J. *A Cross of Iron: Harry S. Truman and the Origins of the National Security State, 1945–1954.* Cambridge: Cambridge University Press, 1998.

Kennan, George F. *Memoirs, 1925–1950.* Boston: Little, Brown, 1967.

May, Ernest R., ed. *American Cold War Strategy: Interpreting NSC 68.* Boston: Bedford Books, 1993.

Miscamble, Wilson D. *George F. Kennan and the Making of American Foreign Policy, 1947–1950.* Princeton, NJ: Princeton University Press, 1992.

Russell, Richard L. *George F. Kennan's Strategic Thought: The Making of an American Realist.* Westport, CT: Praeger, 1999.

Cordier, Andrew Wellington (1901–1975)

Andrew Wellington Cordier was born on March 3, 1901, near Canton, Ohio. After studying at Manchester College in Indiana and the University of Chicago, from 1927 to 1944 he chaired the Department of History and Political Science at Manchester College. In 1944 Cordier joined the U.S. State Department as adviser on international security, drafting early versions of the UN Charter. He also served on the U.S. delegation to the April 1945 San Francisco Conference and the Preparatory Commission for the UN, which met in London. In March 1946 Cordier became executive assistant to the first UN secretary general, Trygve Halvden Lie. Holding the rank of undersecretary, Cordier retained the position until 1962, serving under both Lie and his charismatic successor, Dag Hammarskjöld. In 1962 he left the UN to become dean of the School of International Affairs of Columbia University.

On the night of October 27, while awaiting Soviet premier Nikita Khrushchev's response to President John F. Kennedy's offer of a guarantee that the United States would not invade Cuba in exchange for the removal of the Soviet missiles there, Secretary of State Dean Rusk contacted Cordier, an old friend. He asked Cordier to prepare a proposal that the United States remove NATO Jupiter missiles from Turkey instead. Should Khrushchev reject Kennedy's offer, Rusk and Kennedy intended to ask Cordier to submit this proposal to acting UN secretary general U Thant, whom Cordier knew well. In those circumstances, they hoped that Thant would claim that this fallback suggestion was made on his own initiative. Cordier drafted such a document, but it was never used. That same evening, Attorney General Robert Kennedy, the president's brother, submitted secret proposals on similar lines to Anatoly Dobrynin, Soviet ambassador to the United States. Only in the late 1980s did U.S. officials reveal the existence of this backup plan, which would have represented a

last-ditch attempt to avoid a full-scale invasion of Cuba. Cordier retired from Columbia in 1972. He died in Long Island, New York, on July 11, 1975.

Priscilla Roberts

See also: Dobrynin, Anatoly Fyodorovich; Jupiter Missiles (Turkey and Italy); Kennedy, John Fitzgerald; Kennedy, Robert Francis; Rusk, Dean David; U Thant; United Nations; U.S. Allies

References

Blight, James G., and David A. Welch. *On the Brink: Americans and Soviets Reexamine the Cuban Missile Crisis.* New York: Hill and Wang, 1989.

Firestone, Bernard J. *The United Nations under U Thant, 1961–1971.* Lanham, MD: Scarecrow Press, 2001.

Luard, Evan. *A History of the United Nations.* 2 vols. New York: St. Martin's Press, 1982–1989.

Meisler, Stanley. *The United Nations: The First Fifty Years.* New York: Atlantic Monthly Press, 1995.

Moore, John Alphin, Jr., and Jerry Pubantz. *To Create a New World?: American Presidents and the United Nations.* New York: Peter Lang, 1999.

Ostrower, Gary B. *The United Nations and the United States.* New York: Twayne, 1998.

White, Mark J. *The Cuban Missile Crisis.* London: Macmillan, 1996.

Cuba

Caribbean island nation comprising 42,803 square miles, about the size of the state of Ohio. The largest and western-most island of the West Indies chain, Cuba is in the Caribbean Sea, west of Hispaniola and 90 miles south of Key West, Florida. It had a 1945 population of approximately 5.68 million.

By the early 16th century, Spanish conquistadors and traders had already recognized Havana as an ideal port for trade with Spain. Beginning in the early 1800s, sugarcane production boomed, ensuring a huge influx of black slaves and the institution of a plantation economy. During the 1860s–1870s, a growing independence movement brought armed revolt against Spanish rule. Slavery was outlawed in 1886, and in 1895 Cuban nationalist and poet José Marti led the final struggle against the Spanish, which was fully realized thanks to U.S. involvement in the 1898 Spanish-American War.

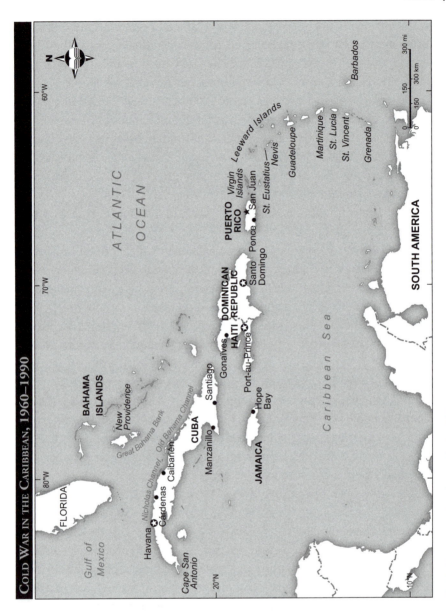

Cold War in the Caribbean, 1960–1990

Cold War in the Caribbean, 1960–1990

The Spanish-Cuban-American War marked a watershed in Cuban-U.S. relations, as it greatly enhanced American influence on the island. However, the event was controversial because Cuban independence fighters saw the island's newfound freedom as an outcome of their 30-year struggle against Spain, whereas many Americans saw Cuban independence as a U.S. victory. The result was an uneasy compromise whereby Cuba became an independent republic with limitations to its sovereignty embodied in the 1901 Platt Amendment, an appendix to the Cuban constitution authorizing U.S. intervention in Cuban affairs at its own discretion. Cuba became a politically independent state on May 20, 1902.

The duality of opinions regarding Cuban sovereignty was central to the crisis that brought down the Cuban republic. For the first half of the 20th century, the United States set the standards to which the Cuban population aspired. In this context, the crisis of the Cuban economic model of dependence on the sugar industry was accompanied by a sympathetic attitude in Washington toward anticommunist dictators.

Gen. Fulgencio Batista's military coup on March 10, 1952, occurred only two months before an election in which nationalist forces were within reach of the presidency. In the context of McCarthyism in the United States, the destruction of the Cuban democracy by Batista's rightist junta generated no significant opposition in Washington. Indeed, the United States backed Batista as an ally in the Cold War. For its part, the Cuban authoritarian Right manipulated the West by presenting itself as a bulwark against communism. In practice, the Batista government actually undermined democracy through its repressive policies. Batista's regime did little, moreover, to improve living standards for poor Cubans, while the middle class and elites enjoyed close and lucrative relationships with American businesses.

A potent popular insurrection against Batista's regime had grown in the eastern and central parts of Cuba by 1958. The revolution's leaders, Fidel Castro and Ernesto "Che" Guevara, questioned both Cuban dependence on the United States and market economy principles. perceiving their movement as part of a developing-world rebellion against the West and as a natural ally of the communist bloc.

The United States was not prepared to deal with the charismatic and doctrinaire Castro. After his takeover, the United States underestimated the profound grievances provoked by U.S. support for the Batista regime. Some of Castro's early measures—such as land reform, the prosecution of Batista's cronies (with no guarantee of due process), and the nationalization of industries—were overwhelmingly popular, but they met stiff U.S. resistance.

Against this backdrop, Castro approached the Soviet Union for support, and in February 1960 a Soviet delegation led by Vice Premier Anastas Mikoyan visited Cuba and signed a trade agreement with Castro's government. The Soviet Union then began to replace the United States as Cuba's main trade and political partner. Soviet leader Nikita Khrushchev soon promised Cuba new machinery, oil, consumer goods, armaments, and a market for Cuban products now subject to U.S. sanctions.

In April 1961, Cuban-U.S. relations collapsed completely after the failed Bay of Pigs invasion by rebel Cuban exiles, sponsored by the U.S. Central Intelligence Agency (CIA). The invasion was doomed from the start, given Castro's popularity in Cuba and the lack of U.S. air support for the rebel force. The botched attack only encouraged closer relations between the Soviet Union and Cuba, especially when the CIA launched additional covert operations. The most important undertaking, Operation MONGOOSE, included 14 attempts to assassinate Castro. Khrushchev subsequently proposed installing nuclear-capable missiles in Cuba to gain a better bargaining position with the United States while offering protection to Cuba. Castro was elated. Khrushchev naively assumed that the missiles could be installed without U.S. detection. U.S. intelligence quickly discovered them, however, provoking the Cuban Missile Crisis, the most dangerous confrontation between the two Cold War superpowers. President John F. Kennedy declared a naval quarantine of the island in October 1962. For nearly two weeks the world stood at the edge of a nuclear abyss. Ultimately, Kennedy and Khrushchev worked out an agreement whereby the Soviets removed the missiles in return for U.S. promises not to invade Cuba and to withdraw Jupiter missiles from Turkey.

The end of Kennedy's quarantine did not conclude strife between Cuba and the United States, however. In addition to an embargo still in force in 2012, the United States mounted further covert operations against Castro's government. U.S. hostility was reinforced by the Cuban revolution's transformation from a nationalist rebellion against authoritarianism to a totalitarian state aligned with the Soviet Union, with serious shortcomings in civil and political liberties.

The resolution of the Cuban Missile Crisis also created serious strains between Havana and Moscow. Cuba's foreign policy was made in Havana, so Castro refused to accept Moscow's or Beijing's directives. In 1968, he cracked down on a group of Cuban communists, accusing them of working with Soviet agents in Havana. Eventually, he used the 1968 Soviet intervention in Czechoslovakia against the Prague Spring to broker a compromise by which Cuba preserved its autonomy but promised

not to criticize the Soviet Union publicly. Cuba thus became a Comecon member, receiving significant additional economic aid from the communist bloc.

In Latin America, the Cuban government actively supported revolutionary movements with leftist or nationalist agendas, especially those that challenged U.S. hegemony in the region. But the 1960s witnessed successive failed Cuban attempts to export revolution. Guevara's 1967 murder in Bolivia concluded a series of subversive projects encouraged by Havana. Cuban revolutionary attempts were part of Cubans' core revolutionary beliefs and also a response to the rupture of diplomatic relations with Havana by all Latin American countries except Mexico.

From the 1970s to 1990, as part of the Cold War conflict, Cuba played a major international role. A high point of Castro's foreign policy came at the 1979 Sixth Summit of the Non-Aligned Movement in Havana. Cuba became a major conduit of alliance between the developing world and the communist bloc. Havana's diplomatic success and military involvement were accompanied by massive civilian involvement in health and education aid programs to African, Latin American, and Asian countries.

Cuba adopted a foreign policy suited to a medium-sized power. Castro sent 40,000 troops to Angola to support the pro-Soviet Popular Movement for the Liberation of Angola (MPLA) government in its struggle against the National Union for the Total Independence of Angola (UNITA) forces backed by South Africa and the United States. He also dispatched troops to aid the pro-Soviet government of Ethiopia. In all, Cuba deployed more than 300,000 troops or military advisers to Angola, Ethiopia, the Congo, Guinea-Bissau, Algeria, Mozambique, Syria, and South Yemen. The fight in southern Africa was ended through a skillfully designed tripartite agreement signed by Cuba, Angola, and South Africa and mediated by President Ronald Reagan's administration that led to Namibia's independence.

Paradoxically, due in part to these Cold War commitments, Cuba missed its best chance to solve its conflict with the United States. In the 1970s U.S. leaders sought serious negotiations with Cuba. Efforts at negotiation began during Richard Nixon's administration (1969–1974) and seemed most promising during Jimmy Carter's presidency (1977–1981). Carter demonstrated that he was serious in his desire to improve hemispheric relations and promote human rights. In 1977, Carter even stated that the United States did not consider a Cuban retreat from Angola a precondition for beginning negotiations. Castro, however, insisted on continuing what he defined as "revolutionary solidarity" and "proletarian internationalism."

The Cuban government was interested in negotiations with the United States but insisted on a radical leftist solution to problems. Castro took significant steps in releasing political prisoners and allowing Cuban exiles to visit the island as goodwill gestures toward the United States. In the international arena, in May 1978 Castro informed Lyle Lane, head of the State Department's U.S. Interest Section, that Cuba had no involvement in the Katangese invasion and rebellion in Zaire. Nevertheless, Castro gave priority to Cuban relations with other revolutionary movements, especially in Africa. In 1977, he sent 17,000 Cuban troops to Ethiopia to support the dictator Mengistu Haile Mariam in his territorial conflict with Somalia. This development, despite progress on several bilateral issues, represented a major blow to the prospect of improved Cuban-U.S. relations, as did Castro's support for the Sandinista government of Nicaragua in the 1980s.

A new development came in 1976 when Ricardo Boffill, Elizardo Sanchez, and Gustavo Arcos founded the first human rights group in Cuba since 1959. A new generation of opposition groups based on strategies of civil disobedience slowly emerged, gaining strength in the 1990s. Equally, during the 1970s Cuban civil society began to emerge from totalitarian ostracism that had reduced its religious communities to a minimum. This evolution continued, and by the late 1980s religious groups were growing rapidly.

The collapse of the communist bloc beginning in 1989 was a catastrophe for Castro's government, as Cuba lost its major benefactors. Simultaneously, the international community, particularly Latin America and the former communist countries, adopted general norms of democratic governance opposed to the Cuban leadership's goals and behavior. Without Soviet backing, Cuba adjusted its economy and foreign policy to survive in a world that was no longer safe for revolution. In 1988 Castro withdrew Cuban troops from Angola and reduced the Cuban military presence in the Horn of Africa.

Cuba's gross domestic product fell by almost one-third between 1989 and 1993. The collapse of the Cuban economy was particularly hard on imports, which fell from 8.6 billion pesos in 1989 to about 2 billion pesos in 1993. In response to the economic collapse, Castro permitted limited private enterprise, allowed Cubans to hold foreign currencies, and pushed for foreign investment, particularly in tourism. His reforms, however, did little to stem economic hemorrhaging. In addition, Cuban troops were withdrawn from wherever they were posted. In 2008, almost 20 years after the Cold War wound down, Castro, one of the last leaders of the old-style communist order, retired for reasons of ill health, handing his offices to his younger brother Raúl.

Arturo Lopez-Levy

References

Dominguez, Jorge I. *To Make a World Safe for Revolution: Cuba's Foreign Policy.* Cambridge, MA: Harvard University Press, 1989.

Font, Mauricio A., with Scott Larson, eds. *Cuba: In Transition? Pathways to Renewal, Long-Term Development and Global Reintegration.* New York: The Bildner Center for Western Hemisphere Studies, City University of New York, 2006.

Gleijeses, Piero. *Conflicting Missions: Havana, Washington, and Africa, 1959–1976.* Chapel Hill: University of North Carolina Press, 2002.

Morley, Morris H. *Imperial State and Revolution: The United States and Cuba, 1952–1986.* Cambridge: Cambridge University Press, 1987.

Morley, Morris, and Chris McGillion, eds. *Cuba, the United States, and the Post-Cold War World: The International Dimensions of the Washington-Havana Relationship.* Gainesville: University Press of Florida, 2005.

Morley, Morris, and Chris McGillion. *Unfinished Business: America and Cuba After the Cold War, 1989–2001.* Cambridge: Cambridge University Press, 2002.

Pastor, Robert. *The Carter Administration and Latin America.* Occasional Paper Series, Vol. 2, No. 3. Atlanta, GA: Carter Center of Emory University, 1992.

Pérez, Louis A., Jr. *Cuba and the United States: Ties of Singular Intimacy.* 2nd ed. Athens: University of Georgia Press, 1997.

Pérez, Louis A. *Cuba: Between Reform and Revolution.* 4th ed. New York: Oxford University Press, 2011.

Pérez-Stable, Marifeli. *The Cuban Revolution: Origins, Course, and Legacy.* New York: Oxford University Press, 1993.

Pérez-Stable, Marifeli. *The United States and Cuba: Intimate Enemies.* New York: Routledge, 2011.

Smith, Wayne. *The Closest of Enemies: A Personal and Diplomatic History of the Castro Years.* New York: Norton, 1987.

Staten, Clifford L. *The History of Cuba.* Westport, CT: Greenwood Press, 2003.

Wright, Thomas C. *Latin America in the Era of the Cuban Revolution.* Rev. ed. Westport, CT: Praeger, 2001.

D

Dillon, C(larence) Douglas (1909–2003)

U.S. secretary of the treasury, 1961–1965. C. Douglas Dillon was born on August 21, 1909, in Geneva, Switzerland, the only son of Clarence Douglas Dillon, self-made financier and founder of the prominent New York investment bank Dillon Read. After attending the elite Groton School, Massachusetts, and Harvard University, the younger Dillon became a stockbroker and investment banker, joining Dillon Read in 1938. He served in the U.S. Navy during World War II, then returned to Dillon Read as board chairman. Active in Republican politics, during 1951–1952 he campaigned actively for Dwight D. Eisenhower, the successful presidential candidate, who appointed Dillon ambassador to France in 1953. Joining the State Department in Washington as deputy undersecretary for economic affairs in January 1957, Dillon rose first to undersecretary for economic affairs and eventually, from April 1959 to January 1961, to undersecretary for political affairs, the department's second-highest position. Dillon, a dedicated internationalist, concentrated on promoting trade and economic development, coordinating mutual security assistance programs, and enhancing foreign aid's scope and effectiveness. His efforts contributed to founding the Inter-American Development Bank in 1959 and in 1960 to establishing the Act of Bogotá economic development program, a forerunner of the Alliance for Progress, and the European-backed Organization for Economic Cooperation and Development.

In December 1960 Democratic president-elect John F. Kennedy, seeking to reassure the financial community that he would not adopt "easy money" policies, named Dillon secretary of the treasury, a post he held until March 1965. Dillon also sat on the National Security Council. In

August 1961 he headed the U.S. delegation to the Punta del Este conference that created the Latin American Alliance for Progress program. Dillon served on the Executive Committee (ExComm) that decided policies during the Cuban Missile Crisis. He initially favored a quick air strike, without any warning, against Soviet missile facilities in Cuba. By October 20 Dillon had come around to favoring the announcement of a blockade, an ultimatum that might be followed by air strikes within three days if Soviet construction of missile bases continued. After Russian SA-2 surface-to-air missile batteries shot down a U-2 reconnaissance plane over Cuba on October 27, Dillon favored a quick, unannounced strike against them, one that would probably also target nearby missile sites. Although he considered the Jupiter nuclear missiles the United States had placed in Turkey strategically worthless, Dillon clearly found unpalatable the prospect of trading these publicly for Soviet missiles in Cuba.

Dillon returned to banking in March 1965. In March 1968, after the Tet Offensive, as one of President Lyndon B. Johnson's Senior Advisory Group on Vietnam he was among the "wise men" who urged Johnson to seek withdrawal from Vietnam. On January 10, 2003, following several weeks of illness, Dillon died at Presbyterian Hospital, New York.

Priscilla Roberts

See also: Alliance for Progress; Eisenhower, Dwight David; Jupiter Missiles (Turkey and Italy); Kennedy, John Fitzgerald; U-2 Overflights

References

Katz, Bernard S., and C. Daniel Vencill. *Biographical Dictionary of the United States Secretaries of the Treasury, 1789–1995.* Westport, CT: Greenwood Press, 1996.

May, Ernest R., and Philip D. Zelikow, eds. *The Kennedy Tapes: Inside the White House during the Cuban Missile Crisis.* Cambridge, MA: Harvard University Press, 1997.

Sobel, Robert. *The Life and Times of Dillon Read.* New York: Dutton, 1991.

Dobrynin, Anatoly Fyodorovich (1919–2010)

Soviet diplomat and ambassador to the United States. Born on November 16, 1919, in Krasnaya Gorka, Anatoly Dobrynin studied engineering at the Ordzhonikidze Moscow Aviation Institute and worked as a designer at

Experimental Aircraft Plant No. 115 in Moscow before being selected by the Personnel Department of the Communist Party of the Soviet Union (CPSU) Central Committee to attend the Higher Diplomatic School in 1944. He joined the CPSU the following year. In 1946 he graduated with a doctorate in history.

Dobrynin joined the Ministry of Foreign Affairs as assistant chief of the Education Department, serving simultaneously as an assistant professor of U.S. foreign policy at the Institute of International Relations. From 1947 to 1952 he worked on the staff of Deputy Foreign Minister Valerian Zorin, ultimately becoming his first assistant. Dobrynin was posted to Washington as counselor at the Soviet embassy in 1952, serving as minister-counselor from 1954 to 1955. Returning to Moscow in 1955, he was promoted to the rank of ambassador extraordinary and plenipotentiary in the Foreign Ministry before becoming an assistant to Foreign Minister Dmitri T. Shepilov. In 1957, Dobrynin was posted to the United Nations (UN) Secretariat as an undersecretary general, becoming director of the Department of Political and Security Council Affairs the next year.

In February 1960 Dobrynin was recalled to Moscow to head the Foreign Ministry's American Department, where he served until January 1962, returning briefly to the UN in summer 1960 to help Foreign Minister Andrey Gromyko lodge complaints regarding U.S. U-2 overflights of the Soviet Union. In January 1962 Dobrynin was appointed ambassador to the United States. Dobrynin served in this post until 1986, playing a critical role in almost every aspect of Soviet-U.S. relations. Kremlin officials did not inform Dobrynin of the Presidium's May 1962 decision to install nuclear-capable missiles on

Anatoly F. Dobrynin, appointed Soviet ambassador to the United States in April 1962, within months took part in secret behind-the-scenes negotiations during the Cuban Missile Crisis that were vitally important to its resolution. A highly effective diplomat, Dobrynin remained ambassador until 1986, becoming a fixture in Soviet-American relations. (Getty Images)

Cuba, leading him to misinform U.S. Attorney General Robert F. Kennedy on September 4 that only defensive weaponry was reaching the island and the Soviets would not introduce offensive weapons, including ballistic missiles. His private and secret discussions with Robert Kennedy on proposals to remove NATO Jupiter nuclear missiles from Turkey soon after Soviet nuclear-capable weapons left Cuba were instrumental to the peaceful resolution of the resulting Cuban Missile Crisis. During Richard Nixon's presidency, Dobrynin worked with National Security Adviser Henry Kissinger to resolve disputes in the SALT I negotiations and became an informal channel for U.S. communications with North Vietnam leading to the Paris Peace Talks. During the presidencies of Jimmy Carter and Ronald Reagan, Dobrynin provided a degree of stability in deteriorating Soviet-U.S. relations following the 1979 Soviet invasion of Afghanistan.

Dobrynin became a candidate member of the CPSU Central Committee in 1966 and a full member in 1977. In March 1986, new Soviet leader Mikhail Gorbachev recalled Dobrynin to join the CPSU Central Committee as secretary for foreign affairs and head of the International Department. He was also elected a deputy to the Supreme Soviet, serving until 1989. Dobrynin retired from the Central Committee in 1988 but continued to serve as a foreign policy adviser to Gorbachev until the collapse of the Soviet Union in late 1991. Beginning in 1995, Dobrynin became a consultant to the Russian Foreign Ministry. He died in Moscow on April 6, 2010.

Steven W. Guerrier

See also Gromyko, Andrey Andreyevich; Jupiter Missiles (Turkey and Italy); Kennedy, John Fitzgerald; Kennedy, Robert Francis; Khrushchev, Nikita Sergeyevich; Rusk, Dean David; United Nations; U-2 Overflights; Zorin, Valerian Aleksandrovich

References

Brugioni, Dino A. *Eyeball to Eyeball: Inside the Cuban Missile Crisis.* Edited by Robert F. McCort. New York: Random House, 1993.

Dobrynin, Anatoly. *In Confidence: Moscow's Ambassador to America's Six Cold War Presidents (1962–1986).* Rev ed. Seattle: University of Washington Press, 2001.

Friedman, Norman. *The Fifty-Year War: Conflict and Strategy in the Cold War.* Annapolis, MD: Naval Institute Press, 2000.

Gelman, Harry. *The Brezhnev Politburo and the Decline of Détente.* Ithaca, NY: Cornell University Press, 1984.

Dulles, Allen Welsh (1893–1969)

Director of the U.S. Central Intelligence Agency (CIA), 1953–1961. Born in Watertown, New York, on April 7, 1893, Allen Dulles obtained a BA and an MA in international law from Princeton University and in 1916 joined the U.S. Foreign Service. Assigned first to Vienna, by the time the United States entered World War I Dulles was in Bern, Switzerland, where he nurtured U.S. embassy contacts with Austro-Hungarian and Balkan exiles. He served on the U.S. delegation to the 1919 Paris Peace Conference and in various positions overseas, but in 1926 financial considerations caused him to join the prominent New York law firm of Sullivan and Cromwell, where his brother John Foster Dulles was a leading partner. Allen Dulles remained deeply interested in foreign affairs, focusing on international business and becoming active in the New York–based Council on Foreign Relations.

A strong supporter of U.S. intervention in World War II, in 1942 Dulles joined the newly created U.S. intelligence agency, the Office of Strategic Services (OSS), headed by Col. William J. Donovan, and spent most of the war based in Bern in neutral Switzerland, running a network of German intelligence agents. By 1944 the prospect of communist and Soviet expansion in Europe troubled Dulles.

In spring 1945 Dulles helped negotiate the surrender of Germany's remaining forces in northern Italy. In what some have perceived as the opening move of the Cold War, U.S. and British forces initiated the surrender talks without involving their ally the Soviet Union, leading Soviet leader Joseph Stalin to believe that they intended to negotiate a separate peace with Germany. In late 1945, President Harry S. Truman disbanded the OSS. Dulles remained a strong advocate of a permanent U.S. foreign intelligence service and helped to draft the 1947 National Security Act, which created the CIA. In 1950 Dulles became CIA deputy director, and from 1953 to 1961 he served as the agency's third director. He deliberately publicized his agency's existence and accomplishments and was responsible for building its permanent headquarters in Langley, Virginia. President Dwight D. Eisenhower's 1953 appointment of John Foster Dulles as secretary of state, a post he held until his death in 1959, further enhanced the CIA director's official influence.

Besides analyzing intelligence, under Dulles the CIA mounted extensive covert operations, among them successful antileftist coups against the governments of Mohammed Mossadegh in Iran in 1953 and Jacobo Arbenz in Guatemala in 1954. Dulles later authorized a comparable effort

to overthrow the radical new regime headed by Fidel Castro in Cuba. In March 1961 a poorly planned and botched U.S.-backed invasion attempt by Cuban exiles landing at the Bay of Pigs ended in highly publicized failure, a major international humiliation for the United States. President John F. Kennedy publicly accepted full responsibility but privately blamed Dulles, who resigned a few months later. In the early 1970s congressional investigations uncovered evidence on some of the CIA's past excesses overseas during the Dulles years that severely damaged the organization's reputation.

Dulles subsequently served on the Warren Commission that investigated Kennedy's assassination, undercutting its credibility when he admitted that to safeguard what they considered to be national security, CIA operatives might well lie even when giving evidence before the commission. In retirement Dulles wrote several books on intelligence. He died in Washington, D.C., on April 7, 1969.

Priscilla Roberts

See also: Bay of Pigs Invasion; Bissell, Richard Mervin, Jr.; Castro, Fidel; Central Intelligence Agency; Containment, Doctrine and Course of; Dulles, John Foster; Eisenhower, Dwight David; Kennedy, John Fitzgerald

References

Grose, Peter. *Gentleman Spy: The Life of Allen Dulles.* Boston: Houghton Mifflin, 1994.

Lucas, Scott. *Freedom's War: The American Crusade against the Soviet Union.* New York: New York University Press, 1999.

Ranelagh, John. *The Agency: The Rise and Decline of the CIA.* New York: Simon and Schuster, 1986.

Srodes, James. *Allen Dulles: Master of Spies.* Washington, DC: Regnery, 1999.

Zegart, Amy B. *Flawed by Design: The Evolution of the CIA, JCS, and NSC.* Stanford, CA: Stanford University Press, 1999.

Dulles, John Foster (1888–1959)

U.S. secretary of state (1953–1959). Born in Washington, D.C., on February 25, 1888, John Foster Dulles studied under Woodrow Wilson at Princeton University and at the Sorbonne, earned a law degree from George

Washington University, and in 1911 joined the prestigious Wall Street law firm of Sullivan and Cromwell. Appointed to the U.S. delegation at the 1919 Paris Peace Conference, Dulles unsuccessfully sought to restrain Allied reparations demands on Germany.

Active between the wars in internationalist organizations, during World War II Dulles focused intensely on postwar planning and became prominent in Republican politics. Seeking to secure bipartisan political support on foreign policy, President Harry S. Truman included Dulles in virtually all major international meetings, beginning with the 1945 San Francisco Conference that drafted the final United Nations Charter. Briefly appointed Republican senator for New York in 1948–1949, Dulles strongly supported creation of the North Atlantic Treaty Organization (NATO). He also favored European integration as a means of strengthening the continent's economies and militaries. By the late 1940s Dulles had become a dedicated anticommunist.

As a foreign affairs adviser to the Republican presidential campaign in 1952, Dulles argued that the Truman administration had been timorous in merely containing Soviet communism when it should have moved to roll back Soviet influence in Eastern Europe.

Named secretary of state by President Dwight D. Eisenhower in 1953, Dulles deferred to the president's leadership, although the two men were very different in style. A supporter of Eisenhower's New Look defense policy of heavy reliance on nuclear weapons, in tactics that came to be known as "brinkmanship" Dulles rhetorically threatened "massive retaliation" against the United States' enemies. In practice, he was often more cautious and followed pragmatic policies, effectively respecting established Soviet interests in Europe. When discontented East Berlin workers triggered an uprising in the German Democratic Republic (GDR) (East Germany) in 1953 and again when Hungarians rebelled against Soviet rule in 1956, Dulles and Eisenhower welcomed refugees but offered no further support.

Dulles and Eisenhower ended the Korean War in 1953, pressuring both sides to accept an armistice, and established a series of alliances around Asia and the Middle East. When possible, Eisenhower avoided direct major military interventions, preferring to rely on covert operations orchestrated by the Central Intelligence Agency (CIA), headed by Dulles's younger brother Allen. The CIA played key roles in coups that overthrew Left-leaning governments in Iran in 1953 and Guatemala in 1954. These were precursors of subsequent CIA-orchestrated efforts to overthrow the radical government Fidel Castro established in Cuba in 1959.

The emergence of Nikita Khrushchev as top Soviet leader in the mid-1950s seemed to promise relaxation of U.S.-Soviet tensions, as Khrushchev openly repudiated Stalinist tactics and called for peaceful coexistence between communist and noncommunist nations. Eisenhower hoped to conclude substantive disarmament agreements with Khrushchev. In practice, however, Khrushchev was often far from accommodating. The Soviet Union's success in launching the first space satellite (*Sputnik*) in 1957, Soviet possession of nuclear and thermonuclear weapons, and Khrushchev's seeming readiness from late 1958 onward to provoke an international crisis over Berlin all alarmed U.S. leaders, including the ailing Dulles, diagnosed in 1957 with cancer. When his health deteriorated, he resigned as secretary on April 15, 1959. Dulles died in Washington, D.C., on May 24, 1959.

Priscilla Roberts

See also: Berlin Crises; Central Intelligence Agency; Containment, Doctrine and Course of; Dulles, Allen Welsh; Eisenhower, Dwight David; Khrushchev, Nikita Sergeyevich; Military Balance; Nuclear Arms Race

References

Hoopes, Townsend. *The Devil and John Foster Dulles.* Boston: Little, Brown, 1973.

Immerman, Richard H. *John Foster Dulles: Piety, Pragmatism, and Power in U.S. Foreign Policy.* Wilmington, DE: Scholarly Resources, 1999.

Marks, Frederick W., III. *Power and Peace: The Diplomacy of John Foster Dulles.* Westport, CT: Praeger, 1993.

Toulouse, Mark G. *The Transformation of John Foster Dulles: From Prophet of Realism to Priest of Nationalism.* Macon, GA: Mercer University Press, 1985.

Tudda, Chris. *The Truth is Our Weapon: The Rhetorical Diplomacy of Dwight D. Eisenhower and John Foster Dulles.* Baton Rouge: Louisiana State University Press, 2006.

E

Eisenhower, Dwight David (1890–1969)

U.S. Army general, president of the United States (1953–1961). Born in Denison, Texas, on October 14, 1890, Dwight Eisenhower grew up in Abilene, Kansas, and graduated from the U.S. Military Academy, West Point, in 1915. In December 1943 he was named to command the Allied forces scheduled to invade Western Europe in 1944, and in spring 1945 he was promoted to general of the army. Military success translated into political viability. In 1952 the Republican Party, desperate to choose a candidate assured of victory, turned to Eisenhower, who won the subsequent election.

As president, Eisenhower largely endorsed existing Cold War policies, staunchly opposing global communism. He solidified U.S. defense commitments around the world into a network of bilateral and multilateral alliances. A fiscal conservative uneasy with high defense budgets, Eisenhower introduced the New Look strategy of relying heavily on nuclear weapons rather than on conventional forces. Alarmed by the increasing destructiveness of nuclear armaments, however, Eisenhower was the first president to attempt, albeit rather unsuccessfully, to reach arms-control agreements with the Soviet Union.

As the Bandung Non-Aligned Movement gained strength around the developing world—especially in decolonizing Asia, Africa, and the Middle East, where nationalist sentiments frequently ran high—Eisenhower sought to entice Third World nations into the U.S. camp. As president, Eisenhower was generally cautious in risking American troops in overseas interventions. Instead, he relied heavily on covert activities, authorizing the Central Intelligence Agency (CIA) to back coups in both Iran

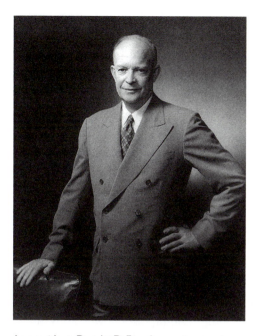

As president, Dwight D. Eisenhower imposed sanctions on Fidel Castro's revolutionary regime and set in motion plans to overthrow Castro. Eisenhower's actions did much to set Cuba and the United States on a collision course and impelled Castro to turn to the Soviet Union for assistance. (Library of Congress)

and Guatemala in 1953 and 1954 and encouraging it to undertake numerous other secret operations.

After leftist insurgents led by Fidel Castro overthrew the government of Fulgencia Batista in Cuba in January 1959, there followed policies of radical land reform and nationalization that often expropriated American businesses in Cuba. The Eisenhower administration quickly turned against the new regime, with assorted economic sanctions. From spring 1959 Castro, despite public declarations that he was not a communist, therefore covertly sought Soviet aid and military protection, and U.S. economic pressure and commercial boycotts soon impelled him to move openly into the Soviet camp. In response, in March 1960 Eisenhower authorized the CIA to devise a scheme to train Cuban exiles based in Guatemala to invade the island and overthrow Castro. Eisenhower had no schedule for such an invasion, but he did want a plan to be in place and ready to execute at his decision. In early January 1961, shortly before leaving office, Eisenhower took the measure of ending U.S. recognition of Castro's government.

After the failure of the April 1961 Bay of Pigs invasion attempt, President John F. Kennedy consulted Eisenhower, who criticized his successor's non-authorization of air cover for the invading force and his reluctance to reveal the extent of U.S. backing for the exiles. While promising to support Kennedy's efforts to exclude communism from the Western Hemisphere, Eisenhower also warned that the American people would support intervention by U.S. military forces only when clear and serious provocation existed.

On October 17, 1962, CIA director John McCone briefed Eisenhower on the presence of Soviet nuclear-capable missiles in Cuba. The former president characterized the situation as "intolerable," pledged his support

to Kennedy, and recommended prompt and decisive military action. On October 20, McCone again briefed Eisenhower on potential options: air strikes alone, air strikes plus invasion, and a naval blockade against Cuba. Consulted by Kennedy in person two days later, Eisenhower advised against air strikes alone but refused to choose between the other alternatives. Informed by Kennedy of his intention to impose a naval blockade, Eisenhower offered his support. A week later, Kennedy spoke to him again, outlining Soviet premier Nikita Khrushchev's agreement to withdraw the missiles in return for a U.S. commitment not to invade Cuba. Eisenhower warned Kennedy to exercise caution over the precise wording of the non-invasion pledge. In November 1962 he also urged McCone to insist that U.S. inspection teams enter Cuba to ensure all missiles had been removed, something Castro adamantly refused to sanction and on which Kennedy, to Eisenhower's private annoyance, was unwilling to insist. Eisenhower died in Washington, D.C., on March 28, 1969.

Priscilla Roberts

See also: Batista y Zaldívar, Fulgencio; Bay of Pigs Invasion; Berlin Crises; Castro, Fidel; Central Intelligence Agency; Containment, Doctrine and Course of; Dulles, Allen Welsh; Dulles, John Foster; Kennedy, John Fitzgerald; Khrushchev, Nikita Sergeyevich; McCone, John Alex; Missile Gap; Military Balance; Nuclear Arms Race; U-2 Overflights

References

Ambrose, Stephen E. *Eisenhower: The President.* 2 vols. New York: Simon and Schuster, 1984.

Ambrose, Stephen E., and Richard H. Immerman. *Ike's Spies: Eisenhower and the Espionage Establishment.* Garden City, NY: Doubleday, 1981.

Bowie, Robert R., and Richard H. Immerman. *Waging Peace: How Eisenhower Shaped an Enduring Cold War Strategy.* New York: Oxford University Press, 1998.

Dockrill, Saki. *Eisenhower's New Look: National Security Policy, 1953–1961.* New York: St. Martin's Press, 1996.

Korda, Michael. *Ike: An American Hero.* New York: HarperCollins, 2007.

Newton, Jim. *Eisenhower: The White House Years.* New York: Doubleday, 2011.

Perret, Geoffrey. *Eisenhower.* New York: Random House, 1999.

Rabe, Stephen G. *Eisenhower and Latin America: The Foreign Policy of Anticommunism.* Chapel Hill: University of North Carolina Press, 1988.

Smith, Jean Edward. *Eisenhower in War and Peace.* New York: Random House, 2012.

Welch, Richard E., Jr. *Response to Revolution: The United States and the Cuban Revolution, 1959–1961.* Chapel Hill: University of North Carolina Press, 1985.

F

Feklisov (Fomin), Aleksandr (1914–2007)

KGB officer, head of Soviet intelligence, Washington, D.C., 1960–1963. Aleksandr Feklisov was born in Moscow on March 9, 1914, the son of a railway signalman. In 1939 he joined the NKVD—the Soviet intelligence service, predecessor of the KGB—taking the cover name "Fomin" and specializing in gathering foreign scientific and technological information. Based in New York from 1941 to 1947 and then in London, he helped recruit and run highly effective espionage networks of scientists working on nuclear technology, electronic devices, radio equipment, and jet aircraft, including the now infamous spies Klaus Fuchs and Julius and Ethel Rosenberg. On Fuchs's arrest in 1950, Feklisov returned to Moscow, served in Czechoslovakia, and from 1955 to 1960 headed the KGB First Chief Directorate, responsible for overseas espionage.

From 1960 to 1964 Feklisov, officially counselor at the Soviet embassy in Washington, D.C., headed its KGB operations. In March 1962 he reported that an outright U.S. invasion of Cuba was unlikely unless the Cubans attacked the U.S. naval base at Guantánamo Bay or the Soviets installed nuclear-capable missiles on the island. Once the Cuban Missile Crisis became public, gossip circulated by American journalists convinced Feklisov that a U.S. invasion of Cuba was imminent. Acting apparently on his own volition, without KGB or Politburo authorization, on October 26, 1962, he contacted John Scali, an ABC News State Department correspondent with good contacts in the Kennedy administration, to discuss a potential settlement. During their lunchtime conversation, Feklisov reportedly warned Scali that, should the United States invade Cuba, Soviet forces would attack West Berlin, and suggested a settlement whereby the

Soviet Union would remove its missiles from Cuba, whose leader, Fidel Castro, would agree not to accept any further offensive weaponry, in exchange for a U.S. pledge not to invade Cuba. Later that day Scali reported this conversation to the State Department, where Secretary of State Dean Rusk interpreted it, however unauthorized, as a positive indication of Soviet willingness to compromise. Scali and Feklisov met again that evening, when Scali confirmed these terms might represent an acceptable basis for a settlement. U.S. officials believed that Feklisov's initiative marked a shift in the original intransigent Soviet position, and a letter Premier Nikita Khrushchev dispatched on October 26, conveying similar proposals, seemed to confirm this. Although Feklisov was effectively freelancing, his report to Moscow helped convince top Soviet officials that an arrangement along these lines might prove feasible.

In further conversations with Scali on October 29 and November 3, Feklisov warned that Soviet officials found it very hard to control Castro, who deeply resented that they had conducted settlement negotiations with the United States without consulting him and was proving intransigent over accepting the terms agreed. Scali assured Feklisov that Kennedy did not seek to humiliate Khrushchev, and then relayed Feklisov's information to ExComm.

Reassigned to Moscow in 1964, Feklisov trained spies at the KGB's Red Banner Institute until his retirement 10 years later. In later life he earned a doctorate in history, wrote several volumes of memoirs—which critics alleged exaggerated his significance in the Cuban Missile Crisis and other events—and hinted at his involvement in other secret operations "too recent to be told." He died in Moscow on October 26, 2007.

Priscilla Roberts

See also: Castro, Fidel; Guantánamo Bay Naval Base; Kennedy, John Fitzgerald; Khrushchev, Nikita Sergeyevich; Rusk, Dean David

References

Andrew, Christopher, and Oleg Gordievsky. *The KGB: The Inside Story of Its Foreign Operations from Lenin to Gorbachev.* London: Hodder and Stoughton, 1990.

Feklisov, Alexander. *The Man behind the Rosenbergs.* Translated by Catherine Dop. New York: Enigma Books, 2001.

Fursenko, Aleksandr, and Timothy Naftali. *One Hell of a Gamble: Khrushchev, Castro, and Kennedy, 1958–1964.* New York: Norton, 1997.

Salinger, Pierre. *With Kennedy.* New York: Avon Books, 1966.

G

Gilpatric, Roswell Leavitt (1906–1996)

Roswell Gilpatric was born in Brooklyn on November 4, 1906. In 1931 he joined the premier New York law firm Cravath, Swaine & Moore (then Cravath, de Gersdorff, Swaine & Wood). As legal representative for the Finnish government and large industrial clients, during World War II Gilpatric acquired a lifelong interest in defense policy and government service. In May 1951, during the Korean War, Gilpatric became assistant secretary of the Air Force for matériel, directing aircraft procurement and production; in October 1951 he was promoted to undersecretary, a position he held until January 1953. Gilpatric served on the 1956–1957 Rockefeller Brothers Fund panel on defense, which produced the Gaither report, recommending major increases in weapons research and spending.

In January 1961 President John F. Kennedy appointed Gilpatric, who had advised him on national security issues during his campaign, deputy secretary of defense. Serving under Robert McNamara, Gilpatric supervised procurement and overseas weapons sales, successfully persuading European allies to strengthen their defenses and narrow the dollar gap through massive purchases of U.S. military supplies.

As one of the Executive Committee (ExComm) of top-level advisers Kennedy created to handle the Cuban Missile Crisis, Gilpatric usually accompanied McNamara to meetings. Although he habitually said little, he made one important intervention on October 20, when ExComm debated whether to launch direct air strikes on Cuban missile sites or merely impose a naval blockade on Cuba. McNamara and Gilpatric consistently favored the second, less risky option. Gilpatric finally summed

up: "Essentially, Mr. President, this is a choice between limited action and unlimited action; and most of us think that it's better to start with limited action." Kennedy followed his advice. Once the crisis was resolved, Gilpatric took part in lengthy negotiations with Soviet deputy prime minister Vasily V. Kuznetsov on the settlement's detailed implementation.

After leaving office in late 1963, Gilpatric wrote extensively on disarmament, military policy, and international affairs, consistently endorsing successive disarmament treaties and urging rationalization of the defense establishment. On March 15, 1996, he died of prostate cancer in Manhattan.

Priscilla Roberts

See also: Kennedy, John Fitzgerald; Kuznetsov, Vasili Vasilyevich; McNamara, Robert Strange; Nuclear Arms Race; U.S. Allies

References

Borklund, Carl W. *The Department of Defense.* New York: Praeger, 1968.

Borklund, Carl W. *Men of the Pentagon: From Forrestal to McNamara.* New York: Praeger, 1966.

Nalty, Bernard C., ed. *Winged Shield, Winged Sword: A History of the USAF.* 2 vols. Washington, DC: Air Force History and Museums Program, United States Air Force, 1997.

Shapley, Deborah, *Promise and Power: The Life and Times of Robert McNamara.* Boston: Little, Brown, 1993.

Gribkov, Anatoli Ivanovich (1919–2008)

Soviet major general, deputy head of the Main Operations Directorate, Soviet General Staff. Anatoli Gribkov was born on March 23, 1919, in Dukhovoye, in the Liskinsky District of Voronezh Province in Russia, one of ten children of a peasant family. He served as a tank officer in the Russo-Finnish War and then in Latvia. When German forces invaded Russia in June 1941, Gribkov fought in Belarus, Smolensk, and the defense of Moscow, and then spent five months studying at the J. V. Stalin Armored Troops School. He saw combat service on the Kalinin front, took part in the Battle of Kursk, and fought on the southern front in the Ukraine, winning numerous decorations. After the war Gribkov studied at the General Staff Academy, receiving high honors, and served in the Leningrad and

Kiev military districts, winning promotion to major general in 1958. In early 1961 Gribkov became chief of operations in the Main Operations Directorate of the Soviet General Staff.

In May 1962 Col. Gen. Semyon Pavlovich Ivanov, head of the Main Operations Directorate, instructed Gribkov to prepare detailed plans for Operation ANADYR, the deployment to Cuba of over 50,000 Soviet combat troops, equipped with conventional and nuclear-capable weapons, together with a substantial naval force of cruisers, destroyers, and submarines, some of which would likewise carry nuclear armaments. Under considerable pressure, between May and October 1962 Gribkov and his subordinates planned and implemented this operation, observing great secrecy. In September 1962, after U.S. President John F. Kennedy warned publicly against any Soviet installation of nuclear-capable weapons on Cuba, Soviet leaders reduced the naval component to four nuclear-armed submarines but supplemented the nuclear-capable weaponry with a squadron of Il-28 light bombers, equipped with six atomic bombs, and three detachments of Luna short-range missiles, with a total of 12 two-kiloton warheads.

In October 1962, growing Soviet fears that the U.S. government was likely to discover and react strongly to the presence of these forces in Cuba impelled Soviet defense minister Rodion Malinovsky to dispatch Gribkov to Cuba, heading a military mission whose purpose was to accelerate the construction of military installations and the deployment of Soviet weapons. A second objective of Gribkov's presence was to underline the Kremlin's insistence that Gen. Issa Alexandrovich Pliyev, who commanded Soviet forces in Cuba, refrain from any use of R-12 medium-range or R-14 intermediate-range nuclear-armed ballistic missiles against U.S. targets without specific Kremlin authorization and employ only tactical Luna and FKR short-range tactical nuclear-armed weapons in actual battlefield situations if he lost contact with superiors in Moscow. On October 22, Gribkov later recalled, as Kennedy publicly demanded the withdrawal of Soviet nuclear-capable missiles from Cuba, Malinovsky tightened Kremlin control when he cabled further instructions to Pliyev that no nuclear-armed weapons whatever should be used even in combat situations. How effective these constraints would have been in battlefield conditions, especially since subsequent instructions from Moscow on the subject over the next week were somewhat ambivalent, has never been entirely clear. When the crisis was resolved, Gribkov remained in Cuba until late November, supervising the removal of the R-12 and R-14 missiles and warheads, the Il-28s, and one batch of short-range missiles before returning to Moscow.

Gribkov was luckier than Colonel General Ivanov, who took the blame for the abortive Cuban venture and was dismissed as head of the General Staff's Operations Directorate. Gribkov, by contrast, flourished, receiving the Order of Lenin in 1963 and promotion to lieutenant general for his accomplishments, and became deputy chief of the Operations Directorate. He later commanded the Seventh Guards Army, stationed in Armenia, and the Leningrad Military District, rising to colonel general in 1973 and general of the army in 1976. From then until 1989 he served simultaneously as chief of staff of the Warsaw Pact armed forces and first deputy chief of the Soviet Armed Forces General Staff. For three additional years he served as inspector general of the Soviet armed forces, retiring in 1992.

Gribkov's revelations, at a 1992 conference of former Soviet, American, and Cuban officials held at Havana, that at the height of the crisis in October 1962 there were almost 42,000 Soviet military personnel on Cuba, together with 36 nuclear warheads for 24 medium-range ballistic missile sites, many of them operational, 80 nuclear warheads for FKR short-range cruise missiles, 12 nuclear warheads for short-range Luna rockets, and six atomic bombs suitable for delivery by specially adapted Il-28s, created a sensation. So, too, did his statement that for substantial periods during the crisis Pliyev had discretionary authority from the Kremlin to use the short-range tactical weapons in battlefield combat against any U.S. attackers. In retirement Gribkov wrote his memoirs, published in German in 1992, and numerous other works. He died in Moscow on February 12, 2008.

Priscilla Roberts

See also: ANADYR, Operation; Castro, Fidel; Kennedy, John Fitzgerald; Khrushchev, Nikita Sergeyevich; Malinovsky, Rodion Yakovlevich; Pliyev, Issa Alexandrovich

References

Blight, James G., Bruce J. Allyn, and David A. Welch. *Cuba on the Brink: Castro, the Missile Crisis, and the Soviet Collapse.* New York: Pantheon Books, 1993.

Fursenko, Aleksandr, and Timothy Naftali. *One Hell of a Gamble: Khrushchev, Castro, and Kennedy, 1958–1964.* New York: Norton, 1997.

Gribkov, Anatoli I. *Im Dienste der Sowjet-Union: Erinnerungen eines Armeegenerals* [In the Service of the Soviet Union: Memoirs of a General of the Army]. Berlin: edition q, 1992.

Gribkov, Anatoli I., and William Y. Smith. *Operation ANADYR: U.S. and Soviet Generals Recount the Cuban Missile Crisis.* Edited by Alfred Friendly, Jr. Chicago, Berlin, Tokyo, and Moscow: edition q, 1994.

Gromyko, Andrey Andreyevich (1909–1989)

Soviet diplomat, foreign minister (1957–1985), and president (1985–1988). Born on July 18, 1909, to a peasant family in Starye Gromyki, Belorussia, Andrey Gromyko studied agricultural economics at the Minsk School of Agricultural Technology, earning a degree in 1936. After working as a research associate and economist at the Soviet Academy of Sciences in Moscow, he entered the Foreign Affairs Ministry, where he was named chief of the U.S. division of the People's Commissariat of Foreign Affairs in 1939. That same year he began working at the Soviet embassy in Washington, D.C. In 1943 Soviet leader Josef Stalin appointed Gromyko as Moscow's youngest-ever ambassador to the United States.

Gromyko played an important role in coordinating the wartime alliance between the United States and the Soviet Union, attending the February 1945 Yalta Conference, the July–August 1945 Potsdam Conference, and the October 1945 conference establishing the United Nations (UN). He became Moscow's UN representative in 1946. Gromyko served briefly as ambassador to the United Kingdom during 1952–1953 and then returned to the Soviet Union. In 1956 Gromyko attained full membership on the Central Committee of the Communist Party of the Soviet Union (CPSU). In 1957 he began his 28-year tenure as foreign minister. In 1973 he ascended to the Politburo. During his long career, Gromyko became known as an expert and cunning negotiator. In the West he was dubbed "Mr. Nyet" (Mr. No) because of his hard bargaining and staunch communist views. At home, he exhibited a great talent for adjusting to ruling leaders, failing to develop his own characteristic political line.

From 1958 to 1964 Gromyko readily adapted to Premier Nikita Khrushchev's erratic whims, playing a key role in the Berlin Crises and the Cuban Missile Crisis. Reportedly, Gromyko originally opposed Khrushchev's plan to install nuclear-capable missiles secretly on Cuba, though he later acquiesced in the proposal. Visiting the United States, on October 18, 1962, Gromyko met with U.S. President John F. Kennedy and Secretary of State Dean Rusk, who unbeknown to him were already aware of the presence of Soviet missiles on Cuba. Gromyko's assurances that Cuba possessed no offensive weapons annoyed both men, but neither betrayed this. Gromyko sent reassuring but inaccurate messages back to Moscow that the Kennedy administration had not discovered the real situation in Cuba.

Soviet leader Leonid Brezhnev, who dominated Soviet politics from Khrushchev's ouster in 1964 to his own death in 1982, gave Gromyko virtual free rein in setting Soviet foreign policy. Under Brezhnev, Gromyko

reached the apogee of his powers. During 1973–1975 Gromyko negotiated on behalf of the Soviet Union during the Conference on Security and Cooperation in Europe, which led to the landmark 1975 Helsinki Final Act. This act recognized Europe's postwar borders and set a political template for further negotiations concerning human rights, science, economics, and cultural exchanges. The Helsinki Final Act marked the full flowering of East-West détente, but because it did not match expectations about liberalization in the Soviet Union and Eastern Europe, it precipitated mounting dissent at home and protest abroad.

In 1985 Soviet leader Mikhail Gorbachev appointed his own protégé, Eduard Shevardnadze, as foreign minister and named Gromyko president of the Presidium of the Supreme Soviet of the USSR, by then a purely symbolic position. He remained in this post until 1988. Gromyko died on July 2, 1989, in Moscow.

Beatrice de Graaf

See also: Dobrynin, Anatoly Fyodorovich; Kennedy, John Fitzgerald; Khrushchev, Nikita Sergeyevich; Rusk, Dean David; United Nations

References

Gromyko, Anatoli. *Andrey Gromyko: In the Kremlin's Labyrinth.* Moscow: Avtor, 1997.

Gromyko, Andrei. *Memories.* New York: Arrow Books, 1989.

Guantánamo Bay Naval Base

The only U.S. military base on communist-held territory and the site of much East-West discord during the Cold War. Located on both sides of an impressive harbor on the southwestern coast of Cuba, the Guantánamo Bay naval base (officially termed Naval Station Guantánamo Bay) has been occupied by the United States since the early 20th century.

U.S. troops first landed at Guantánamo Bay in June 1898, during the Spanish-American War. In a 1903 agreement, the United States leased 28,817 acres, or about 45 square miles of land and water, around Guantánamo Bay from the new Republic of Cuba. A 1934 treaty modified the original lease, stipulating that the base would revert to Cuban sovereignty only if both nations agreed to the change.

Cuba's post-1959 government, led by communist dictator Fidel Castro, steadfastly refused to accept the legality of the base or the payments stipulated in the lease. Cubans argued that the original lease was forced on a weak, newly independent Cuba as part of the 1902 Platt Amendment, which gave the United States the right to intervene in Cuban affairs indefinitely.

U.S. strategic justifications for retaining the base have undergone various permutations. Guantánamo was initially built as a coaling station to resupply the U.S. fleet. As coal-fueled ships became obsolete, the United States sought other pretexts to keep the base. Guantánamo, it was subsequently argued, gave the United States control over Atlantic entry to the Caribbean as well as sea routes between its Atlantic coast ports and the Panama Canal. When changes in military technology and the end of the Cold War inspired a debate over the base's future in the 1990s, Washington argued that the base was vital to U.S. efforts to interdict drug smugglers from Central and South America.

Cuban critics have condemned the U.S. government's use of the base to interfere in the economic and political affairs of Cuba. Indeed, Guantánamo was used to stage U.S. interventions in Cuba in 1906 and 1912 and during 1917–1919, ostensibly to stabilize political disturbances and to protect U.S.-owned sugar properties in the region.

Following the 1959 Cuban Revolution, Guantánamo was at the center of the Cold War conflict between the United States and communist Cuba, supported by the Soviet Union. During John F. Kennedy's presidency, his brother, Attorney General Robert F. Kennedy, intermittently contemplated faking an attack on the base by Cuban revolutionary forces to provide a pretext for a U.S. invasion of the island. During the Cuban Missile Crisis, U.S. officials anticipated that one response to any U.S. moves against the island would be Soviet and Cuban attacks on Guantánamo. They therefore ordered the evacuation from the base of U.S. dependants and nonessential personnel, while airlifting an additional 3,600 Marine troops and 3,200 tons of military equipment into the base to reinforce its defenses. On October 26 and 27, with the crisis still unresolved, several hundred Soviet troops moved nuclear-capable cruise missiles to advance positions from which they could launch an attack on Guantánamo. One truck bearing a missile overturned, crushing two soldiers and a Cuban bystander to death. In the immediate aftermath of the crisis, as Soviet and U.S. representatives negotiated details of the removal of Soviet missiles in November and December 1962, Castro unavailingly sought to include the return of Guantánamo as part of the crisis settlement.

In subsequent years the base remained a U.S.-Cuban flashpoint. Defecting Cubans entering Guantánamo, a 1964 attempt by the Cuban government to cut water supplies to the base, and clashes between U.S. and Cuban troops along the fence surrounding the base all created tension. The Cubans also interpreted naval maneuvers conducted from Guantánamo during the Jimmy Carter, Ronald Reagan, and George H. W. Bush administrations as assaults on Cuban sovereignty.

In 1992, Camp X-Ray was built at the base to house Haitian refugees seeking entrance to the United States. In 1994, Guantánamo received thousands of Cubans who wished to leave the island. Eight years later, prisoners captured in the U.S. invasion of Afghanistan began to be ferried to the base for indefinite detention. Evidence of ill treatment of prisoners at the base provoked a wide-ranging debate within the United States and abroad during 2002–2007.

Priscilla Roberts

See also: ANADYR, Operation; Castro, Fidel; Kennedy, John Fitzgerald; Kennedy, Robert Francis

References

Dobbs, Michael. *One Minute to Midnight: Kennedy, Khrushchev, and Castro on the Brink of Nuclear War.* New York: Knopf, 2008.

Hansen, Jonathan M. *Guantánamo: An American History.* New York: Hill and Wang, 2011.

Lipman, Jana K. *Guantánamo: A Working-Class History between Empire and Revolution.* Berkeley: University of California Press, 2008.

Mason, Theodore. *Across the Cactus Curtain: The Story of Guantánamo Bay.* New York: Dodd, Mead, 1984.

Ricardo, Roger. *Guantánamo: The Bay of Discord.* Melbourne, Australia: Ocean Press, 1994.

Schwab, Stephen Irving Max. *Guantánamo, USA: The Untold History of America's Cuban Outpost.* Lawrence: University Press of Kansas, 2009.

Strauss, Michael J. *The Leasing of Guantanamo Bay.* Westport, CT: Praeger Security International, 2009.

Guevara de la Serna, Ernesto "Che" (1928–1967)

Argentine Marxist revolutionary and contributor to the doctrine of revolutionary warfare, Cuban minister of the interior, 1959–1965. Born on

June 14, 1928, to a middle-class family in Rosario, Argentina, Ernesto "Che" Guevara de la Serna trained as a medical doctor at the University of Buenos Aires, graduating in 1953. That same year he traveled throughout Latin America, witnessing the early months of the Bolivian National Revolution and the last months of the October Revolution in Guatemala during the presidency of Jacobo Arbenz. America's covert 1954 operation that ousted the leftist Arbenz from power radicalized Guevara, as did his later encounter in Mexico with several Cuban revolutionaries, including Fidel Castro. Guevara subsequently joined Castro's expedition to Cuba in December 1956 and fought with his July 26 Movement until it triumphed in January 1959.

Guevara became Cuba's first president of the National Bank and then minister of industry in Cuba's early postrevolutionary government. With Fidel Castro's brother Raúl, he was among the strongest proponents of communism within the Cuban government. He developed close ties with Aleksandr Alekseev, a Soviet KGB espionage agent who first came to Havana in October 1959 and was appointed Soviet ambassador in May 1962. Guevara and Raúl Castro both believed that a July 1960 Soviet declaration warning the United States against attacking Cuba had deterred an anticipated U.S.-backed invasion attempt in October 1960. In November 1960, Guevara visited Moscow, Prague, and Beijing, celebrating the November 7 anniversary of the Russian Revolution with Soviet leaders. At this time, he reportedly broached the idea of basing Soviet nuclear-capable missiles in Cuba with Party Secretary Nikita Khrushchev, a suggestion that may have sown the seeds of the Cuban Missile Crisis. Visiting Moscow in August 1962, Guevara initialed the secret Cuban-Soviet defense agreement governing the installation and operation of nuclear-capable missiles and other Soviet forces in Cuba.

Guevara, like Fidel Castro, deplored Khrushchev's decision to make concessions to the United States in October 1962 and remove Soviet missiles from Cuba. He warned Soviet officials that their actions during the crisis had weakened the Soviet Union's credibility around the world as a leader of international revolutionary movements. After the crisis had been resolved, Guevara told Anastas Mikoyan, a senior member of the Soviet Presidium, who visited Cuba in November 1962 to supervise the removal of the missiles, of his deep skepticism that the United States would honor its pledge not to invade Cuba in the future. In the economic sphere, he subsequently rejected the counsel of more orthodox Marxist and Soviet advisers and followed Chinese Communist developmental teachings as propounded by Chairman Mao Zedong, which proved largely unsuccessful in Cuba as in China.

Guevara left Cuba in 1965, possibly motivated by disagreement with its political leadership and certainly because of a long-standing commitment to promoting worldwide revolution. Guevara traveled to the Congo in 1965 and then to Bolivia in 1966, in the hope of initiating an insurrection that would become a focus for the transformation of neighboring countries. Guevara's overwhelming goal was to provide a diversion that would weaken U.S. resolve and resources then dedicated to waging war in Vietnam.

A Bolivian Army unit captured Guevara in the Yuro ravine on October 8, 1967, and summarily executed him the next day at La Higuera, Villagrande. One of his hands was removed to facilitate identification by U.S. intelligence. Guevara's body was uncovered in an unmarked site in Bolivia in 1997 and, together with the remains of a number of other Cuban revolutionaries who died in Bolivia, repatriated to Cuba for interment in a monument in Santa Clara City.

Priscilla Roberts

See also: Alekseev (Shitov), Aleksandr Ivanovich; Castro, Fidel; Castro, Raúl; China, People's Republic of; Khrushchev, Nikita Sergeyevich; Mikoyan, Anastas Ivanovich

References

Anderson, Jon Lee. *Che Guevara: A Revolutionary Life.* Rev. ed. New York: Grove Press, 2010.

Castañeda, Jorge. *Companero: The Life and Death of Che.* New York: Vintage, 1998.

Fursenko, Aleksandr, and Timothy Naftali. *One Hell of a Gamble: Khrushchev, Castro, and Kennedy, 1958–1964.* New York: Norton, 1997.

Guevara, Ernest Che. *Che: The Diaries of Ernesto Che Guevara.* New York: Ocean Press, 2009.

Löwy, Michael. *The Marxism of Che Guevara: Philosophy, Economics and Revolutionary Warfare.* New York: Monthly Review Press, 1974.

Reid-Henry, Simon. *Fidel* and *Che: A Revolutionary Friendship.* London: Sceptre, 2008.

Harriman, William Averell (1891–1986)

Ambassador-at-large, 1961; assistant secretary of state for Far Eastern affairs, 1962–1963; undersecretary of state for political affairs, 1963–1964. William Averell Harriman was born in New York City on November 15, 1891. He inherited the massive fortune of his father, the railroad tycoon E. H. Harriman. During World War II Harriman served as President Franklin D. Roosevelt's special envoy to British prime minister Winston Churchill and Soviet leader Joseph Stalin (1941–1943), and then as U.S. ambassador to the Soviet Union (1943–1946). Under President Harry S. Truman, he was ambassador to Great Britain (1946), secretary of commerce (1946–1948), special representative in Europe for the Economic Cooperation Administration (1948–1950), special assistant to the president (1950–1951), and head of the Mutual Security Administration (1951–1953). In 1954 he was elected governor of New York, serving one four-year term.

Harriman considered himself a Russian expert. In 1959 he toured the Soviet Union, where he had lengthy interviews with Soviet premier Nikita Khrushchev. When Khrushchev visited the United States later that year, Harriman reciprocated his hospitality. The two men fundamentally agreed on the need for arms-control agreements. Although not initially close to John F. Kennedy, in 1960 the office-hungry Harriman made strenuous efforts to win a foreign policy post. Beginning as ambassador-at-large, he became assistant secretary of state for Far Eastern affairs in 1962 and in March 1963 worked his way up to undersecretary of state for political affairs, third in seniority in the Department of State. In these years he developed a warm relationship with both the president and his brother Robert, the attorney general.

W. Averell Harriman, former U.S. ambassador to the Soviet Union and a close friend of Attorney General Robert F. Kennedy, was not formally a member of the Executive Committee (ExComm) of the National Security Council. During the Cuban Missile Crisis he made his views known and was a voice for moderation. (National Archives)

Initially, Kennedy largely ignored the advice Harriman was eager to offer him: to remain cool, calm, and relaxed when Khrushchev blustered and threatened and maintain a firm line on such issues as the status of Berlin, but do so through negotiations rather than military demonstrations. During the Cuban Missile Crisis, Harriman was not one of the Executive Committee (ExComm) inner circle of presidential advisers who deliberated over the U.S. response. As matters hung in the balance after Kennedy's public announcement on October 22 of the U.S. naval blockade of Cuba, Harriman worried that the United States might be forcing the beleaguered Khrushchev into a confrontation he wished to avoid. He shared these concerns with Arthur Schlesinger, Jr., Kennedy's special assistant, in the hope that they would reach the president. He also wrote to Robert Kennedy on October 22, warning that Khrushchev found particularly galling the presence of NATO Jupiter missiles in Turkey. In July 1963, Khrushchev agreed to resume negotiations for a nuclear test ban treaty, as Kennedy requested in his final public exchange of letters during the crisis. Harriman headed the delegation that negotiated an agreement whereby both powers as well as Britain agreed to halt atmospheric nuclear tests.

Harriman viewed with apprehension growing U.S. involvement in Indochina. In 1961–1962 he brokered a settlement between warring factions in Laos that sought to neutralize that country's participation in the burgeoning insurgency in South Vietnam. Harriman believed internal reforms and a negotiated settlement with the Viet Cong represented the best solution to South Vietnam's problems. Demoted by Lyndon B. Johnson, Kennedy's successor, to ambassador-at-large, and excluded from Johnson's inner circle of advisers, Harriman consistently advocated a bombing halt

and the opening of negotiations with North Vietnam. In 1968 he represented the United States when such talks began in Paris, resigning when Richard M. Nixon took office in January 1969. Well into his 80s, Harriman remained active in Democratic Party politics. He died in Yorktown Heights, New York, on July 26, 1986.

Priscilla Roberts

See also: Berlin Crises; Containment, Doctrine and Course of; Jupiter Missiles (Turkey and Italy); Kennedy, John Fitzgerald; Kennedy, Robert Francis; Khrushchev, Nikita Sergeyevich; Johnson, Lyndon Baines; Nuclear Arms Race; Partial Test Ban Treaty; Schlesinger, Arthur Meier, Jr.

References

Abramson, Rudy. *Spanning the Century: The Life of W. Averell Harriman 1891–1986*. New York: Morrow, 1992.

Costigliola, Frank. *Roosevelt's Lost Alliances: How Personal Politics Helped Start the Cold War*. Princeton, NJ: Princeton University Press.

Halberstam, David. *The Best and the Brightest*. New York: Random House, 1973.

Harriman, W. Averell, and Eli Abel. *Special Envoy to Churchill and Stalin, 1941–1946*. New York: Random House, 1975.

Isaacson, Walter, and Evan Thomas. *The Wise Men: Six Friends and the World They Made*. New York: Simon and Schuster, 1986.

Mayers, David. *The Ambassadors and America's Soviet Policy*. New York: Oxford University Press, 1995.

Olson, Lynne. *Citizens of London: The Americans Who Stood with Britain in its Darkest, Finest Hour*. New York: Random House, 2010.

J

Johnson, Lyndon Baines (1908–1973)

Prominent Texas politician who served as 36th president of the United States from 1963 to 1969, succeeding the charismatic John F. Kennedy after his assassination in November 1963. Lyndon Johnson was born in Stonewall in the Texas Hills near Austin, Texas, on August 27, 1908. As a Democratic congressman from 1937 to 1948, senator for Texas from 1949 to 1960, and Senate majority leader from 1955 to 1960, Johnson won a towering political reputation, based on his ability to persuade often balky senators and congressmen to reach consensus on sometimes controversial legislation. During his political career Johnson acquired a respectable understanding of U.S. foreign policies, a perspective informed by the orthodox bipartisan Cold War internationalist consensus on the need to resist the expansion of Soviet communism that most leading American politicians of his time shared. He supported the economic embargo the United States imposed on Cuba in October 1960.

Selected in 1960 as Kennedy's running mate, as vice president Johnson had little input into policy and was excluded from Kennedy's inner circle of advisers. He was left ignorant of planning for the failed April 1961 Bay of Pigs invasion of Cuba. Johnson was, however, a member of the Executive Committee (ExComm) Kennedy established on October 16 to decide how the U.S. government should react to the discovery of Soviet nuclear-capable missile sites in Cuba. Although absent from October 17 to 20, he participated in the final week's deliberations, taking charge when Kennedy was not present.

Johnson initially favored surprise U.S. air strikes to destroy the missile installations and only reluctantly came round to supporting a blockade.

He adamantly opposed suggestions that the United States might consider resolving the Cuban impasse by allowing East Germany to take over West Berlin, a repeated demand of Soviet and East German officials since the late 1950s. He was, however, a strong advocate of removing NATO Jupiter missiles in Turkey in exchange for the dismantling of Soviet missile bases in Cuba, an arrangement that Attorney General Robert F. Kennedy, the president's brother, eventually negotiated as a secret U.S.-Soviet understanding. Johnson also unsuccessfully advised Kennedy against consulting congressional leaders on the crisis, warning that the president would not "get much help out of them." Johnson regarded the outcome of the Cuban Missile Crisis as a U.S. victory. The narrow escape from nuclear war apparently impelled not only President Kennedy but also Johnson actively to seek U.S.-Soviet détente, a policy Johnson supported after becoming president in November 1963.

While still vice president, Johnson concluded that the threat that communist Cuba under Fidel Castro represented to the United States had been "grossly exaggerated." He believed that encouraging Latin American economic development through the Alliance for Progress, a Kennedy administration initiative he strongly supported, was the most productive means of combating radical leftism.

As president, Johnson feared that secret Central Intelligence Agency (CIA) Operation MONGOOSE plots to destabilize Cuba and kill Castro might have impelled Lee Harvey Oswald, a leftist American who belonged to the Free Cuba committee, and Cuban radicals to retaliate by assassinating Kennedy. In late 1963 Johnson ordered the cessation of such operations. Although Johnson initially broke off secret negotiations between Kennedy and Castro, using U.S. and Cuban UN delegates as intermediaries, in early 1964 he began to explore the possibility of normalizing U.S. relations with Cuba, extending highly unofficial secret feelers to Castro while maintaining the economic blockade and continuing to sanction some covert intelligence efforts to sabotage the existing regime. In spring 1964 minor crises—later peacefully resolved—occurred when the U.S. coast guard seized Cuban fishing boats in U.S. waters and Castro retaliated by cutting off the water supply to the U.S. military base at Guantánamo Bay. Johnson's growing preoccupation with the escalating war in Vietnam may have prevented him devoting adequate attention to potential rapprochement with Cuba and also undermined his efforts to improve U.S.-Soviet relations. Ultimately, Johnson's failure to attain victory in Vietnam and growing popular disillusionment with the war destroyed his presidency, and in March 1968 he declared that he would not seek another presidential

term. Johnson died at his Texas ranch on January 22, 1973, four years after leaving office.

Priscilla Roberts

See also: Bay of Pigs Invasion; Castro, Fidel; Central Intelligence Agency; Containment, Doctrine and Course of; Guantánamo Bay Naval Base; Jupiter Missiles; Kennedy, John Fitzgerald; Kennedy, Robert Francis; MONGOOSE, Operation; United Nations; U.S. Allies; U.S. Congress

References

Dallek, Robert. *Flawed Giant: Lyndon Johnson and His Times, 1961–1973.* New York: Oxford University Press, 1998.

Dumbrell, John. *President Lyndon Johnson and Soviet Communism.* Manchester: Manchester University Press, 2004.

Schwartz, Thomas A. *Lyndon Johnson and Europe: In the Shadow of Vietnam.* Cambridge, MA: Harvard University Press, 2003.

Woods, Randall B. *LBJ: Architect of American Ambition.* New York: Free Press, 2006.

Joint Chiefs of Staff

The U.S. Joint Chiefs of Staff (JCS) is a military committee consisting of the chiefs of staff of the U.S. Army and Air Force, the chief of naval operations, and the commandant of the Marine Corps. Its chairman, a separate officer drawn from one of the services, is a U.S. National Security Council member. Originating during World War II, the committee was formalized and codified under the 1947 National Security Act that created a Department of Defense incorporating the former War and Navy departments. The JCS advise the president, the secretary of defense, and the National Security Council and provide guidance to commanders in the field.

President John F. Kennedy's relationship with the JCS was difficult. One of the first decisions he faced when he took office was whether to endorse the plan formulated under his predecessor, President Dwight D. Eisenhower, for a CIA-sponsored invasion of Cuba by refugee Cuban exiles. Kennedy accepted the scheme in principle but insisted that the United States should not provide overt military support for the exiles and moved the projected landing site. He also severely limited the number and nature

of U.S. air strikes and air cover during the operation. In the aftermath of the botched April 1961 Bay of Pigs invasion, which became a humiliating and embarrassing fiasco for the United States, Kennedy and his top civilian aides blamed the JCS for endorsing the plan, albeit with some qualifications, and not pointing out its weaknesses sufficiently forcefully. In his view, the JCS had expected that, should the invasion force encounter problems, Kennedy would drop the pretense of noninvolvement and intervene overtly to assist the rebels, something he was not prepared to sanction. On their side, the JCS considered Kennedy's refusal to give the rebels greater support evidence of weak and irresolute leadership. Adm. Arleigh Burke, chief of naval operations, had since early 1960 supported the overthrow of the Castro government and publicly cast doubt on Soviet premier Nikita Khrushchev's July 1960 pledge that the Soviet Union would if necessary use nuclear weapons to defend Cuba against U.S. attack. As the invading forces encountered greater resistance than anticipated, Burke begged Kennedy to allow him to send naval or air support, but after some wavering Kennedy refused.

One major casualty of the Bay of Pigs was Kennedy's relationship with the JCS. The JCS despised him for failing to escalate U.S. intervention, while Kennedy distrusted them. His relationship with Gen. Lyman Lemnitzer, chairman of the JCS, was particularly bad; the two men could scarcely bear to be in the same room. Burke, who soon leaked to the press information on the Bay of Pigs detrimental to Kennedy, had nothing but contempt for both the president and his secretary of defense, Robert S. McNamara. He retired as chief of naval operations on August 1, 1961, replaced by Adm. George Whelan Anderson, Jr. On June 30, 1961, the forceful Gen. Curtis LeMay also replaced Thomas D. White as chief of staff of the U.S. Air Force. In late April 1961, Kennedy brought in Maxwell D. Taylor, former chief of staff of the U.S. Army under Eisenhower, who had retired four years earlier, to investigate the Bay of Pigs. He soon appointed Taylor his principal military adviser, to serve as liaison with the JCS and as chairman of the Special Group (Augmented) on Cuba. On October 1, 1962, Kennedy appointed Taylor chairman of the Joint Chiefs of Staff, a post he held until mid-1964. Simultaneously, Earle G. Wheeler replaced George Decker as army chief of staff.

During the Cuban Missile Crisis, Taylor generally represented the JCS in the Executive Committee (ExComm) of the president's advisers. Initially he recommended a surgical strike against the missile bases, followed by a naval blockade to prevent the arrival of further weapons. Later that day, after consulting the JCS, he recommended massive air strikes on Cuban

military facilities over several days but hoped to avoid outright U.S. invasion. The JCS met as a group with Kennedy on October 19, recommending massive air strikes against Cuban targets without advance warning, preferably on October 23. With the exception of Taylor, they also favored following this with a full-scale U.S. invasion of the island, measures they further assumed would mean war with the Soviet Union. By October 20 ExComm leaned toward favoring a naval blockade (or "quarantine") of Cuba. Taylor expressed disagreement on behalf of the JCS but pledged their complete backing for the president's decision. After Kennedy's public announcement of the quarantine on October 22, Taylor continued to support massive air strikes targeting all identified nuclear-capable and surface-to-air missile sites, plus all Soviet and Cuban airplanes and airfields. Anderson planned, implemented, and enforced the naval quarantine. On October 27, with negotiations with Khrushchev at a critical stage, the JCS once again recommended launching massive air strikes against Cuba on October 29, followed by an invasion one week later.

The JCS reacted with dismay when Khrushchev and Kennedy reached agreement on October 28, drafting a message to Kennedy characterizing the Soviet response as "an insincere proposal to gain time" that would leave missiles in Cuba and warning against any "relaxation of alert procedures." Anderson told Kennedy, "We have been had." LeMay described the understanding as "the greatest defeat in our history" and continued to urge an invasion. JCS invasion preparations continued into the first week of November. As lengthy negotiations over the removal of the weapons ensued, the JCS deplored Cuba's refusal to allow on-site inspections of missile sites in Cuba. LeMay unavailingly suggested that U.S. naval squadrons and bombers be positioned around Cuba and that, should Castro reject U.S. demands for access, they bomb the Cuban military command center. Castro also sought to retain Soviet Il-28 light bombers in Cuba. Informed of this in mid-November, the Joint Chiefs unanimously recommended that unless these left Cuba, the United States should either bomb them or land military personnel on Cuba to remove them. The dispute was resolved peacefully when Soviet officials agreed to send the Il-28s back to Russia. For the rest of his life Kennedy believed that, had he followed the advice of the JCS, full-scale nuclear war and global devastation would have resulted.

Priscilla Roberts

See also: Bay of Pigs Invasion; Castro, Fidel; Central Intelligence Agency; Eisenhower, Dwight David; Kennedy, John Fitzgerald; McNamara, Robert Strange; Taylor, Maxwell Davenport

References

Brugioni, Dino. *Eyeball to Eyeball: The Inside Story of the Cuban Missile Crisis.* Ed. Robert F. McCort. New York: Random House, 1991.

Dobbs, Michael. *One Minute to Midnight: Kennedy, Khrushchev, and Castro on the Brink of Nuclear War.* New York: Knopf, 2008.

Freedman, Lawrence. *Kennedy's Wars: Berlin, Cuba, Laos, and Vietnam.* New York: Oxford University Press, 2000.

Goduti, Philip A., Jr. *Kennedy's Kitchen Cabinet and the Pursuit of Peace: The Shaping of American Foreign Policy, 1961–1963.* Jefferson, NC: McFarland Press, 2009.

Gribkov, Anatoli I., and Smith, William Y. *Operation ANADYR: U.S. and Soviet Generals Recount the Cuban Missile Crisis.* Edited by Alfred Friendly, Jr. Chicago, Berlin, Tokyo, and Moscow: edition q, 1994.

McMaster, H. R. *Dereliction of Duty: Lyndon Johnson, Robert McNamara, the Joint Chiefs of Staff, and the Lies That Led to Vietnam.* New York: HarperCollins, 1997.

Polmar, Norman, and John D. Gresham. *DEFCON-2: Standing on the Brink of Nuclear War during the Cuban Missile Crisis.* New York: John Wiley, 2006.

Jupiter Missiles (Turkey and Italy)

In the late 1950s the United States developed virtually identical Jupiter and Thor intermediate-range ballistic missiles (IRBMs). Seeking to repair relations with Britain after the previous year's divisive Suez crisis, in March 1957 U.S. President Dwight D. Eisenhower offered such weapons to British prime minister Harold Macmillan, who agreed that 60 Thor missiles should be deployed on British territory, under joint U.S. and British control. They arrived in batches in 1959. In late 1957, in the aftermath of the Soviet launching of *Sputnik,* the first space satellite, the United States decided to offer Jupiter missiles to other U.S. North Atlantic Treaty Organization (NATO) allies in Europe. Following lengthy negotiations, France, West Germany, and Greece declined them, but in 1959 Italy agreed to accept 30 Jupiter missiles and Turkey 15. The warheads were to remain under U.S. control, with launching requiring approval from both U.S. and host governments. Soviet premier Nikita Khrushchev objected particularly strongly to Jupiter deployments in Turkey, because their 1,700-mile range meant these could reach numerous targets in western Soviet territory within a few minutes. Installation of missile bases in Italy was completed during 1961.

By 1961, the liquid-fueled, immobile Jupiters and Thors, highly vulnerable to a Soviet first strike, were already obsolete, as solid-fueled mobile missiles, often based on Polaris submarines, became available. Between February and April 1961, many U.S. officials recommended against installing Jupiters in Turkey, but Turkish leaders resisted cancellation and construction of the installations went ahead, with deployments completed between November 1961 and March 1962. Khrushchev repeatedly assailed the presence of missiles in Turkey, uncomfortably close to his Black Sea dacha. By summer 1962 the United States and Britain had agreed to remove increasingly obsolete Thor missiles within a year. U.S. officials sought similar arrangements with Turkey, but Turkish leaders protested strongly and the missiles remained undisturbed.

When U.S. reconnaissance planes discovered Soviet missile emplacements in Cuba in October 1962, sparking the Cuban Missile Crisis, from the outset President John F. Kennedy and his advisers recognized the possibility that Khrushchev would demand removal of NATO missiles in Turkey as a quid pro quo for dismantling Soviet nuclear-capable missile bases in Cuba. During the crisis, newspaper pundits, including the influential columnist Walter Lippmann and Max Frankel of the *New York Times,* openly suggested such a trade, as did Bruno Kreisky, Austria's foreign minister. Kennedy was reluctant to make a public bargain along these lines but allowed his brother, U.S. Attorney General Robert Kennedy, to explore the possibility with Anatoly Dobrynin, the Soviet ambassador in Washington, and Georgi Bolshakov, a Soviet military intelligence operative. Soviet and U.S. officials informally agreed that the United States would implement the withdrawal of Jupiter missiles in Turkey and Italy within a few months. Had these negotiations failed, Kennedy was ready to encourage U Thant, acting secretary general of the United Nations, to propose a similar arrangement. To sweeten the deal, if necessary Macmillan was also prepared to offer the (already settled) removal of Thor missiles from the United Kingdom, though as events transpired this inducement was not required. There are also some indications that, had the United States launched air strikes against Soviet bases in Cuba, U.S. officials considered not retaliating further should Khrushchev in response order attacks on Turkish Jupiter bases.

Fearful of repercussions, President Kennedy restricted knowledge of the U.S.-Soviet understanding to a very small circle—his brother Robert, Secretary of State Dean Rusk, National Security Adviser McGeorge Bundy, Defense Secretary Robert McNamara, and Ambassador Llewellyn Thompson—that excluded even most ExComm members. Most Soviet

officials likewise remained ignorant of the agreement, since Khrushchev kept his word and maintained great secrecy regarding it. On October 29, 1962, McNamara established an interdepartmental task force to supervise removal of the missiles by April 1, 1963. Turkish officials, who had welcomed the Jupiter missiles enthusiastically, were reluctant to sanction their removal; Italian leaders were readier to relinquish their missiles in return for alternative security arrangements. To encourage Turkish and Italian compliance, the United States offered additional conventional and dual-purpose weapons, including F-104G fighter jets. In February 1963 the Kennedy administration announced the withdrawal of the Jupiters before consulting NATO's governing body, the North Atlantic Council, that supposedly controlled their deployment. By the end of April all Italian and Turkish Jupiter missiles had been dismantled. In their place, nuclear-armed U.S. Polaris submarines patrolled the Mediterranean.

Priscilla Roberts

See also: Bolshakov, Georgi Nikitovich; Bundy, McGeorge; Dobrynin, Anatoly Fyodorovich; Eisenhower, Dwight David; Kennedy, John Fitzgerald; Kennedy, Robert Francis; Khrushchev, Nikita Sergeyevich; McNamara, Robert Strange; Military Balance; Missile Gap; Nuclear Arms Race; Rusk, Dean David; Thompson, Llewellyn Edward, Jr.; U Thant; United Nations; U.S. Allies

References

Frankel, Max. *High Noon in the Cold War: Kennedy, Khrushchev, and the Cuban Missile Crisis.* New York: Ballantine Books, 2004.

Fursenko, Aleksandr, and Timothy Naftali. *One Hell of a Gamble: Khrushchev, Castro, and Kennedy, 1958–1964.* New York: Norton, 1997.

Nash, Philip. *The Other Missiles of October: Eisenhower, Kennedy, and the Jupiters, 1957–1963.* Chapel Hill: University of North Carolina Press, 1997.

K

Kennedy, John Fitzgerald (1917–1963)

U.S. congressman (1946–1952), senator (1953–1961), and president of the United States (1961–1963). John F. Kennedy was born in Brookline, Massachusetts, on May 29, 1917, into a large and wealthy Irish Catholic family. His father, Joseph P. Kennedy, was a multimillionaire with presidential aspirations, and his mother, Rose Fitzgerald, came from a prominent and politically active Boston family. After attending the elite Choate Preparatory School in Wallingford, Connecticut, Kennedy earned his bachelor's degree from Harvard University in 1940. During World War II Kennedy served four years in the U.S. Navy, winning the Navy and Marine Corps Medals and the Purple Heart for action as commander of PT-109, which was rammed and sunk by a Japanese destroyer in the South Pacific.

After the war, Kennedy worked briefly as a newspaper correspondent before entering national politics at the age of 29, winning election as a Democratic congressman from Massachusetts in 1946. Kennedy was elected to the U.S. Senate in 1952. His career there was relatively undistinguished, due in part to several serious health problems, including chronic back problems and Addison's disease. In 1960, he nonetheless won the Democratic nomination for president on the first ballot. As a candidate, Kennedy promised more aggressive defense policies, health care reform, and housing and civil rights programs. He also proposed his New Frontier agenda, designed to revitalize the flagging U.S. economy and to bring young people into government and humanitarian service. Winning by the narrowest of margins, he became the nation's first Roman Catholic president. Only 43 years old, he was also the youngest man ever elected to that office.

Democrat John F. Kennedy, elected president in November 1960, liked to project an image of Cold War toughness. In practice, during the Cuban Missile Crisis, he nonetheless proved flexible and sought to avoid a nuclear conflagration. (John F. Kennedy Presidential Library)

In his inaugural address, Kennedy urged Americans to be active citizens and to sacrifice for the common good. His address, in some respects a rather bellicose call to arms, ended with the now-famous exhortation "ask not what your country can do for you—ask what you can do for your country." As president, Kennedy set out to fulfill his campaign pledges. Once in office, he was forced to respond to the ever-more-urgent demands of civil rights advocates, although he did so rather reluctantly and tardily. By establishing both the Alliance for Progress and the Peace Corps, Kennedy delivered American idealism and goodwill to aid developing countries.

Despite Kennedy's idealism, his presidency witnessed growing tensions in U.S.-Soviet Cold War rivalry. Privately, in 1959 he had suggested that President Dwight Eisenhower's failure to welcome Cuba's revolutionary leader Fidel Castro when he visited the United Nations that year had been a mistake. During the 1960 presidential campaign Kennedy nonetheless excoriated the Eisenhower administration for its failure to eradicate Cuba's communist government. One of his first attempts to address the perceived communist threat was to authorize a band of U.S.-supported Cuban exiles to invade the island in an attempt to overthrow Castro's government. The April 1961 Bay of Pigs invasion, which turned into an embarrassing debacle for the president, had been planned by the Central Intelligence Agency (CIA) during Eisenhower's administration. Although Kennedy harbored reservations about the operation, he nonetheless approved it. Its failure heightened existing Cold War tensions with the Soviet Union and ultimately set the stage for the Cuban Missile Crisis. Kennedy and Castro to some degree became global competitors for the allegiance of idealistic young people around the world.

Cold War confrontation was not limited to Cuba. In spring 1961, the Soviet Union renewed its campaign to control West Berlin. Kennedy spent two days in Vienna in June 1961 discussing the hot-button issue with Soviet premier Nikita Khrushchev. In the months that followed, the construction of the Berlin Wall, which prevented East Berliners from escaping to the West, further intensified the Berlin crisis. Kennedy responded to the provocation by reinforcing troops in the Federal Republic of Germany (FRG) (West Germany) and increasing the nation's military strength. The Berlin Wall, albeit perhaps unintentionally, eased tensions in Central Europe that had nearly resulted in a superpower conflagration. Meanwhile, Kennedy began deploying what would become some 16,000 U.S. military "advisers" to prop up Ngo Dinh Diem's regime in the Republic of Vietnam (RVN) (South Vietnam), a commitment that set the United States on the slippery slope toward full-scale military intervention in Vietnam.

After the Bay of Pigs, Kennedy authorized various CIA and other covert initiatives intended, in tandem with economic sanctions, to sabotage, undermine, and destroy Castro's government. Fearing a second U.S. invasion attempt, and seeking to redress the nuclear strategic balance in their own favor, in May 1962 Soviet leaders decided to clandestinely install nuclear-capable missiles in Cuba. On October 14, 1962, U.S. reconnaissance planes photographed the construction of missile-launching sites in Cuba. The placement of nuclear-capable missiles only 90 miles from U.S. shores threatened to destabilize the Western Hemisphere and undermine the uneasy Cold War nuclear deterrent. Kennedy imposed a naval quarantine on Cuba, designed to interdict any offensive weapons bound for the island. On October 22 U.S. armed forces moved to DEFCON-3, a heightened state of alert, upgraded to DEFCON-2, only one level short of war, on October 25. For several days the outcome hung in the balance, as the two Cold War superpowers appeared close to thermonuclear war, but ultimately Soviet leaders agreed to remove the missiles. In return, the United States pledged not to preemptively invade Cuba and privately agreed to remove obsolete NATO nuclear missiles from Turkey. During the crisis, Kennedy secretly taped the discussions of his Executive Committee (ExComm) of senior advisers. When released in the 1990s, the transcripts revealed a man who, despite his initial belief that U.S. air strikes against the installations on Cuba were almost inevitable, soon leaned to the less confrontational option of a naval quarantine or blockade and was prepared to make substantial concessions in order to avoid escalation into a full-scale nuclear war.

These events sobered both Kennedy and Khrushchev. Following the nerve-wracking crisis, Kennedy took up the causes of civil rights and disarmament. Cold War tensions diminished when the Soviet, British, and

U.S. leaders signed the Partial Test Ban Treaty on August 5, 1963, forbidding atmospheric testing of nuclear weapons and also their testing under water or in outer space. In October 1963, the same three nations agreed to refrain from placing nuclear weapons in orbit. To avoid potential misunderstandings and miscalculations in a future crisis, a hotline was installed that directly linked the Oval Office with the Kremlin.

In July 1963 the U.S. Treasury Department imposed regulations forbidding all U.S. citizens to have any commercial or financial relations with Cuba. Despite his noninvasion pledge, in June 1963 Kennedy endorsed further CIA covert sabotage operations intended to destabilize Castro's government. Paradoxically, working through William Attwood, an adviser to Adlai Stevenson, the U.S. representative at the United Nations (UN), and Carlos Lechuga, Cuba's ambassador to the UN, Kennedy also responded favorably to exploratory feelers from Castro on the possibility of normalizing U.S.-Cuban relations. He suggested that the United States might lift its sanctions on Cuba if Castro dropped his support for revolutionary movements elsewhere in Latin America. On November 22, 1963, Kennedy's assassination in Dallas, Texas, during a political campaign trip cut short these overtures. Kennedy's successor, Lyndon B. Johnson, when informed of the Attwood-Lechuga channel in December 1963, ended the talks, considering them too politically compromising, liable to expose him to Republican charges that he was soft on communism. Lee Harvey Oswald, arrested for murdering the president, held leftist political views that had impelled him to join a Fair Play for Cuba Committee. Oswald, himself shot two days later by a nightclub owner, never stood trial, and it remained unclear how far sympathy for Cuba motivated him to gun down Kennedy. In a great national outpouring of grief, Kennedy was laid to rest in Arlington National Cemetery on November 25, 1963.

Lacie A. Ballinger

See also: Alliance for Progress; Bay of Pigs Invasion; Berlin Crises; Castro, Fidel; Central Intelligence Agency; Containment, Doctrine and Course of; Eisenhower, Dwight David; Johnson, Lyndon Baines; Kennedy, Robert Francis; Khrushchev, Nikita Sergeyevich; Military Balance; Missile Gap; Nuclear Arms Race; Partial Test Ban Treaty; Stevenson, Adlai Ewing II; United Nations; Vienna Conference

References

Beschloss, Michael R. *The Crisis Years: Kennedy and Khrushchev, 1960–1963.* New York: HarperCollins, 1991.

Bradlee, Benjamin C. *Conversations with Kennedy.* New York: Norton, 1975.

Dallek, Robert. *An Unfinished Life: John F. Kennedy, 1917–1963.* Boston: Little, Brown, 2003.

Freedman, Lawrence. *Kennedy's Wars: Berlin, Cuba, Laos, and Vietnam.* New York: Oxford University Press, 2000.

Kennedy, Robert F. *Thirteen Days: A Memoir of the Cuban Missile Crisis.* New York: Norton, 1999.

Lechuga, Carlos M. *In the Eye of the Storm: Castro, Kennedy, Khrushchev, and the Missile Crisis.* Translated by Mary Todd. Melbourne, Victoria, Australia: Ocean Press, 1995.

Rabe, Stephen G. *The Most Dangerous Area in the World: John F. Kennedy Confronts Communist Revolution in Latin America.* Chapel Hill: University of North Carolina Press, 1999.

Schlesinger, Arthur M., Jr. *A Thousand Days: John F. Kennedy in the White House.* New York: Houghton Mifflin, 1965.

White, Mark J. *The Kennedys and Cuba: The Declassified Documentary Record.* Chicago: Ivan R. Dee, 1999.

Kennedy, Robert Francis (1925–1968)

U.S. attorney general (1961–1964), U.S. senator (1965–1968), and chief adviser to his brother, President John F. Kennedy (1961–1963). Born in Boston on November 20, 1925, Robert F. Kennedy was the seventh child of Joseph P. Kennedy, multimillionaire business tycoon and U.S. ambassador to Great Britain. Robert Kennedy served in the U.S. Navy Reserve during 1944–1946 before graduating from Harvard University in 1948. In 1951 he earned a law degree from the University of Virginia. He began his legal career as an attorney in the Criminal Division of the U.S. Department of Justice in 1951 and later served as chief counsel to the Senate Select Committee on Improper Activities in the Labor and Management Field. Robert managed his brother John's successful U.S. senatorial campaign in 1952 and his 1960 presidential campaign.

Following the 1960 election, President-elect Kennedy appointed his younger brother to his cabinet as U.S. attorney general. Robert Kennedy was also President Kennedy's closest adviser on both foreign and domestic policy. Once the president approved the proposed April 1961 Bay of Pigs invasion attempt by U.S.-trained Cuban exiles, his brother enthusiastically endorsed this decision and squelched potential critics. Robert was one

Robert F. Kennedy, attorney general of the United States, was the closest adviser of his brother President John F. Kennedy. During the Cuban Missile Crisis, he and Soviet ambassador Anatoly Dobrynin conducted crucial backstage negotiations over the removal of Jupiter missiles from Turkey that helped to resolve the crisis peacefully. (Lyndon B. Johnson Presidential Library)

of a panel that investigated the reasons for the invasion's failure. He also aggressively backed new measures aimed at Castro's overthrow, including economic sanctions and a wide range of covert sabotage operations within Cuba initiated by both the Central Intelligence Agency (CIA), known as Operation MONGOOSE, and the Special Group (Augment ed) on Cuba, of which he was an influential member and even tually chair. CIA efforts involved cooperation with leading American Mafia figures and repeated attempts to assassinate Castro. It remains unclear exactly how much the attorney general, who was undoubtedly almost obsessively determined to remove Castro, knew of these matters.

From April 1961 onward Robert Kennedy opened an unofficial diplomatic back channel with Georgi Bolshakov, a military intelligence agent based at the Soviet embassy in Washington whose reports went to Soviet premier Nikita Khrushchev. In over 40 meetings and communications, for 18 months he represented the president in efforts to defuse U.S.-Soviet tensions over Berlin, Laos, and Cuba and promote disarmament and superpower cooperation. Ironically, in summer 1962 Khrushchev used Bolshakov to request a cessation of U.S. aerial surveillance of Soviet shipping, facilitating the clandestine installation of nuclear-capable missiles on Cuba.

When the Kennedy administration discovered these missiles in October 1962, Robert Kennedy was a crucial figure in the deliberations of the Executive Committee (ExComm) of senior presidential advisers. Initially, on October 16, he favored immediate air strikes to destroy the missile bases, but within three days he had become the most influential

proponent of a naval quarantine or blockade, the least aggressive course considered and the one that President Kennedy chose. In confidential talks with Anatoly Dobrynin, Soviet ambassador to the United States, Robert Kennedy also negotiated a secret understanding whereby the United States agreed to remove obsolete NATO Jupiter nuclear missiles from Turkey in exchange for Soviet withdrawal of those on Cuba. His posthumously published account of the Cuban missile crisis, *Thirteen Days* (1969), became a bestseller but was by no means entirely accurate in depicting his stance.

Once the missile crisis was resolved, in December 1962 Robert Kennedy concluded an agreement whereby Castro released the Cuban exiles captured at the Bay of Pigs in exchange for $53 million in American medicines, food, and machinery. His hostility to Cuba was still strong, however, and throughout 1963 both Kennedy brothers continued to endorse proposed covert operations intended to facilitate Castro's overthrow and military contingency plans to invade Cuba. The Kennedy administration's dedication to attacking Castro may have been one reason Lee Harvey Oswald, a leftist American who supported Cuba, assassinated the president in November 1963. Some historians have speculated that guilt over the possibility that his near-obsessive crusade against Cuba provoked Oswald's action may have intensified Robert Kennedy's devastating grief over his brother's death. After President Kennedy's assassination, Robert Kennedy resigned his cabinet post in the autumn of 1964 to run for a seat in the U.S. Senate, representing New York. Sworn into the Senate in January 1965, he became a vigorous advocate of social reform and minority rights. Although he had initially supported his brother's increasing military and economic aid to South Vietnam, he became sharply critical of President Lyndon B. Johnson's steep escalation of the war. When Johnson declined to seek renomination for the presidency in March 1968, Kennedy became a candidate for the Democratic presidential nomination, campaigning across the country in the Democratic primaries. On June 4, 1968, just after he had won the California primary, Sirhan B. Sirhan, a Jordanian American, shot Kennedy in the head; he died two days later and was buried in Arlington National Cemetery.

Lacie A. Ballinger

See also: Bay of Pigs Invasion; Bolshakov, Georgi Nikitovich; Castro, Fidel; Central Intelligence Agency; Dobrynin, Anatoly Fyodorovich; Johnson, Lyndon Baines; Jupiter Missiles (Turkey and Italy); Kennedy, Robert Francis; MONGOOSE, Operation; Taylor, Maxwell Davenport

References

Hilty, James W. *Robert Kennedy: Brother Protector.* Philadelphia: Temple University Press, 1997.

Kennedy, Robert F. *Robert Kennedy in His Own Words: The Unpublished Recollections of the Kennedy Years.* New York: Bantam, 1988.

Schlesinger, Arthur M., Jr. *Robert Kennedy and His Times.* 2 vols. Boston: Houghton Mifflin, 1978.

Thomas, Evan. *Robert Kennedy: His Life.* New York: Simon and Schuster, 2000.

Khrushchev, Nikita Sergeyevich (1894–1971)

Soviet politician, first secretary of the Communist Party of the Soviet Union (CPSU), 1953–1964, and premier of the Soviet Union, 1958–1964. Born on April 17, 1894, in Kalinovka, Kursk Province, to a peasant family, Nikita Sergeyevich Khrushchev worked beginning at age 15 as a pipe fitter in various mines near his home. In 1918 he joined the Russian Communist Party, and in 1919 he became a political commissar in the Red Army. Early

Soviet premier Nikita Khrushchev's love of diplomatic braggadocio and brinkmanship did much to precipitate the Cuban Missile Crisis. Fear of nuclear devastation nonetheless ultimately made him willing to concede the withdrawal of Soviet missiles from Cuba. (AP/Wide World Photos)

recognizing the importance of Communist Party Secretary Joseph Stalin, Khrushchev nurtured a friendship with Stalin's associate and party secretary in Ukraine, Lars Kaganovich, who helped him secure a full-time party post in the Moscow city party apparatus in 1931.

By 1935 Khrushchev was secretary general of the Moscow Communist Party, in effect mayor of the capital. In 1938 he became a candidate (nonvoting member) of the Politburo, and in 1939, a full member. He was one of few senior party officials to survive Stalin's Great Purges. After the German invasion of the Soviet Union in June 1941, Khrushchev was made a lieutenant general and placed in charge of resistance in Ukraine and relocating heavy industry eastward.

In 1949, Khrushchev returned to his previous post as head of the Communist Party machinery in Moscow. In 1952, at the 19th Party Congress, Khrushchev received the assignment of drawing up a new party structure, which led to the replacement of the old Politburo by the Presidium of the Central Committee. As one of the powerful committee secretaries, Khrushchev benefited from this change.

Following Stalin's death on March 5, 1953, a brief power struggle ensued, with no one individual on the 10-member Presidium dominating. Khrushchev, chosen as party secretary in 1953, emerged as supreme leader over the next two years, becoming premier in 1958. Khrushchev's greatest—and perhaps most risky—achievement as Soviet leader was to repudiate Stalin and attempt to de-Stalinize Soviet society. The most powerful blow to the Stalinists came during his famous speech at a closed session of the 20th Party Congress on February 25, 1956, in which Khrushchev documented some of the crimes and purges of the Stalinist period. Under Khrushchev, the Soviet Union gradually became more liberal, and oppressive domestic repression relaxed considerably. Soviet success during the 1950s in economic policy, industrial production, and the space program, in which he took special interest, compelled Khrushchev to proclaim that by 1970, the Soviet Union would surpass the United States in per capita production. In 1980, he grandiosely predicted, the United States would embrace communism.

Khrushchev's foreign policies within and beyond the communist bloc tended to be ambivalent. He restored Soviet relations with Yugoslavia in 1955, repairing the Tito-Stalin break of 1948. He promoted de-Stalinization programs in Eastern bloc states and allowed overseas communist parties a certain limited autonomy but was prepared to suppress dissent if he thought this in Soviet best interests. When his secret 1956 speech on Stalin and the ensuing de-Stalinization campaign led to revolts in Poland

and Hungary, he intervened in both cases, ordering the 1956 Hungarian Revolution crushed by brute force. When Albanian and Chinese officials criticized his de-Stalinization policies and rapprochement with the West, this led to crises and permanent schisms in Soviet relations with both countries. Particularly serious was the Sino-Soviet split, which became highly and publicly acrimonious.

Khrushchev generally attempted to ease tensions with the West, particularly with the United States. He rejected Stalin's thesis that wars between capitalist and socialist countries were inevitable and instead sought peaceful coexistence. On the whole, until 1960, Soviet-U.S. relations improved. Khrushchev's 1959 visit to the United States was a remarkable success. His talks with President Dwight D. Eisenhower produced, at least briefly, a warming termed the Spirit of Camp David. But Khrushchev also engaged in some rather dubious and dangerous foreign policy initiatives. He initiated the 1958–1961 Berlin Crises, authorized the construction of the Berlin Wall in 1961, and used the U-2 Affair in 1960 to provoke a showdown and derail the May 1960 Paris summit meeting with Eisenhower.

In 1959, Khrushchev welcomed the emergence of a radical revolutionary regime in Cuba, one whose leader, Fidel Castro, soon sought Soviet economic and military assistance. Fears that U.S. President John F. Kennedy intended forcibly to overthrow Castro's government, and a desire to redress the massive advantage the United States possessed over the Soviet Union in strategic nuclear missiles, impelled Khrushchev in May 1962 to offer to station Soviet military units equipped with short-, medium-, and intermediate-range nuclear-capable ballistic missiles and other conventional weapons on Cuba. The plan was very much Khrushchev's own initiative. He intended to install both men and missiles on the island in great secrecy before publicly announcing their presence there and, he hoped, using them to pressure U.S. officials on Berlin, Cuba, and other issues. In October 1962, when the missile bases were still under construction, the Kennedy administration discovered their existence, and a brief but extremely tense confrontation ensued, as Kennedy demanded the removal of all nuclear warheads and nuclear-capable delivery vehicles from Cuba. For some days, thermonuclear war between the superpowers seemed a distinct possibility. Khrushchev eventually decided to dismantle the missiles and ship them back to Russia, winning in return a public pledge by the United States not to invade Cuba. Secretly, Kennedy also agreed to withdraw NATO Jupiter intermediate-range missiles recently installed in Turkey and Italy, within easy reach of the Soviet Union, a concession that Khrushchev never revealed publicly. The narrow escape from nuclear war sobered leaders on both sides. Nine months later,

on July 25, 1963, the United States, Britain, and the Soviet Union signed a Partial Nuclear Test Ban Treaty.

The debacle in Cuba contributed to the decision of the Soviet Communist Party's Central Committee to oust Khrushchev from power on October 14, 1964, as did his increasingly unpredictable and unstable behavior and his failed agricultural policies. Living quietly in semi-disgrace, he then wrote his memoirs, which were published in the West beginning in 1970. Khrushchev died in Moscow on September 11, 1971, following a massive heart attack.

Magarditsch Hatschikjan

See also: ANADYR, Operation; Bay of Pigs Invasion; Berlin Crises; Castro, Fidel; Eisenhower, Dwight David; Jupiter Missiles (Turkey and Italy); Military Balance; Missile Gap; Nuclear Arms Race; Partial Test Ban Treaty; Vienna Conference

References

Beschloss, Michael R. *The Crisis Years: Kennedy and Khrushchev, 1960–1963.* New York: HarperCollins, 1991.

Fursenko, Aleksandr, and Timothy Naftali. *Khrushchev's Cold War: The Inside Story of an American Adversary.* New York: Norton, 2006.

Haslam, Jonathan. *Russia's Cold War: From the October Revolution to the Fall of the Wall.* New Haven, CT: Yale University Press, 2011.

Khrushchev, Nikita S. *Khrushchev Remembers.* Introduction and commentary by Edward Crankshaw. Translated by Strobe Talbott. Boston: Little, Brown, 1970.

Khrushchev, Nikita S. *Khrushchev Remembers: The Glasnost Tapes.* Translated and edited by Jerrold L. Schecter with Vyacheslav V. Luchkov. Boston: Little, Brown, 1990.

Khrushchev, Nikita S. *Khrushchev Remembers: The Last Testament.* Translated and edited by Strobe Talbott. Boston: Little, Brown, 1974.

Khrushchev, Nikita S. *Memoirs of Nikita Khrushchev.* Edited by Sergei Khrushchev and translated by George Shriver. University Park: Pennsylvania State University Press, 2004.

Medvedev, Roi A. *Khrushchev.* Translated by Brian Pearce. Oxford, UK: Blackwell, 1982.

Taubman, William. *Khrushchev: The Man and His Era.* New York: Norton, 2003.

Zubok, Vladislav M. *A Failed Empire: The Soviet Union in the Cold War from Stalin to Gorbachev.* Chapel Hill: University of North Carolina Press, 2007.

Zubok, Vladislav, and Constantine Pleshakov. *Inside the Kremlin's Cold War: From Stalin to Khrushchev.* Cambridge, MA: Harvard University Press, 1996.

Kohler, Foy David (1908–1990)

U.S. diplomat, ambassador to the Soviet Union, 1962–1966. Foy Kohler was born in Oakwood, Ohio, on February 15, 1908. He attended Toledo University and the University of Ohio before joining the Foreign Service in 1931, undertaking a variety of foreign postings. From 1947 to 1949 he served in the U.S. embassy in Moscow, and from 1949 to 1952 was director of the Voice of America radio broadcasting network. During the 1950s he spent stints with the Policy Planning Staff and the Bureau of Near Eastern Affairs and as counselor in the U.S. embassy in Turkey and was detailed to the International Cooperation Agency. From December 1959 to August 1962, Kohler was assistant secretary of state for European Affairs.

Appointed U.S. ambassador to the Soviet Union in September 1962, Kohler arrived in Moscow only weeks before the Cuban Missile Crisis began. On October 16 Kohler, just arrived in Moscow, reported a conversation with Soviet premier Nikita Khrushchev, in which the latter promised to do nothing to complicate relations with the United States before the approaching early November congressional midterm elections. Kohler was not close to President John F. Kennedy, and during the Cuban Missile Crisis the U.S. embassy in Moscow functioned largely as a conduit and translation bureau for urgent messages between Khrushchev and U.S. officials in Washington. This system proved so slow and clumsy that in June 1963 the Soviet Union and the United States established a dedicated transatlantic telephone "hotline" to enable leaders in both countries to communicate directly with each other. Kohler was present at the August 1963 negotiations in Moscow that resulted in the Partial Nuclear Test Ban Treaty. Retiring from the Foreign Service in 1967 as deputy undersecretary for political affairs, Kohler became a professor of international relations at the University of Miami, Coral Gables, Florida. He died in Jupiter, Florida, on December 23, 1990.

Priscilla Roberts

See also: Kennedy, John Fitzgerald; Khrushchev, Nikita Sergeyevich; Partial Test Ban Treaty

Reference

Fursenko, Aleksandr, and Timothy Naftali. *One Hell of a Gamble: Khrushchev, Castro, and Kennedy, 1958–1964.* New York: Norton, 1997.

Kohler, Foy D. *Understanding the Russians: A Citizen's Primer.* New York: Harper and Row, 1970.

Mayers, David. *The Ambassadors and America's Soviet Policy*. New York: Oxford University Press, 1995.

Kozlov, Frol Romanovich (1908–1965)

Soviet communist leader. Born in Loshchinino, Ryazan, in central Russia on August 18, 1908, Frol Kozlov joined the Communist Party of the Soviet Union (CPSU) and rose steadily in that organization. In 1947 he became second secretary of the Kuybyshev provincial party committee. In 1949 he was assigned to Leningrad, and in 1953 he became first secretary of the CPSU in that city.

Closely allied with Nikita Khrushchev, Kozlov became a full member of the Presidium in 1957. He was briefly premier of the Russian Soviet Federated Socialist Republic (RSFSR) during 1957–1958 but resigned this post to become the deputy chairman of the Council of Ministers of the Soviet Union, or deputy premier. In 1960 he assumed the powerful post of secretary of the CPSU Central Committee.

Kozlov was among Soviet hard-liners who favored an uncompromising stance toward the West. He was a key player in enforcing an uncompromising approach against the June 2, 1962, workers' strike in Novocherkassk that resulted in several deaths when Red Army soldiers fired on demonstrators, an event kept secret for almost 30 years. Kozlov, the Presidium member who followed intelligence activities most closely, likewise endorsed an assertive policy on Cuba. In March 1961 he assured Raúl Castro, younger brother of Cuban leader Fidel Castro, that the Soviet Union was "prepared to give Cuba whatever she needed" militarily, provided "Soviet specialists were sent to Cuba" to supervise the use of such weaponry. In May 1962 Politburo meetings he spoke in favor of Khrushchev's decision to deploy nuclear-capable weapons in Cuba. At the end of October, however, he endorsed the removal of such missiles, acquiescing in Khrushchev's pragmatic recognition that nuclear war over these with the United States was unacceptable.

Kozlov was considered the heir apparent to Khrushchev, whose position with his colleagues in the party hierarchy was weakened following the 1960 U-2 Affair and especially after the Cuban Missile Crisis. This all became moot when Kozlov suffered a stroke in April 1963. Without this health setback, Kozlov and not Leonid Brezhnev might have become the next Soviet leader. Despite his near-complete incapacitation, Kozlov retained his posts

until he was forced to resign in November 1964 after Khrushchev's removal from power. Kozlov died in Moscow on January 30, 1965.

Spencer C. Tucker

See also: Castro, Raúl; Khrushchev, Nikita Sergeyevich

References

Fursenko, Aleksandr, and Timothy Naftali. *Khrushchev's Cold War: The Inside Story of an American Adversary.* New York: Norton, 2006.

Fursenko, Aleksandr, and Timothy Naftali. *One Hell of a Gamble: Khrushchev, Castro, and Kennedy, 1958–1964.* New York: Norton, 1997.

Linden, Carl. *Khrushchev and the Soviet Leadership, 1957–1964.* Baltimore, MD: Johns Hopkins University Press, 1966.

Medvedev, Roi A. *Khrushchev.* Translated by Brian Pearce. Oxford, UK: Blackwell, 1982.

Taubman, William. *Khrushchev: The Man and His Era.* New York: Norton, 2003.

Kuznetsov, Vasili Vasilyevich (1901–1990)

Soviet politician, first deputy foreign minister, 1955–1977. Vasili Kuznetsov was born on February 13, 1901, in Sofilovka, Kostroma Province, Russia. He studied engineering and metal processing, the latter in the United States from 1931 to 1933 at the Carnegie Institute of Technology in Pennsylvania. He joined the Soviet Communist Party in 1927. Rising through various government and party positions, he was chairman of the All-Union Central Council of Trade Unions from 1944 to 1953, and from 1946 to 1950 he also chaired the Soviet of Nationalities. After the death of Soviet leader Joseph Stalin, in 1953 Kuznetsov switched to the foreign ministry, serving briefly as Soviet ambassador to China. He attended the 1954 Geneva conference on Indochina as a Soviet representative. In 1955 Kuznetsov became first deputy foreign minister, a post he held until 1977, working closely with Foreign Minister Andrey Gromyko.

At the end of October 1962, Khrushchev dispatched Kuznetsov to the United Nations (UN) to negotiate the details of the removal of Soviet missiles from Cuba. He worked intensely with UN acting secretary general U Thant and the American John J. McCloy, hammering out bargains whereby the U.S. government accepted that Cuban premier Fidel Castro would not permit on-site inspections in Cuba and thus it would rely on

aerial surveillance and sea inspections of departing freighters to confirm the removal of Soviet weapons. Despite last-ditch efforts by Castro and Soviet defense minister Rodion Malinovsky to leave these in place, at U.S. insistence Soviet Il-28 light bombers and tactical nuclear-capable missiles were also withdrawn from Cuba. The United States did not, as Kuznetsov requested, pledge unequivocally not to invade Cuba, nor did Kuznetsov promise that all Soviet troops would leave the island. In late December 1962, as their negotiations came to an end, Kuznetsov warned McCloy, "we will honor this agreement. But I will tell you something. The Soviet Union is not going to find itself in a position like this ever again." His words signaled Soviet leaders' determination to build up their nuclear forces to something approaching parity with the United States. In May 1963 Kuznetsov nonetheless unsuccessfully opposed Khrushchev's public statement, in a Cuban-Soviet communiqué issued at the end of a visit by Castro, that the Soviet Union would if necessary use nuclear weapons to defend Cuba's independence. In 1977 Kuznetsov became first deputy chairman of the Soviet Presidium, a post he held until he retired in 1986, serving as the Soviet Union's acting head of state after the deaths of Soviet leaders Leonid Brezhnev, Yuri Andropov, and Konstantin Chernenko. He died in Moscow on June 5, 1990.

Priscilla Roberts

See also: Castro, Fidel; Gromyko, Andrey Andreyevich; Khrushchev, Nikita Sergeyevich; Malinovsky, Rodion Yakovlevich; McCloy, John Jay; U Thant; United Nations

References

Bird, Kai. *The Chairman: John J. McCloy and the Making of the American Establishment.* New York: Simon and Schuster, 1992.

Fursenko, Aleksandr, and Timothy Naftali. *One Hell of a Gamble: Khrushchev, Castro, and Kennedy, 1958–1964.* New York: Norton, 1997.

L

Lansdale, Edward Geary (1908–1987)

U.S. Air Force officer, intelligence operative, purportedly the model for the leading characters in two novels—*The Quiet American* by Graham Greene and *The Ugly American* by Eugene Burdick and William Lederer. Born in Detroit, Michigan, on February 6, 1908, Edward Lansdale graduated from the University of California at Los Angeles in 1931 and was commissioned in the army through ROTC. During the Great Depression, he sold advertising in California. He went on active duty during World War II in the U.S. Army, serving with the Office of Strategic Services (OSS) and finishing his wartime service as a major with the U.S. Army Air Forces as chief of the Intelligence Division in the western Pacific. In 1950, at the request of Filipino president Elpidio Quirino, Lansdale became a member of the U.S. Military Assistance Group, undertaking operations to suppress the communist Hukbalahap rebellion. In 1953 Washington dispatched Lansdale to join the U.S. mission in Vietnam as adviser on counter-guerrilla operations. After a brief tour in the Philippines, he returned to Vietnam in 1954 to serve with the U.S. Military Advisory Group there.

After helping solidify South Vietnamese prime minister Ngo Dinh Diem's rule, Lansdale returned to Washington in 1957 and held assorted military and Defense Department positions. He was promoted to brigadier general in 1960 and major general upon his retirement in 1963. From 1959 to 1961, as deputy assistant secretary of defense for special operations he played a prominent role in training Cuban exiles for the disastrous April 1961 Bay of Pigs invasion. Until his retirement in November 1963, he also worked with the Central Intelligence Agency (CIA) and Attorney General

Robert F. Kennedy on various unsuccessful attempts to foment rebellion in Cuba and assassinate Cuban leader Fidel Castro.

Lansdale's convoluted career included two years of service as a consultant to the Food for Peace Program. He returned to South Vietnam in 1965 as senior liaison officer of the U.S. Mission to the Republic of Vietnam and then became assistant to U.S. ambassador Ellsworth Bunker in 1967. Lansdale retired for good in 1968, wrote his memoirs, and died in McLean, Virginia, on February 23, 1987.

Daniel E. Spector

See also: Bay of Pigs Invasion; Castro, Fidel; Central Intelligence Agency; Kennedy, Robert Francis; MONGOOSE, Operation

References

Bohning, Don. *The Castro Obsession: U.S. Covert Operations against Cuba, 1959–1965.* Washington, DC: Potomac Books, 2005.

Currey, Cecil B. *Edward Lansdale: The Unquiet American.* Washington, DC: Brassey's, 1998.

Lansdale, Edward G. *In the Midst of Wars: An American's Mission to Southeast Asia.* New York: Harper and Row, 1972.

Nashel, Jonathan. *Edward Lansdale's Cold War: A Cultural Biography of a Legendary Cold War Figure.* Amherst: University of Massachusetts Press, 2004.

Lovett, Robert Abercrombie (1895–1986)

U.S. secretary of defense (1951–1953), presidential adviser. Born in Huntsville, Texas, on September 14, 1895, Robert Lovett moved in 1909 with his family to New York. He attended Yale University, temporarily dropping out to serve as a naval aviator after the United States entered World War I. In the early 1920s he joined and soon became a partner in the venerable investment bank Brown Brothers, later Brown Brothers Harriman. In 1940 Lovett's continuing interest in aviation and his concern to build up U.S. aerial production capacities led Secretary of War Henry L. Stimson to appoint him assistant secretary of war for air, a post he held for almost five years.

In 1947 Lovett's former superior George C. Marshall, whom President Harry S. Truman had just appointed secretary of state, persuaded Lovett

to become undersecretary of state. He remained in office until late 1948, overseeing the development of the Marshall Plan and the North Atlantic Treaty Organization (NATO). In September 1950, when Marshall became secretary of defense during the Korean War, Lovett once again served as his deputy, supervising a major military buildup and succeeding Marshall when the latter retired in late 1951.

Lovett left office when the Truman administration ended, but successive presidents repeatedly sought his views on assorted foreign policy issues, regarding him as a key member of the "Wise Men," the establishment figures who presided over the mid-20th-century expansion of U.S. international power. In the mid-1950s Lovett presciently warned that the Central Intelligence Agency (CIA) had become overly enamored of covert operations. In 1960 he

Former secretary of defense Robert A. Lovett held no official position in John F. Kennedy's administration but was one of the trusted "Wise Men" of the American foreign policy establishment whose advice Kennedy sought from time to time. By the mid-1950s, Lovett had come to deplore the Central Intelligence Agency's intrusive covert operations in other countries. The CIA's efforts to overthrow Castro's government in Cuba were a prime example of such operations. (Library of Congress)

forcefully attacked CIA plans to invade Cuba and unsuccessfully demanded a complete reassessment of overall covert policies, advice the Eisenhower administration resisted. Afterward Lovett publicly stated, "What right do we have barging into other people's countries, buying newspapers and handing out money to opposition parties or supporting a candidate for this or that office?"

During the Cuban Missile Crisis President John F. Kennedy consulted Lovett, who counseled moderation, favoring the imposition of a naval blockade on Cuba, with gradual increases of pressure if appropriate. He stressed the "desirability of taking a mild and not very bloodthirsty step

first," to give the Soviets an opportunity to retreat. Lovett believed that air strikes would not necessarily succeed in destroying all the missiles. On October 20 he helped Kennedy draft the announcement of a naval quarantine. Lovett died in Locust Valley, Long Island, New York, on September 14, 1986.

Priscilla Roberts

See also: Bay of Pigs Invasion; Central Intelligence Agency; Kennedy, John Fitzgerald

Reference

Isaacson, Walter, and Evan Thomas. *The Wise Men: Six Friends and the World They Made.* New York: Simon and Schuster, 1986.

M

Malinovsky, Rodion Yakovlevich (1898–1967)

Marshal of the Soviet Union, minister of defense, 1957–1967. Born to a poor peasant family near Odessa on November 23, 1898, Rodion Malinovsky enlisted in the Russian Army at the outbreak of World War I, fighting in France and North Africa. Malinovsky returned to Russia via Vladivostok in August 1919, joined the Red Army and fought against the White forces. In 1926 he joined the Communist Party and a year later entered the Frunze Military Academy for a three-year officers' training program. He was a military adviser to the Republican forces during 1937–1938 in the Spanish Civil War. During World War II Malinovsky saw service in the Ukraine, took part in the ill-fated June 1942 Kharkov Offensive, and played a key role in the Battle of Stalingrad, in December defeating Army Group Don, the German relief force under Field Marshal Erich von Manstein.

He also began a long association with Nikita Khrushchev, then a political officer reportedly assigned by Soviet leader Joseph Stalin to watch Malinovsky. He played a major role in the Battle of Kursk in July 1943 and then spearheaded the drive across the Ukraine, taking Odessa in April 1944. From the Ukraine, he led Soviet forces into Romania, Hungary, Austria, and Czechoslovakia. In September 1944 he was promoted to marshal of the Soviet Union. When the war in Europe ended, Malinovsky took command of the Transbaikal Front in the Far East, pushing into Japanese-held Manchuria. A prominent member of the Soviet military hierarchy after the war, he headed the Far East Command during 1947–1953 and the Far East Military District during 1953–1956.

Malinovsky served as deputy minister of defense during 1956–1957, then succeeded Marshal Georgi Zhukov as minister of defense. In this post Malinovsky introduced strategic missiles into the Soviet arsenal and oversaw Soviet military modernization.

From mid-1960 onward, Malinovsky approved the dispatch of increasingly substantial quantities of military assistance to Cuba, including tanks, rifles, pistols, machine guns, field artillery and antitank guns, and antiaircraft guns, plus ammunition. In May 1961, additional supplies earmarked for Cuba included 41 fighter jets and reconnaissance aircraft, 80 additional tanks, 54 antiaircraft guns, and 128 field artillery pieces. By spring 1962, the Soviet Union had sent over $250 million worth of weaponry to Cuba and had promised five rocket batteries and three surface-to-air missile (SAM) batteries, with 196 missiles.

By May 1962, Malinovsky was an enthusiastic advocate of Khrushchev's plan to base nuclear-capable missiles on Cuba, overriding opponents who queried it in meetings. He apparently considered this an excellent opportunity to project Soviet military power into the Western Hemisphere and thereby redress the nuclear balance in the Soviets' favor, deterring U.S. leaders from ever considering a first strike against the Soviet Union. Malinovsky was responsible for implementing the decision, supervising preparations to move and install the missiles and the Soviet military personnel operating them quickly and in great secrecy. He actively discouraged subordinates from suggesting that U-2 surveillance overflights would probably detect the missile bases before they became operational. In August 1962 Malinovsky initialed the secret Soviet-Cuban defense treaty governing the installation and operation of the missiles and other Soviet military facilities and forces on Cuba. After President John F. Kennedy publicly warned the Soviet Union in September 1962 against installing offensive weapons on Cuba, Khrushchev and Malinovsky expanded the program of deliveries to include shipments of short-range Luna missiles and R-11m cruise missiles, plus a squadron of Il-28 light bombers with nuclear bombs. Malinovsky argued that the United States would not react to the missiles when discovered, but he anticipated that, if necessary, a show of Soviet naval power in the Caribbean would suffice to quell U.S. objections; indeed, he hoped to increase permanently the Soviet submarine and surface naval presence there.

On October 22, as apprehensive Kremlin officials waited for Kennedy to make a public statement, Malinovsky urged that the Soviet commander in Cuba, Gen. Issa Pliyev, be instructed to use only conventional weapons in response to any U.S. military action. An authorization to employ

nuclear-capable missiles was held in reserve but never sent. On October 25, Malinovsky remained silent as Khrushchev and the Politburo made the decision to remove the missiles. On October 27, anticipating potential U.S. air strikes, Khrushchev and Malinovsky signed an order authorizing Pliyev to use "all available means of air defense." No such air strikes occurred, however. On October 28, Khrushchev decided to accept Kennedy's proposals, and Malinovsky instructed Pliyev to begin dismantling the missile sites. In the aftermath of the crisis, Malinovsky initially tried to retain 100 short-range tactical nuclear warheads in Cuba, together with several squadrons of Il-28s, and begin training Cubans to use these, but Khrushchev overruled him. Despite the immediate post-crisis acrimony Cuban officials displayed toward the Soviet Union, Malinovsky felt it important to maintain cooperative military relations with Cuba, and he still considered the island an important strategic asset to the Soviet Union. Malinovsky died in office of cancer in Moscow on March 31, 1967.

Michael Share and Spencer C. Tucker

See also: ANADYR, Operation; Castro, Fidel; Gribkov, Anatoli Ivanovich; Kennedy, John Fitzgerald; Khrushchev, Nikita Sergeyevich; Military Balance; Missile Gap; Nuclear Arms Race; Pliyev, Issa Alexandrovich; U-2 Overflights

References

Erickson, John. "Rodion Yakovlevich Malinovsky." Pp. 117–124 in *Stalin's Generals,* edited by Harold Shukman. New York: Grove, 1993.

Fursenko, Aleksandr, and Timothy Naftali. *One Hell of a Gamble: Khrushchev, Castro, and Kennedy, 1958–1964.* New York: Norton, 1997.

Gribkov, Anatoli I., and William Y. Smith. *Operation ANADYR: U.S. and Soviet Generals Recount the Cuban Missile Crisis.* Edited by Alfred Friendly, Jr. Chicago, Berlin, Tokyo, and Moscow: edition q, 1994.

Mann, Thomas C. (1912–1999)

U.S. State Department official and Latin American specialist. Born on November 11, 1912, in Laredo, Texas, Thomas Mann graduated from Baylor University in 1934 with BA and LLB degrees and then practiced law. He began working for the Department of State in 1942 as a special assistant to the U.S. ambassador to Uruguay.

In 1952 as deputy assistant secretary of state for Inter-American Affairs, Mann argued that disparities in wealth between the United States and Latin America would spur anti-Americanism and economic nationalism and that communists would exploit these circumstances. Willing to jettison the U.S. nonintervention pledge, he concluded that Washington must intervene in Latin America if communism threatened to gain a foothold there.

Although he was among the creators of the multilateral Inter-American Development Bank, in 1959 Mann articulated fears that plans for a large U.S. aid program for Latin America would raise unreasonably high expectations that could not be met, resulting in disillusionment and increased anti-Americanism in the region. His misgivings were largely borne out in the Alliance for Progress, launched by President John F. Kennedy in 1961, that disproportionately benefited the wealthy.

Before the April 1961 Bay of Pigs invasion attempt, Mann produced a devastating assessment. Believing that landing Cuban exile paramilitary units on the island was unlikely to trigger a popular uprising against Cuban leader Fidel Castro, he warned that the United States would then face the unpalatable alternatives of abandoning these men or overt military intervention to rescue them and overthrow Castro. Mann also pointed out that the operation violated international law and would damage U.S. credibility. Presented to Kennedy in February 1961, together with a memorandum by CIA deputy director Richard Bissell favoring the invasion, Mann's warnings failed to dissuade Kennedy from sanctioning the operation.

From December 1963, under President Lyndon B. Johnson, Mann was both assistant secretary for Inter-American Affairs and head of the Agency for International Development, which ran the Alliance for Progress. Concurrently, he was made a special assistant to the president. He essentially directed U.S. policy in Latin America. Following Johnson's cue, the so-called Mann Doctrine shifted the emphasis of the Alliance for Progress toward anticommunism and the protection of U.S. investments, promoting cooperation with military or nondemocratic regimes provided they sanctioned U.S. investment on nondiscriminatory terms and adopted anti-Soviet policies. In March 1965 Johnson appointed Mann undersecretary of state for economic affairs.

That same year, however, key congressmen asserted that the administration's April 1965 intervention in the Dominican Republic, which Mann strongly supported, had greatly overstated the communist threat. With the 1966 appointment of Lincoln Gordon as assistant secretary of state for Inter-American Affairs, Mann's influence over Latin American policy effectively ended. He resigned from the Department of State in May 1966, yet future administrations would adopt many of his policies.

From 1967 to 1971 Mann served as president of the Automobile Manufacturers Association. He died on January 23, 1999, in Austin, Texas.

James F. Siekmeier

See also: Alliance for Progress; Bay of Pigs Invasion; Bissell, Richard Mervin, Jr.; Central Intelligence Agency; Johnson, Lyndon Baines; Kennedy, Robert Fitzgerald

References

Lafeber, Walter. "Thomas C. Mann and the Devolution of Latin America Policy: From the Good Neighbor to Military Intervention." Pp. 166–203 in *Behind the Throne: Servants of Power to Imperial Presidents, 1898–1968,* edited by Thomas McCormick and Walter Lafeber. Madison: University of Wisconsin Press, 1993.

Siekmeier, James F. *Aid, Nationalism, and Inter-American Relations: Guatemala, Bolivia, and the United States, 1945–1961.* Lewiston, NY: Edwin Mellen, 1999.

Walker, William O. "The Struggle for the Americas: The Johnson Administration and Cuba." Pp. 97–144 in *The Foreign Policies of Lyndon Johnson: Beyond Vietnam,* edited by H. W. Brands. College Station: Texas A&M University Press, 1999.

McCloy, John Jay (1895–1989)

Presidential arms control adviser, 1961–1974. Born in Philadelphia on March 31, 1895, John J. McCloy attended Amherst College and Harvard Law School. During World War I he interrupted his studies to serve in the U.S. Army, becoming a captain of artillery and acquiring an internationalist outlook. In 1924 McCloy joined the prestigious New York corporate law firm of Cravath, de Gersdorff, Swaine, and Moore, rising to partner in 1929.

In 1940 McCloy joined the War Department as a consultant to Secretary Henry Lewis Stimson, a lifelong hero and role model of McCloy's. Appointed assistant secretary the following year, McCloy was involved in virtually every major political and military wartime decision until he left that position in November 1945. From 1949 to 1952 McCloy was U.S. high commissioner in the Federal Republic of Germany, responsible for implementing that country's return to independent statehood. McCloy was

president of the Chase Manhattan Bank from 1953 to 1960, after which he returned to law. He was one of the "Wise Men," recognized foreign policy experts whom successive presidents consulted on a wide range of international issues. The journalist Richard H. Rovere even termed him the "chairman" of the American Establishment.

In 1961 President John F. Kennedy appointed McCloy director of the new Arms Control and Disarmament Agency, entrusted with formulating broad disarmament policies and revitalizing stalled U.S.-Soviet negotiations for a treaty to ban atmospheric nuclear arms tests. Whether McCloy learned in advance of the Bay of Pigs invasion plan remains unclear. In its aftermath, he criticized the operation for frivolously diverting resources from more serious problems, including Berlin, NATO defense, and disarmament negotiations. Considering Cuba strategically insignificant to the United States, McCloy warned that, by arming Cuban anti-Castro rebels, the U.S. government undermined the legal basis of its protests against Soviet backing of Laotian and South Vietnamese insurgents.

On October 16, when Kennedy learned of the presence of Soviet missile installations in Cuba, McCloy was in Europe. Even before meeting with his Executive Committee (ExComm) of senior officials, Kennedy consulted him by telephone. McCloy recommended an air strike to destroy the missile sites, if necessary followed by a full-scale U.S. invasion of Cuba. While believing the missiles made little practical difference to the U.S.-Soviet nuclear balance, McCloy viewed their presence in Cuba as a test of U.S. international credibility, fearing that if they remained his country's NATO partners would lose all faith in U.S. commitments to Western Europe.

Recalled home on October 21, McCloy briefed United Nations (UN) delegates on the crisis. He remained at the UN for most of the crisis, in part because many ExComm members feared that Adlai Stevenson, U.S. ambassador to the UN, might be too conciliatory when responding to UN initiatives on the crisis. After Kennedy publicly imposed a naval blockade of Cuba on October 22, McCloy resisted suggestions by UN officials that Kennedy agree to temporarily lift the quarantine if Soviet premier Nikita Khrushchev suspended further weapons shipments to Cuba, a position he reiterated at an ExComm meeting on October 26. Returning to the UN, he responded favorably to suggestions from acting secretary general U Thant that the United States might pledge not to invade Cuba in exchange for the removal of Soviet missiles, and he endorsed the president's decision to withdraw NATO missiles from Turkey.

After Khrushchev agreed to dismantle the missiles, throughout November and December 1962 McCloy chaired a three-man UN Special

Coordinating Committee of U.S. officials that handled detailed negotiations with Soviet deputy foreign minister Vasili Kuznetsov and Soviet UN delegate Valerian A. Zorin to facilitate the departure of Soviet weaponry from Cuba. McCloy hoped these talks would give added momentum to subsequent U.S.-Soviet arms-control efforts. McCloy also pragmatically suggested that the United States should respond favorably to any overtures from Cuban leader Fidel Castro to normalize U.S.-Cuban diplomatic relations. McCloy was aware that a small combat brigade of Soviet troops would remain in Cuba. In 1979, when press revelations of the continuing presence of Soviet military personnel in Cuba embarrassed President Jimmy Carter's administration, McCloy defused the crisis when he publicly stated that their deployment on the island did not breach the understandings U.S. and Soviet representatives had reached in late 1962. McCloy continued as a presidential arms control adviser until 1974, welcoming progress on U.S.-Soviet détente and helping negotiate various disarmament agreements. He died in Stamford, Connecticut, on March 11, 1989.

Priscilla Roberts

See also: Bay of Pigs Invasion; Castro, Fidel; Jupiter Missiles (Turkey and Italy); Kennedy, John Fitzgerald; Kuznetsov, Vasili Vasilyevich; Nuclear Arms Race; Stevenson, Adlai Ewing II; U Thant; United Nations; U.S. Allies; Zorin, Valerian Aleksandrovich

References

Bird, Kai. *The Chairman: John J. McCloy and the Making of the American Establishment.* New York: Simon and Schuster, 1992.

Isaacson, Walter, and Evan Thomas. *The Wise Men: Six Friends and the World They Made.* New York: Simon and Schuster, 1986.

McCone, John Alex (1902–1991)

Industrialist and director of the Central Intelligence Agency (CIA), 1961–1965. Born in San Francisco, California, on January 4, 1902, John Alex McCone graduated from the University of California at Berkeley in 1922. A successful businessman who advanced from riveter to vice president of the Consolidated Steel Corporation in the 1920s, McCone made a fortune

in the steel and shipbuilding industries during World War II under the banner of the Bechtel-McCone engineering firm.

In 1950, he became undersecretary of the Air Force, in which position he urged President Harry Truman to begin a program of building guided missiles, which was not immediately done. In 1951, he returned to private business but continued to serve Washington in special missions. In 1958, President Dwight D. Eisenhower appointed him head of the Atomic Energy Commission.

On September 27, 1961, several months after the abortive Bay of Pigs invasion of Cuba, President John F. Kennedy appointed McCone, a conservative Republican with virtually no intelligence experience, to head the CIA, succeeding Allen Dulles. He inherited an agency in considerable turmoil.

McCone proceeded to restore CIA credibility. He immediately convened a study group to identify the duties of the director and submit suggestions on agency reorganization. This substantially improved scientific and technological research and development capabilities, added a cost-analysis system, and created a position of comptroller. In addition, Kennedy publicly strengthened the agency by announcing that the director would be charged with developing policies and coordinating procedures at all levels across the intelligence community. The announcement came less than a month after the president's Foreign Intelligence Advisory Board recommended dismantling the CIA.

Alerted by reports of growing deliveries of Soviet weaponry to Cuba, from August 1962 McCone suspected these might include nuclear armaments and he pressed the White House to authorize surveillance overflights. On October 14 a high-flying U-2 reconnaissance plane produced photographic evidence of potential nuclear-capable missile sites on Cuba. McCone, a longtime advocate of overthrowing Fidel Castro's government in Cuba, an objective he believed would require direct U.S. military intervention, attended many of the subsequent Executive Committee (Ex-Comm) meetings of top U.S. officials convened to handle the situation. His preferred option was a full-scale U.S. invasion of Cuba, preceded by air strikes on the missile installations. Subsequently, his access to the president waned after he bragged too loudly for too long how accurate his predictions of Soviet missiles in Cuba had been.

McCone remained CIA director after Kennedy's November 1963 assassination. His criticism of President Lyndon B. Johnson's escalation of the war in Vietnam as unlikely to prove effective may have hastened his departure from the CIA in 1965. McCone later served on the boards of

several major corporations, including ITT. He died on February 14, 1991, in Pebble Beach, California.

Paul R. Camacho

See also: Bay of Pigs Invasion; Castro, Fidel; Central Intelligence Agency; Dulles, Allen Welsh; Eisenhower, Dwight David; Kennedy, John Fitzgerald; U-2 Overflights

References

Brugioni, Dino. *Eyeball to Eyeball: The Inside Story of the Cuban Missile Crisis.* Edited by Robert F. McCort. New York: Random House, 1991.

Fursenko, Aleksandr, and Timothy Naftali. *One Hell of a Gamble: Khrushchev, Castro, and Kennedy, 1958–1964.* New York: Norton, 1997.

Hersh, Burton. *The Old Boys: The American Elite and the Origins of the CIA.* New York: Charles Scribner's Sons, 1992.

McNamara, Robert Strange (1916–2009)

U.S. secretary of defense, 1961–1968. Born in San Francisco on June 9, 1916, McNamara was an Army Air Corps officer in World War II, when he used statistical techniques acquired at the Harvard Business School to improve the logistics, planning, and analysis of strategic bombing raids over Europe and Japan. Joining the Ford Motor Company after the war, in November 1960 he was appointed president but left almost immediately when President John F. Kennedy recruited him as secretary of defense.

McNamara moved immediately to enlarge his personal staff and centralize decision making in the secretary's office, developing and employing a planning-programming-budgeting system (PPBS) in efforts to enhance cost-effectiveness by eliminating duplication, waste, and overlapping programs among the three services and subjecting proposed weapons systems to close cost-benefit analysis. These and other efficiency measures, including proposals to close unneeded military bases and consolidate the National Guard and Army Reserves into one system, provoked fierce opposition from many military men and from powerful congressional and civilian lobbies.

McNamara made an early mistake in endorsing the disastrous April 1961 Bay of Pigs invasion of Cuba. During the Cuban Missile Crisis,

Secretary of Defense Robert McNamara was one of the key members of the Executive Committee of the National Security Council. As the crisis developed, he oversaw the mobilization of U.S. forces for potential military action against Cuba. In retirement, he participated in several enlightening gatherings of Soviet, Cuban, and American officials involved in the Cuban Missile Crisis. (Yoichi R. Okamoto/Lyndon B. Johnson Presidential Library)

however, he was generally credited with devising the relatively moderate naval quarantine response strategy that Kennedy decided to follow. Determined to avoid nuclear war, McNamara repeatedly stated that the presence of medium- and intermediate-range Soviet nuclear-capable missiles on Cuba made little if any difference to the strategic balance. By October 27, however, the Soviet failure to halt the construction of missile sites and the shooting down of a U-2 reconnaissance plane over Cuba had brought McNamara to endorse massive U.S. air strikes followed by an invasion of the island, a move averted only by Kennedy's determination to allow the Soviet Union additional time before launching such drastic measures.

McNamara supported the 1963 Partial Nuclear Test Ban Treaty, which he hoped would facilitate U.S.-Soviet arms-limitation talks, even as he supported developing a U.S. second-strike capability, the ability to retaliate ferociously even after absorbing a massive nuclear attack. He also broke with President Dwight D. Eisenhower's emphasis on threatening massive retaliation in all crises to support expanding the military by 300,000 personnel to develop flexible-response capabilities, a mobile striking force prepared for conventional or guerrilla warfare. Defense Department budgets rose from $45.9 billion in 1960 to $53.6 billion in 1964. Another reason for this surge was McNamara's early decision to increase land-based U.S. intercontinental ballistic missiles (ICBMs) to 1,000, a move that may have triggered a similar Soviet buildup and arms race. He publicly defended the nuclear strategy of mutually assured destruction (MAD), arguing that it served as a deterrent to nuclear war.

During the Kennedy presidency McNamara's reputation soared, only to fall dramatically and permanently under Kennedy's successor, Lyndon B. Johnson. Growing U.S. involvement in the Republic of Vietnam (RVN) (South Vietnam), which McNamara endorsed, undercut his efforts at rationalization. Military intellectuals later criticized McNamara's decision to permit the demands of the Vietnam War to denude U.S. North Atlantic Treaty Organization (NATO) forces. By 1966 McNamara had become increasingly pessimistic over the war's outcome, especially when antiwar protests intensified and he became a prime target for ferocious criticism, although as late as mid-1967 he seemed on occasion to believe that the war could be won. In late 1967 Johnson rejected his recommendations to freeze U.S. troop levels, cease bombing North Vietnam, and transfer ground combat duties largely to the South Vietnamese Army. McNamara announced his impending resignation in November 1967, leaving three months later to become president of the World Bank.

McNamara remained at the World Bank until 1982, dramatically expanding its lending and development programs. During Ronald Reagan's presidency, McNamara was one of several leading U.S. diplomats who openly sought a pledge by the United States that it would never be the first state to use nuclear weapons. In 1986 he published proposals designed to reduce the risk of conflict. In 1995 he finally published his memoirs and concurrently became heavily involved in continuing efforts by Vietnamese and Western scholars and officials to attain greater understanding of each other's position in the Vietnam conflict. He also participated in several conferences that brought together Soviet, American, and Cuban participants from the 1962 missile crisis. In 2003 he cooperated in producing a documentary, *The Fog of War,* on his experiences from World War II onward, including the Cuban Missile Crisis. He publicly criticized the 2003 U.S. invasion of Iraq.

McNamara remained perennially controversial. His persistent refusal to characterize the U.S. decision to intervene in Vietnam as inherently immoral and unjustified, as opposed to mistaken and unwise, generated passionate and often highly personal criticism from American former opponents of the war. He died peacefully in Washington, D.C., on July 6, 2009.

Priscilla Roberts

See also: Bay of Pigs Invasion; Eisenhower, Dwight David; Johnson, Lyndon Baines; Kennedy, John Fitzgerald; Military Balance; Missile Gap; Nuclear Arms Race; Partial Test Ban Treaty; U-2 Overflights

References

Blight, James G., and Janet M. Lang. *The Fog of War: Lessons from the Life of Robert S. McNamara.* Lanham, MD: Rowman and Littlefield, 2005.

Halberstam, David. *The Best and the Brightest.* New York: Random House, 1972.

McNamara, Robert S., with Brian VanDeMark. *In Retrospect: The Tragedy and Lessons of Vietnam.* New York: Times Books, 1995.

Shapley, Deborah. *Promise and Power: The Life and Times of Robert McNamara.* Boston: Little, Brown, 1993.

Mikoyan, Anastas Ivanovich (1895–1978)

Soviet politician, Politburo member (1926–1966), and chairman of the Presidium of the Supreme Soviet (1964–1965). Born the son of a carpenter in Sanain, Armenia, on November 25, 1895, Anastas Mikoyan joined the revolutionary Bolshevik Party in 1915. He fought in the Russian Civil War. In 1922 Mikoyan was elected to the Soviet Communist Party's Central Committee. A supporter of Joseph Stalin, in 1926 Mikoyan became a candidate member of the Politburo and was appointed commissar for foreign trade. He became a full member of the Politburo in 1935 and was deputy prime minister from 1937 to 1955. There are indications that Stalin, believing that Mikoyan was plotting to unseat him, was planning Mikoyan's death when he himself died in 1953. In the post-Stalin succession struggle in 1953, Mikoyan salvaged his political career by supporting Nikita Khrushchev. Even before Khrushchev's denunciation of Stalin in 1956, Mikoyan often referred to the "evils" of Stalin's dictatorship. He soon became one of Khrushchev's closest advisers.

Mikoyan, who in November 1959 received in person the first reports on Cuba delivered by KGB intelligence agent Aleksandr Alekseev, became an early Kremlin supporter of aid to the Cuban revolution. That same month he recommended that Moscow barter Soviet goods for Cuban sugar. In February 1960 he visited Cuba, the first top Soviet official to do so, had lengthy talks with Fidel Castro and other Cuban leaders, and negotiated a package of trade credits for Cuba. In response to growing U.S. hostility to Cuba, in July 1960, during a visit to Moscow by Castro's brother Raúl, Mikoyan offered the Cubans substantial armaments, including 100,000 automatic rifles and 30 tanks, without expecting payment in return.

Mikoyan nonetheless remained wary of moves the United States might find unduly provocative. In May 1962, Mikoyan was the only Politburo

member who initially opposed Khrushchev's decision to send troops and nuclear-capable missiles secretly to Cuba, warning that U.S. surveillance aircraft would easily detect these. After President John F. Kennedy publicly demanded that the Soviet Union withdraw the missiles, in a Presidium meeting on October 25 Mikoyan endorsed Khrushchev's decision to do so, provided the United States would agree not to invade Cuba.

In November 1962 Khrushchev dispatched Mikoyan to Cuba, where he spent a month on the unenviable task of persuading Castro to accept the terms on which the Cuban Missile Crisis was settled while defusing his anger. Mikoyan—whose wife died just as he arrived in Cuba—bore the brunt of Castro's resentment and was forced to endure repeated lengthy tirades condemning Soviet behavior during the crisis as pusillanimous and a betrayal of Cuba. Castro also attempted to sabotage the settlement by refusing to allow on-site inspections and seeking to shoot down overflying U.S. reconnaissance aircraft verifying the dismantling of the missile sites. Mikoyan bluntly informed Castro that Soviet antiaircraft batteries and personnel would not attack U.S. airplanes. Soviet leaders also refused to allow Il-28 light bombers to remain in Cuba, as Castro demanded. On his own initiative, Mikoyan refused a further request from Castro to allow tactical nuclear-capable cruise missiles to remain in Cuba.

On leaving Cuba, Mikoyan met with United Nations secretary general U Thant, who had brokered many of the arrangements for removing the missiles, and with Kennedy. Kennedy and Mikoyan clashed over the missiles, which Mikoyan claimed had been purely defensive in nature, while Kennedy assailed Soviet behavior in installing the missiles as deliberate deception but assured Mikoyan that his country "would not attack Cuba" though Americans "still consider Castro our adversary."

In July 1964 Mikoyan was elected chair of the Presidium of the Supreme Soviet, making him titular head of state. He timidly supported Khrushchev's ouster from power in October 1964. With new leadership headed by Leonid Brezhnev, Mikoyan found himself increasingly isolated, and he relinquished his chairmanship in December 1965. He retired from the Politburo in April 1966, although he remained a member of the Communist Party Central Committee until 1976. Mikoyan died in Moscow on October 21, 1978.

Paul Wingrove

See also: Alekseev (Shitov), Aleksandr Ivanovich; Castro, Fidel; Castro, Raúl; Kennedy, John Fitzgerald; Khrushchev, Nikita Sergeyevich; U Thant; U-2 Overflights; United Nations

References

Fursenko, Aleksandr, and Timothy Naftali. *One Hell of a Gamble: Khrushchev, Castro, and Kennedy, 1958–1964.* New York: Norton, 1997.

Medvedev, Roy A. *All Stalin's Men.* New York: Doubleday, 1984.

Mikoyan, Anastas. *The Memoirs of Anastas Mikoyan.* Madison, WI: Sphinx, 1988.

Military Balance (1945–1990)

The Cold War military balance was not merely a comparison of U.S. and Soviet military capabilities but just as much a reflection of perceptions, ideas, and assumptions, fueled by the necessity of protecting not just the physical security of a nation but also its core values and way of life. This balance, moreover, was an evolutionary process driven by how leaders on both sides of the Iron Curtain perceived and responded to events on the world stage. While much is known about decision-making dynamics within the U.S. national security establishment during the Cold War, the same cannot be said for the Soviet Union, even after some Soviet archives were opened after the Cold War ended.

The Cold War military balance was defined by three phases. The first phase, marked by the U.S. nuclear monopoly, was ushered in when atomic weapons were used in August 1945 to persuade Japan to surrender. Because the beginning of the Cold War coincided with the dawn of the nuclear age, the history of the two would become inextricably intertwined.

As the postwar period progressed, relations between the United States and the Soviet Union rapidly deteriorated. From the Soviet perspective, U.S. insistence upon free elections in what it considered its sphere of influence in Central and Eastern Europe, the threat of capitalist encirclement by the North Atlantic Treaty Organization (NATO) in 1949, and the U.S. nuclear monopoly combined to convey a hostile picture of the West. In much the same way, Western democracies perceived a growing Soviet threat to liberal capitalist democracies around the globe. Communist threats to both Greece and Turkey in 1947, the communist coup in Czechoslovakia in 1948, and the Berlin Blockade (1948–1949) all seemed to confirm that the Soviets were intent upon world domination.

Yet despite this growing hostility, U.S. officials were reasonably confident that as long as the United States held the nuclear monopoly, the threat of Soviet military aggression against core interests was minimal. In

the immediate postwar period, this monopoly proved vital in counterbalancing the Soviet Union's massive conventional military advantage, itself a by-product of the war against Germany on the Eastern Front. This correlation of forces ensured that relations between the two Cold War powers remained relatively stable.

August 29, 1949, however—when the Soviet Union detonated its first atomic weapon, years ahead of most predictions—marked a crucial shift in the Cold War military balance. U.S. national security planners came to believe, moreover, that by 1954 the Soviets would possess sufficient nuclear capacity to launch a devastating strike against the United States, meaning that the Soviet Union could initiate a conventional assault on Western Europe and rest relatively secure in the knowledge that the threat of a nuclear counter-response from the Kremlin would thwart any U.S. nuclear response. If the United States and NATO chose not to increase their conventional forces, Soviet aggression after 1954 would force either free world appeasement or nuclear devastation. This urgency, combined with the outbreak of the Korean War in June 1950, underpinned President Harry Truman's response to the National Security Council's NSC-68 report, which called for a massive conventional and nuclear military buildup. This policy, driven by the shattering of the U.S. nuclear monopoly and the Korean War, ushered in the second phase of the Cold War military balance: U.S. nuclear superiority.

The underlying fear of the consequences that accompanied Soviet nuclear capabilities in the absence of an adequate conventional deterrent defined the Truman administration's new post-1950 defense posture, which redressed the military balance through a vast conventional rearmament program both at home and in Western Europe. Because conventional forces were generally more expensive than nuclear weapons, the Korean War stalemate and the U.S. preoccupation with rearmament led to budget deficits, inflation, rigid governmental controls on prices and wages, materials shortages, and what many considered to be the beginnings of a U.S. garrison state. Capitalizing on these difficulties, Republican presidential candidate Dwight D. Eisenhower based his 1952 election platform on a more cost-effective national security posture. The Korean War seemed to provide ample evidence that the Truman administration's approach was based too heavily on reaction rather than prevention, allowed the Soviet Union too much initiative, and in the long run would be economically unsustainable. Eisenhower therefore adopted the so-called New Look defense strategy, predicated on massive retaliation.

Eisenhower administration officials believed that the only way to deter the Soviet Union was to create the perception that the United States would

initiate a nuclear response to any level of Soviet aggression, ranging from a limited conventional incursion against a peripheral interest to a full-scale nuclear strike against the United States. To further heighten its perceived credibility, massive retaliation was deliberately cloaked in ambiguity. It was believed that Soviet leaders would refrain from aggression if it remained unclear whether a U.S. nuclear response would be automatic. This could, moreover, be accomplished at a lower cost than the programs prescribed by NSC-68, meaning, in the words of Defense Secretary Charles Wilson, "more bang for a buck." The Eisenhower administration consequently invested deeply in building the U.S. nuclear stockpile, although it did not succeed in implementing major or enduring reductions in defense spending.

Just as the Korean War shaped perceptions of NSC-68, so did the Soviet launching of *Sputnik 1* (October 1957) impact massive retaliation. *Sputnik 1* was propelled into space by an intercontinental ballistic missile (ICBM), demonstrating that the continental United States was vulnerable to direct missile attack.

This event, coupled with the knowledge that the Soviet nuclear stockpile had increased significantly since 1949, forced many defense strategists to rethink the wisdom and prudence of massive retaliation. Although Eisenhower's policy was marginally more cost-effective, the ambiguity upon which much of the deterrent value was based also carried with it a heightened sense of brinkmanship and thus the possibility of nuclear war through miscalculation.

Eisenhower's political opponents, backed by several influential figures within his own military establishment, began calling for a more balanced military capability with a de-emphasis on nuclear weapons. By increasing NATO's conventional strength, the United States and its allies would be able to avoid the unpalatable choices of either nuclear annihilation or appeasement when responding to Soviet aggression. In what represented almost a direct throwback to NSC-68 and the Truman administration, John F. Kennedy's nomination as the Democratic presidential candidate saw him adopt the new doctrine of flexible response as the basis for national security policy.

Flexible response was implemented in 1961 following Soviet premier Nikita Khrushchev's ultimatum to end Western access rights to West Berlin. Conscious that the correlation of forces in conventional terms decidedly favored the Soviet Union and acutely aware that NATO's response to Soviet aggression lay between humiliation and all-out nuclear war, Kennedy employed the sword and shield concept by increasing the

presence of tactical nuclear weapons and initiating a significant buildup of conventional forces in Europe. In turn, Khrushchev quietly dropped his ultimatum.

This shift toward flexible response played a significant role in the Cuban Missile Crisis, since NATO's conventional deterrent and its arsenal of tactical nuclear weapons allowed time for pauses in the escalatory process, maximized the possibility of a diplomatic settlement, and minimized the threat of war by miscalculation. Although the conflict was resolved peacefully, it highlighted the dangers of brinkmanship and the threat of full-scale nuclear conflict. With these lessons fresh in their minds, both the United States and the Soviet Union began to seek a Cold War détente. The Partial Test Ban Treaty, signed in August 1963, imposed mutual restraint on large-scale atmospheric nuclear tests, and perhaps most significantly, a direct hotline was established between the White House and the Kremlin.

By the early 1970s, the Cold War military balance entered its third and final stage: rough nuclear parity. As the decade progressed and both the United States and the Soviet Union increased their nuclear stockpiles, both sides recognized that a nuclear war was unwinnable. This underlay the concept of mutually assured destruction (MAD) and, paradoxically, the belief that mutual vulnerability was the key to stability and deterrence. This balance of strategic nuclear parity coupled with the Warsaw Pact's massive conventional forces and the sword and shield concept embraced by NATO gave rise to the Strategic Arms Limitation Talks (SALT) that began in November 1969 and set the tone for much of the remaining Cold War.

Josh Ushay

See also: Berlin Crises; Containment, Doctrine and Course of; Eisenhower, Dwight David; Kennedy, John Fitzgerald; Khrushchev, Nikita Sergeyevich; Missile Gap; Nuclear Arms Race; Partial Test Ban Treaty; U.S. Allies; Warsaw Pact

References

Bundy, McGeorge. *Danger and Survival: Choices about the Bomb in the First Fifty Years.* New York: Vintage, 1990.

Dockrill, Saki. *Eisenhower's New Look: National Security Policy, 1953–1961.* New York: St. Martin's Press, 1996.

Freedman, Lawrence. *The Evolution of Nuclear Strategy.* 3rd ed. Houndmills, UK: Palgrave Macmillan, 2003.

Gaddis, John Lewis. *Strategies of Containment: A Critical Appraisal of Postwar American National Security Policy.* New York: Oxford University Press, 1982.

Garthoff, Raymond L. *Soviet Strategy in the Nuclear Age.* Westport, CT: Greenwood Press, 1974.

Leffler, Melvyn P. *A Preponderance of Power: National Security, the Truman Administration, and the Cold War.* Stanford, CA: Stanford University Press, 1992.

Pierpaoli, Paul G., Jr. *Truman and Korea: The Political Culture of the Early Cold War.* Columbia and London: University of Missouri Press, 1999.

Williamson, Samuel R., Jr., and Steven L. Rearden. *The Origins of U.S. Nuclear Strategy, 1945–1953.* New York: St. Martin's Press, 1993.

Missile Gap

Alleged shortfall of U.S. intercontinental ballistic missiles (ICBMs) as compared to those of the Soviet Union during the late 1950s. Debate on this matter peaked in 1960 but began as early as 1956, when Democratic Missouri senator Stuart Symington charged that the United States lagged behind the Soviet Union in producing guided missiles. President Dwight D. Eisenhower's administration denied the allegations, but the Democrats refused to drop the issue. In August 1957 the Soviet Union launched the world's first ICBM. In October of the same year the Soviet Union launched the first satellite, *Sputnik 1*. *Sputnik 1* was propelled into space by a rocket, leading many Americans to believe the Soviet Union had taken the lead in rocket technology, and thus popular belief in a missile gap between the nations began in earnest. This development not only presented Americans with a public relations problem but also had national security ramifications, since the United States now faced a potential Soviet ICBM attack.

The findings of the 1957 Gaither Committee further increased this sense of technological inferiority and vulnerability. Among other things, the Gaither Report argued that the missile gap not only existed but could be expected to widen, with the Soviet Union moving well ahead of the United States in missile and rocket technology. Still worse, National Intelligence Estimate (NIE) reports seemed to support this evaluation, concluding that the Soviet Union had the capability to manufacture 100 ICBMs in 1960 and some 500 more during 1961–1962. These figures, however, represented nothing more than pure speculation.

Eisenhower tried to downplay *Sputnik 1* and the Gaither Report's findings, but the public reacted with fear and outrage. Furthermore, the matter became a partisan political issue, as the Democrats seized upon it to attack

the president and the Republican Party for "complacency." Hard-line Democratic Cold Warriors viewed these developments as proof that the Eisenhower administration had not spent enough money on national defense. In fact, the Eisenhower administration had spent heavily to develop guided missiles, especially the Titan, Thor, Polaris, and Minuteman, but did so cautiously, seeking to find a middle ground among defense spending, domestic spending, and balanced budgets.

Even when the Central Intelligence Agency (CIA) presented Eisenhower with ominous estimates of the prospects of Soviet missile programs, the president remained unconvinced. The missile gap debate reignited in 1958, when Hanson W. Baldwin, military commentator for the *New York Times,* published the book *The Great Arms Race: A Comparison of Soviet and U.S. Power Today,* which criticized Eisenhower's reaction to *Sputnik 1.* This reinforced some voices from the Pentagon still warning of a missile gap and advocating increased defense spending. Another influential figure who joined the fray was the prominent journalist Joseph Alsop, who charged that the Soviet Union "will have unchallengeable superiority in the nuclear striking power that was once our specialty" and blamed Eisenhower.

Alsop's column provoked a striking reaction, especially given the upcoming 1958 congressional elections. Eisenhower then launched a countercampaign, asserting that no missile gap existed and the United States was still ahead in the missile race, but his efforts failed to convince the public. The missile gap furor helped the Democrats retake both houses of Congress in the November 1958 elections, leaving the Democrats poised to push through higher defense appropriations and thereby embarrass the president. Indeed, in 1959 Congress voted for a defense budget larger than Eisenhower had requested.

The controversy did not end there. Among those convinced of the existence of the missile gap was Massachusetts senator John F. Kennedy, a Democrat, who ran for reelection in 1958 in part by citing the missile gap as proof of Republican bungling. Kennedy easily won a second term but continued his crusade over the gap after his reelection, though much of his evidence for it apparently came from Alsop's columns on the subject, rather than from hard intelligence sources.

Predictably, the missile gap became a major issue in Kennedy's 1960 presidential campaign, when he attempted to portray his opponent, Vice President Richard M. Nixon, as soft on defense spending and communism. While Kennedy agreed with Eisenhower that the United States was militarily stronger than the Soviet Union, he was also convinced that the U.S. missile program was lagging behind that of the Soviets, which would pose

grave future consequences. Reportedly, Eisenhower possessed fairly reliable intelligence data—much of it gathered by clandestine U-2 reconnaissance overflights of the Soviet Union—suggesting that the United States actually enjoyed superiority over the Soviets in ICBMs, but national security imperatives bound him to secrecy. Kennedy won a perilously thin victory over Nixon in the 1960 presidential election.

Once Kennedy became president, he quickly learned the truth: the missile gap was only a myth. Kennedy did not, however, reveal this information immediately. Robert McNamara, Kennedy's secretary of defense, quietly resolved the controversy during a February 1961 press conference, when he casually mentioned that no missile gap existed, whereupon the subject sank into relative obscurity. In practice, Kennedy conducted his national security policy on the basis that the United States enjoyed considerable strategic nuclear superiority over the Soviet Union. Soviet premier Nikita Khrushchev's desire to redress the imbalance between Soviet and U.S. missiles was probably one factor in the attempt to install Soviet short- and medium-range nuclear-capable missiles on Cuba, precipitating the Cuban Missile Crisis.

David Tal

See also: Central Intelligence Agency; Eisenhower, Dwight David; Kennedy, John Fitzgerald; Khrushchev, Nikita Sergeyevich; McNamara, Robert Strange; Military Balance; Nuclear Arms Race; U-2 Overflights

References

Divine, Robert. *The Sputnik Challenge.* New York: Oxford University Press, 1993.

Preble, Christopher A. *John F. Kennedy and the Missile Gap.* DeKalb: Northern Illinois University Press, 2004.

Roman, Peter J. *Eisenhower and the Missile Gap.* Ithaca, NY: Cornell University Press, 1996.

Snead, David L. *The Gaither Committee, Eisenhower, and the Cold War.* Columbus: Ohio State University Press, 1999.

MONGOOSE, Operation

U.S. covert operation, begun in 1961, to overthrow the Cuban government and assassinate Cuban leader Fidel Castro. Following the failed April 1961 Bay of Pigs invasion, communications between Castro and Soviet premier Nikita Khrushchev increased dramatically. Castro requested additional

Soviet military support, and the Kremlin responded to his appeal. Within a year, Moscow had approved a $148 million arms package, although Khrushchev stalled the support.

After a clandestine meeting between Richard Goodwin, President John F. Kennedy's representative to the Inter-American Economic and Social Council in Uruguay, and Ernesto "Che" Guevara, Cuban minister of the interior, on August 22, 1961, in which Goodwin laid out ways that Cuba could improve relations with the United States, he reported that he saw Guevara's views as symptomatic of a deteriorating Cuban economy and impatience with Moscow. Various U.S. agencies therefore started discussing programs to sabotage the Cuban economy, and Kennedy began exploring options to eliminate Castro. Kennedy's brother and attorney general, Robert Kennedy, did not want to involve the Central Intelligence Agency (CIA) because of the Bay of Pigs debacle. In November 1961, he approached President Kennedy with a plan to establish an interagency project against Cuba that would not rely on CIA experts. On November 30, President Kennedy named Brig. Gen. Edward Lansdale chief of operations for the project.

The interagency committee, known as Special Group, included Robert Kennedy and Treasury Secretary C. Douglas Dillon. The inclusion of Kennedy and Dillon changed the group's name to the Special Group Augmented (SGA). SGA members were CIA director John McCone, National Security Adviser McGeorge Bundy, Alexis Johnson from the State Department, Roswell Gilpatric from the Defense Department, Gen. Lyman Lemnitzer of the Joint Chiefs of Staff, and Gen. Maxwell D. Taylor. Also in attendance at meetings, although they were not members, were President Kennedy, Secretary of State Dean Rusk, and Secretary of Defense Robert McNamara.

In February 1962, Khrushchev finally agreed to provide enhanced arms support to Cuba after receiving intelligence reports that the White House was planning to destroy Castro.

Lansdale devised a two-phase plan to implement Operation MONGOOSE that included paramilitary, sabotage, and political propaganda programs. The SGA ordered an intensification of sabotage and intelligence activity, while President Kennedy continued to waver on the need for military action. Lacking support from U.S. forces, the stability of Operation MONGOOSE began to weaken. Instead, the CIA turned to the Mafia for assistance in assassination plots, and Lansdale used his experience in psychological warfare to devise propaganda strategies. Plans for sabotage and counterintelligence included the injection of untraceable poison into Castro's favorite brand of cigars, the poisoning of Castro's food and drinks, the retrofitting of Castro's fountain pen with a hidden needle capable of injecting a lethal toxin, airdropping anti-Castro propaganda over Cuba, spraying

a television studio where Castro was about to appear with a hallucinogenic drug to undermine his popularity, contaminating Cuban sugar, and counterfeiting Cuban money and ration books.

In spring 1962, Robert Kennedy asked the SGA to consider the role of the Soviet Union as a factor in determining the outcome of Operation MONGOOSE. The group did not, however, act on this directive, viewing the idea of a Soviet military base on Cuba as too remote to consider. Yet only a few months earlier, Khrushchev had agreed to begin building up Cuban forces. Ultimately, SGA's nonchalance was a factor in the development of the Cuban Missile Crisis.

Lansdale's project was shut down in October 1962 following the Cuban Missile Crisis, but similar CIA psychological warfare projects against Castro continued well into 1963. These operations failed to win over a skeptical Cuban population.

Lacie A. Ballinger

See also: Bay of Pigs Invasion; Bundy, McGeorge; Castro, Fidel; Central Intelligence Agency; Dillon, C. Douglas; Gilpatric, Roswell Leavitt; Guevara de la Serna, Ernesto "Che"; Joint Chiefs of Staff; Kennedy, John Fitzgerald; Kennedy, Robert Francis; Khrushchev, Nikita Sergeyevich; Lansdale, Edward Geary; McCone, John Alex; McNamara, Robert Strange; Rusk, Dean David; Taylor, Maxwell Davenport

References

Beschloss, Michael R. *The Crisis Years: Kennedy and Khrushchev, 1960–1963.* New York: HarperCollins, 1991.

Bohning, Don. *The Castro Obsession: U.S. Covert Operations against Cuba, 1959–1965.* Washington, DC: Potomac Books, 2005.

Brugioni, Dino A. *Eyeball to Eyeball: Inside the Cuban Missile Crisis.* New York: Random House, 1993.

Fursenko, Aleksandr, and Timothy Naftali. *"One Hell of a Gamble": Khrushchev, Castro, and Kennedy, 1958–1964.* New York: Norton, 1997.

Monroe Doctrine (1823)

Promulgated on December 2, 1823, by U.S. President James Monroe, the Monroe Doctrine was a public declaration that the United States would

oppose any efforts by European nations to obtain further colonial territory in the Americas or to reestablish control of colonies that had won independence. The statement, a unilateral announcement, effectively defined the Western Hemisphere as a U.S. sphere of influence. Throughout the 19th century, the United States tacitly relied heavily on the far stronger British fleet to enforce these principles. U.S. leaders nonetheless repeatedly invoked the Monroe Doctrine against British efforts to form alliances or acquire territory in the Americas. In 1842 President John Tyler extended the doctrine to the mid-Pacific islands of Hawai'i, then coveted by Britain. During the 1895 Venezuela Crisis U.S. Secretary of State Richard W. Olney cited the Monroe Doctrine when publicly exhorting Britain to submit to mediation a territorial dispute between its colony, British Guiana, and neighboring Venezuela. The Monroe Doctrine was also evoked to justify U.S. intervention against continued Spanish rule in Cuba in 1898.

Under the 1904 Roosevelt Corollary to the Monroe Doctrine, President Theodore Roosevelt asserted the right of the United States to intervene in the affairs of any Latin American nation that had fallen into disorder, a proviso the United States frequently used to prevent European naval expeditions collecting debts owed their nationals by insolvent Latin American governments. The United States invoked the Corollary to justify numerous unilateral interventions in Latin American nations, including Mexico, Nicaragua, Guatemala, Honduras, Cuba, Chile, the Dominican Republic, Panama, El Salvador, and Grenada. Critics characterized the Monroe Doctrine and Corollary as assertions of exclusive U.S. hegemony over the Americas. During the 1930s, President Franklin D. Roosevelt supposedly replaced these with a less intrusive "Good Neighbor Policy." In World War II and the Cold War years, extensive U.S. interventions in Latin America nonetheless occurred, usually combining the broad rubric of the Monroe Doctrine with the Cold War principle of containment of communism. Although President John F. Kennedy doubted the validity of the Monroe Doctrine as international law, he sought to apply its principles to U.S. actions against Cuba.

Priscilla Roberts

See also: Containment, Doctrine and Course of; Kennedy, John Fitzgerald; Organization of American States

References

Livingston, Grace. *America's Backyard: The United States and Latin America from the Monroe Doctrine to the War on Terror.* London: Zed Books, 2009.

May, Ernest R. *The Making of the Monroe Doctrine.* Cambridge, MA: Belknap Press, 1975.

Murphy, Gretchen. *Hemispheric Imaginings: The Monroe Doctrine and Narratives of U.S. Empire.* Durham, NC: Duke University Press, 2005.

Sexton, Jay. *The Monroe Doctrine: Empire and Nation in Nineteenth-Century America.* New York: Hill and Wang, 2011.

Smith, Gaddis. *The Last Years of the Monroe Doctrine, 1945–1993.* New York: Hill and Wang, 1994.

N

Nitze, Paul Henry (1907–2004)

Assistant secretary of defense for international security affairs, 1961–1963. Paul Nitze was born in Amherst, Massachusetts, on January 16, 1907. He entered investment banking in 1928, and during and after World War II held several government positions related to international trade and economics. In late 1949 he became director of the State Department's Policy Planning Staff. In January 1950, responding to the Soviet detonation of an atomic bomb and the fall of China to communism, Secretary of State Dean Acheson asked Nitze to chair an interdepartmental study group to conduct a full review of U.S. foreign and defense policy, the first such comprehensive survey. Nitze largely wrote its report, NSC-68, which was handed to President Harry S. Truman in April 1950, and argued that the Soviets were bent on world domination. Nitze recommended that, to meet this challenge, the United States should rebuild the West economically, while assuming primary responsibility for the entire non-Communist world's defense and security against outside attack. NSC-68 envisaged doubling to quadrupling U.S. defense spending, estimating that the United States could devote up to 20 percent of its gross national product to defense expenditures without major economic disruptions. When the Korean War began two months later, these recommendations were implemented. The U.S. defense budget rose from $13 billion to $50 billion. The broad framework of U.S. defense capabilities, commitments, and objectives laid out in NSC-68 would in many respects characterize U.S. strategy for the subsequent 40 years.

In 1961 President John F. Kennedy made Nitze assistant secretary of defense for international security affairs. Nitze participated in deliberations

during crises over Berlin, in October 1961 even contemplating a preemptive strategic nuclear strike against the Soviet Union should West Berlin be threatened. During the Cuban Missile Crisis Nitze attended meetings of the Executive Committee (ExComm) of the president's advisers, but most of his work was done in small groups, on contingency planning related to Berlin and the potential withdrawal of NATO missiles from Turkey and Italy. Together with deputy undersecretary of state U. Alexis Johnson, he prepared detailed plans to implement a blockade. The existence of this blueprint helped tip the balance in favor of the quarantine option, even though Nitze himself believed this initial strategy might ultimately require reinforcement with air strikes and possibly a U.S. invasion of Cuba. Nitze strongly opposed the idea of removing NATO missiles in Turkey in return for the dismantling of Soviet missiles in Cuba, and he remained ignorant of the secret U.S.-Soviet understanding to this effect negotiated by Attorney General Robert F. Kennedy.

From 1963 to 1967 Nitze was secretary of the Navy, in which position he became a proponent of a negotiated Vietnam peace settlement and the de-escalation of the ground war. Nitze was one of the "Wise Men," the members of the President's Ad Hoc Task Force on Vietnam which in March 1968 recommended U.S. withdrawal from the Vietnam conflict. He was deputy secretary of defense from 1967 to 1969 and a leading figure in arms-control negotiations under Republican presidents Richard M. Nixon and Ronald Reagan. In the 1970s Nitze was a founder of the second Committee on the Present Danger, which argued that U.S. defenses were dangerously inadequate and attacked the SALT II arms-limitation treaty negotiated under Gerald Ford as ineffective. He died of pneumonia at his Georgetown, Washington, home on October 19, 2004.

Priscilla Roberts

See also: Berlin Crises; Containment, Doctrine and Course of; Jupiter Missiles (Turkey and Italy); Kennedy, John Fitzgerald; Kennedy, Robert Francis; Military Balance; Nuclear Arms Race

References

Callahan, David. *Dangerous Capabilities: Paul Nitze and the Cold War.* New York: Harper Collins, 1990.

Nitze, Paul H., with Ann M. Smith and Steven L. Rearden. *From Hiroshima to Glasnost at the Center of Decision: A Memoir.* New York: Grove Weidenfeld, 1989.

Rearden, Steven L. *The Evolution of American Strategic Doctrine: Paul H. Nitze and the Soviet Challenge.* Boulder, CO: Westview Press, 1984.

Talbott, Strobe. *The Master of the Game: Paul Nitze and the Nuclear Peace.* New York: Knopf, 1988.

Thompson, Nicholas. *The Hawk and the Dove: Paul Nitze, George Kennan, and the History of the Cold War.* New York: Henry Holt, 2009.

Nuclear Arms Race

General term for the undeclared Cold War contest in which the United States and the Soviet Union developed, tested, and deployed increasingly advanced nuclear weapons and delivery systems. The strategic motivation behind the arms race was each nation's drive to ensure that its adversary did not gain any measurable advantage in nuclear-strike capability. Also at play was the evolving concept of nuclear deterrence, which held that a nation must retain adequate nuclear capabilities to deter the enemy from launching a preemptive nuclear attack. This concept became known as mutually assured destruction (MAD) and held that any preemptive attack would result in an overwhelming and catastrophic retaliatory strike.

The nuclear arms race traces its origins to World War II, when the U.S. government learned that Germany had the capacity and desire to build an atomic bomb. Spurred by this threat, the Americans raced the Germans to build the first nuclear weapon, although it was hardly a competitive endeavor. The Germans paid less attention to atomic weapons development than the Americans, who poured considerable sums into their Manhattan Project, while Germany focused on apparently more pragmatic weapons systems.

The race continued beyond World War II. With its first test explosion in July 1945, the United States possessed an atomic monopoly, and the Soviet Union, with which the Americans found themselves increasingly at odds, understandably feared the U.S. nuclear threat, especially given the demonstrated ability of the United States to conduct long-range strategic bombing. Thus, the Soviets pursued their own atomic bomb extremely vigorously. Soviet spies who had infiltrated the Manhattan Project and a skilled scientific community allowed the Soviet Union to detonate its first nuclear weapon in August 1949.

The Americans sought to retain their nuclear lead and, in an action-reaction cycle that would typify the arms race, pursued the next nuclear

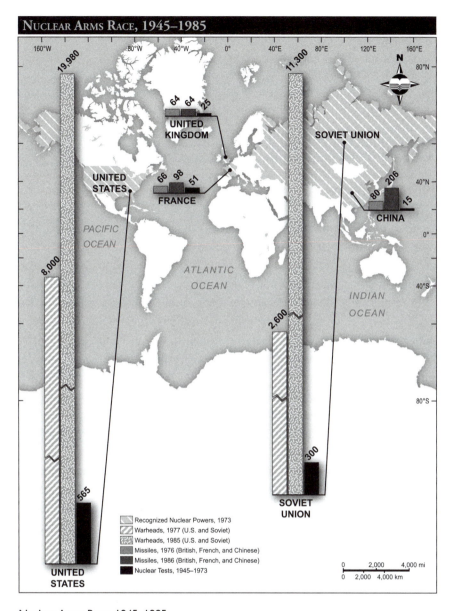

Nuclear Arms Race, 1945–1985

development—in this case, a thermonuclear (or hydrogen) bomb. U.S. success in developing the hydrogen bomb in 1952 was followed by Soviet success in 1955. The nuclear arms race now entered its most recognizable form, wherein the superpowers pursued weapons that were smaller in size, more powerful, and increasingly accurate, while delivery systems became faster, more accurate, and more difficult for enemy surveillance to locate.

During the late 1940s and early 1950s, the primary delivery vehicle for nuclear weapons was the strategic bomber. More advanced aircraft were needed to carry more than one nuclear weapon, and indeed, nuclear weapons needed to be smaller to enable a variety of aircraft to carry them. The U.S. B-29 bomber was matched by the Soviet TU-4, but neither proved adequate, and ultimately the B-52 and the TU-20 were developed, both intercontinental bombers capable of delivering large payloads to multiple targets.

The next step in the nuclear arms race was missile development. Advances in rocketry led to the development of ballistic missiles in both the United States and the Soviet Union. The first U.S. intercontinental ballistic missile (ICBM), the Atlas D, was deployed on October 31, 1959. The Soviets followed suit with their own ICBM, the SS-6 Sapwood of North Atlantic Treaty Organization (NATO) designation, on January 20, 1960. ICBMs were a step up from their cousins, medium-range ballistic missiles (MRBMs) and intermediate-range ballistic missiles (IRBMs), and became the most popular delivery system because of their range and relative invulnerability to enemy air defenses. ICBMs had a maximum range of 10,000 miles and could be stationed on the other side of the world from their targets.

In the 1950s, both superpowers came to rely on nuclear weapons as the primary weapon for any major Cold War engagement. The nuclear arms race created ever-larger arsenals and increasingly effective delivery systems, leaving both sides vulnerable to an enemy attack. This vulnerability perpetuated the arms race during the decade and beyond. Neither side was willing to give up its weapons, and the newer weapons now meant that the nation that launched a first strike might be able to avoid a retaliatory strike if its nuclear advantage were enough to allow it to destroy most of the enemy's nuclear forces in the first blow. Any large gap in nuclear arms made one nation vulnerable, and only nuclear parity could ensure nuclear stability. Scientific advances by one nation consequently had to be matched by the other, since otherwise a gap would result, advantaging one side. The Cuban Missile Crisis can be understood as an attempt by the Soviet Union to take a shortcut and reduce an asymmetrical nuclear balance greatly favoring the United States, by stationing assorted tactical, intermediate-range, and medium-range nuclear-capable missiles within 100 miles of the United States.

In the 1960s the evolution of the counterforce (or no cities) doctrine aggravated this situation. Advocates of the doctrine suggested a general agreement between the superpowers to use nuclear weapons only against

military installations, sparing population centers. Adopting this policy meant accepting the reality that in order to sustain the ability to launch an effective counterstrike, a nation must deploy sufficient weapons to ensure that the enemy could not destroy them all in a preemptive strike, mandating more and better weapons.

Arms-control talks and treaties during the 1970s and arms-reduction agreements during the 1980s slowed but did not halt the nuclear arms race. When the Cold War ended, so did the nuclear arms race in its original form. Because nuclear weapons remain a strategic force for some nations, a new and different nuclear arms race can be anticipated.

Brian Madison Jones

See also: Containment, Doctrine and Course of; Military Balance; Missile Gap; Partial Test Ban Treaty

References

Bottome, Edgar M. *The Balance of Terror: A Guide to the Arms Race.* Boston: Beacon, 1971.

Powaski, Ronald E. *March to Armageddon: The United States and the Nuclear Arms Race, 1939 to the Present.* New York: Oxford University Press, 1987.

Powaski, Ronald E. *Return to Armageddon: The United States and the Nuclear Arms Race, 1981–1999.* New York: Oxford University Press, 2000.

Organization of American States

Multinational institution established in 1948 by the U.S. and Latin American governments to promote international cooperation within the Western Hemisphere. The concept of an organization to encourage cooperation among Western Hemispheric nations originated in the early 19th century, when the South American revolutionary war hero Simón Bolívar unsuccessfully proposed a league of Latin American republics. Decades later, the United States revived the idea with more success and with a different agenda: the promotion of trade. At a conference in Washington, D.C., during 1889–1890, 18 Western Hemispheric nations founded the Commercial Bureau of the American Republics (later transformed into the Pan-American Union), with headquarters in Washington, D.C.

After 1945 various pressures, many related to the Cold War, led the U.S. and Latin American governments to seek closer cooperation through new institutions. Latin American leaders, worried by declining U.S. economic engagement following World War II, sought to open new channels to encourage U.S. aid and investment. President Harry Truman's administration, anxious about worsening Cold War tensions, hoped to consolidate U.S. authority in the hemisphere.

In 1947 the United States and 19 Latin American governments signed the Rio Pact, a mutual defense treaty that advanced the long-standing U.S. effort to make enforcement of the 1823 Monroe Doctrine a multilateral responsibility. A year later, 21 Western Hemispheric nations gathered in Bogotá, Colombia, to discuss economic and political relations. On April 30, 1948, the attending nations signed the Charter of the Organization of American States (OAS).

The OAS called for efforts to promote peace, prosperity, and democracy in the hemisphere and established mechanisms for resolving disputes among member states. Members were committed to opposing communism within the Western Hemisphere. At the insistence of Latin American governments keenly aware of the long record of U.S. intervention in their nations, the OAS also declared the principle of nonintervention. Adopted over U.S. objections, Article 15 of the OAS Charter asserted that "no State or group of States has the right to intervene, directly or indirectly, for any reason whatever, in the internal or external affairs of any other State."

In subsequent decades, U.S. leaders repeatedly overcame this limitation by using the OAS as a means to attain U.S. geopolitical objectives behind a façade of regional solidarity. President Dwight Eisenhower's administration established this pattern in 1954 when it used the OAS to help oust the left-leaning government of Jacobo Arbenz in Guatemala, in the following way. In March 1954, at an OAS meeting in Caracas, U.S. officials successfully pushed for a resolution committing OAS members to take joint action against any communist regime in the Western Hemisphere. The Eisenhower administration had calculated that an OAS resolution condemning Arbenz as a communist would give a veneer of legitimacy to U.S. action against his regime. The U.S. government told Latin American governments that the episode was a "test case" of the OAS's ability to defend the hemisphere and threatened to act alone if the organization failed to take a stand. With only Guatemala in opposition, 16 Latin American governments grudgingly supported the United States. In June 1954, as a military operation sponsored by the Central Intelligence Agency (CIA) overthrew Arbenz, U.S. leaders claimed to be acting in the interests of the OAS.

The OAS performed a similar function when the United States sought to apply pressure on Cuba during 1959 and the early 1960s. One reason why Cuban leader Fidel Castro was initially cagey about committing himself openly to the communist camp was his apprehension that this would allow the United States to invoke the Caracas Resolution and cloak any action against his government in OAS legitimacy. Similar reasons impelled Cuban officials to conceal how from mid-1959 onward they received substantial quantities of arms from Czechoslovakia, Poland, and eventually the Soviet Union. When Cuban leaders complained to the United Nations (UN) about U.S. hostility, U.S. officials convinced the UN Security Council that the OAS, not the UN, was the appropriate body to consider the issue. Under the guise of regional cooperation, the United States then maneuvered to exclude Cuba from the OAS. At a ministerial meeting in Punta del Este, Uruguay, in January 1962, President John Kennedy's administration

won OAS approval—by a one-vote margin—of a statement declaring Marxism-Leninism incompatible with the American system. Technically, Cuba remained a member state, but its existing government was excluded from attending OAS meetings and participating in the body's activities.

During the Cuban Missile Crisis, after several days' deliberations Kennedy decided to impose a naval quarantine or blockade to prevent any further Soviet weapons shipments reaching Cuba. The Kennedy administration decided to do so under OAS auspices, entrusting Secretary of State Dean Rusk and Edwin Martin, undersecretary of state for Latin American affairs, with steering the resolution through the OAS, which they did on October 23, winning unanimous support for the quarantine. The blockade became operative at 10:00 a.m. on October 24 and remained in force until November 20, 1962.

Despite periodic protests from Castro's government, Cuba's suspension from the OAS lasted much longer, in part because he openly promoted revolution in other Latin American states. In 1964, after Cuba began supporting revolutionary movements in Venezuela and elsewhere, all Latin American nations except Mexico broke diplomatic relations with Cuba. In June 2009 the OAS Assembly voted to lift Cuba's suspension, but made this conditional on Cuban compliance with all treaties signed by OAS member states, including the Inter-American Democratic Charter of 2001.

Mark Atwood Lawrence

See also: Castro, Fidel; Central Intelligence Agency; Containment, Doctrine and Course of; Eisenhower, Dwight David; Kennedy, John Fitzgerald; Monroe Doctrine; Rusk, Dean David; United Nations

References

Herz, Mônica. *The Organization of American States (OAS): Global Governance Away from the Media.* New York: Routledge, 2011.

Schoultz, Lars. *Beneath the United States: A History of U.S. Policy toward Latin America.* Cambridge, MA: Harvard University Press, 1998.

Shaw, Carolyn M. *Cooperation, Conflict, and Consensus in the Organization of American States.* New York: Palgrave Macmillan, 2004.

Smith, Gaddis. *The Last Years of the Monroe Doctrine, 1945–1993.* New York: Hill and Wang, 1994.

Smith, Peter H. *Talons of the Eagle: Dynamics of U.S.–Latin American Relations.* 3rd ed. New York: Oxford University Press, 2007.

P

Partial Test Ban Treaty

Treaty banning all nuclear tests, except underground trials. The Partial Test Ban Treaty (PTBT), also known as the Limited Test Ban Treaty (LTBT), was signed in Moscow on August 5, 1963, by representatives of Great Britain, the United States, and the Soviet Union and entered into force on October 10, 1963, with unlimited duration. The PTBT was the result of five years of intense negotiations concerning the limiting of nuclear weapons tests. Some 125 nations have since signed the document, although France and the People's Republic of China (PRC) refused to sign, arguing that the test ban was a means of preserving the superiority of the three initial nuclear powers.

The PTBT was clearly an attempt to make nuclear weapons programs more difficult to sustain, thus limiting nuclear proliferation. Signatories agreed that they would no longer carry out any nuclear test explosion in the atmosphere, underwater, in outer space, or in any other environment that would allow radioactive fallout to spread beyond the territorial borders of the state conducting the test. There was a precedent for an agreement of this kind, namely the 1959 Antarctic Treaty, the first major international arms-control treaty following World War II. Its goal was to prevent the use of Antarctica for military purposes in the belief that it was in humankind's interest to keep the continent pristine and open to scientific research.

World public opinion was already attuned to the dangers of atmospheric nuclear testing as a result of the 1954 *Castle Bravo* incident, when a thermonuclear weapons test at Bikini Island in the Pacific unwittingly exposed to nuclear fallout 28 Americans, 236 Marshall Islanders, and 23 crew members of the Japanese fishing boat *Castle Bravo*. France's decision to conduct atmospheric tests in Polynesia in 1962 further inflamed public opinion.

Furthermore, in the United States support for a test ban increased throughout the summer of 1963. In early July that year, 52 percent of Americans signaled unqualified support for a test ban. After the treaty had been signed, 81 percent of those polled approved the ban. During the early 1960s, two developments were influential in pushing forward a test ban. Considerable radioactive materials were being poured into the atmosphere as a result of atmospheric nuclear testing, and the world's nuclear states had advanced their nuclear technology to the point where a combination of underground tests and physical calculations gave them sufficient information to design and test their strategic weapons without risking radioactive fallout.

In 1962, the newly established Eighteen-Nation Disarmament Committee (ENDC) within the United Nations (UN) became the principal forum for discussions concerning a test ban. After protracted negotiations, an agreement emerged on the use of seismic stations and on-site inspections for verification purposes, but disagreement on the acceptable number of inspections continued. In July 1963 the United States, Britain, and the Soviet Union initiated tripartite talks on the cessation of nuclear tests in the atmosphere, in outer space, and underwater. Agreement on a partial test-ban treaty emerged from those discussions after about three weeks of talks.

The PTBT seemed to offer hope for future disarmament agreements. In 1968 the Nuclear Non-Proliferation Treaty (NPT) was signed, restricting the flow of weapons, technical knowledge, and fissile materials to states that did not already have nuclear weapons. The United States and the Soviet Union went a step further in 1974 when they signed the Threshold Test Ban Treaty (TTBT), limiting underground testing, which entered into force in 1990.

Jérôme Dorvidal and Jeffrey Larsen

See also: Kennedy, John Fitzgerald; Khrushchev, Nikita Sergeyevich; Military Balance; Nuclear Arms Race; U.S. Allies

References

Dean, Arthur H. *Test Ban and Disarmament: The Path of Negotiation.* New York: Harper and Row, 1966.

Oliver, Kendrick. *Kennedy, Macmillan, and the Nuclear Test-Ban Debate, 1961–63.* New York: St. Martin's Press, 1998.

Seaborg, Glenn, with Benjamin S. Loeb. *Kennedy, Khrushchev, and the Test Ban.* Berkeley: University of California Press, 1981.

Sobel, Lester A. *Disarmament and Nuclear Tests, 1960–1963.* New York: Facts on File Series, Library of Congress, 1964.

Terchek, Ronald J. *The Making of the Test Ban Treaty.* The Hague: Martinus Nijhoff, 1970.

Walker, John R. *British Nuclear Weapons and the Test Ban 1954–73.* Farnham, Surrey, UK: Ashgate, 2010.

Pliyev, Issa Alexandrovich (1903–1979)

Soviet general, commander of Soviet forces on Cuba, July–December 1961. Issa Pliyev was born on November 25, 1903, in Stari Batakoyurt, North Ossetia, in the Russian Empire. After fighting in the Russian Civil War, he joined the Red Army in 1922, graduating from the Leningrad Cavalry School in 1926, the Frunze Military Academy in 1933, and the Soviet General Staff Academy in 1941. He joined the Soviet Communist Party in 1926. A cavalry and tank commander, during World War II Pliyev took part in the battles of Moscow, Stalingrad, and Debrecen (Hungary), and the Budapest and Prague offensives. In August 1945 he commanded the Soviet-Mongolian Cavalry-Mechanized Group in Manchuria, fighting the Japanese Kwantung Army. For his wartime service, Pliyev was twice named a Hero of the Soviet Union. After World War II, Pliyev held several important military commands. From 1955 to 1962 he served as deputy commander and then commander of the North Caucasus Military District. In 1962, after suppressing popular riots in Novocherkassk in the Caucasus, he was appointed general of the army.

In July 1962 the Soviet Presidium selected Pliyev, a longtime associate of Defense Minister Rodion Malinovsky, under whom he had served in Hungary and Manchuria during World War II, to command the forces selected to install nuclear-capable missiles in Cuba. Bearing a false passport under the assumed name Pavlov, he left by air for Cuba on July 10. Pliyev, who suffered from a recurrent kidney ailment, possessed a dour personality and few diplomatic skills. He developed little rapport with Cuban officials, especially Premier Fidel Castro. Maj. Gen. Aleksei Alekseyevich Dementyev, head of the group of Soviet military advisers in Cuba, largely handled relations with Cuban authorities. Pliyev was also on poor terms with many of his subordinates. Under his supervision, 41,000 Soviet personnel nonetheless moved swiftly to construct 24 R-12 medium-range ballistic missile (MRBM) (range 1,100–1,400 miles) sites and 16 R-14 intermediate-range ballistic missile (IRBM) (range up to 2,800 miles) sites, together with 16 coastal batteries, each equipped with 5 short-range FKR cruise missiles.

In a verbal briefing in July 1962, Soviet premier Nikita Khrushchev reportedly gave Pliyev permission to use battlefield nuclear weapons, namely the cruise missiles, should he be unable to contact Moscow in a combat situation, but emphasized that he should not employ any of the strategic MRBMs or IRBMs without explicit Kremlin orders. In early September 1962, however, Malinovsky failed to confirm this authorization when sending Pliyev written instructions, in connection with further deployments of a squadron of Il-28 light bombers, equipped with six atomic bombs, and three detachments of Luna short-range missiles, with a total of 12 two-kiloton warheads. In mid-October the Soviet Ministry of Defense, concerned that the U.S. government appeared increasingly suspicious of the presence of Soviet forces in Cuba, dispatched a mission headed by Maj. Gen. Anatoli I. Gribkov, deputy head of the Soviet General Staff's Main Operations Directorate. On Malinovsky's orders Gribkov, who arrived on the island on October 18, reiterated and emphasized Kremlin insistence that the R-12 and R-14 missiles must not be used. Even the short-range Luna missiles were to be employed only if U.S. forces actually attacked and invaded, and there should be no haste to do so. Malinovsky also stressed the need to maintain strict control of all missiles.

On October 22, when President John F. Kennedy publicly announced that the United States would not tolerate the presence of Soviet missiles in Cuba, Pliyev had completed construction of the R-12 sites but not the R-14 installations. He controlled 36 R-12 warheads, all the Luna missiles, the Il-28s and their bombs, and 36 cruise missile FKR warheads. After Kennedy's speech, construction of missile sites continued at full speed, and one Soviet ship, the *Alexandrovsk,* carrying 24 nuclear warheads for R-14 IRBMs and 44 warheads for FKR land-based cruise missiles, reached Cuba just before the United States imposed a naval blockade, though several other vessels bearing R-14 missiles turned back. The Presidium tentatively considered allowing Pliyev to use tactical nuclear-armed missiles to resist a U.S. invasion, while forbidding him to launch the MRBMs against targets in the United States without direct authorization from Moscow. On October 22 Pliyev received instructions "to be in full readiness" but not to employ any nuclear weapons, including the Lunas and FKR cruise missiles, in combat situations, effectively a tightening of Kremlin control.

On October 23 Pliyev stepped up preparations for war, accelerating the uncrating and assembly of Il-28s capable of carrying nuclear payloads. It seems likely that on October 26 he moved nuclear warheads on or close to missile sites, though it is uncertain whether any missiles were actually armed. On the night of October 26–27 Pliyev informed Moscow

of his intention to use "all available means of air defense" against anticipated U.S. air strikes. Malinovsky and Khrushchev approved this decision. Shortly afterward, however, as a negotiated settlement with the United States seemed likely, the Presidium instructed Pliyev to refrain from installing nuclear warheads on short-range cruise missiles or atomic bombs on the Il-28s without specific authorization.

On the morning of October 27, a U.S. U-2 reconnaissance plane piloted by Maj. Rudolf Anderson overflew Cuba, where a Soviet SA-2 surface-to-air missile (SAM) battery spotted it. The commander, Capt. N. Antonyets, tried to call Pliyev at his headquarters but failed to reach him. Unable to contact Pliyev by telephone, his deputy, Lt. Gen. Stepan Grechko, authorized Antonyets to fire at the U-2, which he did, downing it and killing Anderson. On learning of the incident, Pliyev sent a report to the Ministry of Defense, and although Malinovsky characterized the response as "too hasty," given that negotiations to resolve the crisis peacefully were already under way, no reprimands were subsequently issued. On October 28 the Presidium, still concerned that the United States might launch air strikes on the missile sites, decided to permit Pliyev to use force to defend himself in such an eventuality, leaving it ambivalent whether or not he might employ tactical nuclear-armed weapons. Later that day, as the outlines of a settlement with the United States became clearer, Khrushchev sent Pliyev a warning forbidding him to use either missiles or fighter jets to attack U-2s. Shortly afterward, Pliyev was ordered to begin dismantling the MRBM sites, which were already operational. On October 30, he received instructions to load all the R-12 warheads onto the *Alexandrovsk,* to be returned to the Soviet Union together with the R-14s. Between November 20 and 22, Malinovsky ordered Pliyev to ship out all remaining tactical nuclear warheads on Cuba, an operation completed on December 25, 1962.

Pliyev soon followed, though around 18,000 Soviet troops remained on Cuba. The Soviet government awarded Pliyev the Order of Lenin for his service in Cuba. He subsequently wrote two volumes of memoirs on his World War II service. In 1968 the Defense Ministry appointed him a military inspector and adviser to its General Inspectors Group. Pliyev died on February 2, 1979.

Priscilla Roberts

See also: ANADYR, Operation; Castro, Fidel; Gribkov, Anatoli Ivanovich; Kennedy, John Fitzgerald; Khrushchev, Nikita Sergeyevich; Malinovsky, Rodion Yakovlevich; U-2 Overflights

References

Blight, James G., Bruce J. Allyn, and David A. Welch. *Cuba on the Brink: Castro, the Missile Crisis, and the Soviet Collapse.* New York: Pantheon Books, 1993.

Fursenko, Aleksandr, and Timothy Naftali. *One Hell of a Gamble: Khrushchev, Castro, and Kennedy, 1958–1964.* New York: Norton, 1997.

Gribkov, Anatoli I., and William Y. Smith. *Operation ANADYR: U.S. and Soviet Generals Recount the Cuban Missile Crisis.* Edited by Alfred Friendly, Jr. Chicago, Berlin, Tokyo, and Moscow: edition q, 1994.

Polmar, Norman, and John D. Gresham. *DEFCON-2: Standing on the Brink of Nuclear War During the Cuban Missile Crisis.* New York: John Wiley, 2006.

R

Rostow, Walt Whitman (1916–2003)

Chairman, State Department Policy Planning Council, 1961–1966. Walt Rostow was born in New York City on October 7, 1916, and studied economics at Yale University and as a Rhodes Scholar at Oxford University. During World War II, he served in the Office of Strategic Services (OSS), and from 1945 to 1949 he held positions in the State Department and the Economic Commission for Europe. Returning to academic life in 1950, for a decade he taught economics at the Massachusetts Institute of Technology. He was also associated with the Institute's Central Intelligence Agency–supported Center for International Studies. Rostow's research centered upon modernization theory and sought to provide an alternative to Marxist models and historical theories of economic development.

Rostow informally advised Sen. John F. Kennedy during his presidential campaign. As deputy special assistant to the president for national security affairs, from early February 1961 onward Rostow enthusiastically supported substantially expanding U.S. programs in South Vietnam. Immediately after the failed April 1961 Bay of Pigs invasion of Cuba, Rostow warned Kennedy against allowing resentment of Cuba to dominate U.S. foreign policymaking to the detriment of U.S. interests in Southeast Asia. In August 1961 he nonetheless urged that, to safeguard its own credibility and standing in the Western Hemisphere, the United States should employ covert means to overthrow Fidel Castro's government while providing massive developmental aid to Latin American nations.

Appointed chairman of the State Department's Policy Planning Council in November 1961, Rostow was only indirectly involved in resolving the Cuban Missile Crisis. Rostow counseled National Security Adviser

McGeorge Bundy—who differed strongly with him—against offering the Soviet Union any concessions or bargains in order to avoid nuclear warfare and recommended air strikes on Cuba, hoping that these would overturn Castro's regime. On October 25, he also unsuccessfully recommended that the United States embargo all petroleum imports to Cuba. Rostow further proposed deploying tactical nuclear weapons in Berlin, though this suggestion never reached the president. Unaware of Kennedy's secret understanding with the Soviets to remove NATO Jupiter nuclear missiles from Turkey, Rostow thought that U.S. firmness alone had forced the Soviets to back down, a belief that reinforced his existing proclivity to advocate the continuing expansion of U.S. commitments in South Vietnam. During Lyndon B. Johnson's presidency, Rostow—who succeeded Bundy as national security adviser in March 1966—became the administration's staunchest advocate of this position.

In January 1969, Rostow moved to the University of Texas at Austin, teaching economics and history. In voluminous writings, he consistently defended U.S. involvement in the Vietnam War, arguing that this gave other Southeast Asian nations the breathing space needed to develop strong economies and become staunch regional bastions of anticommunism. He died in Austin, Texas, on February 14, 2003.

Priscilla Roberts

See also: Bay of Pigs Invasion; Berlin Crises; Bundy, McGeorge; Castro, Fidel; Central Intelligence Agency; Johnson, Lyndon Baines; Jupiter Missiles (Turkey and Italy); Kennedy, John Fitzgerald

References

Halberstam, David. *The Best and the Brightest.* New York: Random House, 1973.

Milne, David. *America's Rasputin: Walt Rostow and the Vietnam War.* New York: Hill and Wang, 2008.

Peace, Charles Kimber. *Rostow, Kennedy, and the Rhetoric of Foreign Aid.* Lansing: Michigan State University Press, 2001.

Rostow, Walt W. *The Diffusion of Power, 1957–1972: An Essay in Recent History.* New York: Macmillan, 1972.

Rusk, Dean David (1909–1994)

U.S. secretary of state (1961–1969). Born in Cherokee County, Georgia, on February 9, 1909, Dean Rusk graduated from Davidson College, then

won a Rhodes Scholarship to Oxford University. In 1934 he became professor of government and dean at Mills College, California. An Army Reserve officer, he was called to active duty in 1940, ending the war as a colonel on the War Department General Staff. He then became special assistant to Secretary of War Robert P. Patterson. In 1947 incoming secretary of state George C. Marshall invited Rusk to head the State Department's Office of Special Political Affairs. In spring 1949 Rusk became deputy undersecretary of state. Major policy initiatives during his tenure included the Marshall Plan, the establishment of a separate West German state, and negotiating the North Atlantic Treaty.

In March 1950 Rusk became assistant secretary of state for Far Eastern affairs, formulating policy on the People's Republic of China (PRC), the Republic of China (ROC) (Taiwan), and the Koreas. When the Democratic People's Republic of Korea (DPRK) (North Korea) invaded the Republic

President John F. Kennedy's Executive Committee (ExComm) of top advisers met daily during the Cuban Missile Crisis, discussing and trying to decide on the best policies to pursue. The meeting of October 29, 1962, included President Kennedy and (*clockwise*) Secretary of Defense Robert S. McNamara; Deputy Secretary of Defense Roswell Gilpatric; Chairman of the Joint Chiefs of Staff Gen. Maxwell Taylor; Assistant Secretary of Defense Paul Nitze; Deputy USIA Director Donald Wilson; Special Counsel Theodore Sorensen; Special Assistant McGeorge Bundy; Secretary of the Treasury Douglas Dillon; Attorney General Robert F. Kennedy; Vice President Lyndon B. Johnson (*hidden*); Ambassador Llewellyn Thompson; Arms Control and Disarmament Agency Director William C. Foster; CIA Director John McCone (*hidden*); Undersecretary of State George Ball; and Secretary of State Dean Rusk. (John F. Kennedy Presidential Library)

of Korea (ROK) (South Korea) in June 1950, Rusk recommended firm action and military intervention under international United Nations (UN) auspices. His varied experiences reinforced his conviction that aggressive totalitarian powers, whether leftist or rightist, must be uncompromisingly opposed. During 1951–1961 Rusk headed the Rockefeller Foundation, greatly expanding aid programs to the developing world.

In 1961 President John F. Kennedy appointed Rusk secretary of state. Rusk placed special emphasis on improving relations with the Soviet Union, pushing arms-control agreements—including the 1963 Partial Test Ban Treaty (PTBT) and the 1968 Non-Proliferation Treaty (NPT)—and increasing aid to developing countries.

Although he had reservations regarding the feasibility of the April 1961 Bay of Pigs invasion attempt against Cuba, doubts he privately shared with Kennedy, to his later regret Rusk failed to express these forcefully in meetings of Kennedy's advisers or to coordinate potential opposition to the scheme within the Kennedy administration. As the invasion encountered major resistance, Rusk refused requests from its Central Intelligence Agency (CIA) planners to permit further U.S. air strikes against Cuban airfields. In January 1962, Rusk headed the U.S. delegation that persuaded the Organization of American States (OAS) to suspend Cuba's participation and impose economic and diplomatic sanctions on Castro's government.

Generally speaking, Rusk counseled moderation during both the ongoing Berlin Crisis and the Cuban Missile Crisis. Although often silent during the deliberations of the Executive Committee (ExComm) of presidential advisers that debated how best to counter the Soviet installation of nuclear-capable missiles in Cuba, Rusk favored the naval quarantine/blockade approach rather than immediate air strikes and helped develop a consensus for it. Unannounced air strikes would, he warned forcibly, contravene international law. Rusk led the delegation that obtained OAS endorsement of the blockade on October 23. Rusk was among the few Kennedy advisers privy to efforts by the president's brother, Attorney General Robert F. Kennedy, to negotiate an understanding with Soviet officials whereby the United States would decommission NATO Jupiter nuclear missiles in Turkey in exchange for the withdrawal of Soviet missiles from Cuba. Had this approach failed, he and John Kennedy were ready to ask the secretary general of the United Nations to propose a similar arrangement.

Initially skeptical of Kennedy's growing troop commitments to South Vietnam, under President Lyndon B. Johnson, who relied far more heavily

on his advice, Rusk became increasingly convinced that the United States must resist communist aggression there. He soon became the war's most ardent official defender, backing subsequent troop increases and heavy U.S. bombing raids on North Vietnam. His reputation tarnished by exhausting years in office, a deeply scarred Rusk left the State Department in 1969, teaching international law at the University of Georgia until 1984 and eventually writing his memoirs. He died in Athens, Georgia, on December 20, 1994.

Priscilla Roberts

See also: Bay of Pigs Invasion; Berlin Crises; Central Intelligence Agency; Johnson, Lyndon Baines; Jupiter Missiles (Turkey and Italy); Kennedy, John Fitzgerald; Kennedy, Robert Francis; Organization of American States; Partial Test Ban Treaty; United Nations

References

Cohen, Warren I. *Dean Rusk.* Totowa, NJ: Cooper Square, 1980.

Papp, Daniel S., ed. *As I Saw It: By Dean Rusk As Told to Richard Rusk.* New York: Norton, 1990.

Schoenbaum, Thomas J. *Waging Peace and War: Dean Rusk in the Truman, Kennedy, and Johnson Years.* New York: Simon and Schuster, 1988.

Zeiler, Thomas W. *Dean Rusk: Defending the American Mission Abroad.* Wilmington, DE: Scholarly Resources, 2000.

S

Schlesinger, Arthur Meier, Jr. (1917–2007)

U.S. historian, special assistant to the president, 1960–1964. Arthur Schlesinger, Jr., was born on October 15, 1917, in Columbus, Ohio, the son of a distinguished professor of history who moved to Harvard University in 1924. Educated at Phillips Exeter Academy, Harvard University, and Peterhouse College, Cambridge, he was appointed a Junior Fellow of Harvard's elite Society of Fellows in September 1939. He served in the Office of War Information from 1942 to 1943 and then transferred to the Office of Strategic Services (OSS) as an analyst, spending two years in Britain and France. Schlesinger, a diligent researcher and prolific writer of highly readable history, rejoined Harvard's History Department in 1947. A committed Democrat, he produced several volumes focusing upon the presidencies of Andrew Jackson and Franklin D. Roosevelt. Schlesinger quickly became a leading figure in the anticommunist U.S. left and in 1947 helped to found Americans for Democratic Action, an organization embodying this outlook.

During the 1960 presidential campaign Schlesinger worked to elect the young, Harvard-educated senator John F. Kennedy, whom he considered the embodiment of pragmatic liberalism. In late 1960, Kennedy appointed Schlesinger to the ill-defined position of special assistant to the president, which he remained until two months after Kennedy's assassination in November 1963. With Kennedy's knowledge, from his vantage point Schlesinger gathered raw material for his subsequent memoir of the Kennedy presidency, *A Thousand Days* (1965). He functioned as the president's contact to intellectuals and his liaison with United Nations (UN) ambassador Adlai Stevenson, whose earlier presidential bids Schlesinger had supported.

Schlesinger also advised Kennedy on Latin America, a long-standing interest of his own, and wrote some of his speeches. In 1961 he was among the few administration officials to oppose the disastrous Bay of Pigs invasion attempt in Cuba, though afterward he publicly defended this venture. Schlesinger did not join the Executive Committee (ExComm) of senior officials that debated U.S. policy during the October 1962 crisis over the installation of Soviet missiles in Cuba. Stevenson, who handled the issue at the United Nations, confided in him and Schlesinger joined Stevenson in New York, assisting the ambassador in drafting speeches for the UN Security Council. On October 24 Schlesinger also passed on to Kennedy advice from W. Averell Harriman, assistant secretary of state for Far Eastern affairs, that Soviet leader Nikita Khrushchev was seeking a peaceful solution and the United States should cooperate with him to achieve this. At this time Schlesinger remained unaware of the secret U.S.-Soviet understanding that NATO Jupiter missiles in Turkey would be removed, negotiated by Attorney General Robert F. Kennedy, the president's younger brother.

Schlesinger, who settled in Manhattan and accepted the Albert Schweitzer Chair in the Humanities at the City University of New York Graduate School in 1967, was closely identified with the Kennedy family. He supported Robert in his 1968 presidential bid, cut short by assassination. Ten years later, Schlesinger published the massive *Robert Kennedy and His Times* (1978), which won the National Book Award. Although important sources, Schlesinger's two somewhat hagiographical volumes on the Kennedy brothers reflected his deep attachment to them and tended to interpret history in their favor while ignoring less flattering evidence. He continued to write prolifically, producing numerous short pieces on history and politics, many later published in book form. Over time, Schlesinger turned against the U.S. military intervention in Vietnam he had originally supported and watched apprehensively the growing strength of U.S. conservatism in the later 20th century. On February 27, 2007, he died of a heart attack in Manhattan.

Priscilla Roberts

See also: Bay of Pigs Invasion; Harriman, William Averell; Jupiter Missiles; Kennedy, John Fitzgerald; Kennedy, Robert Francis; Khrushchev, Nikita Sergeyevich; Stevenson, Adlai Ewing II; United Nations

References

Depoe, Stephen P. *Arthur M. Schlesinger, Jr., and the Ideological History of American Liberalism.* Tuscaloosa: University of Alabama Press, 1994.

Diggins, John Patrick, ed. *The Liberal Persuasion: Arthur Schlesinger, Jr., and the Challenge of the American Past.* Princeton, NJ: Princeton University Press, 1997.

Schlesinger, Arthur M., Jr. *Journals 1952–2000.* Edited by Andrew Schlesinger and Stephen Schlesinger. New York: Penguin Press, 2007.

Schlesinger, Arthur M., Jr. *Robert Kennedy and His Times.* Boston: Houghton Mifflin, 1978.

Schlesinger, Arthur M., Jr. *A Thousand Days: John F. Kennedy in the White House.* Boston: Houghton Mifflin, 1965.

Sorensen, Theodore Chaikin (1928–2010)

Special counsel to President John F. Kennedy, 1961–1963. Theodore Sorensen was born on May 8, 1928, in Lincoln, Nebraska, where his father was active in progressive Republican politics. After earning bachelor's and law degrees from the University of Nebraska, he moved to Washington, D.C., working first for the Farm Security Administration, then as a congressional aide.

In 1953 the youthful senator John F. Kennedy of Massachusetts hired Sorensen as a legislative assistant. Sorensen remained with Kennedy until the latter's death, his duties expanding to include speechwriting; many of Kennedy's best-known lines and jokes originated with him. He also drafted numerous articles for Kennedy, did significant research and writing on Kennedy's prize-winning book *Profiles in Courage* (1956), and accompanied the senator as he traveled across the United States campaigning for the presidency.

Once elected, Kennedy immediately appointed Sorensen special counsel to the president, expecting him to be a major adviser on domestic affairs as well as chief speechwriter. Sorensen had no involvement in planning the abortive April 1961 Bay of Pigs invasion of Cuba. After this event, Kennedy began to consult Sorensen on foreign policies, including such sensitive issues as the ongoing German crisis over the status of West Berlin.

In October 1962 Sorensen attended virtually all deliberations of the Executive Committee (ExComm) of advisers whom Kennedy consulted on the Cuban Missile Crisis. He also joined the smaller group with whom Kennedy discussed concurrent secret negotiations with Soviet officials regarding the removal of NATO Jupiter missiles from Turkey in exchange

for dismantling of Soviet missile installations in Cuba. Kennedy entrusted Sorensen with drafting several presidential letters to Soviet premier Nikita Khrushchev. His failure to produce an acceptable draft of an initial communication on October 18 may have helped tip the balance toward the imposition of a U.S. naval blockade (quarantine) on Cuba, rather than air strikes against missile installations. Sorensen himself favored the quarantine option as less likely "to precipitate general war while still causing the Soviets...to back down."

Sorensen drafted Kennedy's October 22 speech, informing the American people of the presence of Soviet nuclear-capable missiles in Cuba and demanding their withdrawal. Together with Robert F. Kennedy, he helped draft the president's response to Khrushchev's letters of October 26 and 27, setting out terms on which the Soviet Union would remove the Cuban missiles. He also joined in drafting a secret letter to Khrushchev on the scrapping of the Turkish missiles. Robert McNamara, Kennedy's secretary of defense, later credited him with helping hold the members of ExComm together.

Three months after Kennedy's assassination in November 1963, a devastated Sorensen submitted his resignation to President Lyndon B. Johnson, who had asked him to remain and utilized Sorensen's speechwriting talents for his first State of the Union Address. Sorensen wrote a memoir of the Kennedy administration and had a successful career with a prominent international law firm. He also remained active in Democratic Party politics, a recognized standard-bearer of liberal values, and wrote extensively on domestic and international affairs. On October 31, 2010, he died of a stroke in Manhattan.

Priscilla Roberts

See also: Bay of Pigs Invasion; Berlin Crises; Johnson, Lyndon Baines; Jupiter Missiles (Turkey and Italy); Kennedy, John Fitzgerald; Kennedy, Robert Francis; Khrushchev, Nikita Sergeyevich; McNamara, Robert Strange

References

Goduti, Philip A., Jr. *Kennedy's Kitchen Cabinet and the Pursuit of Peace: The Shaping of American Foreign Policy, 1961–1963.* Jefferson, NC: McFarland Press, 2009.

Sorensen, Theodore C. *Counselor: A Life at the Edge of History.* New York: Harper, 2008.

Sorensen, Theodore C. *Kennedy.* With new preface. New York: Harper, 2009.

Stevenson, Adlai Ewing, II (1900–1965)

U.S. politician, 1952 and 1956 Democratic Party presidential candidate, and ambassador to the United Nations (UN), 1961–1965. Born in Los Angeles on February 5, 1900, Adlai Stevenson attended Princeton University and Northwestern University Law School. Joining the leading Chicago law firm of Cutting, Moore and Sidley, he rapidly won social prominence and a wide circle of intellectual friends, serving on many public service organizations, most notably the Chicago Council on Foreign Relations, becoming its president in 1935. He soon won a reputation as a stellar public speaker.

From 1941 to 1944, Stevenson worked in the U.S. Navy Department. He then spent three years in the State Department as a special assistant to the secretary of state, serving on the U.S. team at the 1945 San Francisco conference that created the UN and attending several UN General Assemblies. In 1948 he was elected governor of Illinois on the Democratic ticket. In 1952 and again in 1956 Stevenson ran unsuccessfully as the Democratic candidate for the U.S. presidency, losing twice by wide margins to the Republican Dwight D. Eisenhower.

In 1961 the newly elected Democratic president, John F. Kennedy, made Stevenson ambassador to the UN, a position he held for the rest of his life. The president and his closest adviser, his brother Robert, both considered Stevenson overly liberal, weak, and indecisive, and treated him rather contemptuously. Left ignorant of planning for the April 1961 Bay of Pigs invasion of Cuba, Stevenson at first erroneously informed the UN that his country had played no part in it, a humiliating indication of his exclusion from the administration's inner circle.

Stevenson's finest hour came during the Cuban Missile Crisis. Speaking before the UN Security Council in an emergency debate on October 25, he displayed photographic evidence of Soviet missile bases on Cuba and aggressively demanded that Valerian Zorin, the Soviet UN representative, confirm whether or not his country had deployed nuclear-capable missiles there. Participating sporadically in the deliberations of the Executive Committee (ExComm) of Kennedy's senior advisers, sometimes in person, sometimes by telephone from New York, during the crisis Stevenson consistently counseled moderation and resolving issues through negotiations. Shown pictures of the missile installations by Kennedy on October 16, Stevenson advised against air strikes on them. By October 20, he supported the option of a blockade of Cuba, which he hoped would lead to negotiations "in an atmosphere free of threat." Even if Soviet premier Nikita

Khrushchev remained intransigent, Stevenson still hoped to avoid resorting to air strikes against Cuba. More conciliatory than other U.S. officials, on October 24 he inclined to favor a proposal by UN secretary general U Thant suggesting that the Soviet Union suspend all further nuclear and other weaponry shipments for two or three weeks while the United States dropped its quarantine and both sides embarked on peaceful discussions. Once the Soviet Union had agreed to withdraw the missiles, Stevenson participated in lengthy UN-supervised negotiations with Soviet representatives settling the details of these arrangements.

In a sour aftermath, in December 1962 the *Saturday Evening Post* published an article by the journalists Stewart Alsop and Charles Bartlett depicting Stevenson as so eager to conciliate the Soviets during the crisis by jettisoning NATO missiles in Italy and Turkey in exchange for those in Cuba that he "wanted a Munich," a reference to the 1938 agreement whereby Britain and France pressured Czechoslovakia to cede much of its territory to Nazi Germany. Ironically, Robert Kennedy, who had secretly negotiated an arrangement along these lines with Soviet officials, was the unnamed source for this story. It probably represented an attempt on his part to force Stevenson, whom he disliked intensely, to resign from his brother's administration. Stevenson retained his post until July 14, 1965, when he died suddenly of a heart attack in London.

Priscilla Roberts

See also: Bay of Pigs Invasion; Eisenhower, Dwight David; Jupiter Missiles (Turkey and Italy); Kennedy, John Fitzgerald; Kennedy, Robert Francis; Khrushchev, Nikita Sergeyevich; Schlesinger, Arthur M., Jr; U Thant; United Nations; Zorin, Valerian Aleksandrovich

References

Broadwater, Jeff. *Adlai Stevenson and American Politics: The Odyssey of a Cold War Liberal.* New York: Twayne, 1994.

Johnson, Walter, ed. *The Papers of Adlai E. Stevenson.* 8 vols. Boston: Little, Brown, 1972–1979.

Liebling, Alvin, ed. *Adlai Stevenson's Lasting Legacy.* New York: Palgrave Macmillan, 2007.

Martin, John Bartlow. *Adlai Stevenson and the World: The Life of Adlai E. Stevenson.* Garden City, NY: Doubleday, 1977.

McKeever, Porter. *Adlai Stevenson: His Life and Legacy.* New York: William Morrow, 1989.

T

Taylor, Maxwell Davenport (1901–1987)

U.S. military officer, chairman of the Joint Chiefs of Staff, 1962–1964. Maxwell Taylor was born on August 26, 1901, in Keytesville, Missouri. He graduated from the U.S. Military Academy, West Point, in 1922. In February 1955 he became chief of staff of the U.S. Army. Although Taylor served out his four-year term and did not, as often alleged, resign in protest, he differed with President Dwight D. Eisenhower over army policy: whereas Taylor favored building up conventional forces to enable the United States to fight limited wars—the strategy of "flexible response"— the budget-conscious president preferred to rely on massive but probably unusable "New Look" nuclear retaliation. In his 1959 book *The Uncertain Trumpet* Taylor publicly aired his views, winning the attention and approval of Eisenhower's successor, John F. Kennedy, and a reputation as a "political general."

The 1961 Bay of Pigs fiasco left Kennedy disillusioned with the Joint Chiefs of Staff (JCS), who had, he believed, left him inadequately briefed on the risks of the operation, assuming that, faced with potential failure, the president would simply authorize direct assistance by U.S. military forces. Shortly afterward, Kennedy brought Taylor in to investigate that episode and then appointed Taylor his principal military adviser, to serve as liaison with the JCS and as chairman of the Special Group (Augmented) on Cuba. Taylor also developed an extremely close relationship with Attorney General Robert F. Kennedy, the president's brother. In August 1962 Taylor, commenting on Operation MONGOOSE proposals to destabilize Cuba devised by Edward Lansdale, deputy assistant secretary of defense for special operations, in collaboration with the Central Intelligence Agency,

recognized that internal opposition to Fidel Castro's government was unlikely to overthrow his regime. Taylor favored an expanded program of intelligence gathering and economic warfare against Cuba, together with efforts to discredit Castro domestically and internationally. On October 1, 1962, Kennedy appointed Taylor chairman of the Joint Chiefs of Staff, a post he held until mid-1964.

Once photographic evidence revealed the presence of nuclear-capable missile launching sites in Cuba, Taylor was a key member of the Executive Committee (ExComm) of senior officials the Kennedy administration established on October 16, 1962, to handle the crisis. Initially he recommended a surgical strike against the bases, followed by a naval blockade to prevent the arrival of further weapons. Later that day, after speaking to the Joint Chiefs of Staff (JCS), he recommended massive air strikes on Cuban military facilities over several days but hoped to avoid outright U.S. invasion. By October 19 the rest of the JCS unanimously supported the full program of air strikes plus invasion, a position to which Taylor eventually converted as evidence of numerous additional Soviet missile sites on Cuba emerged. Both Kennedy brothers initially leaned toward the option of air strikes, rather than a less provocative limited naval blockade of Cuba, but by October 20 they had come around to favoring the blockade (or "quarantine"). Taylor expressed disagreement on behalf of the JCS but pledged their complete backing for the president's decision. After Kennedy's public announcement of the quarantine on October 22, Taylor continued to support massive air strikes targeting all identified nuclear-capable and surface-to-air missile sites, plus all Soviet and Cuban airplanes and airfields.

In late 1961 Taylor was an early advocate of the expansion of U.S. troop commitments in South Vietnam, together with military and economic aid. As JCS chairman from 1962 to 1964, and then as U.S. ambassador to South Vietnam, Taylor opposed the commitment of further U.S. ground forces to Vietnam but supported escalation of the war through U.S. air strikes within Vietnam and bombing raids on North Vietnam. In March 1968 Taylor was one of only three senior advisers or "Wise Men" to dissent from the view that the United States should seek a negotiated settlement to end the war. For the rest of his life Taylor continued to defend U.S. policies in Vietnam and to blame his country's defeat largely upon criticism by the media and public opinion, which in his view had sapped American resolve to win. He died in Washington, D.C., on April 19, 1987.

Priscilla Roberts

See also: Bay of Pigs Invasion; Castro, Fidel; Central Intelligence Agency; Eisenhower, Dwight David; Joint Chiefs of Staff; Kennedy,

John Fitzgerald; Kennedy, Robert Francis; Lansdale, Edward Geary; Military Balance; MONGOOSE, Operation; U-2 Overflights

References

Buzzanco, Robert. *Masters of War: Military Dissent and Politics in the Vietnam Era.* New York: Cambridge University Press, 1996.

Goduti, Philip A., Jr. *Kennedy's Kitchen Cabinet and the Pursuit of Peace: The Shaping of American Foreign Policy, 1961–1963.* Jefferson, NC: McFarland Press, 2009.

Kinnard, Douglas. *The Certain Trumpet: Maxwell Taylor and the American Experience in Vietnam.* Washington, DC: Brassey's, 1991.

McMaster, H. R. *Dereliction of Duty: Lyndon Johnson, Robert McNamara, the Joint Chiefs of Staff, and the Lies That Led to Vietnam.* New York: HarperPerennial, 1998.

Taylor, John M. *General Maxwell Taylor: The Sword and the Pen.* New York: Doubleday, 1989. Reissued as *An American Soldier: The Wars of General Maxwell Taylor.* Novato, CA: Presidio, 2001.

Taylor, Maxwell D. *Swords and Plowshares.* New York: Norton, 1972.

Thompson, Llewellyn Edward, Jr. (1904–1972)

U.S. career diplomat and one of the premier Cold War Soviet experts. Born the son of a sheep rancher on August 24, 1904, in Las Animas, Colorado, Llewellyn Thompson graduated from the University of Colorado in 1928 and joined the Foreign Service the following year. His first appointment to Moscow came in 1941. He endeared himself to Muscovites by staying on during the grim Nazi siege of 1941–1942. In 1944 he was sent to London, and in 1946 he returned to Washington to take on senior posts in Eastern European and European affairs.

In 1950 Thompson went to Rome and was then appointed high commissioner and ambassador to Austria (1952–1956). He went on to serve during 1957–1961 as ambassador to the Soviet Union, where he secured Soviet leader Nikita Khrushchev's personal trust. This served Thompson well as an adviser to presidents Dwight D. Eisenhower and John F. Kennedy during Cold War crises over Berlin and Cuba between 1958 and 1962.

Thompson facilitated Khrushchev's visit to the United States in 1959 as well as U.S.-Soviet summits in Paris (1960) and Vienna (1961). Thompson returned to Washington in 1962 and was appointed ambassador-at-large. During the Cuban Missile Crisis, he exerted a moderating

influence in White House Executive Committee (ExComm) meetings, in which President Kennedy relied particularly heavily on his expertise on the Soviet Union. In 1966 President Lyndon B. Johnson appointed Thompson—who was involved in many crucial nuclear arms talks—ambassador to the Soviet Union for a second time, a post he held until 1969, making him the longest-serving U.S. ambassador to the Soviet Union in history. Thompson died in Bethesda, Maryland, on February 6, 1972.

Günter Bischof

See also: Berlin Crises; Eisenhower, Dwight David; Johnson, Lyndon Baines; Kennedy, John Fitzgerald; Nuclear Arms Race

References

Beschloss, Michael R. *The Crisis Years: Kennedy and Khrushchev, 1960–1963.* New York: HarperCollins, 1991.

Garthoff, Raymond L. *A Journey through the Cold War: A Memoir of Containment and Coexistence.* Washington, DC: Brookings Institution Press, 2001.

Mayers, David. *The Ambassadors and America's Soviet Policy.* New York: Oxford University Press, 1995.

U

U Thant (1909–1974)

Burmese politician, secretary general of the United Nations (UN), 1961–1971. Born in Pantanaw, Burma, on January 22, 1909, U Thant worked as an educator and freelance journalist before going into government service. During 1947–1957 he served as press director of the government of Burma, director of national broadcasting, secretary to the Ministry of Information, secretary of projects in the Prime Minister's Office, and executive secretary of Burma's Economic and Social Board. In 1957 he became Burma's representative to the UN. He quickly became a leading figure in the UN effort to broker a solution to the war in Algeria. As a moderate neutralist, he was elected to complete the term of UN secretary general Dag Hammarskjöld, who died in a September 1961 plane crash. He served two further terms in his own right, from November 1962 until December 1971.

As secretary general, Thant preferred quiet diplomacy and tended to rely more heavily on superpower initiatives than had his predecessor. But he could also be quite forceful in policy implementation, sending UN forces in November 1961 and again in December 1962 to end the secession crisis involving the Congolese province of Katanga.

His most notable successes included sending UN peacekeeping forces to Cyprus in 1964 and his 1965 brokering of a cease-fire in the 1965 Indo-Pakistani war over Kashmir.

At the height of the Cuban Missile Crisis, Thant sent identical appeals to U.S. president John F. Kennedy and Soviet leader Nikita Khrushchev to end the dispute through negotiations, suggesting that the United States lift the naval quarantine and the Soviet Union halt work on the missile sites. Those appeals were ignored. It seems, however, that if U.S.-Soviet

negotiations for a peaceful resolution failed, Kennedy intended to seek UN mediation, a strategy he considered greatly preferable to outright nuclear warfare. Once a settlement was reached in principle, on October 30 and 31, 1962, Thant led a delegation that visited Cuba and inspected some of the missile installations. As a conciliatory gesture, the United States ceased surveillance overflights during his visit. Thant also allowed U.S. and Soviet representatives to work under UN auspices in finalizing the sometimes contentious details of the agreement to remove the missiles and other weaponry from Cuba.

Thant's attempts after 1963 to sponsor negotiations among the United States, the Democratic Republic of Vietnam (DRV) (North Vietnam), and the Soviet Union were less successful. He retired from the UN in December 1971, when his term of office ended. Thant died on November 25, 1974, in New York City.

Lise Namikas

See also: Kennedy, John Fitzgerald; Khrushchev, Nikita Sergeyevich; U-2 Overflights; United Nations

References

Firestone, Bernard J. *The United Nations under U Thant, 1961–1971.* Lanham, MD: Scarecrow Press, 2001.

Fursenko, Aleksandr, and Timothy Naftali. *One Hell of a Gamble: Khrushchev, Castro, and Kennedy, 1958–1964.* New York: Norton, 1997.

May, Ernest R., and Philip D. Zelikow, eds. *The Kennedy Tapes: Inside the White House during the Cuban Missile Crisis.* Cambridge, MA: Harvard University Press, 1997.

Nassif, Ramses. *U Thant in New York, 1961–1971: Portrait of the Third U.N. General-Secretary.* New York: St. Martin's Press, 1988.

U Thant. *View from the UN.* New York: Doubleday, 1977.

U-2 Overflights

In the 1950s, the U.S. defense contractor and aircraft manufacturer Lockheed developed light jet-powered sailplanes that could undertake photographic reconnaissance missions at high altitude, designated U-2s. As part of a program beginning in 1956 under direction from the Central Intelligence Agency (CIA), pilots who came from the U.S. military but were

officially employed by Lockheed and attached to a Weather Observation Squadron based in Turkey and making heavy use of bases in Pakistan flew 24 U-2 surveillance flights over Soviet territory along an arc running from Pakistan to Norway. These clandestine flights, which violated Soviet airspace, provided the CIA with vital information on the number, strength, and location of Soviet nuclear missiles and other weapons. The program was ended with the 24th such flight in 1960, after the U-2 Affair, in which Soviet surface-to-air missiles (SAMs) shot down a U-2 deep over Soviet territory, capturing the pilot, Francis Gary Powers, alive and obtaining his public confession that he had been engaged in an espionage mission. One casualty of the U-2 Affair was a summit meeting in Paris between U.S. president Dwight D. Eisenhower and Soviet premier Nikita Khrushchev, an encounter originally intended to defuse international tensions and make some progress toward halting the nuclear arms race.

No further flights were made over Soviet territory, but U-2s still undertook reconnaissance missions over other hostile states, such as China

At the height of the Cuban Missile Crisis, on October 27, 1962, a Soviet missile battery shot down a U-2 surveillance aircraft conducting reconnaissance over Cuba. The pilot, Rudolph Martin Anderson, Jr., was killed. Fearing that any retaliation would further escalate the situation and possibly result in outright war, President John F. Kennedy deliberately chose not to retaliate with an air strike against the antiaircraft battery responsible for downing the U-2. (Getty Images)

and Cuba, where the danger of interception was considered small. From August 1962, CIA director John McCone, who had heard reports that unusual quantities of Soviet military equipment were arriving in Cuba and rumors that these included nuclear warheads, pressed to resume U-2 missions over Cuba. This was allowed in October 1962. At the insistence of Secretary of Defense Robert S. McNamara, uniformed military officers rather than civilians piloted the airplanes involved.

Analysis of photographic data collected by several flights on October 14 and 15 revealed the existence of several nuclear-capable missile sites in Cuba, some equipped for intermediate-range ballistic missiles (IRBMs) and others intended for medium-range ballistic missiles (MRBMs), as well as crates holding Il-28 medium-range light bombers. On the evening of October 15 Ray Cline, the CIA's deputy director of intelligence, passed on this information to McGeorge Bundy, President John F. Kennedy's national security adviser. The following morning Bundy in turn told Kennedy. The news marked the beginning of the Cuban Missile Crisis, triggering 13 days of deliberations among Kennedy and his senior diplomatic and military advisers.

Further U-2 sorties over the next week identified numerous additional missile sites on Cuba, with no certainty that the reconnaissance revealed all existing installations. On October 25, in an emergency debate at the United Nations, U.S. ambassador Adlai Stevenson displayed sample photographs and demanded that Valerian Zorin, his Soviet counterpart, confirm or deny the presence of Soviet nuclear-capable missiles on Cuba. When French newspapers expressed doubts over the validity of the photographic evidence, CIA officials flew to France bearing sets of the photographs to verify their allegations.

U-2 overflights had the potential to escalate the crisis. Soviet forces tracked overflights on October 14, 15, and 17, but had been ordered not to fire on U.S. aircraft unless attacked. On October 27, as negotiations between U.S. and Soviet officials continued, a Soviet SAM battery in Cuba shot down a U-2, killing the pilot, Maj. Rudolph Anderson. Other lower-flying naval reconnaissance aircraft over Cuba also came under fire; one was damaged but returned safely to base. Kennedy and other U.S. officials had previously agreed that any attacks on U.S. airplanes would trigger U.S. air strikes against the batteries responsible for these. In the event, Kennedy and McNamara decided against immediate retaliation, choosing instead to assume that lower-level Soviet military personnel in Cuba had acted without specific authorization from their superiors in Moscow.

The same day, another U-2 collecting atmospheric samples from Soviet nuclear testing near the North Pole strayed off course into Soviet airspace. Soviet MiG fighter jets tried to intercept it, and nuclear-armed U.S. fighter jets based in Alaska escorted the U-2 back once it reentered U.S. airspace. All these incidents revealed the potential for trigger-happy military forces to spark an incident that could easily spiral into a full-scale nuclear exchange. The Pentagon hastily stated that any interference with U.S. surveillance would provoke a response. Khrushchev—who apparently initially believed that Cuban rather than Soviet troops had shot down the U-2—instructed his military commanders in Cuba to exercise restraint and avoid further attacks on U.S. aircraft. At this point the bellicose Cuban leader Fidel Castro was urging Khrushchev to initiate a nuclear first strike against the United States. Fearful that Castro might try to incite Soviet and Cuban military officers manning missile batteries to further hostile action against U.S. targets, Khrushchev begged him to resist the temptation to respond forcibly to U.S. overflights.

Once Soviet officials had agreed to remove the missiles from Cuba, throughout November and December 1962 U-2 overflights as well as lower-level air reconnaissance flights monitored the progress of these operations, provoking sharp protests from Castro. The Soviet government bluntly warned him that Soviet troops would no longer assist in shooting down such aircraft. Eventually, U.S. officials decided to suspend the noisy and disruptive low-level flights and restrict their surveillance to high-altitude U-2 missions. U-2 flights over Cuba continued until the late 1970s, and thereafter were reintroduced during times of tension in U.S.-Cuban relations.

Priscilla Roberts

See also: Bundy, McGeorge; Castro, Fidel; Central Intelligence Agency; Eisenhower, Dwight David; Kennedy, John Fitzgerald; Khrushchev, Nikita Sergeyevich; McCone, John Alex; McNamara, Robert Strange; Stevenson, Adlai Ewing II; United Nations; U.S. Allies; Zorin, Valerian Aleksandrovich

References

Brugioni, Dino. *Eyeball to Eyeball: The Inside Story of the Cuban Missile Crisis.* Edited by Robert F. McCort. New York: Random House, 1991.

Dobbs, Michael. *One Minute to Midnight: Kennedy, Khrushchev, and Castro on the Brink of Nuclear War.* New York: Knopf, 2008.

Pedlow, Gregory W., and Donald E. Welzenbach. *The CIA and the U-2 Program 1954–1974.* Washington, DC: Central Intelligence Agency, Center for the Study of Intelligence, 1998.

Pocock, Chris. *The U-2 Spyplane: Toward the Unknown: A New History of the Early Years.* Atglen, PA: Schiffer Publishing, 2000.

Polmar, Norman, and John D. Gresham. *DEFCON-2: Standing on the Brink of Nuclear War during the Cuban Missile Crisis.* New York: John Wiley, 2006.

Prados, John. *Presidents' Secret Wars: CIA and Pentagon Covert Operations from World War II through the Persian Gulf.* Rev. ed. Chicago: Ivan R. Dee, 1996.

United Nations

Multinational organization established in 1945 and designed to promote four primary objectives: collective security, international economic and cultural cooperation, multilateral humanitarian assistance, and human rights. The creation of the United Nations (UN) represented an attempt by the World War II Allies to establish an international organization more effective than the interwar League of Nations, which had failed to mitigate the worldwide economic depression of the 1930s or prevent a second world war. UN architects were heavily influenced by the belief that during the 1930s, nationalist policies, economic and political rivalries, and the absence of international collaboration to help resolve outstanding disputes had contributed substantially to the outbreak of World War II.

The UN soon became an arena for Cold War contests and disputes in which the major powers tested their strength, while Third World nations came to see the UN as a forum where, given their growing numbers, the concerns of less-developed countries could be voiced and made effective, especially in the General Assembly, which was empowered to discuss all international questions of interest to members. In the Cold War context, the UN became a venue where communist and Western-led camps contended for power. Despite its stated security role, the organization proved largely unsuccessful in defusing the growing tensions that, during the second half of the 1940s, rapidly came to divide the former World War II Allies, with the Western powers—Britain, France, and the United States— soon fiercely at odds with the Soviet Union.

When the UN was founded, it was anticipated that peacekeeping and the restoration of international security and order, if necessary by military means, would be among its major functions. Under Article 43 of the

Debate on the Cuban Missile Crisis at the United Nations (UN) on October 25, 1962. During the meeting, U.S. ambassador to the UN Adlai Stevenson dramatically confronted his Soviet counterpart Valerian Zorin, challenging him to confirm or deny the presence of Soviet missiles in Cuba. Stevenson displayed U-2 surveillance photographs documenting the existence of these missiles. (United Nations)

UN's charter, member states were originally expected to agree to make specified military forces available to the UN for deployment under the organization's control, for use on occasions when military intervention was required to maintain or reestablish international peace and security. In practice, no nation signed any such agreement relinquishing control of any military forces to UN authority.

The UN General Assembly was the stage for some of the most significant pronouncements and dramatic confrontations of the Cold War, providing a backdrop to the saga of Cuba in the late 1950s and 1960s. U.S. diplomats soon noted that under Fidel Castro Cuba frequently voted with the Soviet bloc, a disturbing indication of its new international alignment. On September 26, 1960, Castro addressed the UN General Assembly in New York, denouncing U.S. policies toward Cuba. The audience included Soviet premier Nikita Khrushchev, who loudly affirmed his country's support for Cuba. A month later, on October 25, 1960, as fears that the United States was covertly planning military intervention against Cuba mounted, both Cuban and Soviet representatives appealed to the United Nations to prevent this. Washington convinced the UN Security Council that the

Organization of American States, not the UN, was the appropriate body to consider the issue. Embarrassingly for the United States, during the U.S.-backed Bay of Pigs invasion attempt against Cuba in April 1961, U.S. ambassador to the UN Adlai Stevenson initially denied that his country was involved, a statement he was later forced to retract.

Eighteen months later, in an emergency debate in the Security Council on October 25, 1962, Stevenson dramatically challenged his Soviet counterpart Valerian Zorin to confirm the presence of Soviet nuclear-capable missiles in Cuba, displaying photographic evidence of these installations. One day earlier, UN secretary general U Thant sent identical messages to both parties, suggesting that the Soviet Union suspend all further nuclear and conventional weapons shipments for two or three weeks while the United States dropped its quarantine and both sides embarked on peaceful negotiations. He offered to mediate a settlement, an offer that President John F. Kennedy might well have accepted had his own efforts for a peaceful resolution proved futile. On October 30 and 31, 1962 a UN delegation headed by U Thant visited Havana to inspect the missile sites. Initially, Soviet and U.S. negotiators anticipated UN inspectors would provide verification once the missiles had left, but the resentful Castro refused to allow such inspections on Cuban soil. After the broad lines of an agreement to remove the missiles and other assorted weaponry in exchange for a U.S. pledge not to invade Cuba had been reached, U.S. representatives led by arms-control negotiator John J. McCloy and Soviet deputy foreign minister Vasili Kuznetsov spent two months working under UN auspices to finalize details of these arrangements, completing their work in late December 1962. In late 1963 William Attwood, an adviser to Stevenson, and Carlos Lechuga, Cuban ambassador to the UN, served as conduits for preliminary feelers from Castro to Kennedy on a possible normalization of Cuban-U.S. relations, approaches cut short by Kennedy's assassination in November 1963.

Priscilla Roberts

See also: Bay of Pigs Invasion; Castro, Fidel; Cordier, Andrew Wellington; Kennedy, John Fitzgerald; Khrushchev, Nikita Sergeyevich; Kuznetsov, Vasili Vasilyevich; McCloy, John Jay; Organization of American States; Stevenson, Adlai Ewing II; U Thant; Zorin, Valerian Aleksandrovich

References

Firestone, Bernard J. *The United Nations under U Thant, 1961–1971.* Lanham, MD: Scarecrow Press, 2001.

Heller, Peter B. *The United Nations under Dag Hammarskjöld, 1953–1961.* Lanham, MD: Scarecrow Press, 2001.

Kennedy, Paul. *The Parliament of Man: The Past, Present, and Future of the United Nations.* New York: Random House, 2006.

Lechuga, Carlos M. *In the Eye of the Storm: Castro, Kennedy, Khrushchev, and the Missile Crisis.* Translated by Mary Todd. Melbourne, Victoria, Australia: Ocean Press, 1995.

Luard, Evan. *A History of the United Nations.* 2 vols. New York: St. Martin's Press, 1982–1989.

Meisler, Stanley. *The United Nations: A History.* 2nd ed. New York: Grove, 2011.

Ostrower, Gary B. *The United Nations and the United States.* New York: Twayne, 1998.

U.S. Allies

The emergence in Cuba in January 1959 of a radical revolutionary government led by Fidel Castro had implications for U.S. relations with its allies, particularly those in the North Atlantic Treaty Organization (NATO). Most U.S. allies considered U.S. hostility toward Castro's Cuba excessive. The British Conservative government under Prime Minister Harold Macmillan thought U.S. economic sanctions against Cuba liable to prove counterproductive by inclining Castro toward the communist bloc, though during 1959–1960 U.S. pressure impelled Britain to refuse to sell Hunter warplanes or other arms to Castro. Canadian prime minister John Diefenbaker, reluctant to simply endorse U.S. policies toward Cuba and elsewhere, refused to end trade or break diplomatic relations with revolutionary Cuba and also rejected Canadian membership in the Organization of American States (OAS).

By mid-1960 British officials sympathized with U.S. president Dwight D. Eisenhower's desire to oust Castro, but urged caution in avoiding the appearance of U.S. interventionism. In April 1961 Macmillan loyally backed President John F. Kennedy's actions during the abortive U.S.-sponsored Bay of Pigs invasion attempt—in which NATO allies played no official role—but the episode drew widespread condemnation from the British press, public, and political elite. Internationally, popular and media reaction from most U.S. allies in Western Europe and Canada was generally unfavorable, especially when U.S. officials sought to deceive the United Nations over their country's involvement.

During the Cuban Missile Crisis, NATO states in Western Europe were acutely conscious that U.S. aerial bombing or invasion of Cuba might easily bring Soviet retaliation against West Berlin and the escalation of the dispute into a full-scale nuclear conflict. On October 19, the CIA formally briefed British officials on the developing crisis, and from then onward Kennedy consulted frequently with Macmillan by telephone and in person with his old friend Sir David Ormsby-Gore, the British ambassador in Washington. Asked whether he preferred the options of U.S. air strikes against Cuban missile bases or the imposition of a naval blockade, Ormsby-Gore selected the latter, the alternative Kennedy ultimately chose. On October 22 Kennedy dispatched personal emissaries to inform Macmillan, President Charles de Gaulle of France, West German chancellor Konrad Adenauer, and the North Atlantic Council of his anticipated response to the Soviet missiles in Cuba. With some reservations over the blockade's legality and fears the confrontation might escalate into full-scale war involving both Berlin and British thermonuclear forces, Macmillan offered his support, as did de Gaulle, though much British and French media opinion was initially skeptical of U.S. allegations that nuclear-capable missiles were present on Cuba.

As the crisis developed, U.S. and Soviet officials secretly agreed that the United States would within a few months remove obsolete NATO Jupiter nuclear missiles in Turkey and Italy, close to Soviet borders, in exchange for Soviet withdrawal of nuclear-capable weapons in Cuba. Soviet diplomats in London apparently suggested a bargain on these lines. Before offering this concession, Kennedy consulted Macmillan, who was willing to contribute 60 Thor intermediate-range ballistic missiles (IRBMs), based in Eastern England and already scheduled for removal in 1963. Eventually, it proved unnecessary to add these to the package. Formally, the Turkish and Italian missiles were under NATO control, requiring the United States to convince its allies, especially the reluctant Turks, that relinquishing these weapons would not affect those countries' security. U.S. defense officials, fearful of diminishing the credibility of their commitment to Europe's defense, agreed to compensate for their loss by stationing nuclear-armed Polaris submarines in the Mediterranean, a deployment Soviet premier Nikita Khrushchev eventually but unavailingly protested. Turkey and Italy also received substantial quantities of substitute U.S. conventional and dual-purpose weaponry.

In some respects, the Cuban Missile Crisis encouraged anti-American tendencies among U.S. allies. Kennedy's failure to notify Canada before taking action during the crisis led Diefenbaker, angered by this omission,

to refuse U.S. requests that Canada participate in the blockade of Cuba or place the Canadian armed forces in heightened readiness. President de Gaulle's sense that U.S. officials had informed rather than consulted him during the crisis intensified his conviction that French policy should be more independent of both NATO and the United States. The U.S. decision to remove Jupiter missiles from Turkey and Italy likewise impelled France to develop its own independent nuclear deterrent, free from U.S. control. Although Britain, the United States, and the Soviet Union, all sobered by the crisis, negotiated a Partial Nuclear Test Ban Treaty in spring 1963, an agreement that most U.S. allies quickly signed, France refused to be a party to it. The fact that Western Europe came uncomfortably close to enduring thermonuclear devastation over distant bases on a Caribbean island helped boost European peace organizations, including the Campaign for Nuclear Disarmament.

Most U.S. allies greeted the peaceful resolution of the crisis with relief. Yet when news of the crisis became public on October 22, many in the South Korean military were eager to see it escalate into full-scale war, as they believed this would offer an ideal opportunity to invade North Korea and unify the country. U.S. forces in the Demilitarized Zone separating the two Koreas turned their artillery south toward their own ally, and on the insistence of the U.S. government South Korean air force planes were grounded, to prevent any attack on the north. The episode was one example of just how far the implications of the Cuban Missile Crisis extended and how volatile and explosive its impact on the international situation might easily have become.

Priscilla Roberts

See also: Acheson, Dean Gooderham; Bay of Pigs Invasion; Berlin Crises; Castro, Fidel; Eisenhower, Dwight David; Kennedy, John Fitzgerald; Jupiter Missiles (Turkey and Italy); Military Balance; Nuclear Arms Race; Organization of American States; Partial Test Ban Treaty; United Nations

References

Glazov, Jamie. *Canadian Policy toward Khrushchev's Soviet Union.* Montreal and Kingston: McGill-Queen's University Press, 2002.

Mahan, Erin R. *Kennedy, de Gaulle, and Western Europe.* New York: Palgrave Macmillan, 2002.

Mayer, Frank A. *Adenauer and Kennedy: A Study in German-American Relations, 1961–1963.* New York: St. Martin's Press, 1996.

McMahon, Patricia I. *Essence of Indecision: Diefenbaker's Nuclear Policy, 1957–1963*. Montreal: McGill-Queen's University Press, 2009.

Scott, L. V. *Macmillan, Kennedy and the Cuban Missile Crisis: Political, Military and Intelligence Aspects*. New York: St. Martin's Press, 1999.

U.S. Congress

When dealing with Cuban issues, U.S. president John F. Kennedy was always conscious that he needed to maintain congressional support for his policies. Usually, strongly anticommunist senators and congresspersons tended to attack his administration for being too weak on Cuba. An exception to this pattern came when the president informed J. William Fulbright, chairman of the Senate Foreign Relations Committee, of the planned April 1961 Bay of Pigs invasion. Fulbright forcefully condemned the venture as a hypocritical affront to stated American principles of national self-determination.

As Cuba moved ever further into the Soviet camp, Republican criticism of Kennedy's policies mounted, spearheaded by such conservative stalwarts as Arizona senator Barry Goldwater. News that massive Soviet shipments of arms were reaching Cuba provoked allegations by New York senator Kenneth Keating, a Republican, made on the Senate floor on August 31, 1962, that Soviet troops were building nuclear-capable missile bases in Cuba. Indiana senator Homer Capehart, also a Republican, made similar charges, suggesting that the United States should move to impose a blockade on Cuba. In response, on September 4 Kennedy, Secretary of State Dean Rusk, and Defense Secretary Robert McNamara met with 15 congressional leaders and stated that U.S. surveillance had so far revealed only defensive weaponry on Cuba. Kennedy then issued a public statement that the United States would take action should Soviet combat troops, military bases, or offensive ground-to-ground or nuclear-capable missiles be present on Cuba. Recognizing that the forthcoming midterm congressional elections exposed Kennedy to political pressures to take a tough anti-Soviet line, on October 4 Soviet premier Nikita Khrushchev informally sent a message that he would do nothing provocative until mid-November, after these had taken place. A few days later, on October 10, as the Kennedy administration accelerated its U-2 surveillance overflights of Cuba, Keating again claimed to possess evidence that six launching pads for intermediate-range ballistic missiles (IRBMs) were under construction there.

On October 16, Kennedy and his chief advisers began discussing how best to respond to the discovery that these allegations were true. On October 22 Kennedy publicly announced the presence of Soviet nuclear-capable missiles on Cuba. Two hours earlier, he had briefed 20 Republican and Democratic congressional leaders on the situation and informed them he initially intended to impose a blockade. Most—including Fulbright, Richard Russell (D-GA), chairman of the Senate Armed Services Committee, and Carl Vinson (D-GA), chairman of the House Armed Services Committee—tended to favor air strikes or an invasion, the more provocative options. After Kennedy's speech that evening, Congress adopted a resolution supporting his policies, especially his unequivocal demand that the Soviets remove the missiles. The following day Central Intelligence Agency (CIA) director John McCone met again with selected congressional leaders, including Fulbright and Russell. On October 24—as U.S.-Soviet negotiations continued, the blockade came into force, and U.S. officials waited to see whether Soviet ships would turn back—Kennedy once more met congressional leaders, who were broadly supportive. The successful resolution of the crisis rebounded to Kennedy's political advantage. Noting with some satisfaction that hardline Republicans fared poorly in the November 1962 midterm congressional elections, while former vice president Richard Nixon, a strong anticommunist, lost his gubernatorial race in California, and Democrats gained four Senate seats overall, Khrushchev congratulated Kennedy on this political outcome of recent events.

Fears of adverse political repercussions were a major reason Kennedy administration officials insisted on keeping secret the informal U.S.-Soviet agreement that NATO would remove nuclear missiles from Turkey. In February 1963, Kennedy faced renewed allegations from suspicious Republican congressmen, especially Keating, that up to 40 Soviet medium-range nuclear-capable ballistic missiles remained concealed on Cuba. On February 7 McNamara publicly denied these allegations, providing U-2 surveillance photographic evidence. He was less forthcoming over continued stationing of Soviet troops in Cuba, which lasted throughout the Cold War, provoking congressional complaints in 1979. Congressional pressure was one factor limiting Kennedy's options during the Cuban Missile Crisis, since failure on his part to ensure the withdrawal of Soviet missiles from the island would almost certainly have been extremely politically damaging to him.

Priscilla Roberts

See also: Bay of Pigs Invasion; Castro, Fidel; Central Intelligence Agency; Jupiter Missiles (Turkey and Italy); Kennedy, John Fitzgerald; Khrushchev,

Nikita Sergeyevich; McCone, John Alex; McNamara, Robert Strange; Rusk, Dean David; U-2 Overflights

References

Freedman, Lawrence. *Kennedy's Wars: Berlin, Cuba, Laos, and Vietnam.* New York: Oxford University Press, 2000.

Fursenko, Aleksandr, and Timothy Naftali. *One Hell of a Gamble: Khrushchev, Castro, and Kennedy, 1958–1964.* New York: Norton, 1997.

George, Alice L. *Awaiting Armageddon: How Americans Faced the Cuban Missile Crisis.* Chapel Hill: University of North Carolina Press, 2006.

May, Ernest R., and Philip D. Zelikow, eds. *The Kennedy Tapes: Inside the White House during the Cuban Missile Crisis.* Cambridge, MA: Harvard University Press, 1997.

V

Vienna Conference (June 3–4, 1961)

Summit meeting between U.S. president John F. Kennedy and Soviet premier Nikita Khrushchev in Vienna, Austria, on June 3–4, 1961. Shortly after Kennedy took office in January 1961, Khrushchev suggested a meeting with his American counterpart. After the embarrassing and abortive Cuban Bay of Pigs invasion in April, Kennedy's advisers adamantly opposed the conference, believing that Khrushchev would exploit the failed invasion either by berating the president or by using it as a propaganda ploy. Kennedy rejected their advice.

Kennedy wanted the meeting to focus on a nuclear test ban treaty and the neutralization of Laos, where a communist insurgency was threatening the government. The president believed that these agreements would be important steps toward easing Cold War tensions, which had intensified since the May 1960 U-2 Affair. He also hoped that the summit might encourage a wider détente.

Khrushchev had little interest in a test ban and almost none in Laos, however. His primary concern was the fate of Berlin. He wanted an agreement that would stanch the flow of East Germans fleeing to the West via the divided city. His earlier attempt to pressure President Dwight D. Eisenhower into accepting a settlement on Berlin by threatening to sign a peace treaty with the German Democratic Republic (GDR) (East Germany), which would have given the GDR full control of the city, had failed embarrassingly.

Following President Kennedy's death in 1963, his brother, Attorney General Robert F. Kennedy, reported that he had laid the groundwork for the summit during secret meetings with Khrushchev's conduit Georgi

Bolshakov, a Soviet intelligence officer who worked undercover as a reporter. Kennedy later claimed that Khrushchev had used this channel to trick his brother into believing that he would limit the Vienna discussions to Laos and the test ban treaty, which Khrushchev hinted could be verified by numerous on-site inspections. Robert Kennedy had not saved the messages, but the Soviets had. Their records verified that Khrushchev was not interested in either Laos or a nuclear test ban and that he had never agreed to on-site inspections. Instead, Khrushchev's notes to Kennedy focused on Berlin, reiterating his earlier threats.

Khrushchev's recalcitrance alarmed the president. Hoping to make the summit a success, President Kennedy sent the attorney general to Bolshakov, offering concessions and assurances that he wanted a good working relationship. Shortly before leaving for Vienna, Khrushchev met with his advisers, berating those who suggested that he work seriously with Kennedy and telling them that the president was weak and would buckle under his threats.

During the conference the president was in constant pain from a recent back injury, which many suggested meant he was not in top form. The summit had no formal agenda, allowing the two men to roam from topic to topic. Kennedy told aides that when he broached the subject of the dangers of war through miscalculation, Khrushchev became almost uncontrollably hostile. The Soviet leader also rebuffed Kennedy's efforts to discuss the nuclear test ban, responding that it "meant nothing" outside the context of total nuclear disarmament. As predicted by Kennedy's advisers and ignoring the president's earlier request, Khrushchev taunted Kennedy over Cuba. On Berlin, Khrushchev again threatened to sign a peace treaty if Kennedy did not agree to neutralize the city. Although badgered, Kennedy did not back down.

The following day, Khrushchev hinted at possible future discussions on Laos, although no progress was made on the test ban. In his last meeting with the president that day, Khrushchev told Kennedy that he intended to give East Germany control over West Berlin's access routes, adding that if the United States used force to keep them open, war would result. Kennedy icily replied, "Then there will be war, Mr. Chairman. It's going to be a very cold winter." Despite Kennedy's bold counterpunch, Khrushchev believed that he had sufficiently cowed the president.

Although Kennedy's aides told him that the meeting had been typical for Khrushchev, the president refused to believe it and began to prepare for war over Berlin. In a July 25, 1961, speech, Kennedy announced that he was dramatically expanding the armed forces, reinforcing Berlin, and

seeking increased congressional appropriations for civil defense. The administration even advised Americans to build backyard bomb shelters.

Khrushchev soon realized that he had badly miscalculated by bullying Kennedy. Believing that Kennedy had lost control of his government to militarists, Khrushchev concluded that the only way to solve the Berlin Crisis and avoid a war was to construct a wall separating the halves of the city. Nevertheless, largely because of Vienna, Khrushchev continued to view Kennedy as weak. This probably contributed to his decision in summer 1962 to offer to install nuclear-capable missiles in Cuba.

Robert Anthony Waters, Jr.

See also: Bay of Pigs Invasion; Berlin Crises; Bohlen, Charles Eustis; Bolshakov, Georgi Nikitovich; Eisenhower, Dwight David; Kennedy, John Fitzgerald; Kennedy, Robert Francis; Khrushchev, Nikita Sergeyevich; Partial Test Ban Treaty; U.S. Allies

References

Beschloss, Michael R. *The Crisis Years: Kennedy and Khrushchev, 1960–1963.* New York: HarperCollins, 1991.

Dallek, Robert. *An Unfinished Life: John F. Kennedy, 1917–1963.* Boston: Little, Brown, 2003.

Fursenko, Aleksandr, and Timothy Naftali. *One Hell of a Gamble: Khrushchev, Castro, and Kennedy, 1958–1964.* New York: Norton, 1997.

Kempe, Frederick. *Berlin 1961: Kennedy, Khrushchev, and the Most Dangerous Place on Earth.* New York: G. P. Putnam's Sons, 2011.

Reeves, Richard. *President Kennedy: Profile of Power.* New York: Simon and Schuster, 1993.

Reynolds, David. *Summits: Six Meetings That Shaped the Twentieth Century.* New York: Basic Books, 2007.

Warsaw Pact

Politico-military alliance among the Soviet Union and its Eastern European satellite states. The multilateral Treaty of Friendship, Cooperation, and Mutual Assistance signed on May 14, 1955, in Warsaw, Poland, formally institutionalized the Eastern European alliance system, the Warsaw Treaty Organization, known as the Warsaw Pact. The Warsaw Treaty was identical to bilateral treaties concluded during 1945–1949 between the Soviet Union and its Eastern European client states to assure Moscow's continued military presence on their territory. The Soviet Union, Albania, Bulgaria, Romania, the German Democratic Republic (GDR) (East Germany), Hungary, Poland, and Czechoslovakia pledged to defend each other if one or more of the members were attacked.

The Warsaw Pact was created as a political instrument for Soviet leader Nikita S. Khrushchev's Cold War policy in Europe. The immediate trigger was the admission of the Federal Republic of Germany (FRG) (West Germany) into the North Atlantic Treaty Organization (NATO) on May 5, 1955, and the Austrian State Treaty of May 15, 1955, which provided for Austrian neutrality and the withdrawal of Soviet troops. The creation of the Warsaw Pact sent important signals to both Eastern Europe and the West. On the one hand, the Soviet Union made clear to its satellite states that Austria's neutral status would not likewise be granted to them. On the other hand, Khrushchev allured the West with a standing offer to disband the Warsaw Pact in conjunction with the dissolution of NATO, contingent upon East-West agreement on a new collective security system in Europe.

The Political Consultative Committee (PCC) was established as the alliance's highest governing body, consisting of the member states' party

leaders. The PCC met almost annually in one of the capitals of the Warsaw Pact states. On the military side, a unified command and a joint staff were created to organize the actual defense of the Warsaw Treaty states.

Behind the façade of unity, however, growing differences hounded the Eastern alliance. Following Khrushchev's campaign of de-Stalinization, Poles and Hungarians in the fall of 1956 demanded a reform of the Warsaw Pact to reduce overwhelming Soviet dominance within the alliance. Polish generals issued a memorandum that proposed modeling the Warsaw Pact more after NATO, while Hungary's new Communist Party leader, Imre Nagy, declared his country's neutrality and plans to leave the Warsaw Pact. In November 1956, the Soviet Army invaded Hungary and soon crushed all resistance.

In 1958, Romania demanded the withdrawal from its territory of all Soviet troops and military advisers. To cover Soviet embarrassment, Khrushchev termed this a unilateral troop reduction contributing to greater European security. At the height of the Berlin Crisis (1961), the Warsaw Pact's weakest and least strategically important country, Albania, stopped supporting the pact and formally withdrew from the alliance in 1968.

From December 1958 onward Fidel Castro's revolutionary government in Cuba sought to purchase substantial armaments from Czechoslovakia, Poland, and other Warsaw Pact countries, requests that those states carefully cleared with the Soviet Union before dispatching any military equipment. The Warsaw Pact was left in ignorance when Khrushchev provoked the Cuban Missile Crisis. Only after the crisis ended did Eastern European leaders learn, in a secret meeting, that nuclear war had been narrowly avoided. Romania reacted promptly to Moscow's nonconsultation in such a serious matter. In 1963, the Romanian government gave secret assurances to the United States that it would remain neutral in the event of a confrontation between the superpowers. In 1963 Castro, seeking additional assurance that the United States would not invade Cuba in future, asked Khrushchev to admit Cuba as a Warsaw Pact member, a request the Soviet leader rejected.

Christian Nuenlist

See also: Berlin Crises; Castro, Fidel; Khrushchev, Nikita Sergeyevich

References

Heiss, Mary Ann, and S. Victor Papacosma, eds. *NATO and the Warsaw Pact: Intrabloc Conflicts.* Kent, OH: Kent State University Press, 2008.

Holden, Gerard. *The Warsaw Pact: The WTO and Soviet Security Policy.* Oxford, UK: Blackwell, 1989.

Jones, Christopher D. *Soviet Influence in Eastern Europe: Political Autonomy and the Warsaw Pact.* Brooklyn: Praeger, 1981.

Mastny, Vojtech, and Malcolm Byrne, eds. *A Cardboard Castle? An Inside History of the Warsaw Pact, 1955–1991.* Budapest, Hungary, and New York: Central European Press, 2005.

Mastny, Vojtech, Sven Holtsmark, and Andreas Wenger, eds. *War Plans and Alliances in the Cold War: Threat Perceptions in the East and West.* New York: Routledge, 2006.

Z

Zorin, Valerian Aleksandrovich (1902–1986)

Soviet diplomat. Born in Novocherkassk in the Rostov Oblast on January 14, 1902, Valerian Zorin joined the Communist Party of the Soviet Union (CPSU) in 1922. He taught and served as a party official in several posts until joining the People's Commissariat of Foreign Affairs in 1941. He served as assistant secretary general during 1941–1942, deputy commissar during 1942–1943, and head of the Fourth (Central European) Department during 1943–1945.

In March 1945, Zorin was appointed Soviet ambassador to Czechoslovakia, where he served until the spring of 1947. He then served as Soviet representative to the United Nations (UN) Economic Commission for Europe and later served on the Soviet delegation to the UN before returning to Moscow in November 1947 as deputy foreign minister, a post he held until 1955. He was dispatched to Prague to help oversee the February 1948 coup that installed a communist government.

From October 1952 to April 1953, Zorin was Soviet ambassador to the UN while retaining his foreign ministry post. In 1955 he was named Soviet ambassador to the Federal Republic of Germany (FRG) (West Germany) before returning as deputy foreign minister the following year, a position he held until 1965. In 1959, when the new radical government of Cuba sought to buy arms from Poland and Czechoslovakia, both Soviet satellites, the two Eastern European governments consulted Soviet officials. Speaking for the Foreign Ministry, Zorin expressed misgivings that such arms sales might harm the recent rapprochement negotiated by U.S. president Dwight D. Eisenhower and Soviet premier Nikita Khrushchev. Cuba nonetheless soon received substantial Soviet arms shipments.

From 1960 to 1963 Zorin also served once more as Soviet ambassador to the UN, representing his country in inconclusive 1961 disarmament negotiations with the United States for a nuclear test ban treaty. In October 1960, with rumors rife that the United States planned to invade Cuba and overthrow Castro, Zorin urged all nations to implement "urgent measures to prevent military action against Cuba." Two years later, during the Cuban Missile Crisis, he engaged in a dramatic exchange with U.S. ambassador to the UN Adlai Stevenson on October 25, 1962, as Stevenson pressed the recalcitrant Zorin to confirm or deny the presence of Soviet nuclear-capable missiles in Cuba. Once the Soviet Union had agreed to remove the missiles, Zorin participated in negotiations with U.S. and UN representatives to hammer out the details of implementation.

In 1965, Zorin was named Soviet ambassador to France, where he served until retiring in 1971. Subsequently, he served occasionally as an ambassador-at-large with responsibility for human rights issues. Elected a candidate member of the CPSU Central Committee in 1956, he became a full member in 1965. He died in Moscow on January 14, 1986.

Steven W. Guerrier

See also: Castro, Fidel; Eisenhower, Dwight David; Khrushchev, Nikita Sergeyevich; Stevenson, Adlai Ewing II; United Nations; Warsaw Pact

References

Brugioni, Dino A. *Eyeball to Eyeball: Inside the Cuban Missile Crisis.* Edited by Robert F. McCort. New York: Random House, 1993.

Dobrynin, Anatoly. *In Confidence: Moscow's Ambassador to America's Six Cold War Presidents, 1962–1986.* New York: Times Books, 1995.

Friedman, Norman. *The Fifty-Year War: Conflict and Strategy in the Cold War.* Annapolis, MD: Naval Institute Press, 2000.

Fursenko, Aleksandr, and Timothy Naftali. *One Hell of a Gamble: Khrushchev, Castro, and Kennedy, 1958–1964.* New York: Norton, 1997.

Meisler, Stanley. *The United Nations: A History.* 2nd ed. New York: Grove, 2011.

Primary Documents

1. President John F. Kennedy, Report to the American People on the Soviet Arms Buildup in Cuba, October 22, 1962

**The first public acknowledgment that the United States govern-
ment knew of the presence of Soviet nuclear-capable missiles in
Cuba came when President John F. Kennedy addressed the nation on
October 22, 1962. He demanded the withdrawal of these weapons
and announced the imposition of a naval blockade (or "quarantine")
on Cuba.**

This Government, as promised, has maintained the closest surveillance of
the Soviet military buildup on the island of Cuba. Within the past week,
unmistakable evidence has established the fact that a series of offensive
missile sites is now in preparation on that imprisoned island. The purpose
of these bases can be none other than to provide a nuclear strike capability
against the Western Hemisphere.

Upon receiving the first preliminary hard information of this nature last
Tuesday morning at 9 A.M., I directed that our surveillance be stepped up.
And having now confirmed and completed our evaluation of the evidence
and our decision on a course of action, this Government feels obliged to
report this new crisis to you in fullest detail.

The characteristics of these new missile sites indicate two distinct
types of installations. Several of them include medium range ballistic missiles, capable of carrying a nuclear warhead for a distance of more than
1,000 nautical miles. Each of these missiles, in short, is capable of striking

Washington, D.C., the Panama Canal, Cape Canaveral, Mexico City, or any other city in the southeastern part of the United States, in Central America, or in the Caribbean area.

Additional sites not yet completed appear to be designed for intermediate range ballistic missiles—capable of traveling more than twice as far—and thus capable of striking most of the major cities in the Western Hemisphere, ranging as far north as Hudson Bay, Canada, and as far south as Lima, Peru. In addition, jet bombers, capable of carrying nuclear weapons, are now being uncrated and assembled in Cuba, while the necessary air bases are being prepared.

This urgent transformation of Cuba into an important strategic base—by the presence of these large, long-range, and clearly offensive weapons of sudden mass destruction—constitutes an explicit threat to the peace and security of all the Americas, in flagrant and deliberate defiance of the Rio Pact of 1947, the traditions of this Nation and hemisphere, the joint resolution of the 87th Congress, the Charter of the United Nations, and my own public warnings to the Soviets on September 4 and 13. This action also contradicts the repeated assurances of Soviet spokesmen, both publicly and privately delivered, that the arms buildup in Cuba would retain its original defensive character, and that the Soviet Union had no need or desire to station strategic missiles on the territory of any other nation.

The size of this undertaking makes clear that it has been planned for some months. Yet only last month, after I had made clear the distinction between any introduction of ground-to-ground missiles and the existence of defensive antiaircraft missiles, the Soviet Government publicly stated on September 11 that, and I quote, "the armaments and military equipment sent to Cuba are designed exclusively for defensive purposes," that, and I quote the Soviet Government, "there is no need for the Soviet Government to shift its weapons. for a retaliatory blow to any other country, for instance Cuba," and that, and I quote their government, "the Soviet Union has so powerful rockets to carry these nuclear warheads that there is no need to search for sites for them beyond the boundaries of the Soviet Union." That statement was false.

Only last Thursday, as evidence of this rapid offensive buildup was already in my hand, Soviet Foreign Minister Gromyko told me in my office that he was instructed to make it clear once again, as he said his government had already done, that Soviet assistance to Cuba, and I quote, "pursued solely the purpose of contributing to the defense capabilities of

Cuba," that, and I quote him, "training by Soviet specialists of Cuban nationals in handling defensive armaments was by no means offensive, and if it were otherwise," Mr. Gromyko went on, "the Soviet Government would never become involved in rendering such assistance." That statement also was false.

Neither the United States of America nor the world community of nations can tolerate deliberate deception and offensive threats on the part of any nation, large or small. We no longer live in a world where only the actual firing of weapons represents a sufficient challenge to a nation's security to constitute maximum peril. Nuclear weapons are so destructive and ballistic missiles are so swift, that any substantially increased possibility of their use or any sudden change in their deployment may well be regarded as a definite threat to peace.

For many years, both the Soviet Union and the United States, recognizing this fact, have deployed strategic nuclear weapons with great care, never upsetting the precarious status quo which insured that these weapons would not be used in the absence of some vital challenge. Our own strategic missiles have never been transferred to the territory of any other nation under a cloak of secrecy and deception; and our history—unlike that of the Soviets since the end of World War II—demonstrates that we have no desire to dominate or conquer any other nation or impose our system upon its people. Nevertheless, American citizens have become adjusted to living daily on the bull's-eye of Soviet missiles located inside the U.S.S.R. or in submarines.

In that sense, missiles in Cuba add to an already clear and present danger—although it should be noted the nations of Latin America have never previously been subjected to a potential nuclear threat.

But this secret, swift, and extraordinary buildup of Communist missiles—in an area well known to have a special and historical relationship to the United States and the nations of the Western Hemisphere, in violation of Soviet assurances, and in defiance of American and hemispheric policy—this sudden, clandestine decision to station strategic weapons for the first time outside of Soviet soil—is a deliberately provocative and unjustified change in the status quo which cannot be accepted by this country, if our courage and our commitments are ever to be trusted again by either friend or foe.

The 1930's taught us a clear lesson: aggressive conduct, if allowed to go unchecked, ultimately leads to war. This nation is opposed to war. We are also true to our word. Our unswerving objective, therefore, must be to

prevent the use of these missiles against this or any other country, and to secure their withdrawal or elimination from the Western Hemisphere.

Our policy has been one of patience and restraint, as befits a peaceful and powerful nation, which leads a worldwide alliance. We have been determined not to be diverted from our central concerns by mere irritants and fanatics. But now further action is required—and it is under way; and these actions may only be the beginning. We will not prematurely or unnecessarily risk the costs of worldwide nuclear war in which even the fruits of victory would be ashes in our mouth—but neither will we shrink from that risk at any time it must be faced.

Acting, therefore, in the defense of our own security and of the entire Western Hemisphere, and under the authority entrusted to me by the Constitution as endorsed by the Resolution of the Congress, I have directed that the following *initial* steps be taken immediately:

First: To halt this offensive buildup, a strict quarantine on all offensive military equipment under shipment to Cuba is being initiated. All ships of any kind bound for Cuba from whatever nation or port will, if found to contain cargoes of offensive weapons, be turned back. This quarantine will be extended, if needed, to other types of cargo and carriers. We are not at this time, however, denying the necessities of life as the Soviets attempted to do in their Berlin blockade of 1948.

Second: I have directed the continued and increased close surveillance of Cuba and its military buildup. The foreign ministers of the OAS, in their communiqué of October 6, rejected secrecy on such matters in this hemisphere. Should these offensive military preparations continue, thus increasing the threat to the hemisphere, further action will be justified. I have directed the Armed Forces to prepare for any eventualities; and I trust that in the interest of both the Cuban people and the Soviet technicians at the sites, the hazards to all concerned of continuing this threat will be recognized.

Third: It shall be the policy of this Nation to regard any nuclear missile launched from Cuba against any nation in the Western Hemisphere as an attack by the Soviet Union on the United States, requiring a full retaliatory response upon the Soviet Union.

Fourth: As a necessary military precaution, I have reinforced our base at Guantanamo, evacuated today the dependents of our personnel there, and ordered additional military units to be on a standby alert basis.

Fifth: We are calling tonight for an immediate meeting of the Organ of Consultation under the Organization of American States, to consider this threat to hemispheric security and to invoke articles 6 and 8 of the Rio Treaty in support of all necessary action. The United Nations Charter

allows for regional security arrangements-and the nations of this hemisphere decided long ago against the military presence of outside powers. Our other allies around the world have also been alerted.

Sixth: Under the Charter of the United Nations, we are asking tonight that an emergency meeting of the Security Council be convoked without delay to take action against this latest Soviet threat to world peace. Our resolution will call for the prompt dismantling and withdrawal of all offensive weapons in Cuba, under the supervision of U.N. observers, before the quarantine can be lifted.

Seventh and finally: I call upon Chairman Khrushchev to halt and eliminate this clandestine, reckless, and provocative threat to world peace and to stable relations between our two nations. I call upon him further to abandon this course of world domination, and to join in an historic effort to end the perilous arms race and to transform the history of man. He has an opportunity now to move the world back from the abyss of destruction—by returning to his government's own words that it had no need to station missiles outside its own territory, and withdrawing these weapons from Cuba—by refraining from any action which will widen or deepen the present crisis-and then by participating in a search for peaceful and permanent solutions.

This Nation is prepared to present its case against the Soviet threat to peace, and our own proposals for a peaceful world, at any time and in any forum—in the OAS, in the United Nations, or in any other meeting that could be useful-without limiting our freedom of action. We have in the past made strenuous efforts to limit the spread of nuclear weapons. We have proposed the elimination of all arms and military bases in a fair and effective disarmament treaty. We are prepared to discuss new proposals for the removal of tensions on both sides—including the possibilities of a genuinely independent Cuba, free to determine its own destiny. We have no wish to war with the Soviet Union—for we are a peaceful people who desire to live in peace with all other peoples.

But it is difficult to settle or even discuss these problems in an atmosphere of intimidation. That is why this latest Soviet threat—or any other threat which is made either independently or in response to our actions this week—must and will be met with determination. Any hostile move anywhere in the world against the safety and freedom of peoples to whom we are committed—including in particular the brave people of West Berlin—will be met by whatever action is needed.

Finally, I want to say a few words to the captive people of Cuba, to whom this speech is being directly carried by special radio facilities. I speak to you as a friend, as one who knows of your deep attachment to

your fatherland, as one who shares your aspirations for liberty and justice for all. And I have watched and the American people have watched with deep sorrow how your nationalist revolution was betrayed—and how your fatherland fell under foreign domination. Now your leaders are no longer Cuban leaders inspired by Cuban ideals. They are puppets and agents of an international conspiracy which has turned Cuba against your friends and neighbors in the Americas—and turned it into the first Latin American country to become a target for nuclear war—the first Latin American country to have these weapons on its soil.

These new weapons are not in your interest. They contribute nothing to your peace and well-being. They can only undermine it. But this country has no wish to cause you to suffer or to impose any system upon you. We know that your lives and land are being used as pawns by those who deny your freedom. Many times in the past, the Cuban people have risen to throw out tyrants who destroyed their liberty. And I have no doubt that most Cubans today look forward to the time when they will be truly free-free from foreign domination, free to choose their own leaders, free to select their own system, free to own their own land, free to speak and write and worship without fear or degradation. And then shall Cuba be welcomed back to the society of free nations and to the associations of this hemisphere.

My fellow citizens: let no one doubt that this is a difficult and dangerous effort on which we have set out. No one can foresee precisely what course it will take or what costs or casualties will be incurred. Many months of sacrifice and self-discipline lie ahead—months in which both our patience and our will will be tested—months in which many threats and denunciations will keep us aware of our dangers. But the greatest danger of all would be to do nothing.

The path we have chosen for the present is full of hazards, as all paths are—but it is the one most consistent with our character and courage as a nation and our commitments around the world. The cost of freedom is always high—but Americans have always paid it. And one path we shall never choose, and that is the path of surrender or submission.

Our goal is not the victory of might, but the vindication of right—not peace at the expense of freedom, but both peace *and* freedom, here in this hemisphere, and, we hope, around the world. God willing, that goal will be achieved.

Source: Kennedy, John F. *Public Papers of the Presidents of the United States: John F. Kennedy, 1962* (Washington, DC: Government Printing Office, 1963).

Available at *The American Presidency Project,* http://www.presidency.ucsb.edu/ws/?pid=8986.

2. Kennedy-Khrushchev Exchanges during the Cuban Missile Crisis, October 22–28, 1962

When he publicly announced that the United States would not accept the presence of Soviet nuclear-capable missiles in Cuba, President John F. Kennedy had already dispatched a letter to Soviet premier Nikita Khrushchev, demanding their withdrawal. For four days, through October 25, Khrushchev and Kennedy traded intransigent letters in which neither showed any sign of backing down. On October 26, Khrushchev dispatched a lengthy letter, suggesting that the Soviets might be willing to remove their missiles if the United States promised not to invade Cuba in the future. The following day, he supplemented this with demands that the United States remove intermediate-range ballistic missiles (IRBMs) recently installed in Turkey, a U.S. NATO ally, which could be used to attack targets in the Soviet Union. On October 27 Kennedy responded publicly to the first letter, accepting its terms in principle. He did not publicize a response to the second letter but privately authorized his brother Robert to explore with Soviet officials the possibility of an informal understanding on the removal of intermediate-range NATO missiles in both Turkey and Italy. On October 27, Soviet surface-to-air batteries shot down a U.S. U-2 reconnaissance plane overflying Cuba, killing the pilot, while another U-2 strayed into Soviet airspace over Siberia but returned safely. U.S. and Soviet officials feared that such these episodes might easily escalate into outright war. In further correspondence on October 28, Khrushchev and Kennedy discussed these incidents. In a message broadcast over Soviet radio to ensure that it would reach the United States as fast as possible, Khrushchev complained of the overflights, pointing out their potential to overturn any peaceful Soviet-U.S. resolution of the crisis. On October 28, Kennedy went so far as to apologize for the October 27 intrusion into Soviet airspace. At this point, neither mentioned the U-2 brought down over Cuba. Instead, both focused upon the need to end the crisis

through negotiations rather than war and expressed their hopes for further progress in this direction.

President Kennedy to Chairman Khrushchev, Washington, October 22, 1962

Dear Mr. Chairman: A copy of the statement I am making tonight concerning developments in Cuba and the reaction of my Government thereto has been handed to your Ambassador in Washington. In view of the gravity of the developments to which I refer, I want you to know immediately and accurately the position of my Government in this matter.

In our discussions and exchanges on Berlin and other international questions, the one thing that has most concerned me has been the possibility that your Government would not correctly understand the will and determination of the United States in any given situation, since I have not assumed that you or any other sane man would, in this nuclear age, deliberately plunge the world into war which it is crystal clear no country could win and which could only result in catastrophic consequences to the whole world, including the aggressor.

At our meeting in Vienna and subsequently, I expressed our readiness and desire to find, through peaceful negotiation, a solution to any and all problems that divide us. At the same time, I made clear that in view of the objectives of the ideology to which you adhere, the United States could not tolerate any action on your part which in a major way disturbed the existing over-all balance of power in the world. I stated that an attempt to force abandonment of our responsibilities and commitments in Berlin would constitute such an action and that the United States would resist with all the power at its command.

It was in order to avoid any incorrect assessment on the part of your Government with respect to Cuba that I publicly stated that if certain developments in Cuba took place, the United States would do whatever must be done to protect its own security and that of its allies.

Moreover, the Congress adopted a resolution expressing its support of this declared policy. Despite this, the rapid development of long-range missile bases and other offensive weapons systems in Cuba has proceeded. I must tell you that the United States is determined that this threat to the security of this hemisphere be removed. At the same time, I wish to point out that the action we are taking is the minimum necessary to remove the threat to the security of the nations of this hemisphere. The fact of this

minimum response should not be taken as a basis, however, for any mis-judgment on your part.

I hope that your Government will refrain from any action which would widen or deepen this already grave crisis and that we can agree to resume the path of peaceful negotiation.

Sincerely,

John F. Kennedy

Source: U.S. Department of State, *Foreign Relations of the United States 1961–1963,* Vol. XI: *The Cuban Missile Crisis and Its Aftermath* (Washington, DC: Government Printing Office, 1996), Document 44, http://www.state.gov/www/about_state/history/frusXI/26_50.html; also Department of State *Bulletin,* November 19, 1973, pp. 635–636.

Chairman Khrushchev to President Kennedy, Moscow, October 23, 1962 [translated by U.S. Embassy, Moscow]

Mr. President.

I have just received your letter, and have also acquainted myself with text of your speech of October 22 regarding Cuba.

I should say frankly that measures outlined in your statement represent serious threat to peace and security of peoples. United States has openly taken path of gross violation of Charter of United Nations, path of violation of international norms of freedom of navigation on high seas, path of aggressive actions both against Cuba and against Soviet Union.

Statement of Government of United States America cannot be evaluated in any other way than as naked interference in domestic affairs of Cuban Republic, Soviet Union, and other states. Charter of United Nations and international norms do not give right to any state whatsoever to establish in international waters control of vessels bound for shores of Cuban Republic.

It is self-understood that we also cannot recognize right of United States to establish control over armaments essential to Republic of Cuba for strengthening of its defensive capacity.

We confirm that armaments now on Cuba, regardless of classification to which they belong, are destined exclusively for defensive purposes, in order to secure Cuban Republic from attack of aggressor.

I hope that Government of United States will show prudence and renounce actions pursued by you, which would lead to catastrophic consequences for peace throughout world.

Viewpoint of Soviet Government with regard to your statement of October 22 is set forth in statement of Soviet Government, which is being conveyed to you through your Ambassador in Moscow.

N. Khrushchev

Source: U.S. Department of State, *Foreign Relations of the United States 1961–1963,* Vol. XI: *The Cuban Missile Crisis and Its Aftermath* (Washington, DC: Government Printing Office, 1996), Document 48, http://www.state.gov/www/about_state/history/frusXI/26_50.html.

President Kennedy to Chairman Khrushchev, Washington, October 23, 1962

Dear Mr. Chairman:

I have received your letter of October twenty-third. I think you will recognize that the steps which started the current chain of events was [sic] the action of your Government in secretly furnishing offensive weapons to Cuba. We will be discussing this matter in the Security Council. In the meantime, I am concerned that we both show prudence and do nothing to allow events to make the situation more difficult to control than it already is.

I hope that you will issue immediately the necessary instructions to your ships to observe the terms of the quarantine, the basis of which was established by the vote of the Organization of American States this afternoon, and which will go into effect at 1400 hours Greenwich time October twenty-four.

Sincerely,

John F. Kennedy

Source: U.S. Department of State, *Foreign Relations of the United States 1961–1963,* Vol. XI: *The Cuban Missile Crisis and Its Aftermath* (Washington, DC: Government Printing Office, 1996), Document 52, http://www.state.gov/www/about_state/history/frusXI/51_75.html.

Chairman Khrushchev to President Kennedy, Moscow, October 24, 1962

Dear Mr. President:

I have received your letter of October 23, have studied it, and am answering you.

Just imagine, Mr. President, that we had presented you with the conditions of an ultimatum which you have presented us by your action. How would you have reacted to this? I think that you would have been indignant at such a step on our part. And this would have been understandable to us.

In presenting us with these conditions, you, Mr. President, have flung a challenge at us. Who asked you to do this? By what right did you do this? Our ties with the Republic of Cuba, like our relations with other states, regardless of what kind of states they may be, concern only the two countries between which these relations exist. And if we now speak of the quarantine to which your letter refers, a quarantine may be established, according to accepted international practice, only by agreement of states between themselves, and not by some third party. Quarantines exist, for example, on agricultural goods and products. But in this case the question is in no way one of quarantine, but rather of far more serious things, and you yourself understand this.

You, Mr. President, are not declaring a quarantine, but rather are setting forth an ultimatum and threatening that if we do not give in to your demands you will use force. Consider what you are saying! And you want to persuade me to agree to this! What would it mean to agree to these demands? It would mean guiding oneself in one's relations with other countries not by reason, but by submitting to arbitrariness. You are no longer appealing to reason, but wish to intimidate us.

No, Mr. President, I cannot agree to this, and I think that in your own heart you recognize that I am correct. I am convinced that in my place you would act the same way.

Reference to the decision of the Organization of American States cannot in any way substantiate the demands now advanced by the United States. This Organization has absolutely no authority or basis for adopting decisions such as the one you speak of in your letter. Therefore, we do not recognize these decisions. International law exists and universally recognized norms of conduct exist. We firmly adhere to the principles of international law and observe strictly the norms which regulate navigation on

the high seas, in international waters. We observe these norms and enjoy the rights recognized by all states.

You wish to compel us to renounce the rights that every sovereign state enjoys, you are trying to legislate in questions of international law, and you are violating the universally accepted norms of that law. And you are doing all this not only out of hatred for the Cuban people and its government, but also because of considerations of the election campaign in the United States. What morality, what law can justify such an approach by the American Government to international affairs? No such morality or law can be found, because the actions of the United States with regard to Cuba constitute outright banditry or, if you like, the folly of degenerate imperialism. Unfortunately, such folly can bring grave suffering to the peoples of all countries, and to no lesser degree to the American people themselves, since the United States has completely lost its former isolation with the advent of modern types of armament.

Therefore, Mr. President, if you coolly weigh the situation which has developed, not giving way to passions, you will understand that the Soviet Union cannot fail to reject the arbitrary demands of the United States. When you confront us with such conditions, try to put yourself in our place and consider how the United States would react to these conditions. I do not doubt that if someone attempted to dictate similar conditions to you—the United States—you would reject such an attempt. And we also say—no.

The Soviet Government considers that the violation of the freedom to use international waters and international air space is an act of aggression which pushes mankind toward the abyss of a world nuclear-missile war. Therefore, the Soviet Government cannot instruct the captains of Soviet vessels bound for Cuba to observe the orders of American naval forces blockading that Island. Our instructions to Soviet mariners are to observe strictly the universally accepted norms of navigation in international waters and not to retreat one step from them. And if the American side violates these rules, it must realize what responsibility will rest upon it in that case. Naturally we will not simply be bystanders with regard to piratical acts by American ships on the high seas. We will then be forced on our part to take the measures we consider necessary and adequate in order to protect our rights. We have everything necessary to do so.

Respectfully,

N. Khrushchev

Source: U.S. Department of State, *Foreign Relations of the United States 1961–1963*, Vol. XI: *The Cuban Missile Crisis and Its Aftermath* (Washington, DC: Government Printing Office, 1996), Document 61, http://www.state.gov/www/about_state/history/frusXI/51_75.html.

President Kennedy to Chairman Khrushchev, Washington, October 25, 1962

Dear Mr. Chairman:

I have received your letter of October 24, and I regret very much that you still do not appear to understand what it is that has moved us in this matter.

The sequence of events is clear. In August there were reports of important shipments of military equipment and technicians from the Soviet Union to Cuba. In early September I indicated very plainly that the United States would regard any shipment of offensive weapons as presenting the gravest issues. After that time, this Government received the most explicit assurance from your Government and its representatives, both publicly and privately, that no offensive weapons were being sent to Cuba. If you will review the statement issued by TASS in September, you will see how clearly this assurance was given.

In reliance on these solemn assurances I urged restraint upon those in this country who were urging action in this matter at that time. And then I learned beyond doubt what you have not denied—namely, that all these public assurances were false and that your military people had set out recently to establish a set of missile bases in Cuba. I ask you to recognize clearly, Mr. Chairman, that it was not I who issued the first challenge in this case, and that in the light of this record these activities in Cuba required the responses I have announced.

I repeat my regret that these events should cause a deterioration in our relations. I hope that your Government will take the necessary action to permit a restoration of the earlier situation.

Sincerely yours,

John F. Kennedy

Source: U.S. Department of State, *Foreign Relations of the United States 1961–1963*, Vol. XI: *The Cuban Missile Crisis and Its Aftermath* (Washington, DC: Government Printing Office, 1996), Document 68, http://www.state.gov/www/about_state/history/frusXI/51_75.html.

Chairman Khrushchev to President Kennedy, Moscow, October 26, 1962 [translated by U.S. Embassy, Moscow]

Dear Mr. President:

I have received your letter of October 25. From your letter, I got the feeling that you have some understanding of the situation which has developed and a sense of responsibility. I value this.

Now we have already publicly exchanged our evaluations of the events around Cuba and each of us has set forth his explanation and his understanding of these events. Consequently, I would think that, apparently, a continuation of an exchange of opinions at such a distance, even in the form of secret letters, will hardly add anything to that which one side has already said to the other.

I think you will understand me correctly if you are really concerned about the welfare of the world. Everyone needs peace: both capitalists, if they have not lost their reason, and, still more, Communists, people who know how to value not only their own lives but, more than anything, the lives of the peoples. We, Communists, are against all wars between states in general and have been defending the cause of peace since we came into the world. We have always regarded war as a calamity, and not as a game nor as a means for the attainment of definite goals, nor, all the more, as a goal in itself. Our goals are clear, and the means to attain them is labor. War is our enemy and a calamity for all the peoples.

It is thus that we, Soviet people, and, together with US, other peoples as well, understand the questions of war and peace. I can, in any case, firmly say this for the peoples of the socialist countries, as well as for all progressive people who want peace, happiness, and friendship among peoples.

I see, Mr. President, that you too are not devoid of a sense of anxiety for the fate of the world and not without an understanding of what war entails. What would a war give you? You are threatening us with war. But you well know that the very least which you would receive in reply would be that you would experience the same consequences as those which you

sent us. And that must be clear to us, people invested with authority, trust, and responsibility. We must not succumb to intoxication and petty passions, regardless of whether elections are impending in this or that country, or not impending. These are all transient things, but if indeed war should break out, then it would not be in our power to contain or stop it, for such is the logic of war. I have participated in two wars and know that war ends when it has rolled through cities and villages, everywhere sowing death and destruction.

In the name of the Soviet Government and the Soviet people, I assure you that your arguments regarding offensive weapons on Cuba are groundless. It is apparent from what you have written me that our conceptions are different on this score, or rather, we have different definitions for these or those military means, indeed, in reality, the same forms of weapons can have different interpretations.

You are a military man and, I hope, will understand me. Let us take for example a simple cannon. What sort of means is this: offensive or defensive? A cannon is a defensive means if it is set up to defend boundaries or a fortified area. But if one concentrates artillery, and adds to it the necessary number of troops, then the same cannons do become an offensive means, because they prepare and clear the way for infantry to advance. The same happens with missile-nuclear weapons as well, with any type of this weapon.

You are mistaken if you think that any of our means on Cuba are offensive. However, let us not argue now, it is apparent that I will not be able to convince you of this, but I say to you: You, Mr. President, are a military man and should understand: can one advance, if one has on one's territory even an enormous quantity of missiles of various effective radiuses and various power, but using only these means. These missiles are a means of extermination and destruction, but one cannot advance with these missiles, even nuclear missiles of a power of 100 megatons because only people, troops, can advance, without people, any means however powerful cannot be offensive.

How can one, consequently, give such a completely incorrect interpretation as you are now giving, to the effect that some sort of means on Cuba are offensive. All the means located there, and I assure you of this, have a defensive character, are on Cuba solely for the purposes of defense, and we have sent them to Cuba at the request of the Cuban Government. You, however, say that these are offensive means.

But, Mr. President, do you really seriously think that Cuba can attack the United States and that even we together with Cuba can advance upon

you from the territory of Cuba? Can you really think that way? How is it possible? We do not understand this. Has something so new appeared in military strategy that one can think that it is possible to advance thus. I say precisely advance, and not destroy, since barbarians, people who have lost their sense, destroy.

I believe that you have no basis to think this way. You can regard us with distrust, but, in any case, you can be calm in this regard, that we are of sound mind and understand perfectly well that if we attack you, you will respond the same way. But you too will receive the same that you hurl against us. And I think that you also understand this. My conversation with you in Vienna gives me the right to talk to you this way.

This indicates that we are normal people, that we correctly understand and correctly evaluate the situation. Consequently, how can we permit the incorrect actions which you ascribe to us? Only lunatics or suicides, who themselves want to perish and to destroy the whole world before they die, could do this. We, however, want to live and do not at all want to destroy your country. We want something quite different: to compete with your country on a peaceful endeavor. We quarrel with you, we have differences in ideological questions. But our view of the world consists in this, that ideological questions, as well as economic problems, should be solved not by military means, they must be solved on the basis of peaceful competition, i.e., as this is understood in capitalist society, on the basis of competition. We have proceeded and are proceeding from the fact that the peaceful co-existence of the two different social-political systems, now existing in the world, is necessary, that it is necessary to assure a stable peace. That is the sort of principle we hold.

You have now proclaimed piratical measures, which were employed in the Middle Ages, when ships proceeding in international waters were attacked, and you have called this "a quarantine" around Cuba. Our vessels, apparently, will soon enter the zone which your Navy is patrolling. I assure you that these vessels, now bound for Cuba, are carrying the most innocent peaceful cargoes. Do you really think that we only occupy ourselves with the carriage of so-called offensive weapons, atomic and hydrogen bombs? Although perhaps your military people imagine that these (cargoes) are some sort of special type of weapon, I assure you that they are the most ordinary peaceful products.

Consequently, Mr. President, let us show good sense. I assure you that on those ships, which are bound for Cuba, there are no weapons at all. The weapons which were necessary for the defense of Cuba are already there. I do not want to say that there were not any shipments of weapons at all.

No, there were such shipments. But now Cuba has already received the necessary means of defense.

I don't know whether you can understand me and believe me. But I should like to have you believe in yourself and to agree that one cannot give way to passions; it is necessary to control them. And in what direction are events now developing? If you stop the vessels, then, as you yourself know, that would be piracy. If we started to do that with regard to your ships, then you would also be as indignant as we and the whole world now are. One cannot give another interpretation to such actions, because one cannot legalize lawlessness. If this were permitted, then there would be no peace, there would also be no peaceful coexistence. We should then be forced to put into effect the necessary measures of a defensive character to protect our interest in accordance with international law. Why should this be done? To what would all this lead?

Let us normalize relations. We have received an appeal from the Acting Secretary General of the UN, U Thant, with his proposals. I have already answered him. His proposals come to this, that our side should not transport armaments of any kind to Cuba during a certain period of time, while negotiations are being conducted—and we are ready to enter such negotiations—and the other side should not undertake any sort of piratical actions against vessels engaged in navigation on the high seas. I consider these proposals reasonable. This would be a way out of the situation which has been created, which would give the peoples the possibility of breathing calmly. You have asked what happened, what evoked the delivery of weapons to Cuba? You have spoken about this to our Minister of Foreign Affairs. I will tell you frankly, Mr. President, what evoked it.

We were very grieved by the fact—I spoke about it in Vienna—that a landing took place, that an attack on Cuba was committed, as a result of which many Cubans perished. You yourself told me then that this had been a mistake. I respected that explanation. You repeated it to me several times, hinting that not everybody occupying a high position would acknowledge his mistakes as you had done. I value such frankness. For my part, I told you that we too possess no less courage; we also acknowledged those mistakes which had been committed during the history of our state, and not only acknowledged, but sharply condemned them.

If you are really concerned about the peace and welfare of your people, and this is your responsibility as President, then I, as the Chairman of the Council of Ministers, am concerned for my people. Moreover, the preservation of world peace should be our joint concern, since if, under

contemporary conditions, war should break out, it would be a war not only between the Soviet Union and the United States which have no contentions between them, but a worldwide cruel and destructive war.

Why have we proceeded to assist Cuba with military and economic aid? The answer is: we have proceeded to do so only for reasons of humanitarianism. At one time, our people itself had a revolution, when Russia was still a backward country, we were attacked then. We were the target of attack by many countries. The USA participated in that adventure. This has been recorded by participants in the aggression against our country. A whole book has been written about this by General Graves, who, at that time, commanded the US Expeditionary Corps. Graves called it "The American Adventure in Siberia."

We know how difficult it is to accomplish a revolution and how difficult it is to reconstruct a country on new foundations. We sincerely sympathize with Cuba and the Cuban people, but we are not interfering in questions of domestic structure, we are not interfering in their affairs. The Soviet Union desires to help the Cubans build their life as they themselves wish and that others should not hinder them.

You once said that the United States was not preparing an invasion. But you also declared that you sympathized with the Cuban counter-revolutionary emigrants, that you support them and would help them to realize their plans against the present Government of Cuba. It is also not a secret to anyone that the threat of armed attack, aggression, has constantly hung, and continues to hang over Cuba. It was only this which impelled us to respond to the request of the Cuban Government to furnish it aid for the strengthening of the defensive capacity of this country.

If assurances were given by the President and the Government of the United States that the USA itself would not participate in an attack on Cuba and would restrain others from actions of this sort, if you would recall your fleet, this would immediately change everything. I am not speaking for Fidel Castro, but I think that he and the Government of Cuba, evidently, would declare demobilization and would appeal to the people to get down to peaceful labor. Then, too, the question of armaments would disappear, since, if there is no threat, then armaments are a burden for every people. Then, too, the question of the destruction, not only of the armaments which you call offensive, but of all other armaments as well, would look different.

I spoke in the name of the Soviet Government in the United Nations and introduced a proposal for the disbandment of all armies and

for the destruction of all armaments. How then can I now count on those armaments?

Armaments bring only disasters. When one accumulates them, this damages the economy, and if one puts them to use, then they destroy people on both sides. Consequently, only a madman can believe that armaments are the principal means in the life of society. No, they are an enforced loss of human energy, and what is more are for the destruction of man himself. If people do not show wisdom, then in the final analysis they will come to a clash, like blind moles, and then reciprocal extermination will begin.

Let us therefore show statesmanlike wisdom. I propose: we, for our part, will declare that our ships, bound for Cuba, are not carrying any armaments. You would declare that the United States will not invade Cuba with its forces and will not support any sort of forces which might intend to carry out an invasion of Cuba. Then the necessity for the presence of our military specialists in Cuba would disappear.

Mr. President, I appeal to you to weigh well what the aggressive, piratical actions, which you have declared the USA intends to carry out in international waters, would lead to. You yourself know that any sensible man simply cannot agree with this, cannot recognize your right to such actions.

If you did this as the first step towards the unleashing of war, well then, it is evident that nothing else is left to us but to accept this challenge of yours. If, however, you have not lost your self-control and sensibly conceive what this might lead to, then, Mr. President, we and you ought not now to pull on the ends of the rope in which you have tied the knot of war, because the more the two of us pull, the tighter that knot will be tied. And a moment may come when that knot will be tied so tight that even he who tied it will not have the strength to untie it, and then it will be necessary to cut that knot. And what that would mean is not for me to explain to you, because you yourself understand perfectly of what terrible forces our countries dispose.

Consequently, if there is no intention to tighten that knot and thereby to doom the world to the catastrophe of thermonuclear war, then let us not only relax the forces pulling on the ends of the rope, let us take measures to untie that knot. We are ready for this.

We welcome all forces which stand on positions of peace. Consequently, I both expressed gratitude to Mr. Bertrand Russell, who manifests alarm and concern for the fate of the world, and readily responded to the appeal of the Acting Secretary General of the UN, U Thant.

There, Mr. President, are my thoughts, which, if you agreed with them, could put an end to that tense situation which is disturbing all peoples.

These thoughts are dictated by a sincere desire to relieve the situation, to remove the threat of war.

Respectfully yours,

N. Khrushchev

Source: U.S. Department of State, Foreign Relations of the United States 1961–1963, Vol. XI: The Cuban Missile Crisis and Its Aftermath (Washington, DC: Government Printing Office, 1996), Document 84, http://www.state.gov/www/about_state/history/frusXI/76_100.html; also printed in Department of State Bulletin, November 19, 1973, pp. 640–643.

Chairman Khrushchev to President Kennedy, Moscow, October 27, 1962 [translation by Language Services, U.S. Department of State]

DEAR MR. PRESIDENT,

I have studied with great satisfaction your reply to Mr. Thant concerning measures that should be taken to avoid contact between our vessels and thereby avoid irreparable and fatal consequences. This reasonable step on your part strengthens my belief that you are showing concern for the preservation of peace, which I note with satisfaction.

I have already said that our people, our Government, and I personally, as Chairman of the Council of Ministers, are concerned solely with having our country develop and occupy a worthy place among all peoples of the world in economic competition, in the development of culture and the arts, and in raising the living standard of the people. This is the most noble and necessary field for competition, and both the victor and the vanquished will derive only benefit from it, because it means peace and an increase in the means by which man lives and finds enjoyment.

In your statement you expressed the opinion that the main aim was not simply to come to an agreement and take measures to prevent contact between our vessels and consequently a deepening of the crisis which could, as a result of such contacts, spark a military conflict, after which all negotiations would be superfluous because other forces and other laws would

then come into play—the laws of war. I agree with you that this is only the first step. The main thing that must be done is to normalize and stabilize the state of peace among states and among peoples.

I understand your concern for the security of the United States, Mr. President, because this is the primary duty of a President. But we too are disturbed about these same questions; I bear these same obligations as Chairman of the Council of Ministers of the U.S.S.R. You have been alarmed by the fact that we have aided Cuba with weapons, in order to strengthen its defense capability—precisely defense capability—because whatever weapons it may possess, Cuba cannot be equated with you since the difference in magnitude is so great, particularly in view of modern means of destruction. Our aim has been and is to help Cuba, and no one can dispute the humanity of our motives, which are oriented toward enabling Cuba to live peacefully and develop in the way its people desire.

You wish to ensure the security of your country, and this is understandable. But Cuba, too, wants the same thing; all countries want to maintain their security. But how are we, the Soviet Union, our Government, to assess your actions which are expressed in the fact that you have surrounded the Soviet Union with military bases; surrounded our allies with military bases; placed military bases literally around our country; and stationed your missile armaments there? This is no secret. Responsible American personages openly declare that it is so. Your missiles are located in Britain, are located in Italy, and are aimed against us. Your missiles are located in Turkey.

You are disturbed over Cuba. You say that this disturbs you because it is 90 miles by sea from the coast of the United States of America. But Turkey adjoins us; our sentries patrol back and forth and see each other. Do you consider, then, that you have the right to demand security for your own country and the removal of the weapons you call offensive, but do not accord the same right to us? You have placed destructive missile weapons, which you call offensive, in Turkey, literally next to us. How then can recognition of our equal military capacities be reconciled with such unequal relations between our great states? This is irreconcilable.

It is good, Mr. President, that you have agreed to have our representatives meet and begin talks, apparently through the mediation of U Thant, Acting Secretary General of the United Nations. Consequently, he to some degree has assumed the role of a mediator and we consider that he will be able to cope with this responsible mission, provided, of course, that each party drawn into this controversy displays good will.

I think it would be possible to end the controversy quickly and normalize the situation, and then the people could breathe more easily, considering

that statesmen charged with responsibility are of sober mind and have an awareness of their responsibility combined with the ability to solve complex questions and not bring things to a military catastrophe.

I therefore make this proposal: We are willing to remove from Cuba the means which you regard as offensive. We are willing to carry this out and to make this pledge in the United Nations. Your representatives will make a declaration to the effect that the United States, for its part, considering the uneasiness and anxiety of the Soviet State, will remove its analogous means from Turkey. Let us reach agreement as to the period of time needed by you and by us to bring this about. And, after that, persons entrusted by the United Nations Security Council could inspect on the spot the fulfillment of the pledges made. Of course, the permission of the Governments of Cuba and of Turkey is necessary for the entry into those countries of these representatives and for the inspection of the fulfillment of the pledge made by each side. Of course it would be best if these representatives enjoyed the confidence of the Security Council, as well as yours and mine—both the United States and the Soviet Union—and also that of Turkey and Cuba. I do not think it would be difficult to select people who would enjoy the trust and respect of all parties concerned.

We, in making this pledge, in order to give satisfaction and hope of the peoples of Cuba and Turkey and to strengthen their confidence in their security, will make a statement within the framework of the Security Council to the effect that the Soviet Government gives a solemn promise to respect the inviolability of the borders and sovereignty of Turkey, not to interfere in its internal affairs, not to invade Turkey, not to make available our territory as a bridgehead for such an invasion, and that it would also restrain those who contemplate committing aggression against Turkey, either from the territory of the Soviet Union or from the territory of Turkey's other neighboring states.

The United States Government will make a similar statement within the framework of the Security Council regarding Cuba. It will declare that the United States will respect the inviolability of Cuba's borders and its sovereignty, will pledge not to interfere in its internal affairs, not to invade Cuba itself or make its territory available as a bridgehead for such an invasion, and will also restrain those who might contemplate committing aggression against Cuba, either from the territory of the United States or from the territory of Cuba's other neighboring states.

Of course, for this we would have to come to an agreement with you and specify a certain time limit. Let us agree to some period of time, but without unnecessary delay—say within two or three weeks, not longer than a month.

The means situated in Cuba, of which you speak and which disturb you, as you have stated, are in the hands of Soviet officers. Therefore, any accidental use of them to the detriment of the United States is excluded. These means are situated in Cuba at the request of the Cuban Government and are only for defense purposes. Therefore, if there is no invasion of Cuba, or attack on the Soviet Union or any of our other allies, then of course these means are not and will not be a threat to anyone. For they are not for purposes of attack.

If you are agreeable to my proposal, Mr. President, then we would send our representatives to New York, to the United Nations, and would give them comprehensive instructions in order that an agreement may be reached more quickly. If you also select your people and give them the corresponding instructions, then this question can be quickly resolved.

Why would I like to do this? Because the whole world is now apprehensive and expects sensible actions of us. The greatest joy for all peoples would be the announcement of our agreement and of the eradication of the controversy that has arisen. I attach great importance to this agreement in so far as it could serve as a good beginning and could in particular make it easier to reach agreement on banning nuclear weapons tests. The question of the tests could be solved in parallel fashion, without connecting one with the other, because these are different issues. However, it is important that agreement be reached on both these issues so as to present humanity with a fine gift, and also to gladden it with the news that agreement has been reached on the cessation of nuclear tests and that consequently the atmosphere will no longer be poisoned. Our position and yours on this issue are very close together.

All of this could possibly serve as a good impetus toward the finding of mutually acceptable agreements on other controversial issues on which you and I have been exchanging views. These views have so far not been resolved, but they are awaiting urgent solution, which would clear up the international atmosphere. We are prepared for this.

These are my proposals, Mr. President.

Respectfully yours,

N. Khrushchev

Source: U.S. Department of State, *Foreign Relations of the United States 1961–1963*, Vol. XI: *The Cuban Missile Crisis and Its Aftermath* (Washington, DC: Government Printing Office, 1996), Document 91, http://www.state.gov/www/

about_state/history/frusXI/76_100.html; also printed in Department of State *Bulletin,* November 19, 1962, pp. 646–649.

President Kennedy to Chairman Khrushchev, Washington, October 27, 1962

Dear Mr. Chairman:

I have read your letter of October 26 with great care and welcomed the statement of your desire to seek a prompt solution to the problem. The first thing that needs to be done, however, is for work to cease on offensive missile bases in Cuba and for all weapons systems in Cuba capable of offensive use to be rendered inoperable, under effective United Nations arrangements.

Assuming this is done promptly, I have given my representatives in New York instructions that will permit them to work out this week and—in cooperation with the Acting Secretary General and your representative—an arrangement for a permanent solution to the Cuban problem along the lines suggested in your letter of October 26. As I read your letter, the key elements of your proposals—which seem generally acceptable as I understand them—are as follows:

1. You would agree to remove these weapons systems from Cuba under appropriate United Nations observation and supervision; and undertake, with suitable safeguards, to halt the further introduction of such weapons systems into Cuba.
2. We, on our part, would agree—upon the establishment of adequate arrangements through the United Nations to ensure the carrying out and continuation of these commitments—(a) to remove promptly the quarantine measures now in effect and (b) to give assurances against an invasion of Cuba and I am confident that other nations of the Western Hemisphere would be prepared to do likewise.

If you will give your representative similar instructions, there is no reason why we should not be able to complete these arrangements and announce them to the world within a couple of days. The effect of such a settlement on easing world tensions would enable us to work toward a more general arrangement regarding "other armaments", as proposed in

your second letter which you made public. I would like to say again that the United States is very much interested in reducing tensions and halting the arms race; and if your letter signifies that you are prepared to discuss a detente affecting NATO and the Warsaw Pact, we are quite prepared to consider with our allies any useful proposals.

But the first ingredient, let me emphasize, is the cessation of work on missile sites in Cuba and measures to render such weapons inoperable, under effective international guarantees. The continuation of this threat, or a prolonging of this discussion concerning Cuba by linking these problems to the broader questions of European and world security, would surely lead to an intensification of the Cuban crisis and a grave risk to the peace of the world. For this reason I hope we can quickly agree along the lines outlined in this letter and in your letter of October 26.

John F. Kennedy

Source: U.S. Department of State, Foreign Relations of the United States 1961–1963, Vol. XI: The Cuban Missile Crisis and Its Aftermath (Washington, DC: Government Printing Office, 1996), Document 95, http://www.state.gov/www/about_state/history/frusXI/76_100.html; also printed in American Foreign Policy: Current Documents, 1962, pp. 441–442.

Chairman Khrushchev to President Kennedy, Moscow, October 28, 1962 [Translated by U.S. Embassy, Moscow]

DEAR MR. PRESIDENT:

I have received your message of October 27. I express my satisfaction and thank you for the sense of proportion you have displayed and for realization of the responsibility which now devolves on you for the preservation of the peace of the world.

I regard with great understanding your concern and the concern of the United States people in connection with the fact that the weapons you describe as offensive are formidable weapons indeed. Both you and we understand what kind of weapons these are.

In order to eliminate as rapidly as possible the conflict which endangers the cause of peace, to give an assurance to all people who crave peace, and to reassure the American people, who, I am certain, also want peace, as do the people of the Soviet Union, the Soviet Government, in addition

to earlier instructions on the discontinuation of further work on weapons construction sites, has given a new order to dismantle the arms which you described as offensive, and to crate and return them to the Soviet Union.

Mr. President, I should like to repeat what I had already written to you in my earlier messages—that the Soviet Government has given economic assistance to the Republic of Cuba, as well as arms, because Cuba and the Cuban people were constantly under the continuous threat of an invasion of Cuba.

A piratic vessel had shelled Havana. They say that this shelling was done by irresponsible Cuban émigrés. Perhaps so, however, the question is from where did they shoot. It is a fact that these Cubans have no territory, they are fugitives from their country, and they have no means to conduct military operations.

This means that someone put into their hands these weapons for shelling Havana and for piracy in the Caribbean in Cuban territorial waters. It is impossible in our time not to notice a piratic ship, considering the concentration in the Caribbean of American ships from which everything can be seen and observed.

In these conditions, pirate ships freely roam around and shell Cuba and make piratic attacks on peaceful cargo ships. It is known that they even shelled a British cargo ship. In a word, Cuba was under the continuous threat of aggressive forces, which did not conceal their intention to invade its territory.

The Cuban people want to build their life in their own interests without external interference. This is their right, and they cannot be blamed for wanting to be masters of their own country and disposing of the fruits of their own labor.

The threat of invasion of Cuba and all other schemes for creating tension over Cuba are designed to strike the Cuban people with a sense of insecurity, intimidate them, and prevent them from peacefully building their new life.

Mr. President, I should like to say clearly once more that we could not remain indifferent to this. The Soviet Government decided to render assistance to Cuba with the means of defense against aggression—only with means for defense purposes. We have supplied the defense means which you describe as offensive means. We have supplied them to prevent an attack on Cuba—to prevent rash acts.

I regard with respect and trust the statement you made in your message of October 27, 1962, that there would be no attack, no invasion of

Cuba, and not only on the part of the United States, but also on the part of other nations of the Western Hemisphere, as you said in your same message. Then the motives which induced us to render assistance of such a kind to Cuba disappear.

It is for this reason that we instructed our officers—these means as I had already informed you earlier are in the hands of the Soviet officers—to take appropriate measures to discontinue construction of the aforementioned facilities, to dismantle them, and to return them to the Soviet Union. As I had informed you in the letter of October 27, we are prepared to reach agreement to enable United Nations Representatives to verify the dismantling of these means.

Thus in view of the assurances you have given and our instructions on dismantling, there is every condition for eliminating the present conflict.

I note with satisfaction that you have responded to the desire I expressed with regard to elimination of the aforementioned dangerous situation, as well as with regard to providing conditions for a more thoughtful appraisal of the international situation, fraught as it is with great dangers in our age of thermonuclear weapons, rocketry, spaceships, global rockets, and other deadly weapons. All people are interested in insuring peace.

Therefore, vested with trust and great responsibility, we must not allow the situation to become aggravated and must stamp out the centers where a dangerous situation fraught with grave consequences to the cause of peace has arisen. If we, together with you, and with the assistance of other people of good will, succeed in eliminating this tense atmosphere, we should also make certain that no other dangerous conflicts which could lead to a world nuclear catastrophe would arise.

In conclusion, I should like to say something about a detente between NATO and the Warsaw Treaty countries that you have mentioned. We have spoken about this long since and are prepared to continue to exchange views on this question with you and to find a reasonable solution.

We should like to continue the exchange of views on the prohibition of atomic and thermonuclear weapons, general disarmament, and other problems relating to the relaxation of international tension.

Although I trust your statement, Mr. President, there are irresponsible people who would like to invade Cuba now and thus touch off a war. If we do take practical steps and proclaim the dismantling and evacuation of the means in question from Cuba, in so doing we, at the same time, want the Cuban people to be certain that we are with them and are

not absolving ourselves of responsibility for rendering assistance to the Cuban people.

We are confident that the people of all countries, like you, Mr. President, will understand me correctly. We are not threatening. We want nothing but peace. Our country is now on the upsurge.

Our people are enjoying the fruits of their peaceful labor. They have achieved tremendous successes since the October Revolution, and created the greatest material, spiritual, and cultural values. Our people are enjoying these values; they want to continue developing their achievements and insure their further development on the way of peace and social progress by their persistent labor.

I should like to remind you, Mr. President, that military reconnaissance planes have violated the borders of the Soviet Union. In connection with this there have been conflicts between us and notes exchanged. In 1960 we shot down your U-2 plane, whose reconnaissance flight over the USSR wrecked the summit meeting in Paris. At that time, you took a correct position and denounced that criminal act of the former U.S. Administration.

But during your term of office as President another violation of our border has occurred, by an American U-2 plane in the Sakhalin area. We wrote you about that violation on 30 August. At that time you replied that that violation had occurred as a result of poor weather, and gave assurances that this would not be repeated. We trusted your assurances, because the weather was indeed poor in that area at that time.

But had not your planes been ordered to fly about our territory, even poor weather could not have brought an American plane into our airspace. Hence, the conclusion that this is being done with the knowledge of the Pentagon, which tramples on international norms and violates the borders of other states.

A still more dangerous case occurred on 28 October, when one of your reconnaissance planes intruded over Soviet borders in the Chukotka Peninsula area in the north and flew over our territory. The question is, Mr. President: How should we regard this? What is this: A provocation? One of your planes violates our frontier during this anxious time we are both experiencing, when everything has been put into combat readiness. Is it not a fact that an intruding American plane could be easily taken for a nuclear bomber, which might push us to a fateful step? And all the more so since the U.S. Government and Pentagon long ago declared that you are maintaining a continuous nuclear bomber patrol.

Therefore, you can imagine the responsibility you are assuming, especially now, when we are living through such anxious times.

I should like to express the following wish; it concerns the Cuban people. You do not have diplomatic relations. But through my officers in Cuba, I have reports that American planes are making flights over Cuba.

We are interested that there should be no war in the world, and that the Cuban people should live in peace. And besides, Mr. President, it is no secret that we have our people in Cuba. Under such a treaty with the Cuban Government we have sent there officers, instructors, mostly plain people: specialists, agronomists, zoo technicians, irrigators, land reclamation specialists, plain workers, tractor drivers, and others. We are concerned about them.

I should like you to consider, Mr. President, that violation of Cuban airspace by American planes could also lead to dangerous consequences. And if you do not want this to happen, it would be better if no cause is given for a dangerous situation to arise.

We must be careful now and refrain from any steps which would not be useful to the defense of the states involved in the conflict, which could only cause irritation and even serve as a provocation for a fateful step. Therefore, we must display sanity, reason, and refrain from such steps.

We value peace perhaps even more than other peoples because we went through a terrible war with Hitler. But our people will not falter in the face of any test. Our people trust their Government, and we assure our people and world public opinion that the Soviet Government will not allow itself to be provoked. But if the provocateurs unleash a war, they will not evade responsibility and the grave consequences a war would bring upon them. But we are confident that reason will triumph, that war will not be unleashed and peace and the security of the peoples will be insured.

In connection with the current negotiations between Acting Secretary General U Thant and representatives of the Soviet Union, the United States, and the Republic of Cuba, the Soviet Government has sent First Deputy Foreign Minister V.V. Kuznetsov to New York to help U Thant in his noble efforts aimed at eliminating the present dangerous situation.

Respectfully yours,

N. Khrushchev

Source: U.S. Department of State, Foreign Relations of the United States 1961–1963, Vol. XI: The Cuban Missile Crisis and Its Aftermath (Washington, DC: Government Printing Office, 1996), Document 102, http://www.state.gov/www/about_state/history/frusXI/101_125.html; also printed in Department of State Bulletin, November 19, 1973, pp. 650–654.

President Kennedy to Chairman Khrushchev, Washington, October 28, 1962

DEAR MR. CHAIRMAN:

I am replying at once to your broadcast message of October twenty-eight even though the official text has not yet reached me because of the great importance I attach to moving forward promptly to the settlement of the Cuban crisis. I think that you and I, with our heavy responsibilities for the maintenance of peace, were aware that developments were approaching a point where events could have become unmanageable. So I welcome this message and consider it an important contribution to peace.

The distinguished efforts of Acting Secretary General U Thant have greatly facilitated both our tasks. I consider my letter to you of October twenty-seventh and your reply of today as firm undertakings on the part of both our governments which should be promptly carried out. I hope that the necessary measures can at once be taken through the United Nations as your message says, so that the United States in turn can remove the quarantine measures now in effect. I have already made arrangements to report all these matters to the Organization of American States, whose members share a deep interest in a genuine peace in the Caribbean area.

You referred in your letter to a violation of your frontier by an American aircraft in the area of the Chukotsk Peninsula. I have learned that this plane, without arms or photographic equipment, was engaged in an air sampling mission in connection with your nuclear tests. Its course was direct from Eielson Air Force Base in Alaska to the North Pole and return. In turning south, the pilot made a serious navigational error which carried him over Soviet territory. He immediately made an emergency call on open radio for navigational assistance and was guided back to his home base by the most direct route. I regret this incident and will see to it that every precaution is taken to prevent recurrence.

Mr. Chairman, both of our countries have great unfinished tasks and I know that your people as well as those of the United States can ask for nothing better than to pursue them free from the fear of war. Modern science and technology have given us the possibility of making labor fruitful beyond anything that could have been dreamed of a few decades ago.

I agree with you that we must devote urgent attention to the problem of disarmament, as it relates to the whole world and also to critical areas. Perhaps now, as we step back from danger, we can together make real

progress in this vital field. I think we should give priority to questions relating to the proliferation of nuclear weapons, on earth and in outer space, and to the great effort for a nuclear test ban. But we should also work hard to see if wider measures of disarmament can be agreed and put into operation at an early date. The United States Government will be prepared to discuss these questions urgently, and in a constructive spirit, at Geneva or elsewhere.

John F. Kennedy

Source: U.S. Department of State, *Foreign Relations of the United States 1961–1963,* Vol. XI: *The Cuban Missile Crisis and Its Aftermath* (Washington, DC: Government Printing Office, 1996), Document 104, http://www.state.gov/www/about_state/history/frusXI/101_125.html.

3. Meeting between U.S. Attorney General Robert F. Kennedy and Soviet Ambassador Anatoly Dobrynin, October 27, 1962

President John F. Kennedy was unwilling to agree publicly to decommission NATO intermediate-range nuclear missile bases in Turkey and Italy in exchange for the removal of Soviet missiles from Cuba. Privately, however, he thought such an arrangement, which Soviet premier Nikita Khrushchev proposed in a letter to Kennedy broadcast over Soviet radio on October 27, an acceptable means of ending the crisis. That same evening Kennedy sent Attorney General Robert F. Kennedy, his brother and closest adviser, to discuss the possibility of such a bargain with Anatoly Dobrynin, the Soviet ambassador in Washington. Robert Kennedy stressed that such an understanding would be strictly contingent on the immediate cessation of further Soviet work on the missile bases in Cuba. Both men left a record of this meeting. Dobrynin immediately cabled a description of it to Soviet leaders in Moscow, while Robert Kennedy, who reported back to his brother and Secretary of State Dean Rusk, set down his recollections of their encounter three days later. All concerned kept their discussions extremely confidential, as they wished the negotiations to remain completely secret.

Ambassador Dobrynin's Cable to the
Soviet Foreign Ministry, October 27, 1962

TOP SECRET Making Copies Prohibited Copy No. I
CIPHERED TELEGRAM

Late tonight R. Kennedy invited me to come see him. We talked alone.

The Cuban crisis, R. Kennedy began, continues to quickly worsen. We have just received a report that an unarmed American plane was shot down while carrying out a reconnaissance flight over Cuba. The military is demanding that the President arm such planes and respond to fire with fire. The US government will have to do this.

I interrupted R. Kennedy and asked him, what right American planes had to fly over Cuba at all, crudely violating its sovereignty and accepted international norms? How would the USA have reacted if foreign planes appeared over its territory?

"We have a resolution of the Organization of American States that gives us the right to such overflights," R. Kennedy quickly replied.

I told him that the Soviet Union, like all peace-loving countries, resolutely rejects such a "right" or, to be more exact, this kind of true lawlessness, when people who don't like the social-political situation in a country try to impose their will on it—a small state where the people themselves established and maintained [their system]. "The OAS resolution is a direct violation of the UN Charter," I added, "and you, as the Attorney General of the USA, the highest American legal entity, should certainly know that."

R. Kennedy said that he realized that we had different approaches to these problems and it was not likely that we could convince each other. But now the matter is not in these differences, since time is of the essence. "I want," R. Kennedy stressed, "to lay out the current alarming situation the way the president sees it. He wants N.S. Khrushchev to know this. This is the thrust of the situation now."

"Because of the plane that was shot down, there is now strong pressure on the president to give an order to respond with fire if fired upon when American reconnaissance planes are flying over Cuba. The US can't stop these flights, because this is the only way we can quickly get information about the state of construction of the missile bases in Cuba, which we believe pose a very serious threat to our national security. But if we start to fire in response—a chain reaction will quickly start that will be very hard to stop. The same thing in regard to the essence of the issue of the missile bases in Cuba. The USA government is determined to get rid of those bases—up to, in the extreme case, of bombing them, since, I repeat, they pose a great threat to the security of the USA. But in response

to the bombing of these bases, in the course of which Soviet specialists might suffer, the Soviet government will undoubtedly respond with the same against us, somewhere in Europe. A real war will begin, in which millions of Americans and Russians will die. We want to avoid that any way we can, I'm sure that the government of the USSR has the same wish. However, taking time to find a way out [of the situation] is very risky (here R. Kennedy mentioned as if in passing that there are many unreasonable heads among the generals, and not only among the generals, who are 'itching for a fight'). The situation might get out of control, with irreversible consequences."

"In this regard," R. Kennedy said, "the president considers that a suitable basis for regulating the entire Cuban conflict might be the letter N.S. Khrushchev sent on October 26 and the letter in response from the President which was sent off today to N.S. Khrushchev through the US Embassy in Moscow. The most important thing for us," R. Kennedy stressed, "is to get as soon as possible the agreement of the Soviet government to halt further work on the construction of the missile bases in Cuba and take measures under international control that would make it impossible to use these weapons. In exchange the government of the USA is ready, in addition to repealing all measures on the "quarantine," to give the assurances that there will not be any invasion of Cuba and that other countries of the Western Hemisphere are ready to give the same assurances—the US government is certain of this."

"And what about Turkey?" I asked R. Kennedy.

"If that is the only obstacle to achieving the regulation I mentioned earlier, then the president doesn't see any unsurmountable difficulties in resolving this issue," replied R. Kennedy. "The greatest difficulty for the president is the public discussion of the issue of Turkey. Formally the deployment of missile bases in Turkey was done by a special decision of the NATO Council. To announce now a unilateral decision by the president of the USA to withdraw missile bases from Turkey—this would damage the entire structure of NATO and the US position as the leader of NATO, where, as the Soviet government knows very well, there are many arguments. In short, if such a decision were announced now it would seriously tear apart NATO."

"However, President Kennedy is ready to come to agree on that question with N.S. Khrushchev, too. I think that in order to withdraw these bases from Turkey," R. Kennedy said, "we need 4–5 months. This is the minimal amount of time necessary for the US government to do this, taking into account the procedures that exist within the NATO framework. On the whole Turkey issue," R. Kennedy added, "if Premier N.S. Khrushchev agrees with what I've said, we can continue to exchange opinions between him and the president, using him, R. Kennedy and the Soviet ambassador.

However, the president can't say anything public in this regard about Turkey," R. Kennedy said again. R. Kennedy then warned that his comments about Turkey are extremely confidential; besides him and his brother, only 2–3 people know about it in Washington.

"That's all that he asked me to pass on to N.S. Khrushchev," R. Kennedy said in conclusion. "The president also asked N.S. Khrushchev to give him an answer (through the Soviet ambassador and R. Kennedy) if possible within the next day (Sunday) on these thoughts in order to have a business-like, clear answer in principle. [He asked him] not to get into a wordy discussion, which might drag things out. The current serious situation, unfortunately, is such that there is very little time to resolve this whole issue. Unfortunately, events are developing too quickly. The request for a reply tomorrow," stressed R. Kennedy, "is just that—a request, and not an ultimatum. The president hopes that the head of the Soviet government will understand him correctly."

I noted that it went without saying that the Soviet government would not accept any ultimatums and it was good that the American government realized that. I also reminded him of N.S. Khrushchev's appeal in his last letter to the president to demonstrate state wisdom in resolving this question. Then I told R. Kennedy that the president's thoughts would be brought to the attention of the head of the Soviet government. I also said that I would contact him as soon as there was a reply. In this regard, R. Kennedy gave me a number of a direct telephone line to the White House.

In the course of the conversation, R. Kennedy noted that he knew about the conversation that television commentator Scali had yesterday with an Embassy adviser on possible ways to regulate the Cuban conflict [one and a half lines whited out]

I should say that during our meeting R. Kennedy was very upset; in any case, I've never seen him like this before. True, about twice he tried to return to the topic of "deception" (that he talked about so persistently during our previous meeting), but he did so in passing and without any edge to it. He didn't even try to get into fights on various subjects, as he usually does, and only persistently returned to one topic: time is of the essence and we shouldn't miss the chance.

After meeting with me he immediately went to see the president, with whom, as R. Kennedy said, he spends almost all his time now.

27/X-62 A. DOBRYNIN

Source: Russian Foreign Ministry archives, translation from copy provided by NHK (Japanese Television), reprinted in Richard Ned Lebow and Janice Gross Stein, *We*

All Lost the Cold War (Princeton, NJ: Princeton University Press, 1994), appendix, pp. 523–526, with minor revisions. The National Security Archives, The George Washington University. Available at: http://www.gwu.edu/~nsarchiv/NSAEBB/ NSAEBB313/Doc01.pdf. Accessed December 1, 2011.

Memorandum from Attorney General Kennedy to Secretary of State Rusk, October 30, 1962

At the request of Secretary Rusk, I telephoned Ambassador Dobrynin at approximately 7:15 p.m. on Saturday, October 27th. I asked him if he would come to the Justice Department at a quarter of eight.

We met in my office. I told him first that we understood that the work was continuing on the Soviet missile bases in Cuba. Further, I explained to him that in the last two hours we had found that our planes flying over Cuba had been fired upon and that one of our U-2's had been shot down and the pilot killed. I said these men were flying unarmed planes.

I told him that this was an extremely serious turn in events. We would have to make certain decisions within the next 12 or possibly 24 hours. There was a very little time left. If the Cubans were shooting at our planes, then we were going to shoot back. This could not help but bring on further incidents and that he had better understand the full implications of this matter.

He raised the point that the argument the Cubans were making was that we were violating Cuban air space. I replied that if we had not been violating Cuban air space then we would still be believing what he and Khrushchev had said—that there were no long-range missiles in Cuba. In any case I said that this matter was far more serious than the air space over Cuba and involved peoples all over the world.

I said that he had better understand the situation and he had better communicate that understanding to Mr. Khrushchev. Mr. Khrushchev and he had misled us. The Soviet Union had secretly established missile bases in Cuba while at the same time proclaiming, privately and publicly, that this would never be done. I said those missile bases had to go and they had to go right away. We had to have a commitment by at least tomorrow that those bases would be removed. This was not an ultimatum, I said, but just a statement of fact. He should understand that if they did not remove those bases then we would remove them. His country might take retaliatory action but he should understand that before this was over, while there might be dead Americans there would also be dead Russians.

He asked me then what offer we were making. I said a letter had just been transmitted to the Soviet Embassy which stated in substance that the missile bases should be dismantled and all offensive weapons should be removed from Cuba. In return, if Cuba and Castro and the Communists ended their subversive activities in other Central and Latin American countries, we would agree to keep peace in the Caribbean and not permit an invasion from American soil.

He then asked me about Khrushchev's other proposal dealing with the removal of the missiles from Turkey. I replied that there could be no quid pro quo—no deal of this kind could be made. This was a matter that had to be considered by NATO and that it was up to NATO to make the decision. I said it was completely impossible for NATO to take such a step under the present threatening position of the Soviet Union. ~~If some time elapsed and per your instructions, I mentioned four or five months—I said I was sure that these matters could be resolved satisfactory.~~ [Deleted in original]

Per your instructions I repeated that there could be no deal of any kind and that any steps toward easing tensions in other parts of the world largely depended on the Soviet Union and Mr. Khrushchev taking action in Cuba and taking it immediately.

I repeated to him that this matter could not wait and that he had better contact Mr. Khrushchev and have a commitment from him by the next day to withdraw the missile bases under United Nations supervision for otherwise, I said, there would be drastic consequences.

Source: U.S. Department of State, *Foreign Relations of the United States 1961–1963*, Vol. XI: *The Cuban Missile Crisis and Its Aftermath* (Washington, DC: Government Printing Office, 1996), Document 96, http://www.state.gov/www/about_state/history/frusXI/76_100.html.

4. Meeting between U.S. Attorney General Robert F. Kennedy and Soviet Ambassador Anatoly Dobrynin, October 28, 1962

With a settlement in sight, on 28 October Soviet officials in Moscow used private exchanges between Ambassador Anatoly Dobrynin and Robert F. Kennedy as a conduit for additional assurances and understandings. Khrushchev sent a message to the president's brother, which Dobrynin passed on the same day, reporting back immediately to Moscow.

Telegram from Soviet Foreign Minister Andrey Gromyko to Ambassador Dobrynin, October 28, 1962

CIPHERED TELEGRAM
EXTRAORDINARY
WASHINGTON
SOVIET AMBASSADOR

Quickly get in touch with R. Kennedy and tell him that you passed on to N.S. Khrushchev the contents of your conversation with him. N.S. Khrushchev sent the following urgent response.

The thoughts which R. Kennedy expressed at the instruction of the President find understanding in Moscow. Today, an answer will be given by radio to the President's message of October 27, and that response will be the most favorable. The main thing which disturbs the President, precisely the issue of the dismantling under international control of the rocket bases in Cuba—meets no objection and will be explained in detail in N.S. Khrushchev's message.

Telegraph upon implementation.

[handwritten]

(A. Gromyko)

Source: Russian Foreign Ministry Archives (AVP RF), copy courtesy of The National Security Archive, The George Washington University. Translation by Mark H. Doctoroff. Available online at Cold War International History Project Virtual Archive,http://legacy.wilsoncenter.org/va2/index.cfm?topic_id=1409&fuseaction= home.document&identifier=5034E33A-96B6-175C-9C8D8C35D3CCF5BE &sort=collection&item=Cuban%20Missile%20Crisis.

Telegram from Ambassador Dobrynin to Soviet Ministry of Foreign Affairs, October 28, 1962

TOP SECRET
Making Copies Prohibited
Copy No. 1
CIPHERED TELEGRAM

R. Kennedy, with whom I met, listened very attentively to N.S. Khrushchev's response. Expressing thanks for the report, he said that he would quickly return to the White House in order to inform the President about the "important response" of the head of the Soviet government. "This is a great

relief," R. Kennedy added further, and it was evident that he expressed his words somehow involuntarily. "I," said R. Kennedy, "today will finally be able to see my kids, for I have been entirely absent from home."

According to everything it was evident that R. Kennedy with satisfaction, it is necessary to say, really with great relief met the report about N.S. Khrushchev's response.

In parting, R. Kennedy once again requested that strict secrecy be maintained about the agreement with Turkey. "Especially so that the correspondents don't find out. At our place for the time being even [White House Press Secretary Pierre] Salinger does not know about it." (It was not entirely clear why he considered it necessary to mention his name, but he did it).

I responded that in the Embassy no one besides me knows about the conversation with him yesterday. R. Kennedy said that in addition to the current correspondence and future exchange of opinions via diplomatic channels, on important questions he will maintain contact with me directly, avoiding any intermediaries.

Before departing, R. Kennedy once again gave thanks for N.S. Khrushchev's quick and effective response.

Your instructions arrived here 1.5 hours after the announcement via radio about the essence of N.S. Khrushchev's response. I explained to R. Kennedy that the tardiness was caused by a delay of telegrams at the telegraph station.

28.X.62 A. DOBRYNIN

Source: Russian Foreign Ministry Archives (AVP RF), copy courtesy of The National Security Archive, The George Washington University. Translation by Mark H. Doctoroff. Available online at Cold War International History Project Virtual Archive, http://legacy.wilsoncenter.org/va2/index.cfm?topic_id=1409& fuseaction=home.document&identifier=5034E405-96B6-175C-9C201F3 F4D387E4B&sort=collection&item=Cuban%20Missile%20Crisis.

5. Chairman Nikita Khrushchev to President John F. Kennedy, Moscow, October 28, 1962

In response to U.S. Attorney General Robert Kennedy's discussions with Soviet ambassador Anatoly Dobrynin on October 27, Soviet premier Nikita Khrushchev dispatched a letter to President John F.

Kennedy, accepting the U.S. offer to remove missiles from Turkey. He promised to keep this arrangement secret. On October 29 Dobrynin forwarded Khrushchev's letter to Robert Kennedy. The president, however, thought the matter so sensitive that he refused to accept this letter, as he preferred that no formal written record of their bargain exist. One day later, his brother Robert therefore returned it to Ambassador Dobrynin.

DEAR MR. PRESIDENT,

Ambassador Dobrynin has apprised me of his conversation with Robert Kennedy which took place on October 27. In this conversation Robert Kennedy said that it is somewhat difficult for you at the present time to publicly discuss the question of eliminating the US missile bases in Turkey because of the fact that the stationing of those bases in Turkey was formalized through a NATO Council decision.

Readiness to agree on this issue that I raised in my message to you of October 27 was also emphasized. In this context Robert Kennedy said that removal of those bases from Turkey would take 4 to 5 months. Furthermore, a wish was expressed that exchanges of views on this matter between you and I should continue through Robert Kennedy and the Soviet Ambassador, and that these exchanges should be considered confidential.

I feel I must state to you that I do understand the delicacy involved for you in an open consideration of the issue of eliminating the US missile bases in Turkey. I take into account the complexity of this issue and I believe you are right about not wishing to publicly discuss it. I agree that our discussion of this subject be pursued confidentially through Robert Kennedy and the Soviet Ambassador in Washington. You may have noticed that in my message to you on October 28, which was to be published immediately, I did not raise this question—precisely because I was mindful of your wish conveyed through Robert Kennedy. But all the proposals that I presented in that message took into account the fact that you had agreed to resolve, [sic] the matter of your missile bases in Turkey consistent with what I had said in my message of October 27 and what you stated through Robert Kennedy in his meeting with Ambassador Dobrynin on the same day.

I express my great appreciation to you for having instructed your brother R. Kennedy to convey those thoughts.

I hope, Mr. President, that agreement on this matter, too, shall be a no small step advancing the cause of relaxation of international tensions and the tensions between our two powers. And that in turn can provide a good

impetus to resolving other issues concerning both the security of Europe and the international situation as a whole.

Mr. President, the crisis that we have gone through may repeat again. This means that we need to address the issues which contain too much explosive material. Not right away, of course. Apparently, it will take some time for the passions to cool down. But we cannot delay the solution to these issues, for continuation of this situation is frought [sic] with many uncertainties and dangers.

Sincerely,

N. Khrushchev

Source: U.S. Department of State, *Foreign Relations of the United States 1961–1963,* Vol. VI: *Kennedy-Khrushchev Exchanges* (Washington, DC: Government Printing Office, 1996), Document 70, http://www.state.gov/www/about_state/history/volume_vi/exchanges.html.

6. Meeting between U.S. Attorney General Robert F. Kennedy and Soviet Ambassador Anatoly Dobrynin, October 30, 1962

On October 30, 1962, Attorney General Robert F. Kennedy met once again with the Soviet ambassador, Anatoly Dobrynin. He refused to accept a letter from Khrushchev, delivered the previous day, setting down in writing the understanding that NATO missiles would be removed from Turkey in exchange for the dismantling of those in Cuba. He promised, however, that the United States would ensure that the Jupiter missiles in both Italy and Turkey were taken out within four or five months. Kennedy's notes for this meeting survive, and Dobrynin sent an account of it to Moscow.

Robert F. Kennedy, Notes for Meeting with Ambassador Dobrynin, October 30, 1962

Read letter—Studied it over night.
No quid pro quo as I told you.
The letter makes it appear that there was.

You asked me about missile bases in Turkey. I told you we would be out of them—4 or 5 months. That still holds.... You have my word on this & that is sufficient.

Take back your letter—Reconsider it & if you feel it is necessary to write letters then we will also write one which you cannot enjoy.

Also if you should publish any document indicating a deal then it is off & also if done afterward will further affect the relationship.

Source: Robert F. Kennedy Papers, John F. Kennedy Presidential Library, Boston. Reprinted in Arthur M. Schlesinger, Jr., *Robert Kennedy and His Times,* 2 vols. (Boston: Houghton Mifflin, 1978), 1:546.

Telegram from Ambassador Dobrynin to the Soviet Foreign Ministry, October 30, 1962

Today Robert Kennedy invited me to meet with him. He said that he would like to talk about N.S. Khrushchev's letter to the President yesterday.

The President, Robert Kennedy said, confirms the understanding [do-govorion-nost] with N.S. Khrushchev on the elimination of the American missile bases in Turkey (Robert Kennedy confirmed that one speaks of an understanding). Corresponding measures will be taken towards fulfilling this understanding within the period of time indicated earlier, in confidential observance of NATO guidelines, but of course without any mention that this is connected to the Cuban events.

We, however, said Robert Kennedy, are not prepared to formulate such an understanding in the form of letters, even the most confidential letters, between the President and the head of the Soviet government when it concerns such a highly delicate issue. Speaking in all candor, I myself, for example, do not want to risk getting involved in the transmission of this sort of letter, since who knows where and when such letters can surface or be somehow published—not now, but in the future—and any changes in the course of events are possible. The appearance of such a document could cause irreparable harm to my political career in the future. This is why we request that you take this letter back.

It is possible, Robert Kennedy continued, that you do not believe us and through letters you want to put the understanding in writing. The issue of Soviet missile bases in Cuba has unfortunately introduced a real element of uncertainty and suspicion even into confidential channels of

contact. We will however live up to our promise, even if it is given in this oral form. As you know, it was in precisely the same oral form that the President made his promise to N.S. Khrushchev regarding the removal of a certain number of American soldiers from Thailand. That promise was kept. So too will this promise be kept.

As a guarantee, Robert Kennedy added, I can only give you my word. Moreover I can tell you that two other people besides the President know about the existing understanding: they are [Secretary of State Dean] Rusk and [advisor on Soviet affairs Llewellyn] Thompson. If you do not believe me, discuss it with them, and they will tell you the same thing. But it is better not to transfer this understanding into a formal, albeit confidential, exchange of letters (as can be noted, the greatest suspicion in the two Kennedy brothers was elicited by the part of Khrushchev's letter which speaks directly of a link between the Cuban events and the bases in Turkey). We hope that N.S. Khrushchev will understand us correctly. In regard to this Robert Kennedy insistently asked to take the letter back without delay.

I told Robert Kennedy that everything said above I would report to N.S. Khrushchev, emphasizing in doing so that even the President and he, Robert Kennedy, could be sure of the fact that the Soviet government is regarding the understanding that has been reached as strictly secret and not for publication. At the same time, in order to confirm Robert Kennedy's statement about the understanding, I asked him again about whether the President really confirms the understanding with N.S. Khrushchev on the elimination of American missile bases in Turkey.

Robert Kennedy said once again that he confirmed it, and again that he hoped that their motivations would be properly understood in Moscow. Taking what they explained into account, I believed it conditionally possible—before receiving any instructions from Moscow—to take this letter [back], since a categorical refusal to do so would, in my opinion, only weaken Robert Kennedy's firm statements on the understanding that has been reached. Moreover, leaving the letter with him, after he had clearly expressed the President's desire not to exchange letters, could scarcely be in the interests of doing business [in the future].

In conclusion Robert Kennedy said that, in his opinion, the events connected with the Cuban issue have been developing quite favorably, and that he hoped that everything would eventually be settled. He added that, on the Turkish issue and other highly confidential issues he was prepared to maintain a direct contact with me as earlier, emphasizing in doing so

that the point was the possible oral considerations of the President and the head of the Soviet government N.S. Khrushchev on the exchange of letters on such delicate issues as missile bases in Turkey, or issues which need to be handled more by the State Department than by him personally, taking into account the delicacy of his situation as the President's brother and as Attorney General of the United States. I do not want, Robert Kennedy added, to claim for myself the function of the State Department, but my "solitary diplomacy" may be needed several more times, and we will be meeting with each other periodically.

I answered to Robert Kennedy that I was prepared to maintain contact with him on highly important issues in the future, passing over the heads, as he himself suggested, of all intermediaries. Robert Kennedy confirmed this. From what Robert Kennedy said it was clear that the President is trying now to avoid exchanging any documents on issues of a highly delicate nature like Turkey which could leave a trace anywhere, but that he favors the continuation of a confidential exchange of opinions between the heads of the two governments.

We believe it expedient to visit Robert Kennedy once again and to issue a statement, in referring to our mission, that the Soviet government and N.S. Khrushchev personally are prepared to take into account the President's desire for maintaining the secrecy of the oral understanding on the removal of the American missile bases from Turkey. It is also expedient to tell of our willingness, if the President is also prepared for this, to continue the confidential exchange of opinions between the heads of the governments on many important unresolved issues, on whose resolution the lessening of international tension, and of the tension between our two countries in particular, is to a very great degree dependent.

I request instructions.

30.X.62 A.DOBRYNIN

Source: Russian Foreign Ministry Archives (AVP RF), copy obtained by NHK (Japanese Television), provided to CWIHP, and on file at The National Security Archive, The George Washington University. Translation by John Henriksen, Harvard University. Available at: http://legacy.wilsoncenter.org/va2/index.cfm?topic_id=1409&fuseaction=home.document&identifier=5034EB58-96B6-175C-9E56519C864C5063&sort=rights&item=cwihp. Accessed January 1, 2012.

7. Letters between Cuban leader Fidel Castro and Soviet Premier Nikita Khrushchev, October 26–31, 1962

As the Cuban Missile Crisis intensified and was then resolved, Cuban Prime Minister Fidel Castro and Soviet premier Nikita Khrushchev exchanged a series of letters, in which Castro showed himself far more bellicose than Khrushchev. Fearing that a U.S. invasion of Cuba was inevitable, on October 26 Castro begged Khrushchev to open hostilities with a nuclear first strike against the United States. When he sent Kennedy two letters, on October 26 and 27, suggesting terms on which the ongoing crisis might be settled, Khrushchev did not consult Castro, an omission that infuriated the Cuban leader. On October 27, Khrushchev wrote to Castro, defending his proposals to Kennedy as the best outcome for Cuba, one that would keep Cuba secure against any future U.S. invasion. Not yet aware that Soviet rather than Cuban military personnel had been responsible for shooting down a U.S. U-2 reconnaissance plane over Cuba on October 27, he also warned Castro against attacking U.S. airplanes. On October 28, Castro asserted Cuba's right to shoot down U.S. aircraft and warned that he was unwilling to accept any outside inspections of Cuban territory in connection with the recent Soviet agreement to remove the missiles in question from the island. Khrushchev replied at length, justifying the recent agreement as one that was in Cuba's best interests, warning that a nuclear war would have brought destruction to Cuba and denying that he had failed to consult Castro during the crisis. His persuasions failed to mollify the deeply resentful Castro, who claimed that not just the Cubans, but also the Soviet soldiers stationed there, had been prepared to fight to the bitter end against the United States. Once again, Castro complained that Soviet officials had not consulted him when negotiating with their U.S. counterparts.

Fidel Castro to Nikita Khrushchev, October 26, 1962

Dear Comrade Khrushchev,

From an analysis of the situation and the reports in our possession, I consider that the aggression is almost imminent within the next 24 or 72 hours.

There are two possible variants: the first and likeliest one is an air attack against certain targets with the limited objective of destroying them; the second, less probable although possible, is invasion. I understand that this variant would call for a large number of forces and it is, in addition, the most repulsive form of aggression, which might inhibit them.

You can rest assured that we will firmly and resolutely resist attack, whatever it may be.

The morale of the Cuban people is extremely high and the aggressor will be confronted heroically.

At this time I want to convey to you briefly my personal opinion.

If the second variant is implemented and the imperialists invade Cuba with the goal of occupying it, the danger that that aggressive policy poses for humanity is so great that following that event the Soviet Union must never allow the circumstances in which the imperialists could launch the first nuclear strike against it.

I tell you this because I believe that the imperialists' aggressiveness is extremely dangerous and if they actually carry out the brutal act of invading Cuba in violation of international law and morality, that would be the moment to eliminate such danger forever through an act of clear legitimate defense, however harsh and terrible the solution would be for there is no other.

It has influenced my opinion to see how this aggressive policy is developing, how the imperialists, disregarding world public opinion and ignoring principles and the law, are blockading the seas, violating our airspace and preparing an invasion, while at the same time frustrating every possibility for talks, even though they are aware of the seriousness of the problem.

You have been and continue to be a tireless defender of peace and I realize how bitter these hours must be, when the outcome of your superhuman efforts is so seriously threatened. However, up to the last moment we will maintain the hope that peace will be safeguarded and we are willing to contribute to this as much as we can. But at the same time, we are ready to calmly confront a situation which we view as quite real and quite close.

Once more I convey to you the infinite gratitude and recognition of our Cuban people to the Soviet people who have been so generous and fraternal with us, as well as our profound gratitude and admiration for you, and wish you success in the huge task and serious responsibilities ahead of you.

Fraternally,

Fidel Castro

Source: The Cuban Missile Crisis, 1962: The 40th Anniversary. The National Security Archive, The George Washington University. Available at: http://www. gwu.edu/~nsarchiv/nsa/cuba_mis_cri/621026%20Castro%20Letter%20to%20 Khrushchev.pdf. Accessed December 1, 2011.

Nikita Khrushchev to Fidel Castro, October 28, 1962

Dear Comrade Fidel Castro,

Our October 27 message to President Kennedy allows for the question to be settled in your favor, to defend Cuba from an invasion and prevent war from breaking out. Kennedy's reply, which you apparently also know, offers assurances that the United States will not invade Cuba with its own forces, nor will it permit its allies to carry out an invasion. In this way the president of the United States has positively answered messages of October 26 and 27, 1962.

We have now finished drafting our reply to the president's message. I am not going to convey it here, for you surely know the text, which is now being broadcast over the radio.

With this motive I would like to recommend to you now, at this moment of change in the crisis, not to be carried away by sentiment and to show firmness. I must say that I understand your feelings of indignation toward the aggressive actions and violation of elementary norms of international law on the part of the United States.

But now, rather than law, what prevails is the senselessness of the militarists at the Pentagon. Now that an agreement is within sight, the Pentagon is searching for a pretext to frustrate this agreement. This is why it is organizing the provocative flights. Yesterday you shot down one of these, while earlier you didn't shoot them down when they overflew your territory. The aggressors will take advantage of such a step for their own purposes.

Therefore, I would like to advise you in a friendly manner to show patience, firmness and even more firmness. Naturally, if there's an invasion it will be necessary to repulse it by every means. But we mustn't allow ourselves to be carried away by provocations, because the Pentagon's unbridled militarists, now that the solution to the conflict is in sight and

apparently in your favor, creating a guarantee against the invasion of Cuba, are trying to frustrate the agreement and provoke you into actions that could be used against you. I ask you not to give them the pretext for doing that.

On our part, we will do everything possible to stabilize the situation in Cuba, defend Cuba against invasion and assure you the possibilities for peacefully building a socialist society.

I send you greetings, extensive to all your leadership group.

N. Khrushchev

Source: The Cuban Missile Crisis, 1962: The 40th Anniversary. The National Security Archive, The George Washington University. Available at: http://www.gwu.edu/~nsarchiv/nsa/cuba_mis_cri/19621028khrlet.pdf. Accessed December 1, 2011.

Fidel Castro to Nikita Khrushchev, October 28, 1962

Dear Comrade Khrushchev,

I have just received your letter.

The position of our government concerning your communication to us is embodied in the statement formulated today, whose text you surely know.

I wish to clear up something concerning the antiaircraft measures we adopted. You say: "Yesterday you shot down one of these [planes], while earlier you didn't shoot them down when they overflew your territory."

Earlier isolated violations were committed without a determined military purpose or without a real danger stemming from those flights.

This time that wasn't the case. There was the danger of a surprise attack on certain military installations. We decided not to sit back and wait for a surprise attack, with our detection radar turned off, when the potentially aggressive planes flying with impunity over targets could destroy them totally. We didn't think we should allow that after all the efforts and expenses incurred and, in addition, because it would weaken us greatly, militarily and morally. For that reason, on October 24 the Cuban forces mobilized 50 antiaircraft batteries, our entire reserve then, to provide support to the Soviet forces' positions. If we sought to avoid the risk of a surprise attack, it was necessary for Cuban artillerymen to have orders to shoot. The Soviet command can furnish you with additional reports of what happened to the plane that was shot down.

Earlier, airspace violations were carried out de facto and furtively. Yesterday the American government tried to make official the privilege of violating our airspace at any hour of the day and night. We cannot accept that, as it would be tantamount to giving up a sovereign prerogative. However, we agree that we must avoid an incident at this precise moment that could seriously harm the negotiations, so we will instruct the Cuban batteries not to open fire, but only for as long as the negotiations last and without revoking the declaration published yesterday about the decision to defend our airspace. It should also be taken into account that under the current tense conditions incidents can take place accidentally.

I also wish to inform you that we are in principle opposed to an inspection of our territory.

I appreciate extraordinarily the efforts you have made to keep the peace and we are absolutely in agreement with the need for struggling for that goal. If this is accomplished in a just, solid and definitive manner, it will be an inestimable service to humanity.

Fraternally,

Fidel Castro Ruz

Source: The Cuban Missile Crisis, 1962: The 40th Anniversary. The National Security Archive, The George Washington University. Available at: http://www.gwu.edu/~nsarchiv/nsa/cuba_mis_cri/19621028caslet.pdf. Accessed December 1, 2011.

Nikita Khrushchev to Fidel Castro, October 30, 1962

Dear Comrade Fidel Castro,

We have received your letter of October 28 and the reports on the talks that you as well as President Dorticós have had with our ambassador.

We understand your situation and take into account the difficulties you now have during this first transitional stage after the liquidation of maximum tension that arose due to the threat of attack on the part of the U.S. imperialists, which you expected would occur at any moment.

We understand that certain difficulties have been created for you as a result of our having promised the U.S. government to withdraw the missile base from Cuba, since it is viewed as an offensive weapon, in exchange

for the U.S. commitment to abandon plans for an invasion of Cuba by U.S. troops or those of its allies in the western hemisphere, and lift the so-called "quarantine," that is, bring the [naval] blockade of Cuba to an end. This led to the liquidation of the conflict in the Caribbean zone which, as you well realize, was characterized by the clash of two superpowers and the possibility of being transformed into a thermonuclear world war using missiles.

As we learned from our ambassador, some Cubans have the opinion that the Cuban people want a declaration of another nature rather than the declaration of the withdrawal of the missiles. It's possible that this kind of feeling exists among the people. But we, political and government figures, are leaders of a people who doesn't know everything and can't really comprehend all that we leaders must deal with. Therefore, we should march at the head of the people and then the people will follow us and respect us.

Had we, yielding to the sentiments prevailing among the people, allowed ourselves to be carried away by certain passionate sectors of the population and refused to come to a reasonable agreement with the U.S. government, then a war could have broken out, in the course of which millions of people would have died and the survivors would pinned the blame on the leaders for not having taken the necessary measures to prevent this war of annihilation.

Preventing the war and an attack on Cuba depended not just on the measures adopted by our governments but also on an estimate of the actions of the enemy's forces deployed near you. Accordingly, the overall situation had to be considered.

In addition, there are opinions that you and we, as they say, failed to engage in consultations concerning these questions before adopting the decisions known to you.

For this reason we believed that we consulted with you, dear Comrade Fidel Castro, receiving your cables, each one more alarming than the next, and finally your cable of October 27, saying you were nearly certain that an attack on Cuba would be launched. You believed it was merely a question of time, that the attack would take place within the next 24 or 72 hours. Upon receiving this alarming cable from you and aware of your courage, we viewed it as a very well-founded alarm.

Wasn't this consultation on your part with us? I have viewed this cable as a signal of extreme alarm. Under the conditions created, also bearing in mind the information that the unabated warmongering group of U.S. militarists wanted to take advantage of the situation that had been created and launch an attack on Cuba, if we had continued our consultations, we would have wasted time and the attack would have been carried out.

We came to the conclusion that our strategic missiles in Cuba became an ominous force for the imperialists: they were frightened and because of their fear that our rockets could be launched, they could have dared to liquidate them by bombing them and launching an invasion of Cuba. And it must be said that they could have knocked them all out. Therefore, I repeat, your alarm was absolutely well-founded.

In your cable of October 27 you proposed that we be the first to launch a nuclear strike against the territory of the enemy. You, of course, realize where that would have led. Rather than a simple strike, it would have been the start of a thermonuclear world war.

Dear Comrade Fidel Castro, I consider this proposal of yours incorrect, although I understand your motivation.

We have lived through the most serious moment when a nuclear world war could have broken out. Obviously, in that case, the United States would have sustained huge losses, but the Soviet Union and the whole socialist camp would also have suffered greatly. As far as Cuba is concerned, it would be difficult to say even in general terms what this would have meant for them. In the first place, Cuba would have been burned in the fire of war. There is no doubt that the Cuban people would have fought courageously or that they would have died heroically. But we are not struggling against imperialism in order to die, but to take advantage of all our possibilities, to lose less in the struggle and win more to overcome and achieve the victory of communism.

Now, as a result of the measures taken, we reached the goal sought when we agreed with you to send the missiles to Cuba. We have wrested from the United States the commitment not to invade Cuba and not to permit their Latin American allies to do so. We have wrested all this from them without a nuclear strike.

We consider that we must take advantage of all the possibilities available to defend Cuba, strengthen its independence and sovereignty, defeat military aggression and prevent a nuclear world war in our time.

And we have accomplished that.

Of course, we made concessions, accepted a commitment, acting according to the principle that a concession on one side be answered by a concession on the other side. The United States also made a concession. It made the commitment before all the world not to attack Cuba.

That's why when we compare aggression on the part of the United States and thermonuclear war with the commitment of a concession in exchange for a concession, the upholding of the inviolability of the Republic of Cuba and the prevention of a world war, I think that the total outcome of this reckoning, of this comparison, is perfectly clear.

Naturally, in defending Cuba as well as the other socialist countries, we can't rely on a U.S. government veto. We have adopted and will continue to adopt in the future all the measures necessary to strengthen our defense and build up our forces, so that we can strike back if needed. At present, as a result of our weapons supplies, Cuba is stronger than ever. Even after the dismantling of the missile installations you will have powerful weapons to throw back the enemy, on land, in the air and on the sea, in the approaches to the island. At the same time, as you will recall, we have said in our message to the president of the United States dated October 28, that at the same time we want to assure the Cuban people that we stand at their side and we will not forget our responsibility to help the Cuban people. It is clear to everyone that this is an extremely serious warning to the enemy on our part.

You also stated during the rallies that the United States can't be trusted. That, of course, is correct. We also view your statements on the conditions of the talks with the United States as correct. The shooting down of a U.S. plane over Cuba turned out to be a useful measure because this operation ended without complications. Let it be a lesson for the imperialists.

Needless to say, our enemies will interpret the events in their own way. The Cuban counterrevolution will also try to raise its head. But we think you will completely dominate your domestic internal enemies without our assistance. The main thing we have secured is preventing aggression on the part of your foreign enemy at present.

We feel that the aggressor came out the loser. He made preparations to attack Cuba but we stopped him and forced him to recognize before world public opinion that he won't do it at the current stage. We view this as a great victory. The imperialists, of course, will not stop their struggle against communism. But we also have our plans and we are going to adopt our measures. This process of struggle will continue so long as there are two political and social systems in the world, until one of these—and we know it will be our communist system—wins and triumphs throughout the world.

Comrade Fidel Castro, I have decided to send this reply to you as soon as possible. A more detailed analysis of everything that has happened will be made in the letter I'll send you shortly. In that letter I will make the broadest analysis of the situation and give you my evaluation of the outcome of the end of the conflict.

Now, as the talks to settle the conflict get underway, I ask you to send me your considerations. For our part, we will continue to report to you on the development of these talks and make all necessary consultations.

I wish you success, Comrade Fidel Castro. You will no doubt have success. There will still be machinations against you, but together with you, we will adopt all the measures necessary to paralyze them and contribute to the strengthening and development of the Cuban Revolution.

Nikita Krushchev

Source: The Cuban Missile Crisis, 1962: The 40th Anniversary. The National Security Archive, The George Washington University. Available at: http://www.gwu.edu/~nsarchiv/nsa/cuba_mis_cri/621030%20Letter%20to%20Castro.pdf. Accessed December 1, 2011.

Fidel Castro to Nikita Khrushchev, October 31, 1962

Dear Comrade Khrushchev,

I received your letter of 30 October. You understand that we indeed were consulted before you adopted the decision to withdraw the strategic missiles. You base yourself on the alarming news that you say reached you from Cuba and, finally, my cable of October 27. I don't know what news you received; I can only respond for the message that I sent you the evening of October 26, which reached you the 27th.

What we did in the face of the events, Comrade Khrushchev, was to prepare ourselves and get ready to fight. In Cuba there was only one kind of alarm, that of battle stations.

When in our opinion the imperialist attack became imminent I deemed it appropriate to so advise you and alert both the Soviet government and command—since there were Soviet forces committed to fight at our side to defend the Republic of Cuba from foreign aggression—about the possibility of an attack that we could not prevent but could resist.

I told you that the morale of our people was very high and that the aggression would be heroically resisted. At the end of the message I reiterated to you that we awaited the events calmly.

Danger couldn't impress us, for danger has been hanging over the country for a long time now and in a certain way we have grown used to it.

The Soviet troops which have been at our side know how admirable the stand of our people was throughout this crisis and the profound brotherhood that was created among the troops from both peoples during the decisive hours. Countless eyes of Cuban and Soviet men who were

willing to die with supreme dignity shed tears upon learning about the surprising, sudden and practically unconditional decision to withdraw the weapons.

Perhaps you don't know the degree to which the Cuban people was ready to do its duty toward the nation and humanity.

I realized when I wrote them that the words contained in my letter could be misinterpreted by you and that was what happened, perhaps because you didn't read them carefully, perhaps because of the translation, perhaps because I meant to say so much in too few lines. However, I didn't hesitate to do it. Do you think, Comrade Khrushchev, that we were selfishly thinking of ourselves, of our generous people ready to sacrifice themselves, and not at all in an unconscious manner, but fully assured of the risk they ran?

No, Comrade Khrushchev. Few times in history, and it could even be said that never before, because no people had ever faced such a tremendous danger, was a people so willing to fight and die with such a universal sense of duty.

We knew, and do not presume that we ignored it, that we would have been annihilated, as you insinuate in your letter, in the event of nuclear war. However, that didn't prompt us to ask you to withdraw the missiles, that didn't prompt us to ask you to yield. Do you believe that we wanted that war? But how could we prevent it if the invasion finally took place? The fact is that this event was possible, that imperialism was obstructing every solution and that its demands were, from our point of view, impossible for the USSR and Cuba to accept.

And if war had broken out, what was one to do with the insane people who unleashed the war? You yourself have said that under current conditions such a war would inevitably have escalated quickly into a nuclear war.

I understand that once aggression is unleashed, one shouldn't concede to the aggressor the privilege of deciding, moreover, when to use nuclear weapons. The destructive power of this weaponry is so great and the speed of its delivery so great that the aggressor would have a considerable initial advantage.

And I did not suggest to you, Comrade Khrushchev, that the USSR should be the aggressor, because that would be more than incorrect, it would be immoral and contemptible on my part. But from the instant the imperialists attack Cuba and while there are Soviet armed forces stationed in Cuba to help in our defense in case of attack from abroad, the imperialists would by this act become aggressors against Cuba and against the USSR, and we would respond with a strike that would annihilate them.

Everyone has his own opinions and I maintain mine about the dangerousness of the aggressive circles in the Pentagon and their preference for a preventive strike. I did not suggest, Comrade Khrushchev, that in the midst of this crisis the Soviet Union should attack, which is what your letter seems to say; rather, that following an imperialist attack, the USSR should act without vacillation and should never make the mistake of allowing circumstances to develop in which the enemy makes the first nuclear strike against the USSR. And in this sense, Comrade Khrushchev, I maintain my point of view, because I understand it to be a true and just evaluation of a specific situation. You may be able to convince me that I am wrong, but you can't tell me that I am wrong without convincing me.

I know that this is a delicate issue that can only be broached in circumstances such as these and in a very personal message.

You may wonder what right I have to broach this topic. I do so without worrying about how thorny it is, following the dictates of my conscience as a revolutionary duty and inspired by the most unselfish sentiments of admiration and affection for the USSR, for what she represents for the future of humanity and by the concern that she should never again be the victim of the perfidy and betrayal of aggressors, as she was in 1941, and which cost so many lives and so much destruction. Moreover, I spoke not as a troublemaker but as a combatant from the most endangered trenches.

I do not see how you can state that we were consulted in the decision you took.

I would like nothing more than to be proved wrong at this moment. I only wish that you were right.

There are not just a few Cubans, as has been reported to you, but in fact many Cubans who are experiencing at this moment unspeakable bitterness and sadness.

The imperialists are talking once again of invading our country, which is proof of how ephemeral and untrustworthy their promises are. Our people, however, maintain their indestructible will to resist the aggressors and perhaps more than ever need to trust in themselves and in that will to struggle.

We will struggle against adverse circumstances, we will overcome the current difficulties and we will come out ahead, and nothing can destroy the ties of friendship and the eternal gratitude we feel toward the USSR.

Fraternally,

Fidel Castro

Source: The Cuban Missile Crisis, 1962: The 40th Anniversary. The National Security Archive, The George Washington University. Available at: http://www.gwu.edu/~nsarchiv/nsa/cuba_mis_cri/621031%20Letter%20to%20Khrushchev.pdf. Accessed December 1, 2011.

Chronology

1823	Monroe Doctrine warns European powers against further territorial acquisitions or interventions in Latin America.
April 1898	The United States and Spain declare war on each other.
December 1898	Spain cedes Cuba to the United States under the Treaty of Paris.
1902	Cuba gains independence, but the Platt Amendment gives the United States the right to intervene in Cuban affairs.
1904	Roosevelt Corollary to the Monroe Doctrine asserts the right of the United States to intervene in the affairs of Latin American nations in order to keep them "stable, orderly and prosperous."
1933	Cuba abrogates the Platt Amendment. President Franklin D. Roosevelt withholds recognition of Ramón Grau's government for a year.
1940–1944	First presidential administration of Fulgencio Batista
1950–1958	Second presidential administration of Fulgencio Batista
1953	Fidel Castro leads an unsuccessful revolution against Batista.
1956	Fidel Castro begins a second rebellion against Batista.
1958	The United States withdraws military aid from Batista.

January 1, 1959	Fidel Castro establishes revolutionary government of Cuba.
February 1959	Castro becomes prime minister of Cuba.
April 1959	Castro visits the United States.
May 1959	Cuban Agrarian Reform Law forbids foreign land ownership and expropriates farm holdings over 1,000 acres.
October 1959	Soviet representative Aleksandr Alekseev arrives in Cuba.
February 1960	Soviet Politburo member Anastas Mikoyan visits Cuba, signs Soviet-Cuban trade agreement.
March 1960	President Dwight D. Eisenhower authorizes a program to fund and train Cuban exiles to overthrow Castro's government.
May 1960	Cuba and the Soviet Union resume diplomatic relations.
July 1960	The United States suspends Cuban sugar import quota. Soviet premier Nikita Khrushchev pledges that Cuba falls under the protection of the Soviet nuclear umbrella.
September 1960	Khrushchev and Castro meet and embrace at the United Nations in New York. Soviet arms shipments begin arriving in Cuba.
October 1960	Cuba nationalizes $1 billion of private American investments in Cuba. The United States imposes a complete economic embargo on Cuba (except for cigars, some foods, and medicines).
December 19, 1960	Cuba aligns itself with the Soviet Union and the communist bloc.
January 3, 1960	The United States ends diplomatic relations with Cuba.
January 20, 1961	John F. Kennedy becomes U.S. president.
April 14, 1961	U.S. B-26 bombers piloted by Cuban exiles attack Cuban airbases.
April 16, 1961	Castro announces he himself is a communist.
April 17–19, 1961	The CIA-backed invasion of Cuba by Cuban exiles ends in failure.

June 3–4, 1961   Kennedy and Khrushchev meet in Vienna.

August 13, 1961   Soviet and East German forces erect the Berlin Wall, dividing East and West Berlin.

November 30, 1961   Kennedy authorizes Operation MONGOOSE to destabilize Castro's government.

December 1, 1961   Castro declares he is a Marxist-Leninist.

January 1962   The Organization of American States excludes Cuba from participation in its activities.

February 1962   Kennedy imposes a full trade embargo—including cigars and food, though not medicines—on Cuba.

April 1962   15 U.S. Jupiter nuclear missiles in Turkey become operational.

May 1962   Khrushchev decides to offer to install nuclear-capable missiles in Cuba.

     Alekseev is appointed Soviet ambassador to Cuba.

July-October 1962   Over 100 Soviet shipments of troops and military equipment reach Cuba.

September 4, 1962   Kennedy states publicly that the United States will not tolerate Soviet offensive weapons in Cuba.

October 2, 1962   Transport of U.S. goods to Cuba is banned.

October 14, 1962   A U-2 surveillance flight over Cuba photographs nuclear-capable missile installations.

October 16, 1962   Kennedy receives photographic evidence of nuclear-capable missile bases on Cuba; summons meeting of Executive Committee (ExComm) of the National Security Council, his senior foreign policy advisers, which meets every day from then to October 28.

October 18, 1962   Kennedy meets Soviet foreign minister Andrey Gromyko, who denies the presence of any Soviet nuclear-capable missiles on Cuba.

October 22, 1962   Kennedy announces publicly that the United States knows Soviet nuclear-capable missiles have been installed on Cuba, demands their withdrawal, and imposes a naval quarantine on the island.

     U.S. forces move to DEFCON-3: high nuclear alert.

October 23, 1962   *Alexandrovsk,* a Soviet ship bearing 68 nuclear warheads, reaches Cuba just before the quarantine becomes operative.

October 24, 1962   The U.S. naval quarantine of Cuba becomes operative. Soviet ships stop at the quarantine line and go no further, while Kennedy delays boarding.

October 25, 1962   U.S. forces move to DEFCON-2: highest nuclear alert short of war.

U.S. ambassador Adlai Stevenson presents photographic evidence of Soviet nuclear-capable missile installations on Cuba to the United Nations.

October 26, 1962   Khrushchev writes to Kennedy, offering to remove the missiles in exchange for a pledge not to invade Cuba. Castro urges Khrushchev to mount a nuclear first strike against the United States.

October 27, 1962   Khrushchev sends a second letter, requesting that the United States remove Jupiter missiles from Turkey. Soviet surface-to-air batteries shoot down a U-2 reconnaissance plane over Cuba. U.S. warships confront nuclear-armed Soviet Foxtrot submarine B-59 in the West Atlantic. Kennedy replies to the first Khrushchev letter, accepting its terms. Robert Kennedy secretly meets Soviet ambassador Anatoly Dobrynin and offers to remove Jupiter missiles from Turkey and Italy within 4–5 months.

October 28, 1962   Khrushchev accepts U.S. terms in letter read over Radio Moscow. Khrushchev writes private third letter to Kennedy setting out terms of agreement on Jupiter missiles.

October 30, 1962   Robert F. Kennedy hands back Khrushchev's private third letter to Kennedy to Ambassador Dobrynin.

November–December 1962   Soviet nuclear-capable missiles and some other weapons are removed from Cuba. Castro refuses to allow on-site inspections. Eighteen thousand Soviet troops remain in Cuba.

November 1962   Mikoyan visits Cuba in an effort to mollify Castro.

November 21, 1962   Kennedy lifts the naval quarantine of Cuba.

April–May 1963   Castro visits the Soviet Union.

May 1963   Khrushchev renews the Soviet nuclear guarantee of Cuba's security.

April 1963   Final Jupiter missiles are removed from Italy and Turkey.

August 5, 1963   The United States, Britain, and the Soviet Union sign the Partial Test Ban Treaty.

November 22, 1963   Kennedy is assassinated in Dallas, Texas, by an American Castro sympathizer.

October 1964   Khrushchev is ousted from power by Soviet Politburo.

December 1976   Fidel Castro becomes president of Cuba.

September 1991   Soviet president Mikhail Gorbachev withdraws all Soviet troops from Cuba.

July 31, 2006   Castro transfers his responsibilities to his brother Raúl Castro.

February 2008   Castro resigns as president of Cuba and Raúl takes over.

Bibliography

Acosta, Tomás Diez. *October 1962: The "Missile" Crisis as Seen from Cuba.* New York: Pathfinder, 2002.

Allison, Graham, and Philip Zelikow. *Essence of Decision: Explaining the Cuban Missile Crisis.* 2nd ed. New York: Longman, 1999.

Allyn, Bruce J., James G. Blight, and David A. Welch. *Cuba on the Brink: Castro, the Cuban Missile Crisis, and the Soviet Collapse.* New York: Pantheon, 1993.

Alterman, Eric. *When Presidents Lie: A History of Official Deception and Its Consequences.* New York: Viking, 2004.

Argote-Freyre, Frank. *Fulgencio Batista: From Revolutionary to Strongman.* New Brunswick, NJ: Rutgers University Press, 2006.

Attwood, William. *The Twilight Struggle: Tales of the Cold War.* New York: Harper and Row, 1987.

Ausland, John C. *Kennedy, Khrushchev, and the Berlin-Cuba Crisis 1961–1964.* Oslo, Norway: Scandinavian University Press, 1996.

Balfour, Sebastian. *Castro.* 3rd ed. Harlow, England: Longmans, 2009.

Barrass, Gordon S. *The Great Cold War: A Journey through the Hall of Mirrors.* Stanford, CA: Stanford University Press, 2009.

Benjamin, Jules R. *The United States and the Origins of the Cuban Revolution: An Empire of Liberty in an Age of National Liberation.* Princeton, NJ: Princeton University Press, 1990.

Beschloss, Michael R. *The Crisis Years: Kennedy and Khrushchev 1960–1963.* New York: Edward Burlingame Books, 1991.

Bethell, Leslie, ed. *Cuba: A Short History.* Cambridge: Cambridge University Press, 1993.

Bissell, Richard M., Jr., with Jonathan E. Lewis and Francis Pudlo. *Reflections of a Cold Warrior: From Yalta to the Bay of Pigs.* New Haven, CT: Yale University Press, 1996.

Blight, James G., and Philip Brenner. *Sad and Luminous Days: Cuba's Struggle with the Superpowers after the Missile Crisis.* Lanham, MD: Rowman and Littlefield, 2002.

Blight, James G., and Peter Kornbluh, eds. *Politics of Illusion: The Bay of Pigs Invasion Reexamined.* Boulder, CO: Lynne Rienner, 1998.

Blight, James G., and Janet M. Lang. *The Fog of War: Lessons from the Life of Robert S. McNamara.* Lanham, MD: Rowman and Littlefield, 2005.

Blight, James G., and David A. Welch, eds. *Intelligence and the Cuban Missile Crisis.* London: Frank Cass, 1998.

Blight, James G., and David A. Welch. *On the Brink: Americans and Soviets Reexamine the Cuban Missile Crisis.* New York: Hill and Wang, 1989.

Bohning, Don. *The Castro Obsession: U.S. Covert Operations against Cuba, 1959–1965.* Washington, DC: Potomac Books, 2005.

Bolender, Keith. *Voices from the Other Side: An Oral History of Terrorism against Cuba.* New York: Pluto Press, 2010.

Brenner, Philip. *From Confrontation to Negotiation: U.S. Relations with Cuba.* Boulder, CO: Westview Press, 1988.

Breuer, William B. *Vendetta: Fidel Castro and the Kennedy Brothers.* New York: John Wiley, 1997.

Brewer, Stewart. *Borders and Bridges: A History of U.S.-Latin American Relations.* Westport, CT: Praeger, 2006.

Brugioni, Dino. *Eyeball to Eyeball: The Inside Story of the Cuban Missile Crisis.* Edited by Robert F. McCort. New York: Random House, 1991.

Brune, Lester H. *The Cuba-Caribbean Missile Crisis of October 1962: A Review of Issues and References.* Claremont, CA: Regina Books, 1996.

Bundy, McGeorge. *Danger and Survival: Choices about the Bomb in the First Fifty Years.* New York: Random House, 1988.

Castro, Fidel. *The Declarations of Havana.* New York: Verso, 2008.

Castro, Fidel, and Ignacio Ramonet. *My Life: A Spoken Autobiography.* Translated by Andrew Hurley. New York: Scribner, 2007.

Chang, Laurence, and Peter Kornbluh, eds. *The Cuban Missile Crisis, 1962: A National Security Archive Documents Reader.* New York: New Press, 1992.

Chun, Clayton K. S. *Thunder over the Horizon: From V-2 Rockets to Ballistic Missiles.* Westport, CT: Praeger, 2005.

Cimbala, Stephen J. *Coercive Military Strategy.* College Station: Texas A & M University Press, 1998.

Cimbala, Stephen J. *Military Persuasion in War and Policy: The Power of Soft.* Westport, CT: Praeger, 2002.

Cline, Ray S. *Secrets, Spies and Scholars: Blueprint of the Essential CIA.* Washington, DC: Acropolis Books, 1976.

Coltman, Leycester. *The Real Fidel Castro.* New Haven, CT: Yale University Press, 2003.

Dallek, Robert. *An Unfinished Life: John F. Kennedy, 1917–1963.* New York: Back Bay Books, 2004.

Dent, David W. *The Legacy of the Monroe Doctrine: A Reference Guide to U.S. Involvement in Latin America and the Caribbean.* Westport, CT: Greenwood Press, 1999.

DePalma, Anthony. *The Man Who Invented Castro: Cuba, Castro, and Herbert L. Matthews of the New York Times.* New York: PublicAffairs, 2006.

Dinerstein, Herbert S. *The Making of a Missile Crisis: October 1962.* Baltimore, MD: Johns Hopkins University Press, 1976.

Dobbs, Michael. *One Minute to Midnight: Kennedy, Khrushchev, and Castro on the Brink of Nuclear War.* New York: Knopf, 2008.

Dobrynin, Anatoly. *In Confidence: Moscow's Ambassador to America's Six Cold War Presidents (1962–1986).* Rev. ed. Seattle: University of Washington Press, 2001.

Dominguez, Esteban Morales, and Gary Prevost. *United States–Cuban Relations: A Critical History.* Lanham, MD: Lexington Books, 2008.

Dominguez, Jorge I. *To Make a World Safe for Revolution: Cuba's Foreign Policy.* Cambridge, MA: Harvard University Press, 1989.

Elliston, Jon, ed. *Psywar on Cuba: The Declassified History of U.S. Anti-Castro Propaganda.* New York: Ocean Press, 1999.

Eubank, Keith. *The Missile Crisis in Cuba.* Malabar, FL: Krieger Publishing, 2000.

Farber, Samuel. *The Origins of the Cuban Revolution Reconsidered.* Chapel Hill: University of North Carolina Press, 2006.

Feklisov, Alexander. *The Man Behind the Rosenbergs.* Translated by Catherine Dop. New York: Enigma Books, 2001.

Foner, Philip S. *A History of Cuba and Its Relations with the United States.* New York: International Publishers, 1962.

Foner, Philip S. *The Spanish-Cuban-American War and the Birth of American Imperialism, 1895–1902.* New York: Monthly Review Press, 1972.

Frankel, Max. *High Noon in the Cold War: Kennedy, Khrushchev, and the Cuban Missile Crisis.* New York: Ballantine Books, 2004.

Freedman, Lawrence. *Kennedy's Wars: Berlin, Cuba, Laos, and Vietnam.* New York: Oxford University Press, 2000.

Fuente, Alejandro de la. *A Nation for All: Race, Inequality, and Politics in Twentieth-Century Cuba.* Chapel Hill: University of North Carolina Press, 2001.

Fursenko, Aleksandr, and Timothy Naftali. *Khrushchev's Cold War: The Inside Story of an American Adversary.* New York: Norton, 2006.

Fursenko, Aleksandr, and Timothy Naftali. *One Hell of a Gamble: Khrushchev, Castro, and Kennedy, 1958–1964.* New York: Norton, 1997.

Gaddis, John Lewis. *The Cold War: A New History.* New York: Penguin, 2006.

Gaddis, John Lewis. *We Now Know: Rethinking Cold War History.* New York: Oxford University Press, 1997.

Gaddis, John Lewis, Philip H. Gordon, Ernest R. May, and Jonathan Rosenberg. *Cold War Statesmen Confront the Bomb: Nuclear Diplomacy Since 1945.* New York: Oxford University Press, 1999.

García, Maria Cristina. *Havana USA: Cuban Exiles and Cuban Americans in South Florida, 1959–1994.* Berkeley: University of California Press, 1996.

Garthoff, Raymond L. *A Journey Through the Cold War: A Memoir of Containment and Coexistence.* Washington, DC: Brookings Institution, 2001.

Garthoff, Raymond L. *Reflections on the Cuban Missile Crisis.* Washington, DC: Brookings Institution, 1987.

Gellman, Irving. *Roosevelt and Batista: Good Neighbor Diplomacy in Cuba, 1933–1945.* Albuquerque: University of New Mexico Press, 1973.

George, Alice L. *Awaiting Armageddon: How Americans Faced the Cuban Missile Crisis.* Chapel Hill: University of North Carolina Press, 2006.

Gibson, David R. *Talk at the Brink: Deliberation and Decision During the Cuban Missile Crisis.* Princeton, NJ: Princeton University Press, 2012.

Gilderhus, Mark T. *The Second Century: U.S.-Latin American Relations Since 1889.* Wilmington, DE: Scholarly Resources, 2000.

Gleijeses, Piero. *Conflicting Missions: Havana, Washington, and Africa, 1959–1976.* Chapel Hill: University of North Carolina Press, 2002.

Goduti, Philip A., Jr. *Kennedy's Kitchen Cabinet and the Pursuit of Peace: The Shaping of American Foreign Policy, 1961–1963.* Jefferson, NC: McFarland Press, 2009.

Gott, Richard. *Cuba: A New History.* New Haven, CT: Yale University Press, 2004.

Grandin, Greg, and Gilbert M, Joseph, eds. *A Century of Revolution: Insurgent and Counterinsurgent Violence during Latin America's Long Cold War.* Durham, NC: Duke University Press, 2010.

Grenier, Guillermo J., and Lisandro Pérez. *The Legacy of Exile: Cubans in the United States.* Boston, MA: Allyn and Bacon, 2003.

Gribkov, Anatoli I., and Smith, William Y. *Operation ANADYR: U.S. and Soviet Generals Recount the Cuban Missile Crisis.* Edited by Alfred Friendly, Jr. Chicago, Berlin, Tokyo, and Moscow: edition q, 1994.

Grow, Michael. *U.S. Presidents and Latin American Interventions: Pursuing Regime Change in the Cold War.* Lawrence: University Press of Kansas, 2008.

Haney, Patrick J., and Walt Vanderbush. *The Cuban Embargo: The Domestic Politics of An American Foreign Policy.* Pittsburgh, PA: University of Pittsburgh Press, 2005.

Haslam, Jonathan. *Russia's Cold War: From the October Revolution to the Fall of the Wall.* New Haven, CT: Yale University Press, 2011.

Hennessy, Alastair, and George Lambie, eds. *The Fractured Blockade: West European-Cuban Relations during the Revolution.* London: Macmillan Caribbean, 1993.

Hersh, Seymour M. *The Dark Side of Camelot.* Boston: Little, Brown, 1997.

Higgins, Trumbull. *The Perfect Failure: Kennedy, Eisenhower, and the CIA at the Bay of Pigs.* New York: Norton, 1987.

Hilsman, Roger. *The Cuban Missile Crisis: The Struggle over Policy.* Westport, CT: Praeger, 1996.

Hilsman, Roger. *To Move a Nation: The Politics of Foreign Policy in the Administration of John F. Kennedy.* Garden City, NY: Doubleday, 1967.

Hinckle, Warren, and William W. Turner. *The Fish is Red: The Story of the Secret War Against Castro.* New York: Harper and Row, 1981.

Horowitz, Louis. *The Long Night of Dark Intent: A Half Century of Cuban Communism.* New Brunswick, NJ: Transaction Books, 2008.

Huchthausen, Peter A. *October Fury.* Hoboken, NJ: John Wiley, 2002.

Huggins, Martha K. *Political Policing: The United States and Latin America.* Durham, NC: Duke University Press, 1998.

Isaacson, Walter, and Evan Thomas. *The Wise Men: Six Friends and the World they Made.* New York: Simon and Schuster, 1986.

Johnson, Dominic D. P. *Overconfidence and War: The Havoc and Glory of Positive Illusions.* Cambridge, MA: Harvard University Press, 2004.

Johnson, Dominic D. P., and Dominic Tierney. *Failing to Win: Perceptions of Victory and Defeat in International Politics.* Cambridge, MA: Harvard University Press, 2006.

Johnson, John J. *A Hemisphere Apart: The Foundations of United States Policy Toward Latin America.* Baltimore, MD: Johns Hopkins University Press, 1990.

Jones, Howard. *The Bay of Pigs.* New York: Oxford University Press, 2008.

Jordan, David C. *Revolutionary Cuba and the End of the Cold War.* Lanham, MD: University Press of America, 1993.

Kaplan, Fred. *1959: The Year That Changed Everything.* New York: John Wiley, 2009.

Kaplowitz, Donna Rich. *Anatomy of a Failed Embargo: U.S. Sanctions Against Cuba.* Boulder, CO: Lynne Rienner, 1998.

Karabell, Zachary. *Architects of Intervention: The United States, the Third World, and the Cold War, 1946–1962.* Baton Rouge: Louisiana State University Press, 1999.

Kempe, Frederick. *Berlin 1961: Kennedy, Khrushchev, and the Most Dangerous Place on Earth.* New York: Putnam, 2011.

Kennedy, Robert F. *Thirteen Days: A Memoir of the Cuban Missile Crisis.* New York: Norton, 1969, 1999.

Khrushchev, Nikita. *Khrushchev Remembers.* Edited by Edward Crankshaw. Translated by Strobe Talbott. Boston: Little, Brown, 1970.

Khrushchev, Nikita. *Khrushchev Remembers: The Glasnost Tapes.* Edited and translated by Jerrold L. Schechter and Vyacheslav V. Luchkov. Boston: Little, Brown, 1990.

Khrushchev, Nikita. *Khrushchev Remembers: The Last Testament.* Edited by Edward Crankshaw and Jerrold L. Schechter. Translated by Strobe Talbott. Boston: Little, Brown, 1974.

Khrushchev, Sergei N. *Nikita Khrushchev and the Creation of a Superpower.* Edited by William Taubman, Sergei Khrushchev, and Abbott Gleason. New Haven, CT: Yale University Press, 2000.

Kolko, Gabriel. *Confronting the Third World: United States Foreign Policy, 1945–1980.* New York: Pantheon, 1980.

Kornbluh, Peter, ed. *Bay of Pigs Declassified: The Secret CIA Report on the Invasion of Cuba.* New York: New Press, 1998.

Latham, Michael E. *Modernization as Ideology: American Social Science and "Nation Building" in the Kennedy Era.* Chapel Hill: University of North Carolina Press, 2000.

Lebow, Richard Ned, and Janice Gross Stein. *We All Lost the Cold War.* Princeton, NJ: Princeton University Press, 1994.

Lechuga, Carlos M. *In the Eye of the Storm: Castro, Kennedy, Khrushchev, and the Missile Crisis.* Translated by Mary Todd. Melbourne, Victoria, Australia: Ocean Press, 1995.

Leffler, Melvyn P. *For the Soul of Mankind: The United States, the Soviet Union, and the Cold War.* New York: Hill and Wang, 2007.

Leffler, Melvyn P., and Odd Arne Westad, eds. *The Cambridge History of the Cold War.* 3 vols. Cambridge: Cambridge University Press, 2010.

Leonard, Thomas M. *Castro and the Cuban Revolution.* Westport, CT: Greenwood Press, 1999.

Lipman, Jana K. *Guantánamo: A Working-Class History between Empire and Revolution.* Berkeley: University of California Press, 2008.

Longley, Kyle. *In the Eagle's Shadow: The United States and Latin America.* 2nd ed. Wheeling, IL: Harlan Davidson, 2009.

Lynch, Grayston L. *Decision for Disaster: Betrayal at the Bay of Pigs.* Washington, DC: Potomac Books, 1998.

Masud-Piloto, Felix Roberto. *From Welcomed Exiles to Illegal Immigrants: Cuban Migration to the U.S., 1959–1995.* Lanham, MD: Rowman and Littlefield, 1996.

May, Ernest R., and Philip D. Zelikow, eds. *The Kennedy Tapes: Inside the White House during the Cuban Missile Crisis.* Cambridge, MA: Harvard University Press, 1997.

McAuliffe, Mary S., ed. *CIA Documents on the Cuban Missile Crisis, 1962.* Washington, DC: Central Intelligence Agency, 1992. https://www.cia.gov/library/center-for-the-study-of-intelligence/csi-publications/books-and-monographs/Cuban%20Missile%20Crisis1962.pdf; also available at http://www.allworldwars.com/Cuban-Missile-Crisis-CIA-Documents.html

McKenna, Peter, and John M. Kirk, eds. *Competing Voices from Revolutionary Cuba.* Westport, CT: Greenwood Press, 2009.

McPherson, Alan. *Intimate Ties, Bitter Struggles: The United States and Latin America Since 1945.* Washington, DC: Potomac Books, 2006.

Medland, William J. *The Cuban Missile Crisis of 1962: Needless or Necessary.* New York: Praeger, 1988.

Montaner, Carlos Alberto. *Cuba, Castro, and the Caribbean: The Cuban Revolution and the Crisis in Western Conscience.* Translated by Nelson Duran. New Brunswick, NJ: Transactions Books, 1985.

Montaner, Carlos Alberto. *Journey to the Heart of Cuba: Life as Fidel Castro.* New York: Algora Publishers, 2001.

Morley, Morris H. *Imperial State and Revolution: The United States and Cuba, 1952–1986.* Cambridge: Cambridge University Press, 1987.

Morley, Morris, and Chris McGillion, eds. *Cuba, the United States, and the Post-Cold War World: The International Dimensions of the Washington-Havana Relationship.* Gainesville: University Press of Florida, 2005.

Morley, Morris, and Chris McGillion. *Unfinished Business: America and Cuba After the Cold War, 1989–2001.* Cambridge: Cambridge University Press, 2002.

Munton, Don, and David A. Welch. *The Cuban Missile Crisis: A Concise History.* New York: Oxford University Press, 2006.

Naftali, Timothy, Philip D. Zelikow, and Ernest R. May, eds. *John F. Kennedy: The Great Crises.* 3 vols. New York: Norton, 2001.

Nash, Philip. *The Other Missiles of October: Eisenhower, Kennedy, and the Jupiters, 1957–1963.* Chapel Hill: University of North Carolina Press, 1997.

Nathan, James A. *Anatomy of the Cuban Missile Crisis.* Westport, CT: Greenwood Press, 2001.

Newsom, David D. *The Soviet Brigade in Cuba: A Study in Political Diplomacy.* Bloomington: University of Indiana Press, 1987.

O'Brien, Michael. *Rethinking Kennedy: An Interpretive Biography.* New York: St. Martin's Press, 2005.

Paterson, Thomas G. *Contesting Castro: The United States and the Triumph of the Cuban Revolution.* New York: Oxford University Press, 2004.

Paterson, Thomas G., ed. *Kennedy's Quest for Victory: American Foreign Policy, 1961–1963.* New York: Oxford University Press, 1989.

Pavia, Peter. *The Cuba Project: Castro, Kennedy, Dirty Business, Double Dealing, and the FBI's Tamale Squad.* New York: Palgrave Macmillan, 2006.

Pedraza, Silvia. *Political Disaffection in Cuba's Revolution and Exodus.* New York: Cambridge University Press, 2007.

Pérez, Louis A., Jr. *Cuba and the United States: Ties of Singular Intimacy.* 2nd ed. Athens: University of Georgia Press, 1997.

Pérez, Louis A. *Cuba: Between Reform and Revolution.* 4th ed. New York: Oxford University Press, 2011.

Pérez, Louis A., Jr. *Cuba in the American Imagination: Metaphor and the Imperial Ethos.* Chapel Hill: University of North Carolina Press, 2008.

Pérez-Stable, Marifeli. *The Cuban Revolution: Origins, Course, and Legacy.* New York: Oxford University Press, 1993.

Pérez-Stable, Marifeli. *The United States and Cuba: Intimate Enemies.* New York: Routledge, 2011.

Polmar, Norman, and John D. Gresham. *DEFCON-2: Standing on the Brink of Nuclear War during the Cuban Missile Crisis.* New York: John Wiley, 2006.

Press, Daryl G. *Calculating Credibility: How Leaders Evaluate Military Threats.* Ithaca, NY: Cornell University Press, 2005.

Priestland, Jane, ed. *Cuba under Castro: The Declassified British Documents.* 5 vols. London: Archival Publications, 2003.

Rabe, Stephen G. *Eisenhower and Latin America: The Foreign Policy of Anticommunism.* Chapel Hill: University of North Carolina Press, 1988.

Rabe, Stephen G. *The Most Dangerous Area in the World: John F. Kennedy Confronts Communist Revolution in Latin America.* Chapel Hill: University of North Carolina Press, 1999.

Rasenberger, Jim. *The Brilliant Disaster: JFK, Castro, and America's Doomed Invasion of Cuba's Bay of Pigs.* New York: Scribner, 2011.

Reid-Henry, Simon. *Fidel and Che: A Revolutionary Friendship.* London: Sceptre, 2008.

Roy, Joaquin. *The Cuban Revolution (1959–2009): Relations with Spain, the European Union, and the United States.* New York: Palgrave Macmillan, 2009.

Russo, Gus, and Stephen Molton. *Brothers in Arms: The Kennedys, the Castros, and the Politics of Murder.* New York: Bloomsbury, 2008.

Sáenz-Rovner, Eduardo. *The Cuban Connection: Drug Trafficking, Smuggling, and Gambling in Cuba from the 1920s to the Revolution.* Translated by Russ Davidson. Chapel Hill: University of North Carolina Press, 2008.

Salinger, Pierre. *P.S., A Memoir.* New York: St. Martin's Press, 1995.

Schlesinger, Arthur M., Jr. *Journals, 1952–2000.* Edited by Andrew Schlesinger and Stephen Schlesinger. New York: Penguin, 2007.

Schlesinger, Arthur M., Jr. *Robert Kennedy and His Times.* Boston: Houghton Mifflin, 1978.

Schlesinger, Arthur M., Jr. *A Thousand Days: John F. Kennedy in the White House.* Boston: Houghton Mifflin, 1965.

Schoultz, Lars. *Beneath the United States: A History of U.S. Policy toward Latin America.* Cambridge, MA: Harvard University Press, 1998.

Schoultz, Lars. *That Infernal Little Cuban Republic: The United States and the Cuban Revolution.* Chapel Hill: University of North Carolina Press, 2009.

Schwab, Peter. *Cuba: Confronting the U.S. Embargo.* New York: St. Martin's Press, 1999.

Scott, L. V. *Macmillan, Kennedy and the Cuban Missile Crisis: Political, Military and Intelligence Aspects.* New York: St. Martin's Press, 1999.

Scott, Len. *The Cuban Missile Crisis and the Threat of Nuclear War: Lessons From History.* New York: Continuum Books, 2007.

Skwiot, Christine. *The Purposes of Paradise: U.S. Tourism and Empire in Cuba and Hawai'i.* Philadelphia, PA: University of Pennsylvania Press, 2010.

Smith, Gaddis. *The Last Years of the Monroe Doctrine, 1945–1993.* New York: Hill and Wang, 1994.

Smith, Joseph. *The United States and Latin America: A History of American Diplomacy, 1776–2000.* New York: Routledge, 2005.

Smith, Peter H. *Talons of the Eagle: Dynamics of U.S.-Latin American Relations.* 3rd ed. New York: Oxford University Press, 2007.

Smith, Robert Freeman. *The United States and Cuba: Business and Diplomacy, 1917–1960.* New York: Bookman Associates, 1961.

Smith, Wayne S. *The Closest of Enemies: A Personal and Diplomatic Account of U.S.-Cuban Relations Since 1957*. New York: Norton, 1987.

Solomon, Daniel F. *Breaking Up with Cuba: The Dissolution of Friendly Relations between Washington and Havana, 1956–1961*. Jefferson, NC: McFarland Press, 2011.

Sorensen, Theodore C. *Counselor: A Life at the Edge of History*. New York: Harper, 2008.

Sorensen, Theodore C. *Kennedy*. With new preface. New York: Harper, 2009.

Staten, Clifford L. *The History of Cuba*. Westport, CT: Greenwood Press, 2003.

Stern, Sheldon M. *Averting 'The Final Failure': John F. Kennedy and the Secret Cuban Missile Crisis Meetings*. Stanford, CA: Stanford University Press, 2003.

Stern, Sheldon M. *The Week the World Stood Still: Inside the Secret Cuban Missile Crisis*. Stanford, CA: Stanford University Press, 2005.

Strauss, Michael J. *The Leasing of Guantanamo Bay*. Westport, CT: Praeger Security International, 2009.

Suchlicki, Jaime. *Cuba: From Columbus to Castro and Beyond*. 5th ed. Washington, DC: Potomac Books, 2002.

Swedin, Eric G. *When Angels Wept: A What-If History of the Cuban Missile Crisis*. Washington, DC: Potomac Books, 2010.

Sweig, Julia E. *Cuba: What Everyone Needs to Know*. New York: Oxford University Press, 2009.

Sweig, Julia E. *Friendly Fire: Losing Friends and Making Enemies in the Anti-American Century*. New York: PublicAffairs, 2006.

Sweig, Julia E. *Inside the Cuban Revolution: Fidel Castro and the Urban Underground*. Cambridge, MA: Harvard University Press, 2002.

Szulc, Tad. *Fidel: A Critical Portrait*. New York: William Morrow, 1986.

Taffet, Jeffrey F. *Foreign Aid as Foreign Policy: The Alliance for Progress in Latin America*. New York: Routledge, 2007.

Taubman, William S. *Khrushchev: The Man and His Era*. New York: Norton, 2003.

Thomas, Evan. *Robert Kennedy: His Life*. New York: Simon and Schuster, 2000.

Thompson, Robert Smith. *The Missiles of October: The Declassified Story of John F. Kennedy and the Cuban Missile Crisis*. New York: Simon and Schuster, 1992.

United States Department of State. *Foreign Relations of the United States 1958–1960,* Vol. VI: *Cuba*. Washington, DC: Government

Printing Office, 1991. http://digicoll.library.wisc.edu/cgi-bin/FRUS/FRUS-idx?id=FRUS.FRUS195860v06

United States Department of State. *Foreign Relations of the United States 1961–1963,* Vol. VI: *Kennedy-Khrushchev Exchanges.* Washington, DC: Government Printing Office, 1996. http://www.state.gov/www/about_state/history/volume_vi/volumevi.html

United States Department of State. *Foreign Relations of the United States 1961–1963,* Vol. X: *Cuba, 1961–1962.* Washington, DC: Government Printing Office, 1997. http://www.state.gov/www/about_state/history/frusX/

United States Department of State. *Foreign Relations of the United States 1961–1963,* Vol. XI: *The Cuban Missile Crisis and Its Aftermath.* Washington, DC: Government Printing Office, 1996. http://www.state.gov/www/about_state/history/frusXI/

Uslu, Nasuh. *The Turkish-American Relationship between 1947 and 2003: The History of a Distinctive Alliance.* New York: Nova Science Publishers, 2003.

Von Tunzelmann, Alex. *Red Heat: Conspiracy, Murder, and the Cold War in the Caribbean.* New York: Henry Holt, 2011.

Waldron, Lamar, with Thom Hartmann. *Ultimate Sacrifice: John and Robert Kennedy, the Plan for a Coup in Cuba, and the Murder of JFK.* New York: Carroll and Graf, 2005.

Weisbrot, Robert. *Maximum Danger: Kennedy, the Missiles, and the Crisis of American Confidence.* Chicago: Ivan R. Dee, 2001.

Welch, Richard E., Jr. *Response to Revolution: The United States and the Cuban Revolution, 1959–1961.* Chapel Hill: University of North Carolina Press, 1985.

Weldes, Jutta. *Constructing National Interests: The United States and the Cuban Missile Crisis.* Minneapolis: University of Minnesota Press, 1999.

Westad, Odd Arne. *The Global Cold War: Third World Interventions and the Making of Our Times.* New York: Cambridge University Press, 2005.

White, Mark J. *The Cuban Missile Crisis.* London: Macmillan, 1996.

White, Mark J. *The Kennedys and Cuba: The Declassified Documentary History.* Chicago: Ivan R. Dee, 1999.

White, Mark J. *Missiles in Cuba: Kennedy, Khrushchev, Castro and the 1962 Crisis.* Chicago: Ivan R. Dee, 1997.

Wright, Thomas C. *Latin America in the Era of the Cuban Revolution.* Rev. ed. Westport, CT: Praeger, 2001.

Zubok, Vladislav M. *A Failed Empire: The Soviet Union in the Cold War from Stalin to Gorbachev.* Chapel Hill: University of North Carolina Press, 2007.

Zubok, Vladislav, and Constantine Pleshakov. *Inside the Kremlin's Cold War: From Stalin to Khrushchev.* Cambridge, MA: Harvard University Press, 1996.

Web Sites

Cold War International History Project: Virtual Archive 2.0 The Cold War in Latin America, Cuba in the Cold War, The Cuban Missile Crisis, and US-Cuban Relations. http://legacy.wilsoncenter.org/va2/index.cfm?topic_id=1409&fuseaction=HOME.browse&sort=Subject&item=Soviet%20Union,%20relations%20with%Cubanet. http://www.cubanet.org

The Cuban Missile Crisis, 40 Years Later. National Public Radio. http://www.npr.org/news/specials/cuban_missile/

CubanMissileCrisis.Info. http://cubanmissilecrisis.info/index.htm

Federation of Atomic Scientists Intelligence Resource Program: The Cuban Missile Crisis. http://www.fas.org/irp/imint/cuba.htm

GlobalSecurity.Org: The Cuban Missile Crisis. http://www.globalsecurity.org/military/ops/cuba-62.htm

HistoryofCuba.Com. http://www.historyofcuba.com/cuba.htm

John F. Kennedy Presidential Library and Museum: The Cuban Missile Crisis. http://www.jfklibrary.org/JFK/JFK-in-History/Cuban-Missile-Crisis.aspx

Miller Center of Public Affairs, University of Virginia: John F. Kennedy—Presidential Recordings. http://millercenter.org/scripps/archive/presidentialrecordings/kennedy

Mount Holyoke College: Resources for the Study of International Relations and Foreign Policy: Documents Relating to the Bay of Pigs Invasion and the Cuban Missile Crisis. http://www.mtholyoke.edu/acad/intrel/cuba.htm

National Security Archive: The Bay of Pigs. http://www.gwu.edu/~nsarchiv/bayofpigs/

National Security Archive: The Cuban Missile Crisis. http://www.gwu.edu/~nsarchiv/nsa/cuba_mis_cri/docs.htm

No Time to Talk: The Cuban Missile Crisis. http://www.october1962.com/

NuclearFiles.Org:CubanMissileCrisis.http://www.nuclearfiles.org/menu/
key-issues/nuclear-weapons/history/cold-war/cuban-missile-crisis/

Films and Television

ABC News Nightline: The JFK Tapes (1994). ABC.
American Experience: Fidel Castro (2005). PBS.
Castro's Cuba (2004). PBS.
Che (2008). Directed by Stephen Soderbergh. Starring Julia Ormond and Benicio del Toro.
Cuba: The 40 Years War (2002). Directed by Peter Melaragno.
The Cold War (1998). BBC/CNN. Directed by Jeremy Isaacs.
Fidel! (1974). Micromedia. Directed by Sam Landau.
Fidel (2002). Starring Victor Huggo Martin, Gael García Bernal, and David Attwood.
Fidel Castro: A Life of Revolution (2008). Canadian Broadcasting Corporation. Directed by Terence McKenna.
The Fog of War: Eleven Lessons from the Life of Robert S. McNamara (2004). Sony. Directed by Errol Morris.
K-19: The Widow Maker (2002). Starring Harrison Ford and Liam Neeson.
Kennedy (1983). NBC. Starring Martin Sheen, Blair Brown, and E. G. Marshall.
Kennedy and Castro: The Secret History (2003). NBC.
The Missiles of October (1974). Starring William Devane, Ralph Bellamy, and Howard Da Silva.
Thirteen Days (2001). Starring Kevin Costner, Bruce Greenwood, and Roger Donaldson.

CD-ROM

Cuban Missile Crisis: CIA-NSA-NSC-State Dept. Files: Audio Recordings. BACM Research: PaperlessArchives.Com. 2008.

About the Editor and Contributors

Editor

Dr. Priscilla Roberts
Associate Professor of History,
School of Humanities
Honorary Director, Centre of
American Studies
University of Hong Kong
Pokfulam, Hong Kong

Contributors

Dr. Valerie Adams
School of Letters and Sciences
Arizona State University—
Polytechnic Campus
Mesa, Arizona

Lacie A. Ballinger
Collections Manager
Fort Worth Museum of Science
and History
Fort Worth, Texas

Dr. Günter Bischof
Department of History
University of New Orleans
New Orleans, Louisiana

Dr. Paul R. Camacho
Director Emeritus, William Joiner
Center for the Study of War and
Social Consequences
University of Massachusetts
Boston, Massachusetts

Dr. Barry Carr
Department of History and
Institute of Latin American Studies
La Trobe University
Melbourne, Australia

Dr. Don M. Coerver
Department of History
Texas Christian University
Fort Worth, Texas

Dr. Jérôme Dorvidal
CRESOI Department of History
University of La Réunion
Réunion Island, Indian Ocean

Dr. Beatrice de Graaf
Centre for Terrorism and
Counterterrorism
Campus The Hague
Leiden University
Netherlands

Dr. Steven W. Guerrier
Department of History
James Madison University
Harrisonburg, Virginia

Dr. Magarditsch Hatschikjan
Institute of East European History
University of Cologne
Cologne, Germany

Dr. Brian Madison Jones
Department of History
Johnson C. Smith University
Charlotte, North Carolina

Dr. Jeffrey Larsen
Senior Policy Analyst
Science Applications International
Corporation
Colorado Springs, Colorado

Dr. Mark Atwood Lawrence
Department of History
University of Texas at Austin
Austin, Texas

Arturo Lopez-Levy
Josef Korbel School of
International Studies
University of Denver
Denver, Colorado

Dr. Lise Namikas
Department of History
Louisiana State University
Baton Rouge, Louisiana

Dr. Caryn E. Neumann
Lecturer in Integrative Studies
History Department
Miami University of Ohio
Oxford, Ohio

Dr. Christian Nuenlist
Lecturer in Contemporary History
University of Zurich
Zurich, Switzerland

Dr. Michael Share
Independent Scholar

Dr. James F. Siekmeier
Assistant Professor of History
West Virginia University
Morgantown, West Virginia

Dr. Daniel E. Spector
Emeritus Professor of History
University of Alabama
Birmingham, Alabama

Dr. David Tal
Kahanoff Chair in Israeli Studies
Department of History
University of Calgary
Calgary, Canada

Dr. Spencer C. Tucker
Senior Fellow
Military History, ABC-CLIO,
LLC

Dr. Josh Ushay
Independent Scholar

Dr. Robert Anthony Waters, Jr.
Department of History
Ohio Northern University
Ada, Ohio

Dr. Paul Wingrove
Department of Politics
University of Greenwich
Greenwich
United Kingdom

Index